Scholastic VISUAL Dictionary

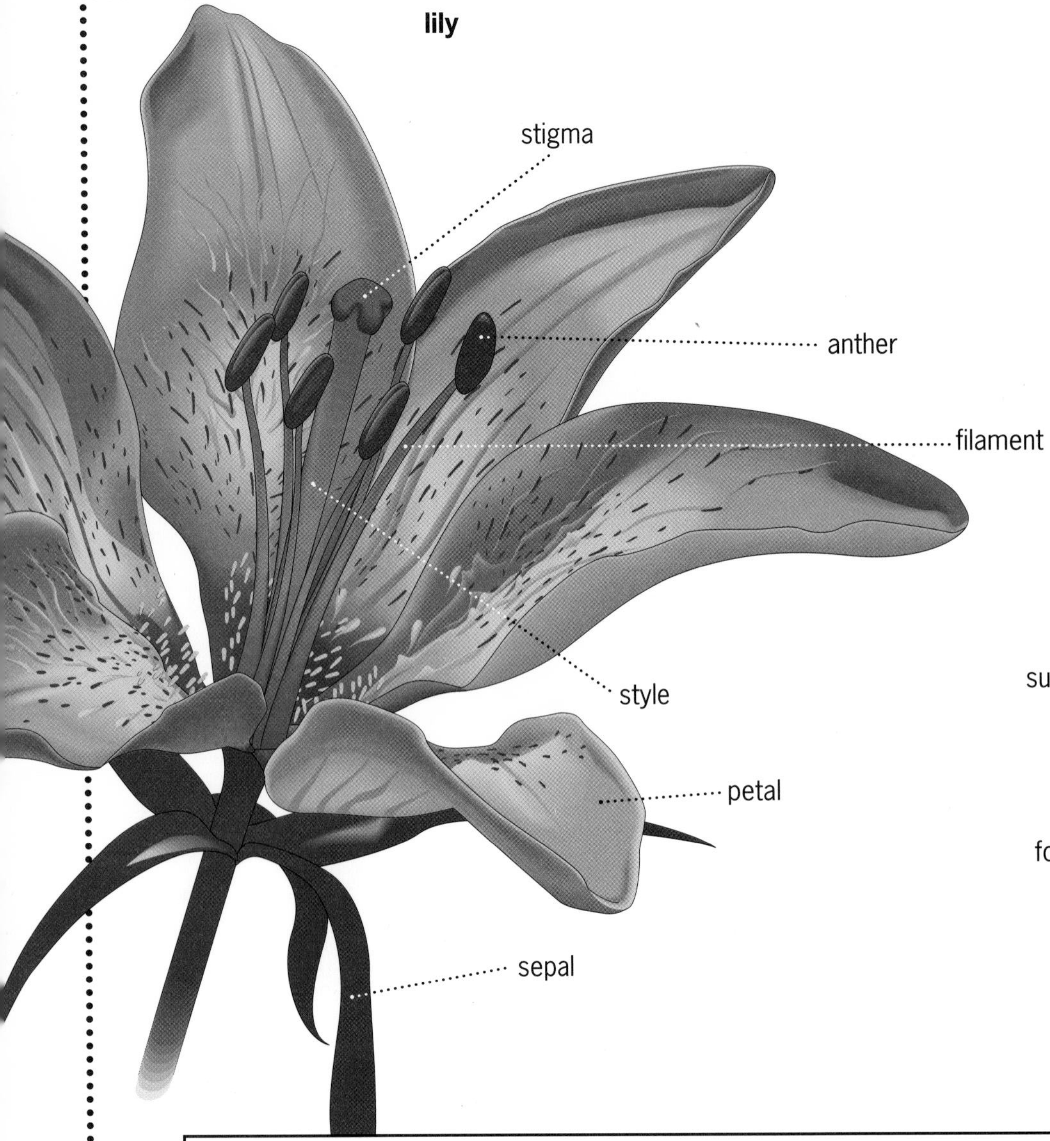
lily
stigma
anther
filament
style
petal
sepal

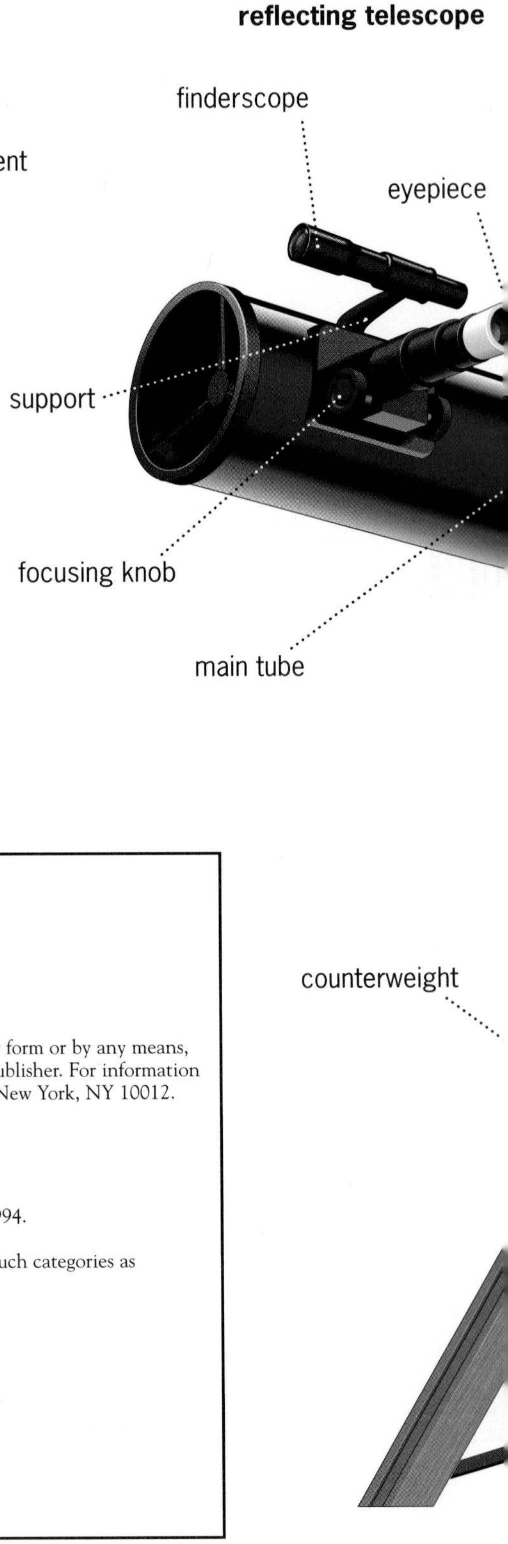
reflecting telescope
finderscope
eyepiece
support
focusing knob
main tube
counterweight

Corbeil, Jean-Claude.
[Junior visual dictionary]
Scholastic visual dictionary / by Jean-Claude Corbeil and Ariane Archambault.
p. cm.
Previously published: Junior visual dictionary. Quebec: Québec/Amérique International, c1994.
Includes index.
Summary: Introduces basic vocabulary in labeled pictures of familiar objects arranged under such categories as "House," "Clothing," and "Animal Kingdom."
ISBN 0-439-05940-2
1. Picture dictionaries, English juvenile literature.
2. English language Textbooks for foreign speakers.
[1. Vocabulary.] I. Archambault, Ariane. II. Title.

PE1629.C635 2000 423'.1—dc21 99-14870 CIP

10 9 8 7 6 5 4 3 2 0/0 01 02 03 04

Printed in the U.S.A. 23
First Scholastic printing, August 2000

Jean-Claude Corbeil • Ariane Archambault

Scholastic VISUAL Dictionary

Art Directors
Jean-Louis Martin
François Fortin

Graphic Designer
Anne Tremblay

Computer Graphic Designers
Marc Lalumière
Jean-Yves Ahern
Rielle Lévesque
Anne Tremblay

Computer Programming
Yves Ferland

Data Capture
Serge D'Amico

Page Make-up
Lucie Mc Brearty
Pascal Goyette

Production
Tony O'Riley

SCHOLASTIC REFERENCE

THEMES AND SUBJECTS

SKY

EARTH

PLANT KINGDOM

FRUITS AND VEGETABLES

GARDENING

ANIMAL KINGDOM

HUMAN BODY

ARCHITECTURE

HOUSE

DO-IT-YOURSELF

CLOTHING

PERSONAL ARTICLES

COMMUNICATIONS

ROAD TRANSPORTATION

RAIL TRANSPORTATION

MARITIME TRANSPORTATION

AIR TRANSPORTATION

SPACE TRANSPORTATION

SCHOOL

MUSIC

TEAM GAMES

WATER SPORTS

WINTER SPORTS

GYMNASTICS

CAMPING

INDOOR GAMES

MEASURING DEVICES

ENERGY

HEAVY MACHINERY

SYMBOLS

SOLAR SYSTEM

planets and moons

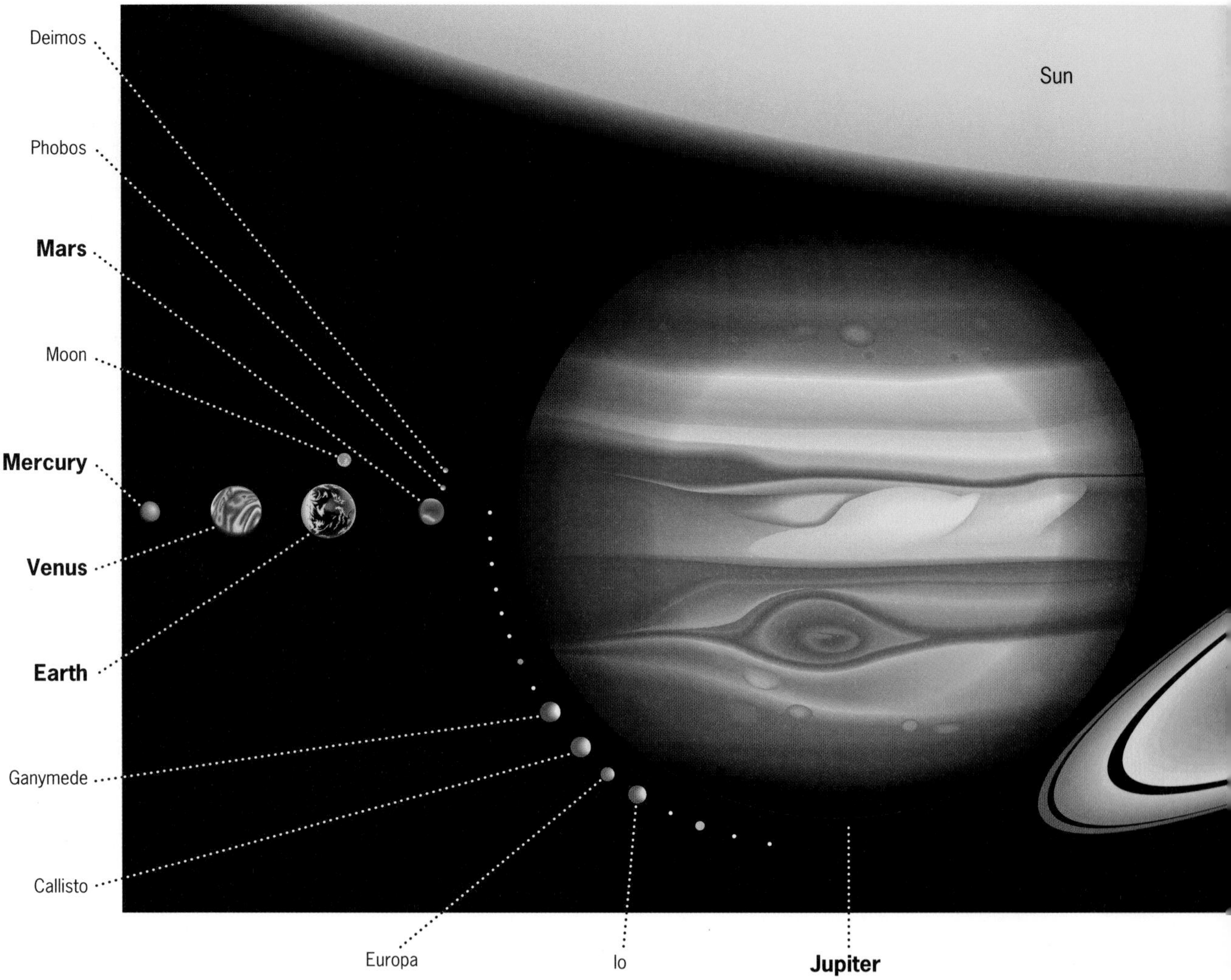
Deimos
Sun
Phobos
Mars
Moon
Mercury
Venus
Earth
Ganymede
Callisto
Europa
Io
Jupiter

orbits of the planets

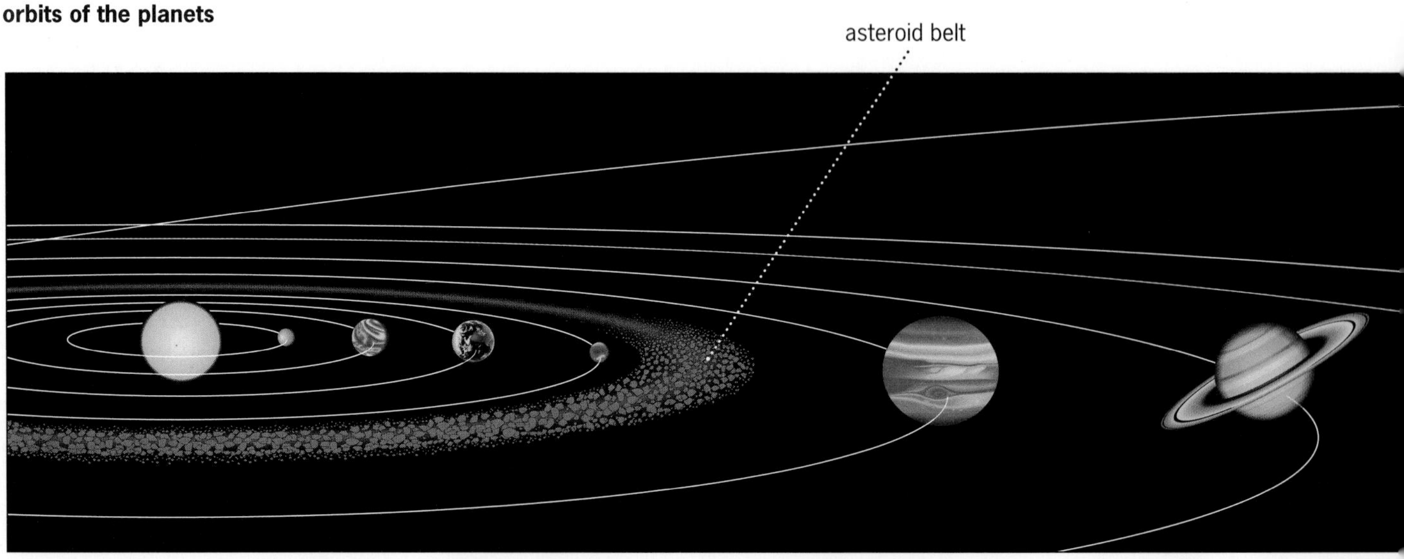
asteroid belt

Neptune
Pluto
Charon
Saturn
Titan
Uranus
Triton

SUN

structure of the Sun

radiation zone
convection zone
Sun's surface
corona
prominence
sunspot
core
flare

MOON

lunar features

bay
cliff
ocean
lake
sea
mountain range
crater
wall
cirque

PHASES OF THE MOON

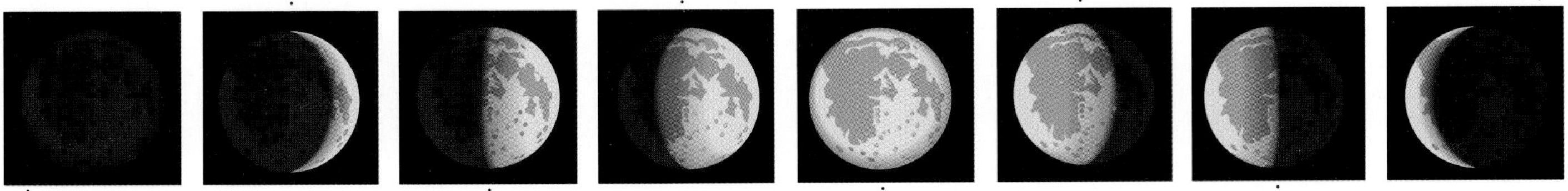
new crescent
waxing gibbous Moon
waning gibbous Moon
old crescent
new Moon
first quarter
full Moon
last quarter

COMET

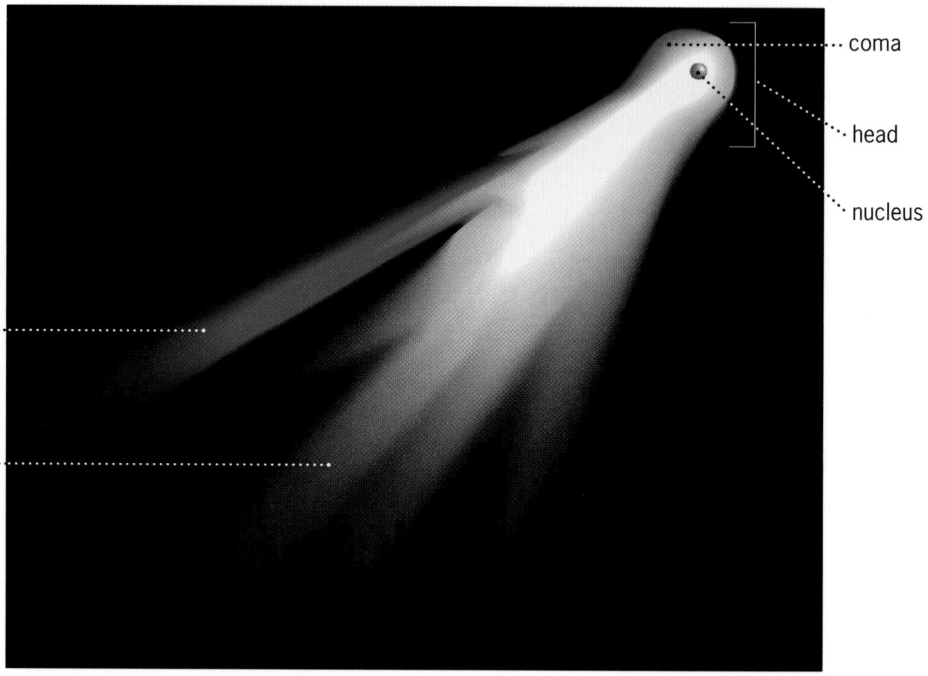
coma
head
nucleus
gas tail
dust tail

SOLAR ECLIPSE

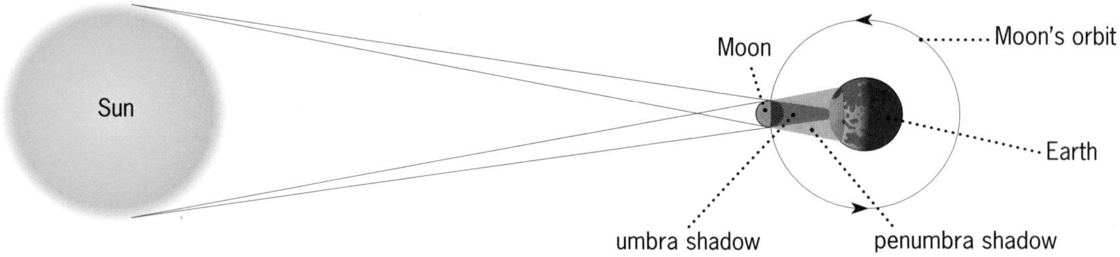
Sun
Moon
Moon's orbit
Earth
umbra shadow
penumbra shadow

TYPES OF SOLAR ECLIPSES

total eclipse

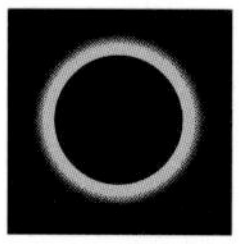
annular eclipse

partial eclipse

LUNAR ECLIPSE

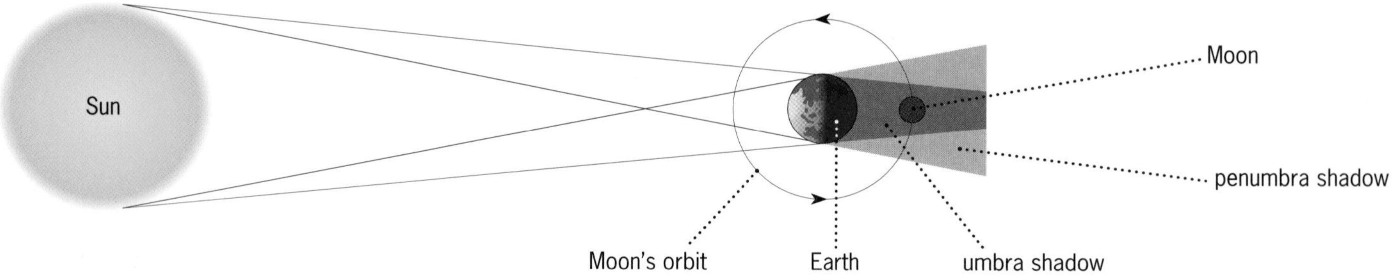
Sun
Moon
penumbra shadow
Moon's orbit
Earth
umbra shadow

TYPES OF LUNAR ECLIPSES

partial eclipse

total eclipse

REFLECTING TELESCOPE

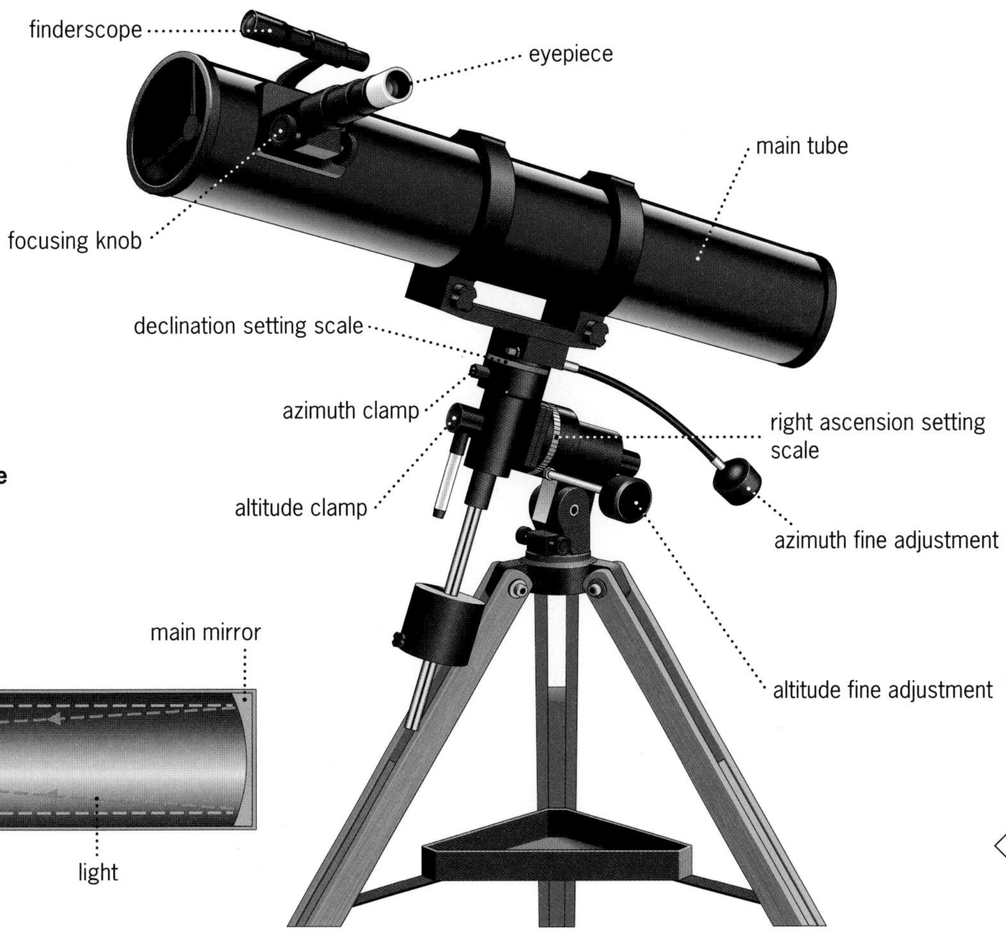
finderscope
eyepiece
main tube
focusing knob
declination setting scale
azimuth clamp
right ascension setting scale
altitude clamp
azimuth fine adjustment
altitude fine adjustment

cross section of a reflecting telescope

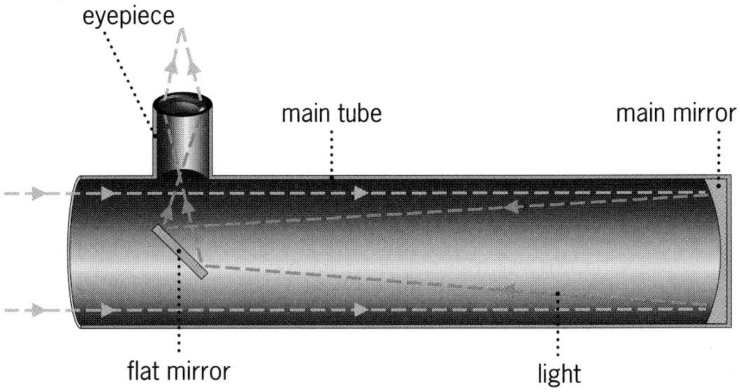
eyepiece
main tube
main mirror
flat mirror
light

REFRACTING TELESCOPE

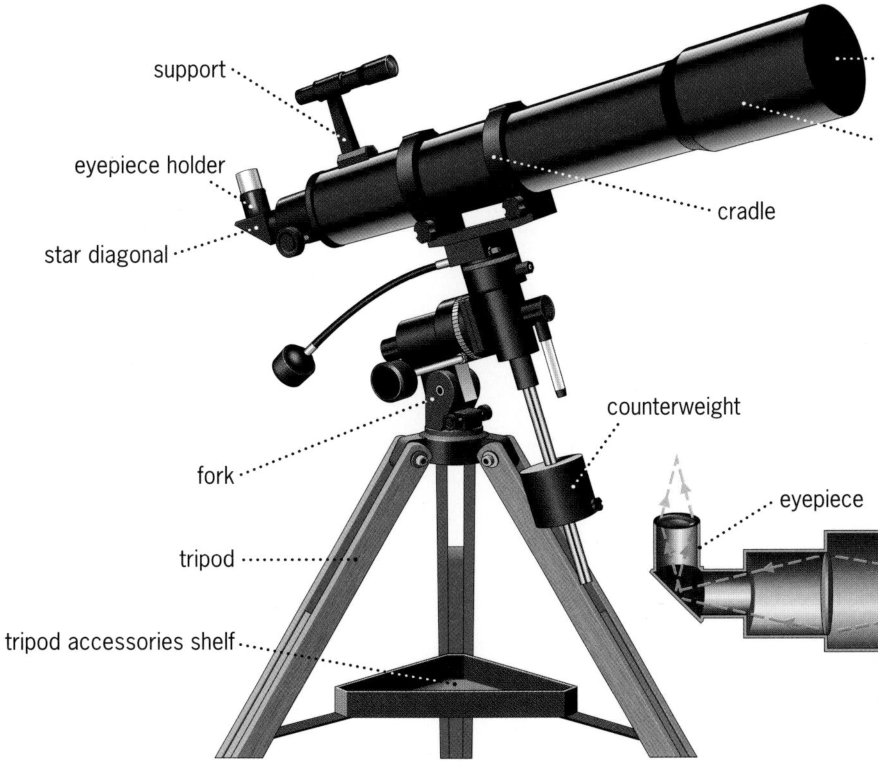
support
objective lens
dew shield
eyepiece holder
cradle
star diagonal
counterweight
fork
tripod
tripod accessories shelf

cross section of a refracting telescope

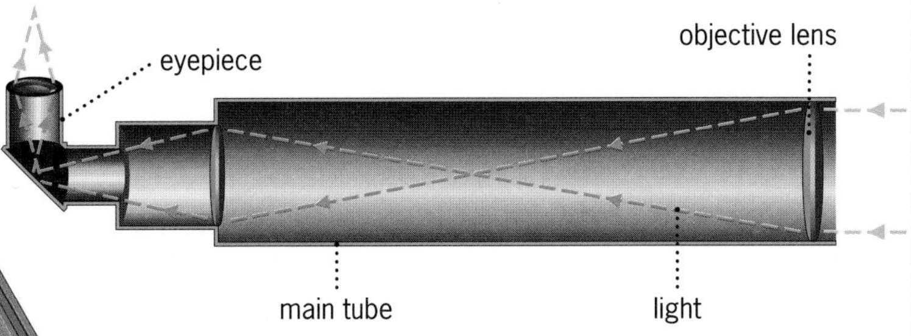
eyepiece
objective lens
main tube
light

EARTH COORDINATE SYSTEM

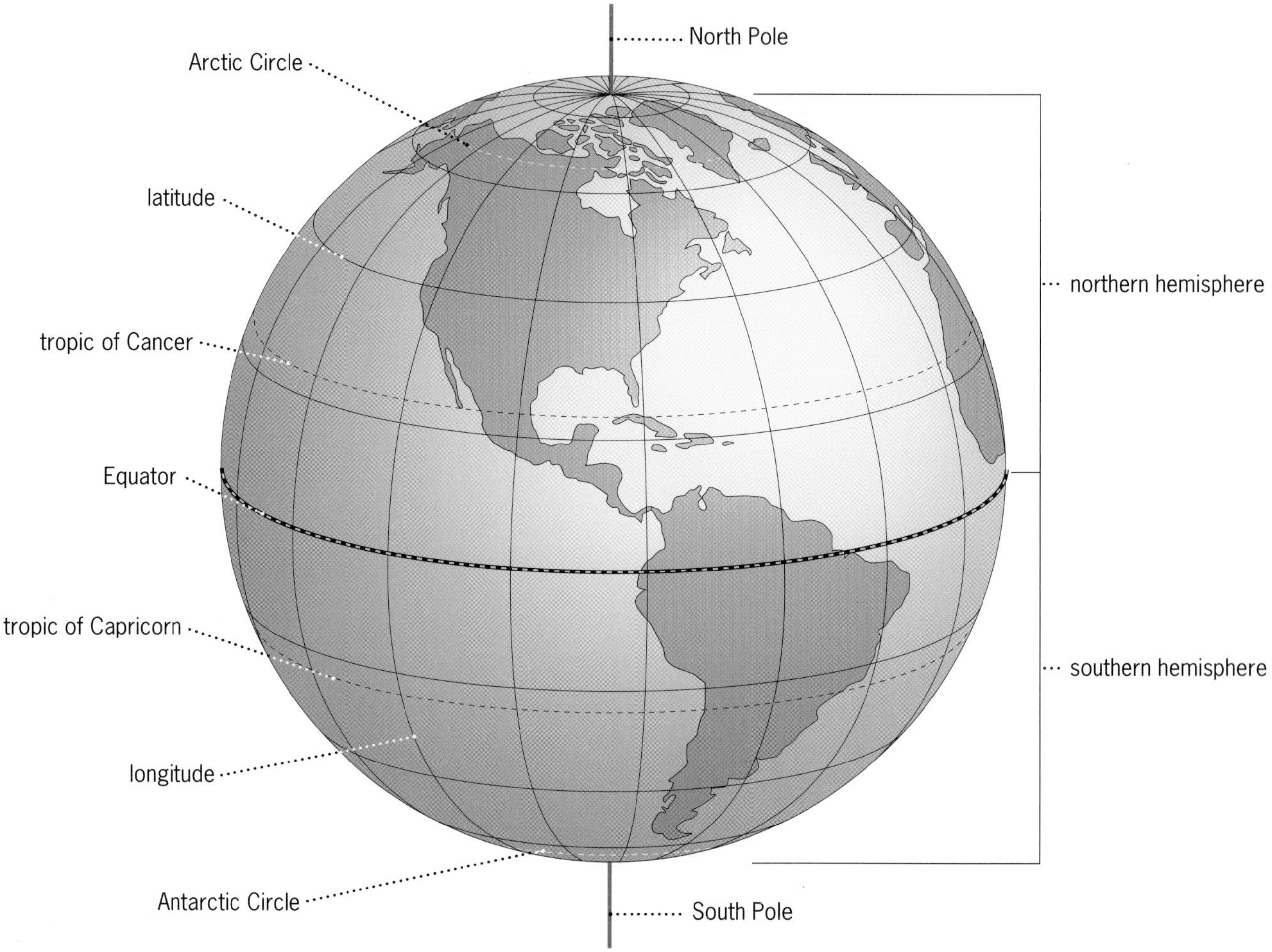
North Pole
Arctic Circle
latitude
tropic of Cancer
Equator
tropic of Capricorn
longitude
Antarctic Circle
South Pole
northern hemisphere
southern hemisphere

STRUCTURE OF THE EARTH

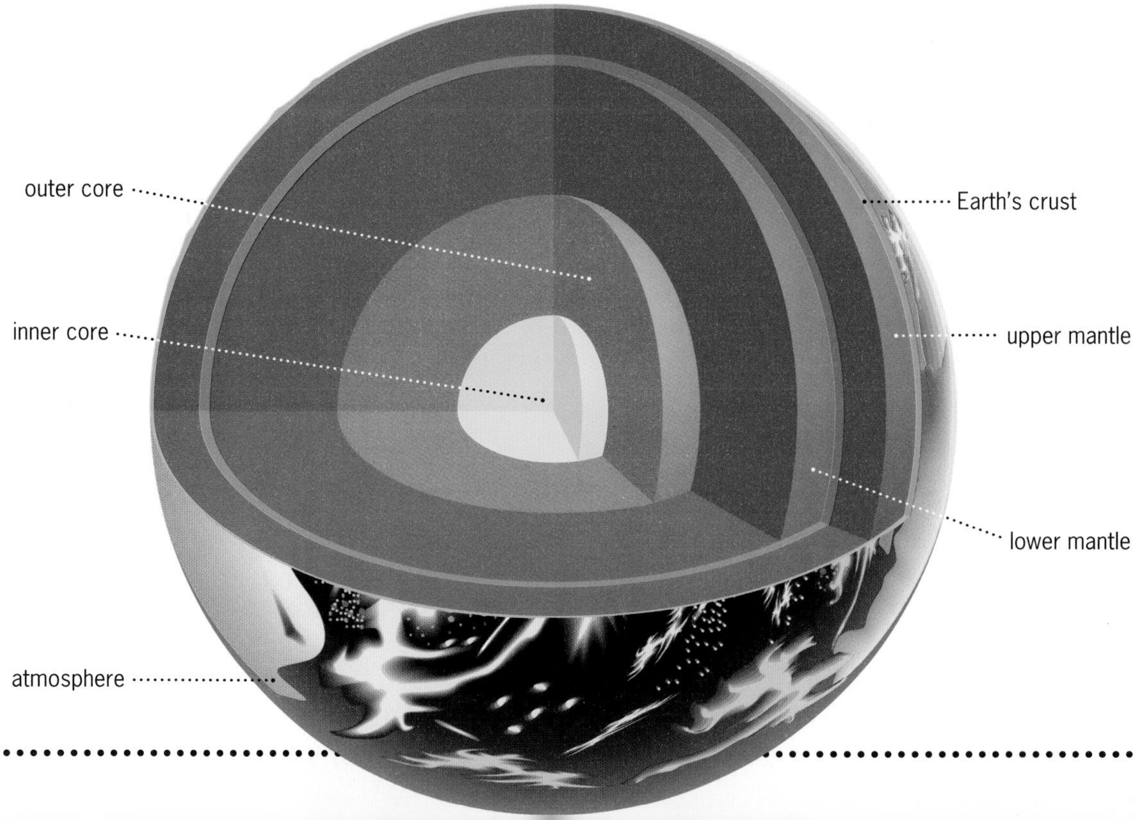
outer core
inner core
atmosphere
Earth's crust
upper mantle
lower mantle

EARTHQUAKE

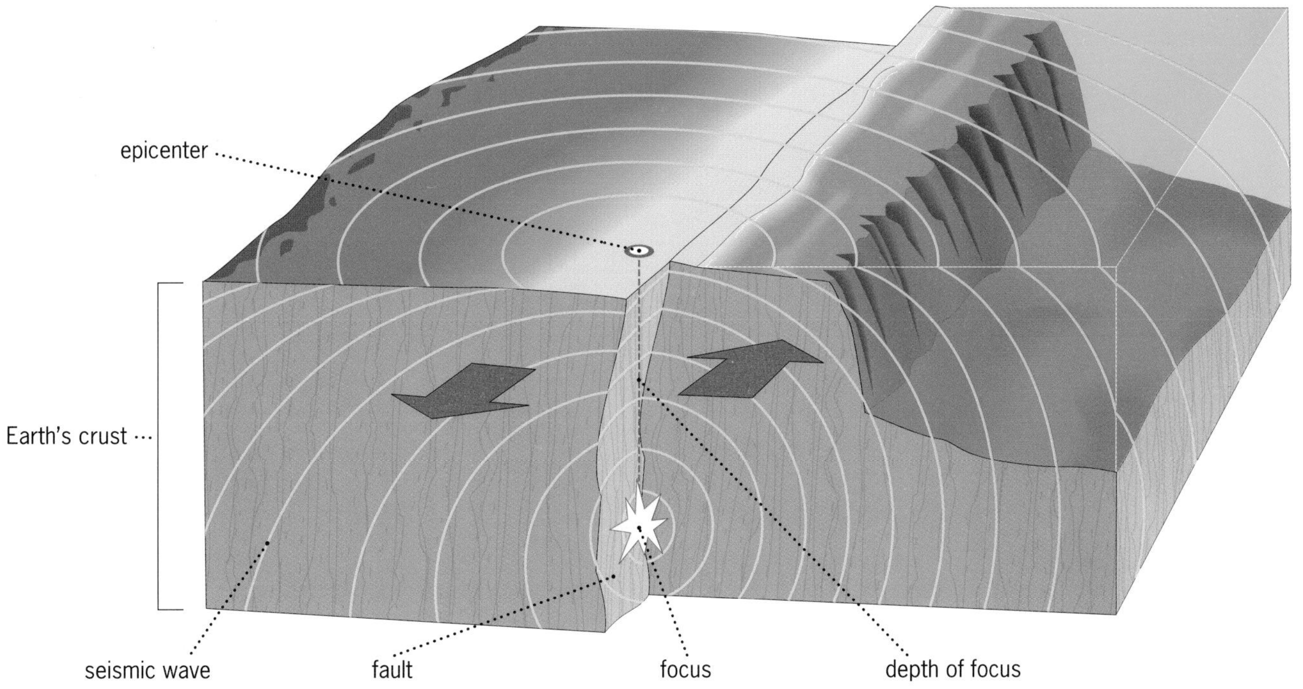
epicenter
Earth's crust
seismic wave
fault
focus
depth of focus

CAVE

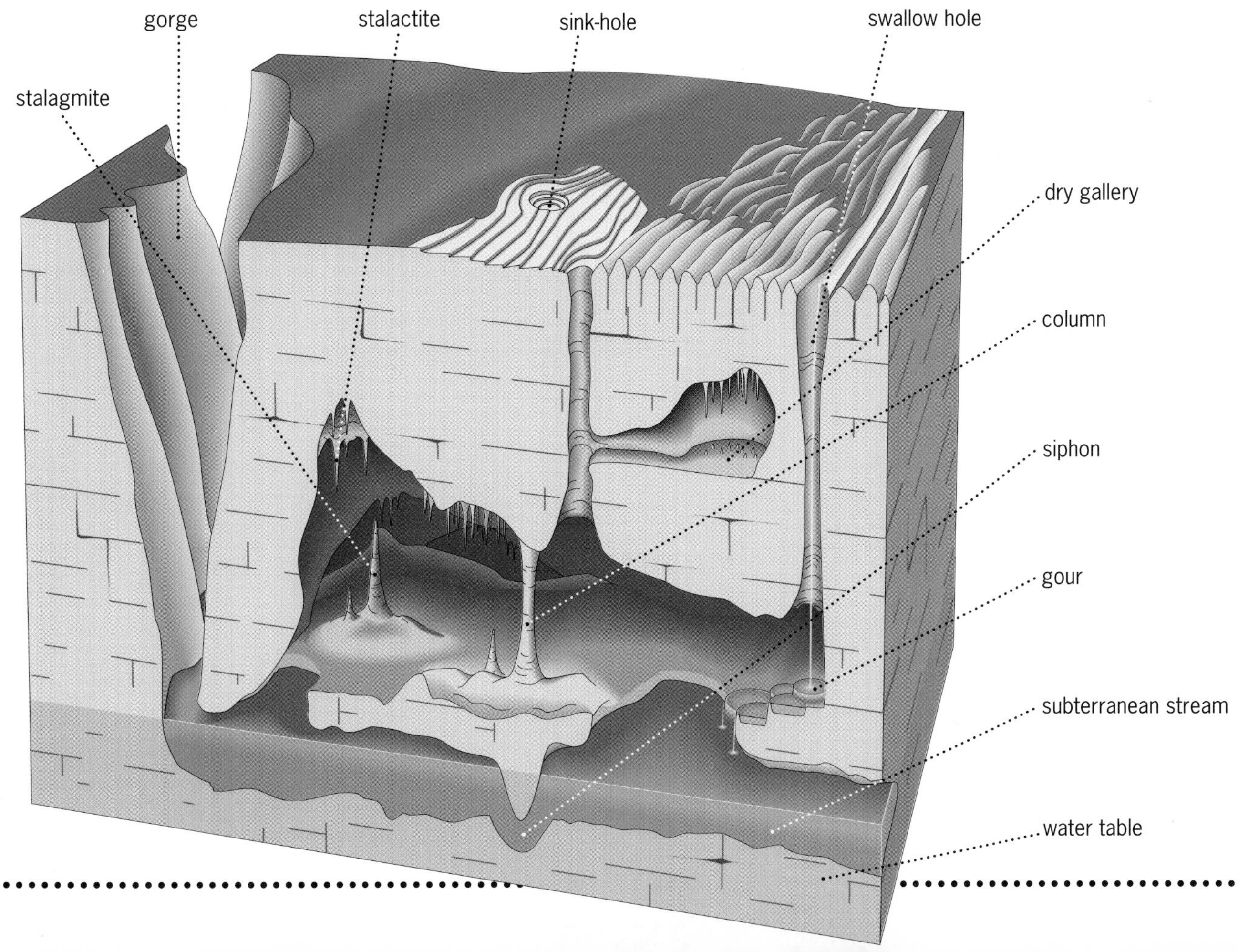
gorge
stalactite
sink-hole
swallow hole
stalagmite
dry gallery
column
siphon
gour
subterranean stream
water table

COASTAL FEATURES

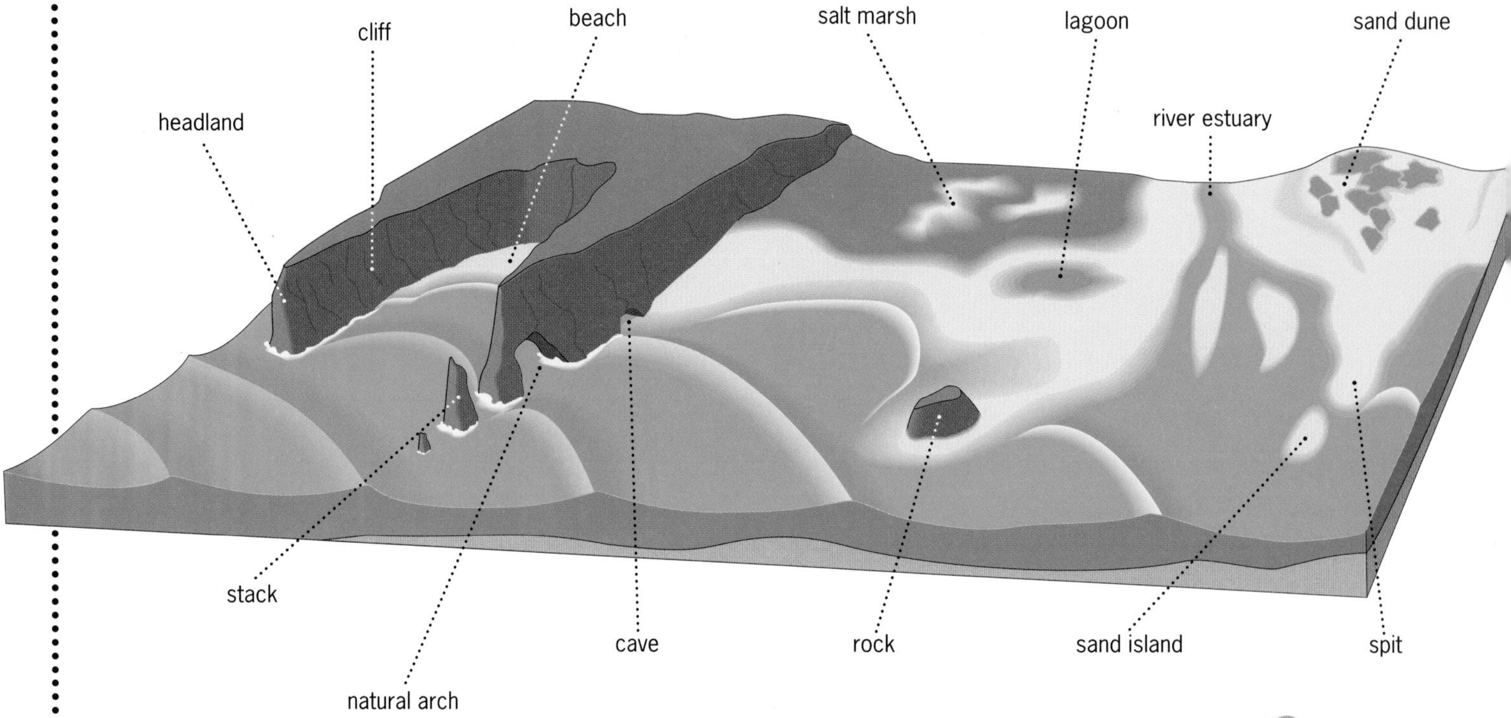
cliff
beach
salt marsh
lagoon
sand dune
headland
river estuary
stack
cave
rock
sand island
spit
natural arch

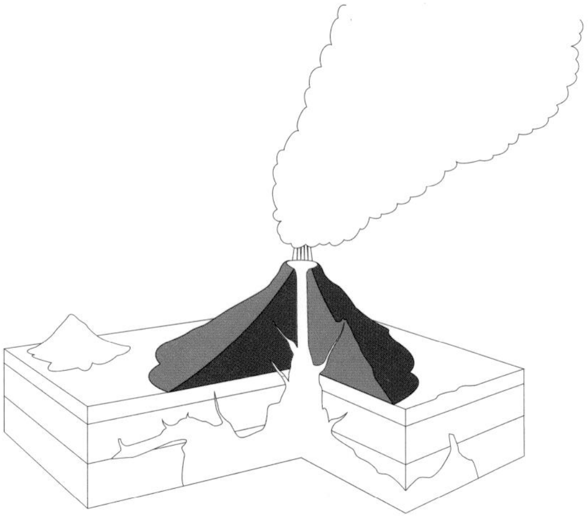

cone

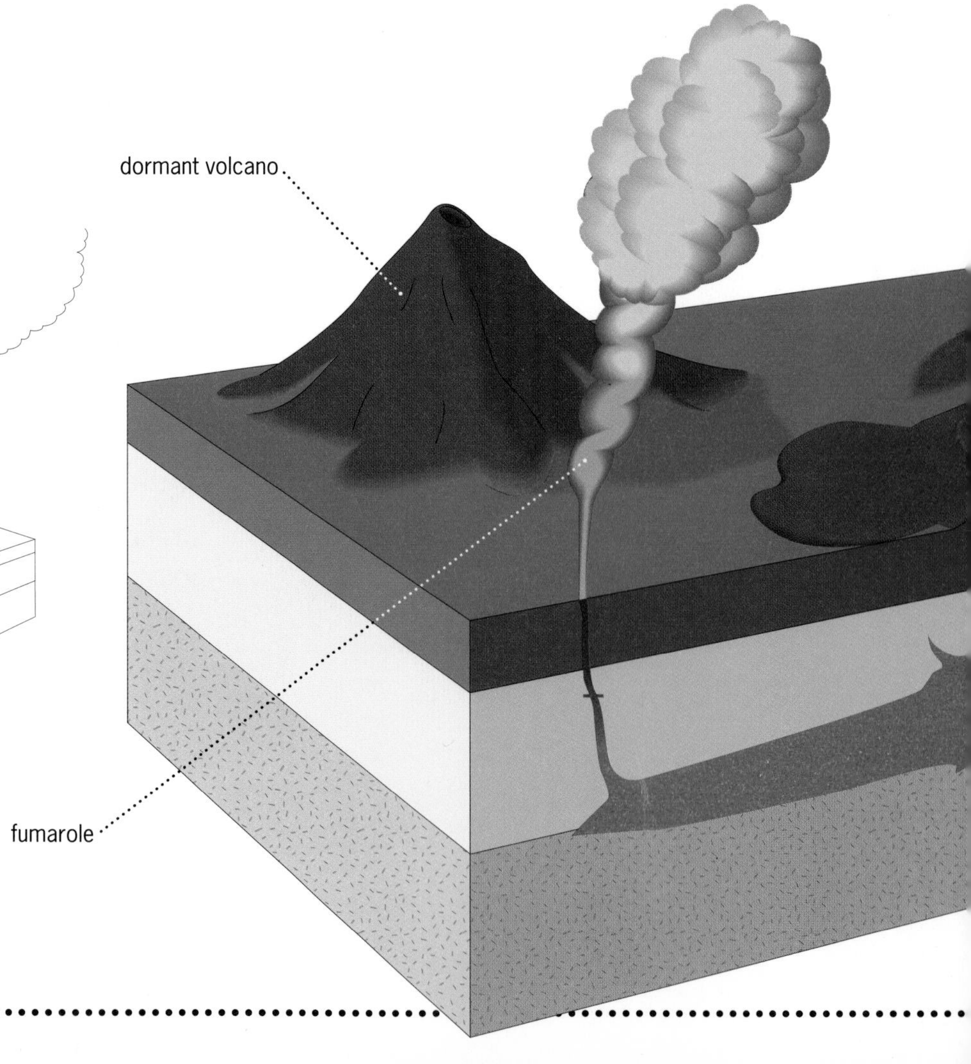
dormant volcano
fumarole

VOLCANO

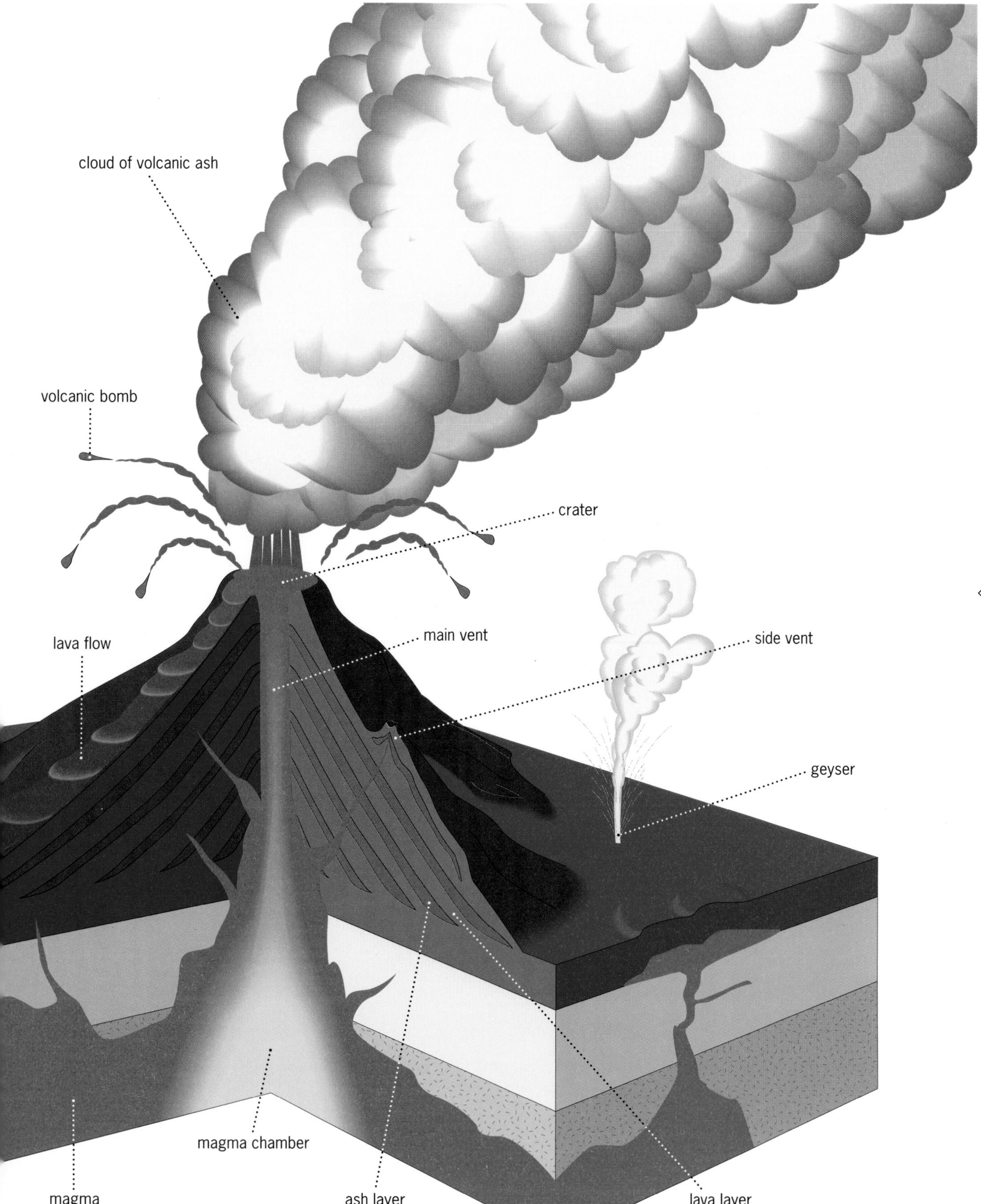
cloud of volcanic ash
volcanic bomb
crater
lava flow
main vent
side vent
geyser
magma
magma chamber
ash layer
lava layer

GLACIER

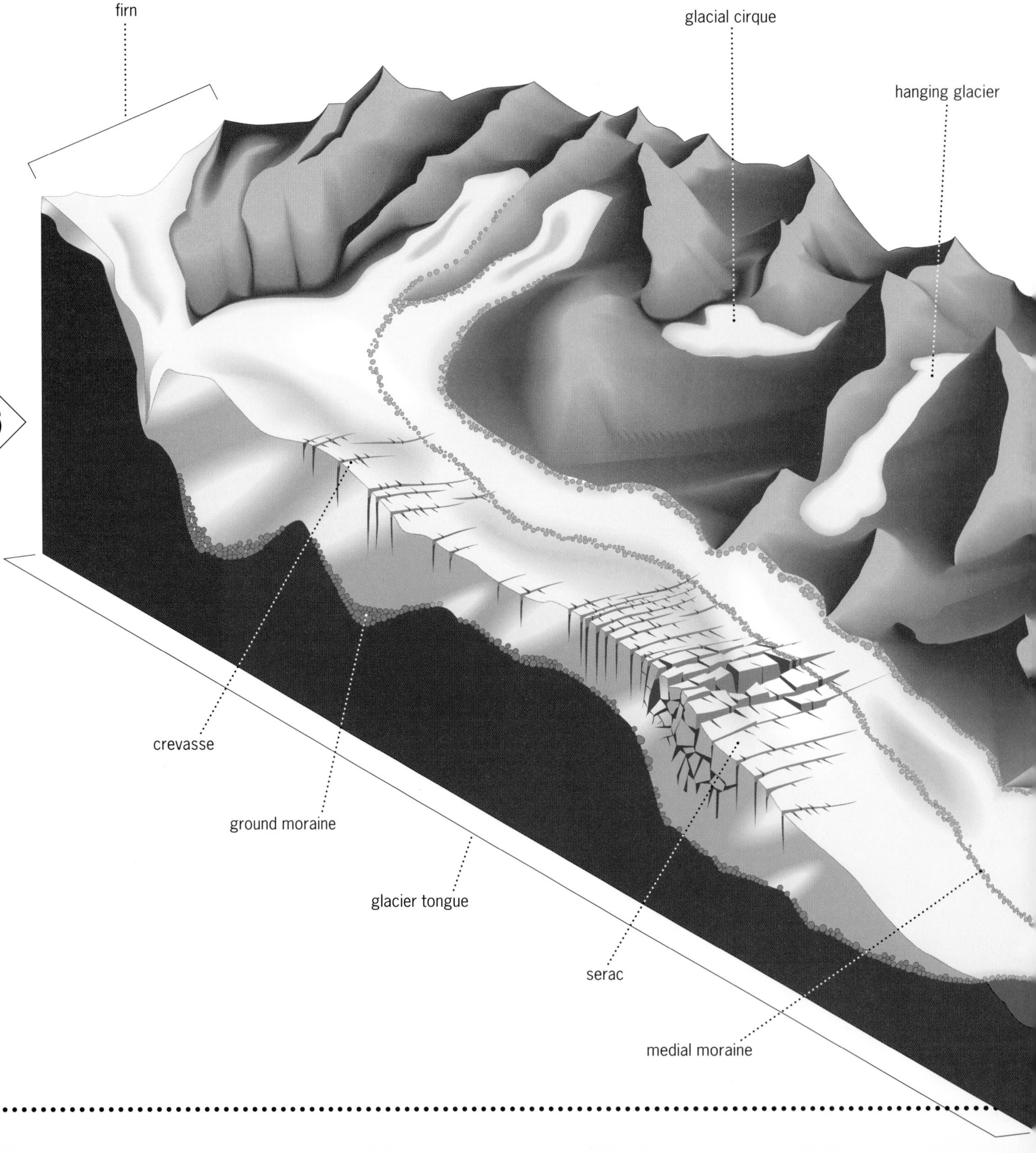
firn
glacial cirque
hanging glacier
crevasse
ground moraine
glacier tongue
serac
medial moraine

MOUNTAIN

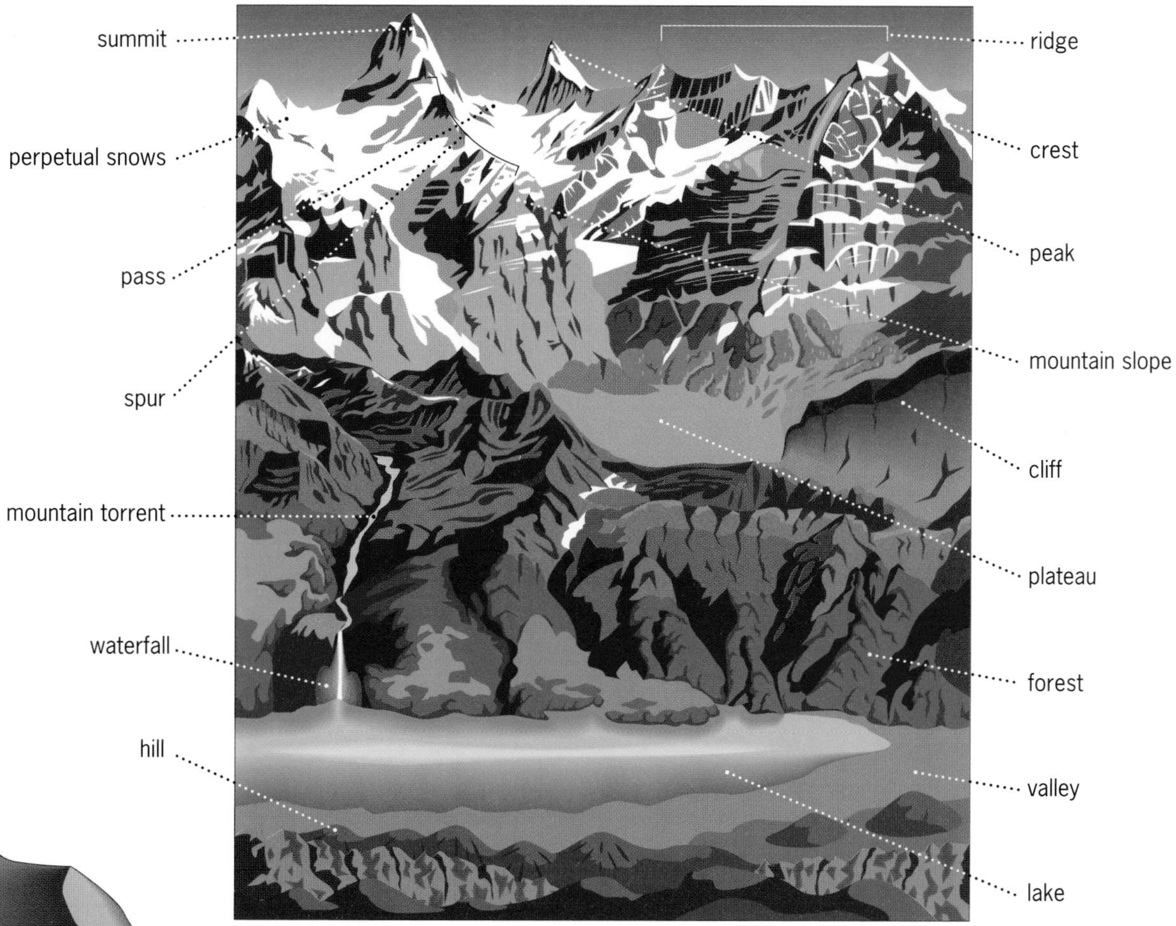
summit
perpetual snows
pass
spur
mountain torrent
waterfall
hill
ridge
crest
peak
mountain slope
cliff
plateau
forest
valley
lake

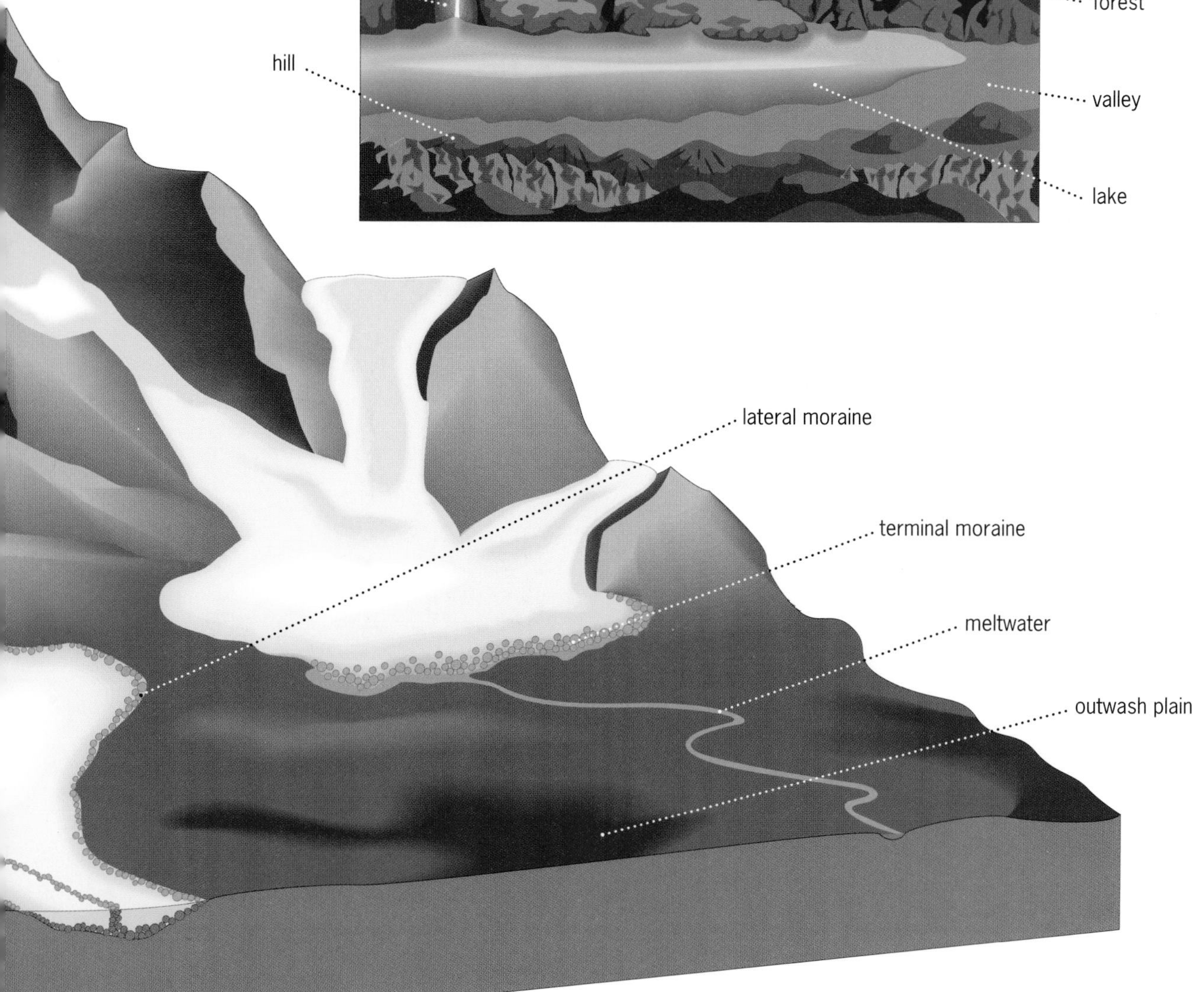
lateral moraine
terminal moraine
meltwater
outwash plain

THE CONTINENTS

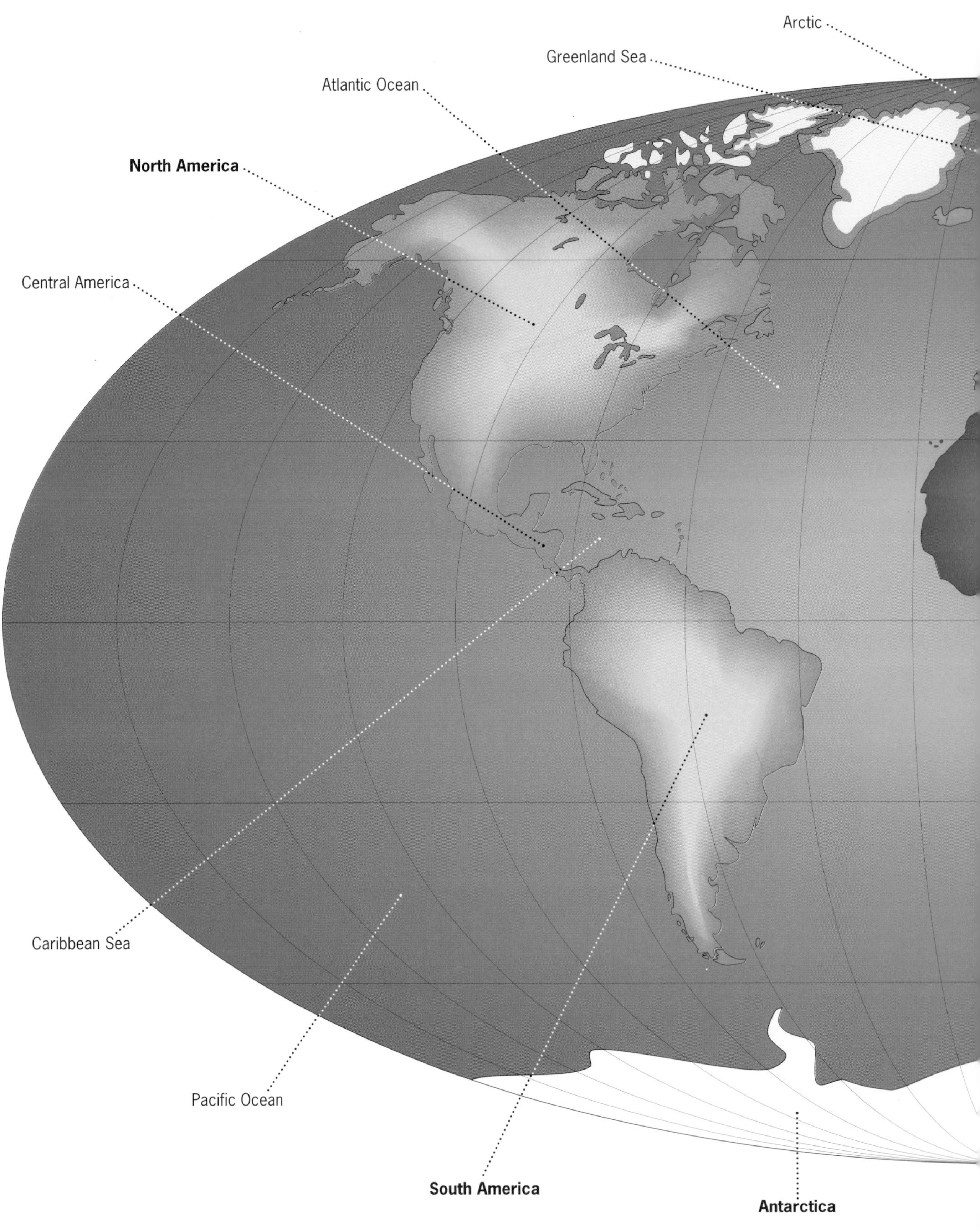

Arctic
Greenland Sea
Atlantic Ocean
North America
Central America
Caribbean Sea
Pacific Ocean
South America
Antarctica

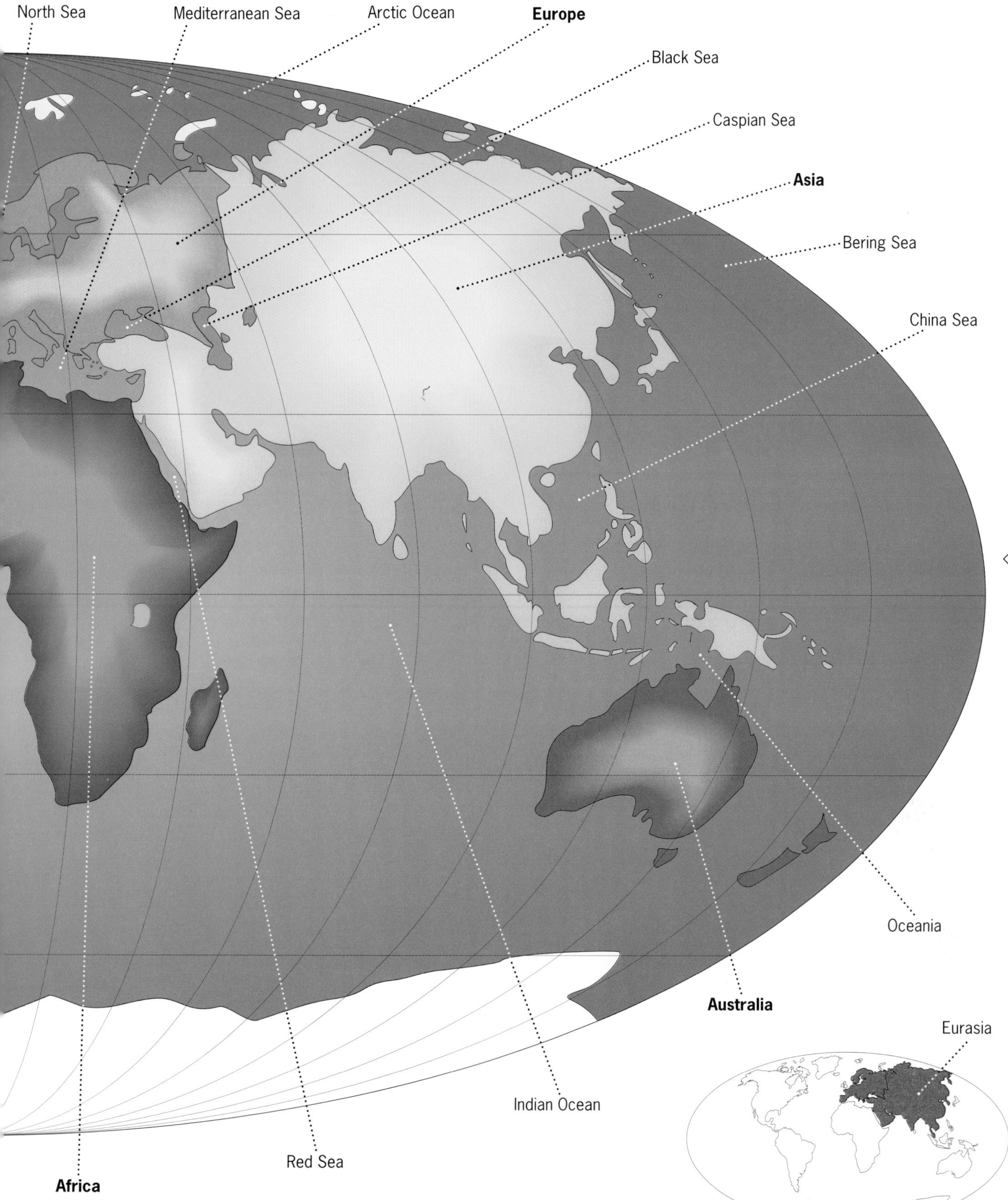
North Sea
Mediterranean Sea
Arctic Ocean
Europe
Black Sea
Caspian Sea
Asia
Bering Sea
China Sea
Oceania
Australia
Eurasia
Indian Ocean
Red Sea
Africa

SEASONS OF THE YEAR

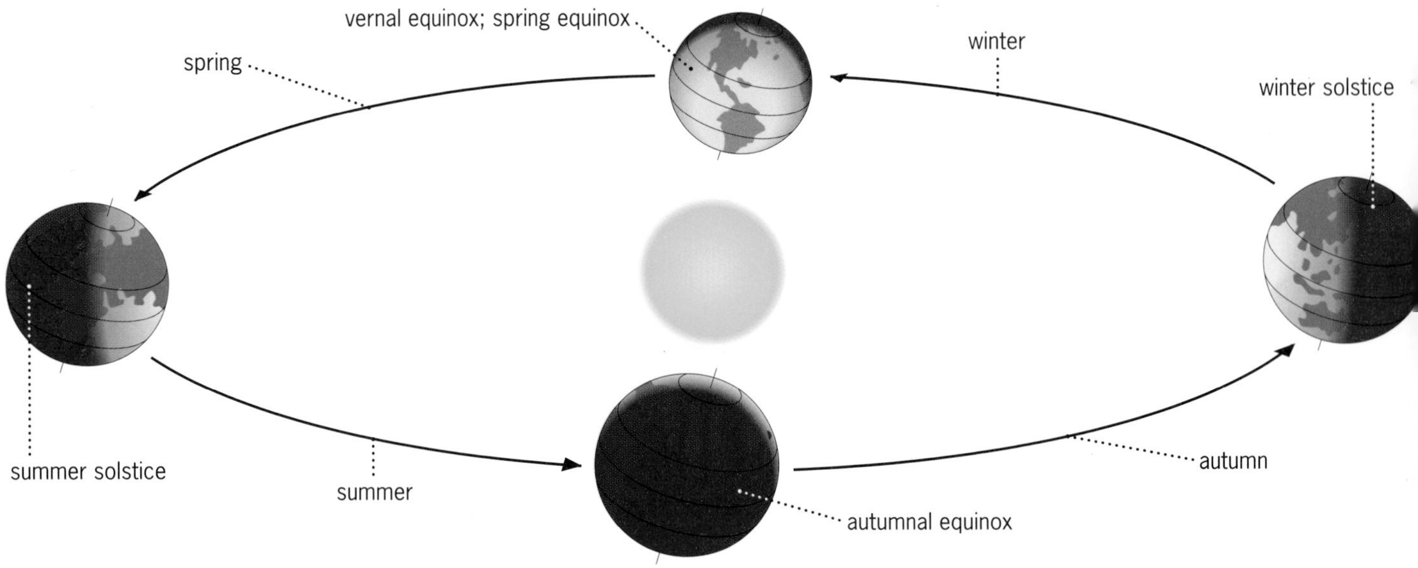
vernal equinox; spring equinox
spring
winter
winter solstice
summer solstice
summer
autumnal equinox
autumn

STRUCTURE OF THE BIOSPHERE

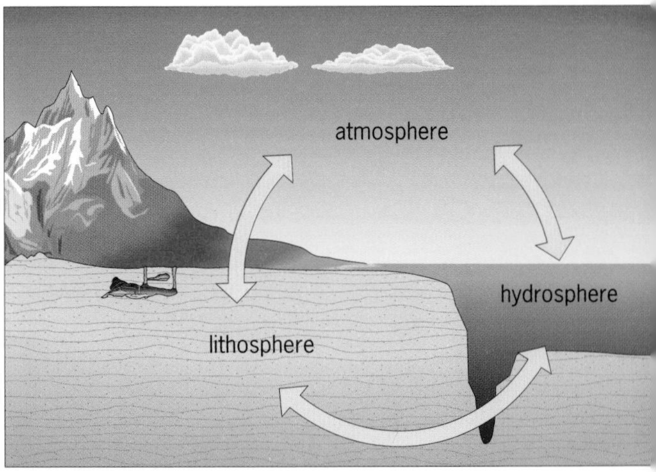
atmosphere
hydrosphere
lithosphere

ELEVATION ZONES AND VEGETATION

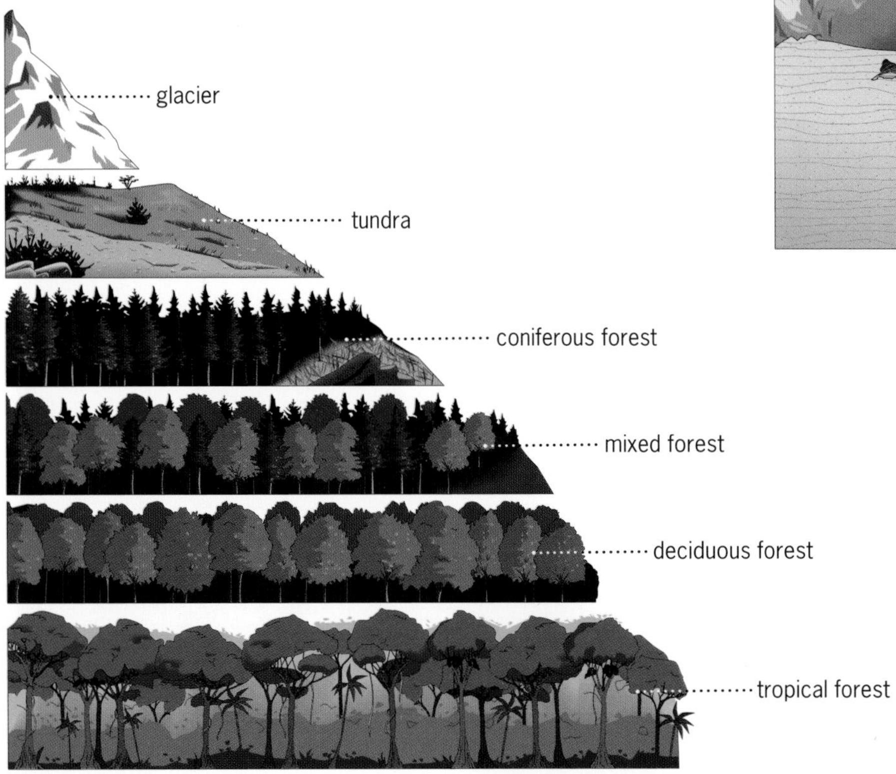
glacier
tundra
coniferous forest
mixed forest
deciduous forest
tropical forest

CLIMATES OF THE WORLD

tropical climates

- tropical rain forest
- tropical savanna
- steppe
- desert

temperate climates

- humid - long summer
- humid - short summer
- marine

polar climates

- polar tundra
- polar ice cap

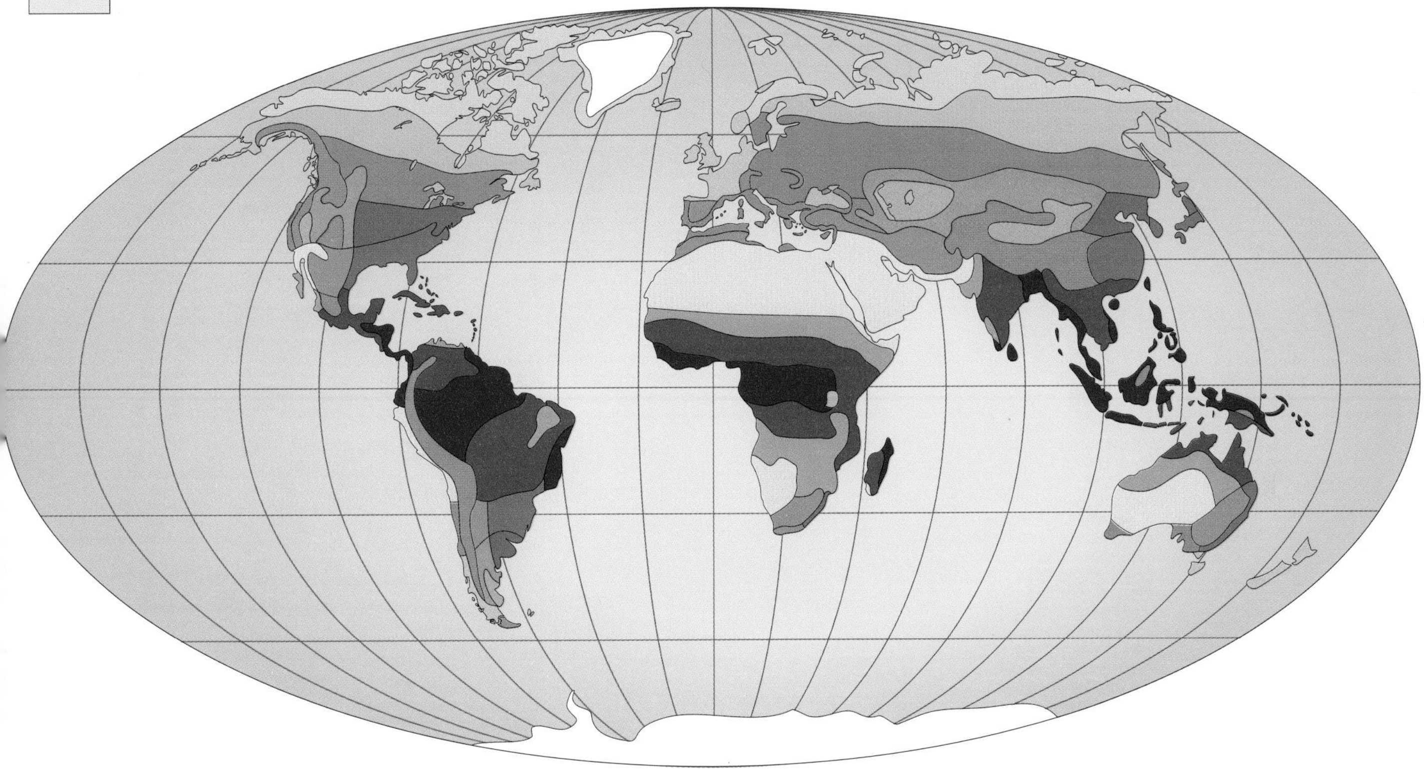

subtropical climates

- Mediterranean subtropical
- humid subtropical
- dry subtropical

continental climates

- dry continental - arid
- dry continental - semiarid

highland climates

- highland climates

subarctic climates

- subarctic climates

WEATHER

mist

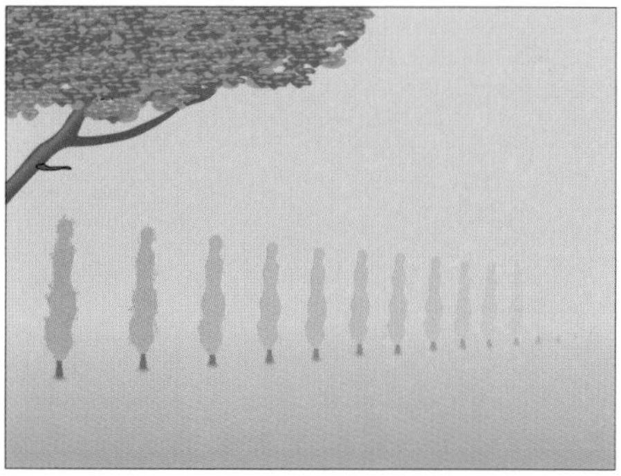
fog

dew

glazed frost

stormy sky

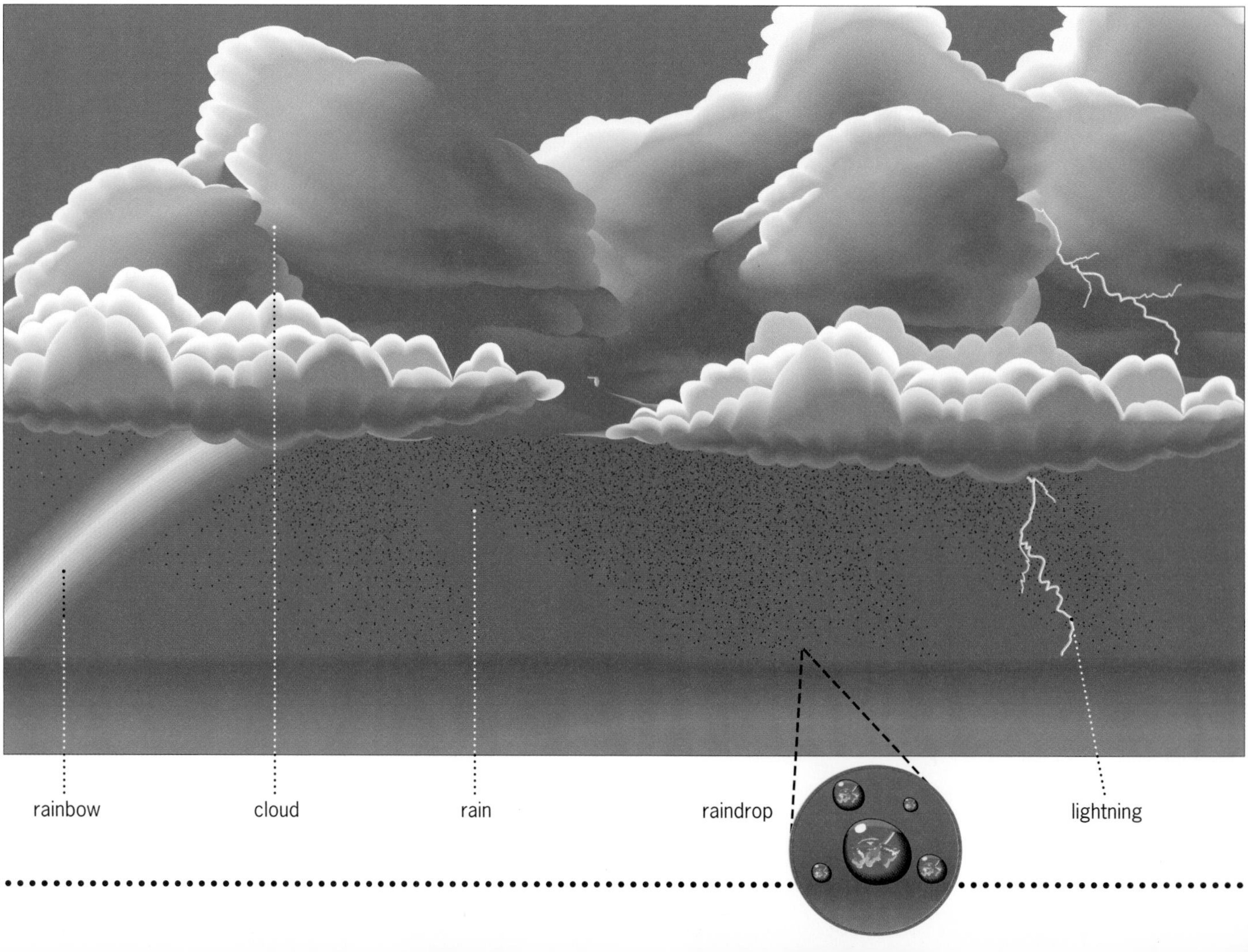
rainbow
cloud
rain
raindrop
lightning

METEOROLOGICAL MEASURING INSTRUMENTS

MEASURE OF WIND DIRECTION

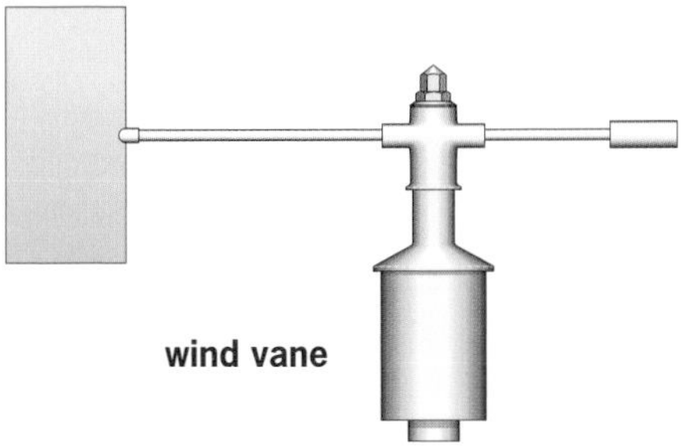

wind vane

MEASURE OF WIND STRENGTH

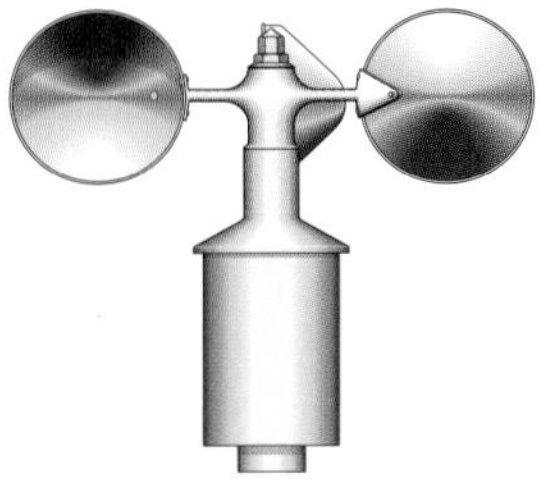

anemometer

MEASURE OF HUMIDITY

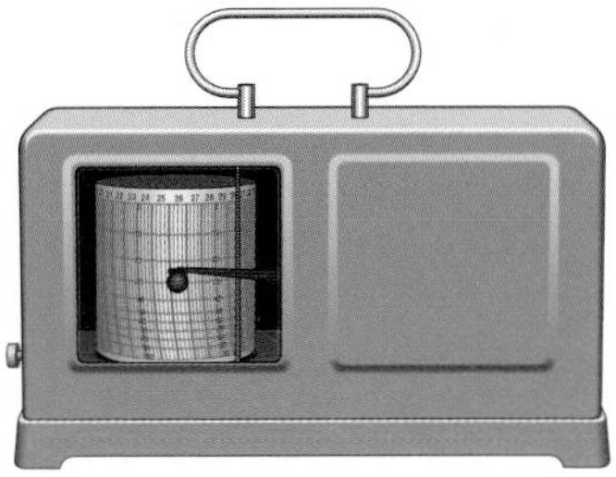

hygrograph

MEASURE OF RAINFALL

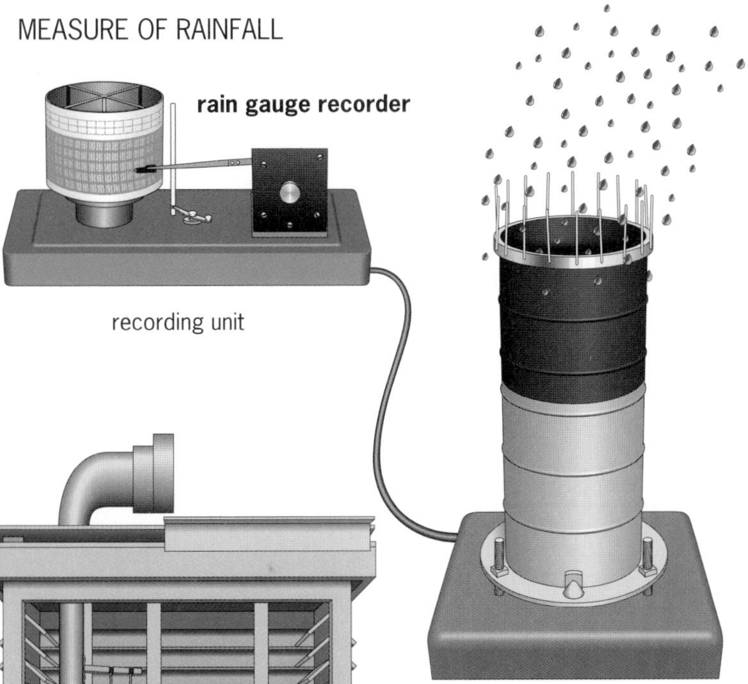

rain gauge recorder

recording unit

collecting vessel

direct-reading rain gauge

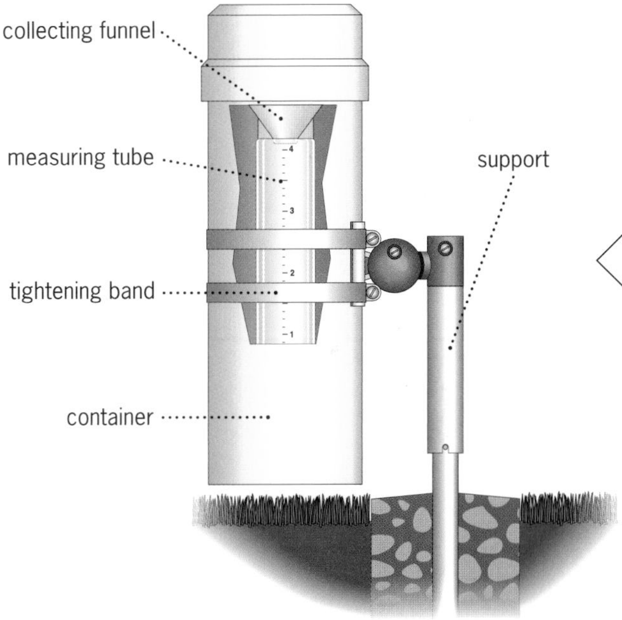
collecting funnel
measuring tube
support
tightening band
container

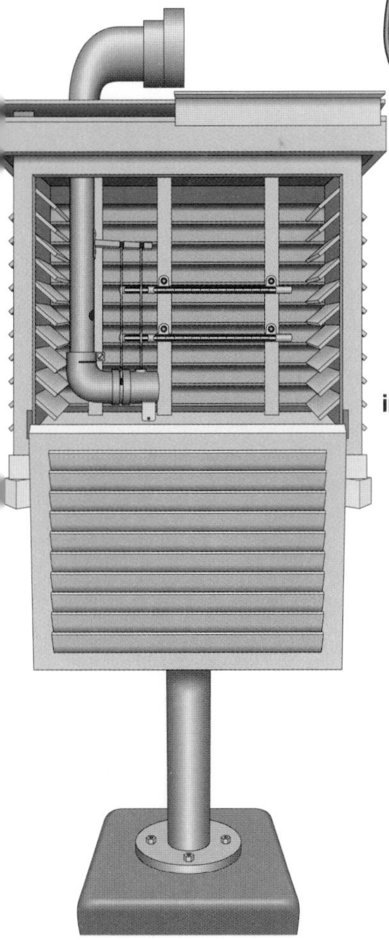

instrument shelter

MEASURE OF TEMPERATURE

minimum thermometer

maximum thermometer

mercury barometer

MEASURE OF AIR PRESSURE

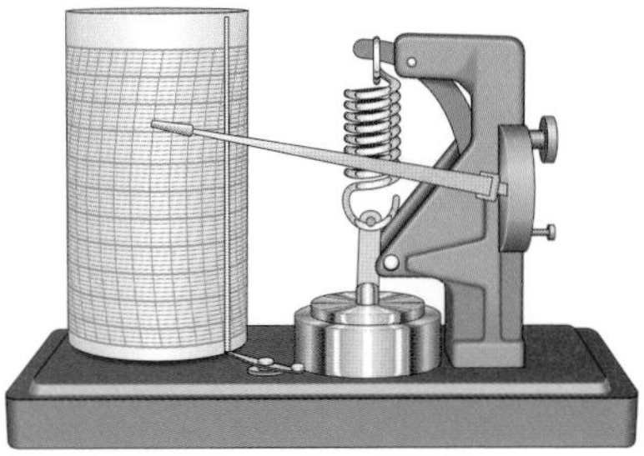

barograph

CARTOGRAPHY

hemispheres

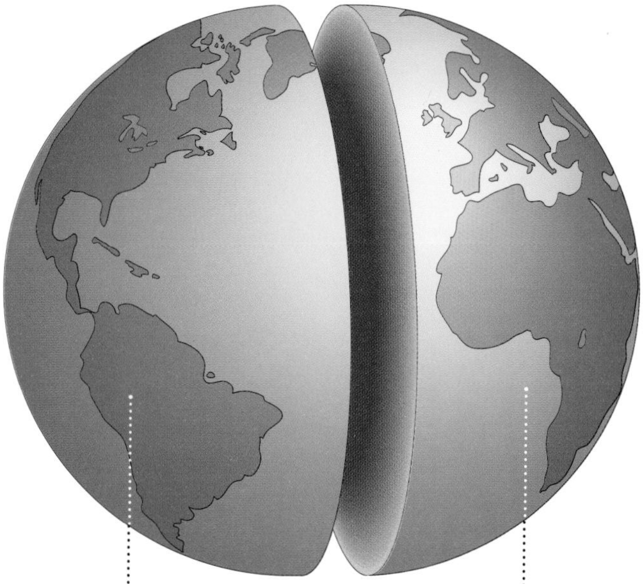
Western hemisphere
Eastern hemisphere

Northern hemisphere
Southern hemisphere

 GRID SYSTEM

lines of latitude

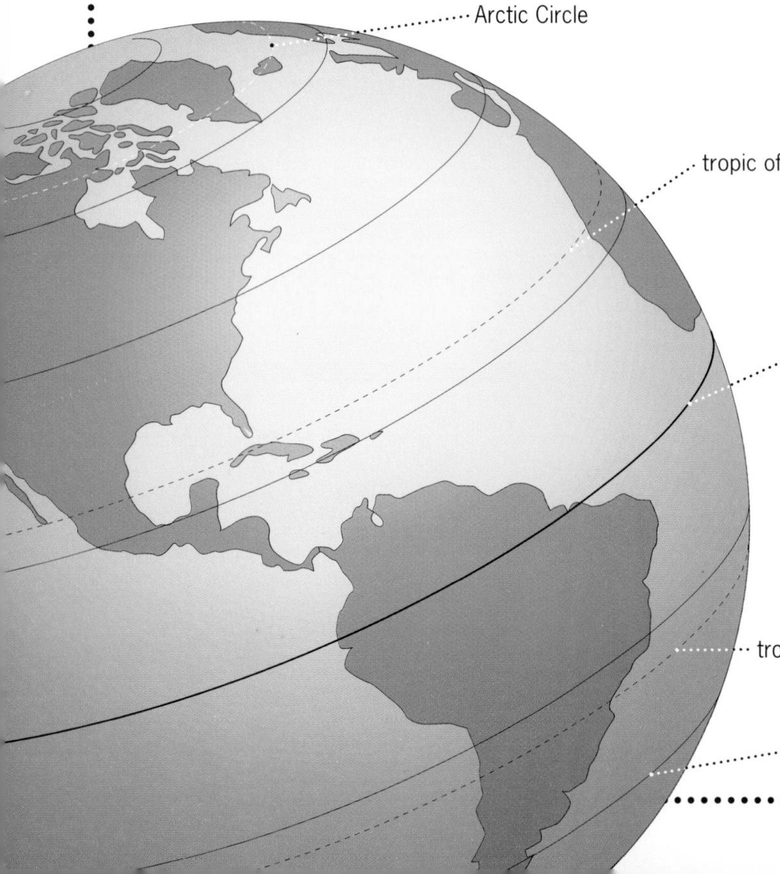
Arctic Circle
tropic of Cancer
Equator
tropic of Capricorn
parallel

lines of longitude

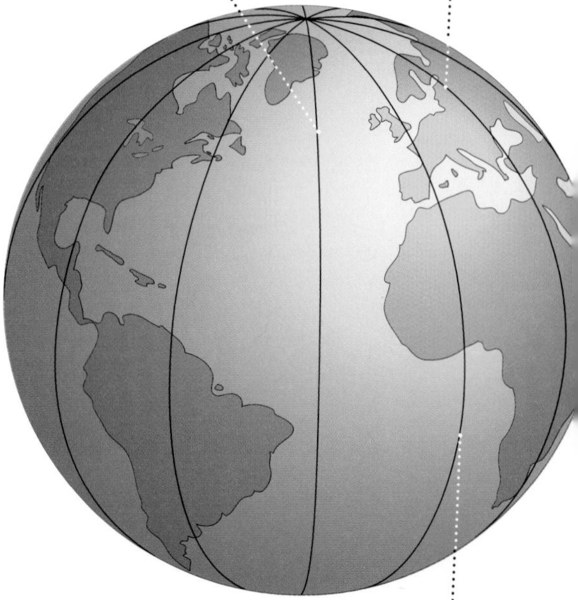
Western meridian
Eastern meridian
prime meridian

MAP PROJECTIONS

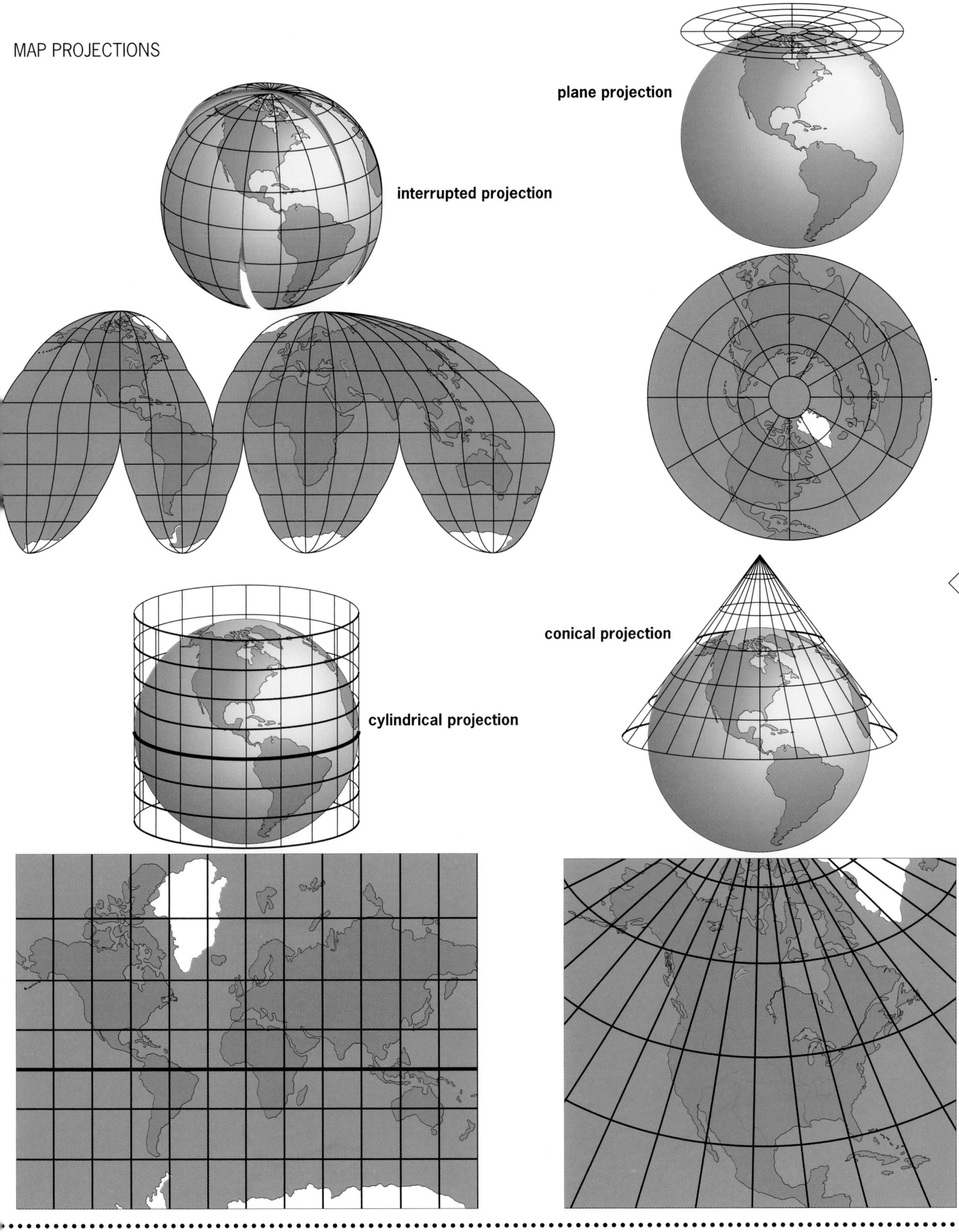
plane projection
interrupted projection
conical projection
cylindrical projection

CARTOGRAPHY

political map

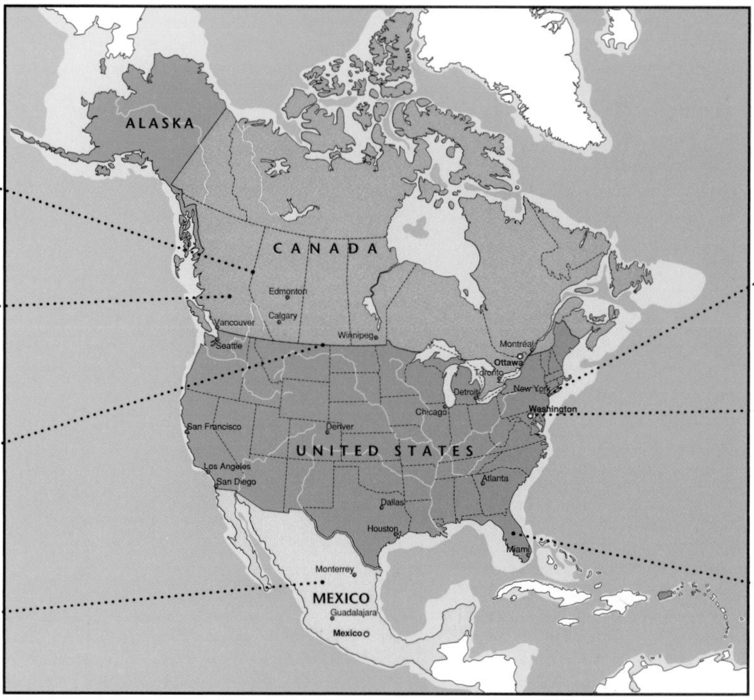
internal boundary
province
international boundary
country
city
capital
state
ALASKA
CANADA
Edmonton
Calgary
Vancouver
Seattle
Winnipeg
Montréal
Ottawa
Toronto
Detroit
New York
Washington
Chicago
Denver
San Francisco
UNITED STATES
Los Angeles
San Diego
Atlanta
Dallas
Houston
Miami
Monterrey
MEXICO
Guadalajara
Mexico

physical map

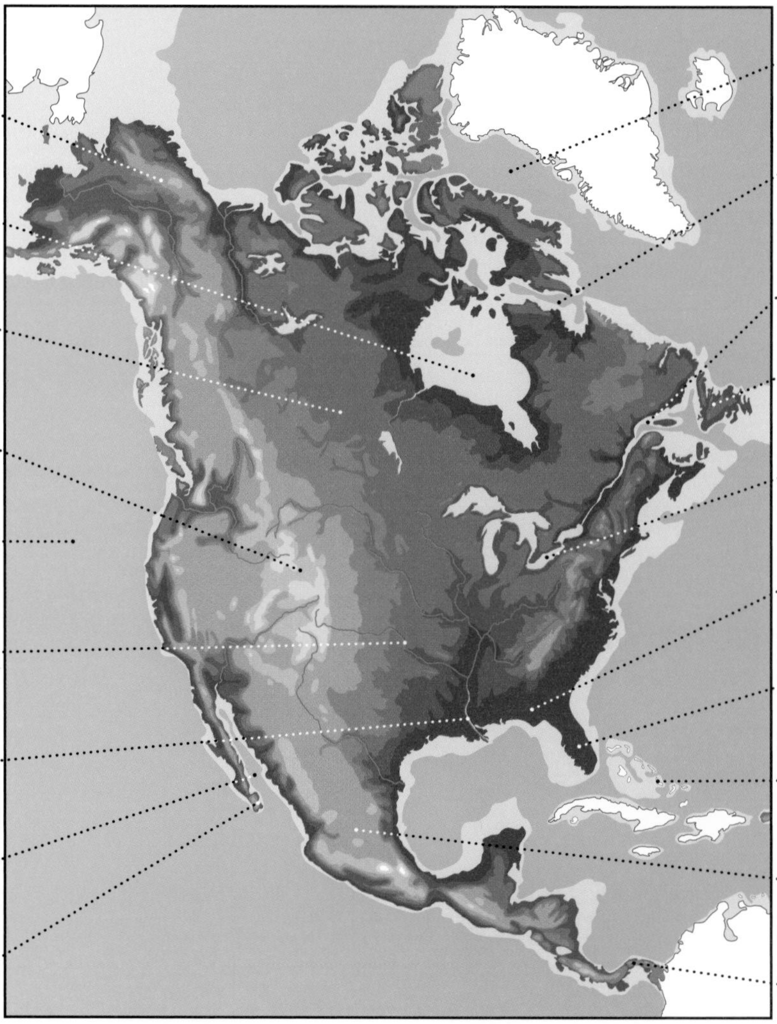
mountain range
bay
prairie
mountain range
ocean
river
river
gulf
cape
sea
strait
river estuary
island
lake
plain
peninsula
archipelago
plateau
isthmus

road map

highway
highway number
rest area
service area
belt highway
secondary road
road
road number
airport
point of interest
national park
scenic route; tourist route
Boston

COMPASS CARD

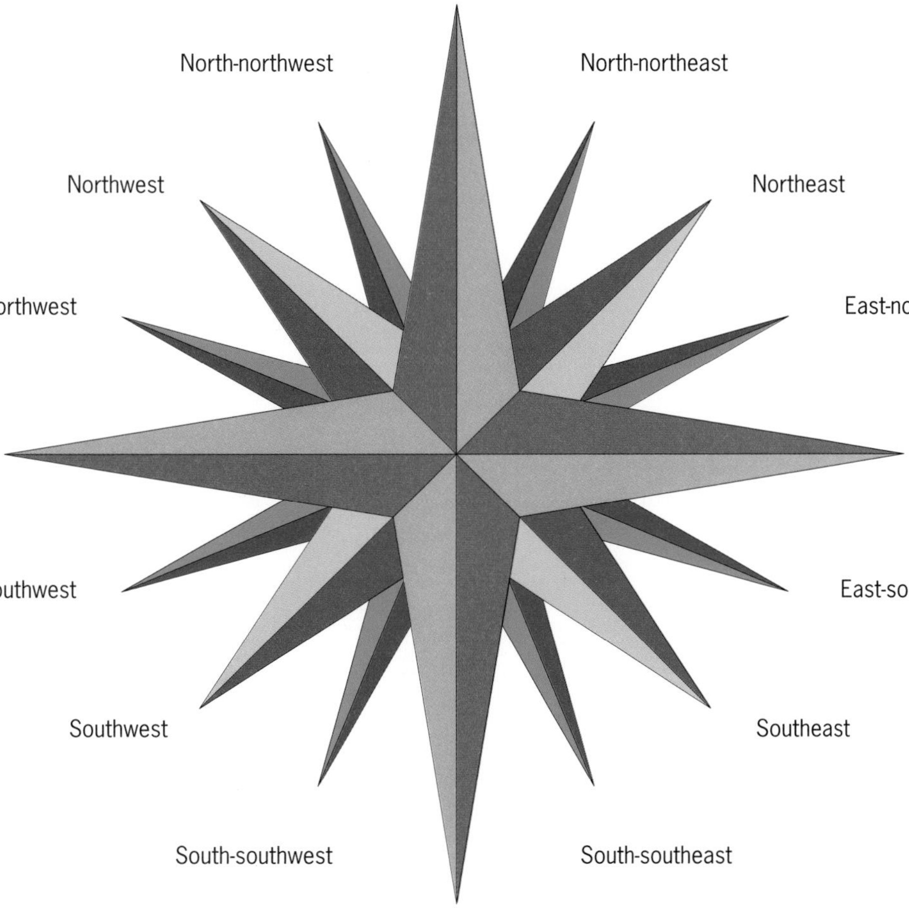
North
North-northeast
Northeast
East-northeast
East
East-southeast
Southeast
South-southeast
South
South-southwest
Southwest
West-southwest
West
West-northwest
Northwest
North-northwest

ECOLOGY

greenhouse effect

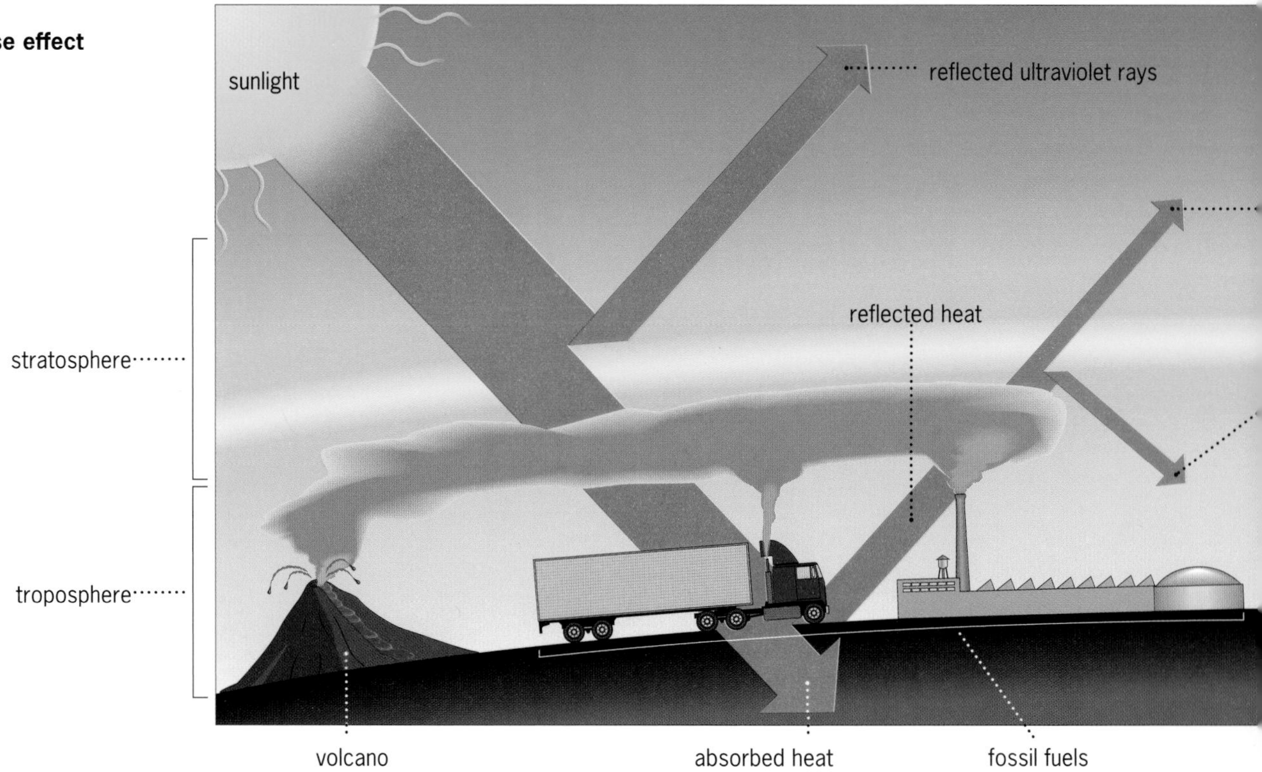
sunlight
reflected ultraviolet rays
reflected heat
stratosphere
troposphere
volcano
absorbed heat
fossil fuels

food chain

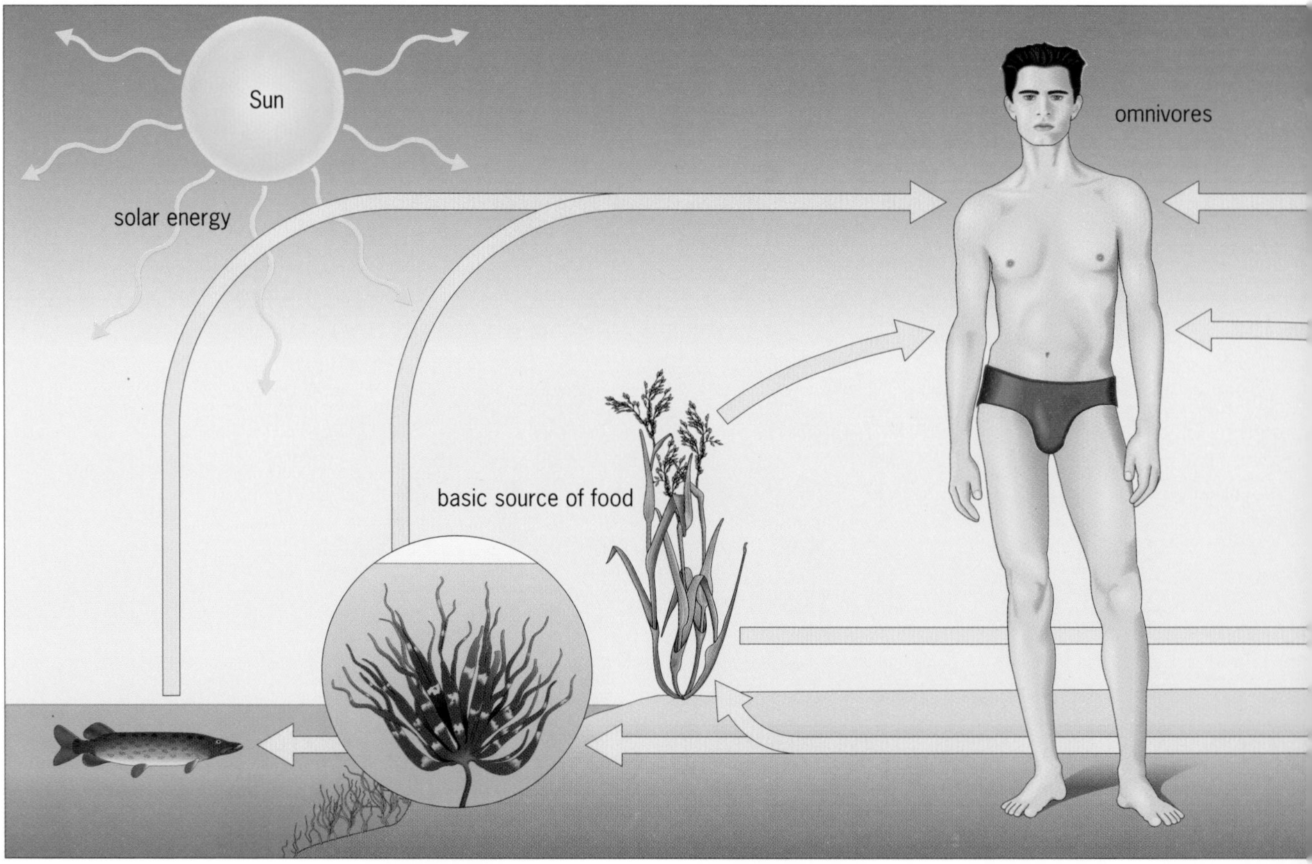
Sun
solar energy
omnivores
basic source of food

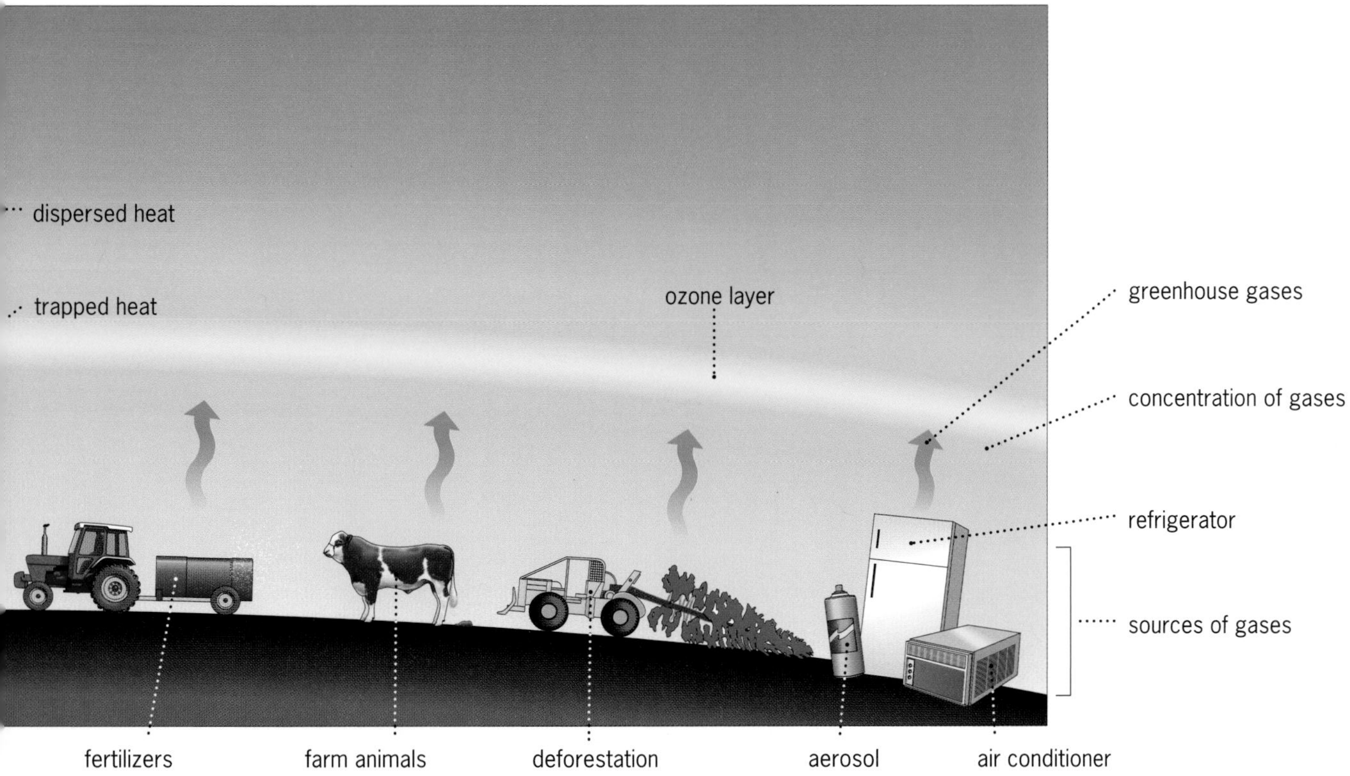
dispersed heat
trapped heat
ozone layer
greenhouse gases
concentration of gases
refrigerator
sources of gases
fertilizers
farm animals
deforestation
aerosol
air conditioner

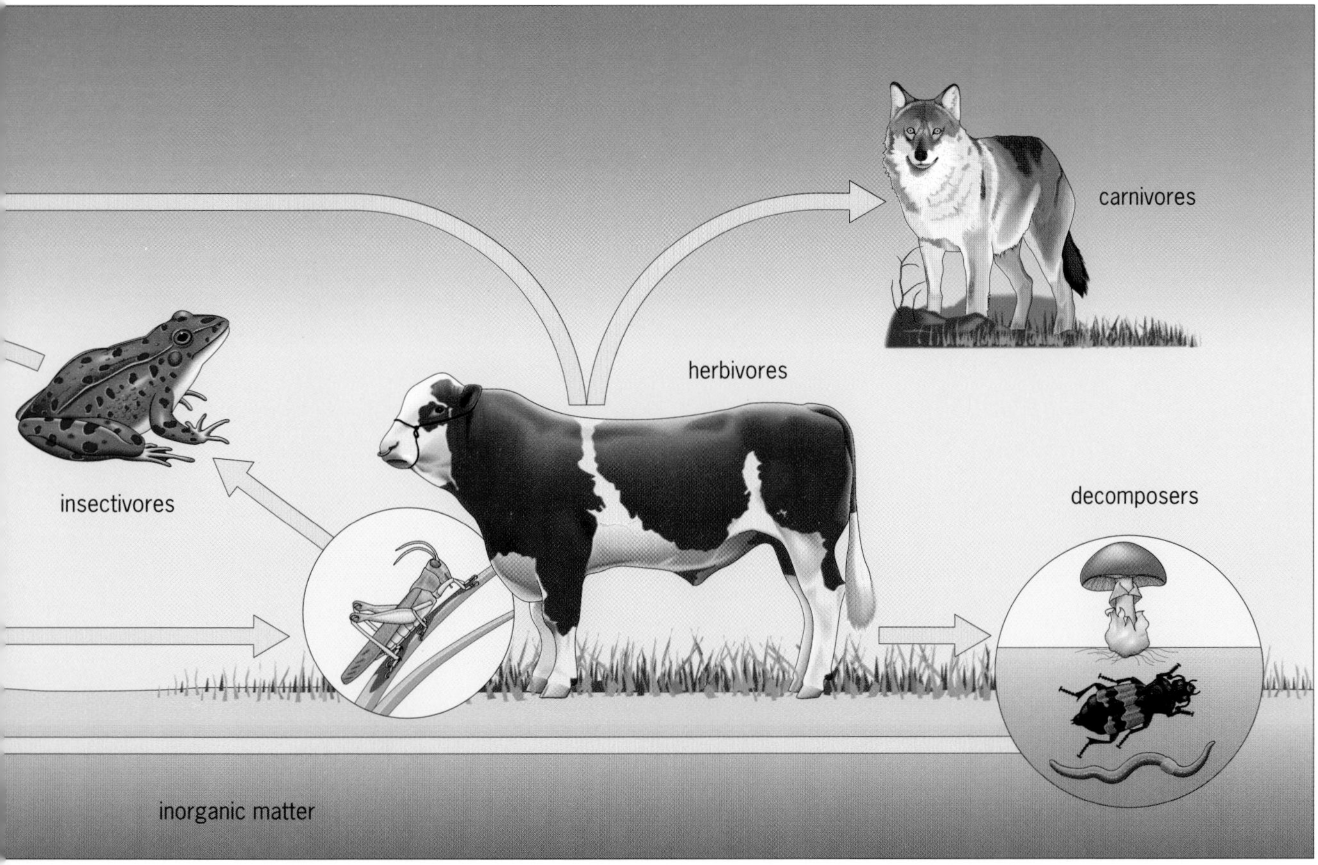
carnivores
herbivores
insectivores
decomposers
inorganic matter

ECOLOGY

atmospheric pollution

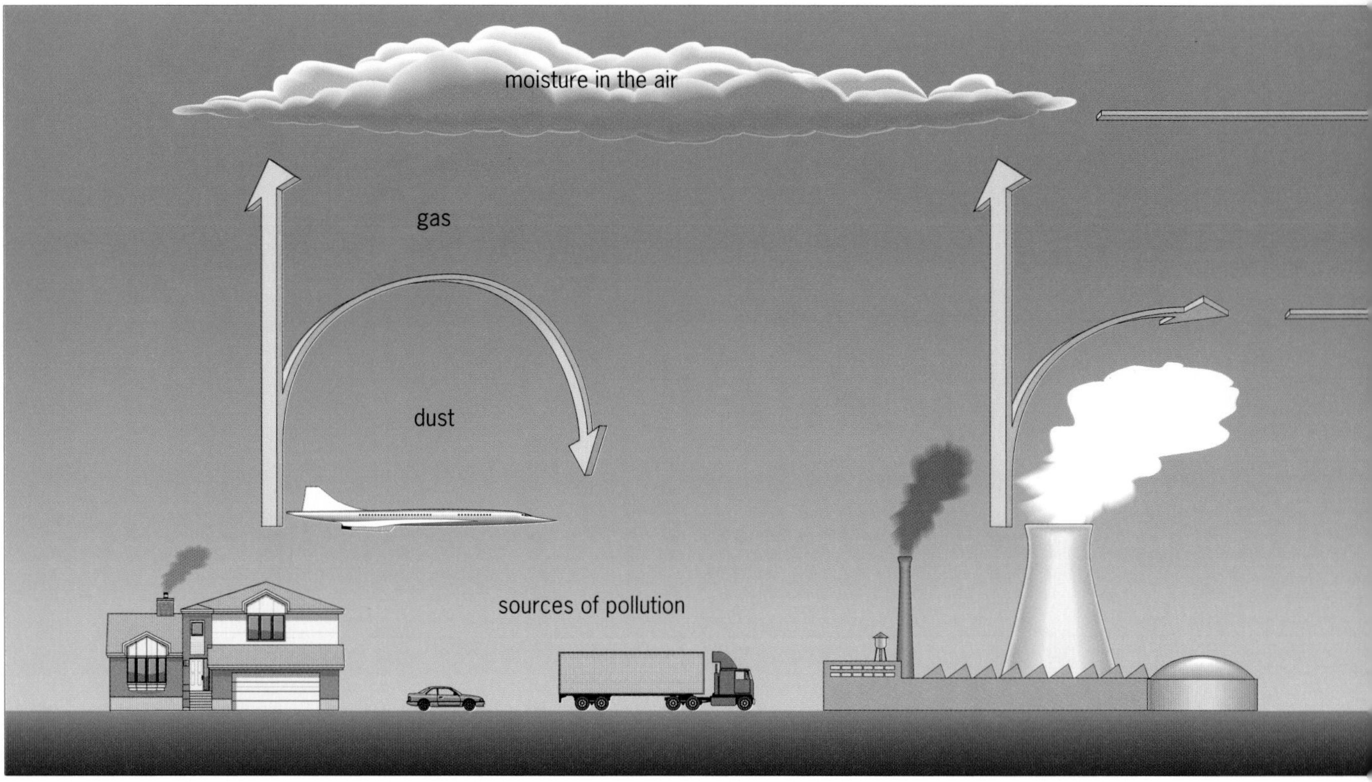
moisture in the air
gas
dust
sources of pollution

water cycle

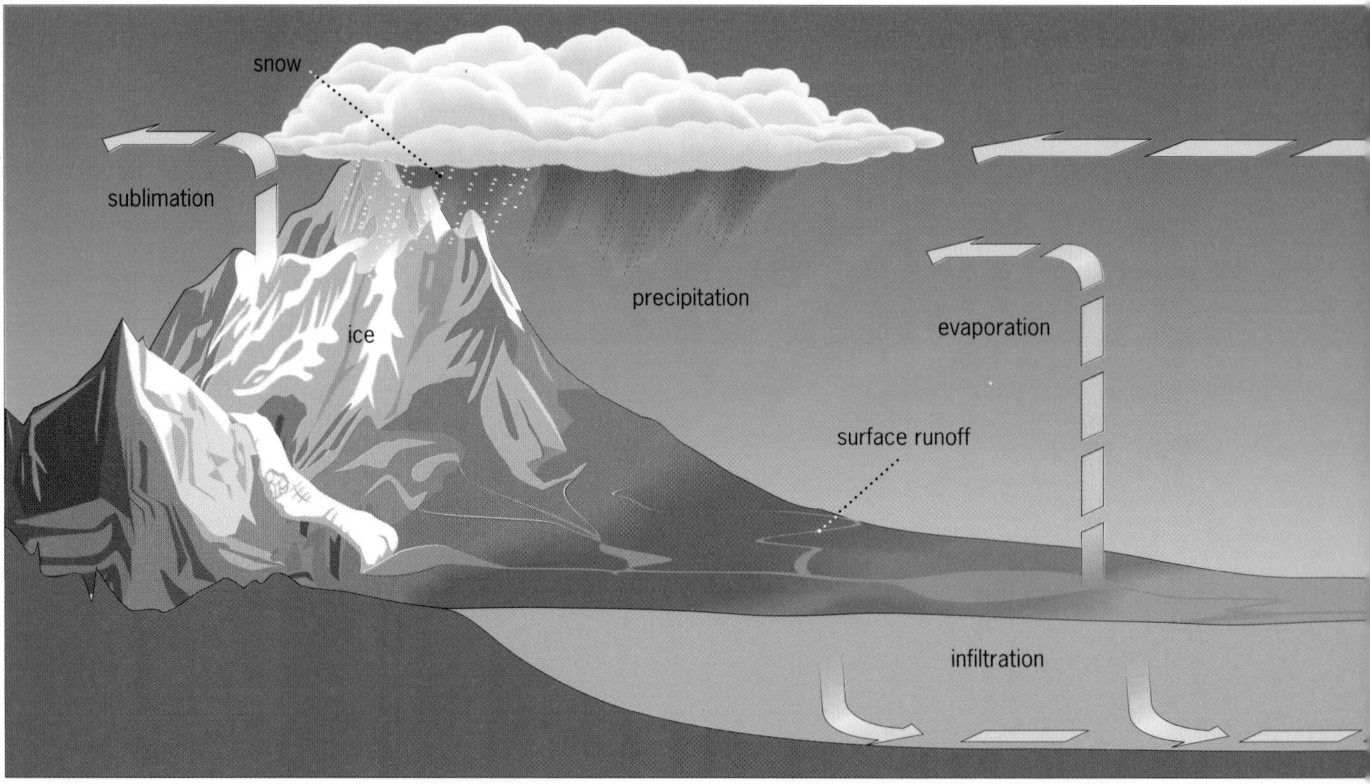
snow
sublimation
precipitation
ice
evaporation
surface runoff
infiltration

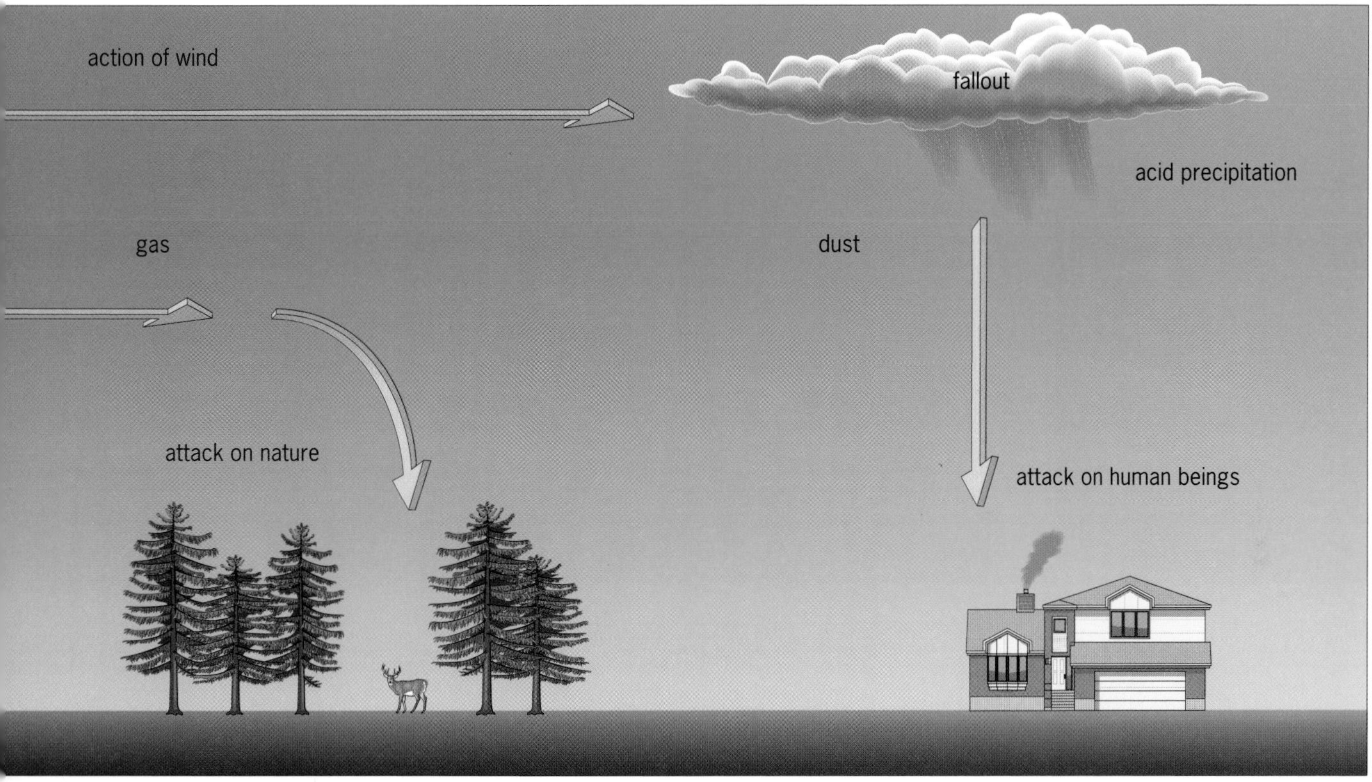
action of wind
fallout
acid precipitation
gas
dust
attack on nature
attack on human beings

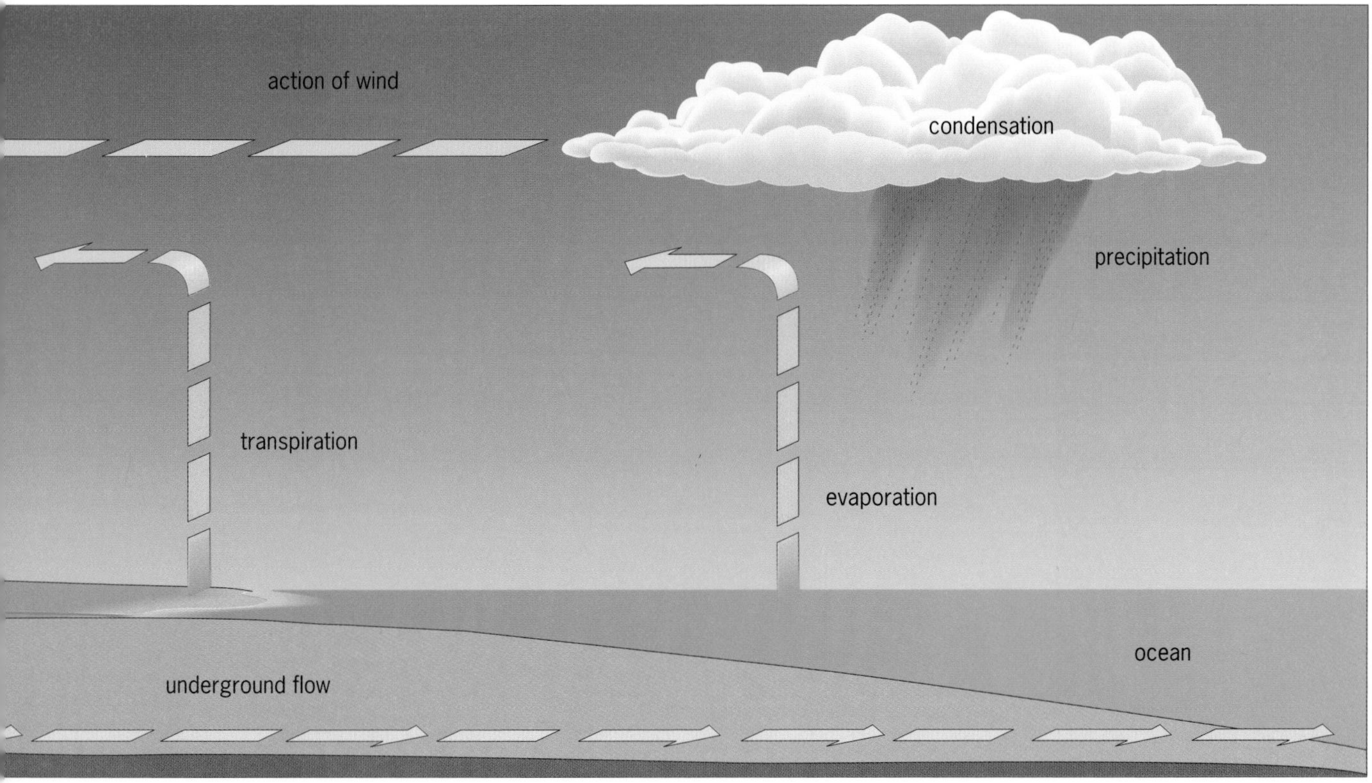
action of wind
condensation
precipitation
transpiration
evaporation
ocean
underground flow

ECOLOGY

food pollution on ground

acid rain
farm pollution
industrial pollution

food pollution in water

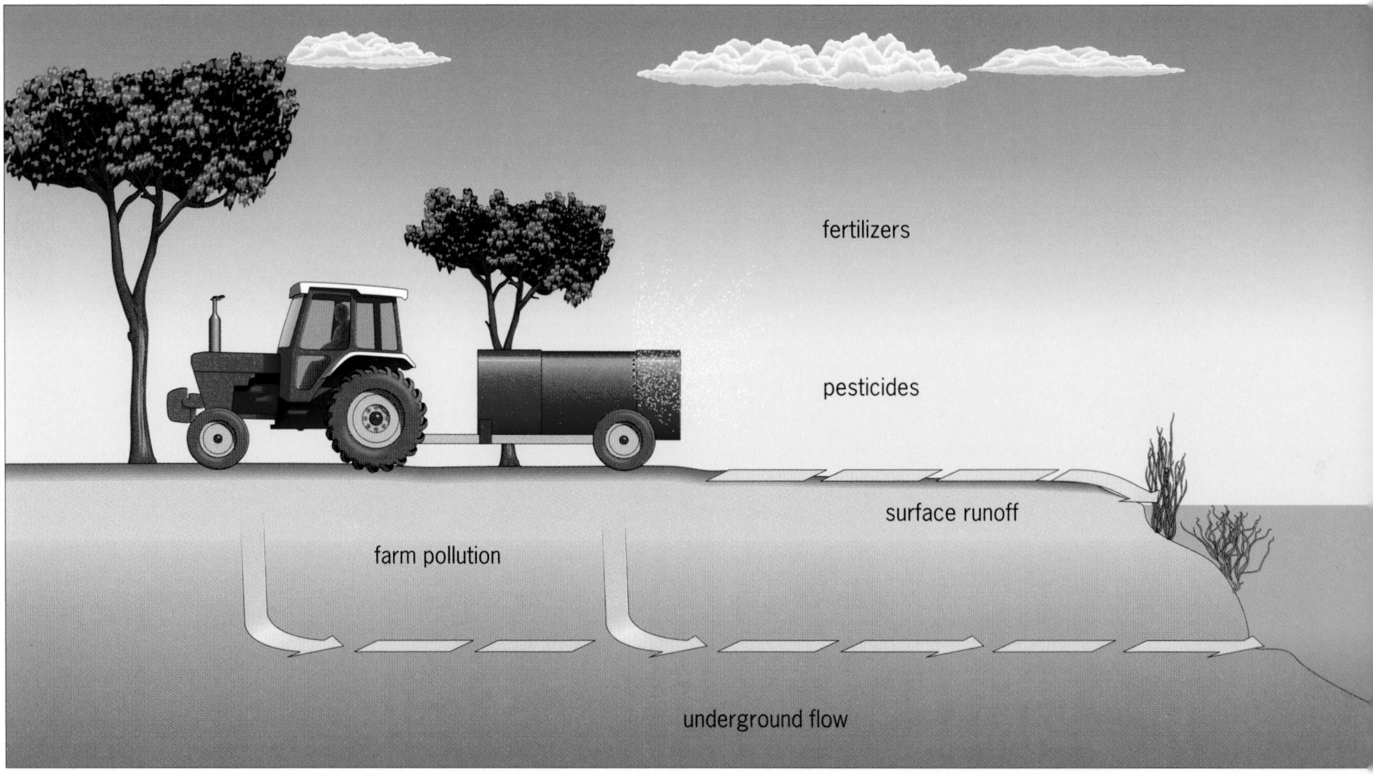
fertilizers
pesticides
surface runoff
farm pollution
underground flow

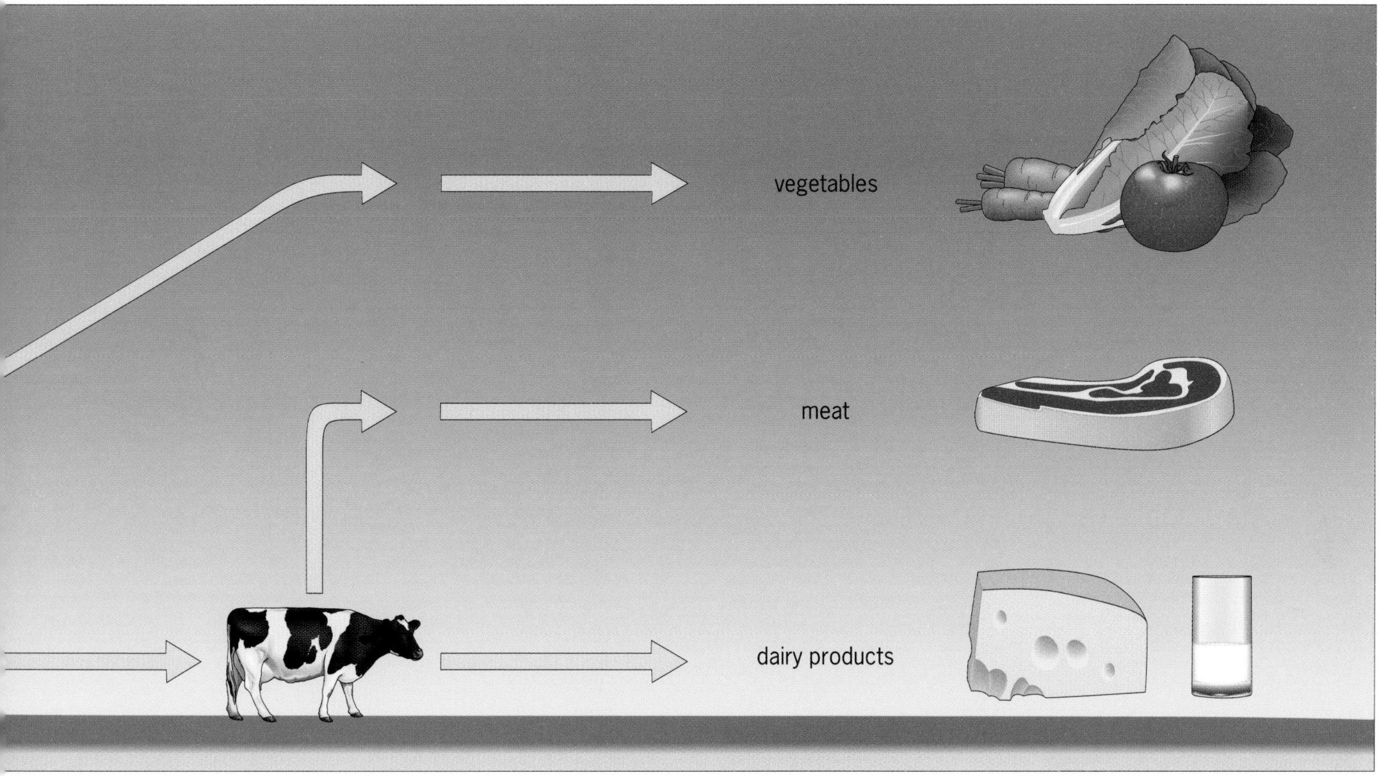
vegetables
meat
dairy products

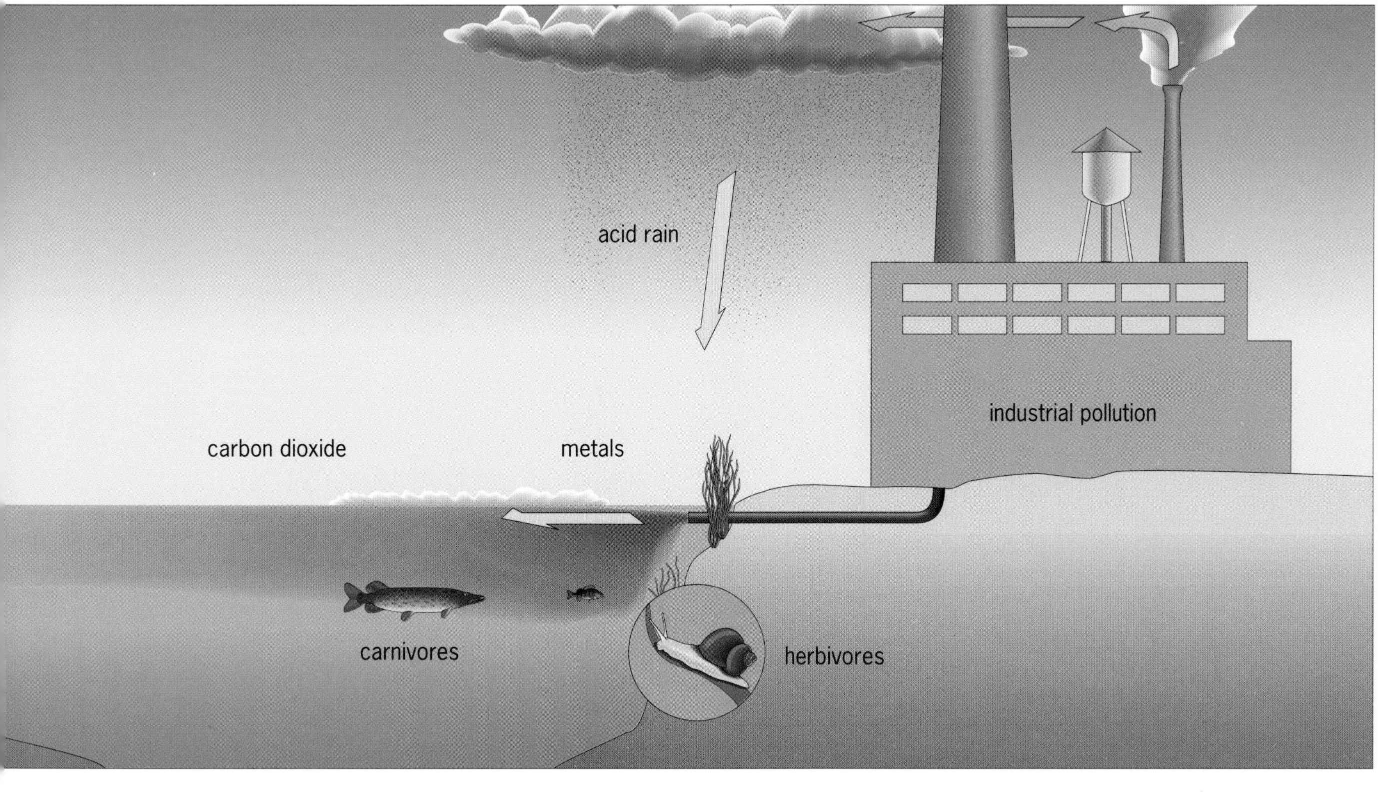
acid rain
industrial pollution
carbon dioxide
metals
carnivores
herbivores

PLANT AND SOIL

SOIL PROFILE

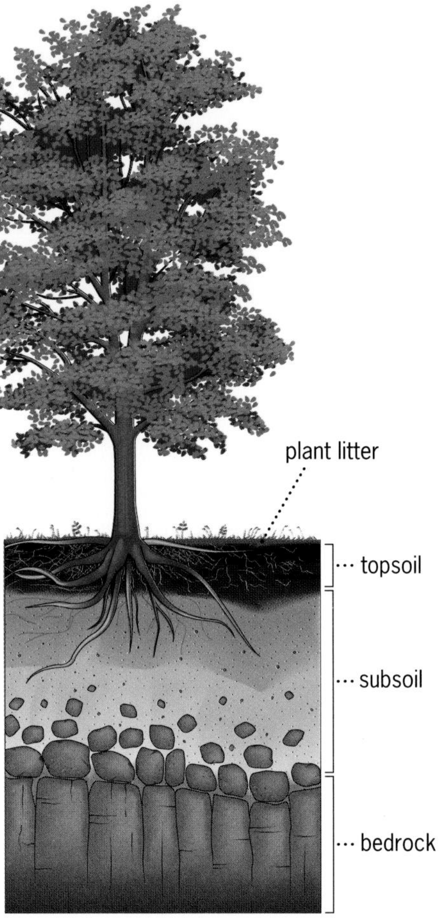
plant litter
topsoil
subsoil
bedrock

GERMINATION

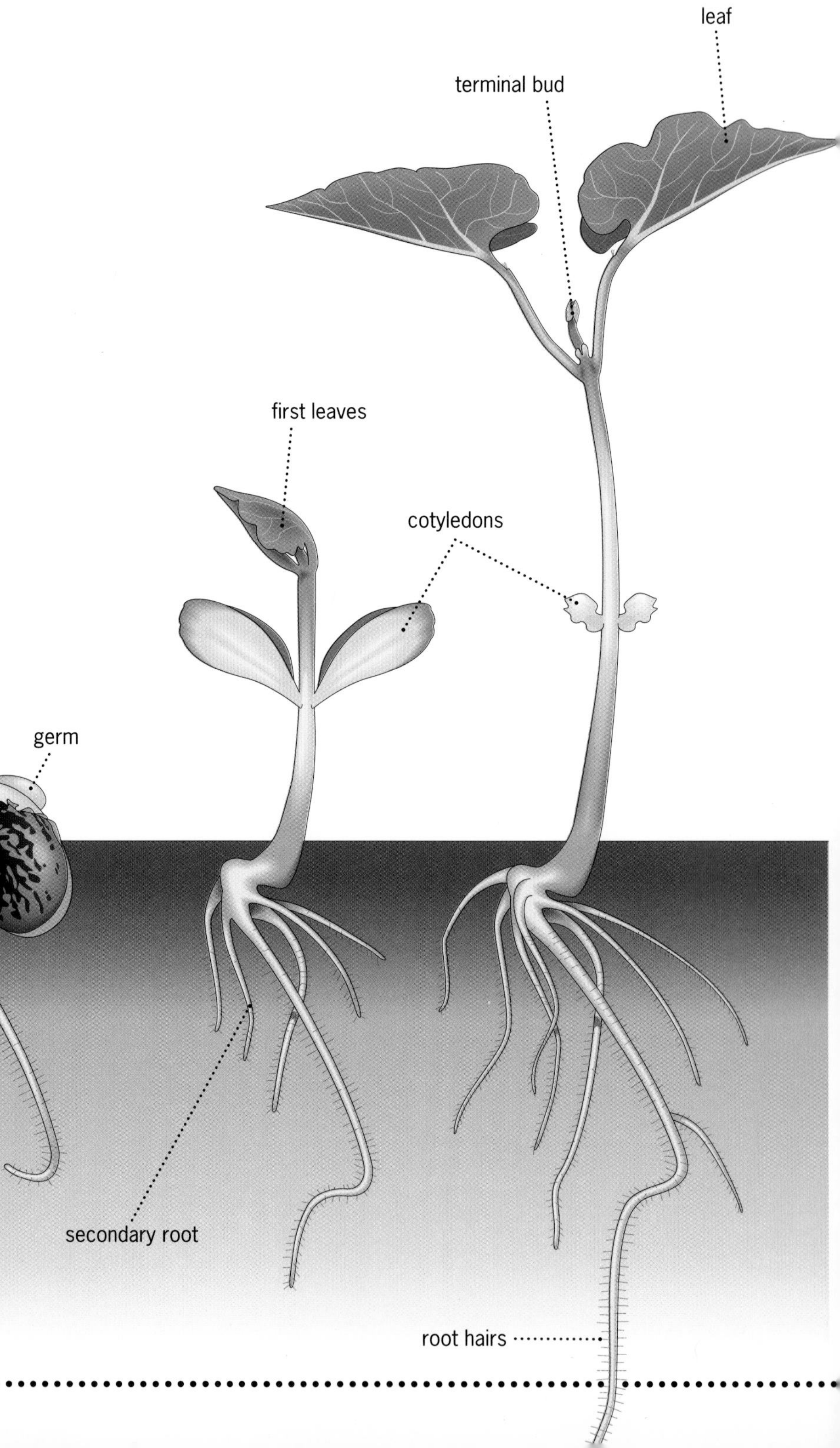
leaf
terminal bud
first leaves
cotyledons
secondary root
root hairs

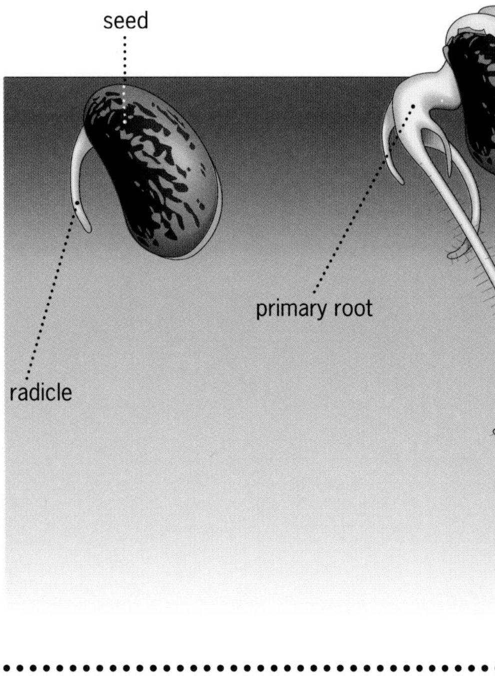
germ
seed
primary root
radicle

MUSHROOM

structure of a mushroom

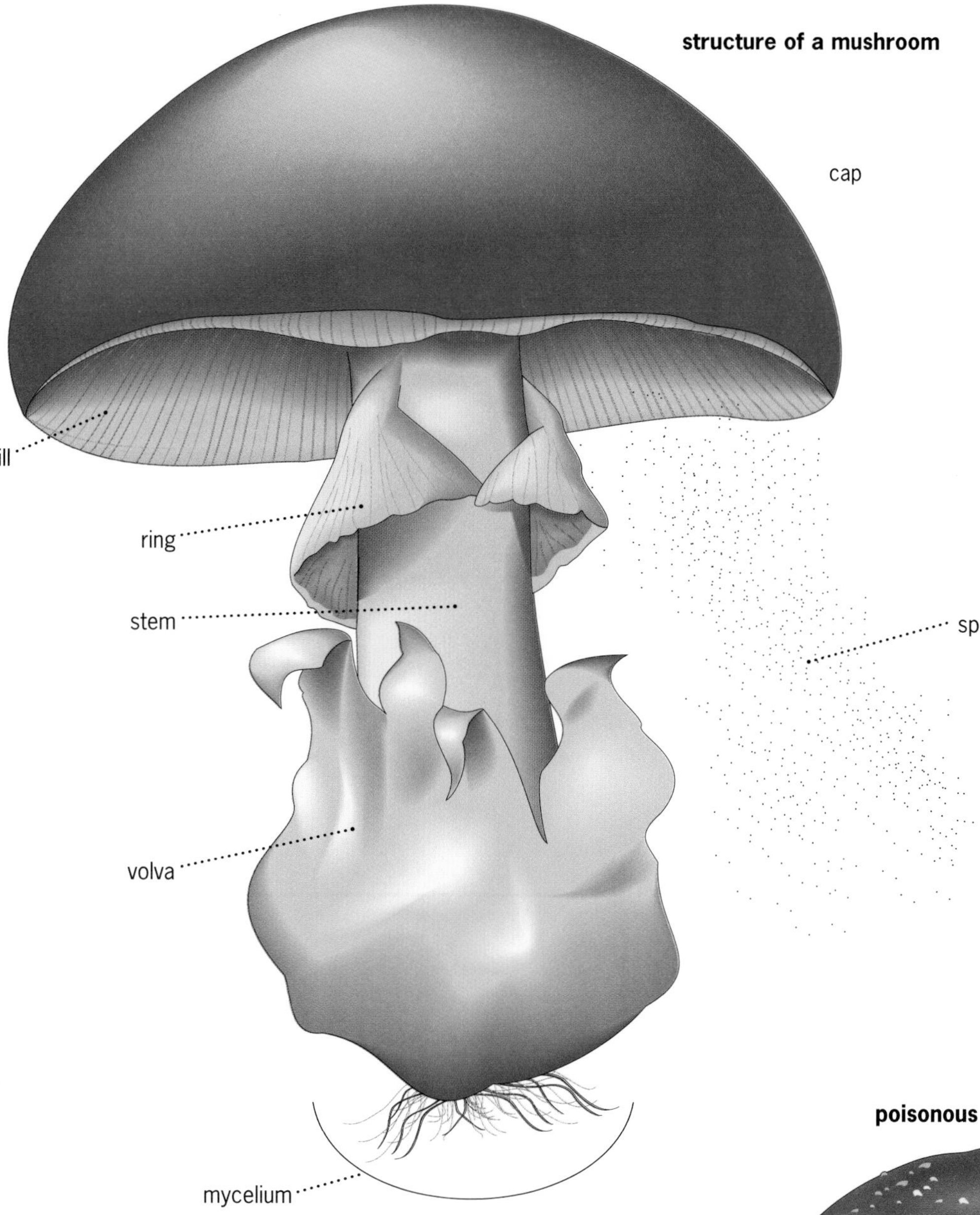
cap
gill
ring
stem
spores
volva
mycelium

edible mushroom

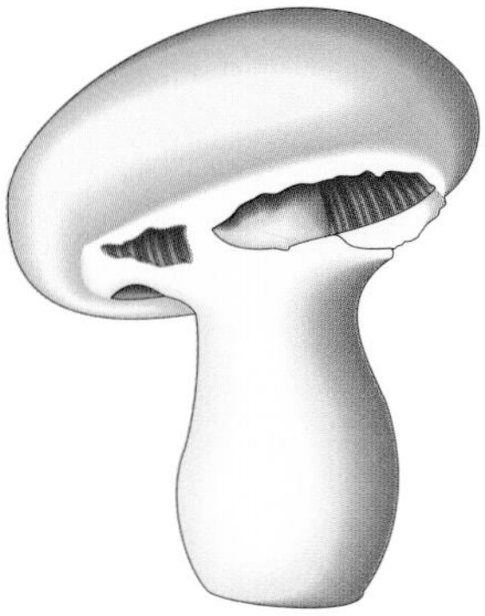

cultivated mushroom

deadly mushroom

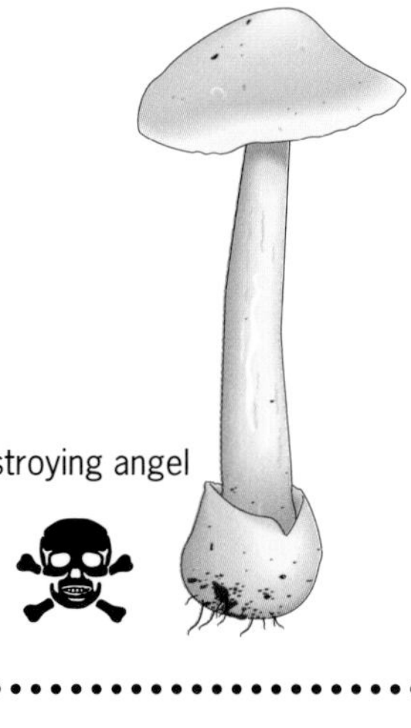
destroying angel

poisonous mushroom

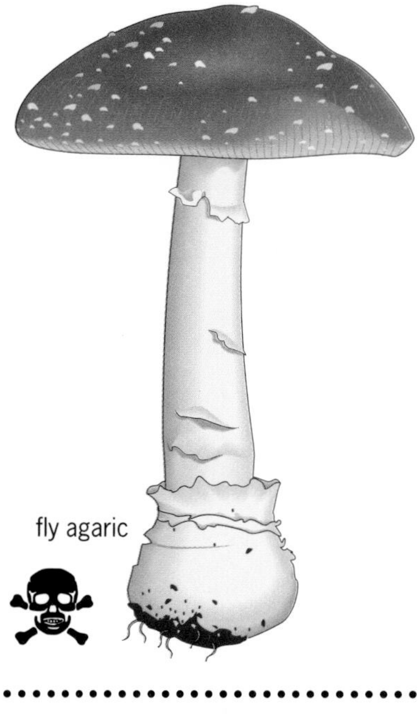
fly agaric

STRUCTURE OF A PLANT

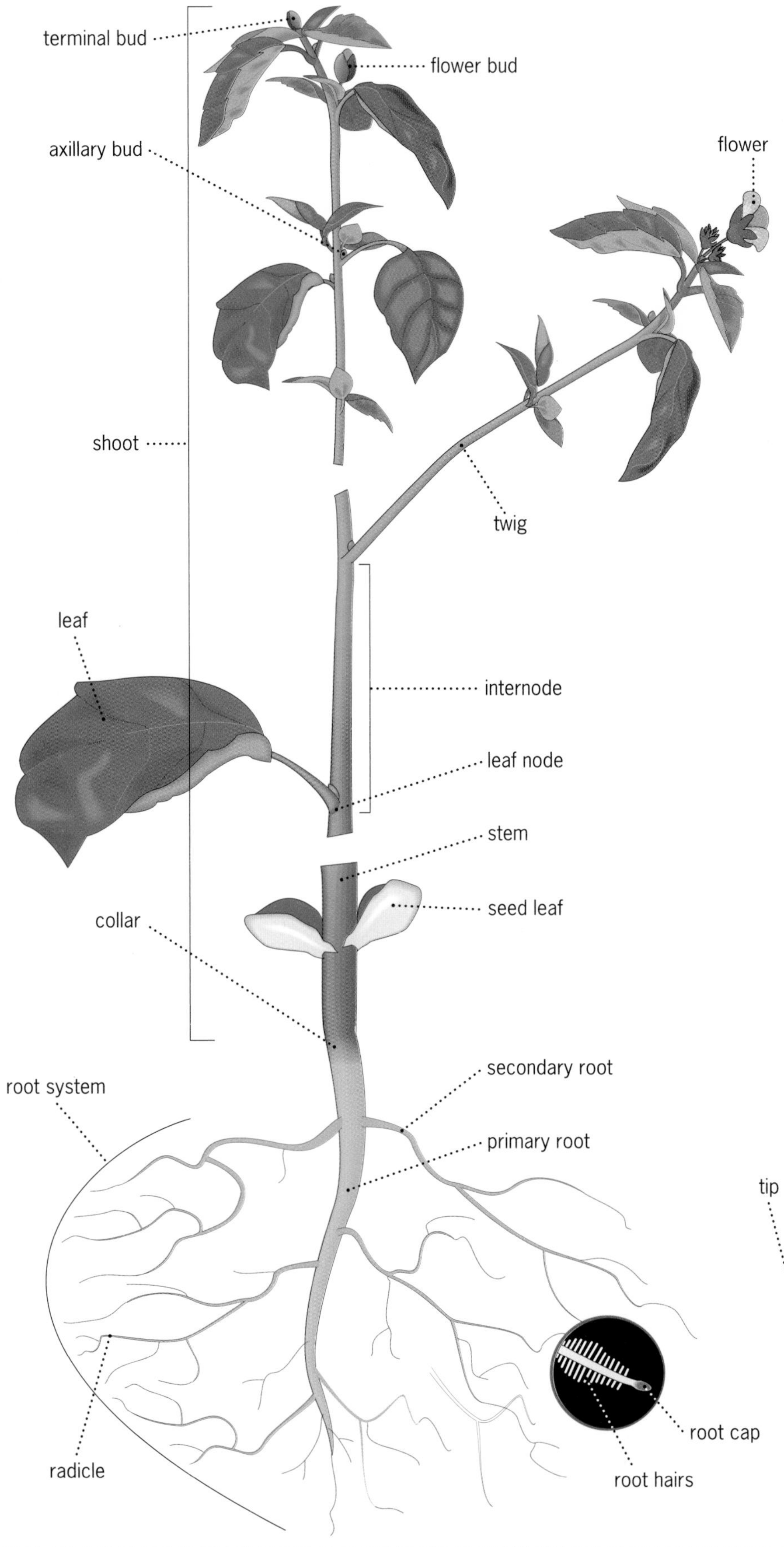
terminal bud
flower bud
axillary bud
flower
shoot
twig
leaf
internode
leaf node
stem
seed leaf
collar
secondary root
root system
primary root
radicle
root cap
root hairs

COMPOUND LEAVES

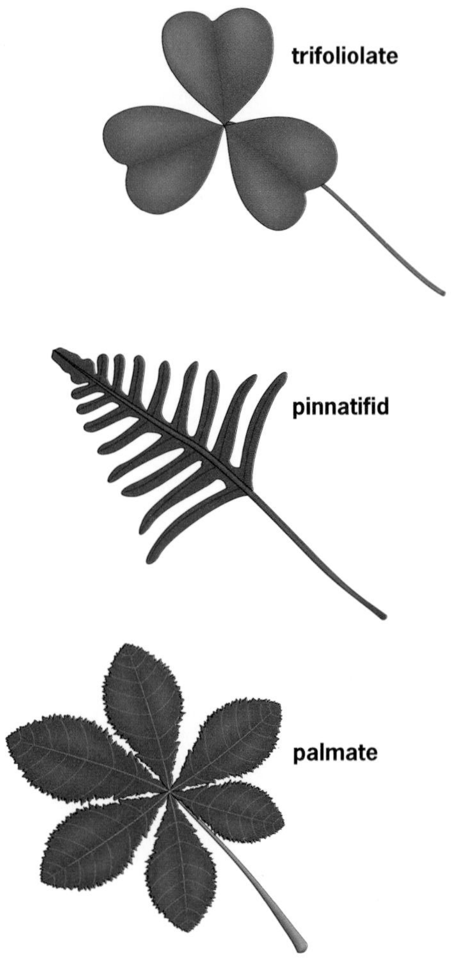
trifoliolate
pinnatifid
palmate

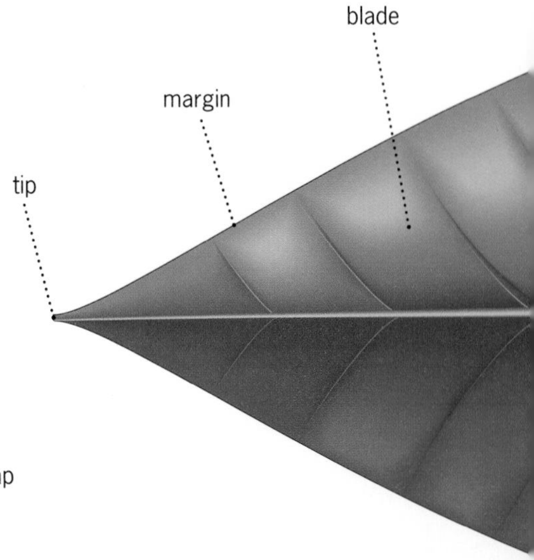
blade
margin
tip

SIMPLE LEAVES

linear

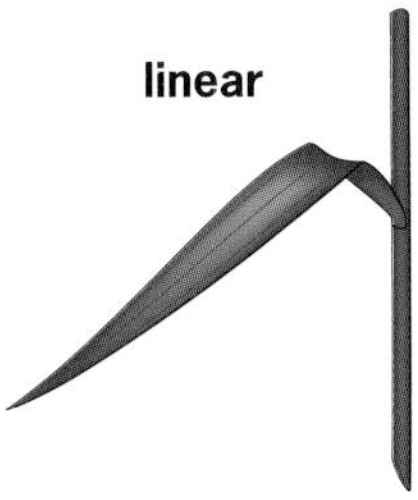

lanceolate

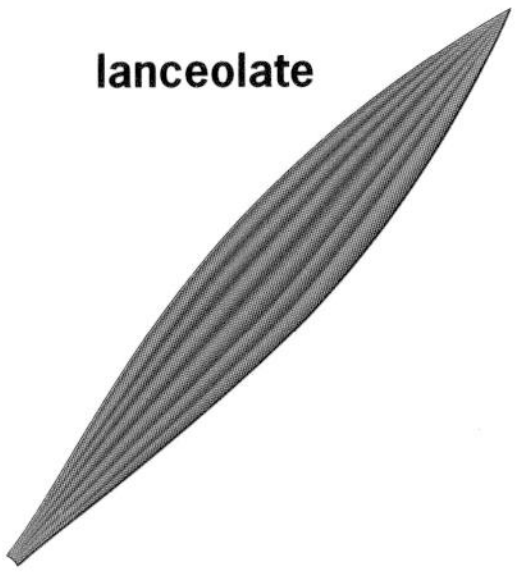

orbiculate

LEAF MARGINS

entire

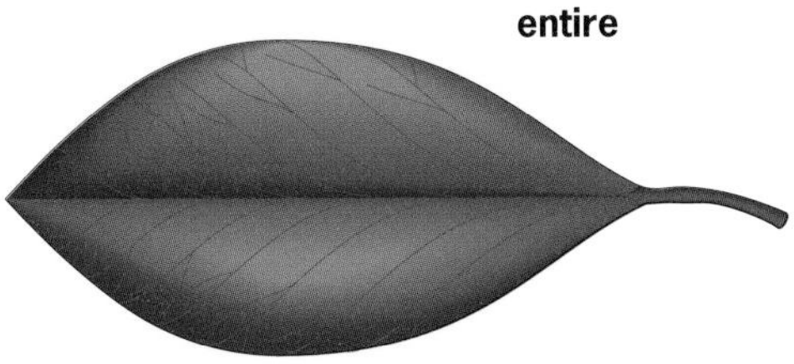

ciliate

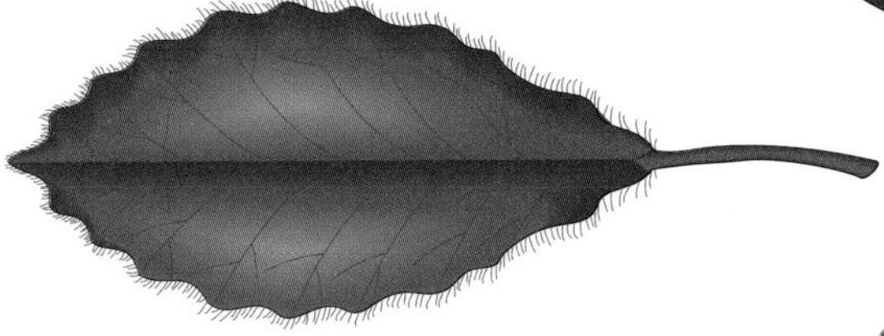

lobate

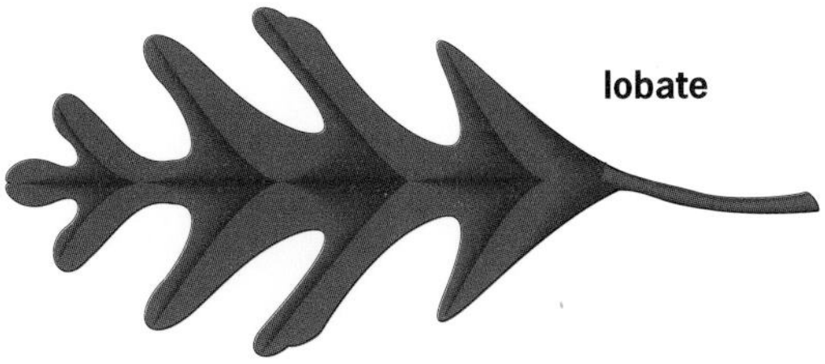

crenate

dentate

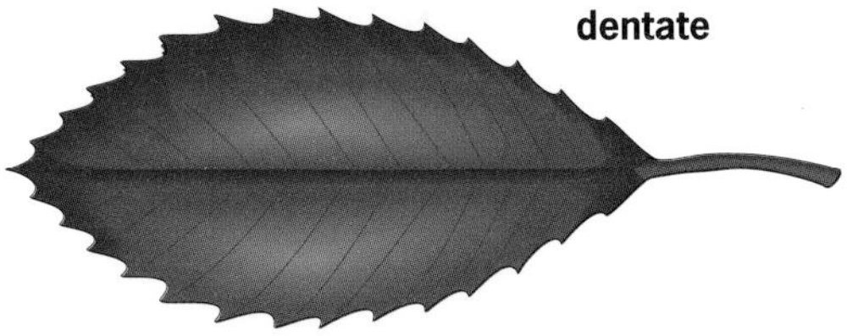

leaf

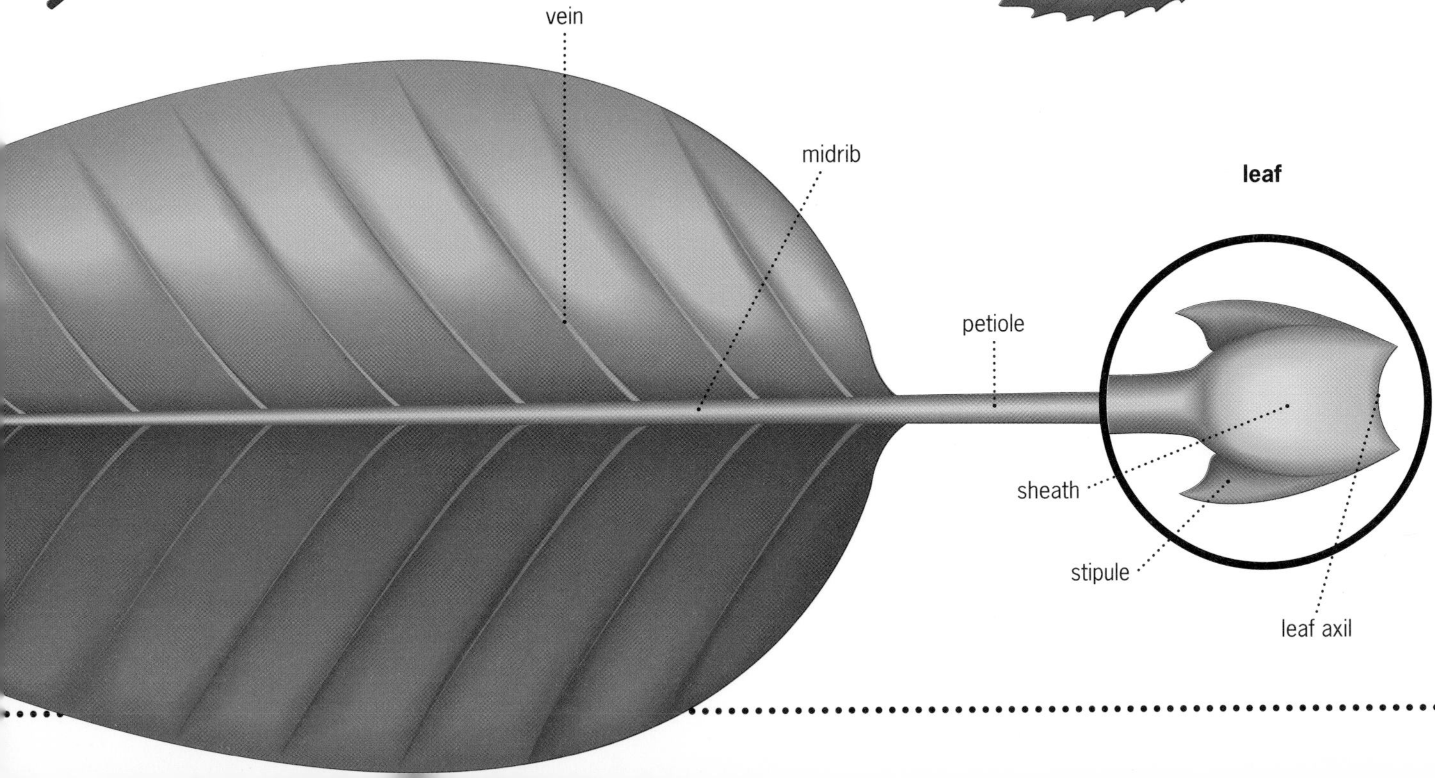
vein
midrib
petiole
sheath
stipule
leaf axil

FLOWERS

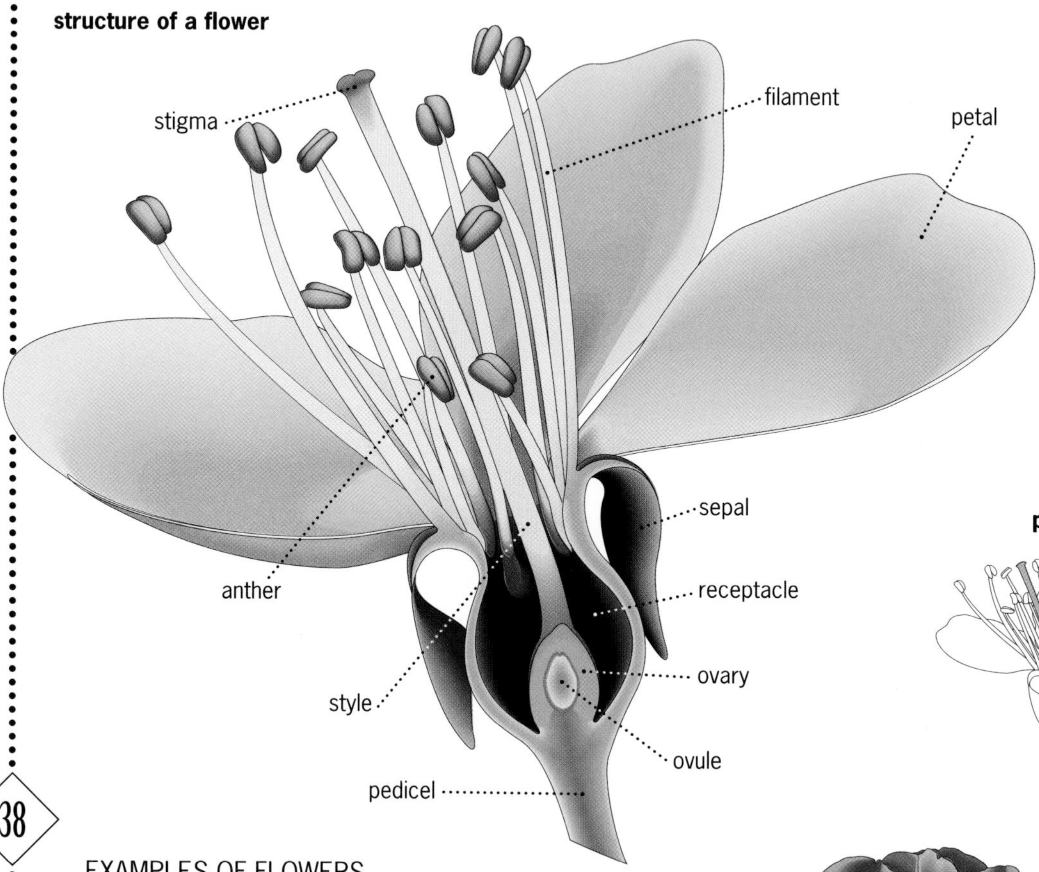
structure of a flower
stigma
filament
petal
anther
sepal
receptacle
style
ovary
ovule
pedicel

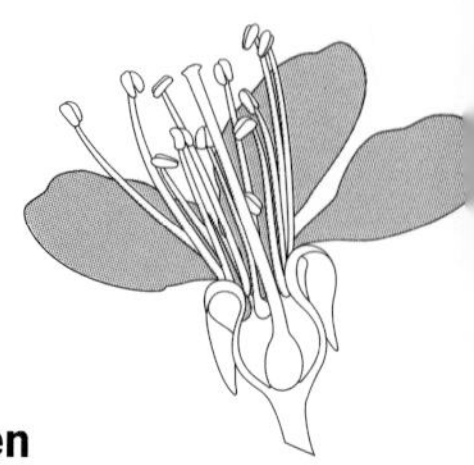
corolla

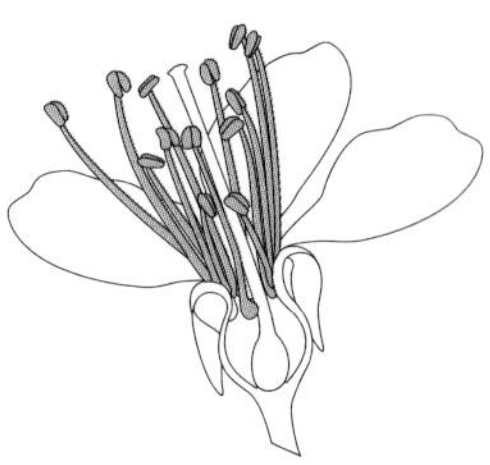
stamen

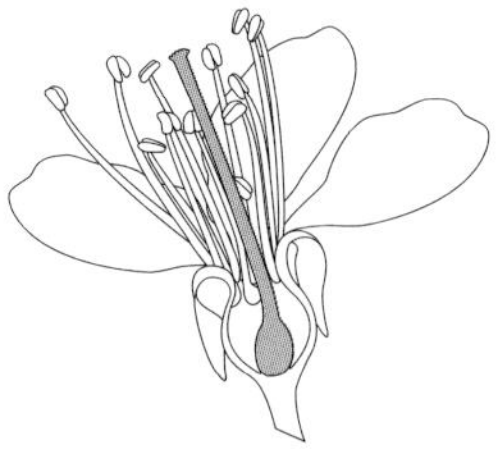
pistil

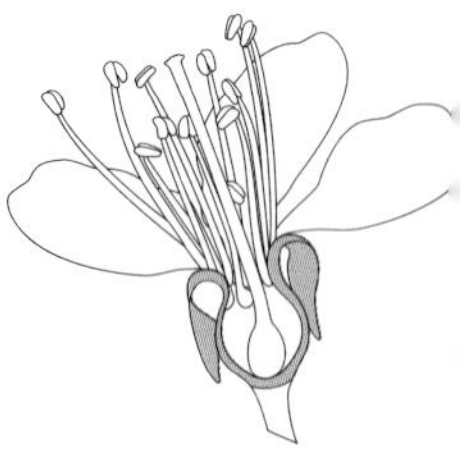
calyx

EXAMPLES OF FLOWERS

orchid

tulip

violet

rose

begonia

poppy

sunflower

lily

lily of the valley

crocus

carnation

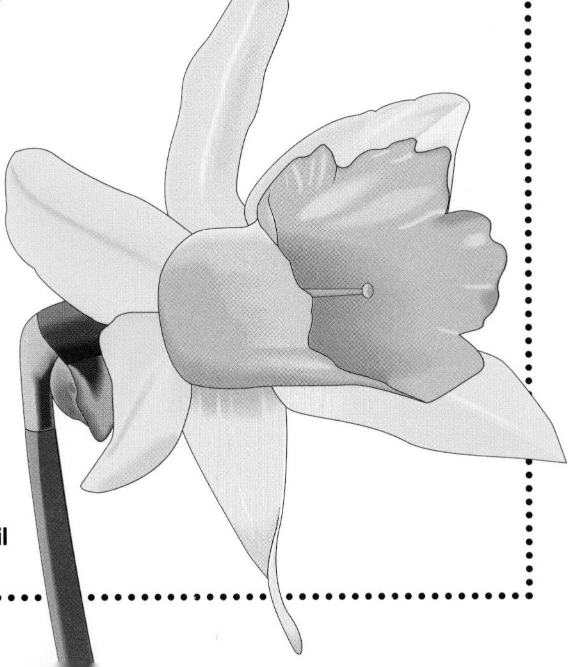

daffodil

TREE

structure of a tree

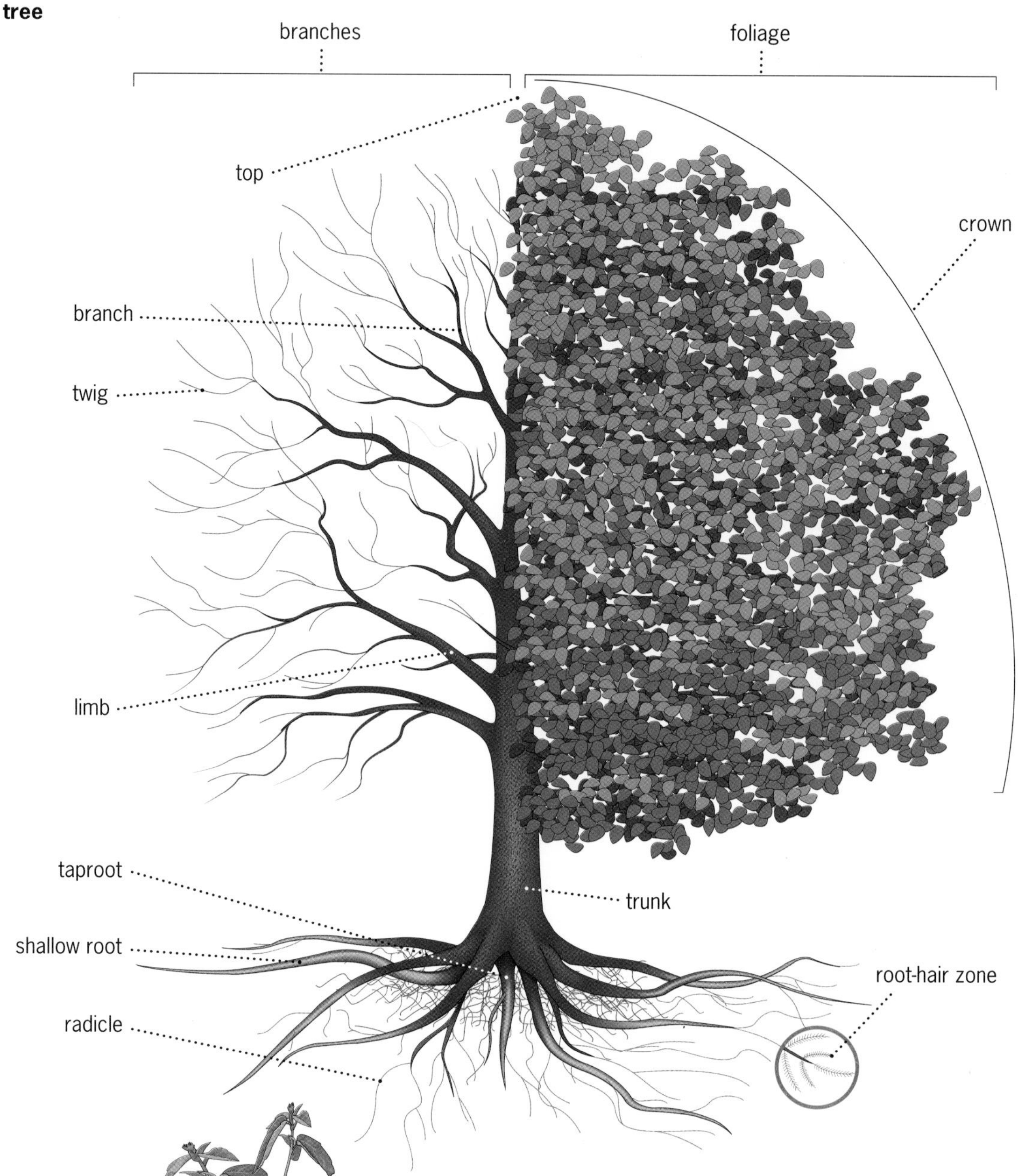
branches
foliage
top
crown
branch
twig
limb
taproot
trunk
shallow root
root-hair zone
radicle

stump

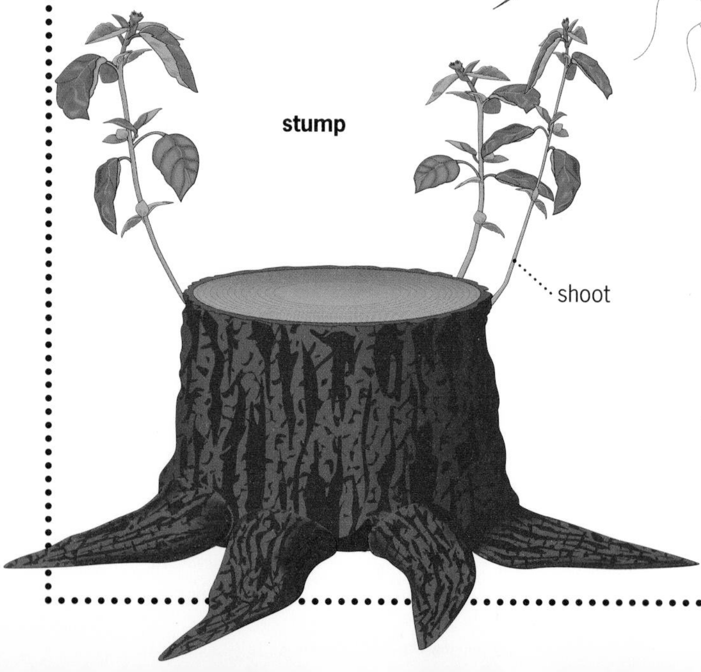
shoot

cross section of a trunk

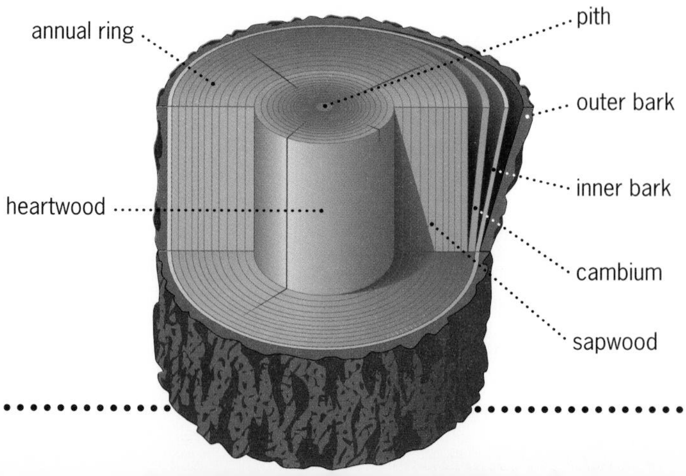
annual ring
pith
outer bark
heartwood
inner bark
cambium
sapwood

EXAMPLES OF TREES

poplar
oak
maple

palm tree

weeping willow

birch

CONIFER

larch
umbrella pine
cone
pine seeds

TYPES OF LEAVES

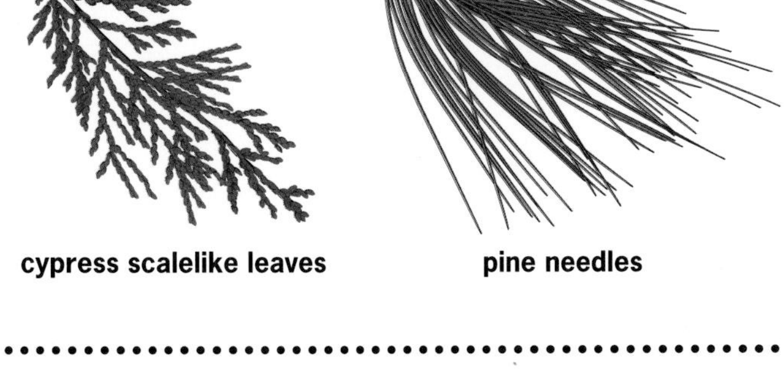
fir needles
cypress scalelike leaves
pine needles

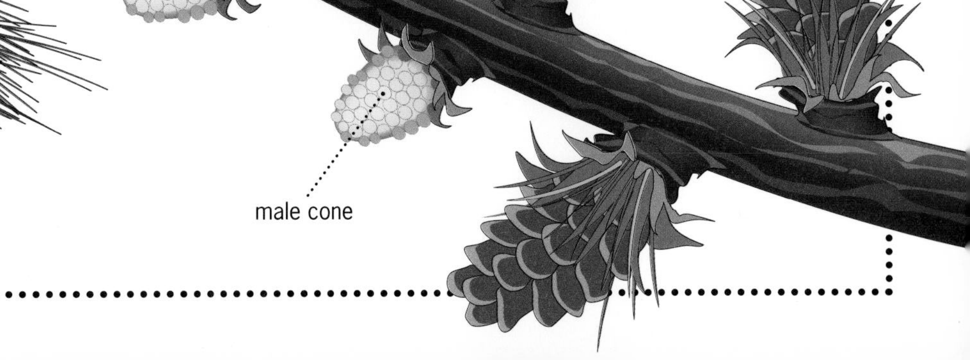
branch
female cone
male cone

FLESHY FRUITS: BERRY FRUITS

section of a berry

grape

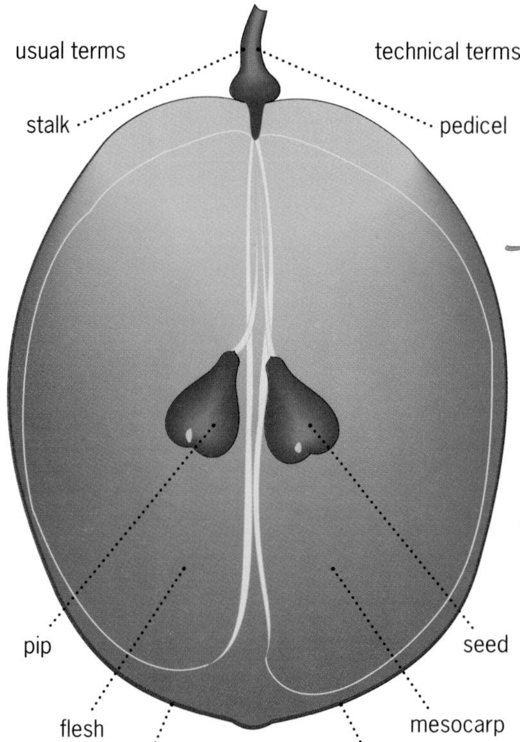
usual terms
technical terms
stalk
pedicel
pip
seed
flesh
mesocarp
skin
exocarp

MAJOR TYPES OF BERRIES

cranberry

blueberry

red currant

grape

black currant

gooseberry

huckleberry

section of a strawberry

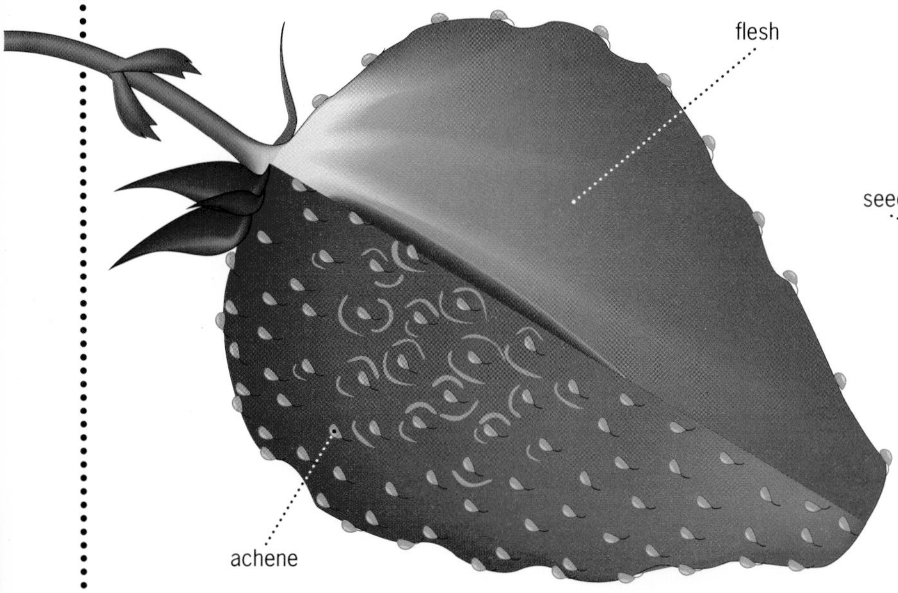
flesh
achene

section of a raspberry

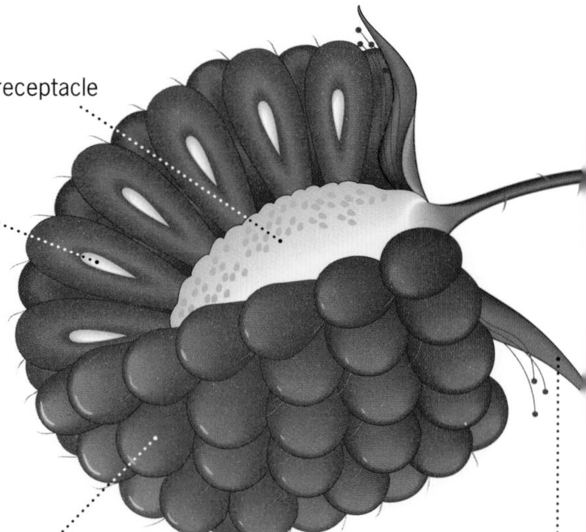
receptacle
seed
drupelet
sepal

FLESHY STONE FRUITS

section of a stone fruit

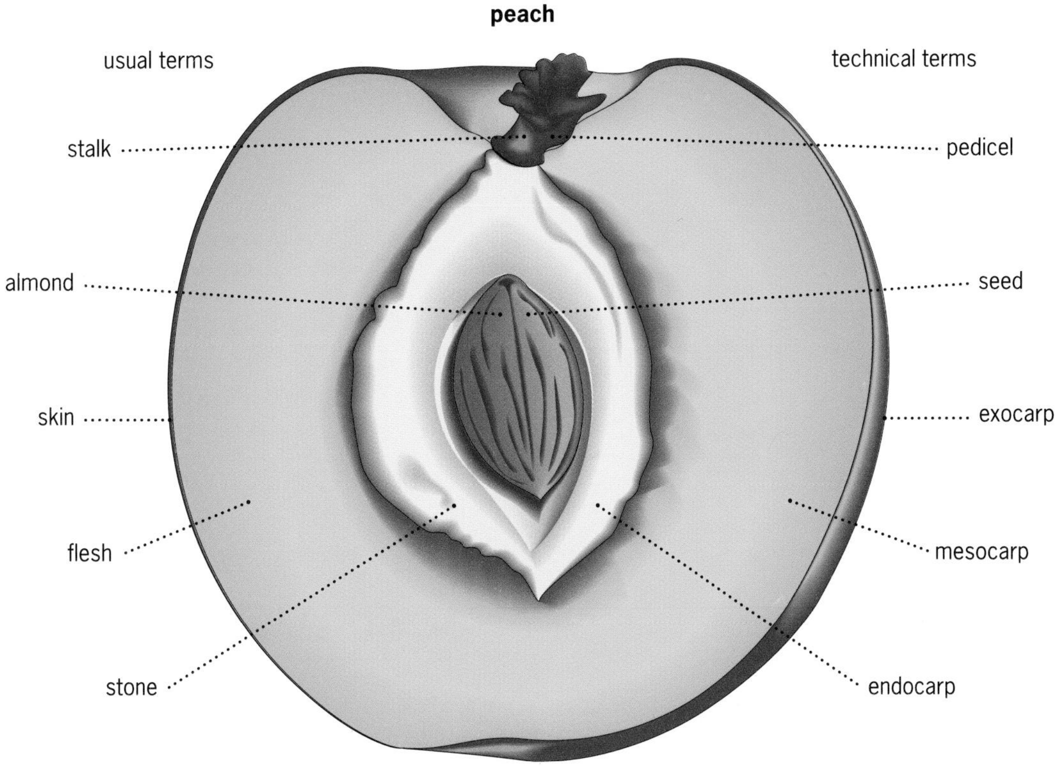
peach
usual terms
technical terms
stalk
pedicel
almond
seed
skin
exocarp
flesh
mesocarp
stone
endocarp

MAJOR TYPES OF STONE FRUITS

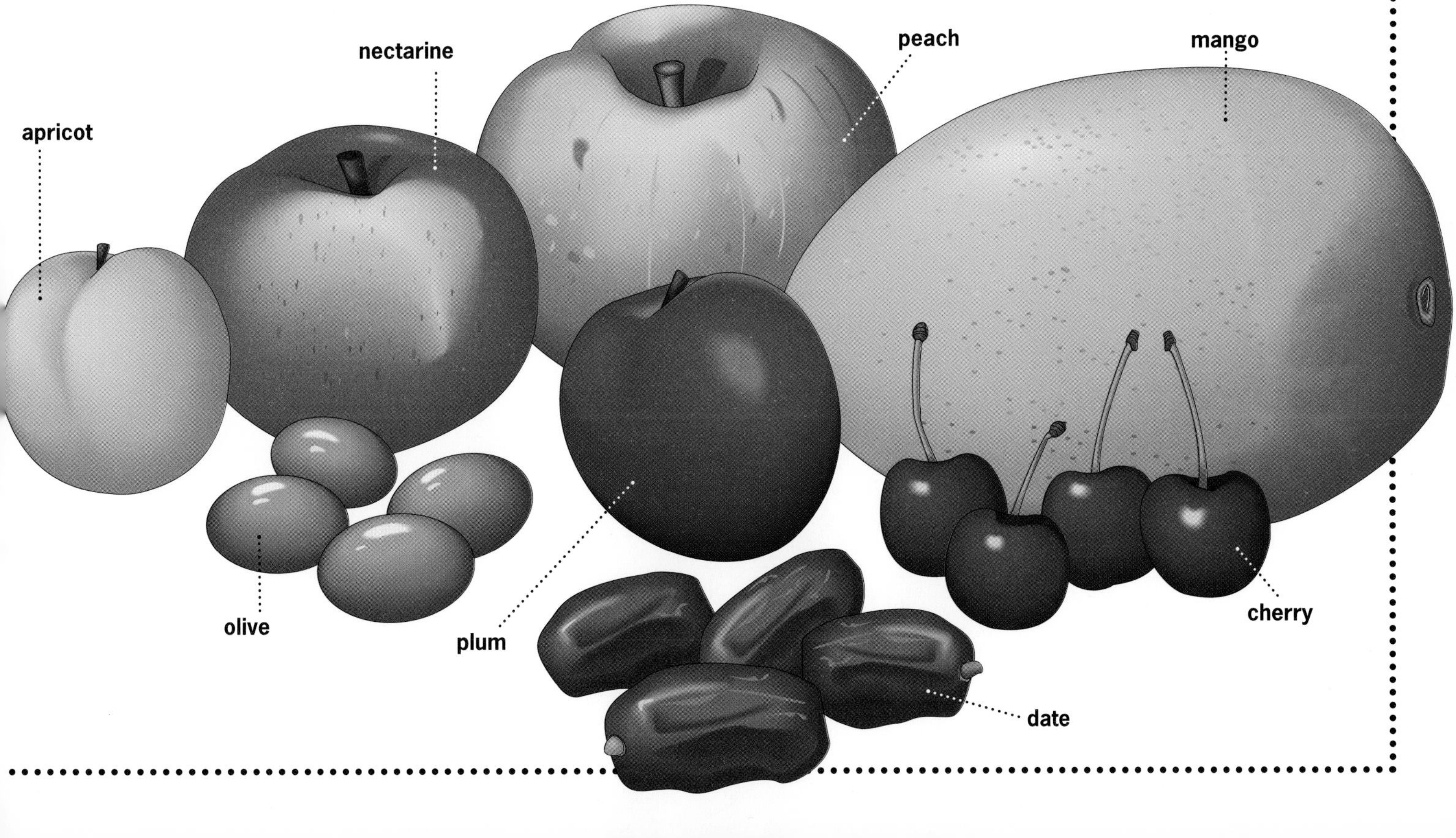
apricot
nectarine
peach
mango
olive
plum
cherry
date

FLESHY POME FRUITS

section of a pome fruit

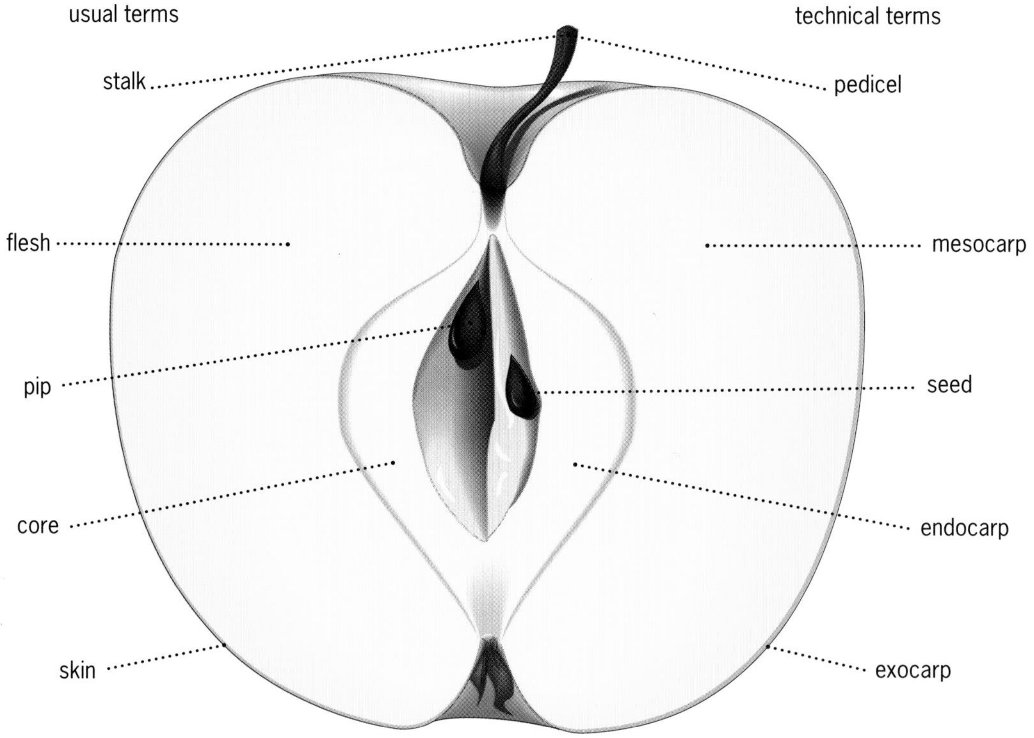
apple
usual terms
technical terms
stalk
pedicel
flesh
mesocarp
pip
seed
core
endocarp
skin
exocarp

MAJOR TYPES OF POME FRUITS

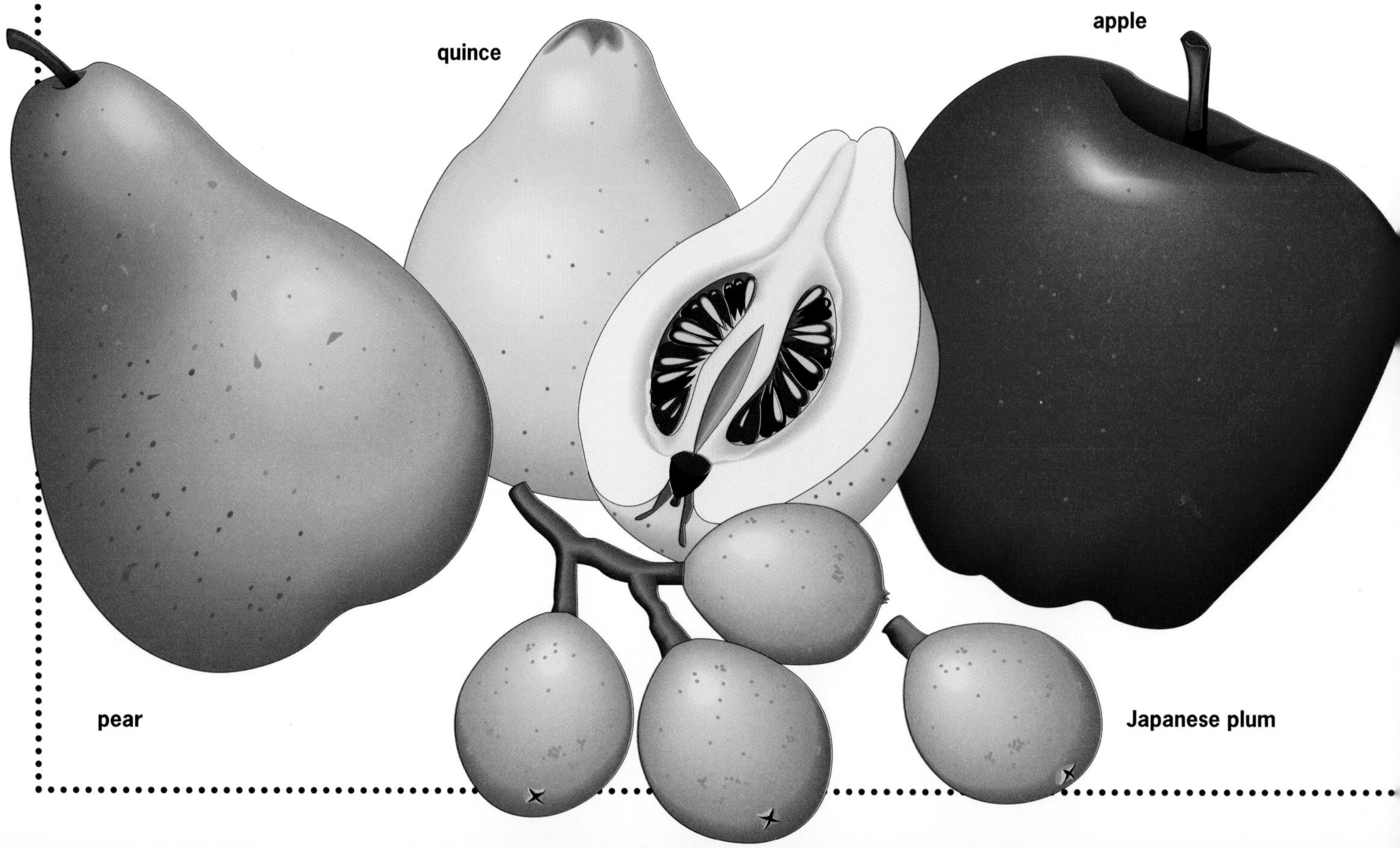
quince
apple
pear
Japanese plum

FLESHY FRUITS: CITRUS FRUITS

section of a citrus fruit

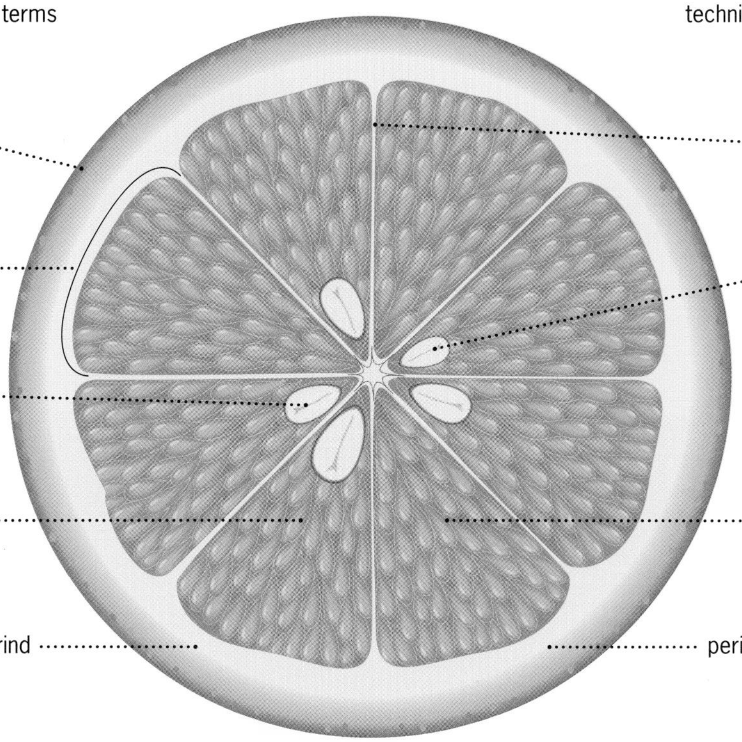
orange
usual terms
technical terms
zest
wall
segment
seed
pip
pulp
mesocarp
rind
pericarp

MAJOR TYPES OF CITRUS FRUITS

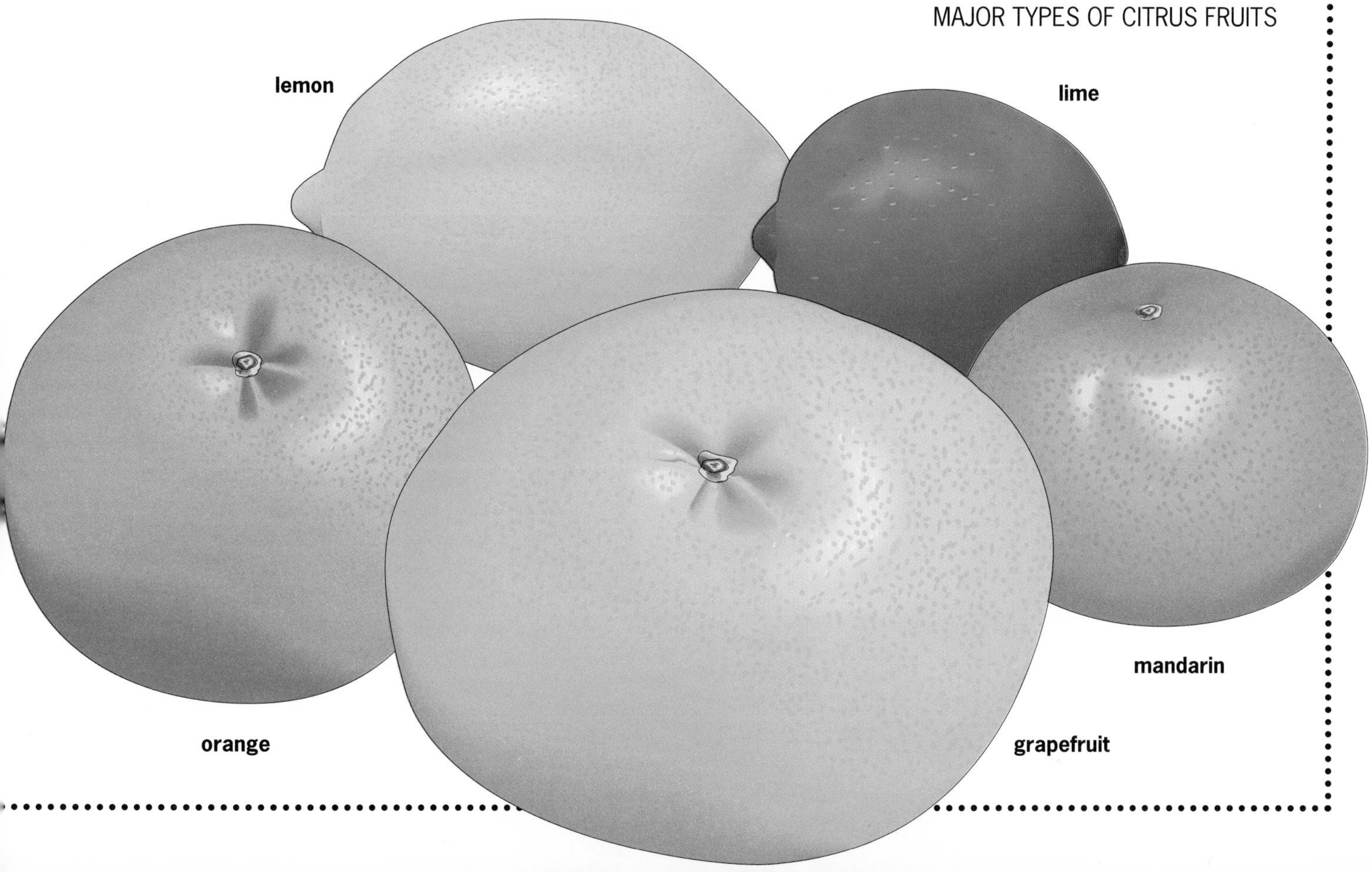
lemon
lime
mandarin
orange
grapefruit

TROPICAL FRUITS

MAJOR TYPES OF TROPICAL FRUITS

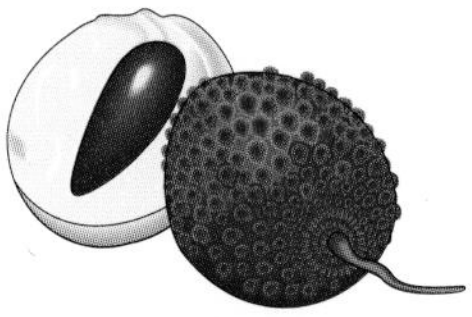
litchi

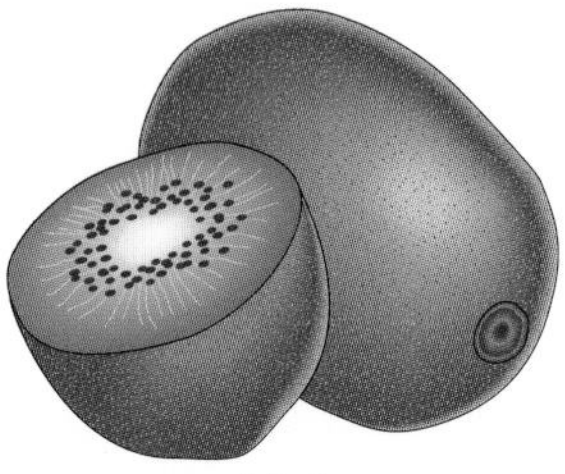
kiwi

guava

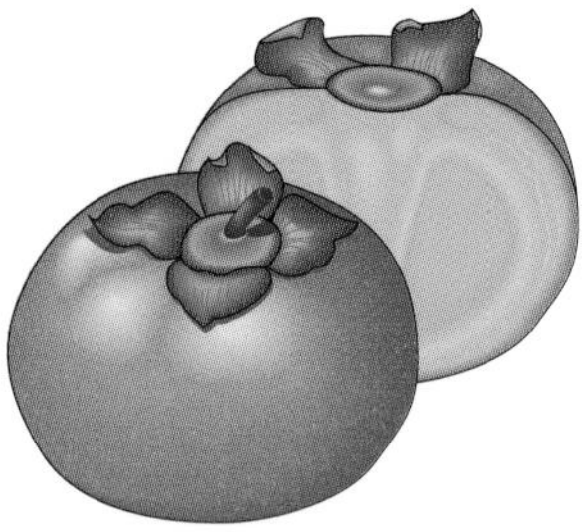
Japanese persimmon

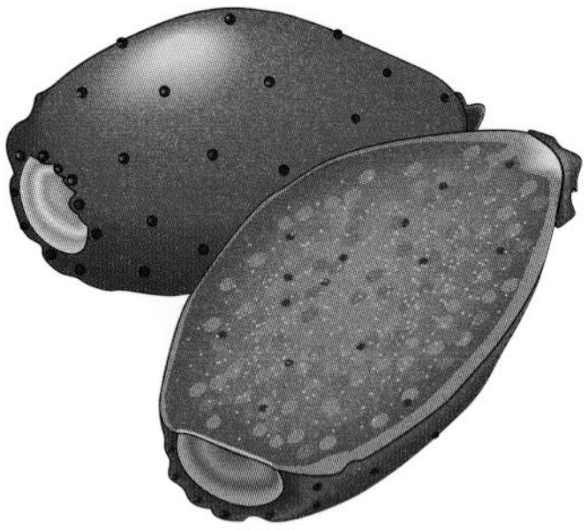
Indian fig

cherimoya

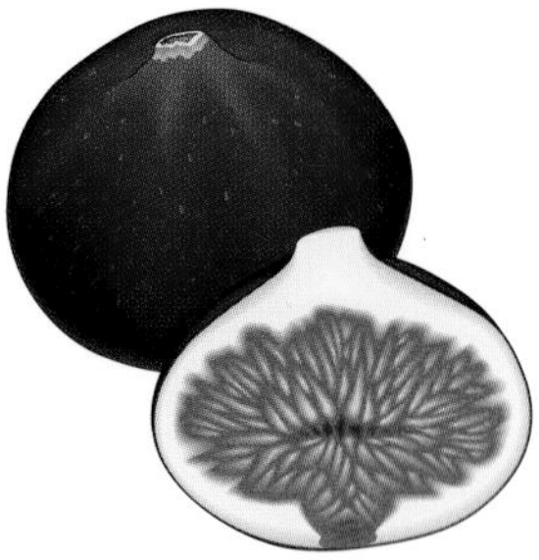
fig

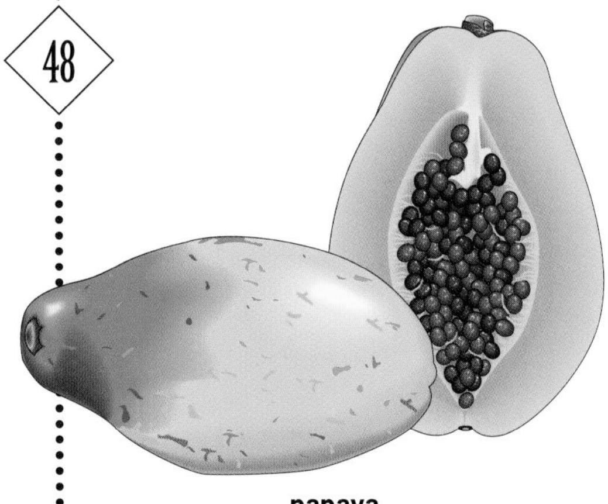
papaya

pomegranate

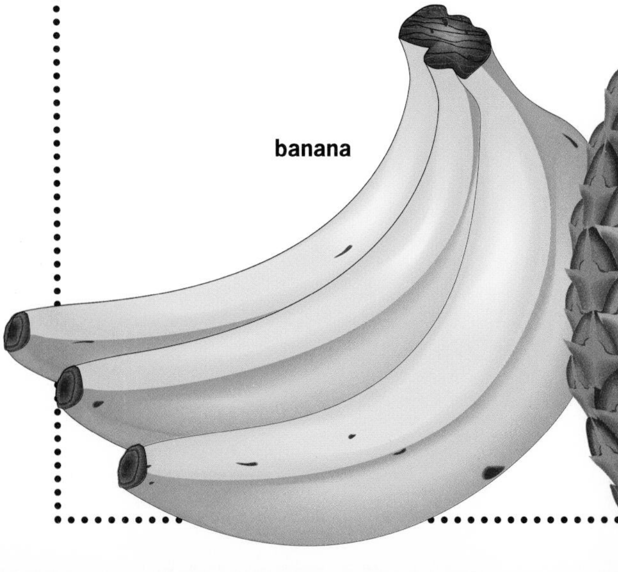
banana

pineapple

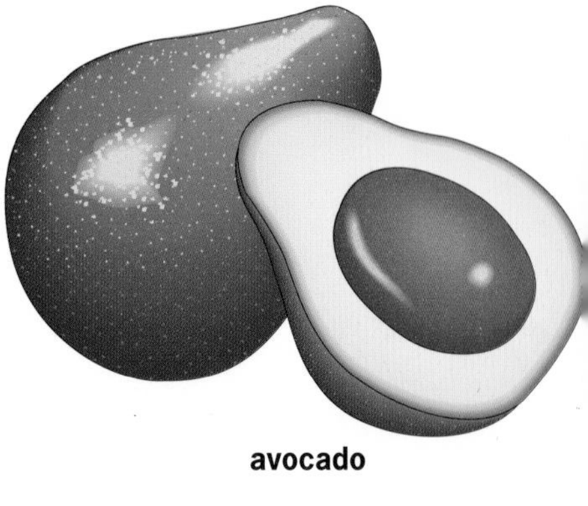
avocado

VEGETABLES

INFLORESCENT VEGETABLES

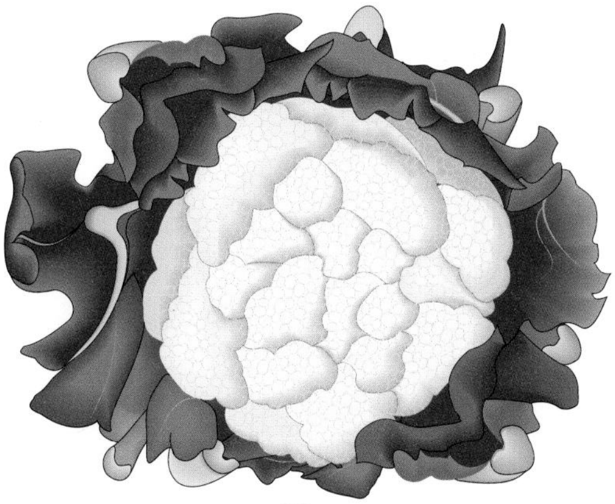

cauliflower

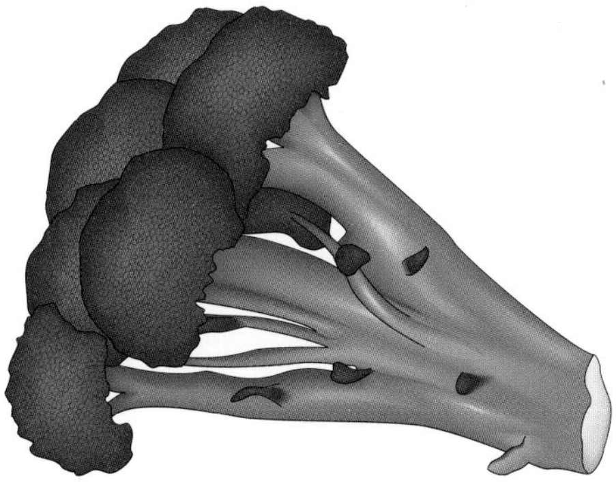

broccoli

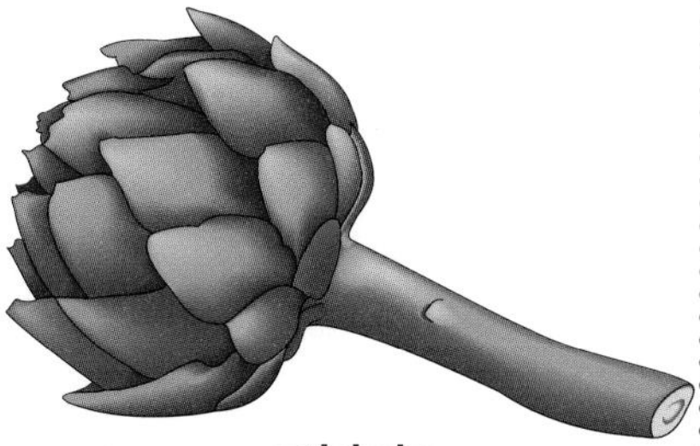

artichoke

FRUIT VEGETABLES

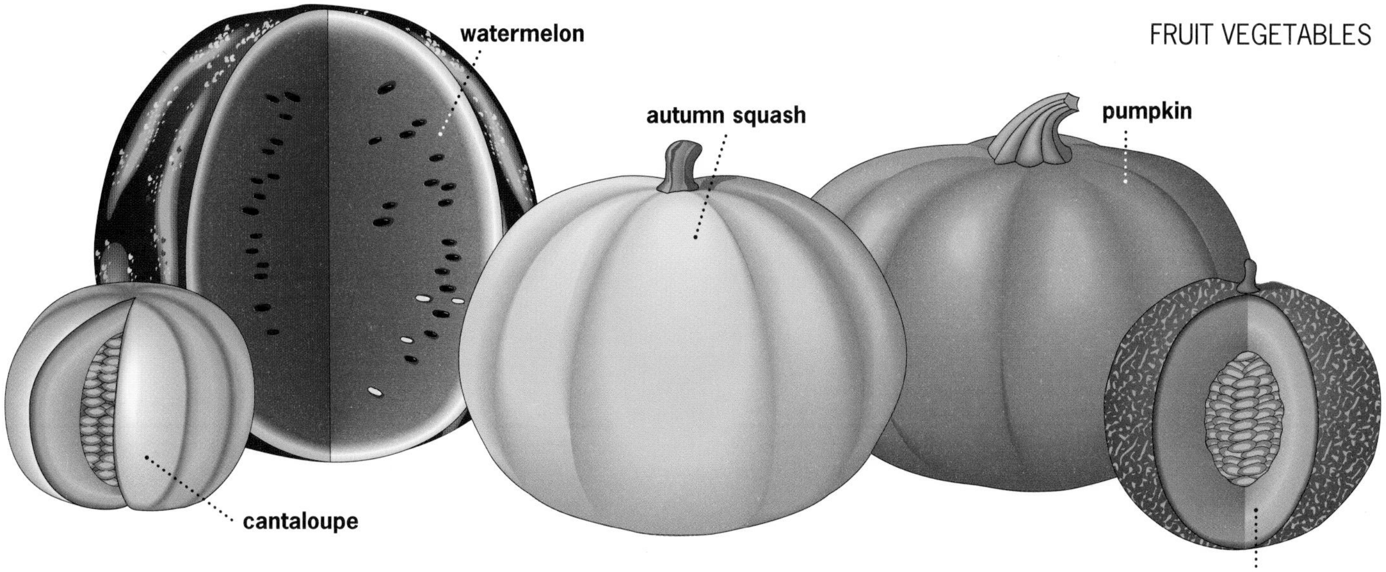
watermelon
autumn squash
pumpkin
cantaloupe
muskmelon

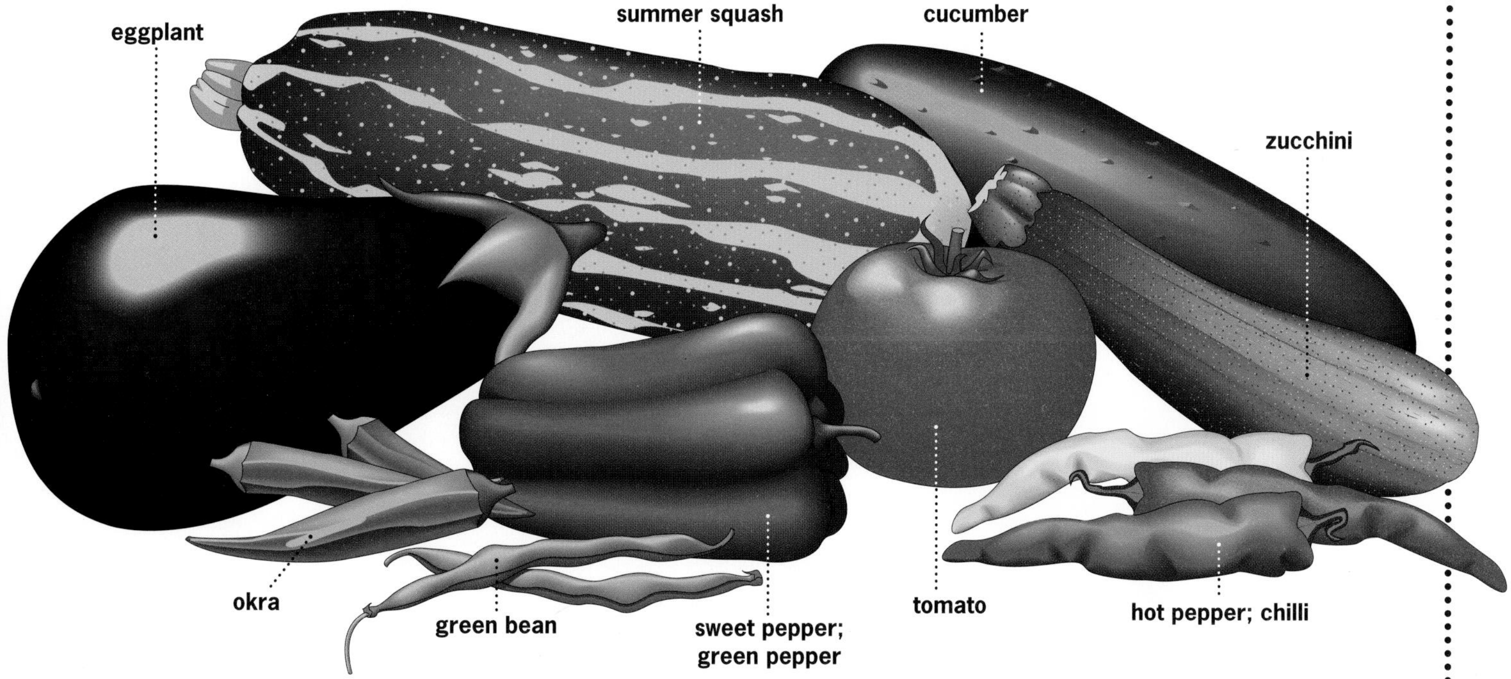
eggplant
summer squash
cucumber
zucchini
okra
green bean
sweet pepper; green pepper
tomato
hot pepper; chilli

VEGETABLES

section of a bulb

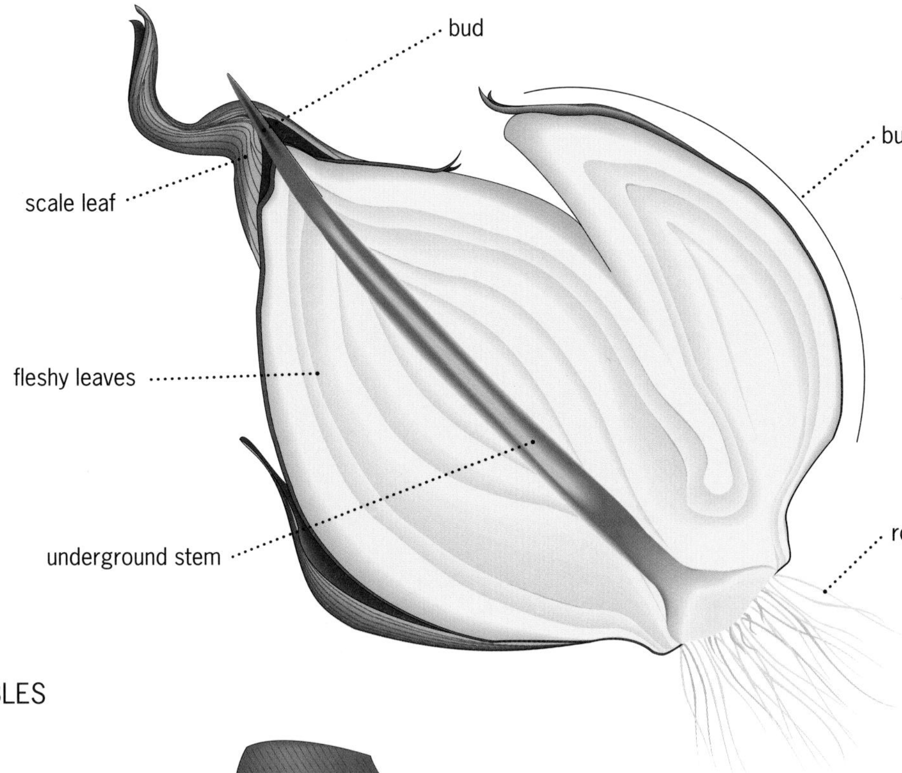
bud
bulbil
scale leaf
fleshy leaves
underground stem
root

BULB VEGETABLES

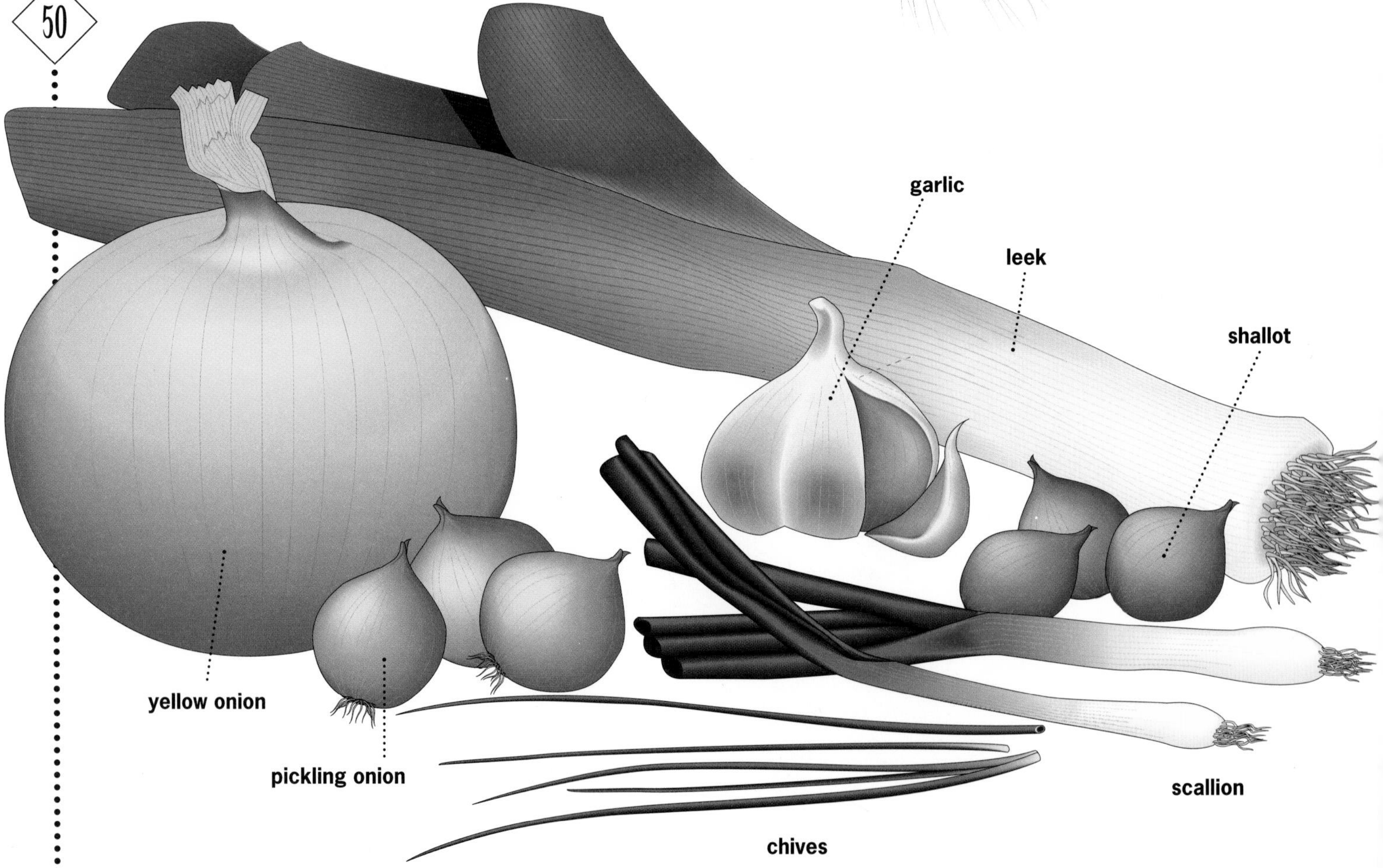
garlic
leek
shallot
yellow onion
pickling onion
scallion
chives

TUBER VEGETABLES

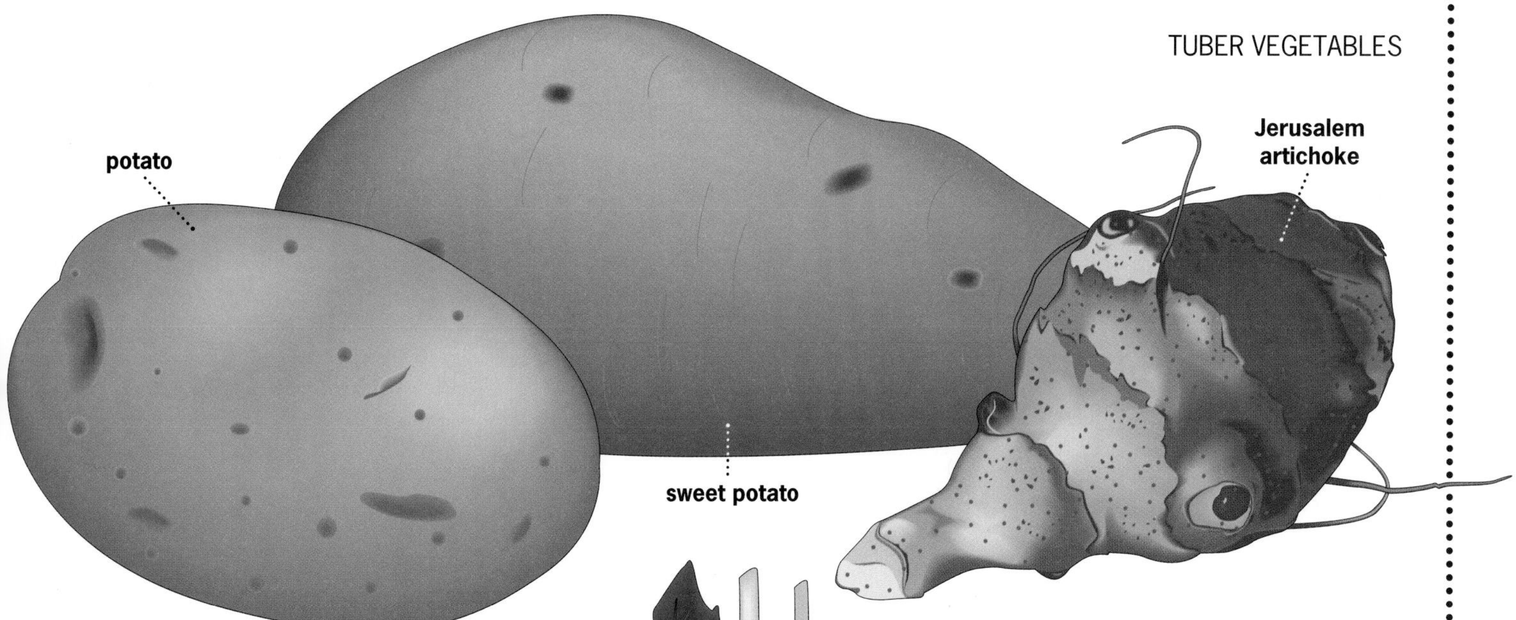
potato
sweet potato
Jerusalem artichoke

ROOT VEGETABLES

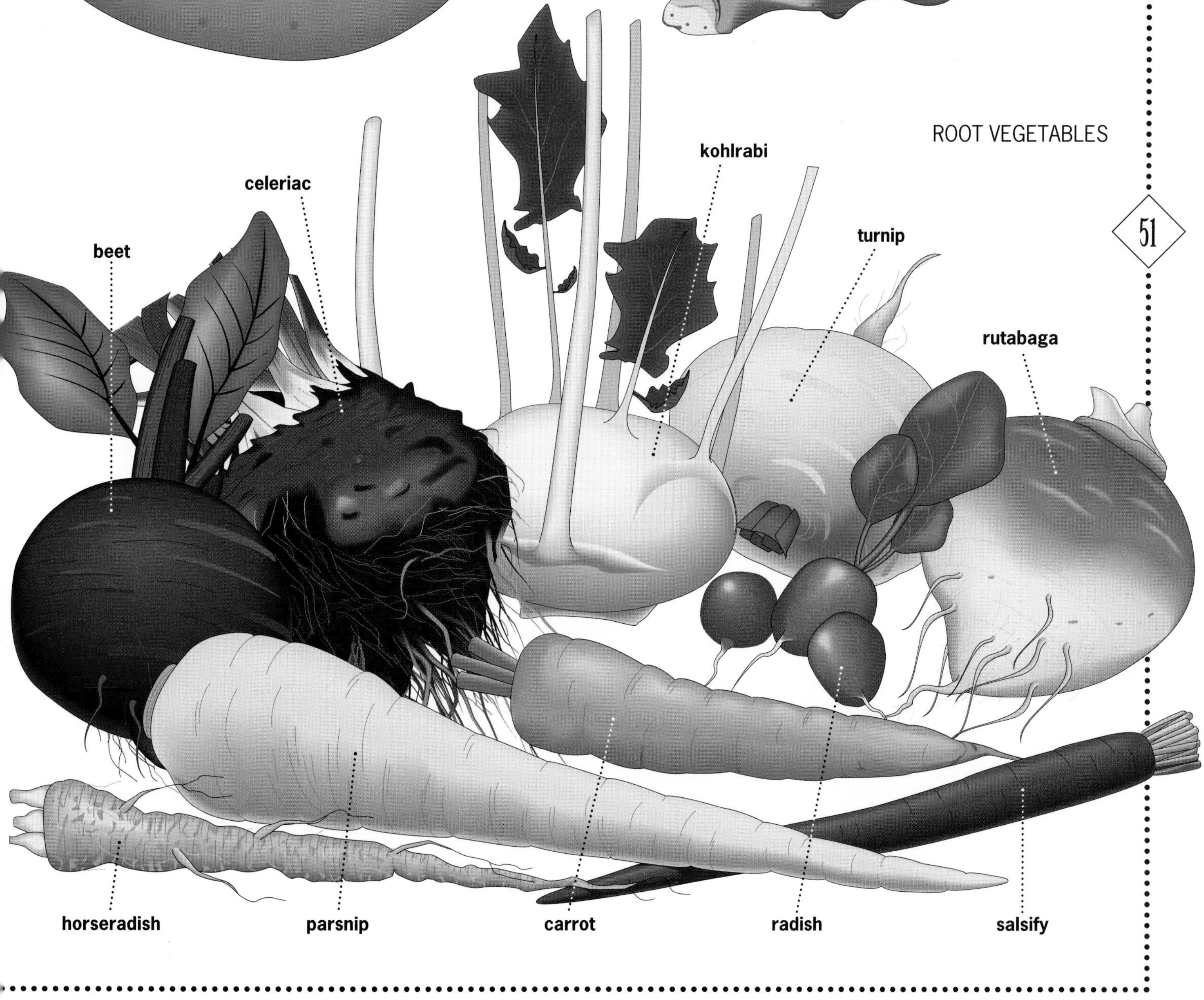
celeriac
kohlrabi
beet
turnip
rutabaga
horseradish
parsnip
carrot
radish
salsify

VEGETABLES

STALK VEGETABLES

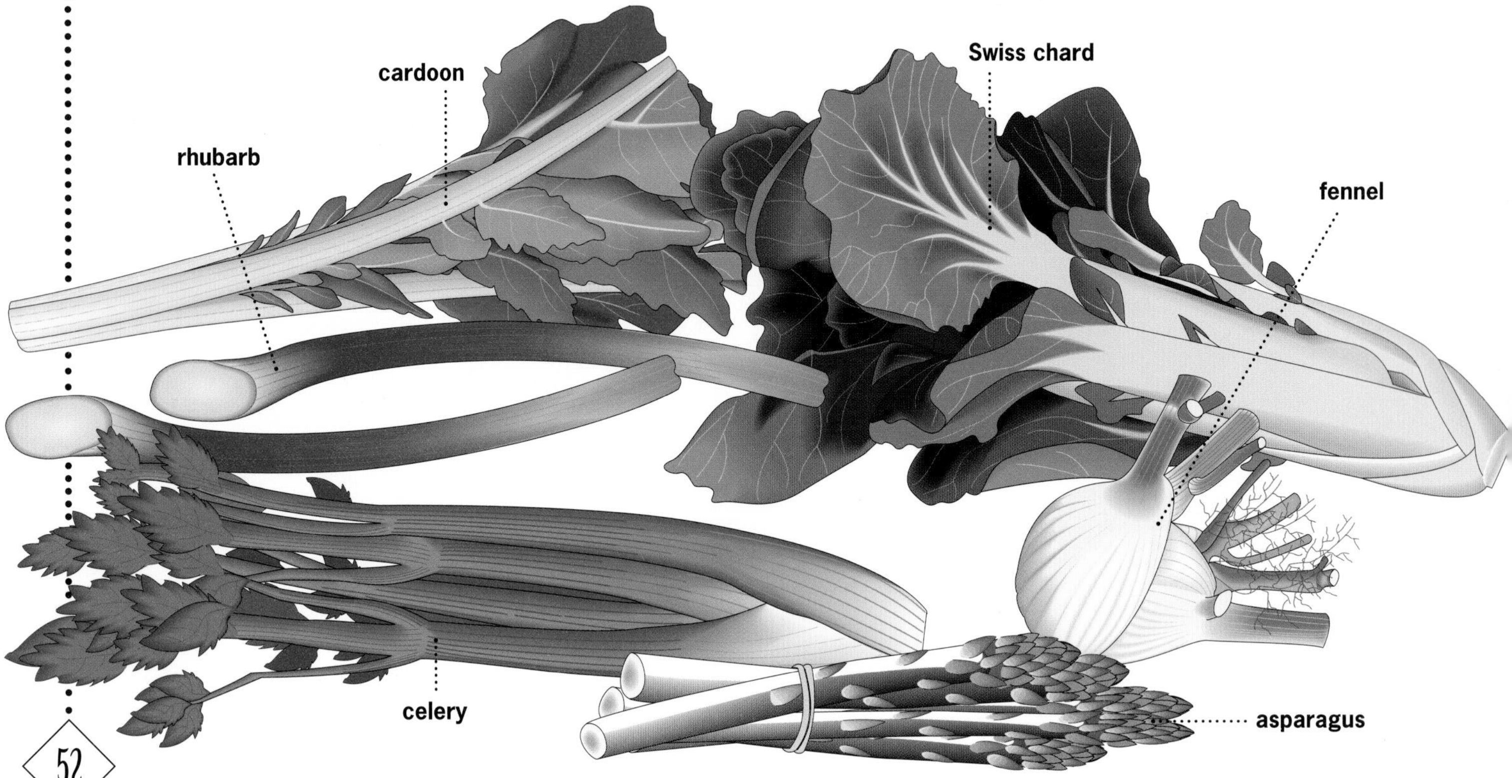
cardoon
rhubarb
Swiss chard
fennel
celery
asparagus

SEED VEGETABLES

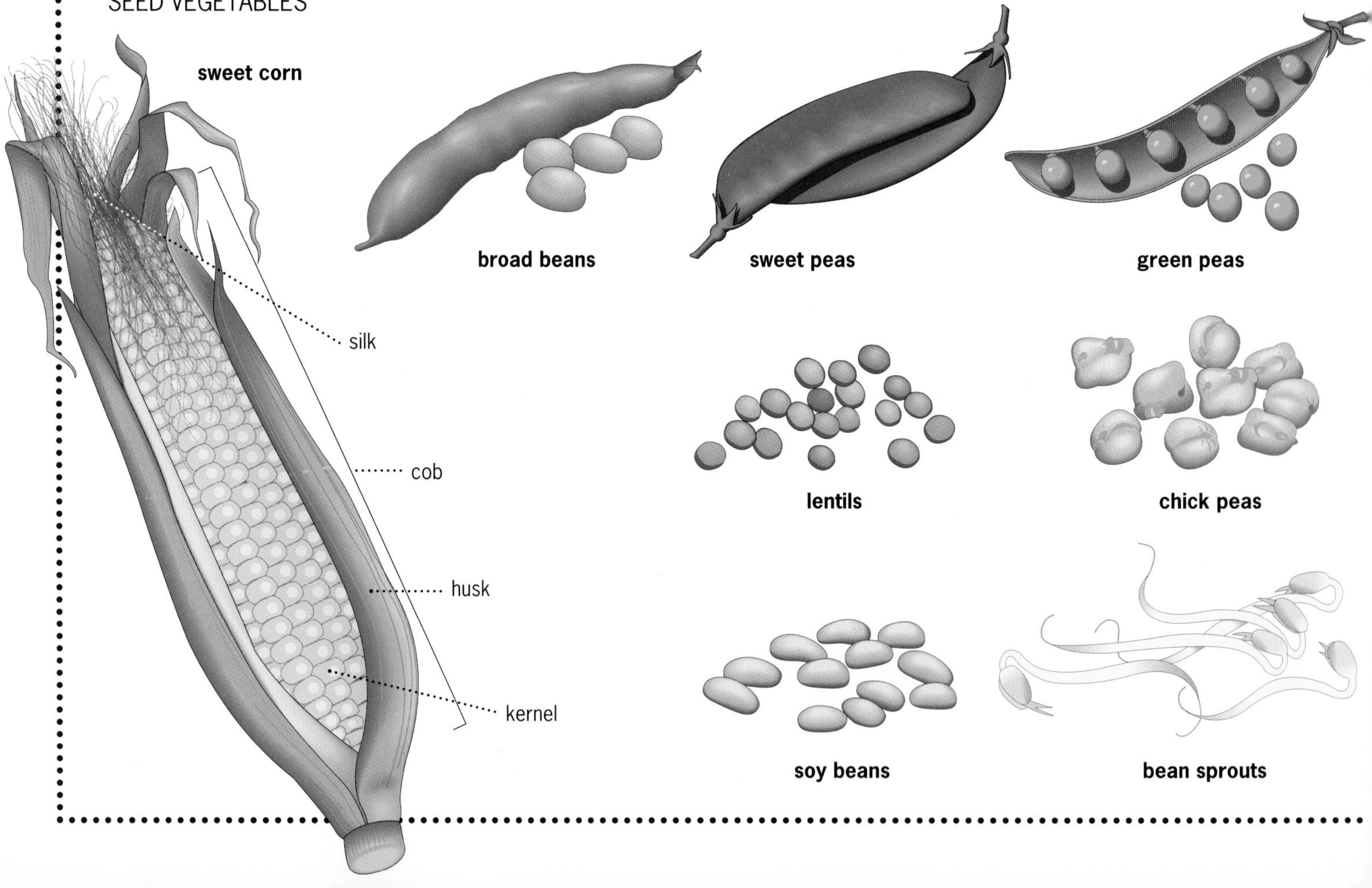
sweet corn
silk
cob
husk
kernel
broad beans
sweet peas
green peas
lentils
chick peas
soy beans
bean sprouts

LEAF VEGETABLES

green cabbage
cabbage lettuce
curly endive
spinach
white cabbage
romaine lettuce
chicory
broad-leaved endive
Chinese cabbage
dandelion
curly kale
Brussels sprouts
garden sorrel
corn salad
watercress
vine leaf

GARDENING

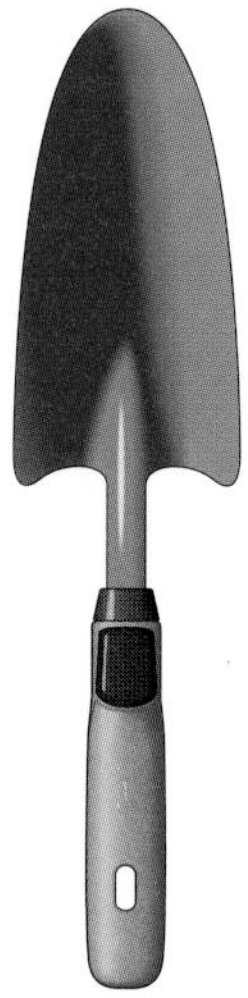

trowel

hand fork

hand cultivator

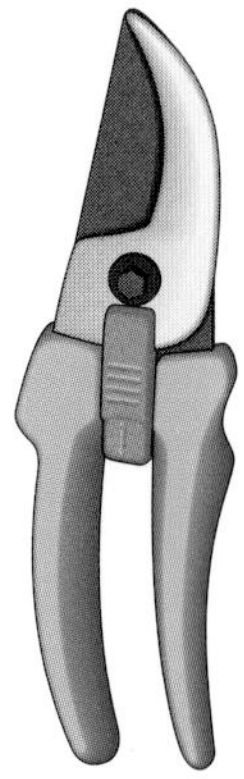

pruning shears

lawnmower

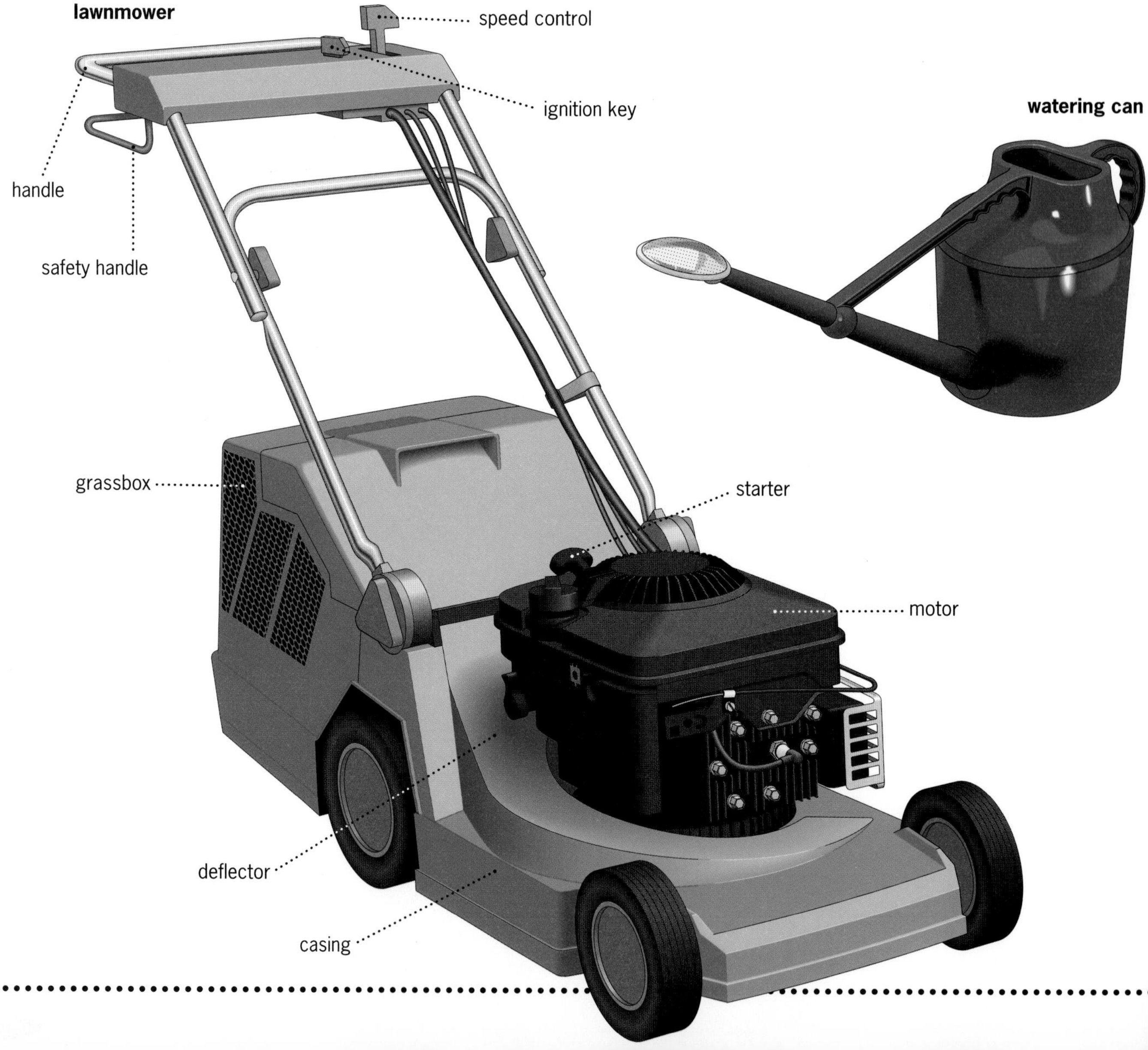
speed control
ignition key
handle
safety handle
grassbox
starter
motor
deflector
casing

watering can

rake

lawn rake

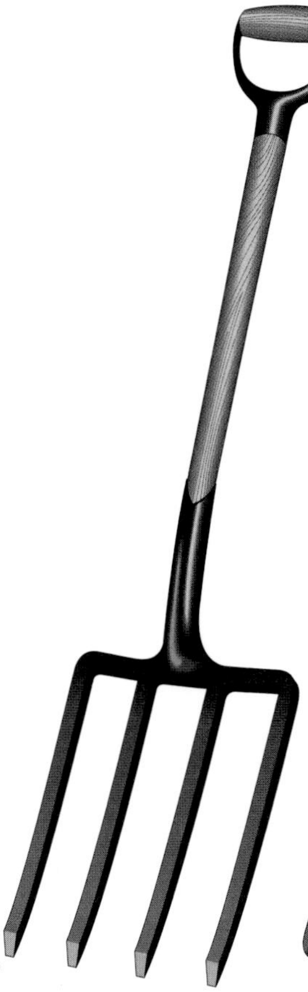

garden fork

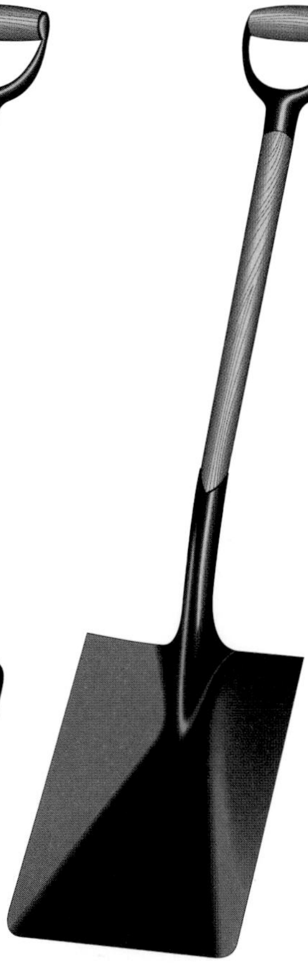

spade

shovel

wheelbarrow

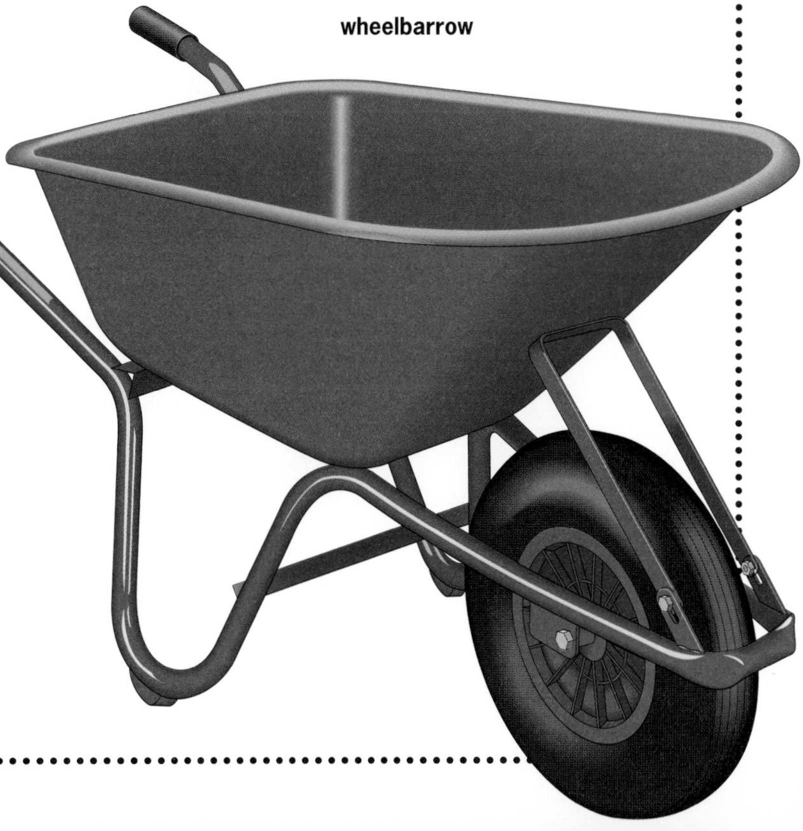

compost bin

INSECTS AND SPIDER

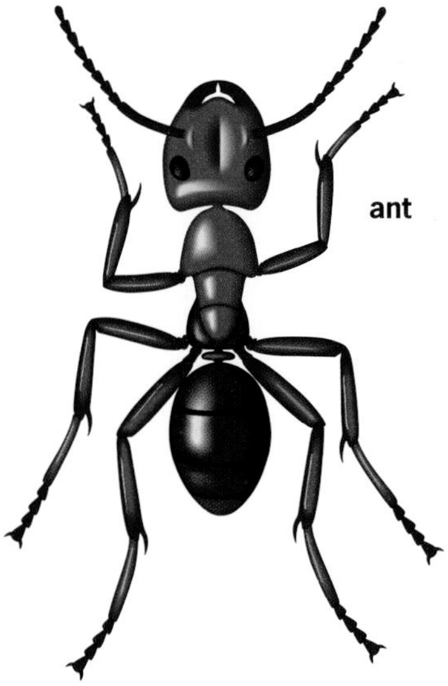

ant

ladybug

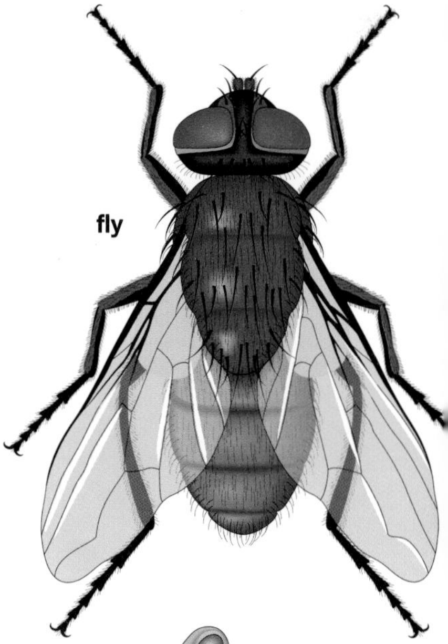

fly

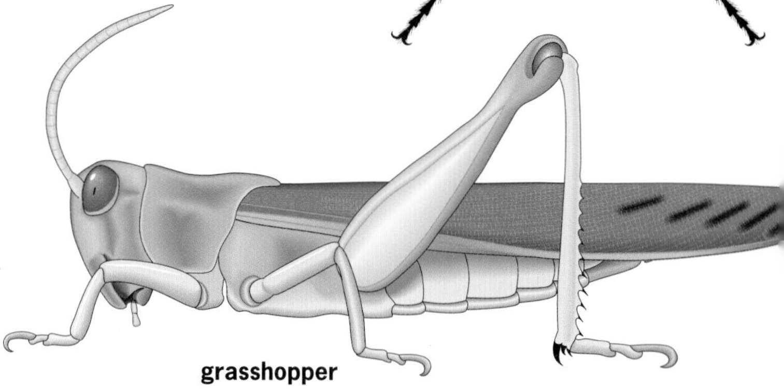

grasshopper

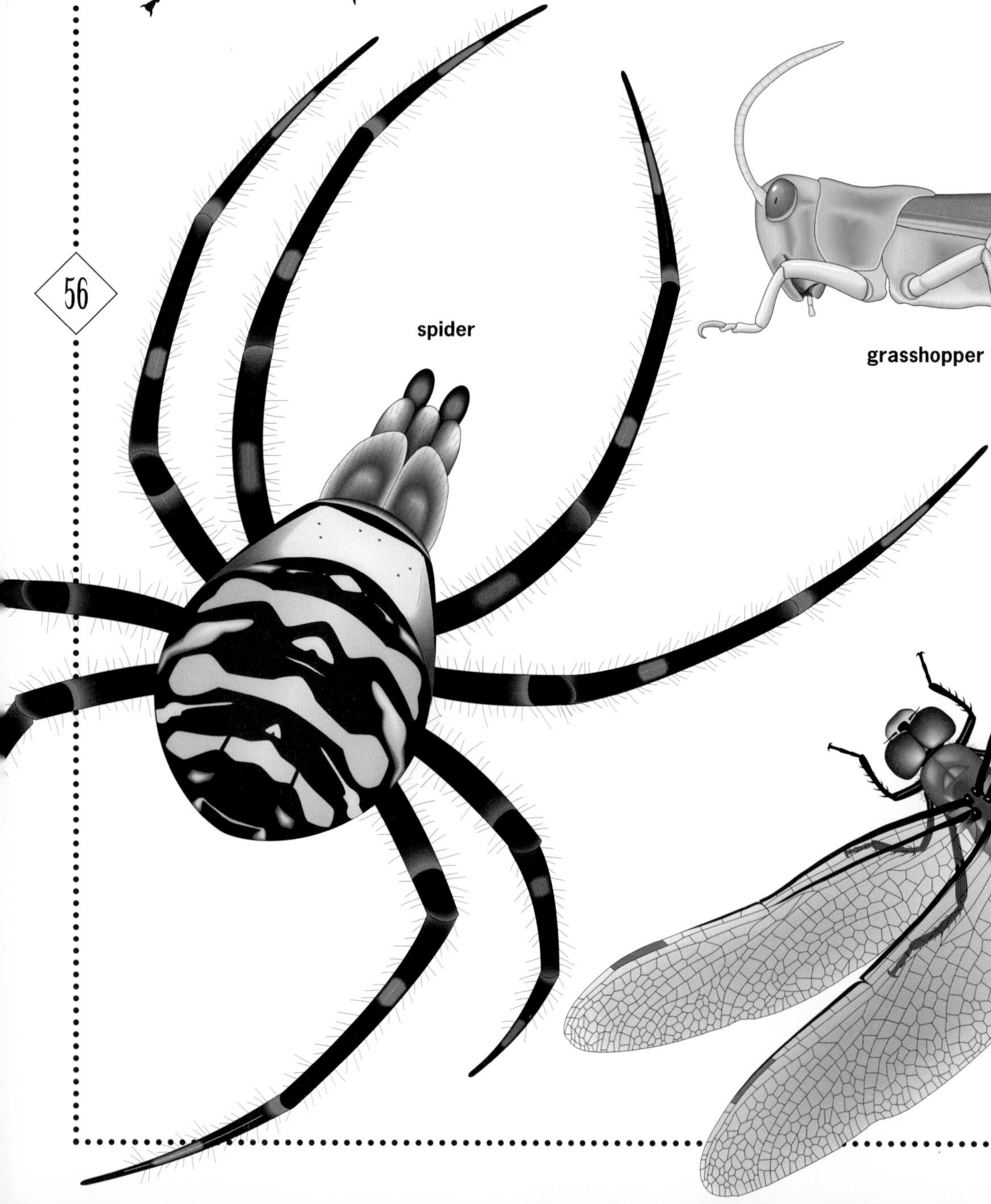

spider

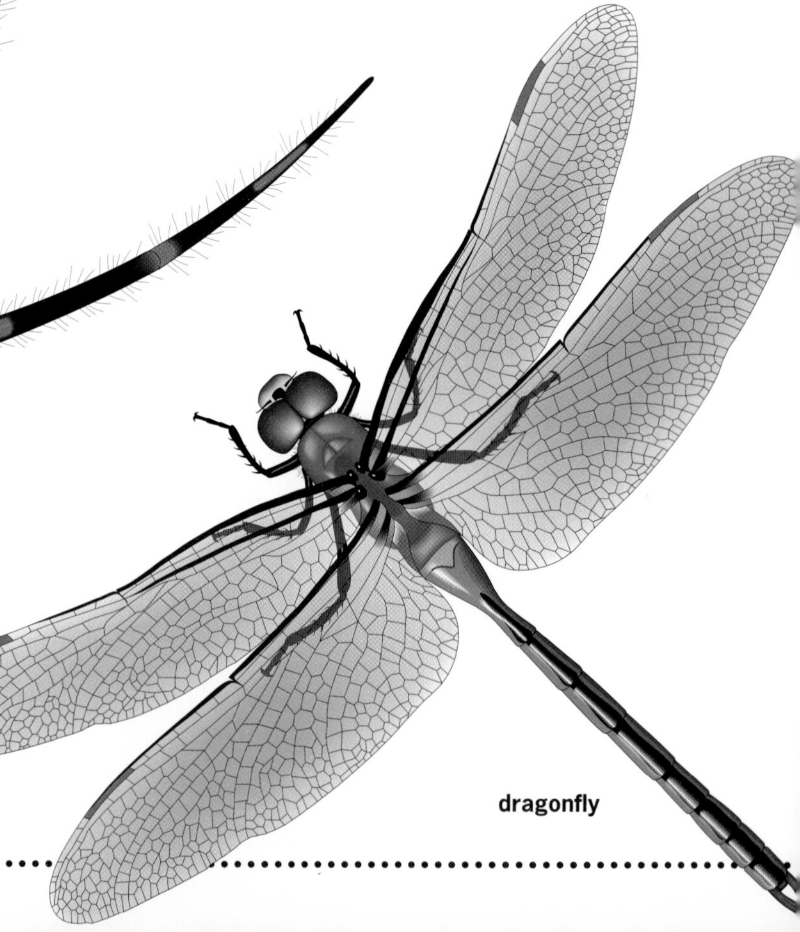

dragonfly

BUTTERFLY

caterpillar
head
simple eye
mandible
walking leg
proleg
chrysalis
forewing
wing vein
cell
thorax
head
antenna
labial palp
compound eye
proboscis
foreleg
middle leg
claw
hind leg
abdomen
hind wing

HONEYBEE

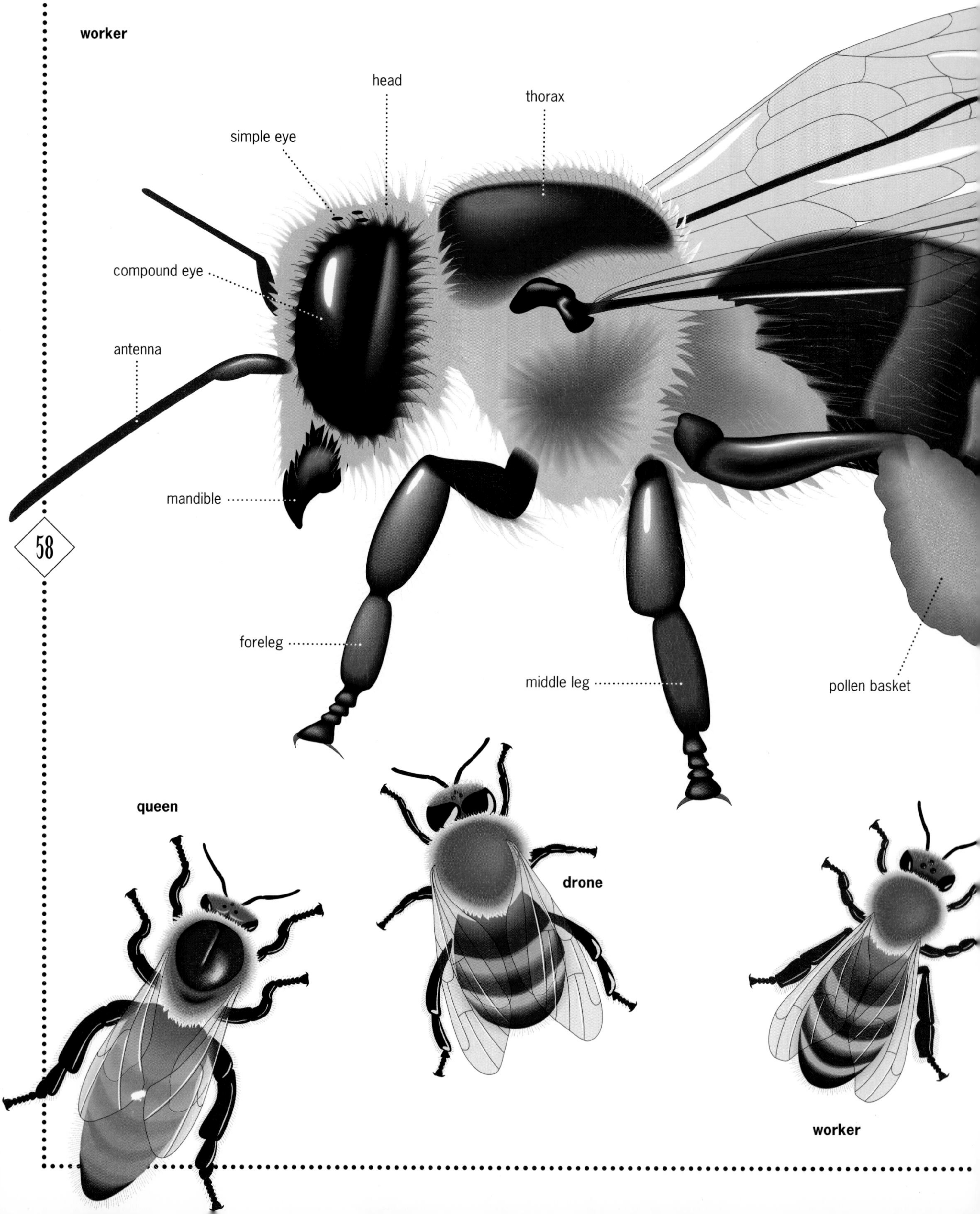
worker
head
thorax
simple eye
compound eye
antenna
mandible
foreleg
middle leg
pollen basket
queen
drone
worker

abdomen
stinger
hind leg

hive

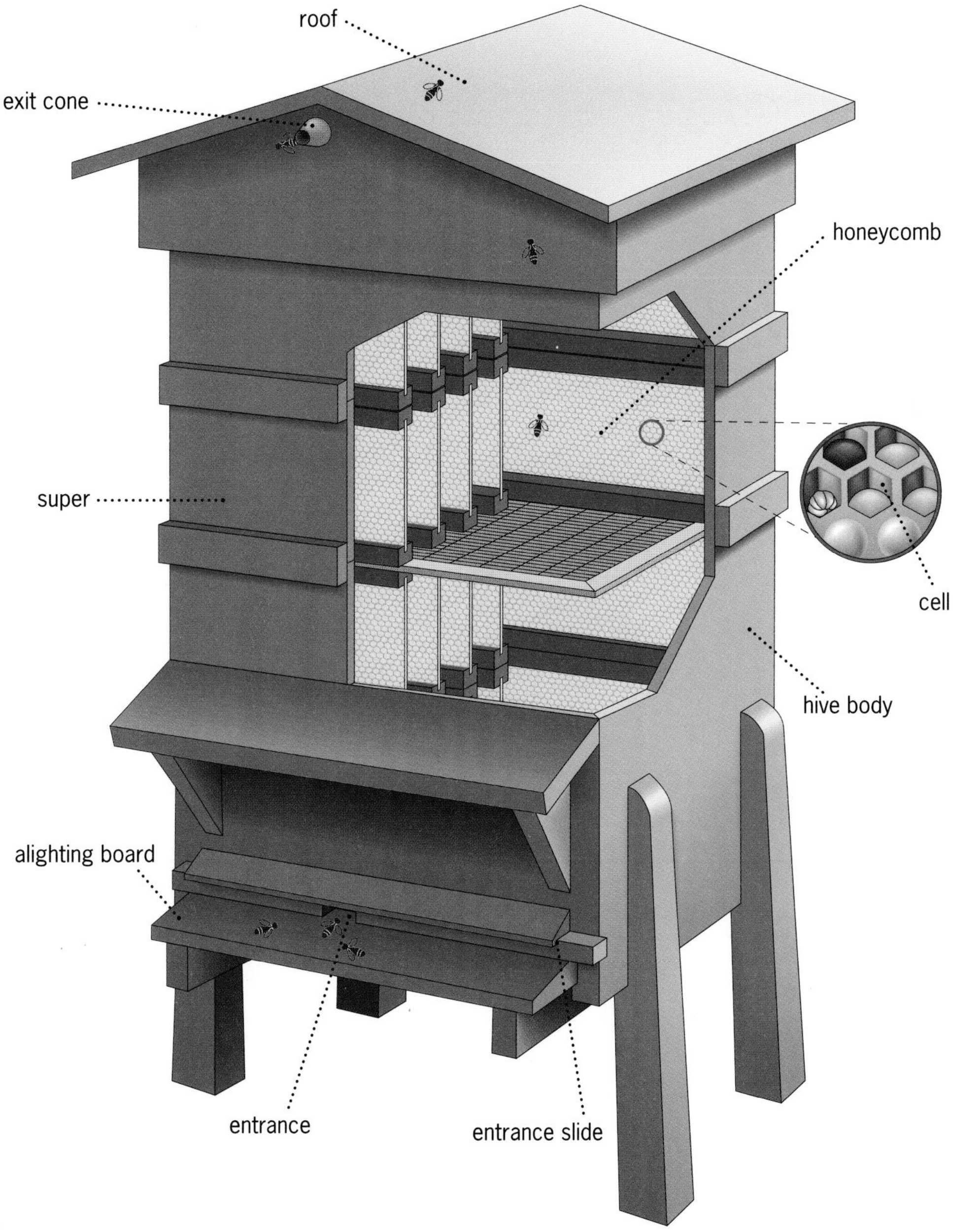
roof
exit cone
honeycomb
super
cell
hive body
alighting board
entrance
entrance slide

honeycomb section

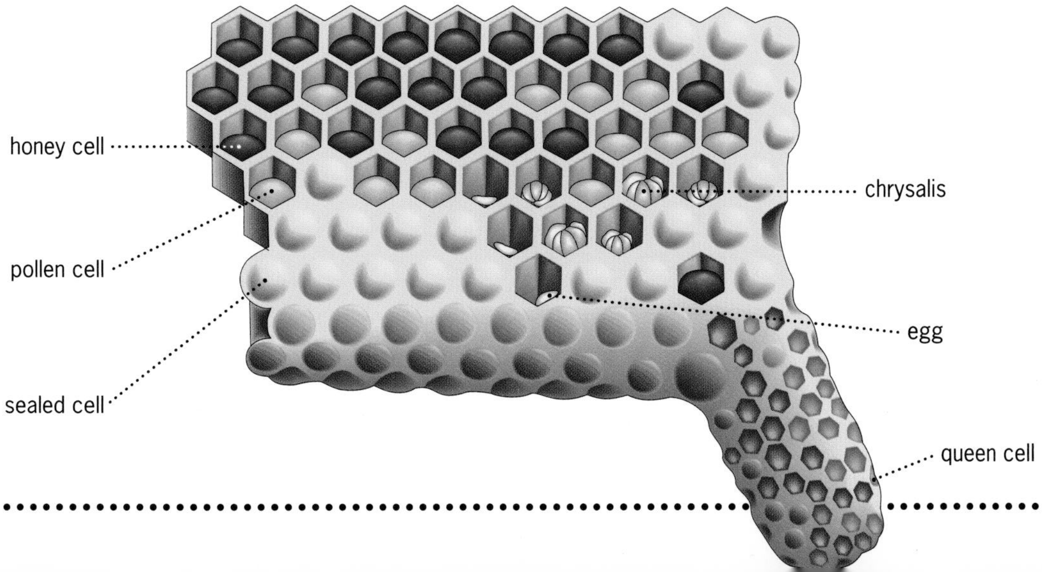
honey cell
chrysalis
pollen cell
egg
sealed cell
queen cell

AMPHIBIANS

frog

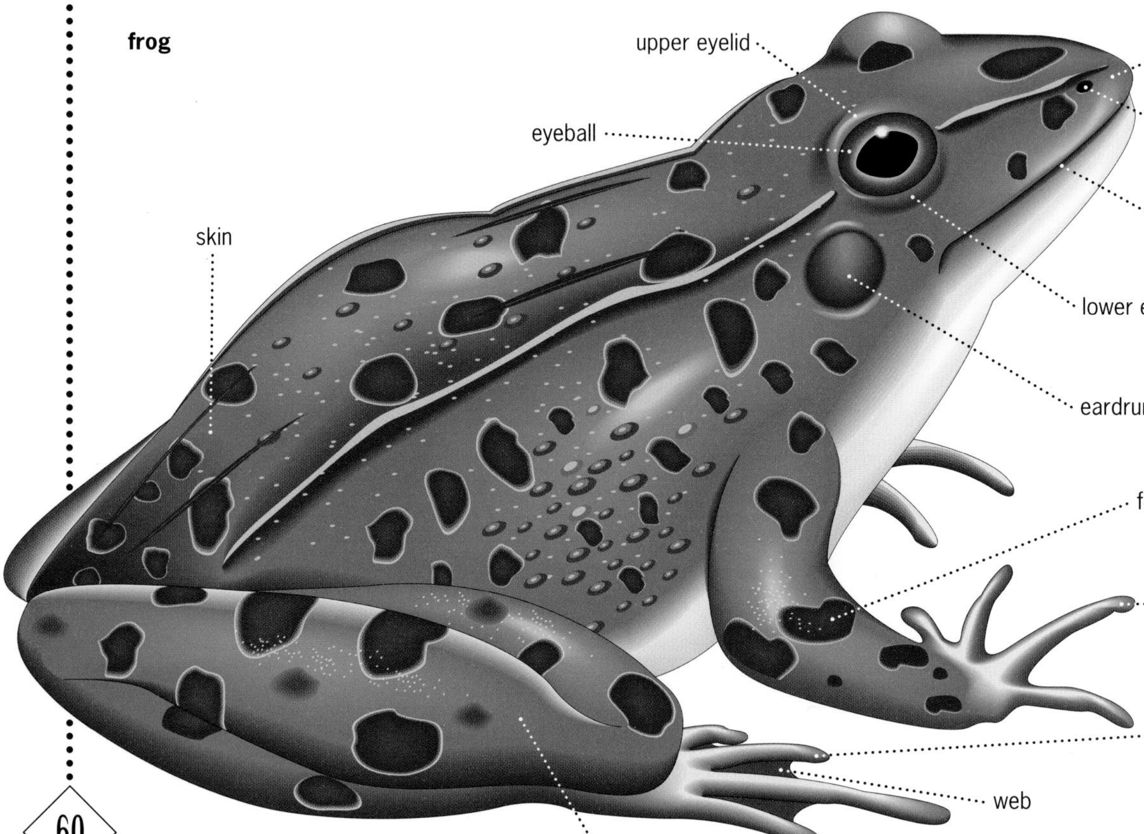
upper eyelid
snout
eyeball
nostril
mouth
skin
lower eyelid
eardrum
forelimb
digit
webbed foot
web
hind limb

LIFE CYCLE OF THE FROG

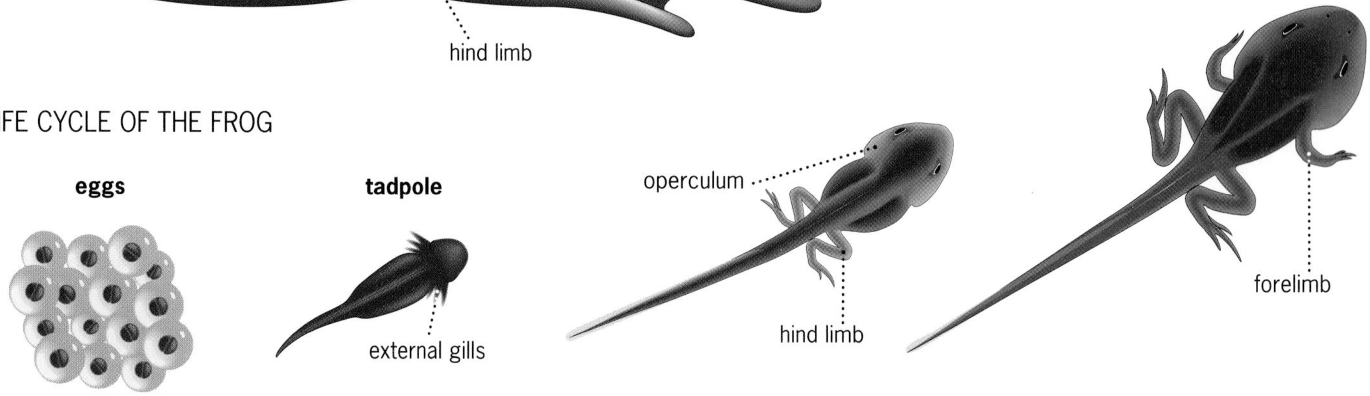
eggs
tadpole
operculum
external gills
hind limb
forelimb

MAJOR AMPHIBIANS

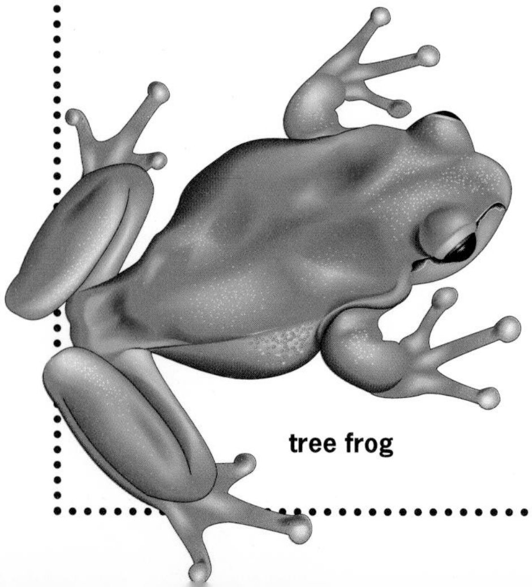

tree frog

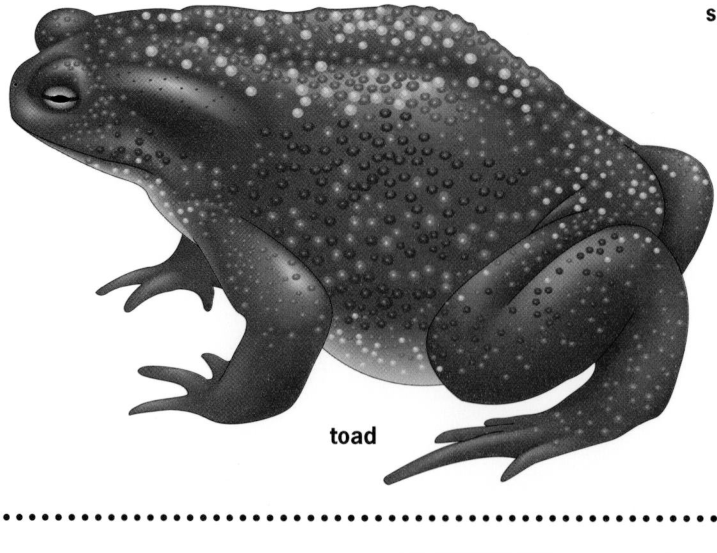

toad

salamander

CRUSTACEANS

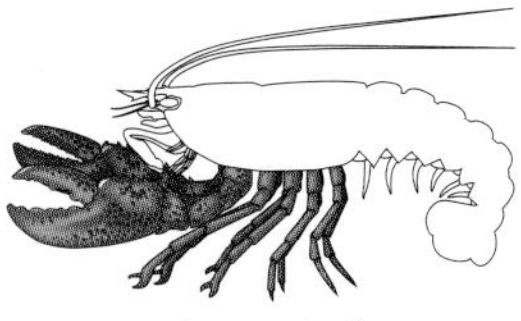

thoracic legs

lobster

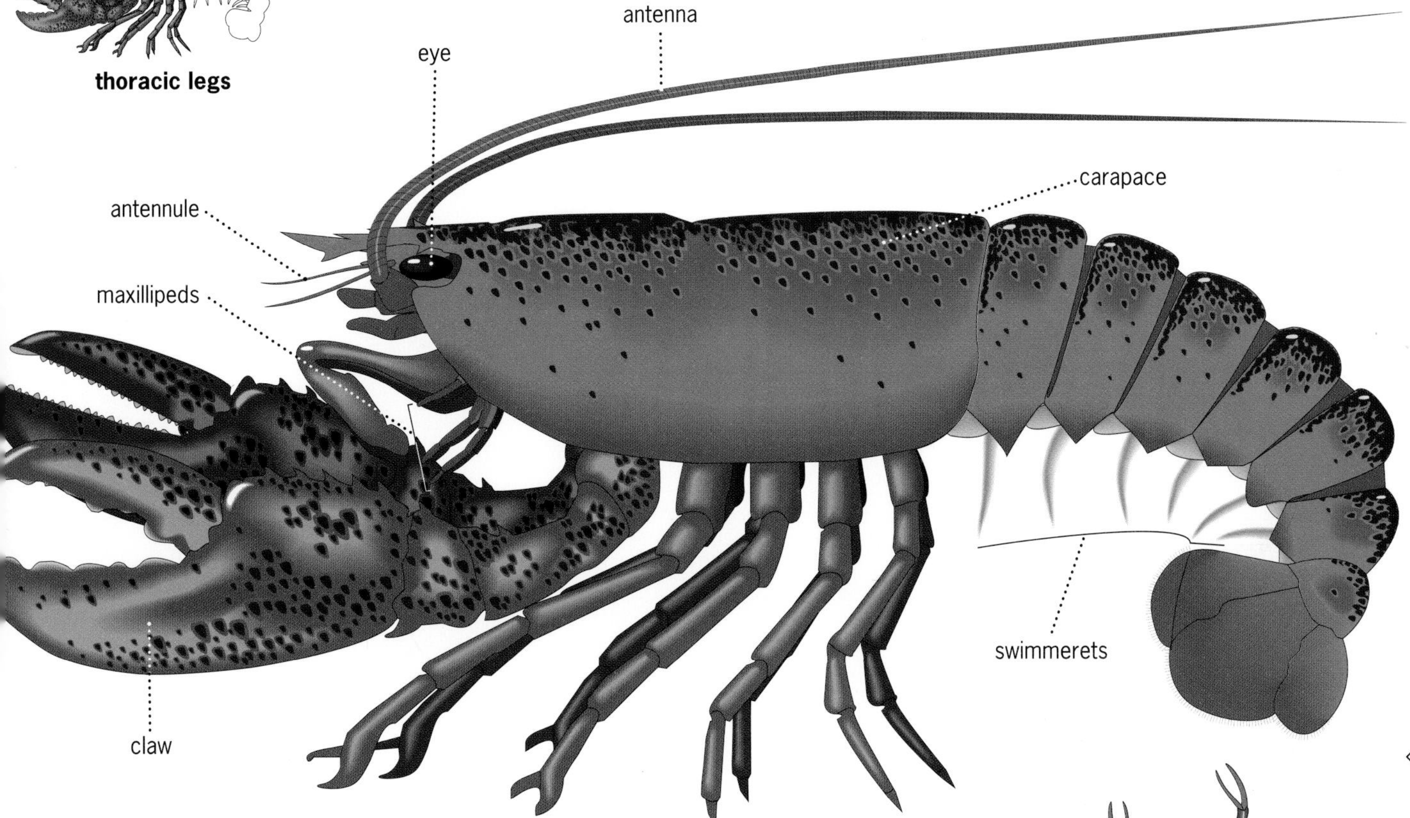
antenna
eye
carapace
antennule
maxillipeds
swimmerets
claw

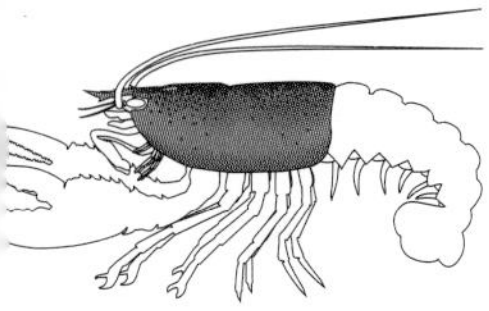

cephalothorax

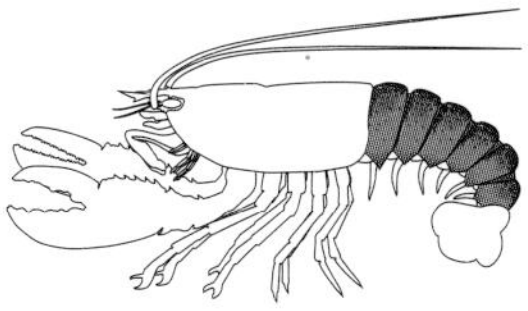

abdomen

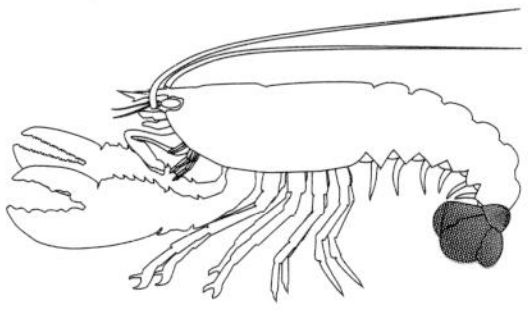

tail

MAJOR EDIBLE CRUSTACEANS

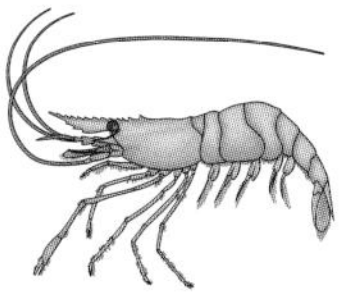

shrimp

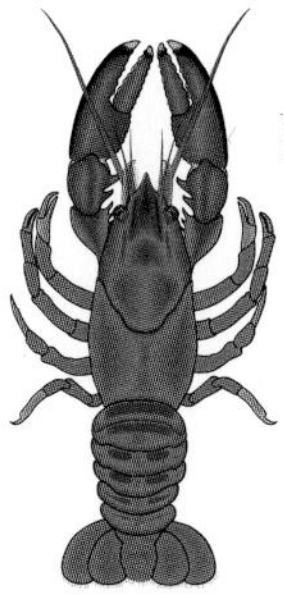

crayfish

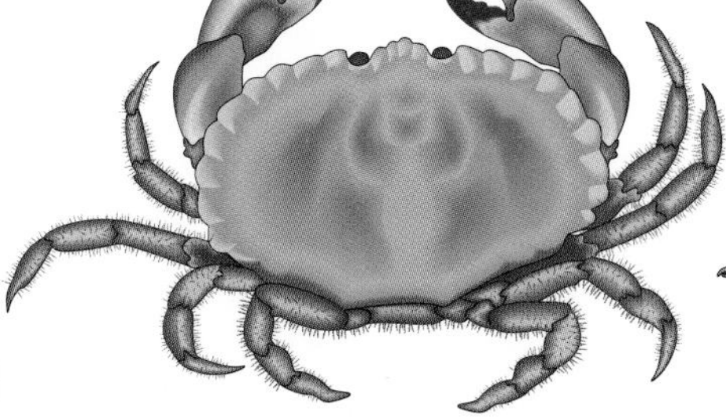

crab

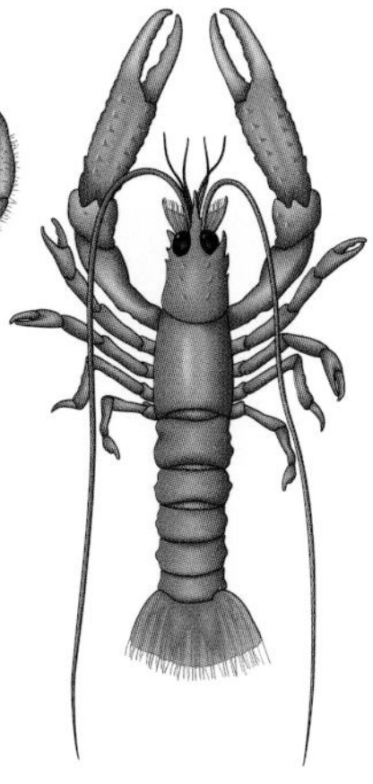

scampi

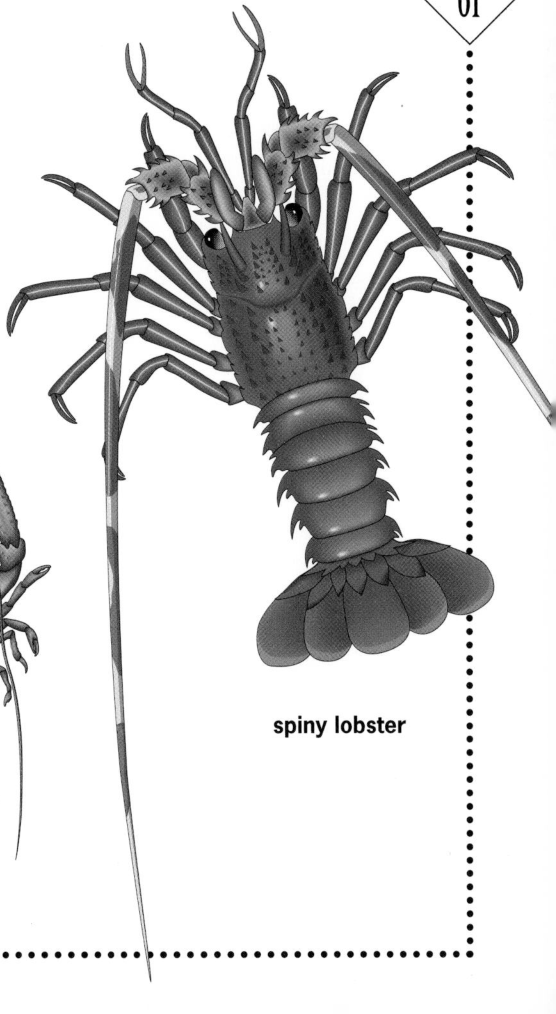

spiny lobster

FISH

MORPHOLOGY

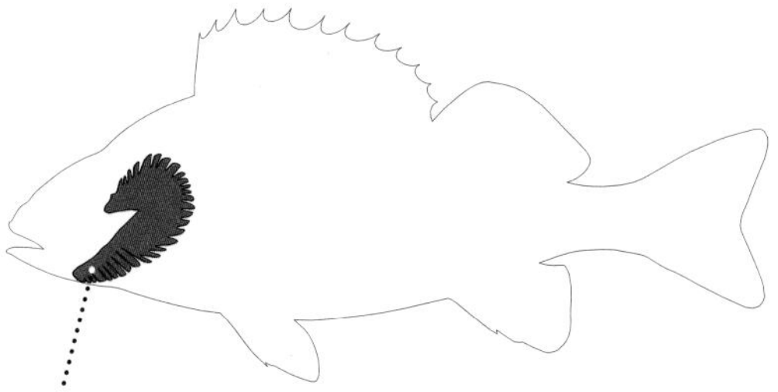
gills

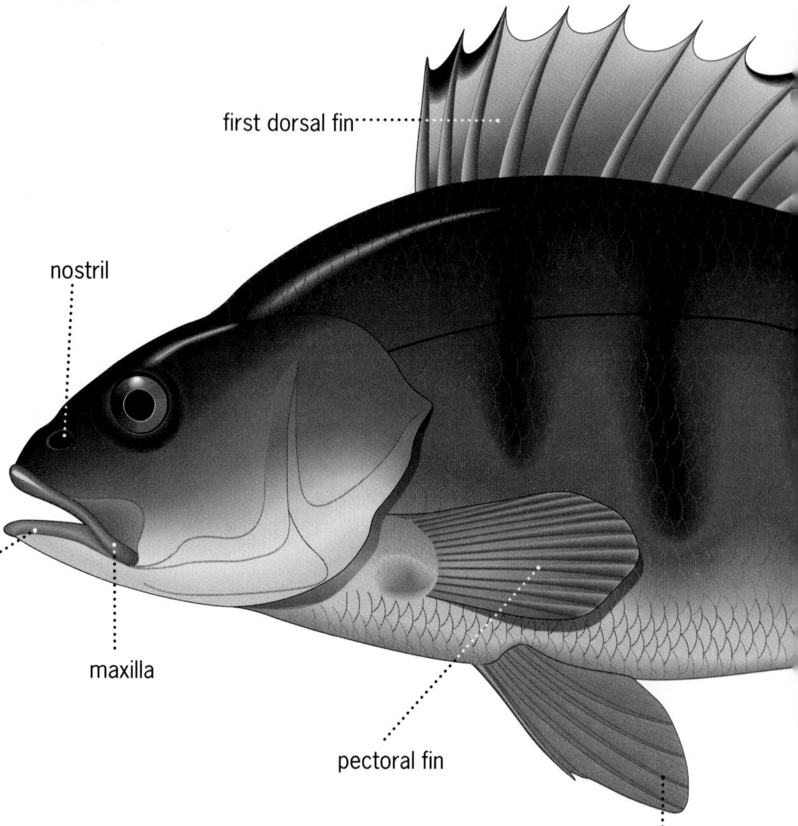
first dorsal fin
nostril
mandible
maxilla
pectoral fin
pelvic fin

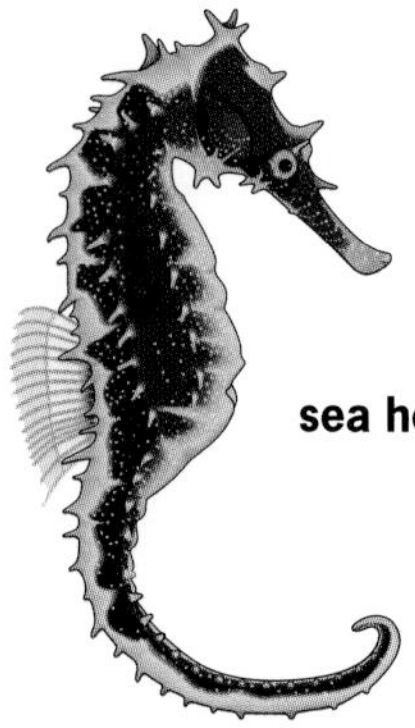

sea horse

trout

swordfish

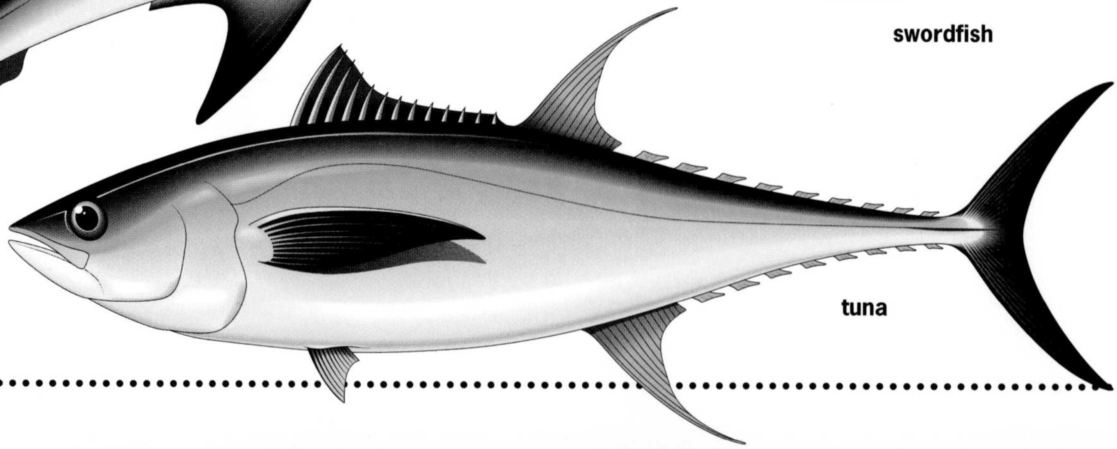

tuna

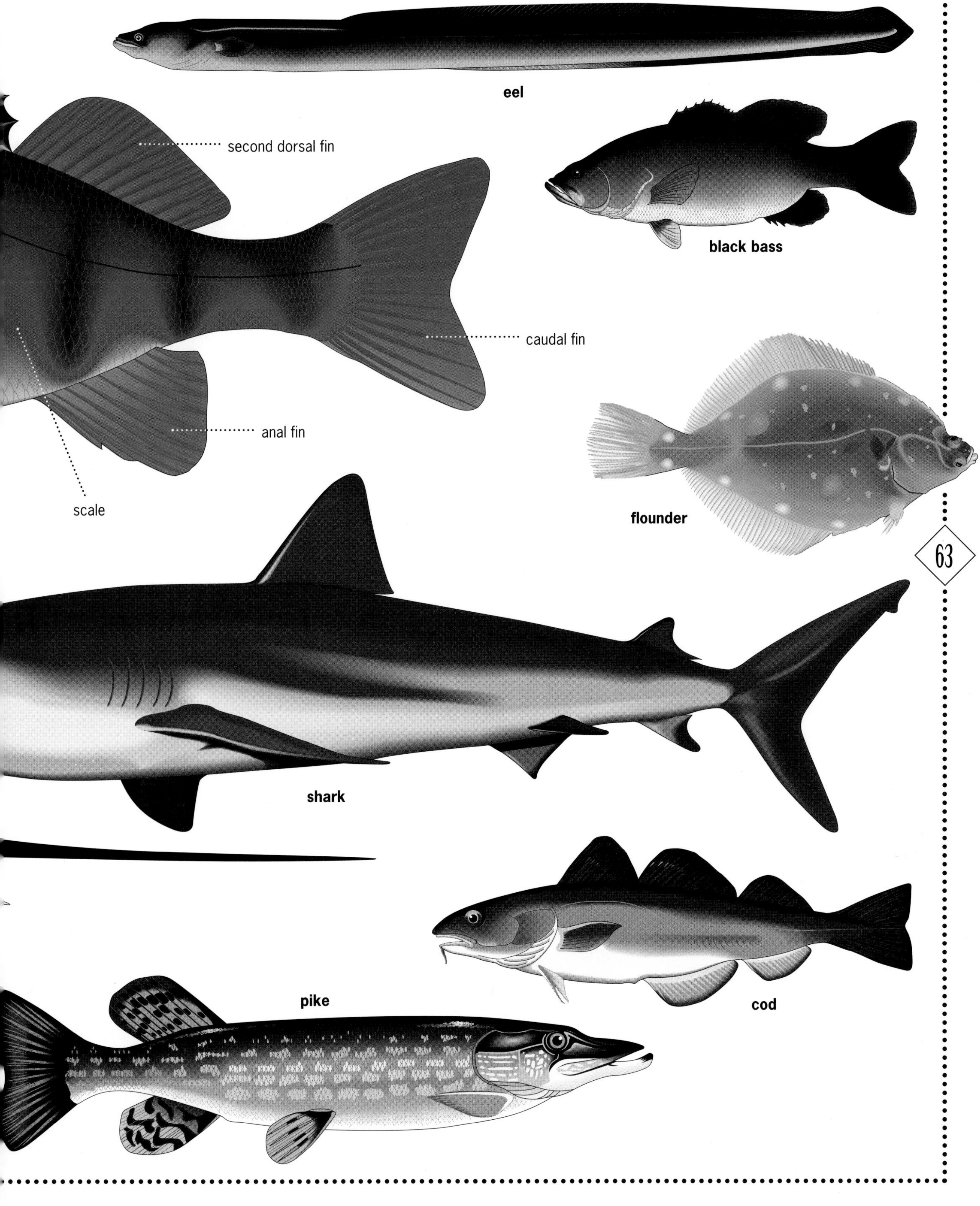
eel
second dorsal fin
black bass
caudal fin
anal fin
flounder
scale
shark
cod
pike

REPTILES

turtle

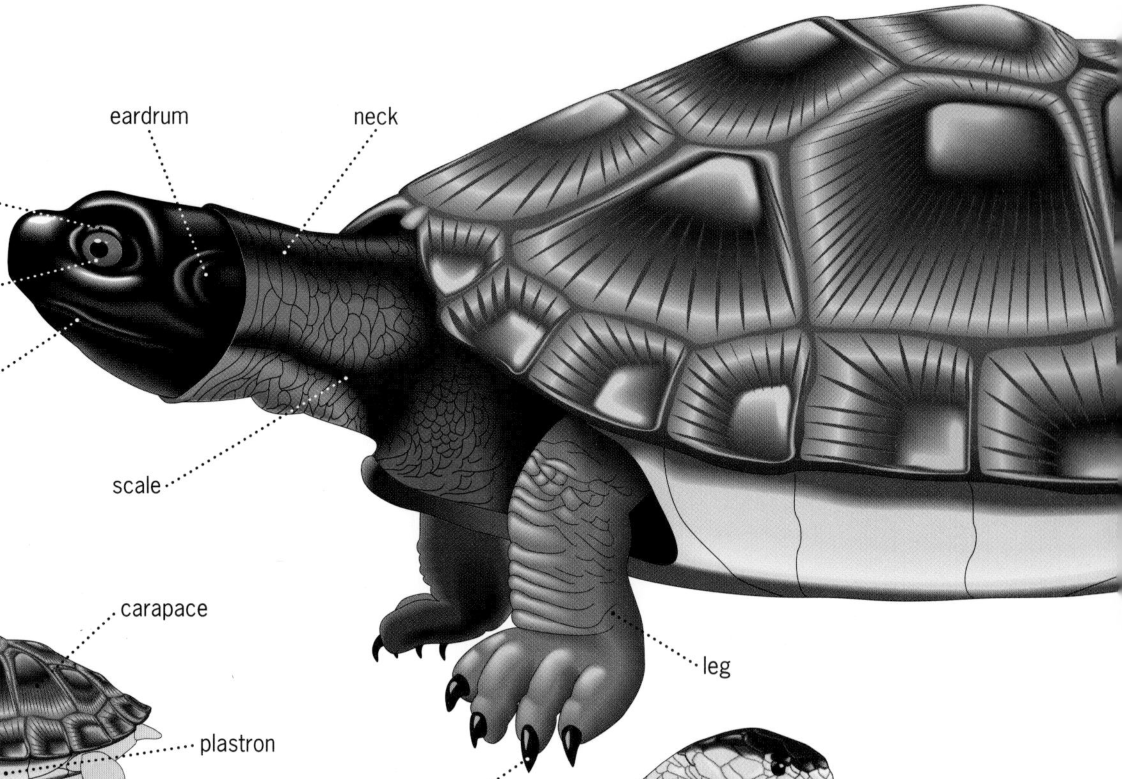
eardrum
neck
eyelid
eye
horny beak
scale
leg
claw

shell

carapace
plastron

venomous snake's head

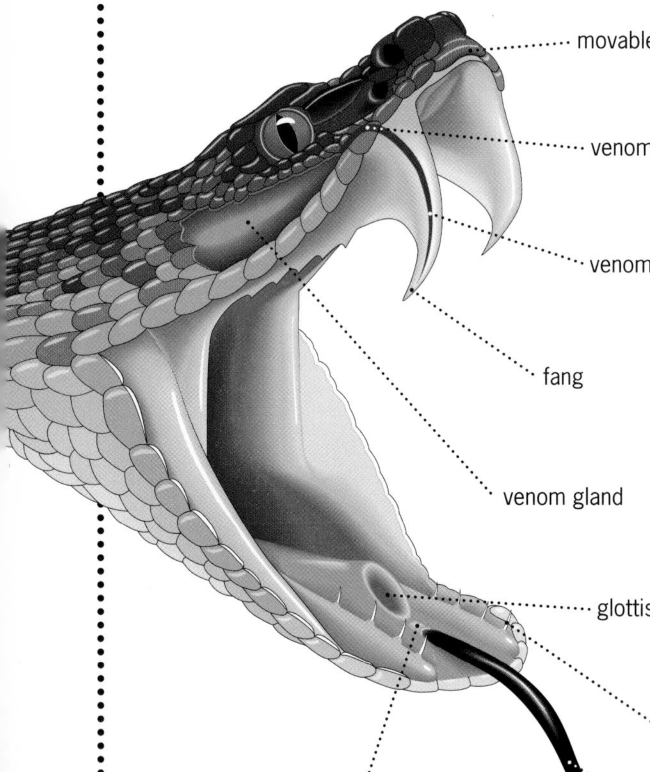
movable maxillary
venom-conducting tube
venom canal
fang
venom gland
glottis
tooth
tongue sheath
forked tongue

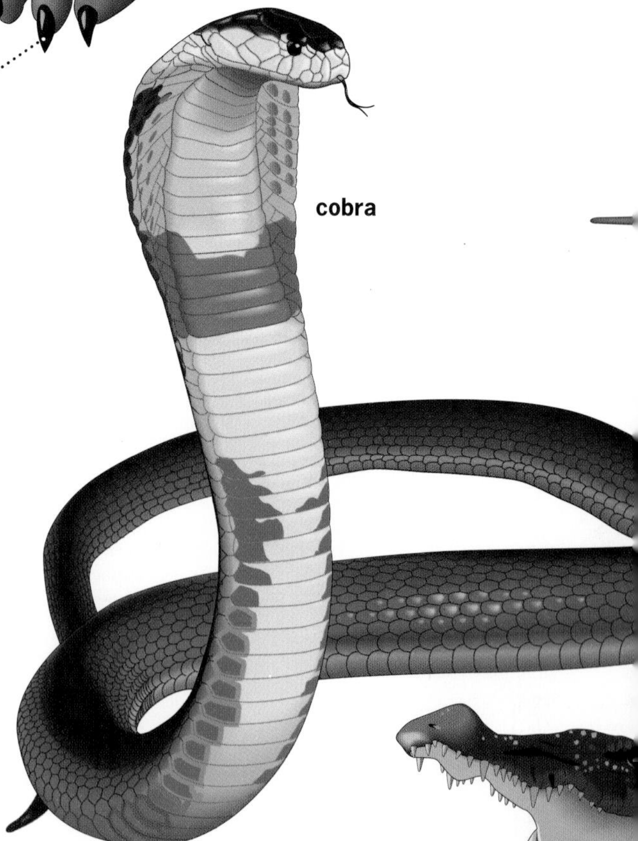

cobra

crocodile

shield
tail
chameleon
lizard
rattlesnake

CAT

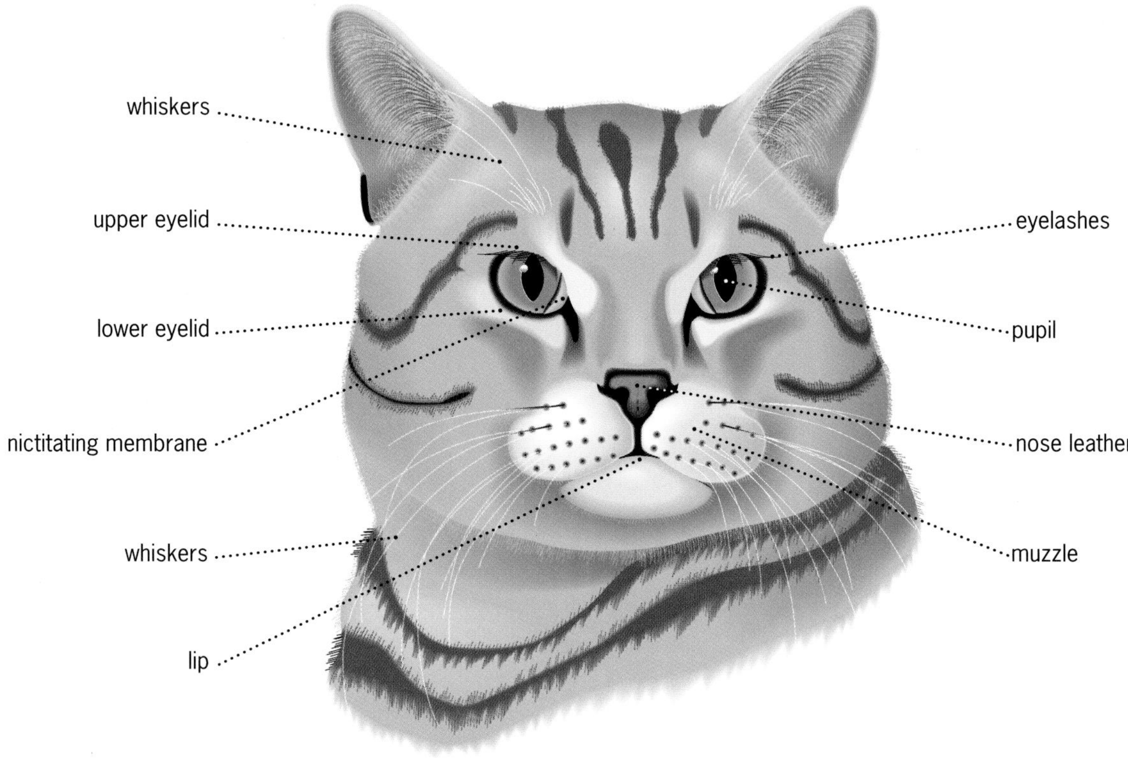
whiskers
upper eyelid
lower eyelid
nictitating membrane
whiskers
lip
eyelashes
pupil
nose leather
muzzle

DOG

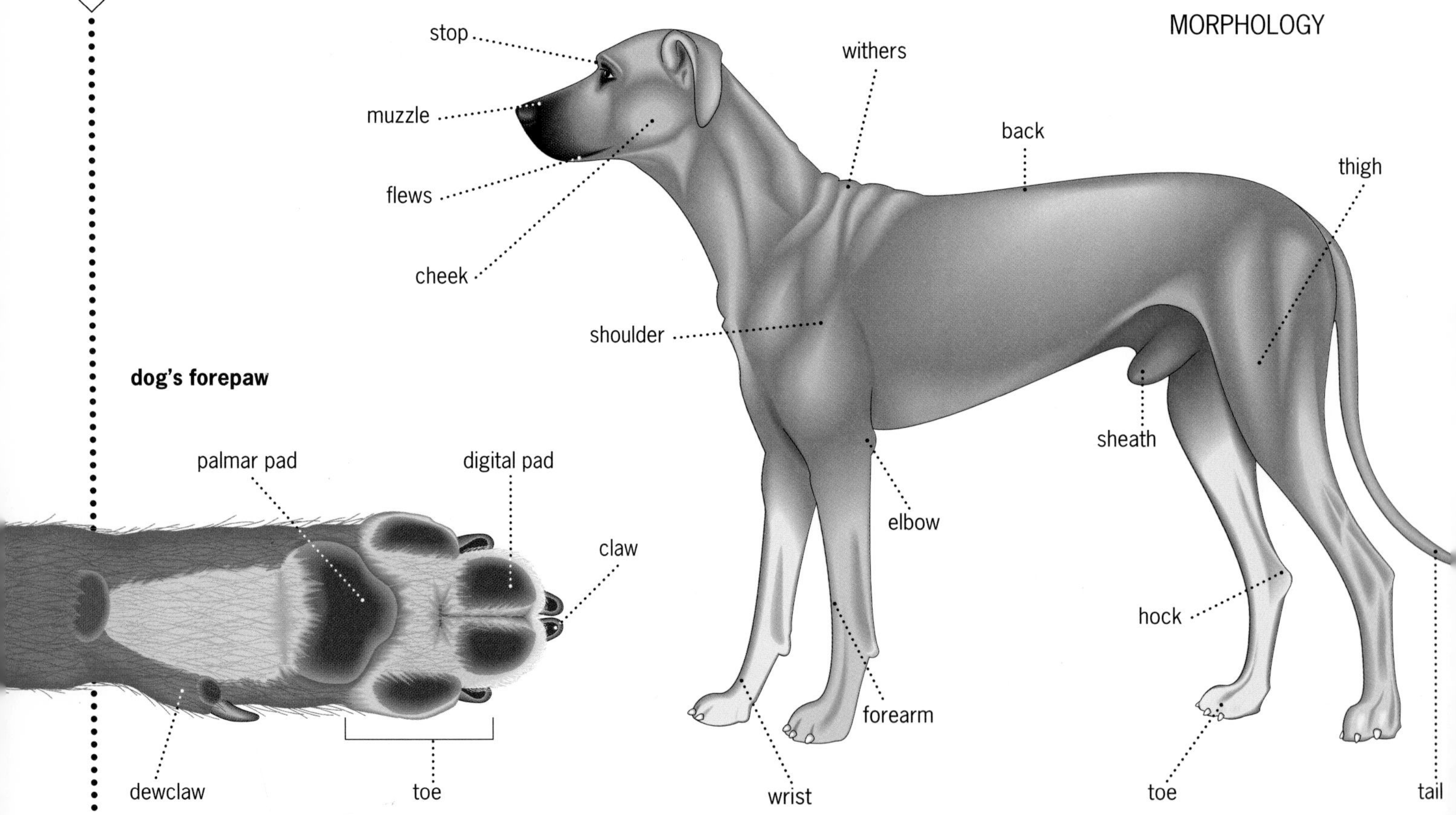
MORPHOLOGY
stop
muzzle
flews
cheek
shoulder
withers
back
thigh
sheath
elbow
hock
forearm
wrist
toe
tail
dog's forepaw
palmar pad
digital pad
claw
dewclaw
toe

HORSE

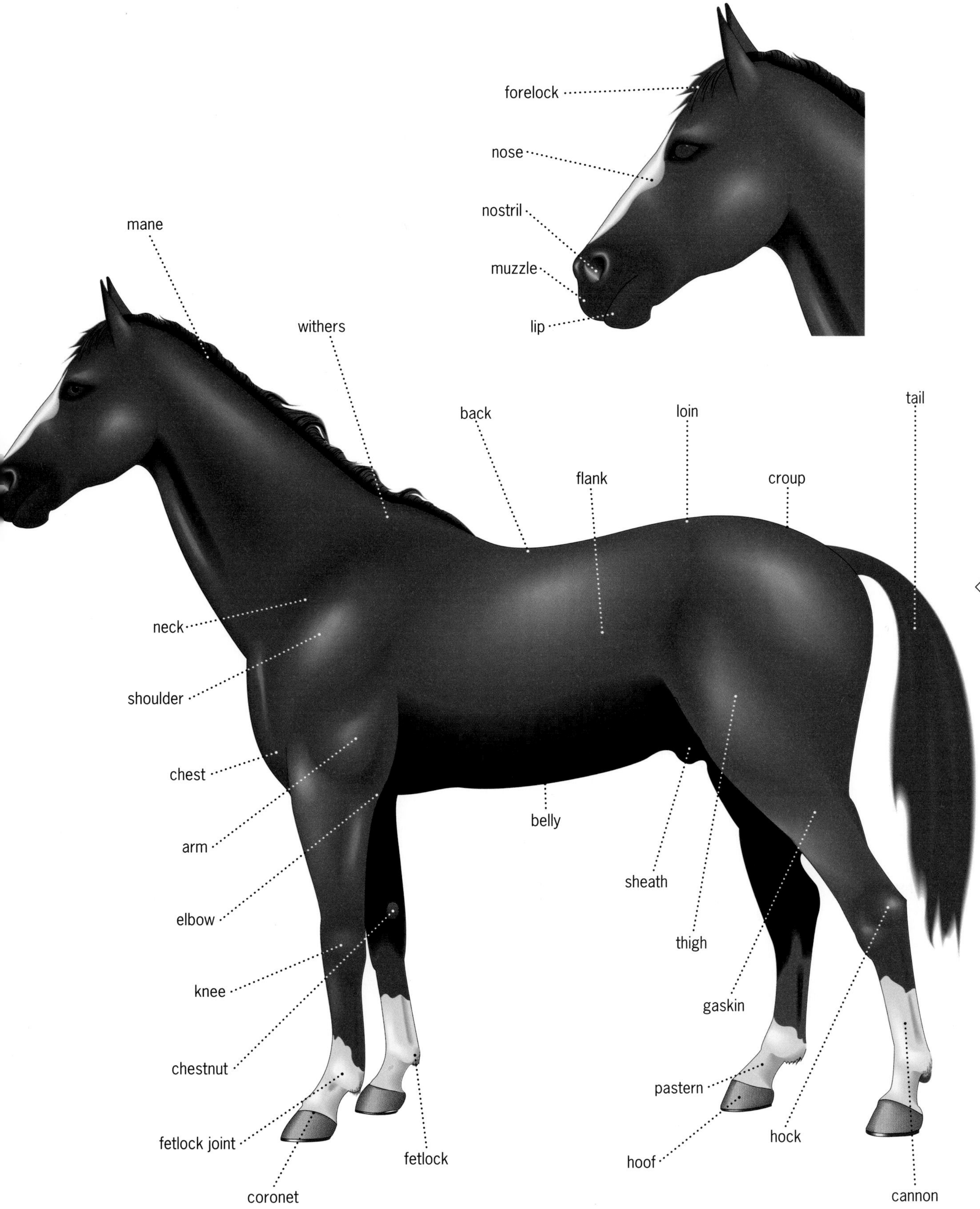
forelock
nose
nostril
muzzle
lip
mane
withers
back
loin
tail
flank
croup
neck
shoulder
chest
arm
belly
elbow
sheath
thigh
knee
gaskin
chestnut
pastern
hock
fetlock joint
fetlock
hoof
coronet
cannon

FARM ANIMALS

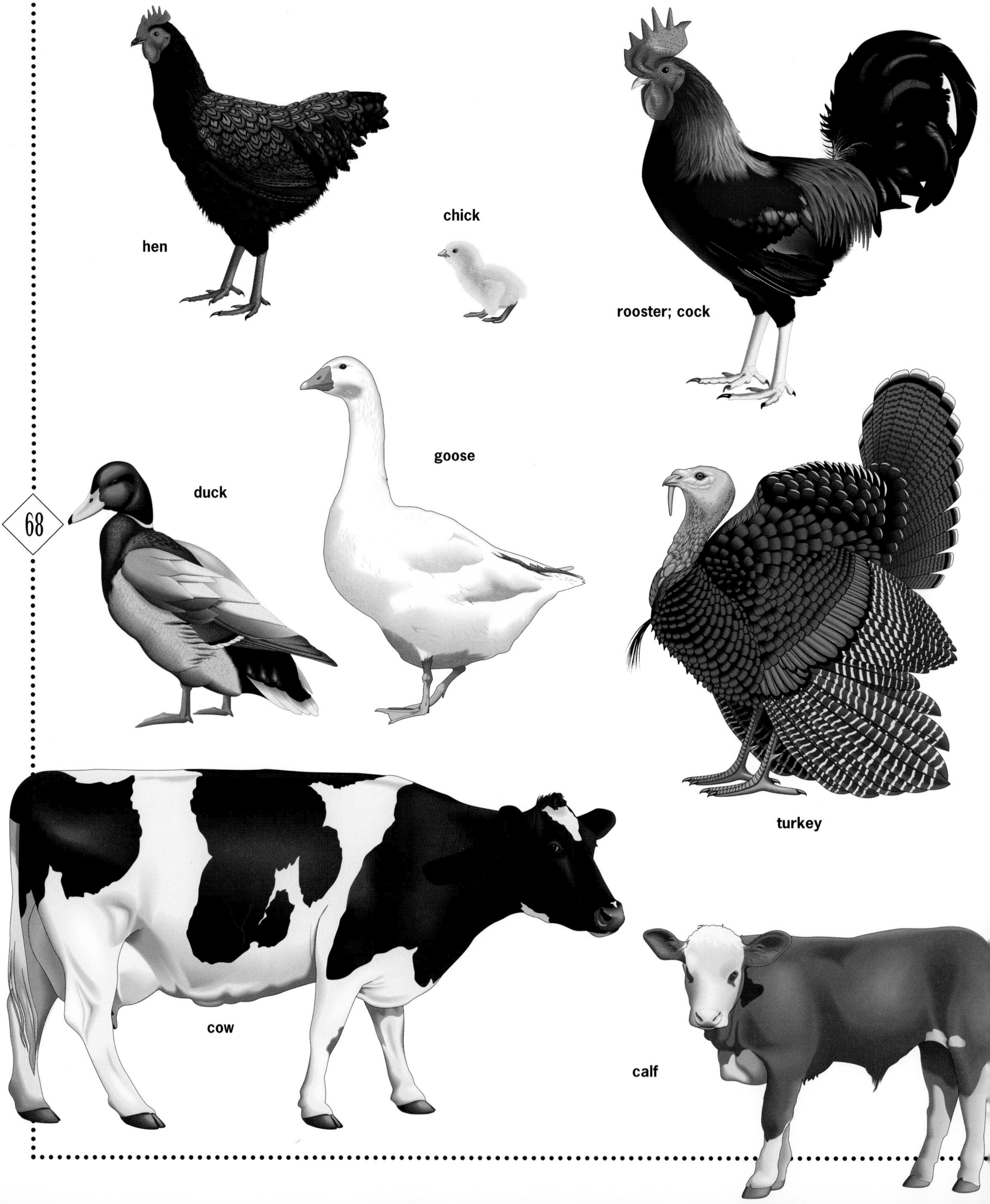
hen
chick
rooster; cock
goose
duck
turkey
cow
calf

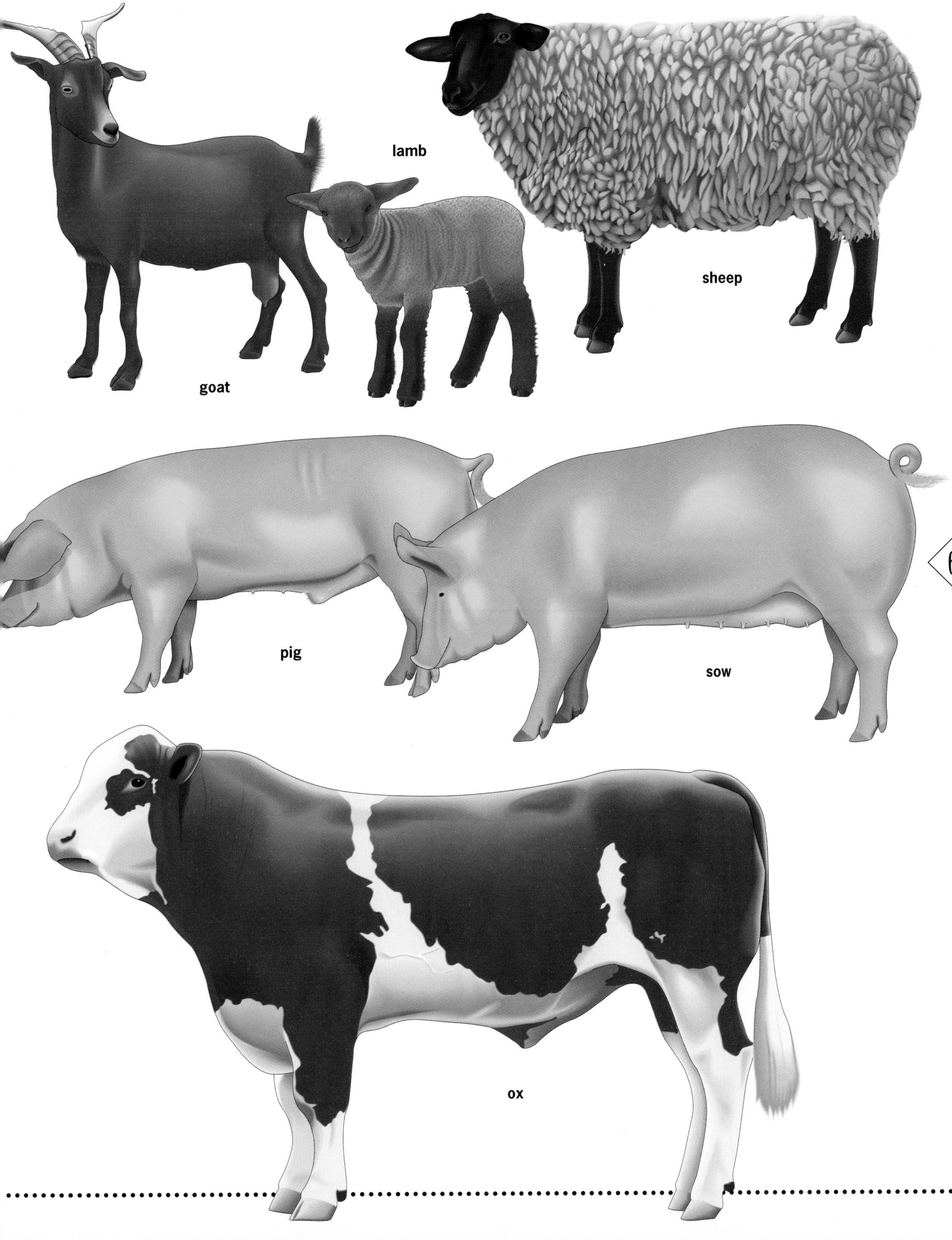
lamb
sheep
goat
pig
sow
ox

TYPES OF JAWS

rodent's jaw

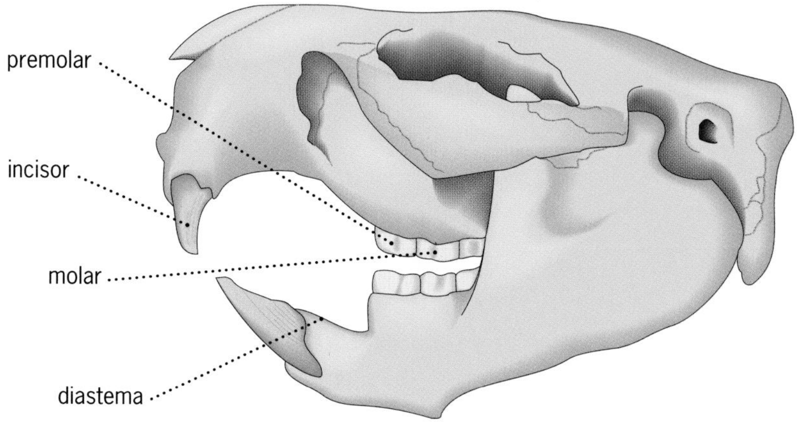
premolar
incisor
molar
diastema

beaver

carnivore's jaw

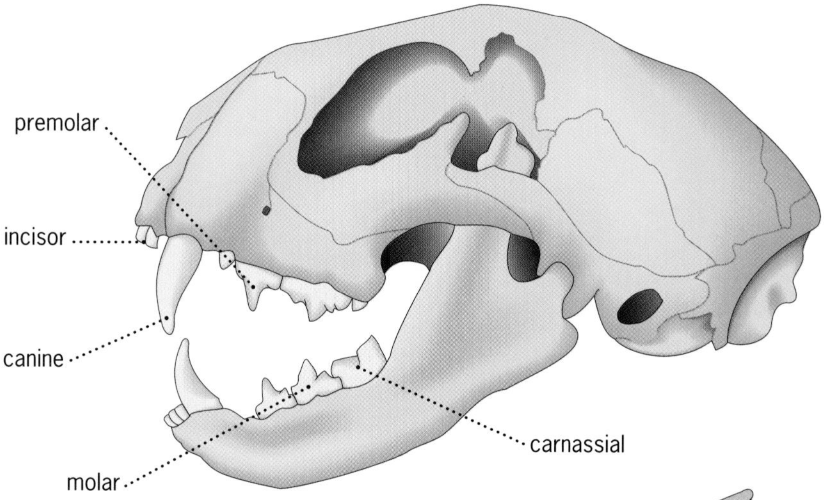
premolar
incisor
canine
molar
carnassial

lion

herbivore's jaw

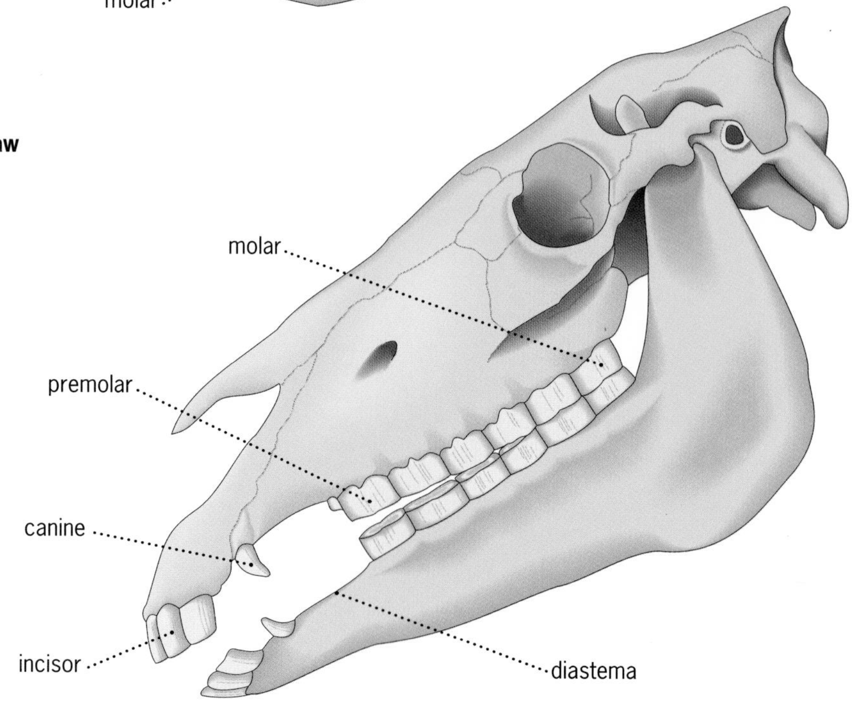
molar
premolar
canine
incisor
diastema

horse

MAJOR TYPES OF HORNS

horns of mouflon

horns of giraffe

horns of rhinoceros

MAJOR TYPES OF TUSKS

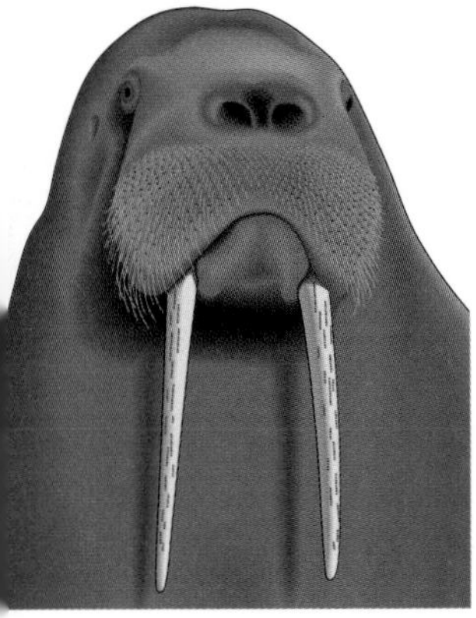

tusks of walrus

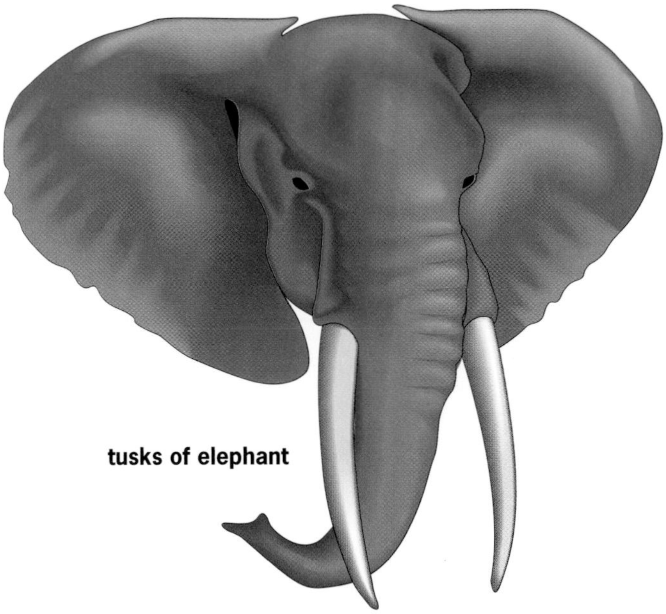

tusks of elephant

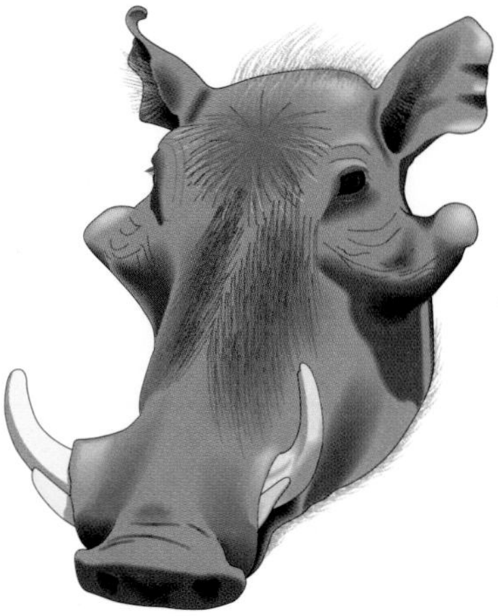

tusks of wart hog

TYPES OF HOOFS

one-toe hoof

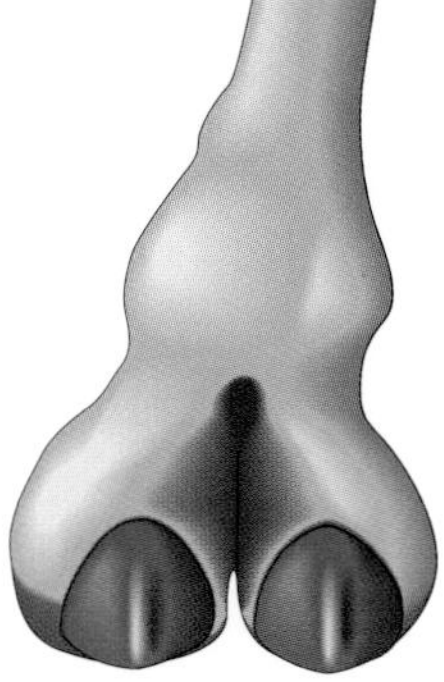

two-toed hoof

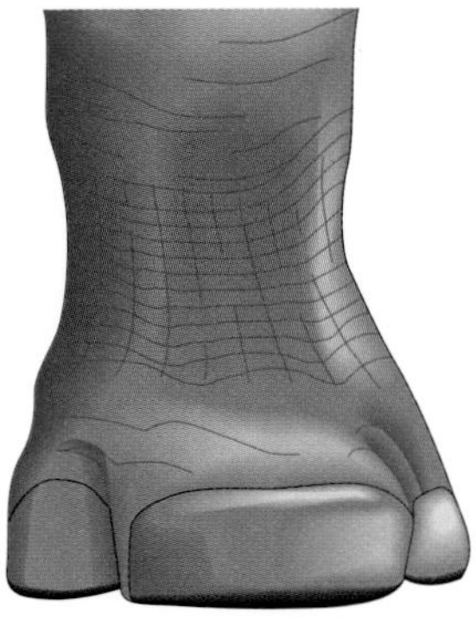

three-toed hoof

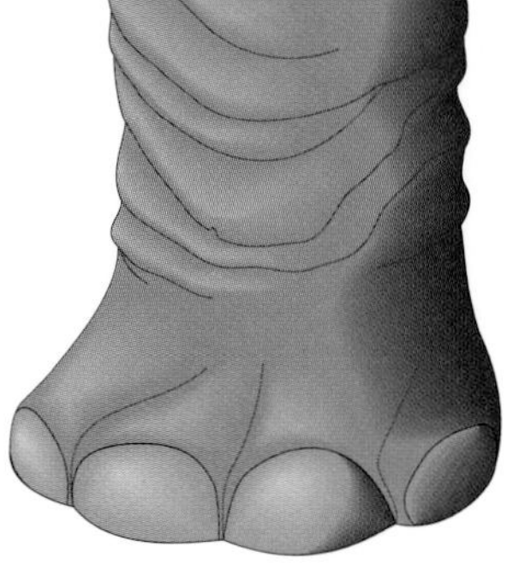

four-toed hoof

WILD ANIMALS

polar bear

giraffe

monkey

lion

dolphin

whale

kangaroo

elephant

dromedary; Arabian camel

zebra

white-tailed deer

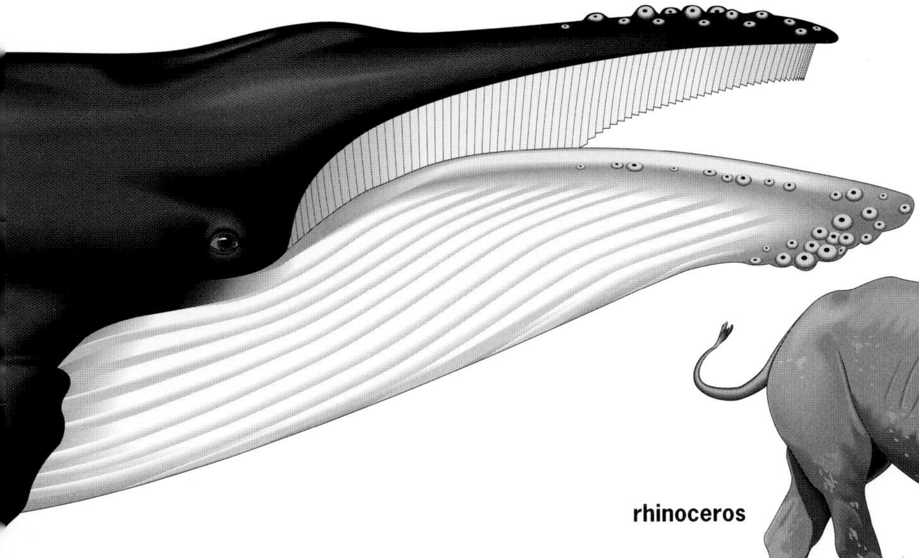

rhinoceros

BIRD

PRINCIPAL TYPES OF BILLS

aquatic bird

insectivorous bird

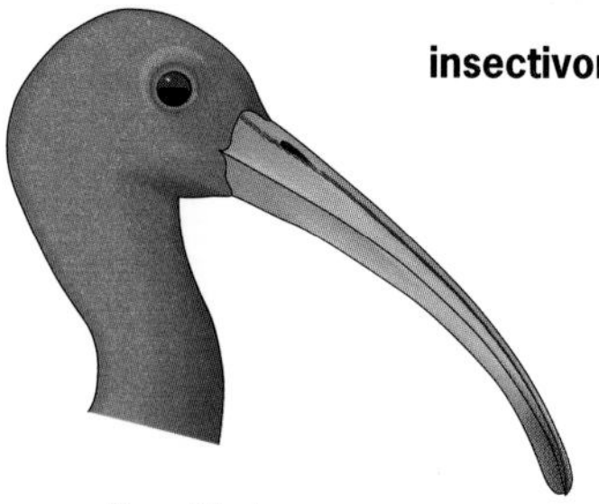

wading bird

granivorous bird

bird of prey

PRINCIPAL TYPES OF FEET

bird of prey

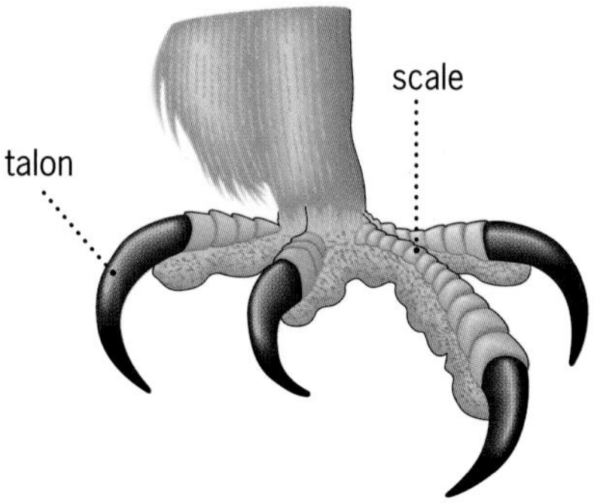
scale
talon

aquatic bird

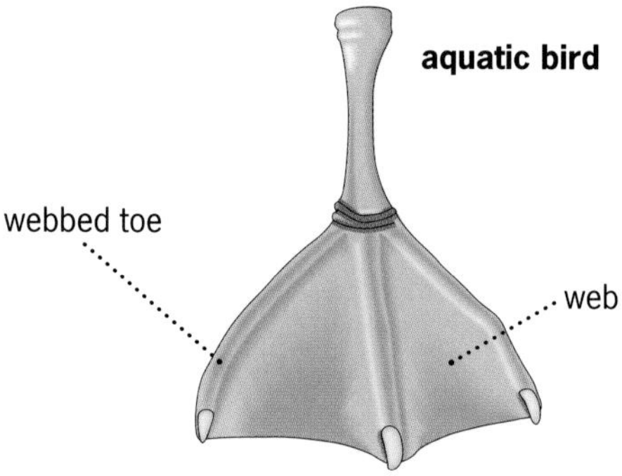
webbed toe
web

aquatic bird

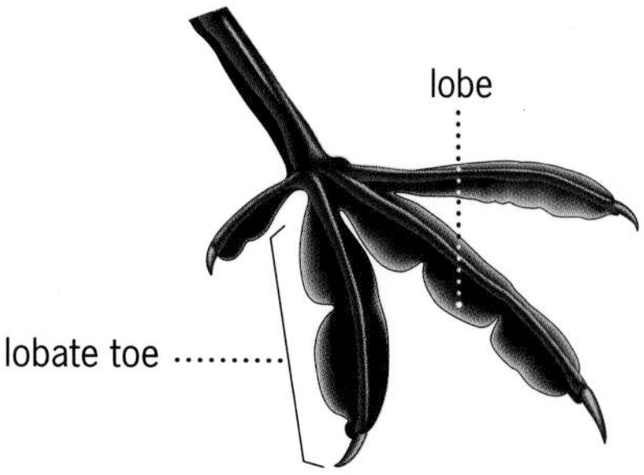
lobe
lobate toe

perching bird

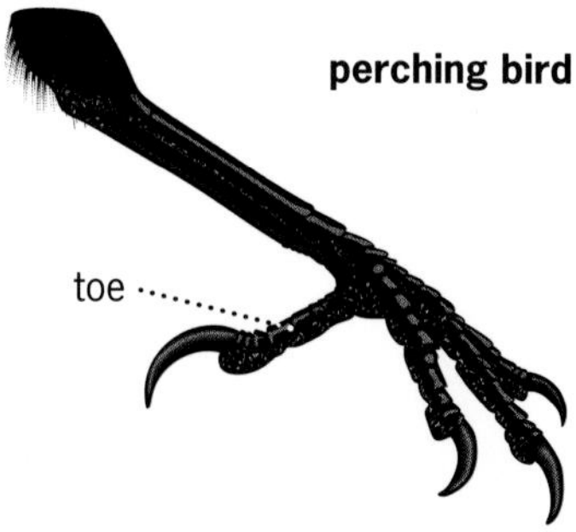
toe

MORPHOLOGY

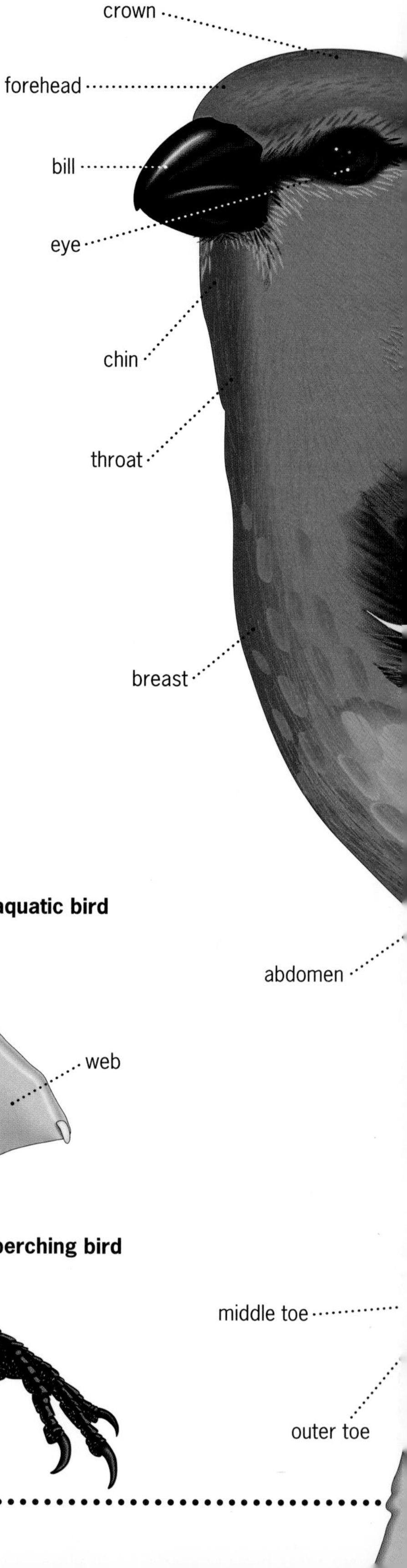
crown
forehead
bill
eye
chin
throat
breast
abdomen
middle toe
outer toe

bird's nest

birdhouse

bird feeder

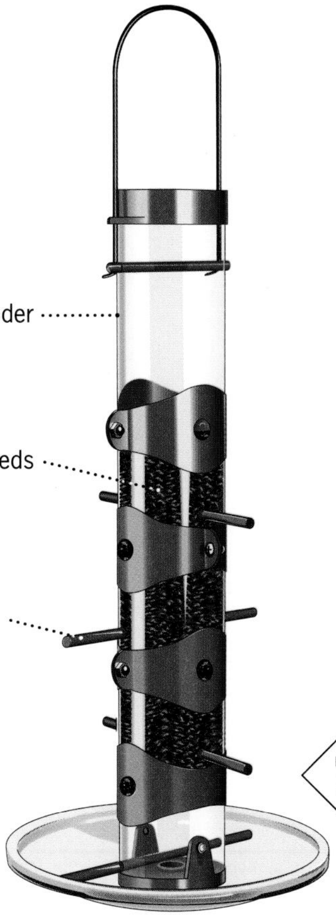
cylinder
seeds
perch

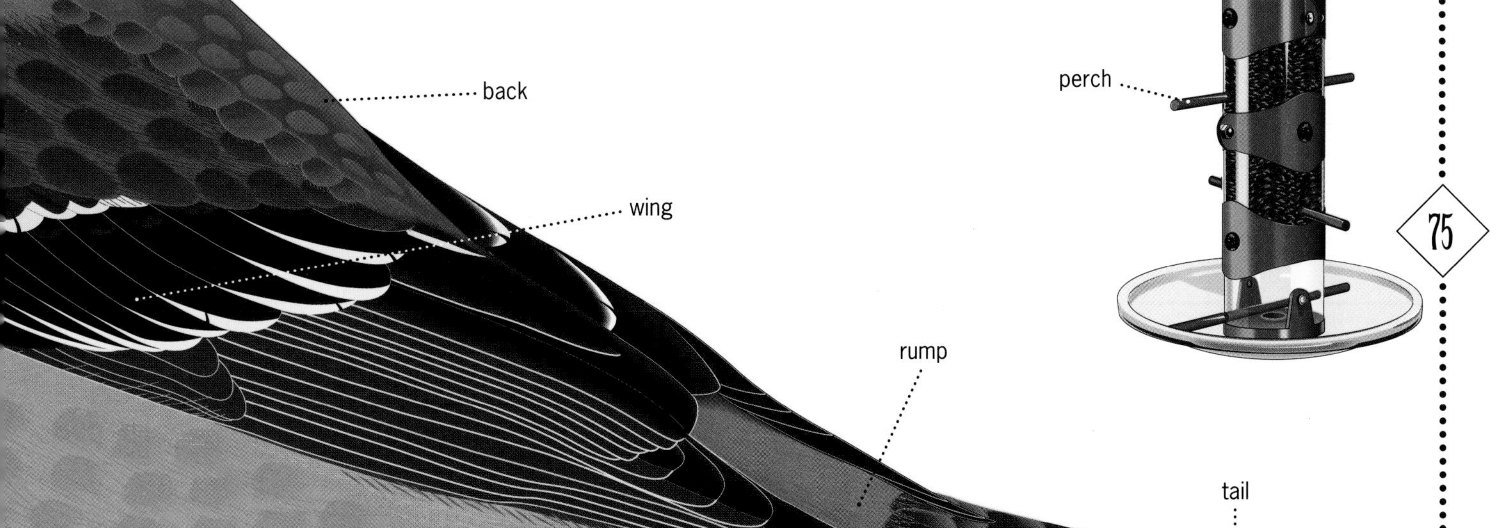
nape
back
wing
rump
tail
under tail covert
upper tail covert
flank
foot
hind toe
claw

egg

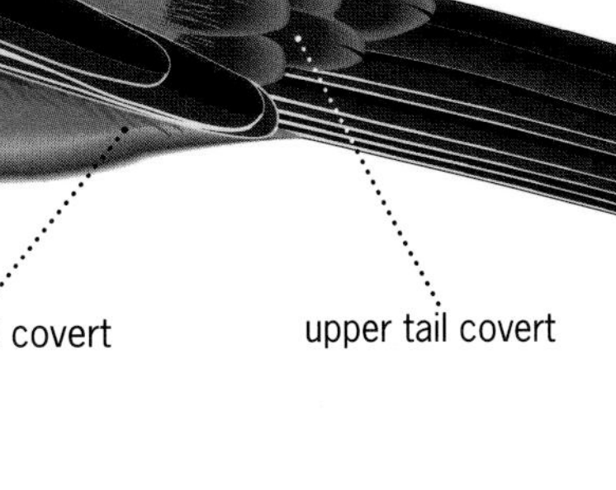
shell
blastodisc
air space
yolk
albumen

EXAMPLES OF BIRDS

crow
parrot
stork
swallow
flamingo
ostrich

robin

blue jay

owl

hummingbird

nightingale

peacock

HUMAN BODY, ANTERIOR VIEW

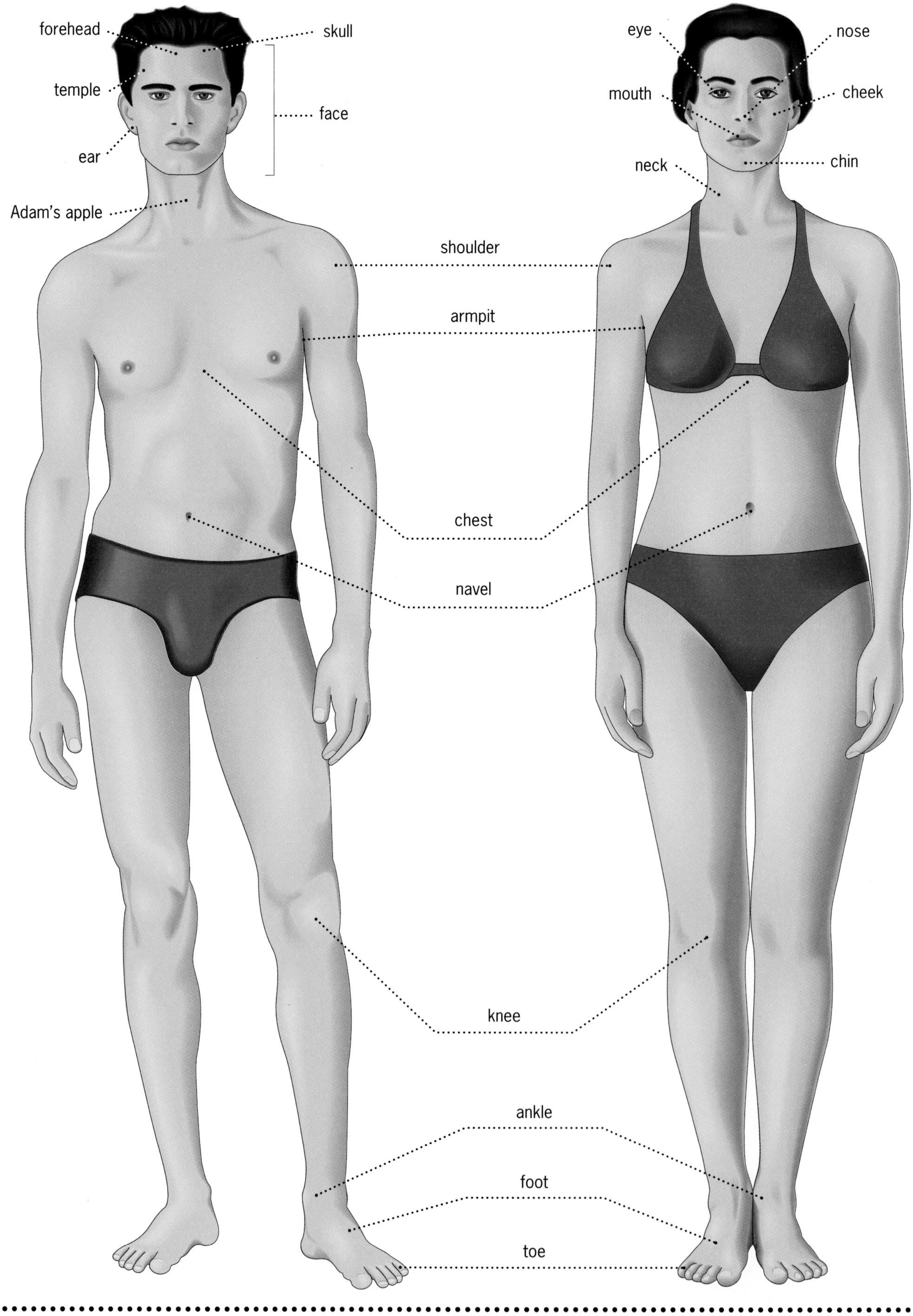
forehead
skull
temple
face
ear
Adam's apple
eye
nose
mouth
cheek
neck
chin
shoulder
armpit
chest
navel
knee
ankle
foot
toe

HUMAN BODY, POSTERIOR VIEW

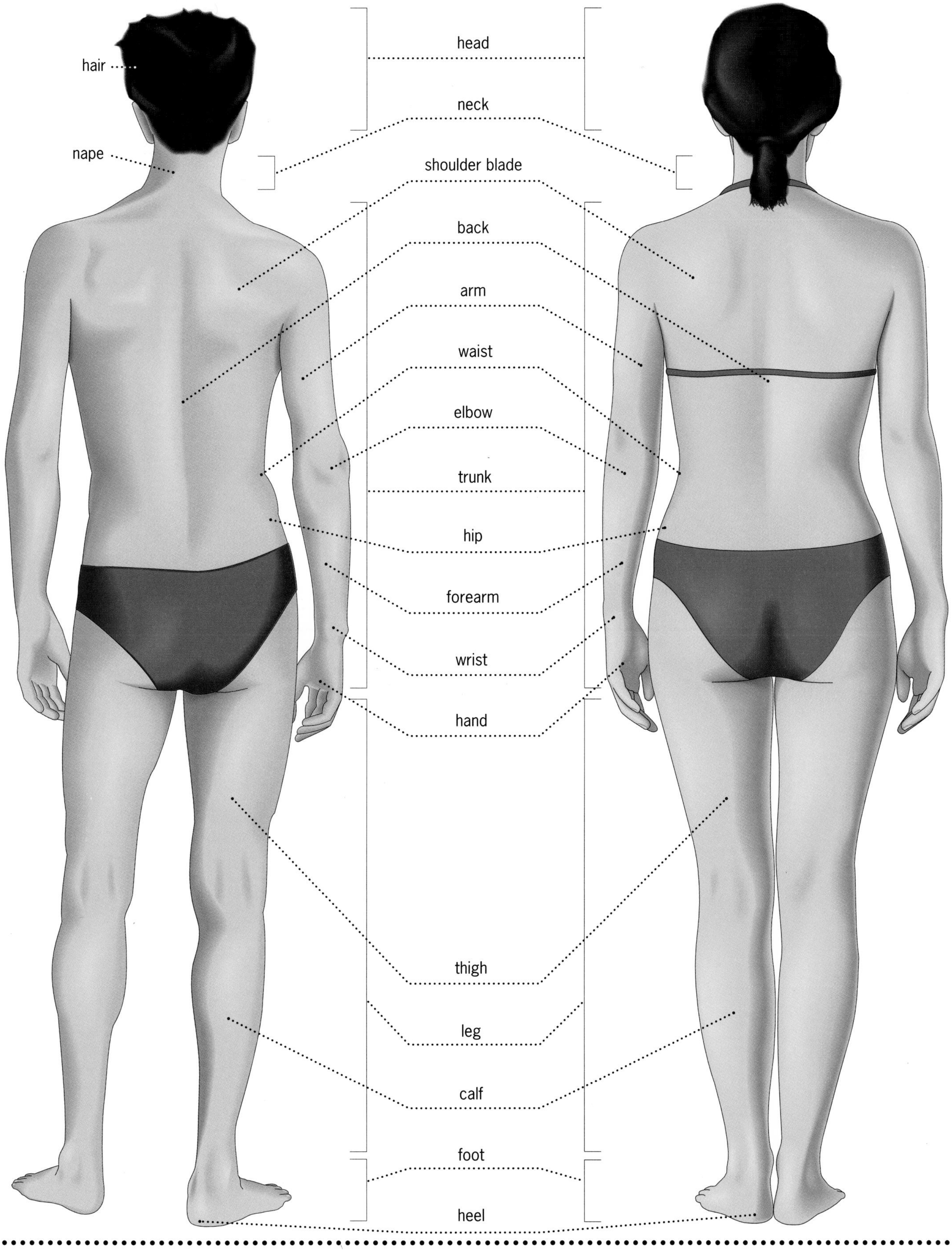
hair
nape
head
neck
shoulder blade
back
arm
waist
elbow
trunk
hip
forearm
wrist
hand
thigh
leg
calf
foot
heel

SKELETON

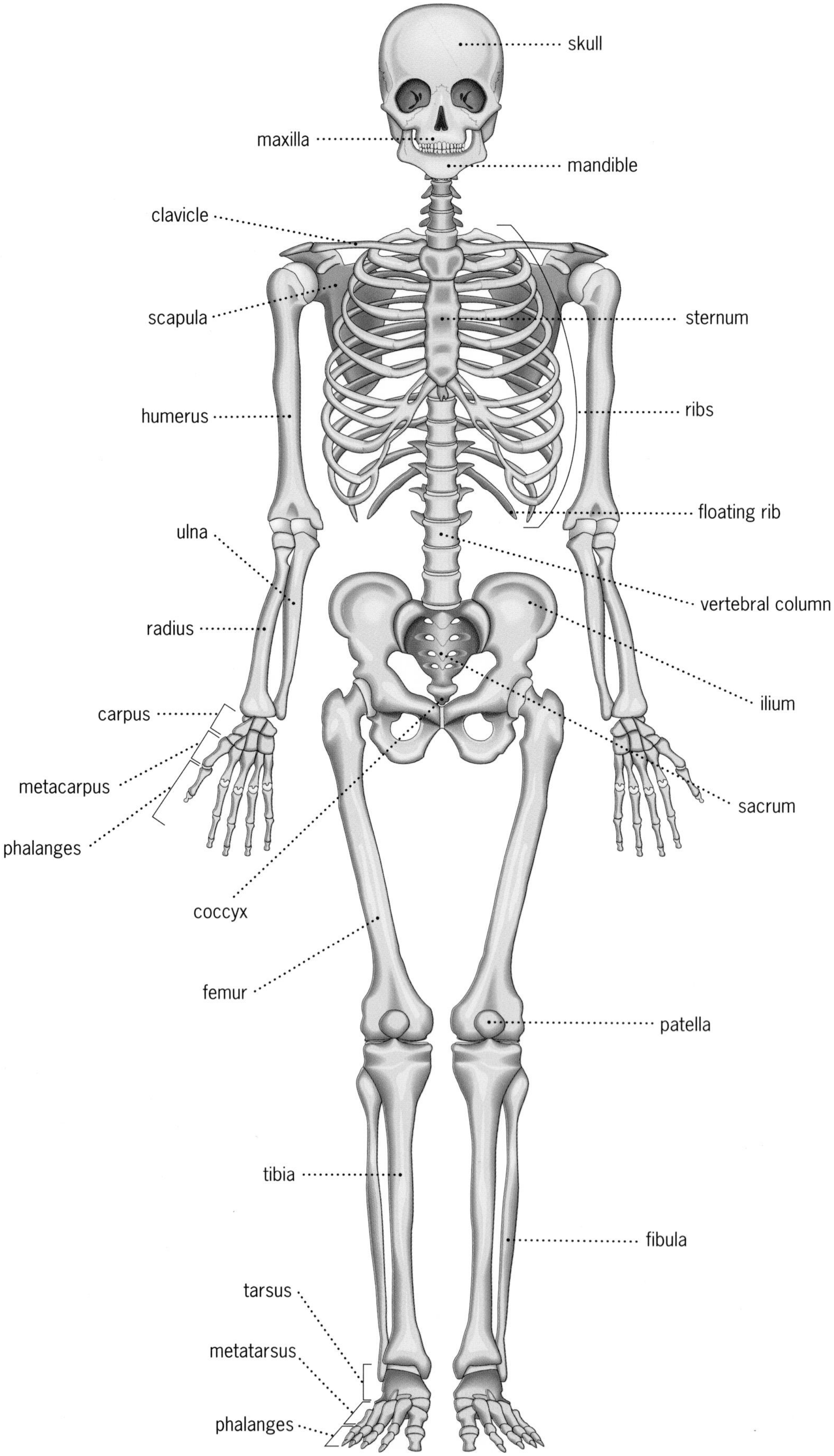
skull
maxilla
mandible
clavicle
scapula
sternum
humerus
ribs
floating rib
ulna
vertebral column
radius
ilium
carpus
metacarpus
sacrum
phalanges
coccyx
femur
patella
tibia
fibula
tarsus
metatarsus
phalanges

HUMAN ANATOMY

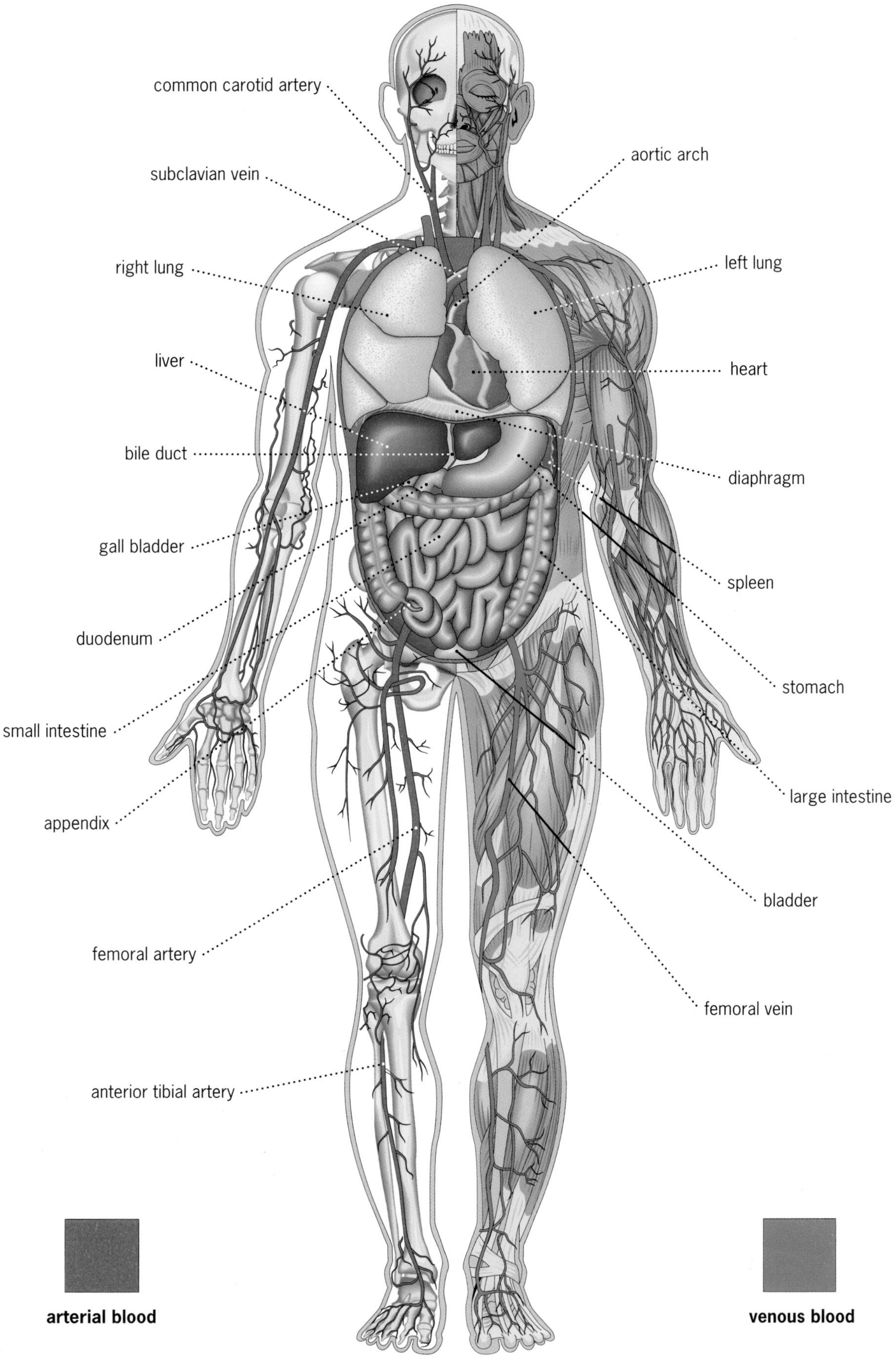
common carotid artery
subclavian vein
right lung
liver
bile duct
gall bladder
duodenum
small intestine
appendix
femoral artery
anterior tibial artery
aortic arch
left lung
heart
diaphragm
spleen
stomach
large intestine
bladder
femoral vein
arterial blood
venous blood

EYE: THE ORGAN OF SIGHT

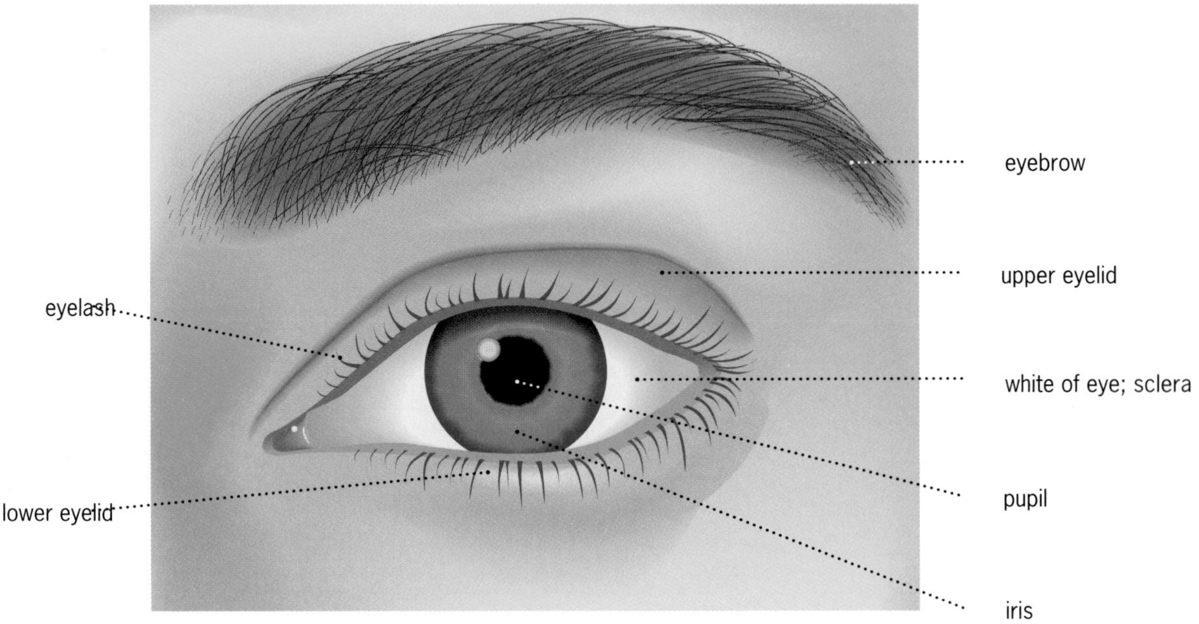
eyebrow
upper eyelid
eyelash
white of eye; sclera
pupil
lower eyelid
iris

HAND: THE ORGAN OF TOUCH

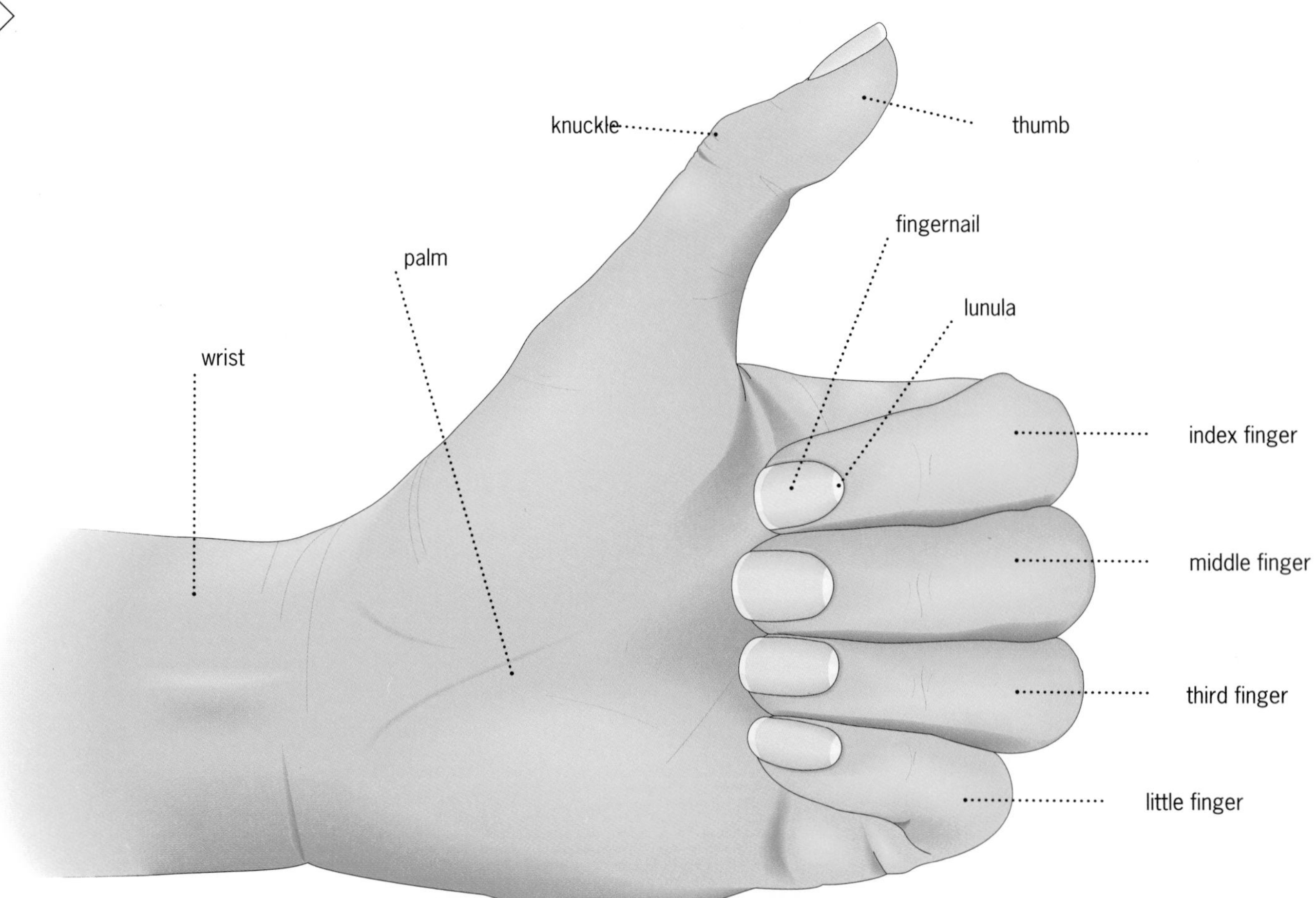
knuckle
thumb
fingernail
palm
lunula
wrist
index finger
middle finger
third finger
little finger

EAR: THE ORGAN OF HEARING

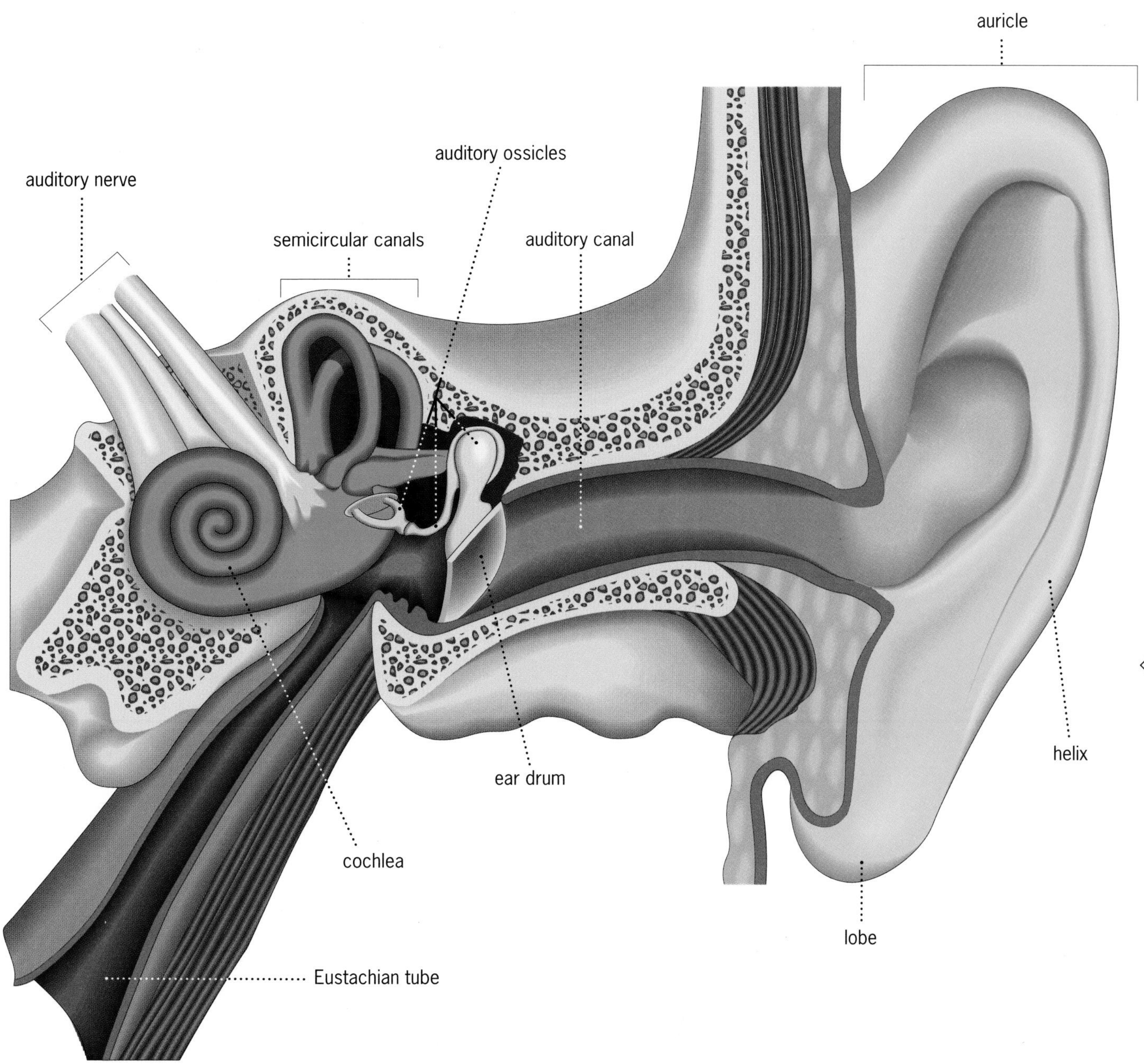
auricle
auditory ossicles
auditory nerve
semicircular canals
auditory canal
helix
ear drum
cochlea
lobe
Eustachian tube

PARTS OF THE EAR

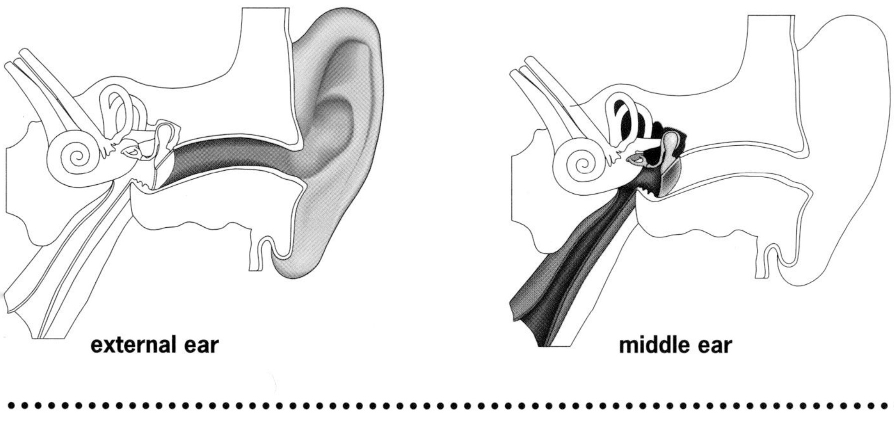
external ear
middle ear
internal ear

NOSE: THE ORGAN OF SMELL

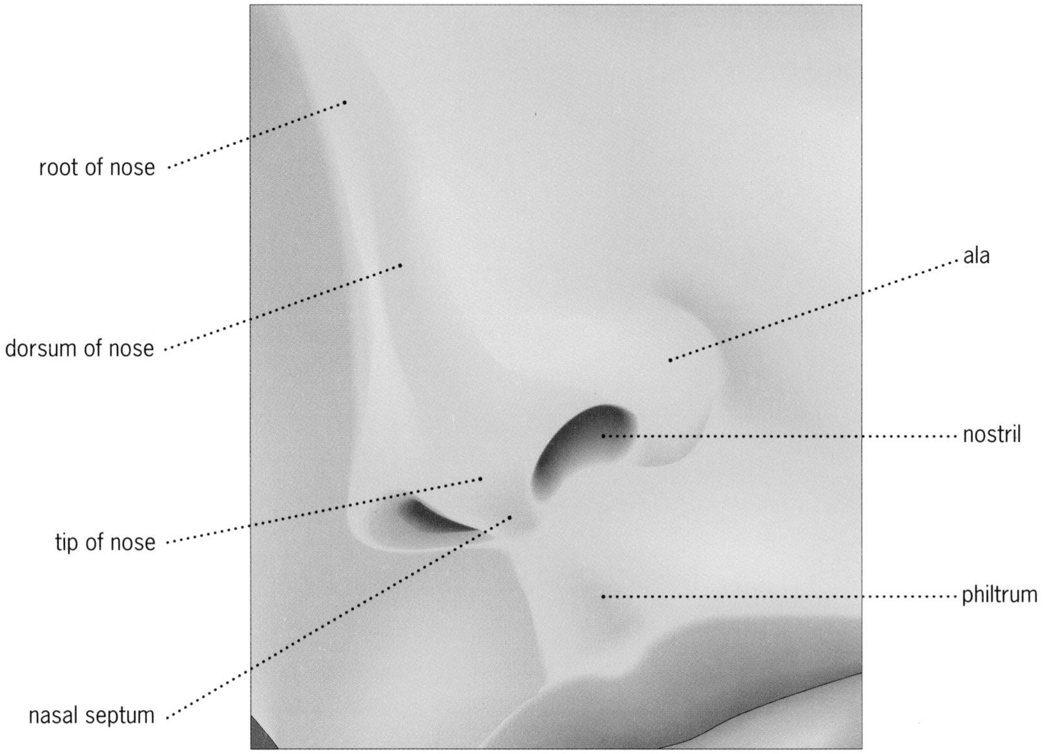
root of nose
dorsum of nose
tip of nose
nasal septum
ala
nostril
philtrum

MOUTH: THE ORGAN OF TASTE

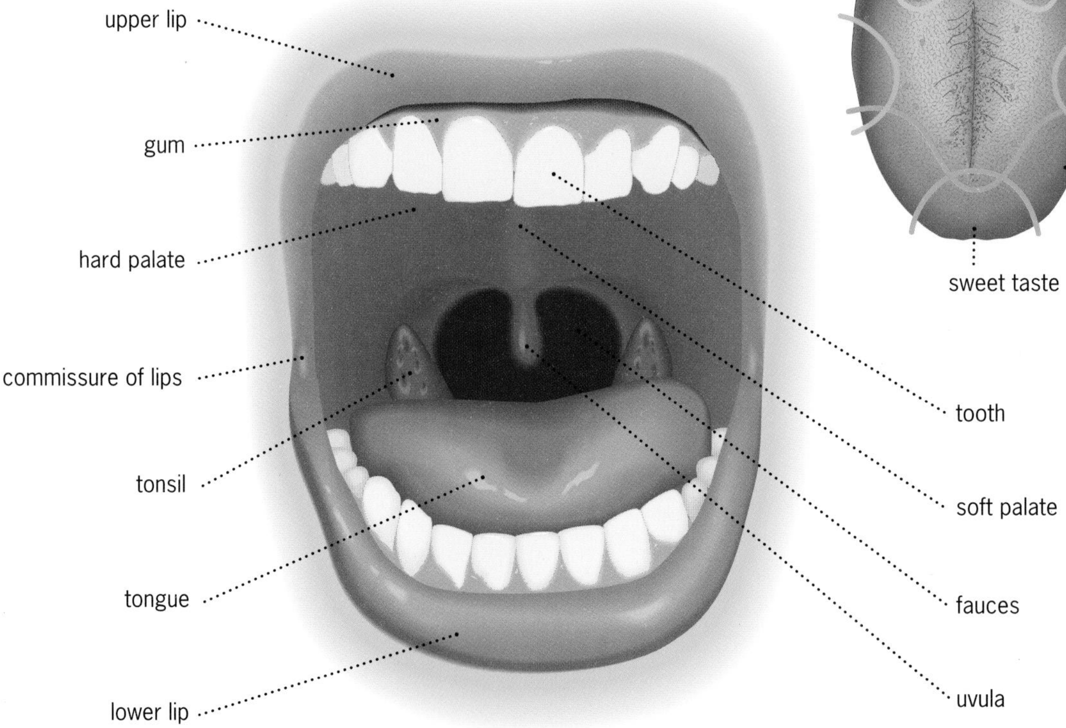
upper lip
gum
hard palate
commissure of lips
tonsil
tongue
lower lip
tooth
soft palate
fauces
uvula

taste sensations

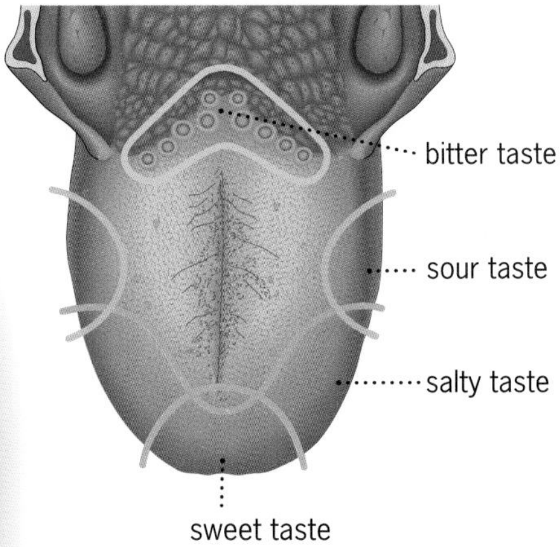
bitter taste
sour taste
salty taste
sweet taste

HUMAN DENTURE

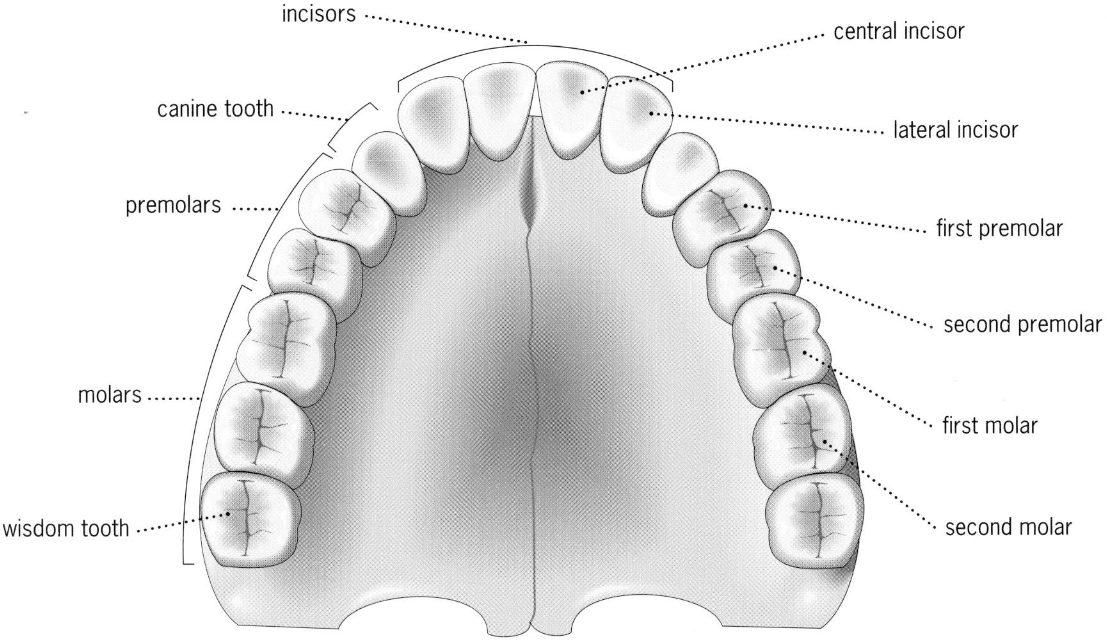
incisors
central incisor
canine tooth
lateral incisor
premolars
first premolar
second premolar
molars
first molar
wisdom tooth
second molar

cross section of a molar

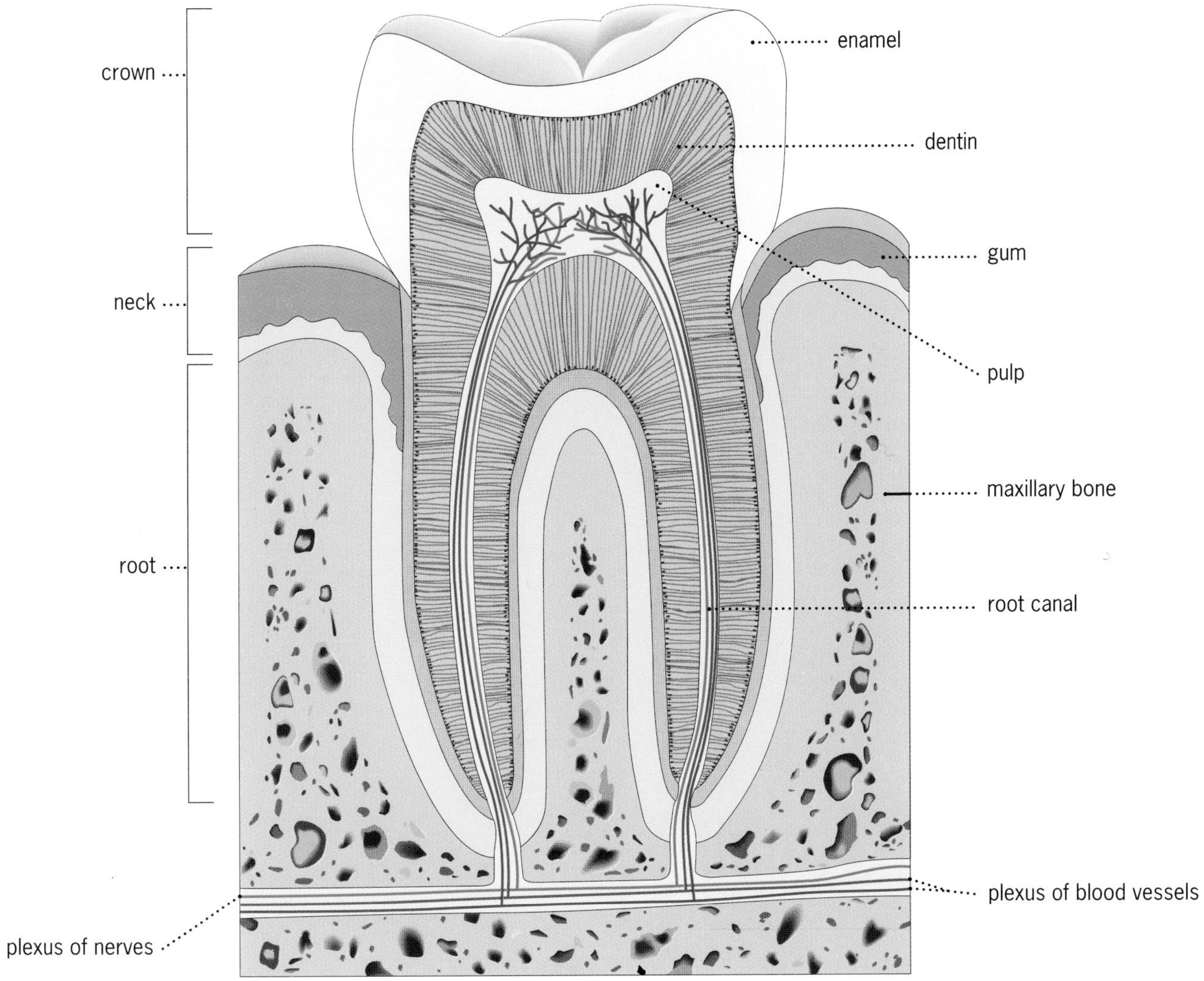
crown
enamel
dentin
gum
neck
pulp
maxillary bone
root
root canal
plexus of blood vessels
plexus of nerves

TRADITIONAL HOUSES

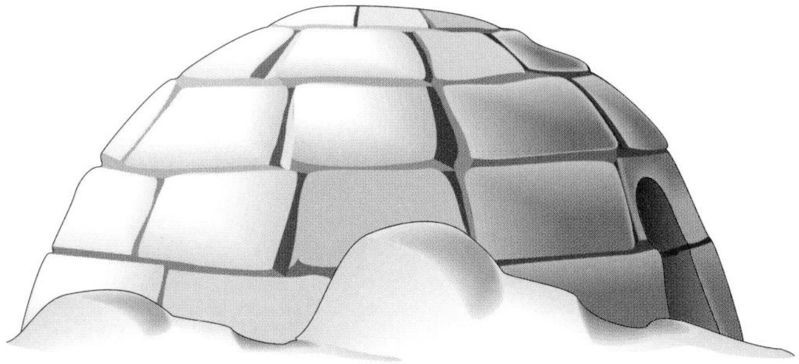

igloo

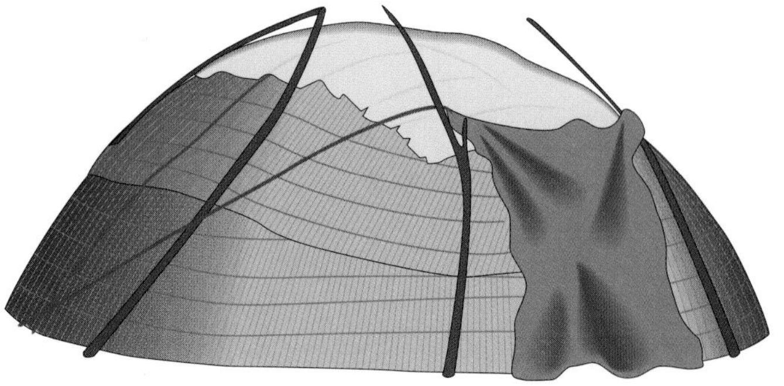

wigwam

log cabin

mud hut

house on stilts

tepee

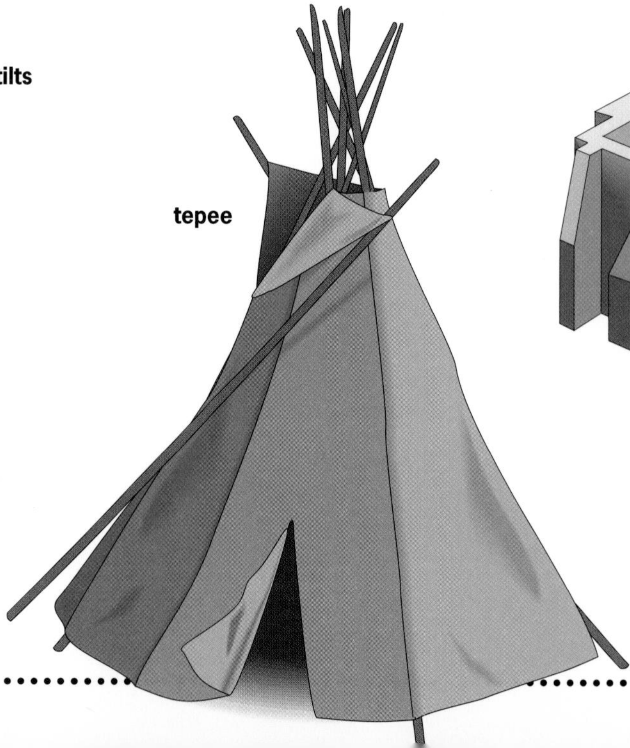

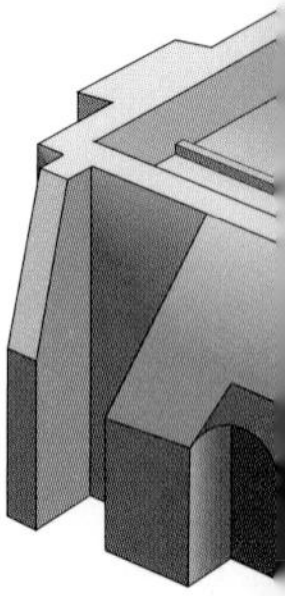

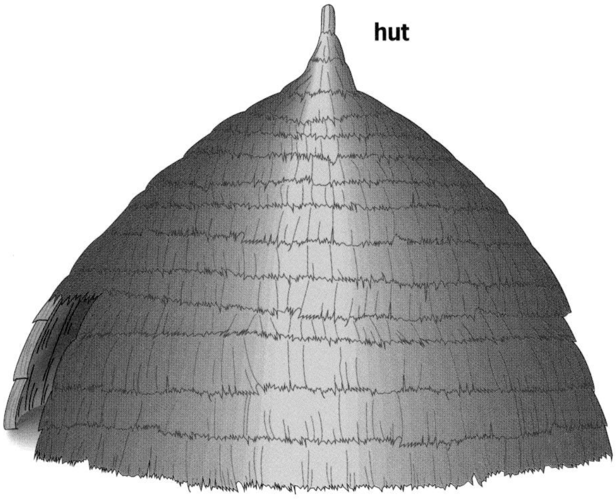
hut

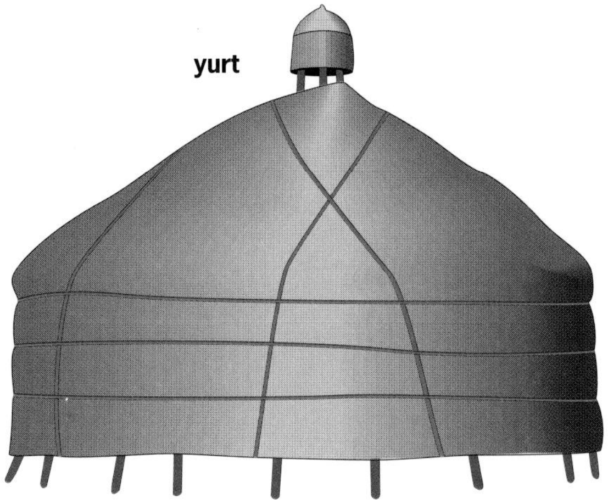
yurt

MOSQUE

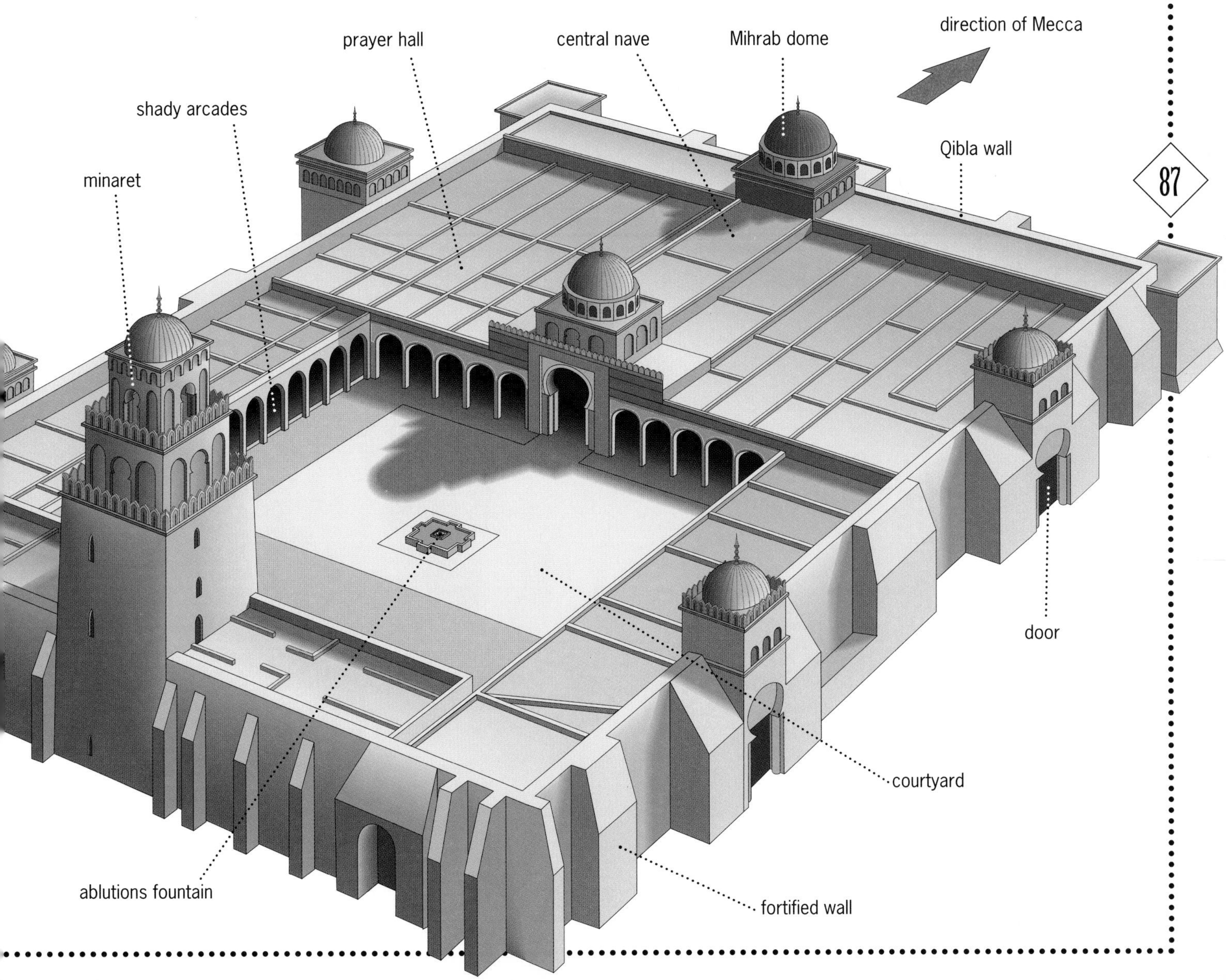
prayer hall
central nave
Mihrab dome
direction of Mecca
shady arcades
Qibla wall
minaret
door
courtyard
ablutions fountain
fortified wall

CASTLE

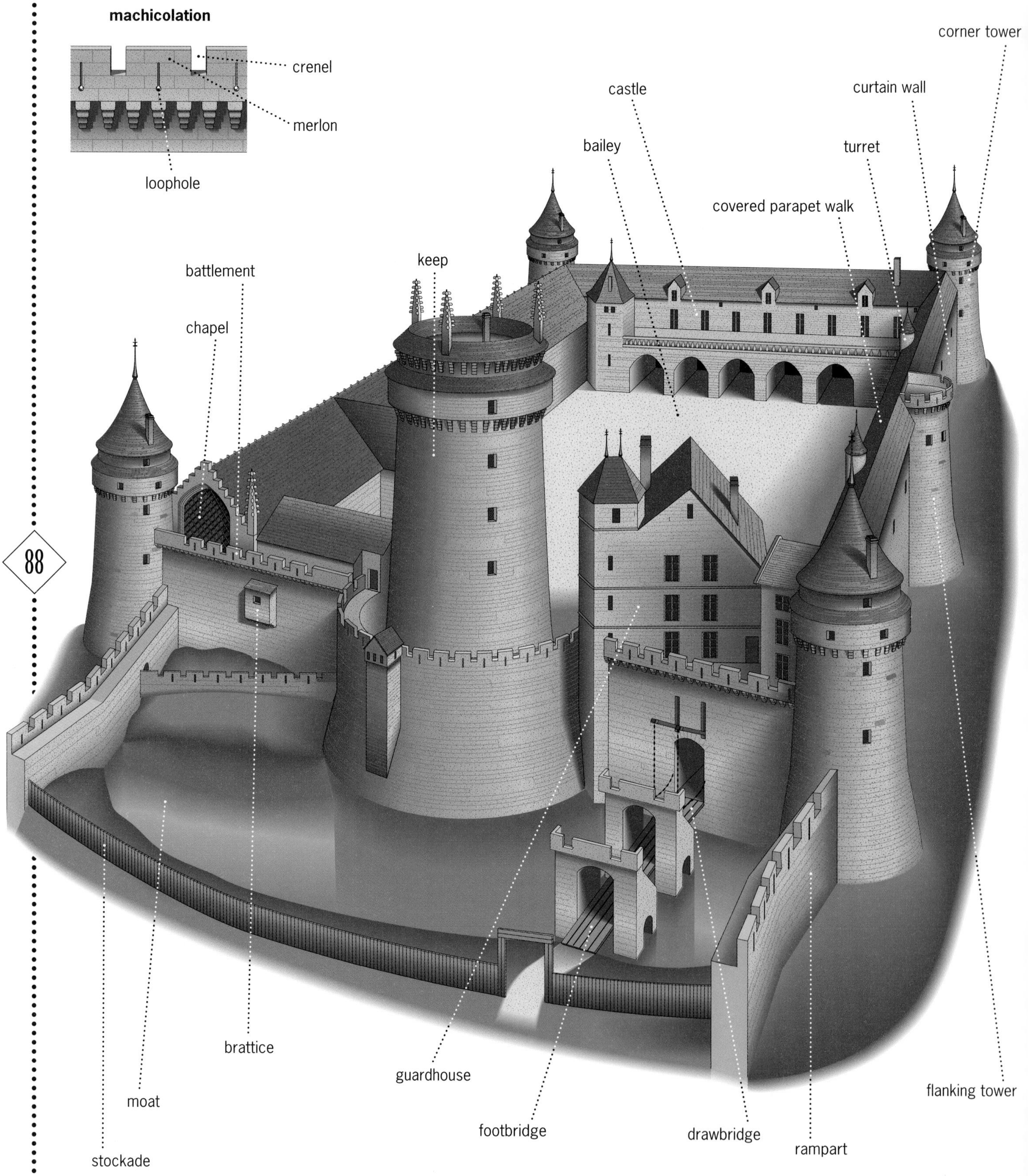
machicolation
crenel
merlon
loophole
corner tower
castle
curtain wall
bailey
turret
covered parapet walk
keep
battlement
chapel
brattice
guardhouse
moat
stockade
footbridge
drawbridge
rampart
flanking tower

GOTHIC CATHEDRAL

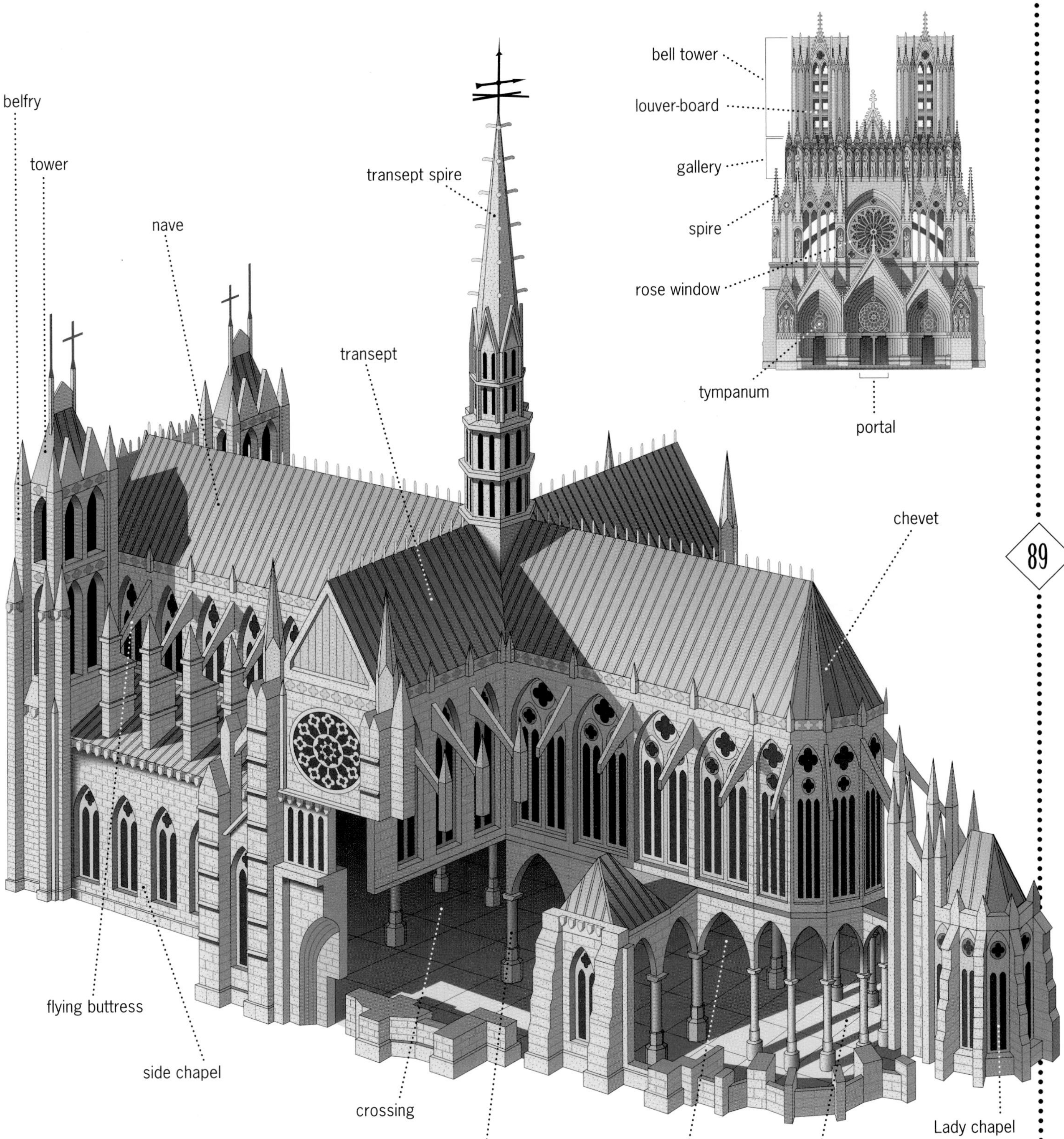
belfry
tower
nave
transept spire
transept
flying buttress
side chapel
crossing
pillar
choir
ambulatory
Lady chapel
chevet
facade
bell tower
louver-board
gallery
spire
rose window
tympanum
portal

DOWNTOWN

park
convention center
office tower
square
cathedral
railroad station
median strip
planetarium
railroad
traffic island
boulevard
street
delivery ramp
freeway

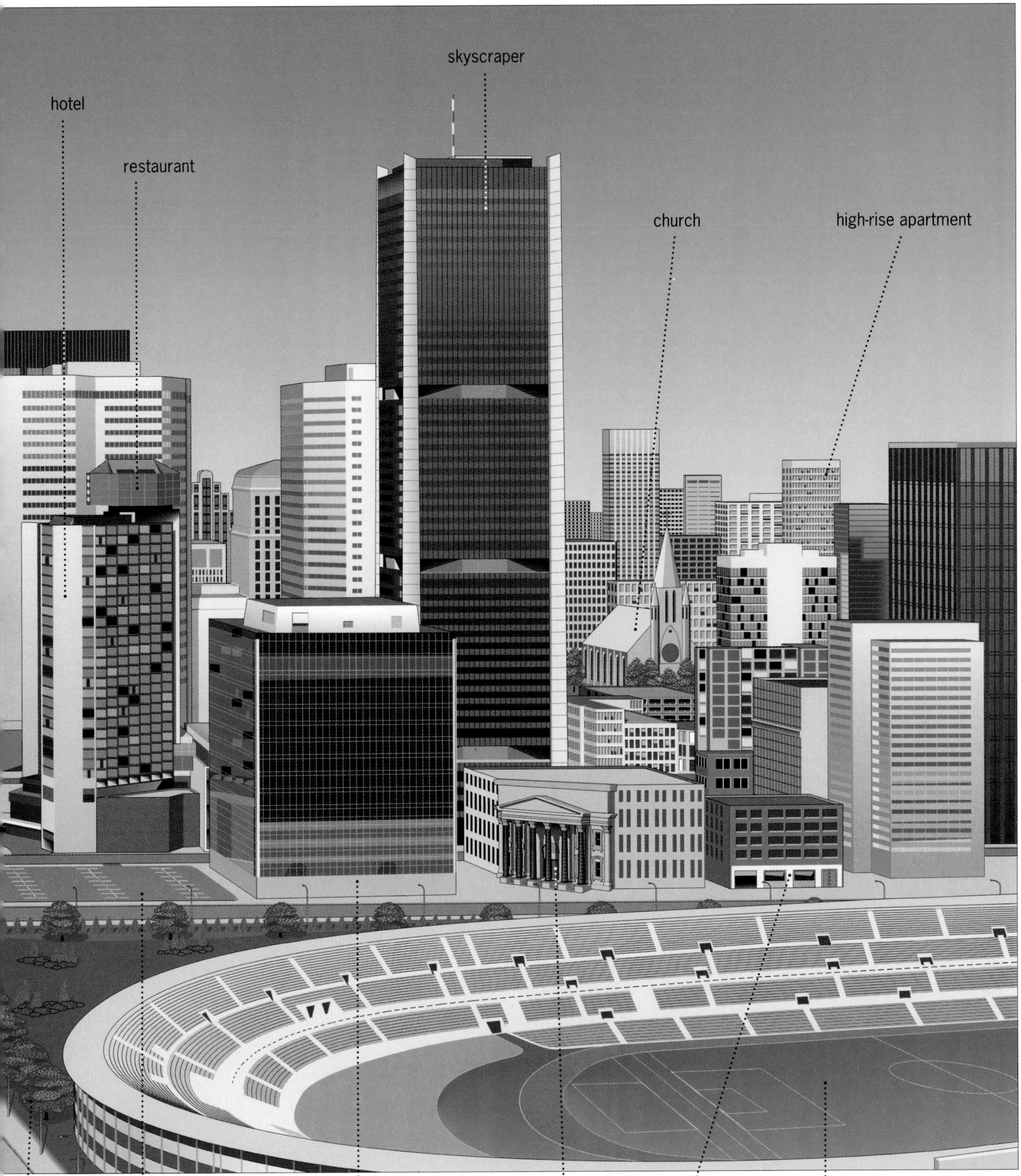
skyscraper
hotel
restaurant
church
high-rise apartment
parking lot
office building
commercial building
street lamp
museum
stadium

HOUSE

exterior of a house

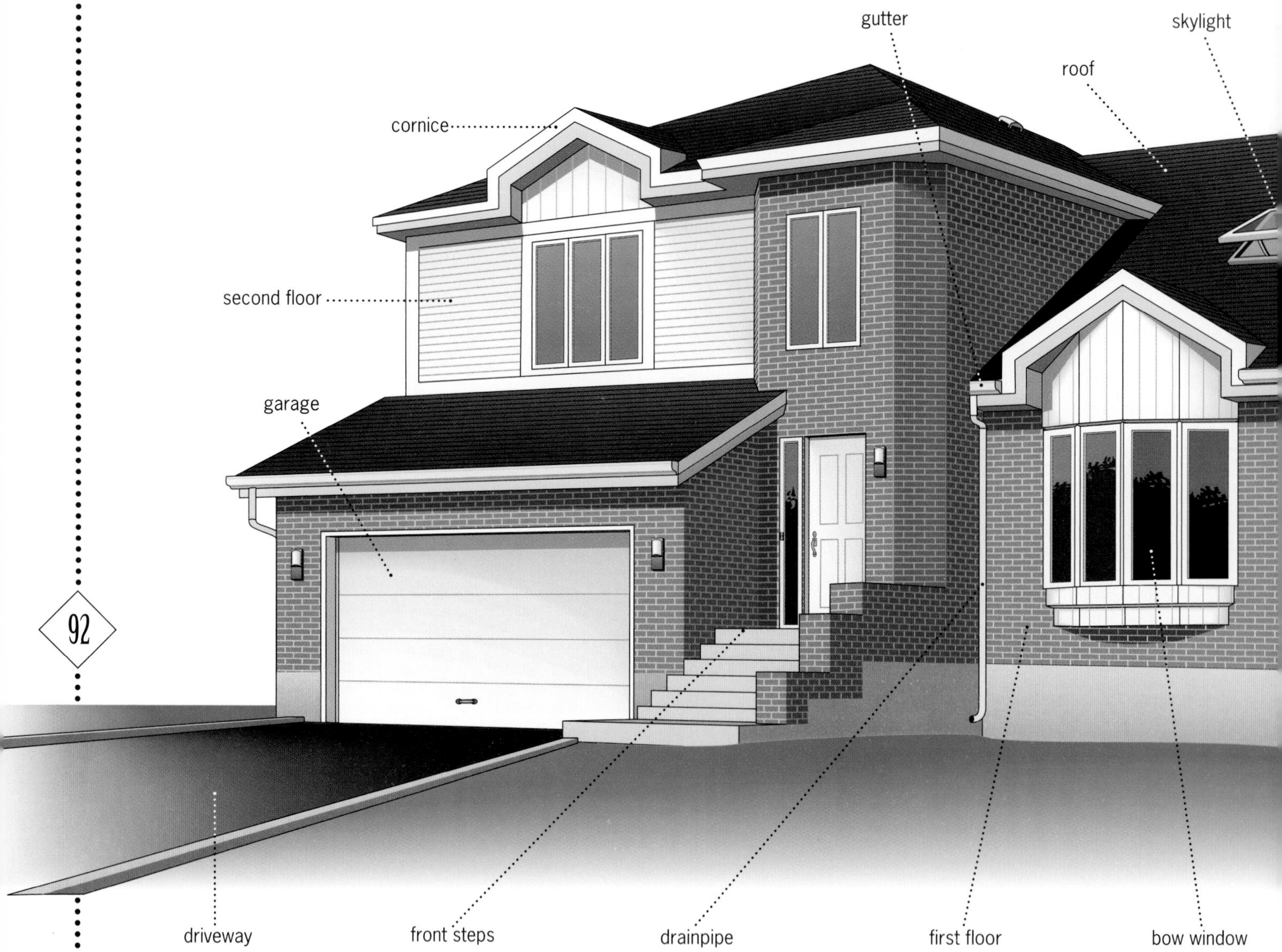
gutter
skylight
roof
cornice
second floor
garage
driveway
front steps
drainpipe
first floor
bow window

TYPES OF DOORS

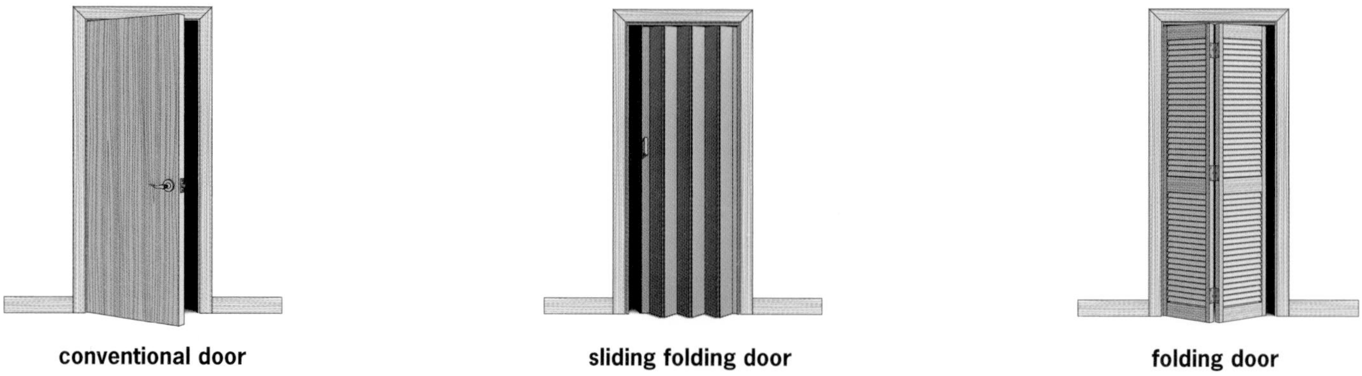
conventional door
sliding folding door
folding door

chimney
lightning rod
gable
bay window
basement window
basement

lock

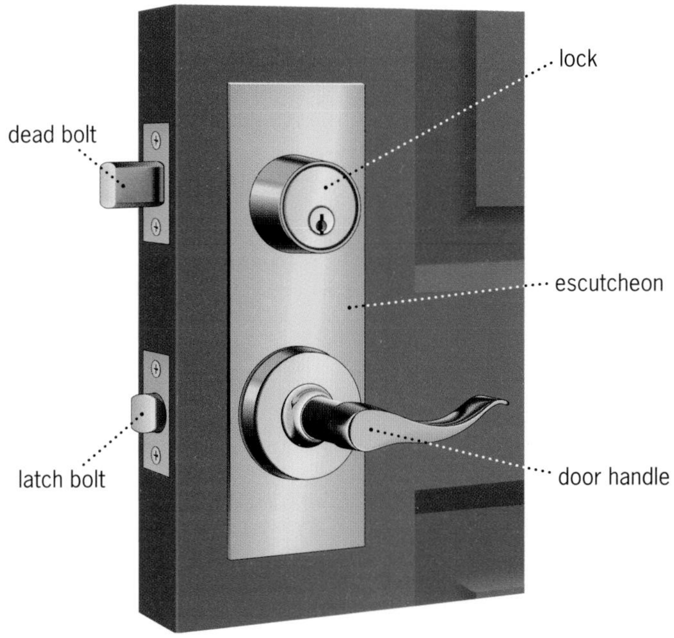
lock
dead bolt
escutcheon
latch bolt
door handle

door

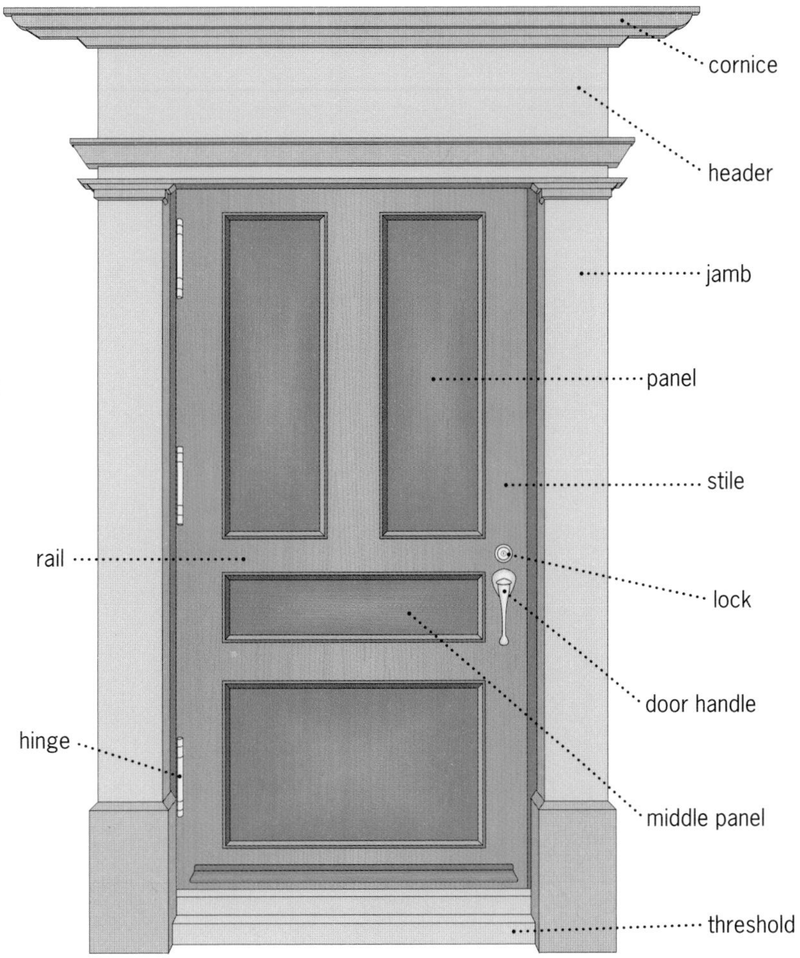
cornice
header
jamb
panel
stile
rail
lock
door handle
hinge
middle panel
threshold

sliding door

WINDOW

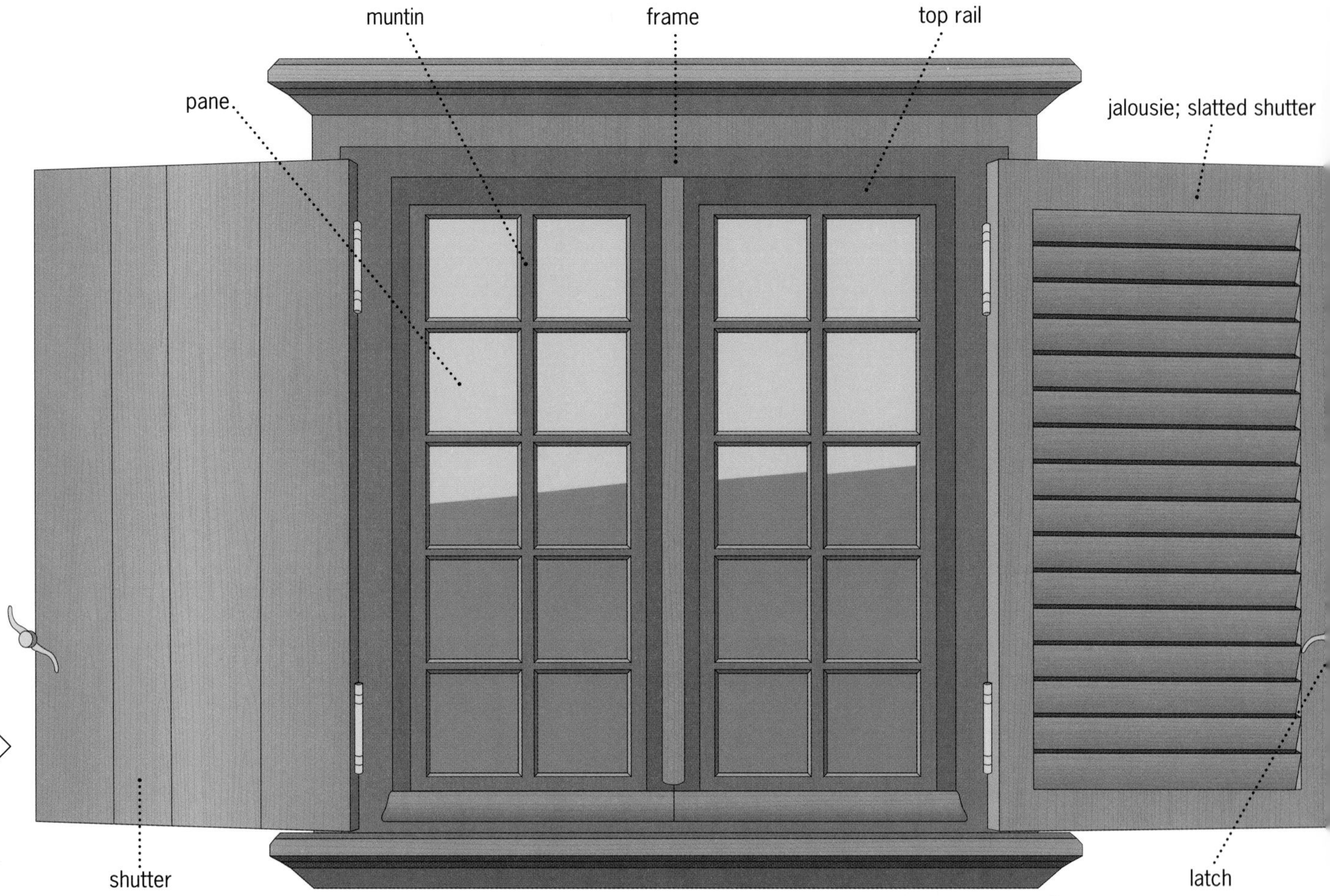
muntin
frame
top rail
pane
jalousie; slatted shutter
shutter
latch

TYPES OF WINDOWS

casement window (inward opening)

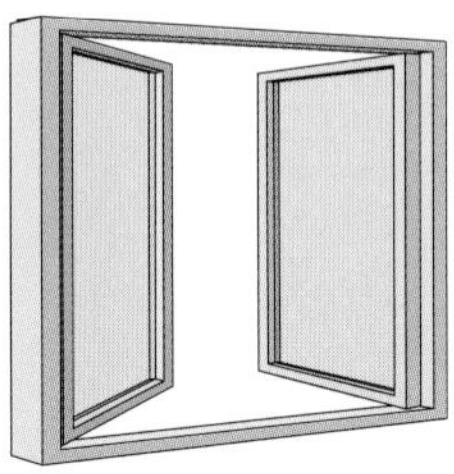

casement window (outward opening)

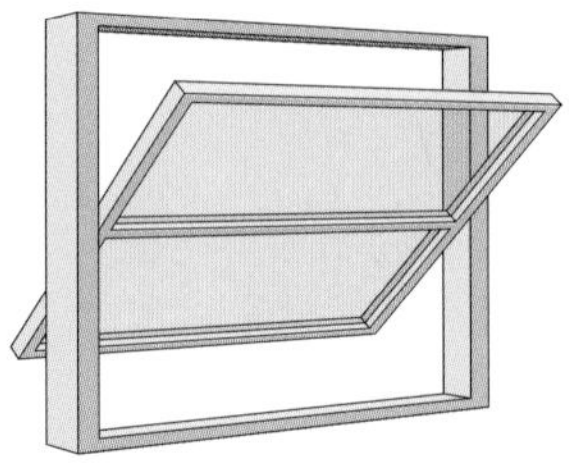

horizontal pivoting window

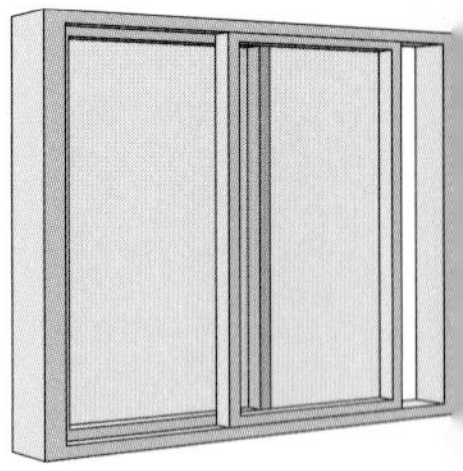

sliding window

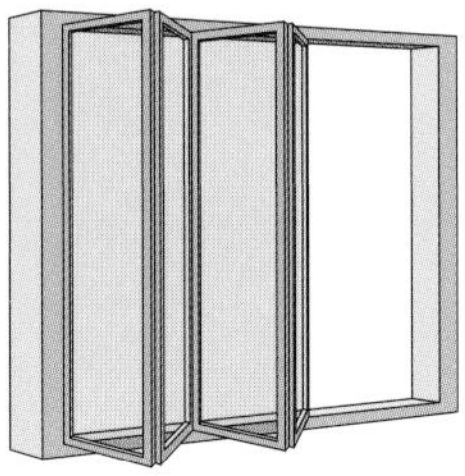

sliding folding window

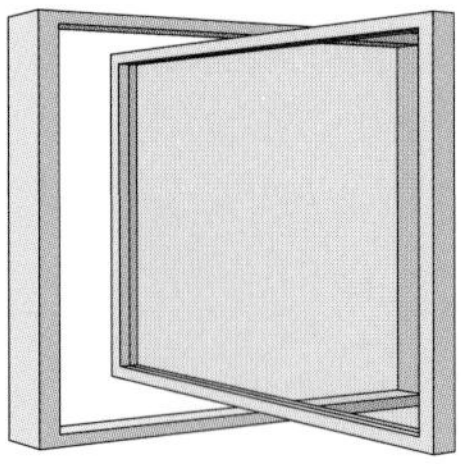

vertical pivoting window

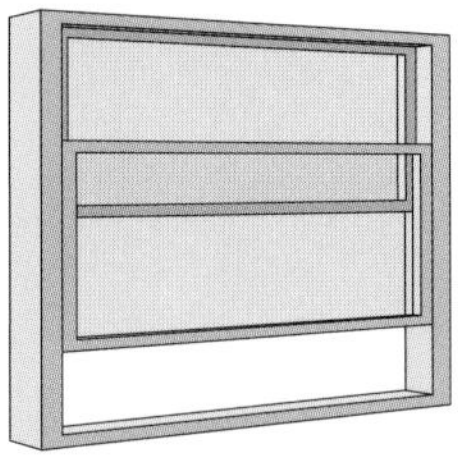

sash window

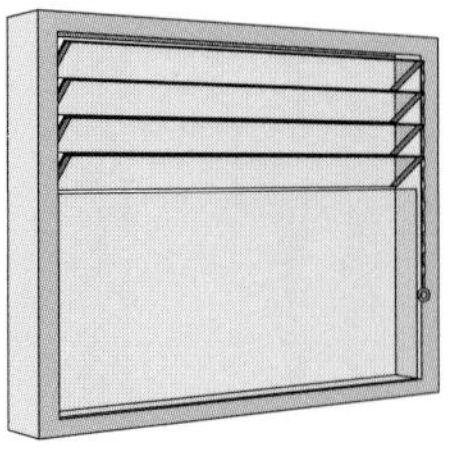

louvred window

BED

parts

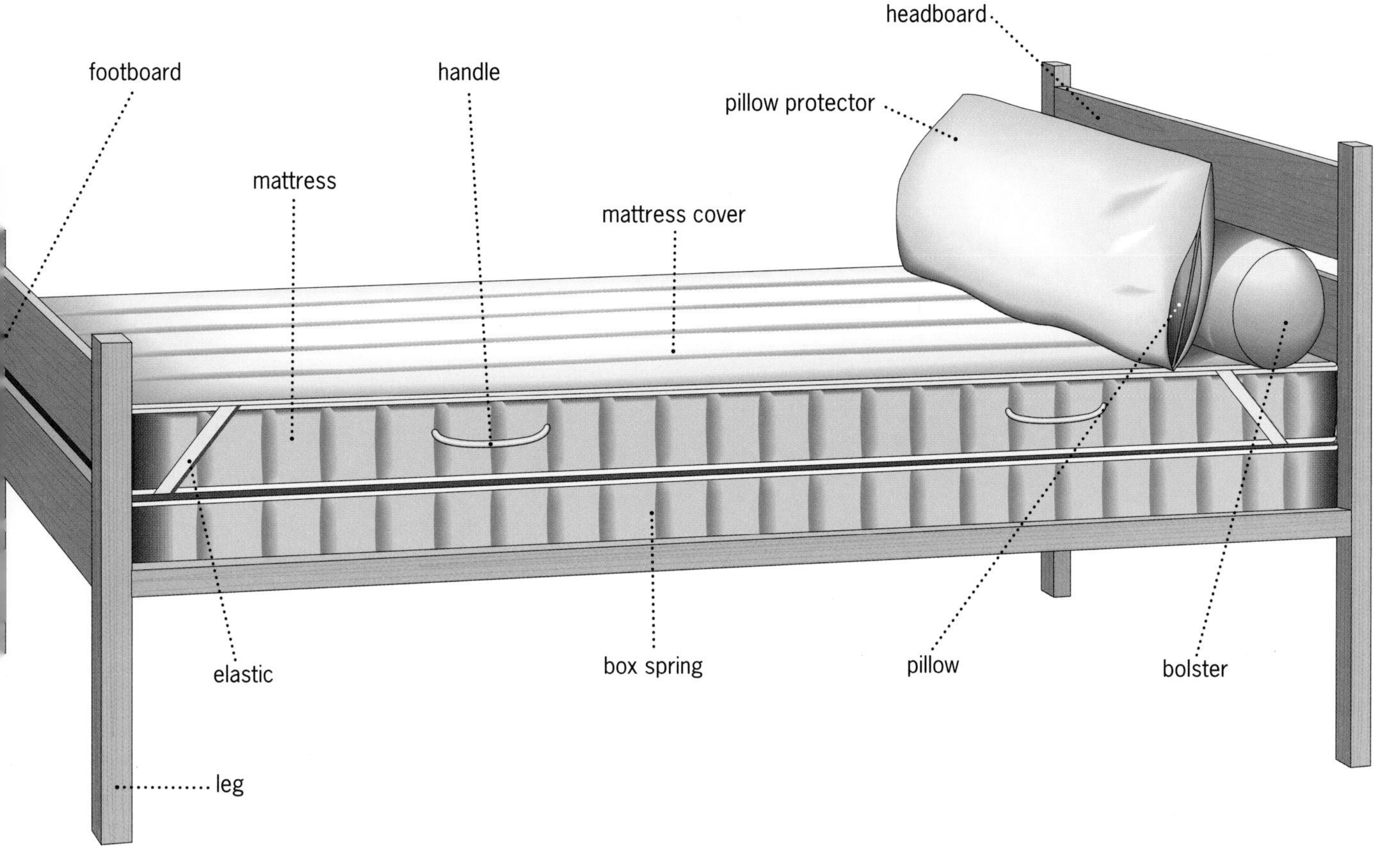
headboard
footboard
handle
pillow protector
mattress
mattress cover
elastic
box spring
pillow
bolster
leg

linen

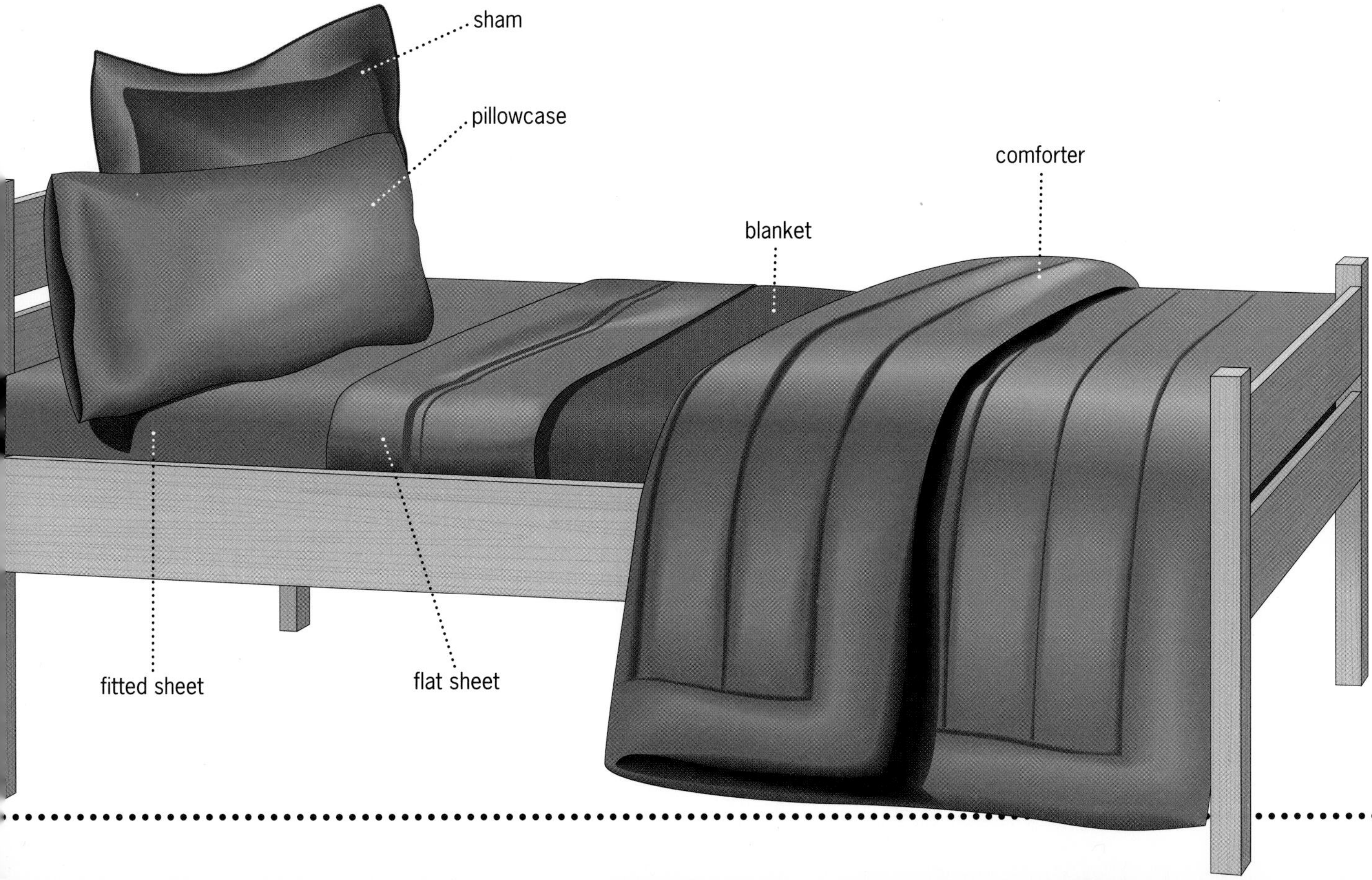
sham
pillowcase
comforter
blanket
fitted sheet
flat sheet

SEATS

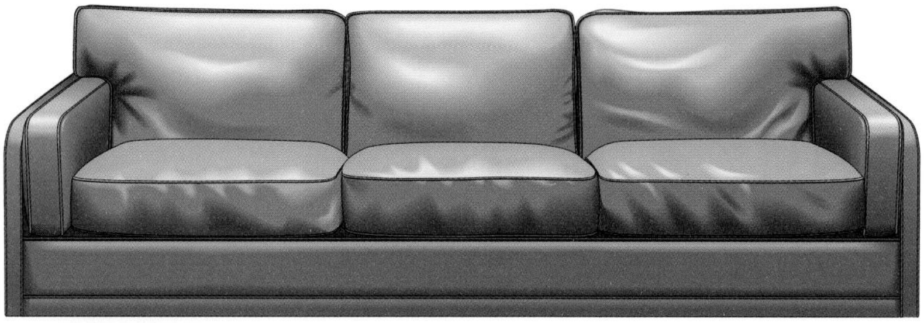

sofa

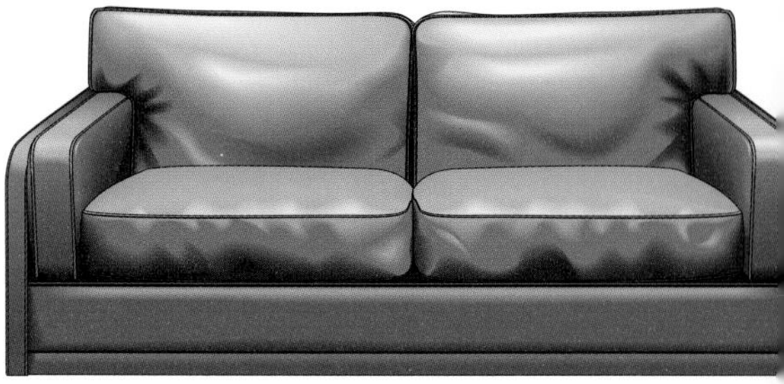

loveseat

armchair

footstool

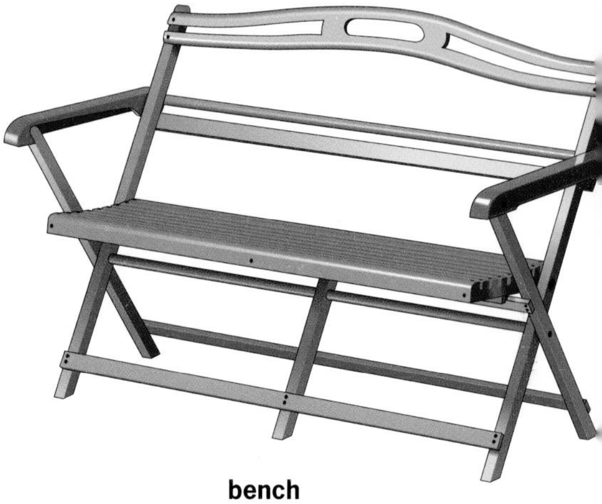

bench

bar stool

stool

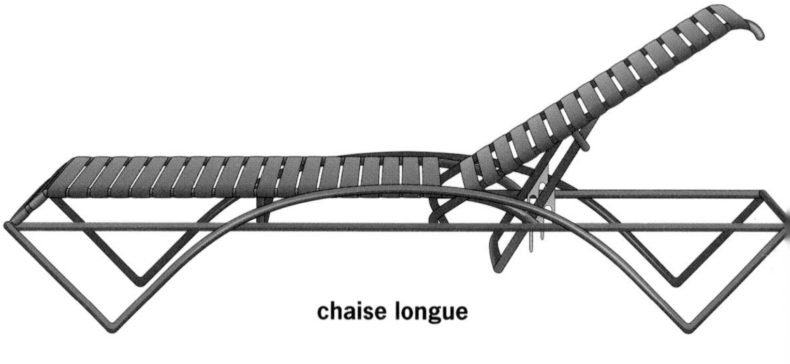

chaise longue

folding chair

rocking chair

stacking chairs

TABLE AND CHAIRS

side chair

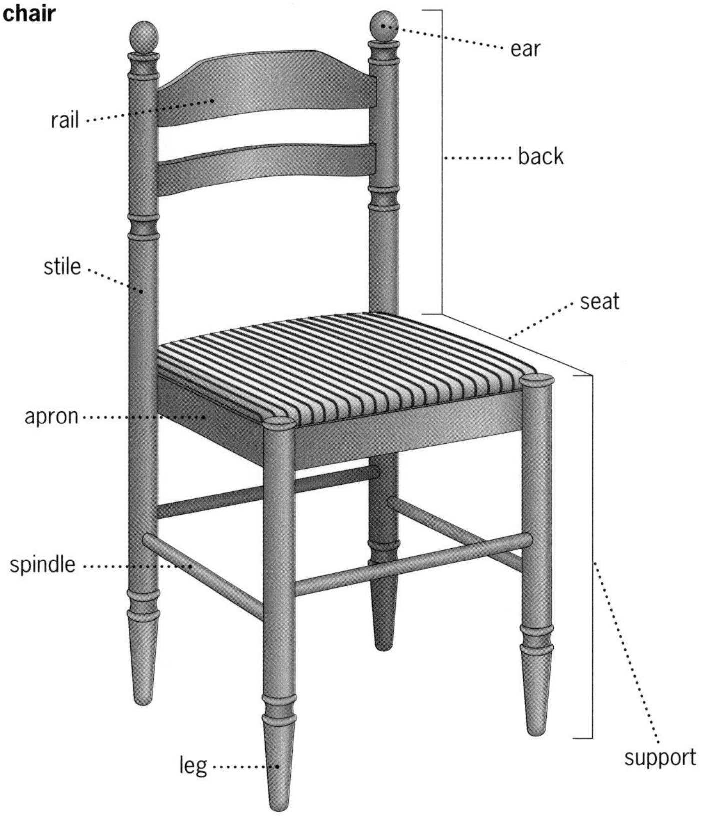
ear
rail
back
stile
seat
apron
spindle
support
leg

armchair

arm

table

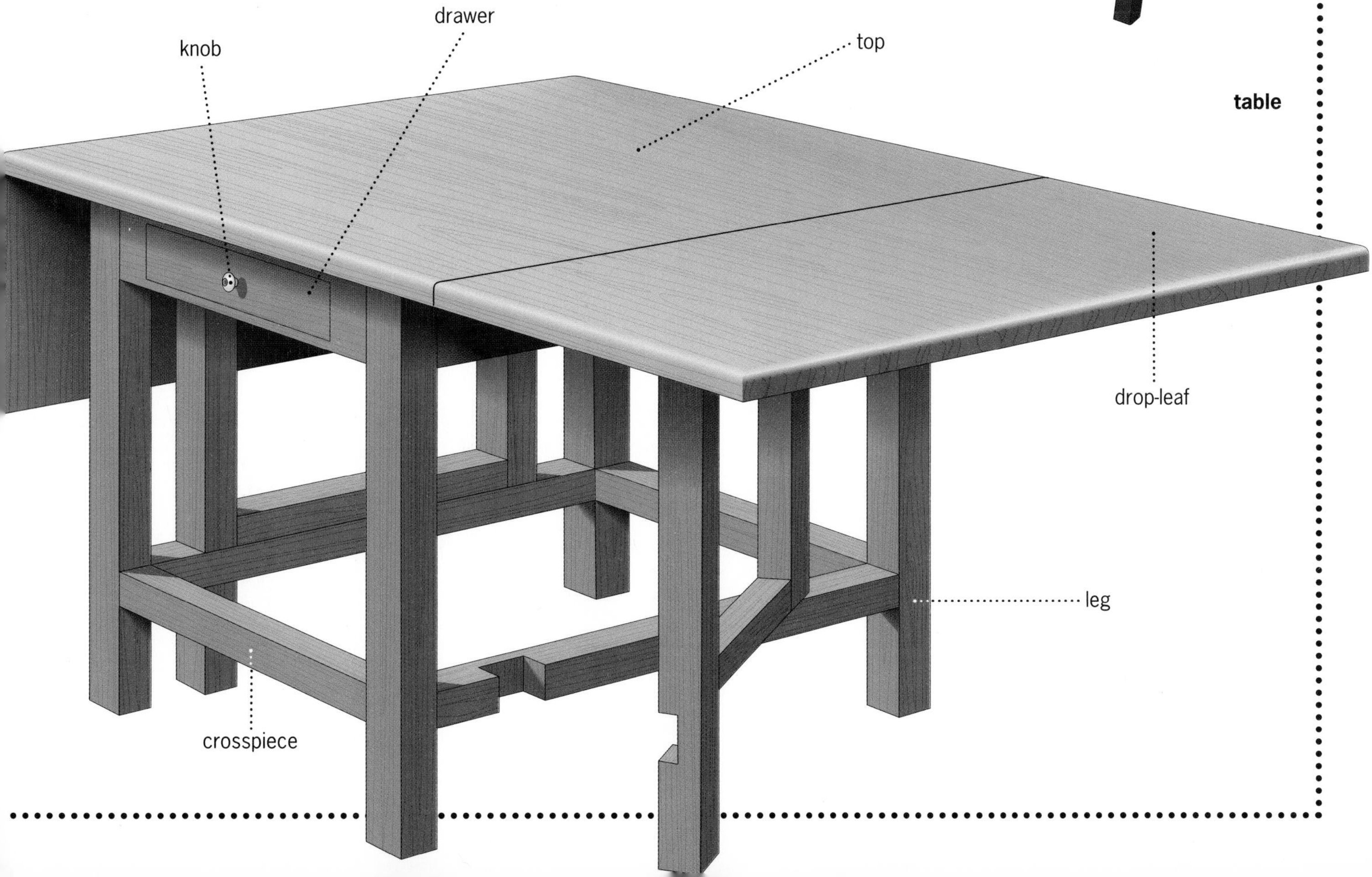
drawer
knob
top
drop-leaf
leg
crosspiece

LIGHTS

track lighting

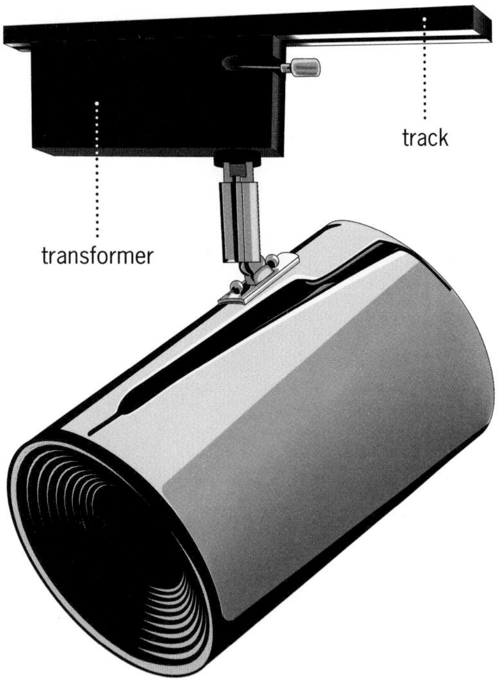
track
transformer

floor lamp

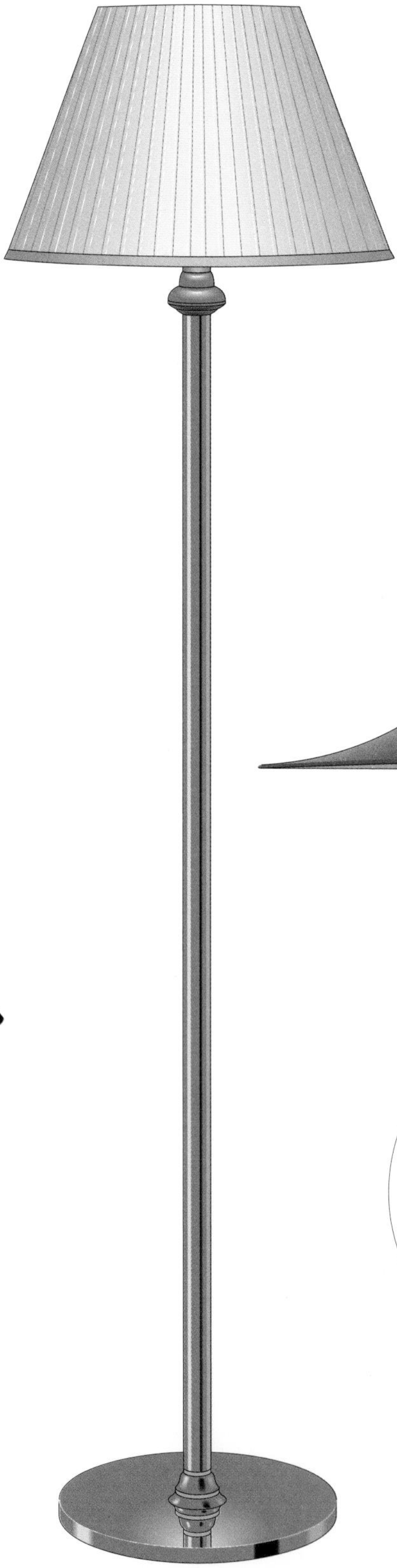

ceiling fixture

hanging pendant

table lamp

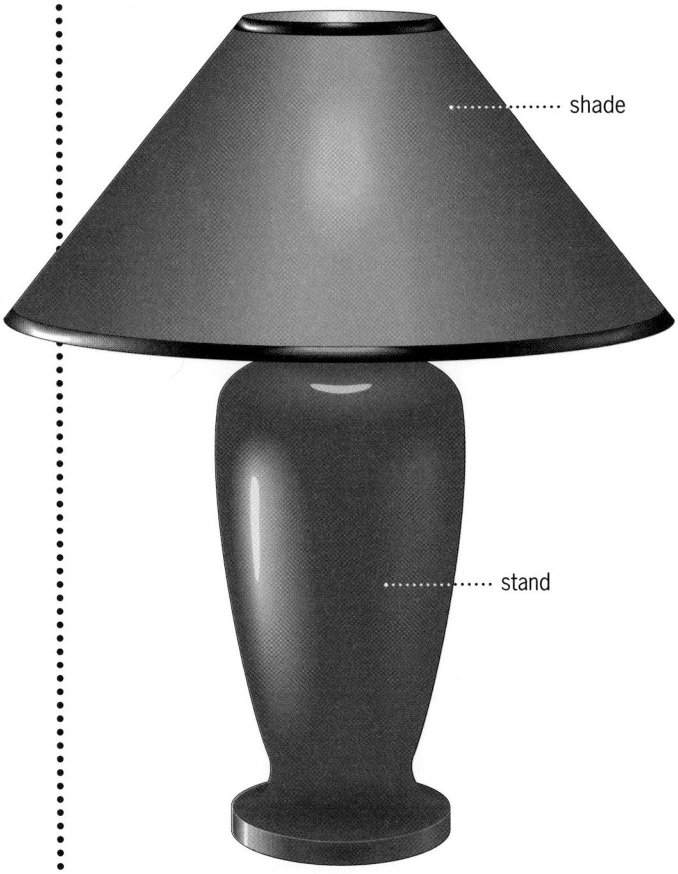
shade
stand

wall fixture

LIGHTING

incandescent lamp

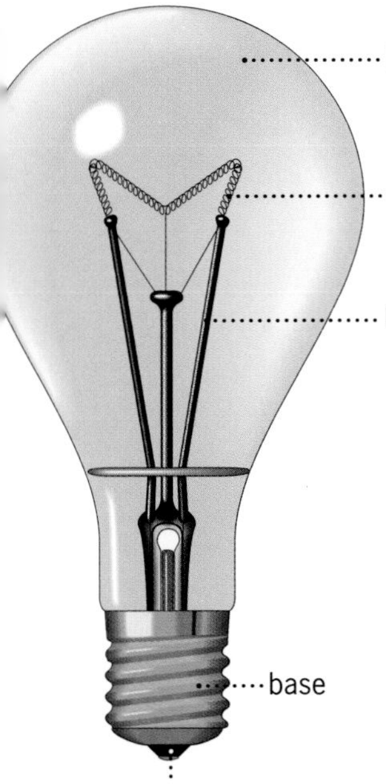
inert gas
filament
lead-in wire
base
contact

bulb

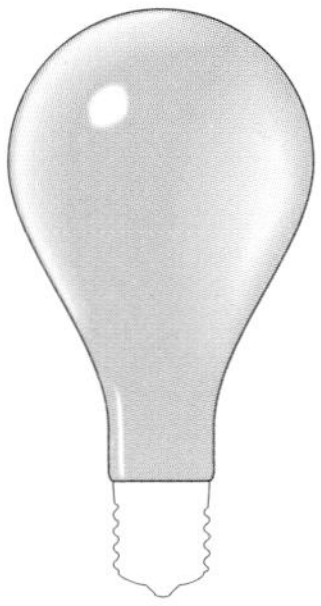

screw base

bayonet base

energy saving bulb

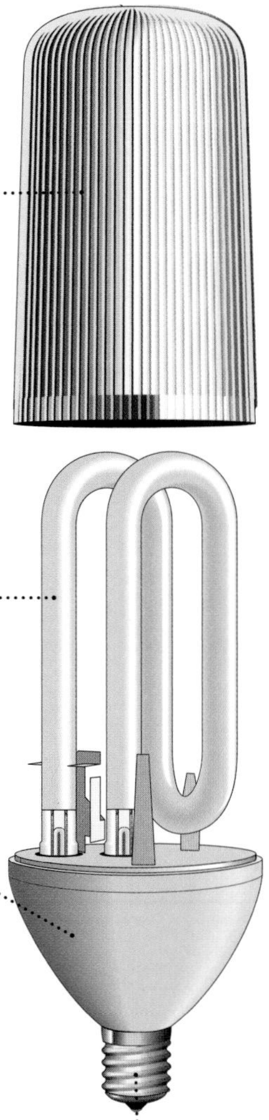
bulb
fluorescent tube
housing
base

tungsten-halogen lamp

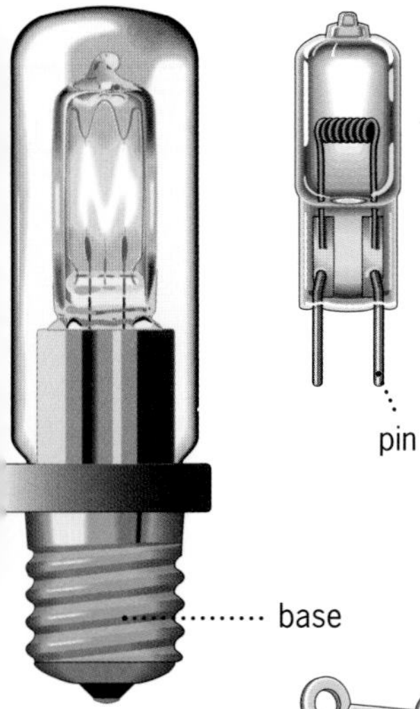
pin
base

fluorescent tube

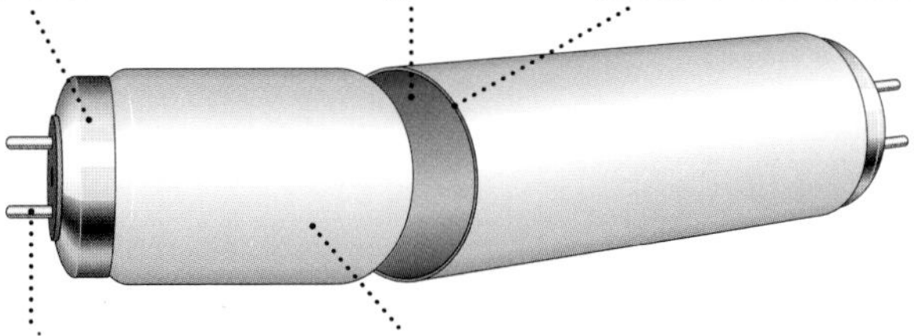
pin base
gas
phosphorescent coating
pin
bulb

European plug

cover
pin

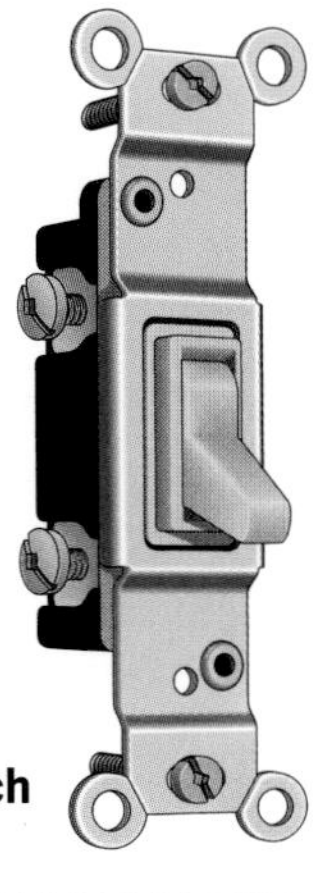

switch

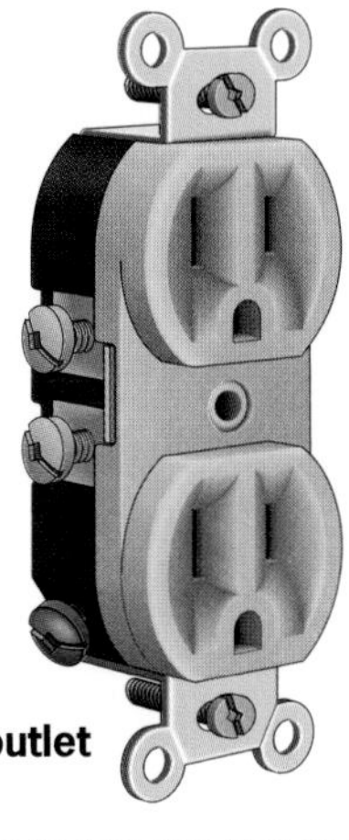

outlet

American plug

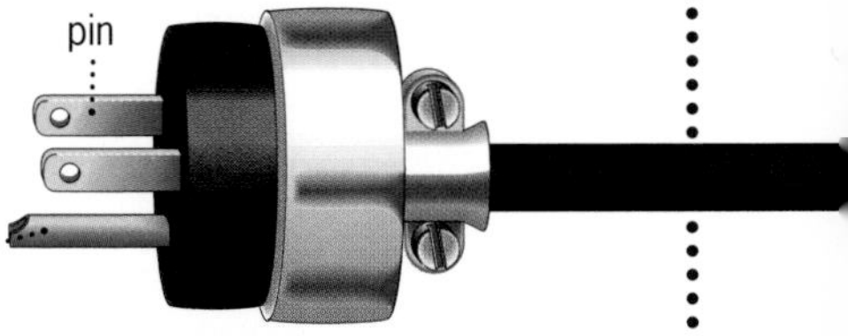
pin
grounding terminal

GLASSWARE

champagne glass
white wine glass
red wine glass
champagne flute
tumbler; glass
beer mug
carafe
decanter

DINNERWARE

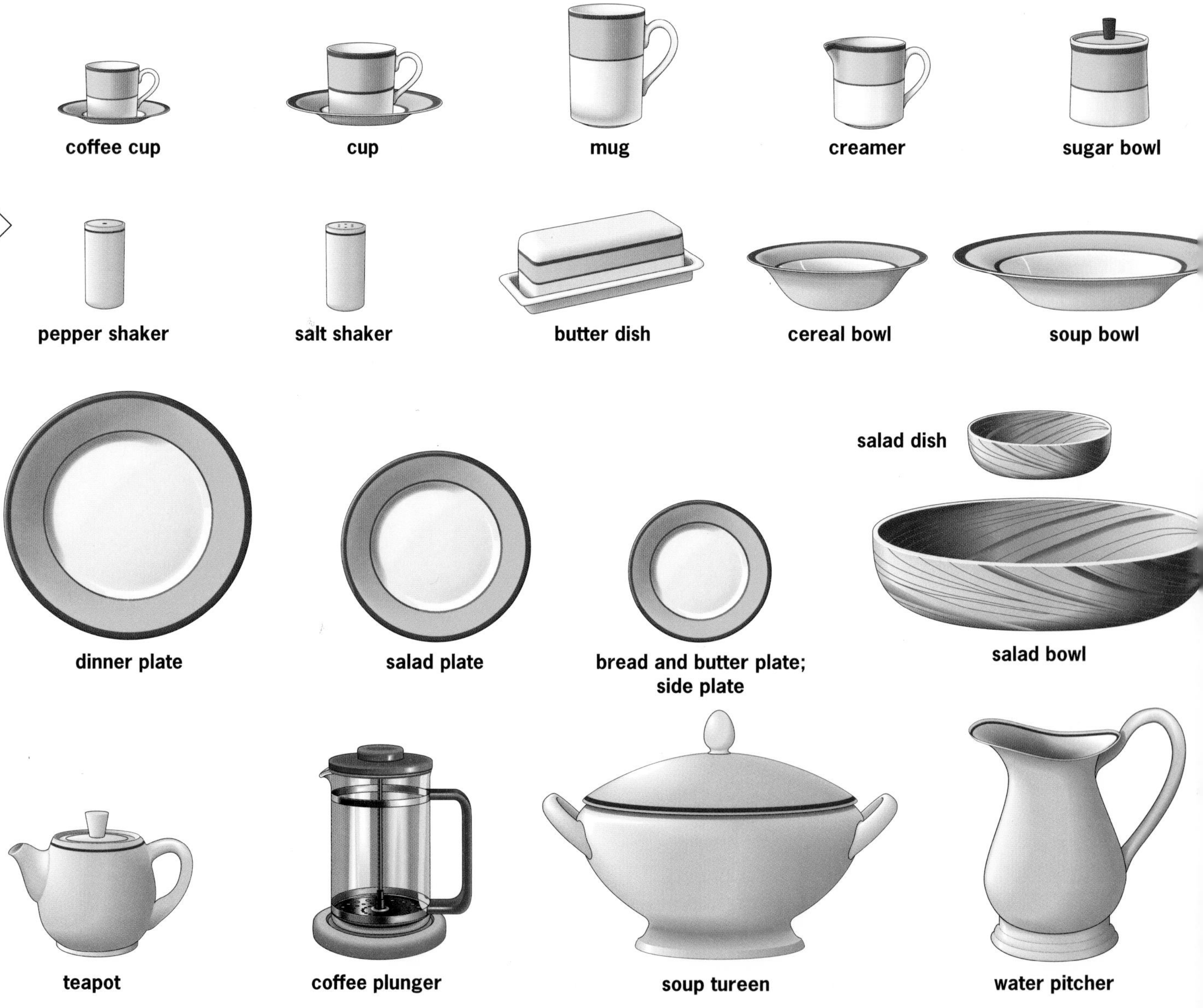
coffee cup
cup
mug
creamer
sugar bowl
pepper shaker
salt shaker
butter dish
cereal bowl
soup bowl
dinner plate
salad plate
bread and butter plate; side plate
salad dish
salad bowl
teapot
coffee plunger
soup tureen
water pitcher

SILVERWARE

knife

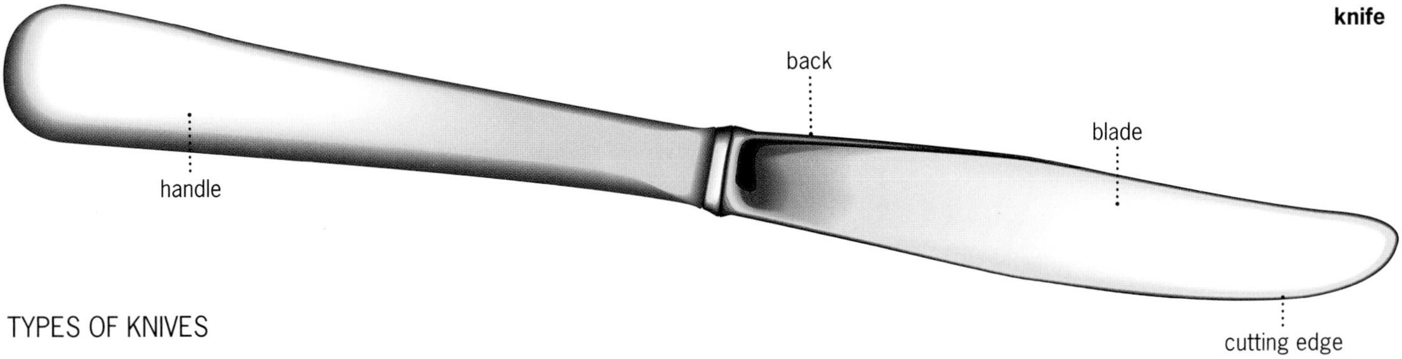
back
blade
handle
cutting edge

TYPES OF KNIVES

butter knife

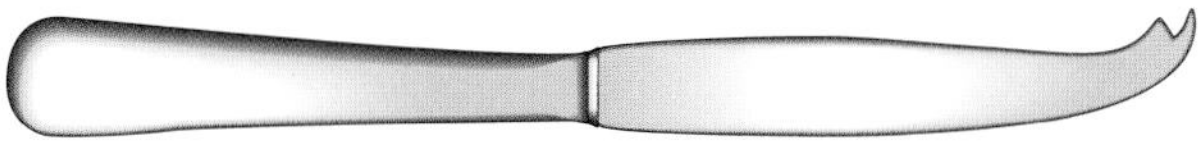

cheese knife

dinner knife

steak knife

fork

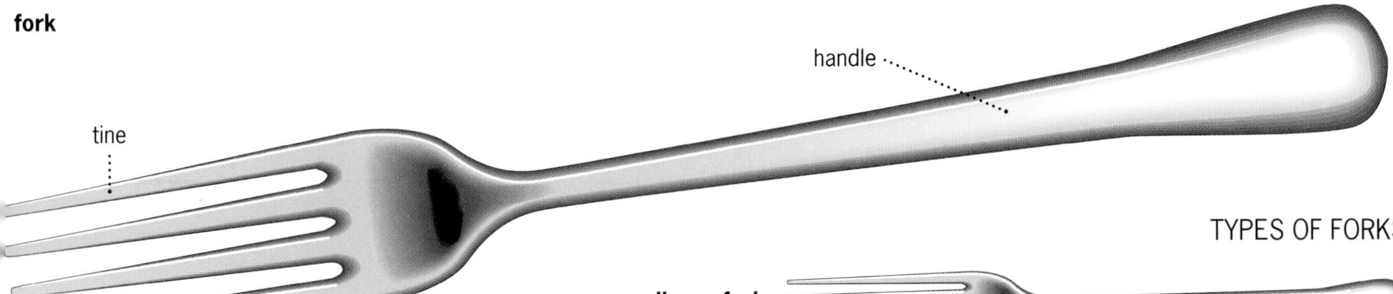
handle
tine
point

TYPES OF FORKS

dinner fork

fondue fork

spoon

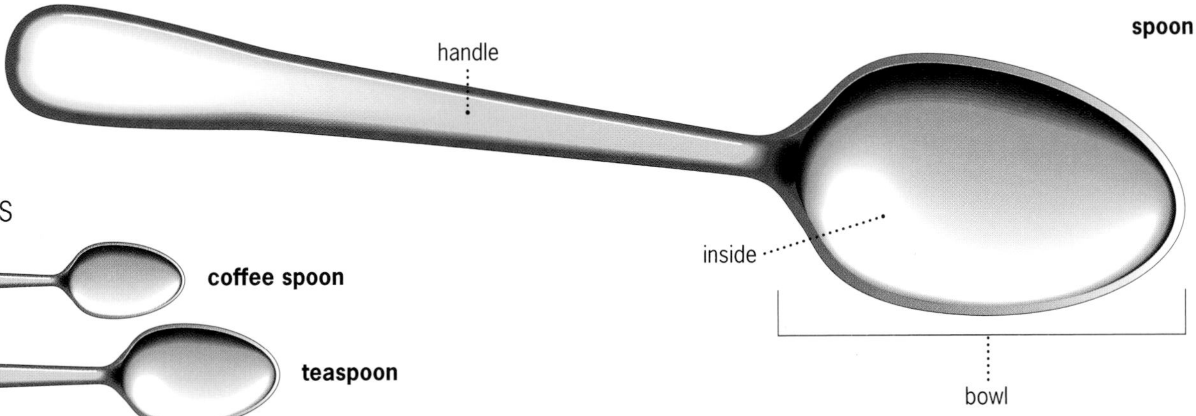
handle
inside
bowl

TYPES OF SPOONS

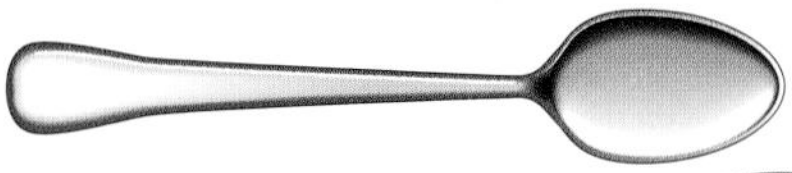

coffee spoon

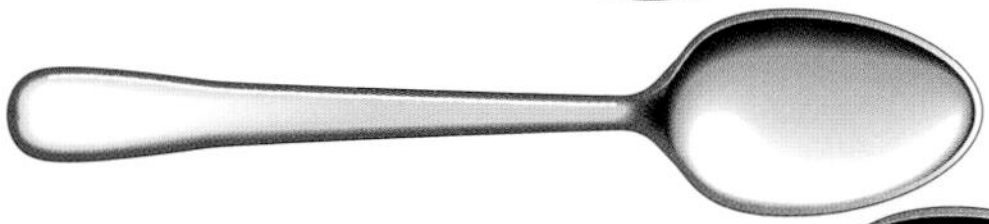

teaspoon

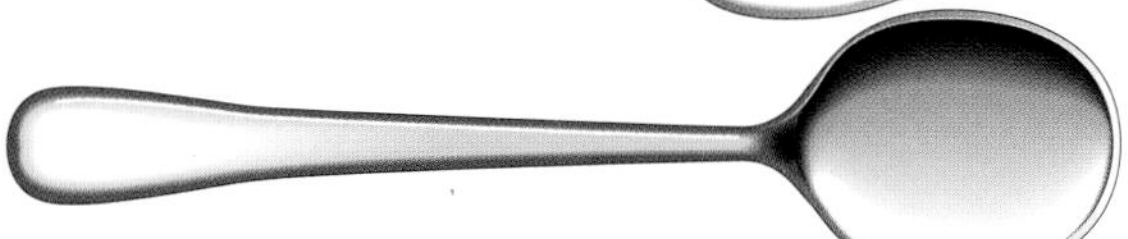

soup spoon

KITCHEN UTENSILS

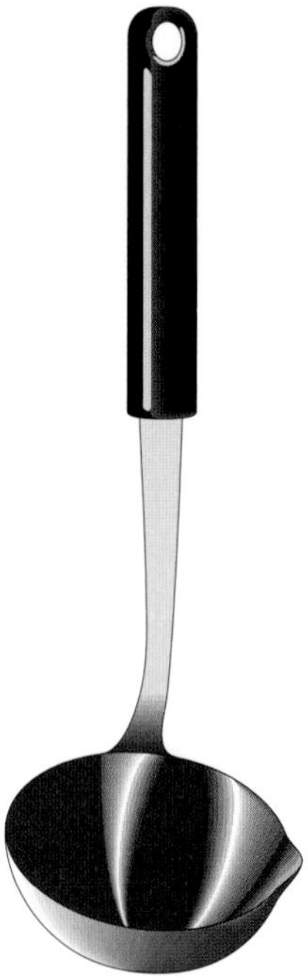
ladle

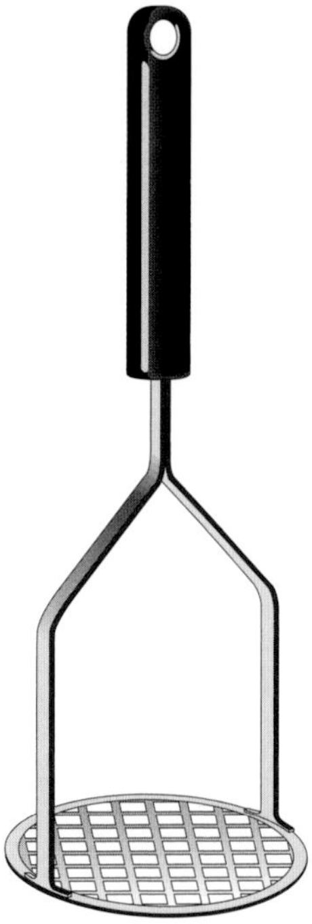
potato masher

spatula

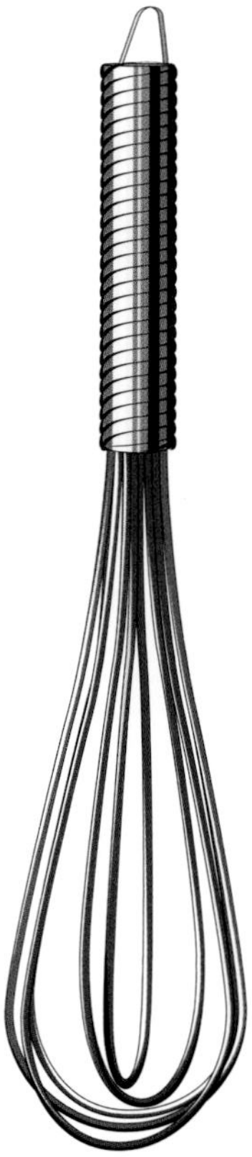
whisk

egg beater

measuring spoons

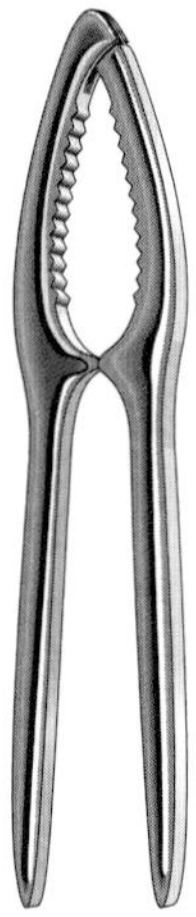
nutcracker

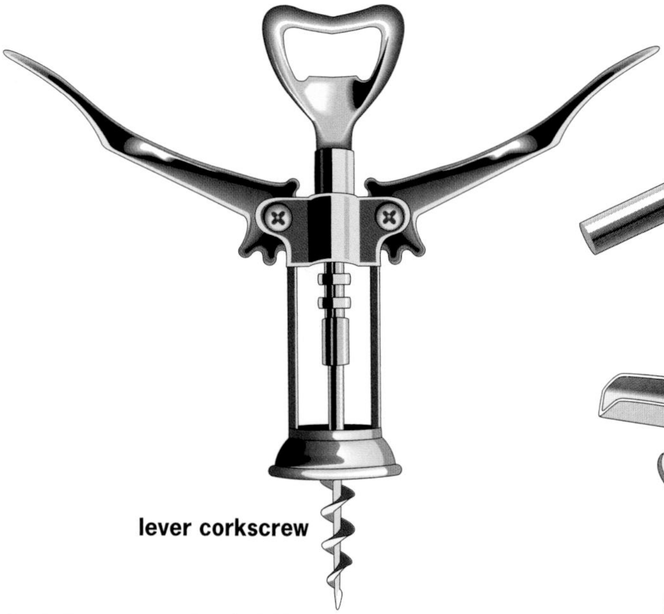
lever corkscrew

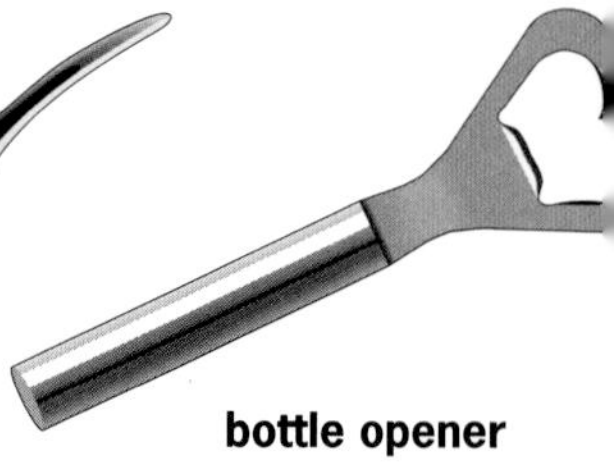
bottle opener

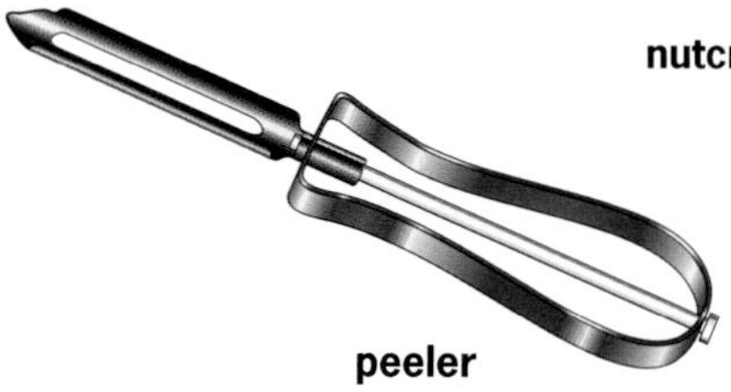
peeler

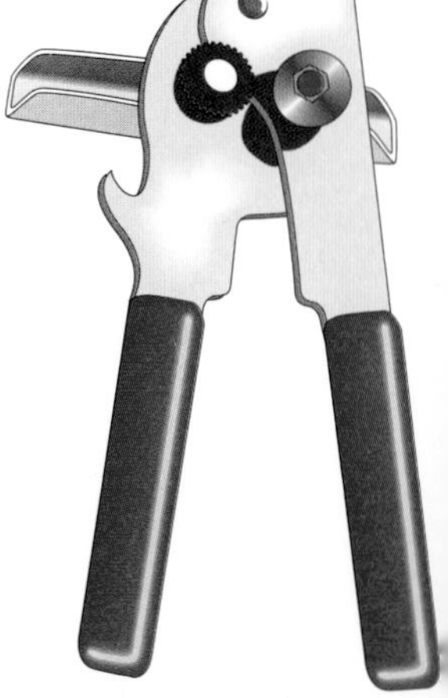
can opener

rolling pin

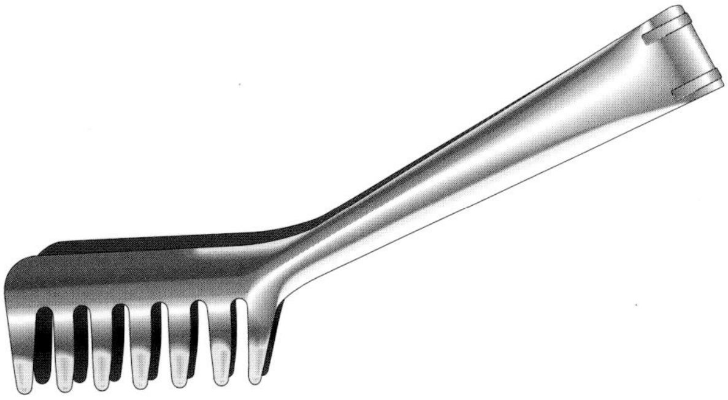

spaghetti tongs

funnel

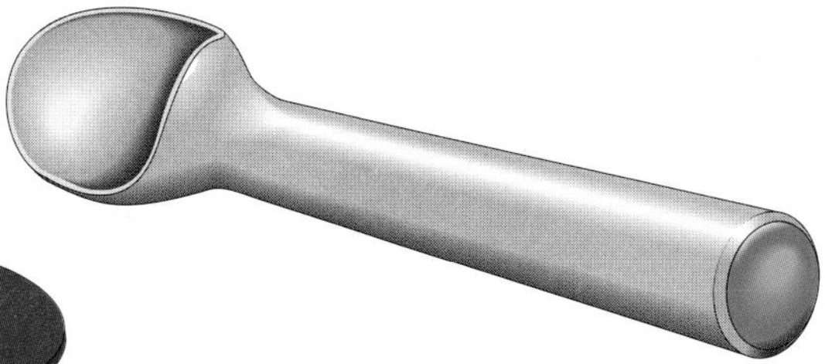

ice–cream scoop

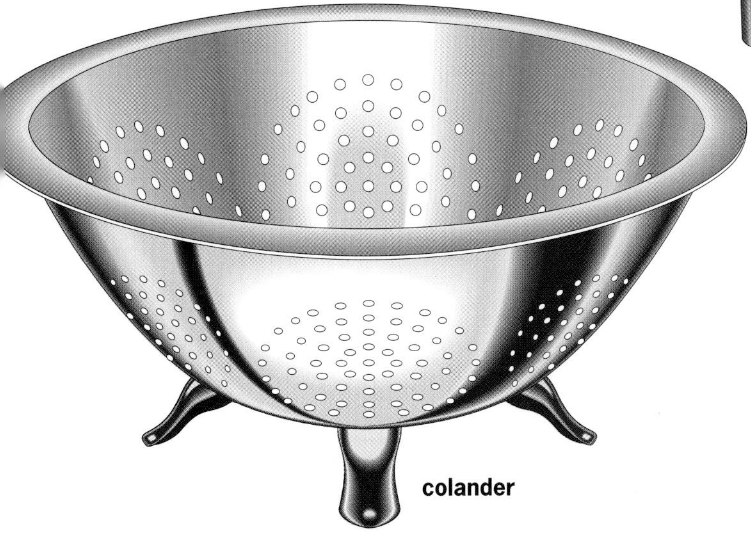

colander

lemon squeezer

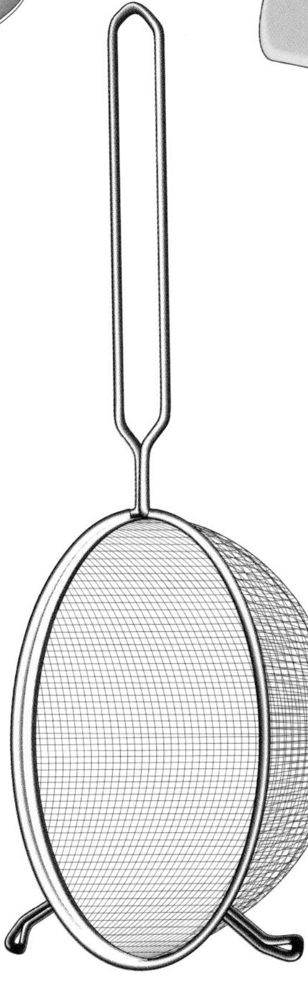

strainer

salad spinner

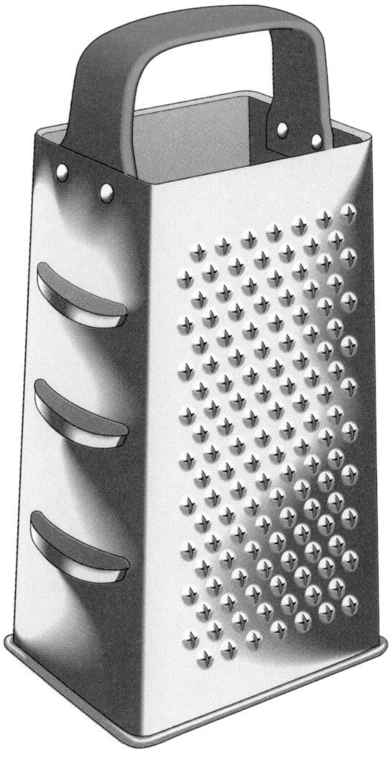

grater

COOKING UTENSILS

stockpot; casserole

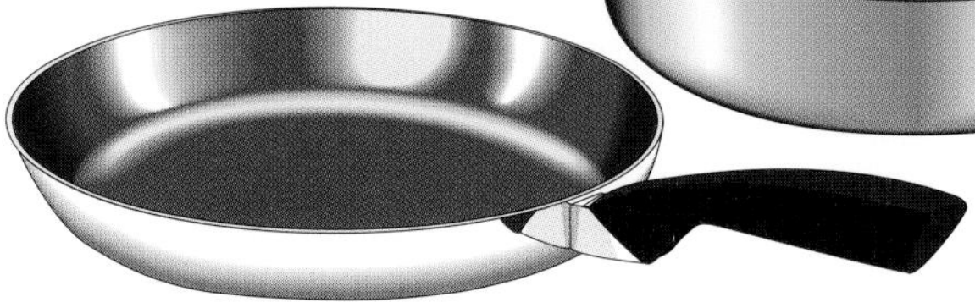
frying pan

sauté pan

wok

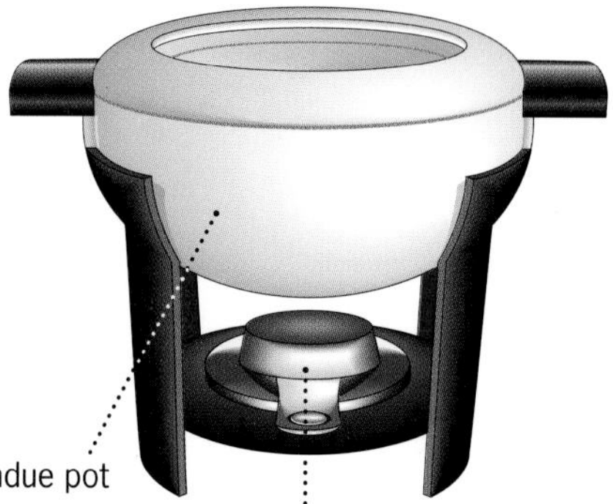
fondue pot
burner
fondue set

double boiler

saucepan

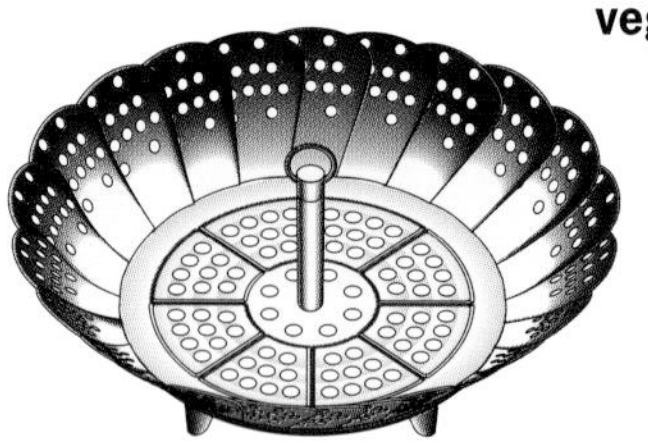
vegetable steamer

roasting pans

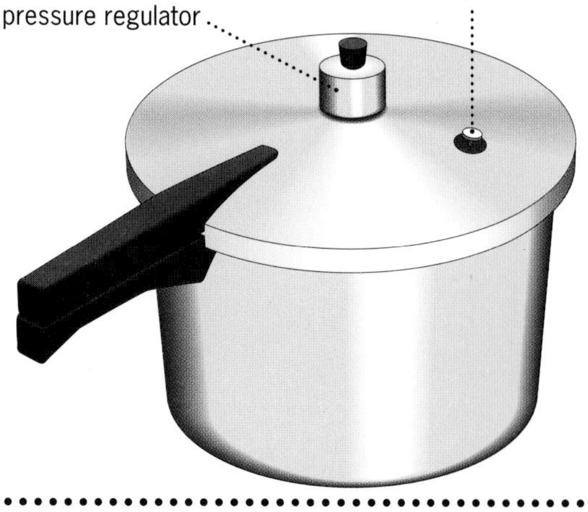
pressure regulator
safety valve
pressure cooker

KITCHEN APPLIANCES

automatic drip coffee maker

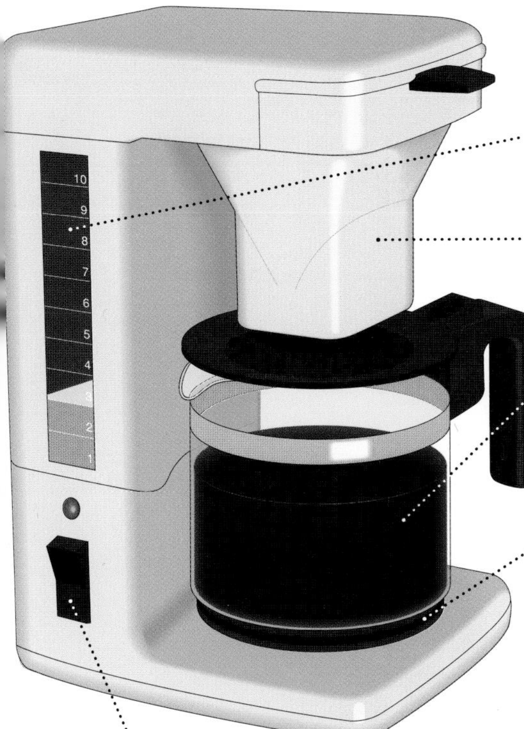
reservoir
basket
carafe
warming plate
on-off switch

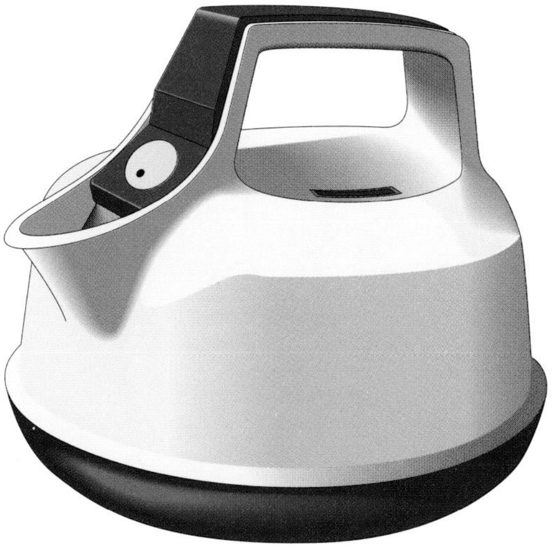

kettle

hand blender

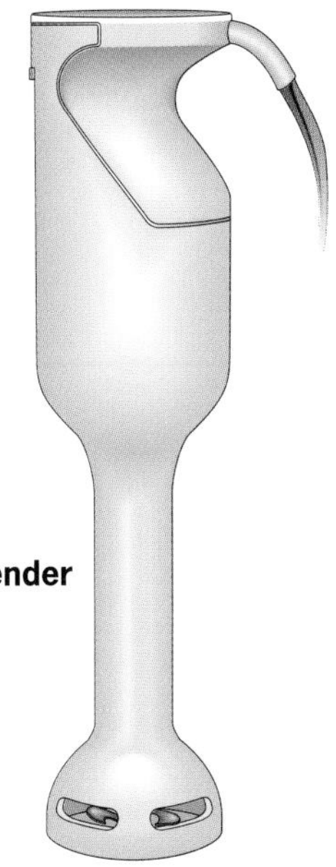

hand mixer

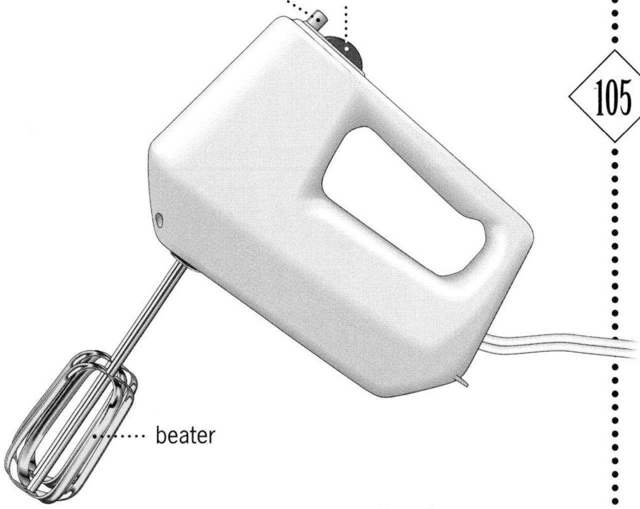
beater ejector
speed control
beater

blender

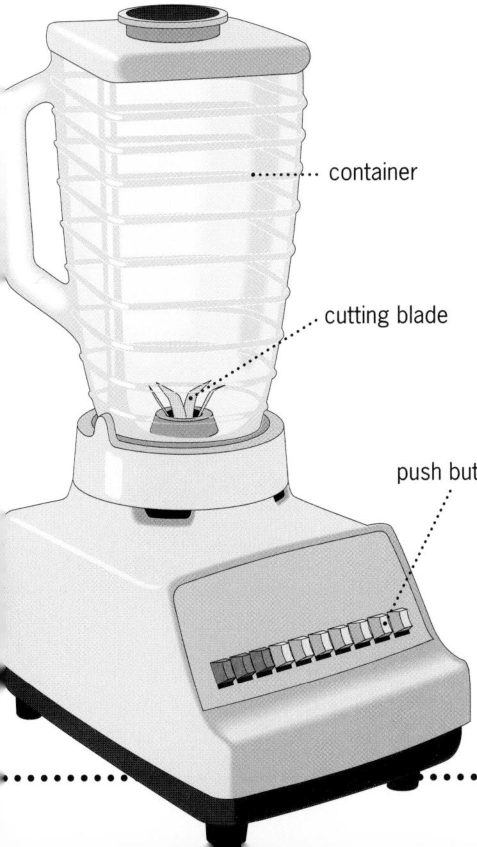
container
cutting blade
push button

toaster

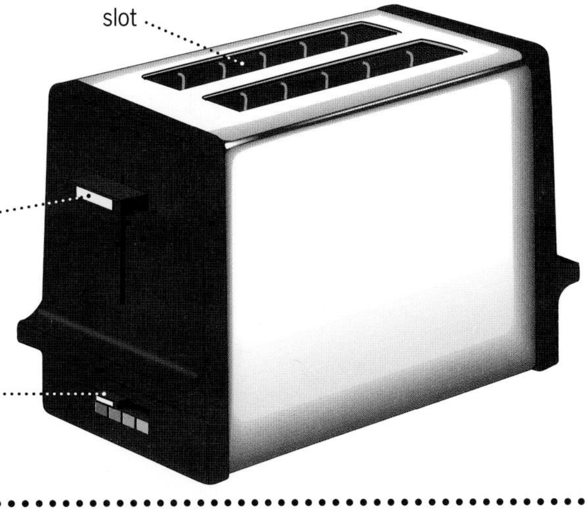
slot
lever
temperature control

REFRIGERATOR

ice cube tray
egg tray
dairy compartment
freezer compartment
thermostat control
butter compartment
crisper
refrigerator compartment
guard rail
meat tray
glass cover
shelf
storage door

COOKING APPLIANCES

microwave oven

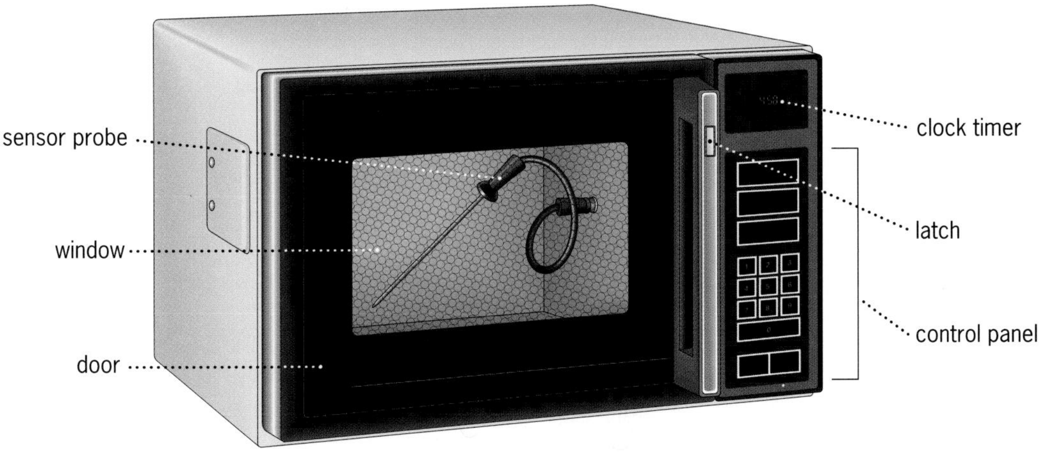
sensor probe
window
door
clock timer
latch
control panel

electric range

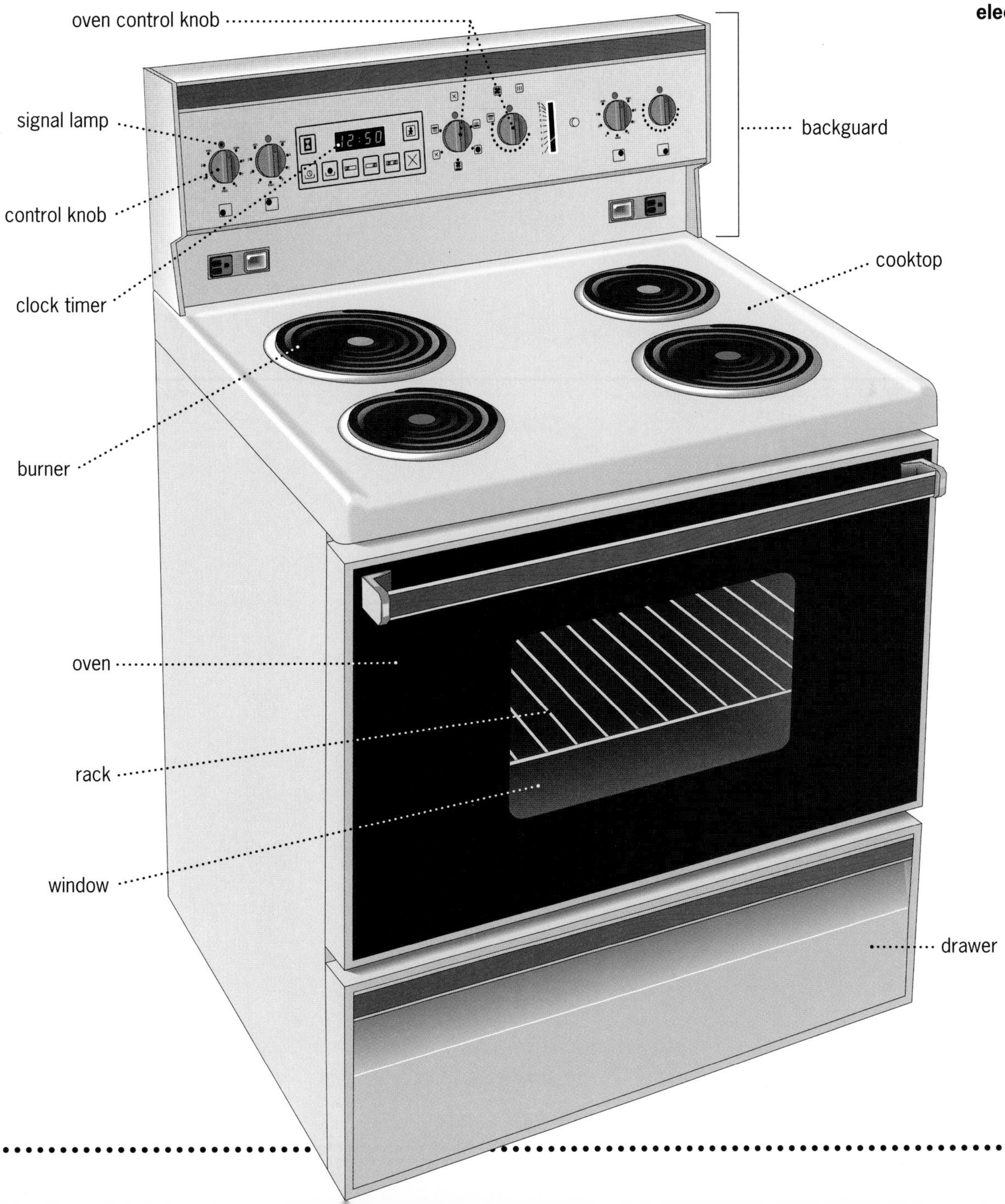
oven control knob
signal lamp
control knob
clock timer
burner
oven
rack
window
backguard
cooktop
drawer

CARPENTRY TOOLS

claw hammer

carpenter's hammer

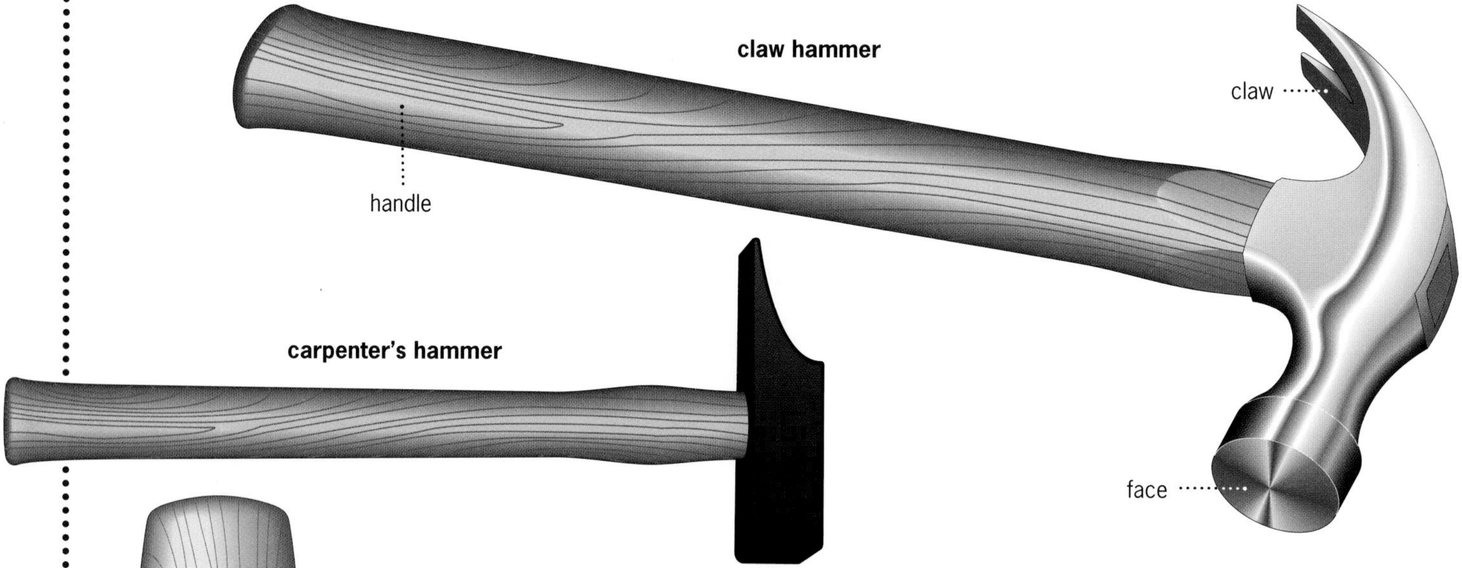
claw
handle
face

mallet

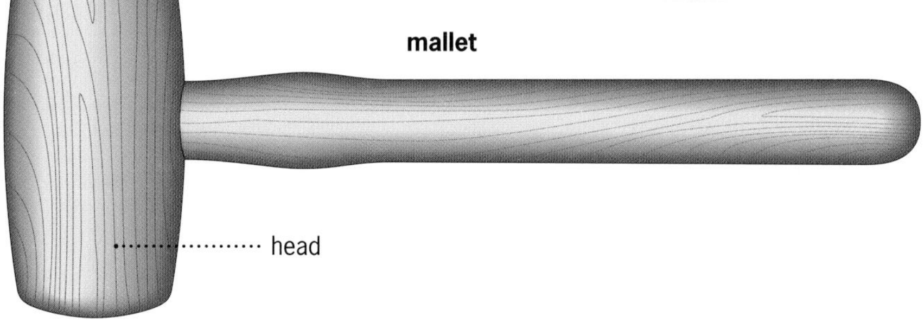
head

tape measure

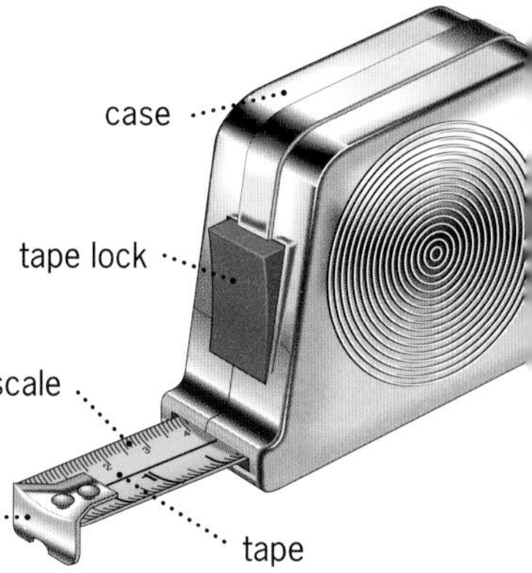
case
tape lock
scale
hook
tape

nail

screw

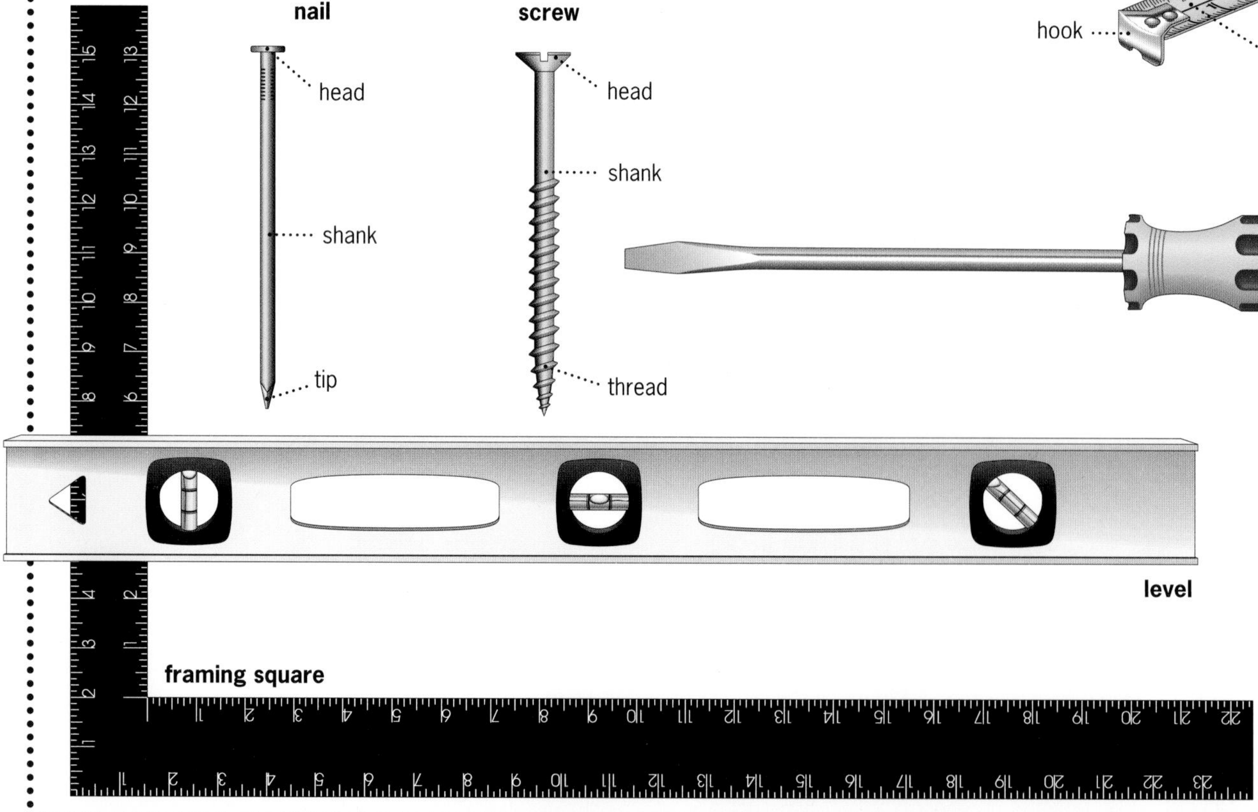
head
shank
tip
head
shank
thread

level

framing square

screwdriver

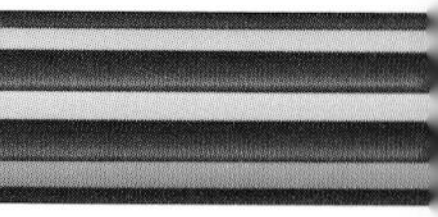

C-clamp

handsaw

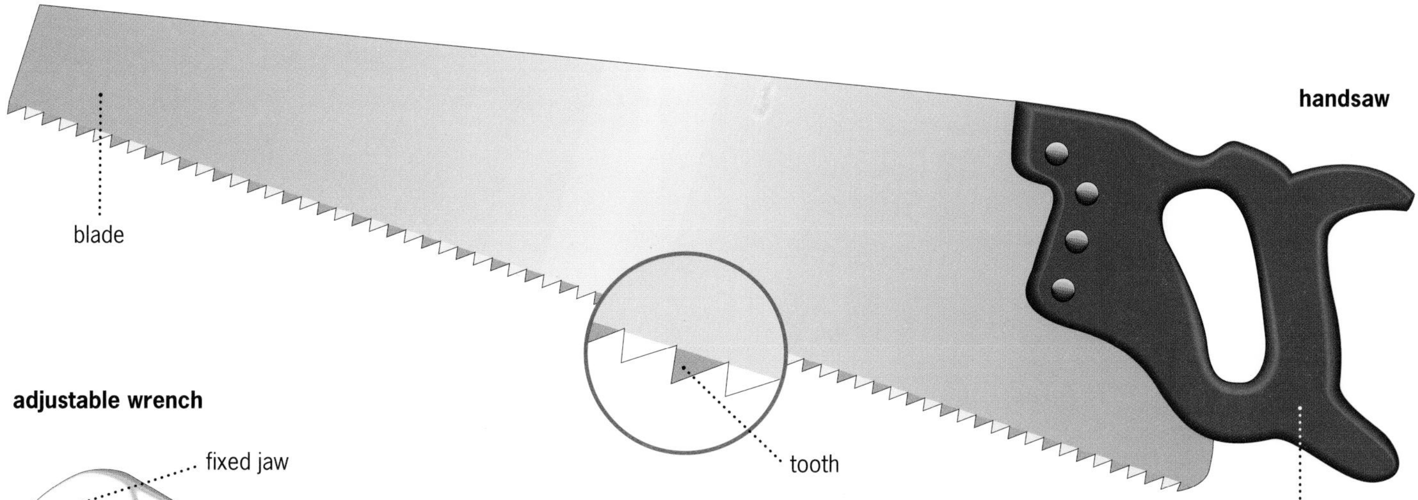
blade
tooth
handle

adjustable wrench

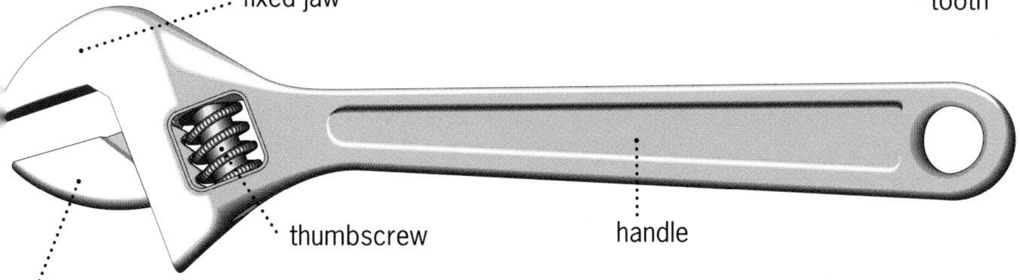
fixed jaw
thumbscrew
handle
movable jaw

locking pliers

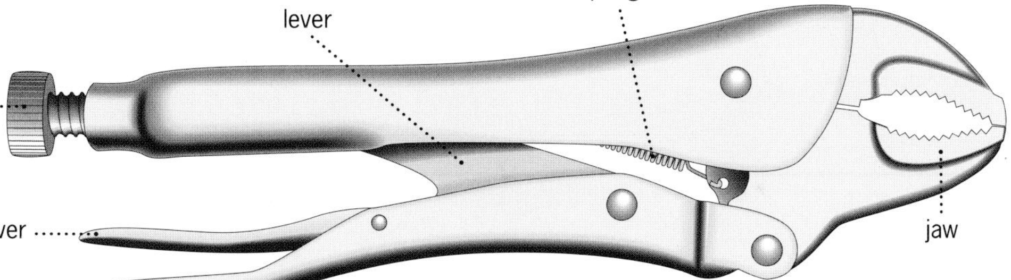
spring
lever
adjusting screw
release lever
jaw

rib joint pliers

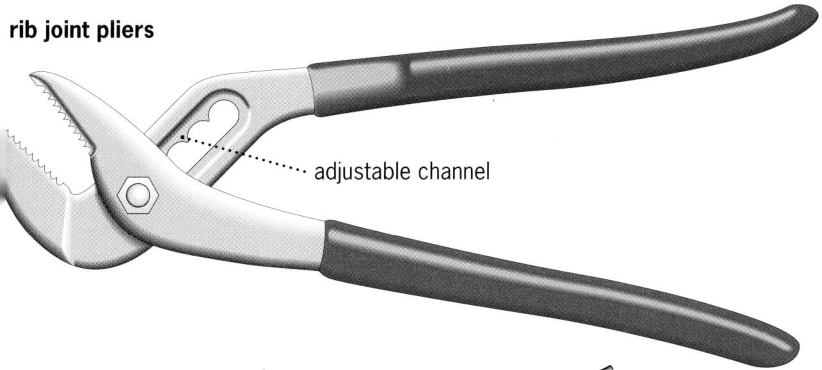
adjustable channel

bolt

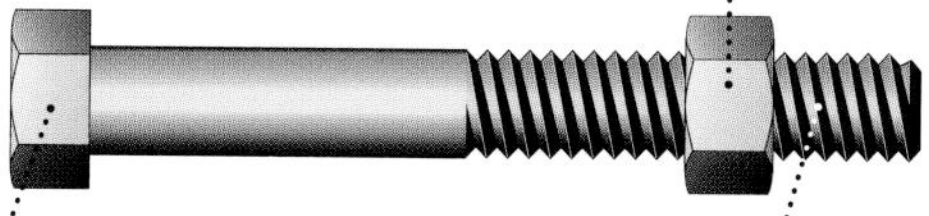
nut
head
threaded rod

long-nose pliers

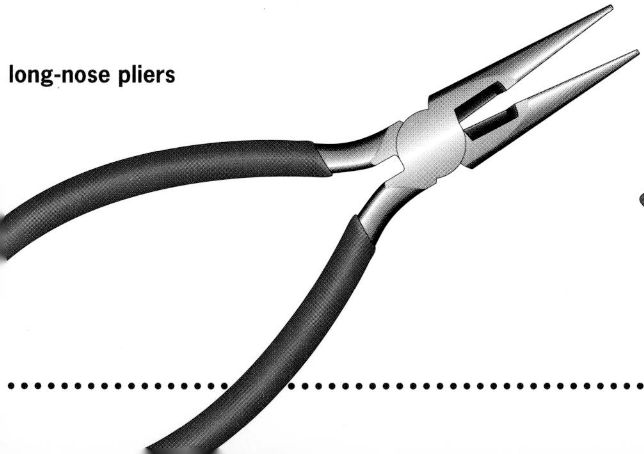

slip joint pliers

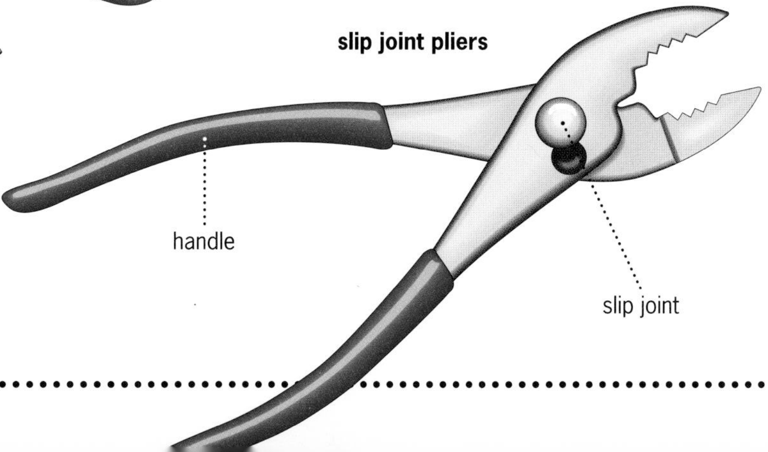
handle
slip joint

ELECTRIC TOOLS

electric drill

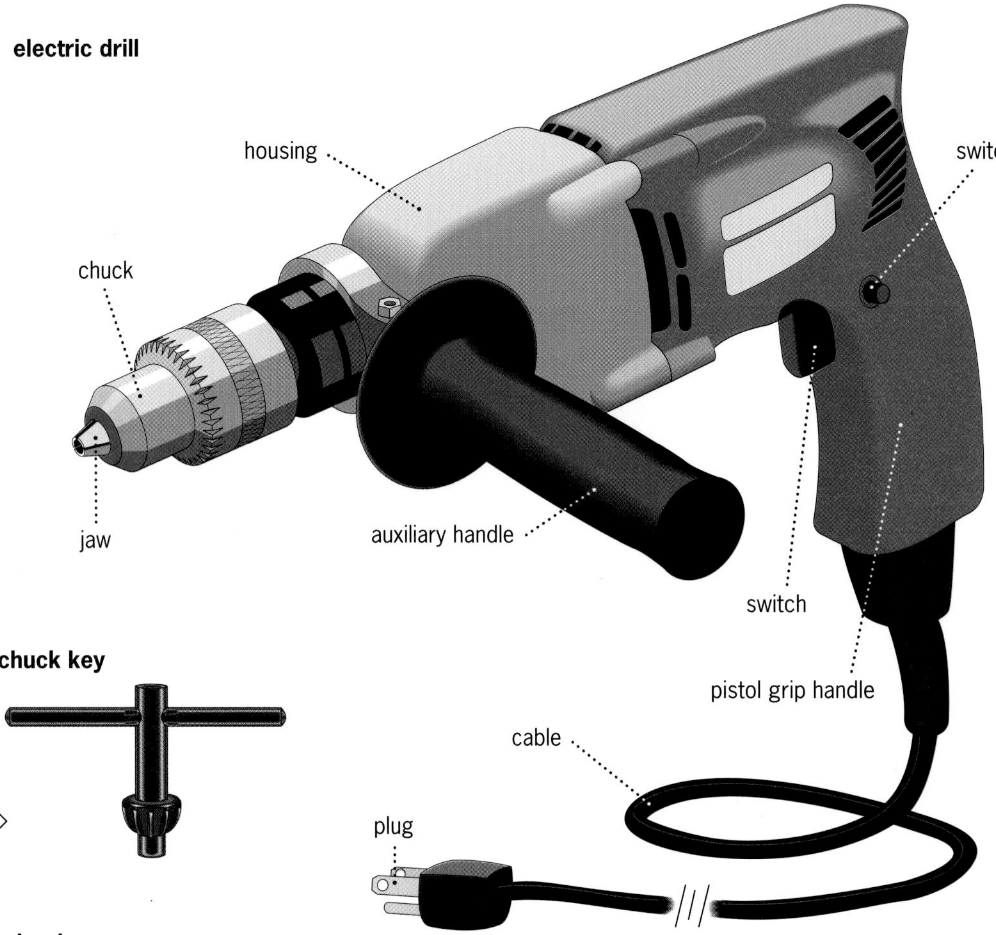
housing
switch lock
chuck
jaw
auxiliary handle
switch
pistol grip handle
cable
plug

chuck key

twist drill

auger bit

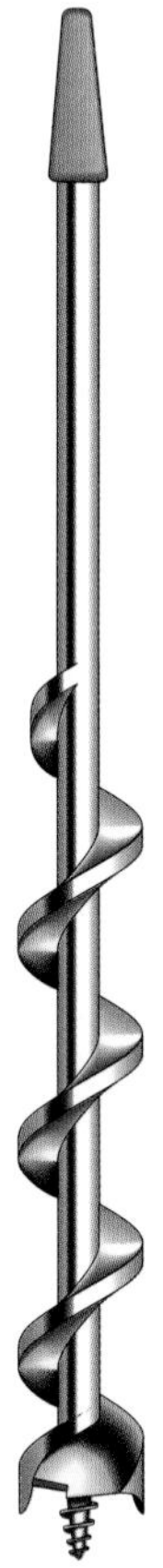

circular saw

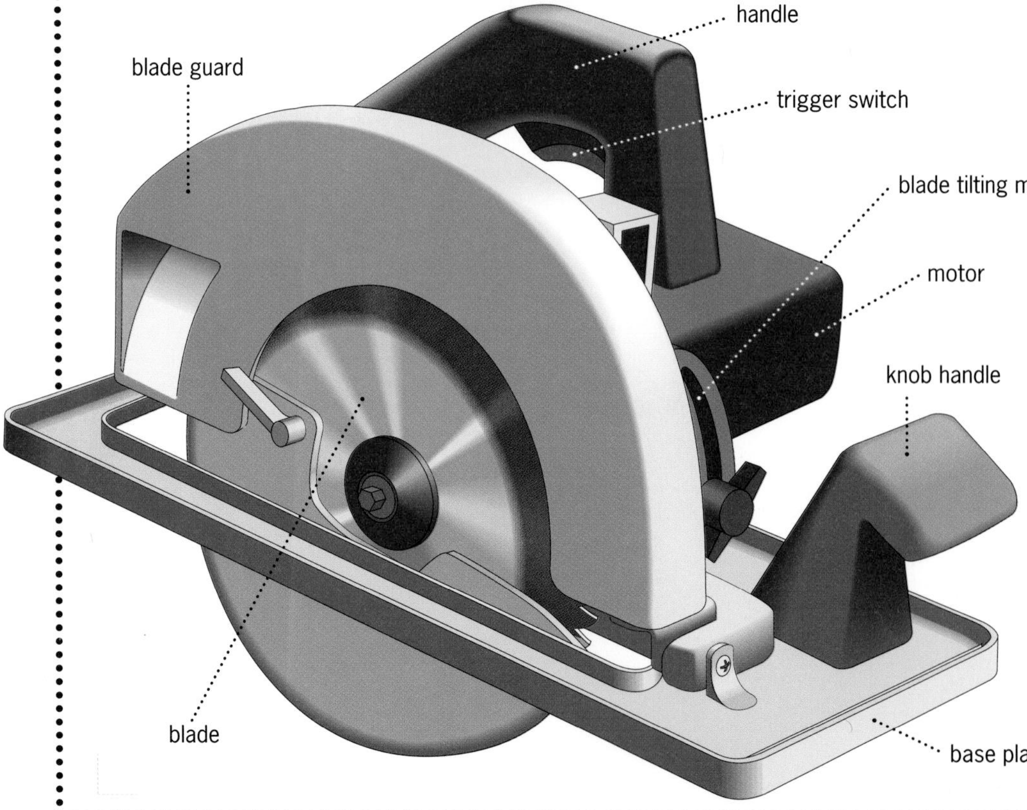
handle
blade guard
trigger switch
blade tilting mechanism
motor
knob handle
blade
base plate

circular saw blade

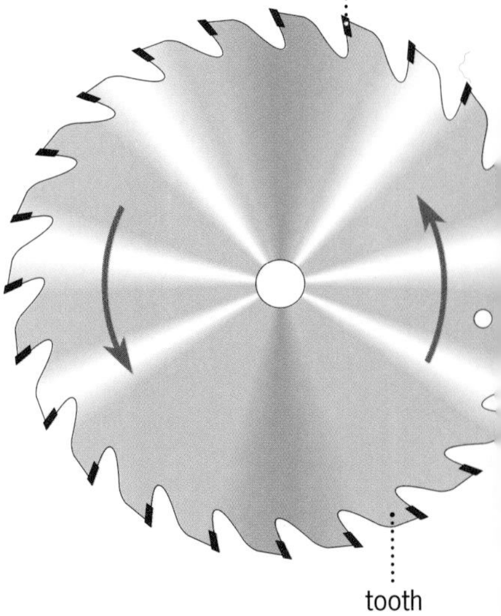
tip
tooth

PAINTING UPKEEP

paint roller

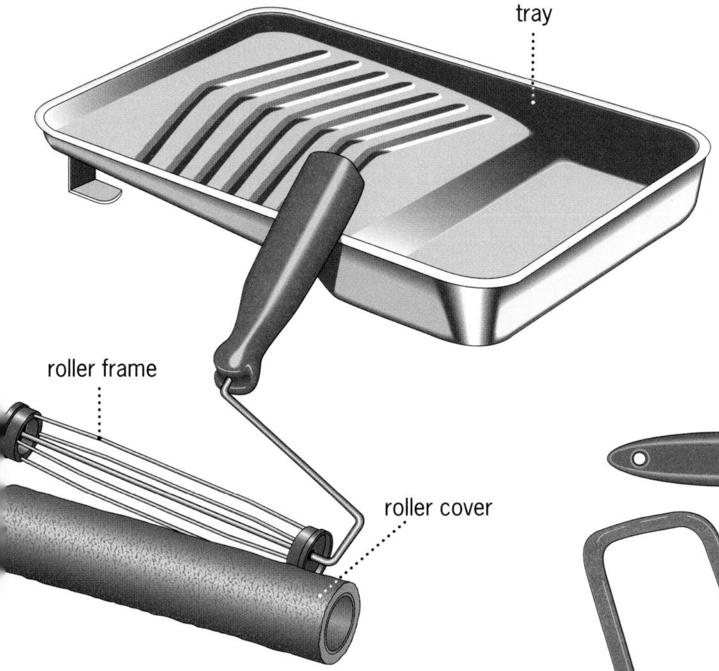
tray
roller frame
roller cover

scraper

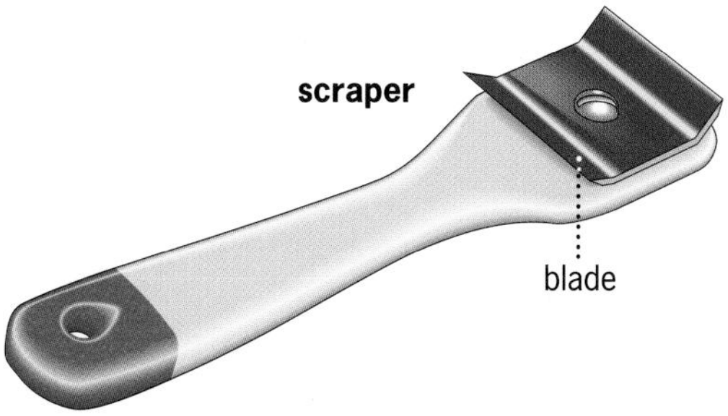
blade

brush

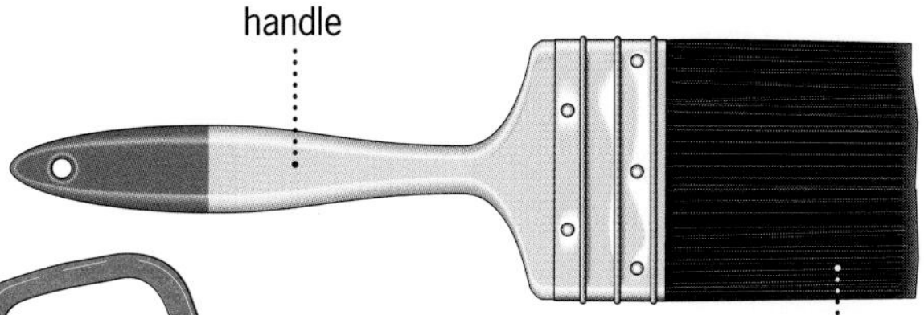
handle
bristles

extension ladder

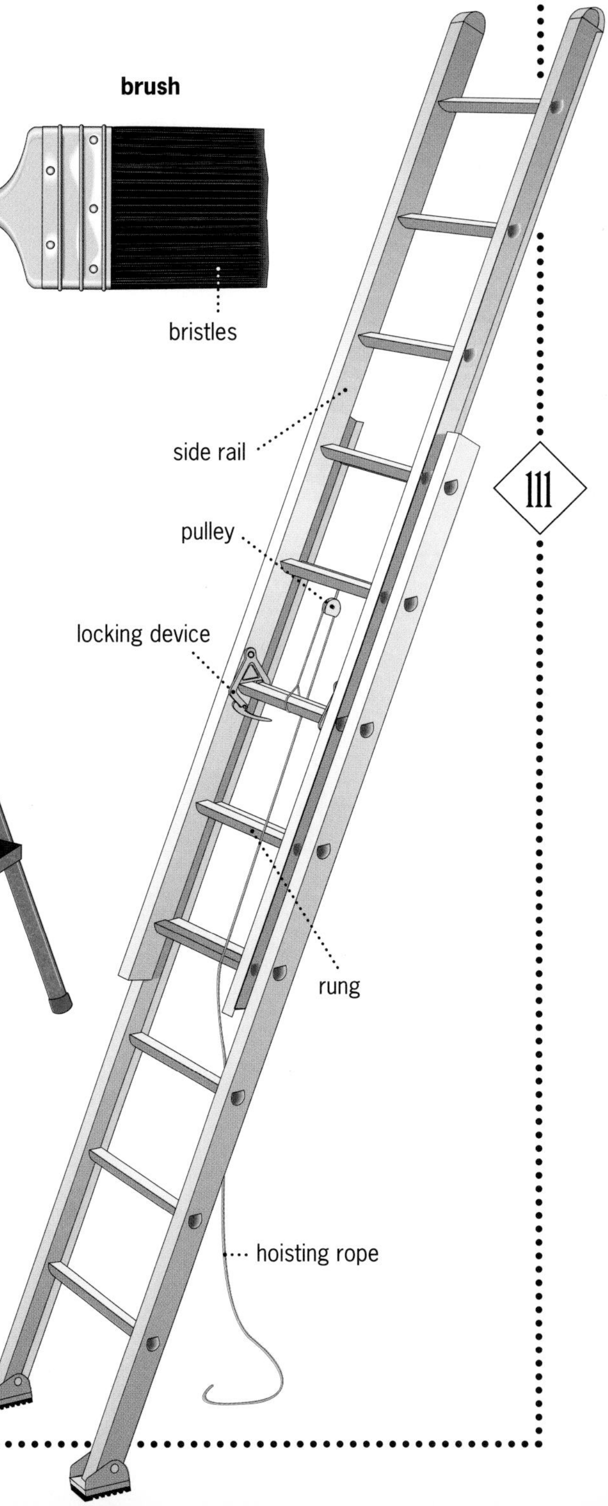
side rail
pulley
locking device
rung
hoisting rope
anti-slip shoe

stepladder

platform ladder

MEN'S CLOTHING

shirt

collar
collar point
placket
breast pocket
front
cuff
button
shirttail

suspenders

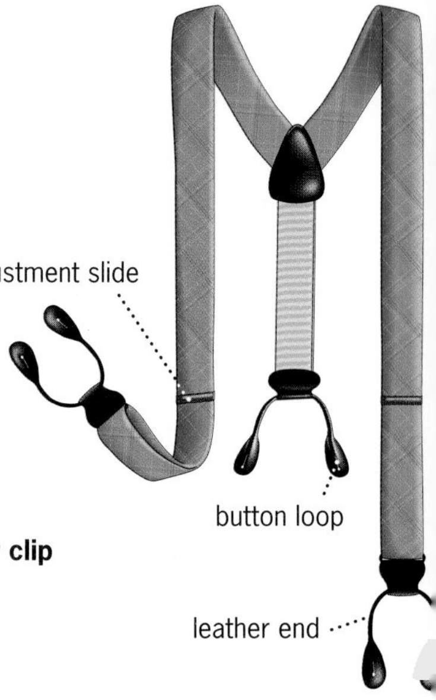
adjustment slide
button loop
leather end

suspender clip

pants

waistband
pocket
fly
crease
cuff

tie

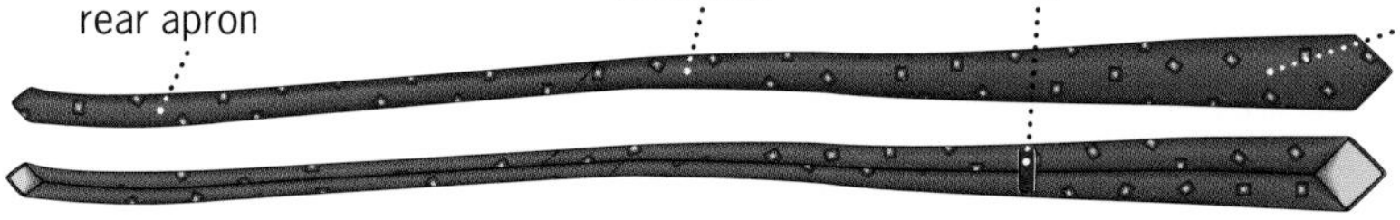
rear apron
neck end
loop
front apron

belt

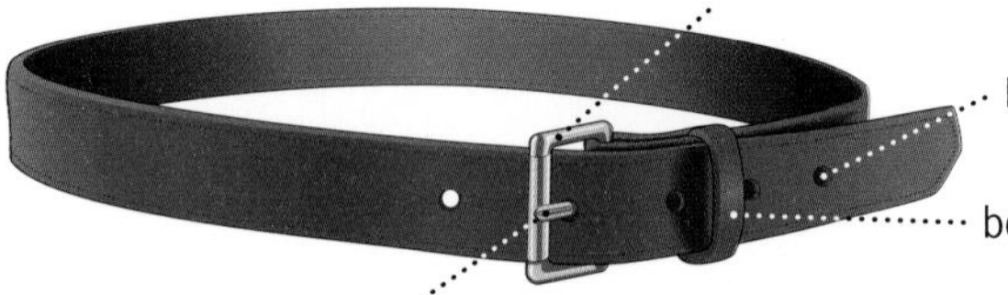
frame
punch hole
belt carrier
tongue

undershirt

boxer shorts

briefs

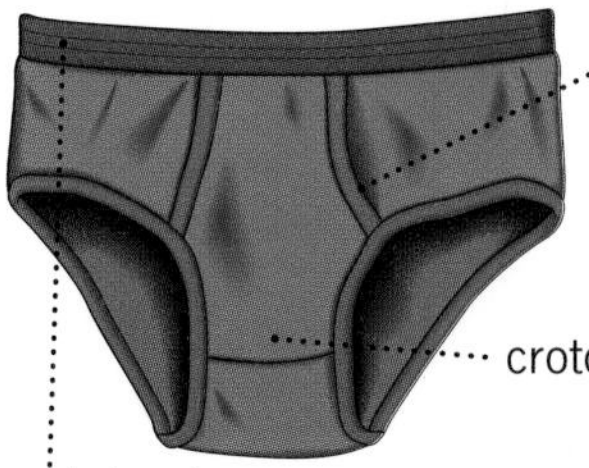
fly
crotch
waistband

double-breasted jacket

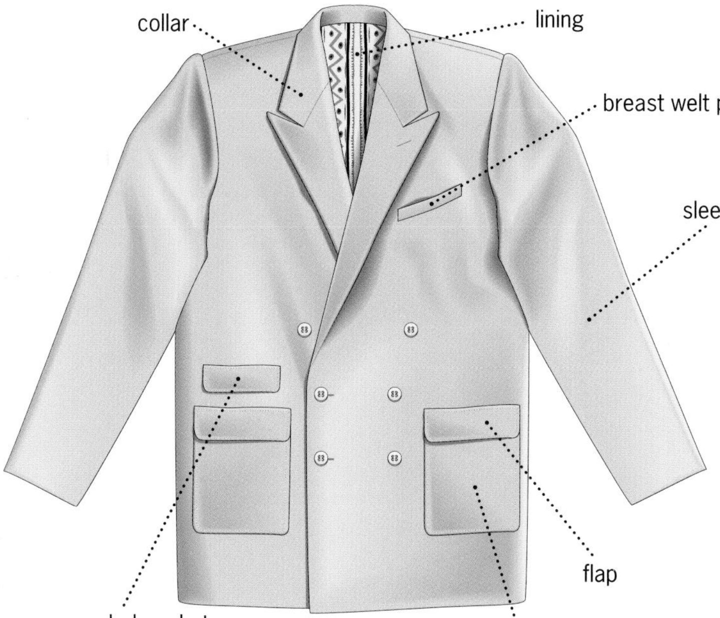
collar
lining
breast welt pocket
sleeve
flap
concealed pocket
patch pocket

duffle coat

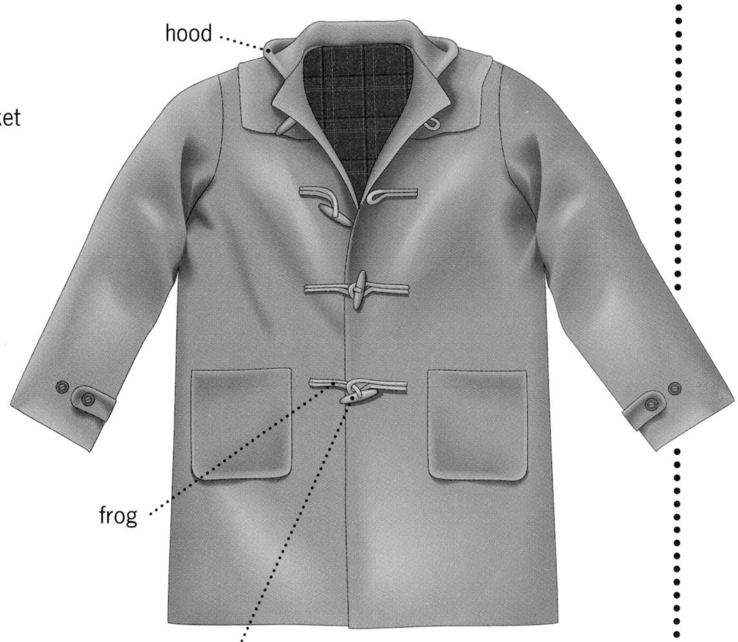
hood
frog
toggle fastening

cap

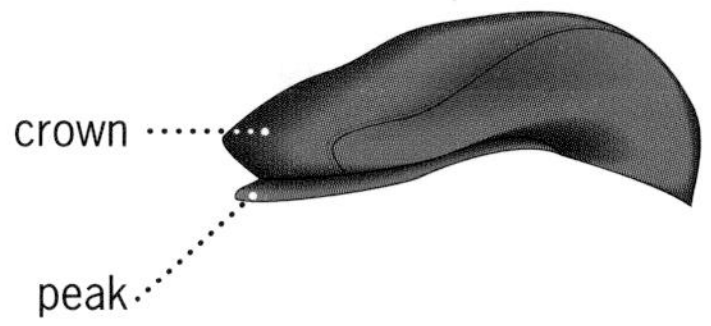
crown
peak

stocking cap

hunting cap

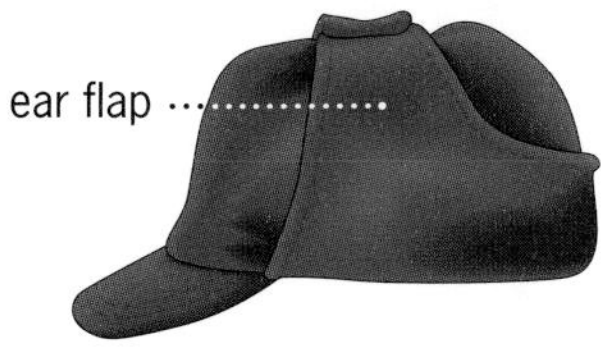
ear flap

jacket

snap fastener
elastic waistband

windbreaker

waistband
drawstring

WOMEN'S CLOTHING

toque

knitted hat

balaclava
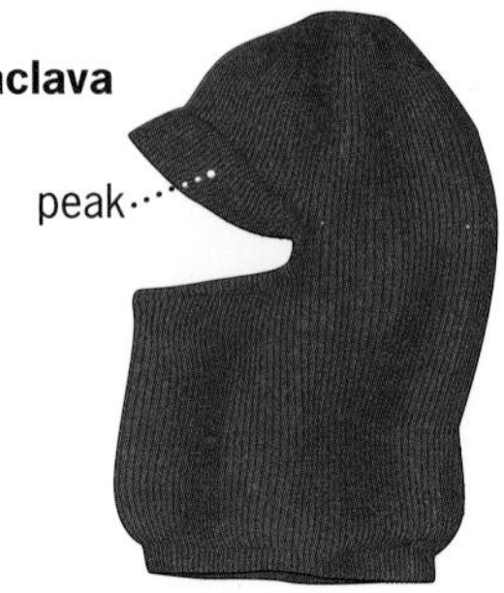

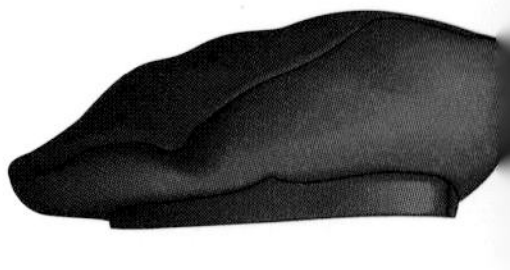
beret

suit

blouse

double-breasted jacket

overcoat

poncho

dress

jeans

ski pants

shorts

Bermuda shorts

straight skirt

culottes

pleated skirt

WOMEN'S CLOTHING

pajamas

bra

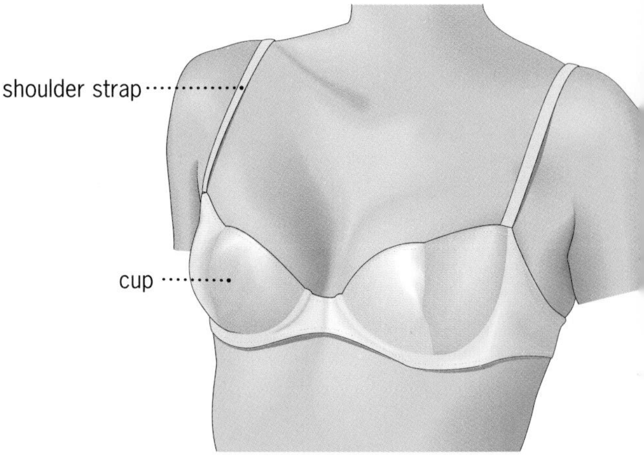
shoulder strap
cup

briefs

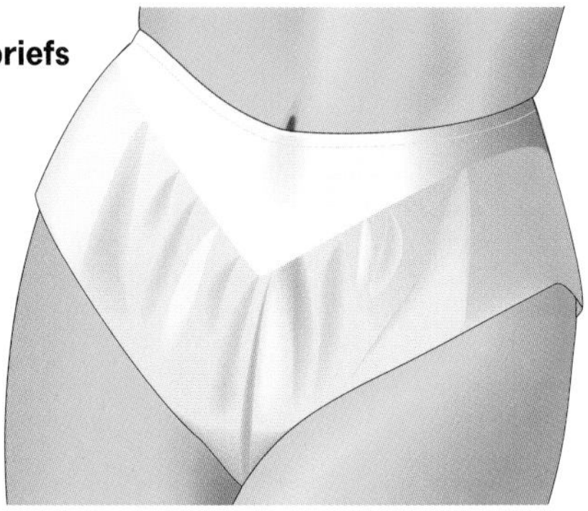

bathrobe

half-slip

SWEATERS

cardigan

crew neck sweater

turtleneck

polo shirt

V-neck cardigan

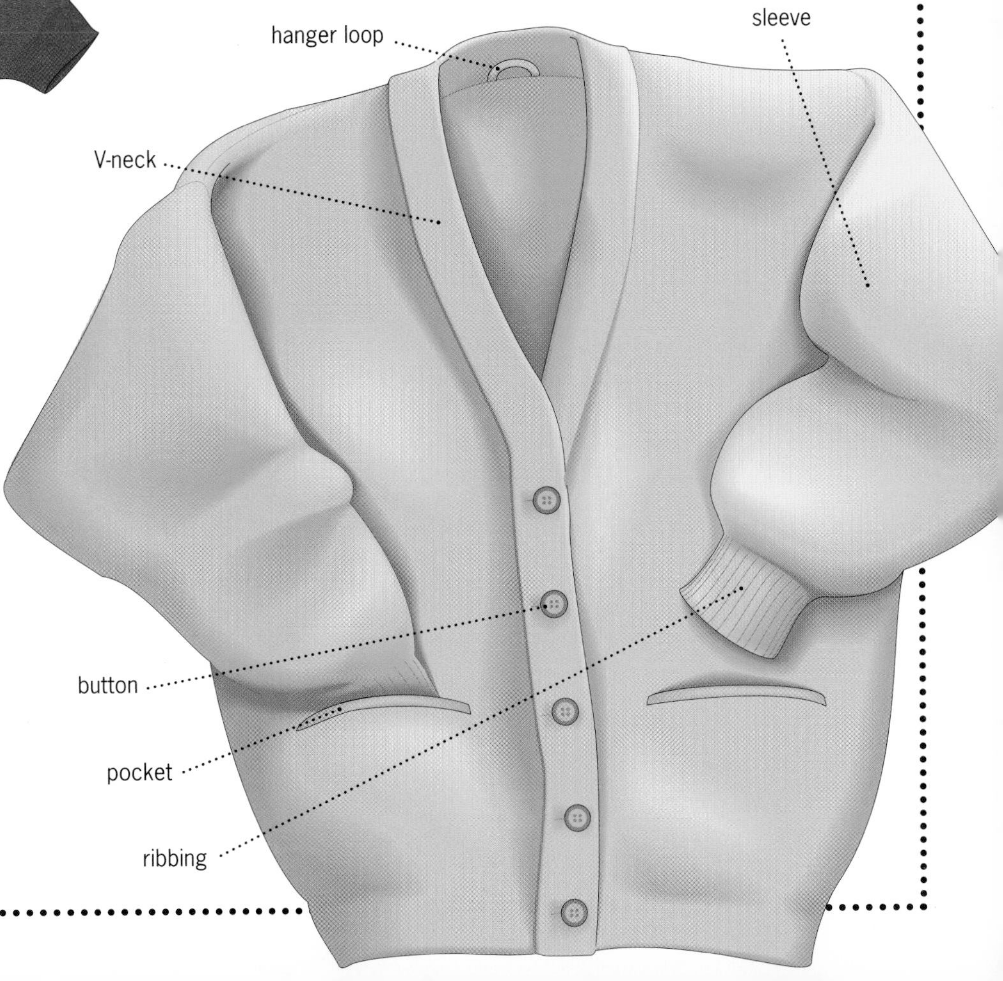
hanger loop
sleeve
V-neck
button
pocket
ribbing

sweater vest

GLOVES AND STOCKINGS

gloves

glove finger
thumb
palm
snap fastener
stitching

driving glove

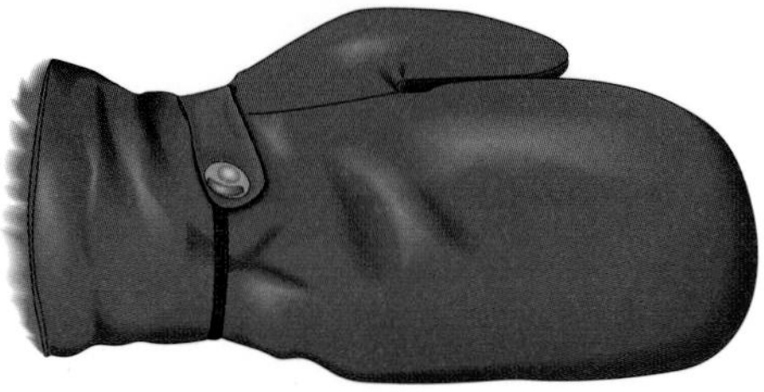

mitten

sock

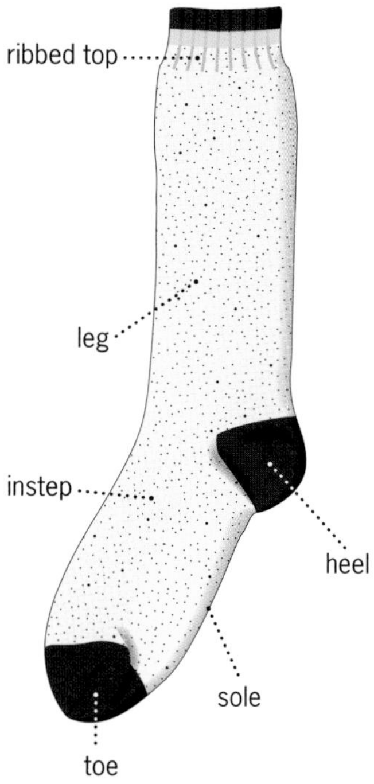
ribbed top
leg
instep
heel
sole
toe

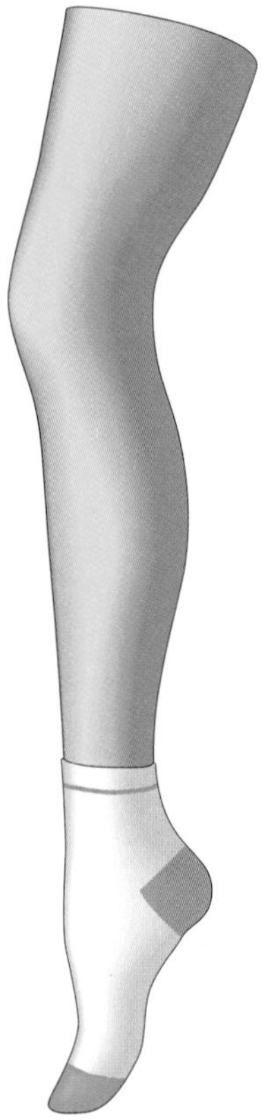

short sock

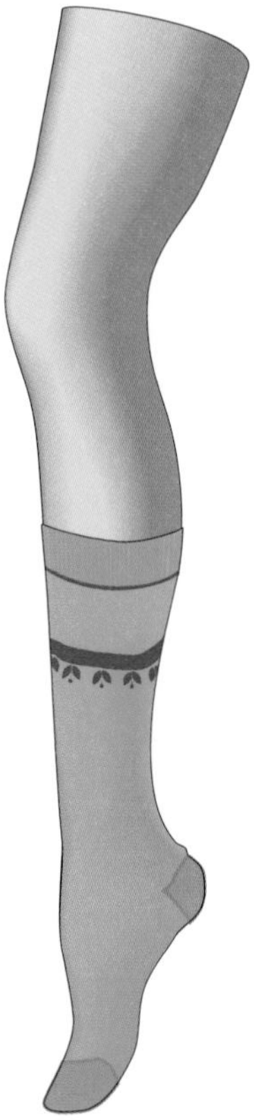

sock

knee-high sock

stocking

tights

SHOES

heavy duty boot
slingback
ballerina
tennis shoe
thigh-boot
pump
espadrille
loafer
moccasin
sandal
boot
ankle boot

SPORTSWEAR

EXERCISE WEAR

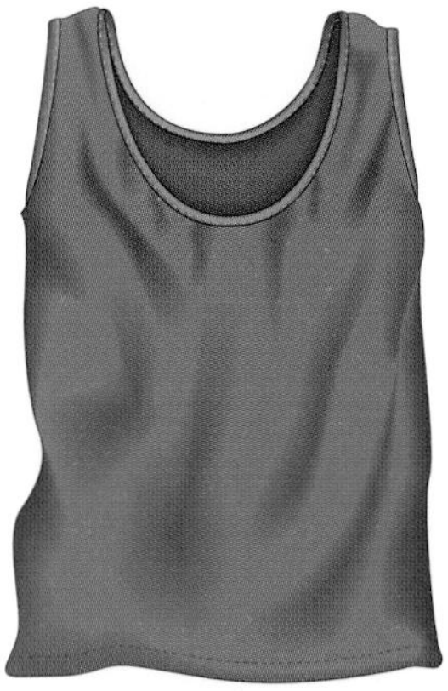

tank top

swimsuit

leotard

TRACK SUIT

sweatshirt

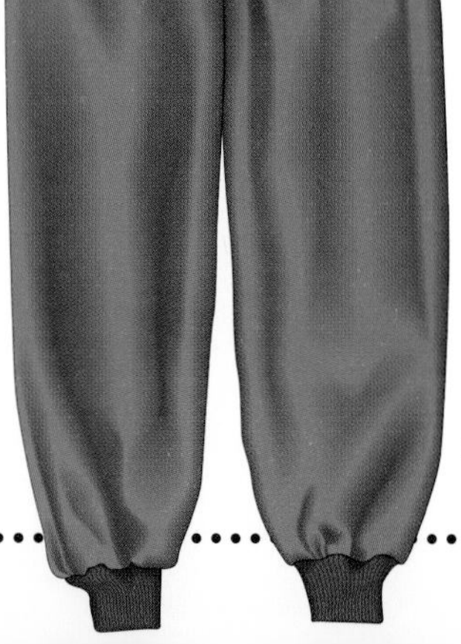

sweatpants

hooded sweatshirt

windbreaker

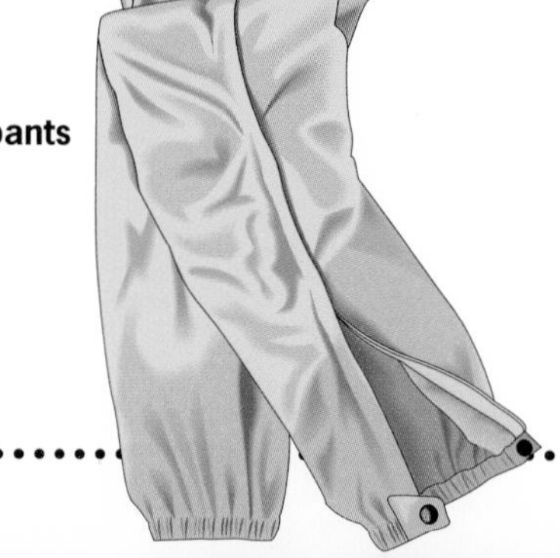

pants

EXERCISE WEAR

footless tights

leg-warmer

swimming trunks

shorts

running shoe

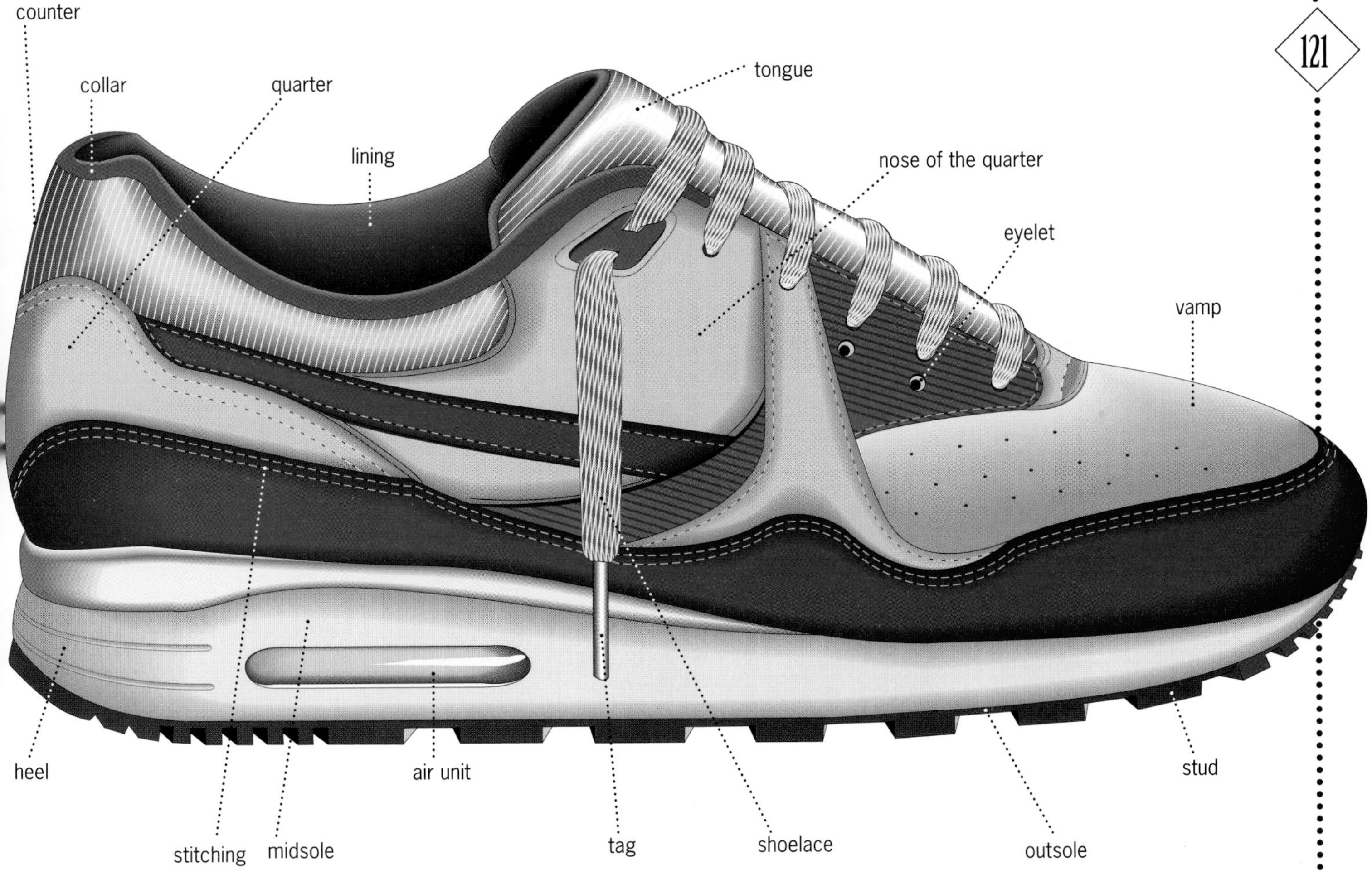
counter
collar
quarter
lining
tongue
nose of the quarter
eyelet
vamp
heel
air unit
stud
stitching
midsole
tag
shoelace
outsole

DENTAL CARE

toothbrush

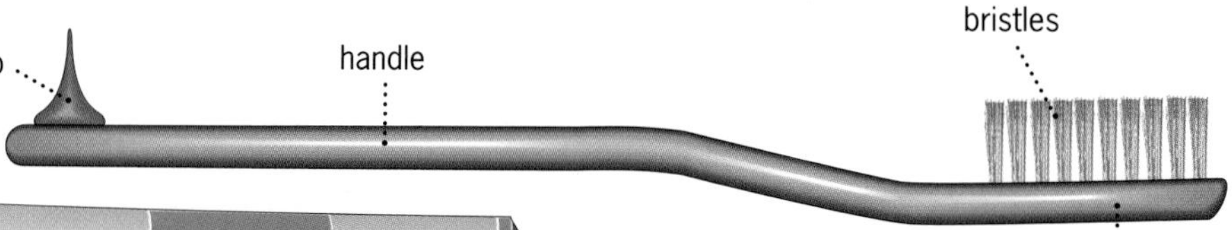
stimulator tip
handle
bristles
head

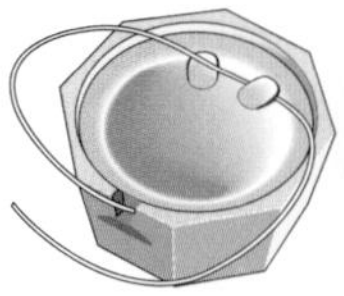

dental floss

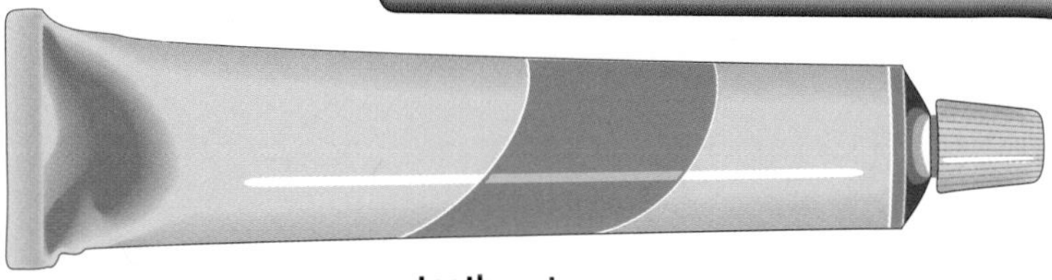

toothpaste

HAIRDRESSING

tail comb

rake comb

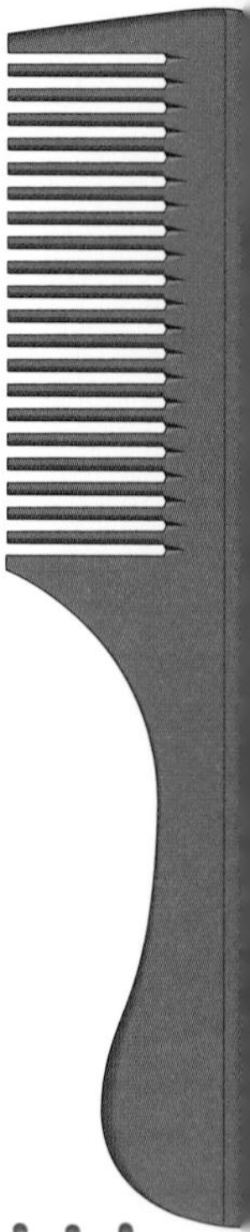

hair-dryer

fan
heat selector switch
barrel
heat
air
0
1
2
1
2
3
chal
air
speed selector switch
on-off switch
air-outlet grille
handle
air concentrator

hairbrush

hair pick

LEATHER GOODS

drawstring bag
drawstring
shoulder strap
front pocket

knapsack

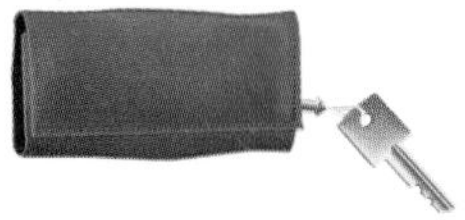
key case

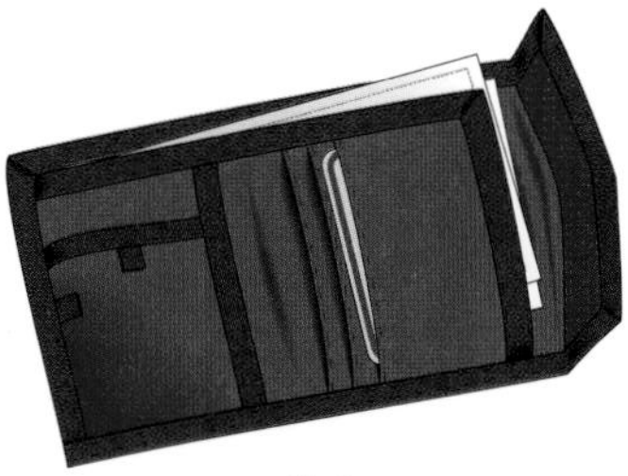
wallet

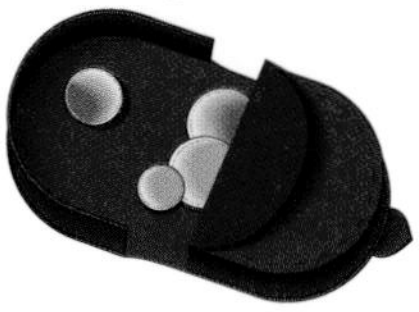
purse

GLASSES

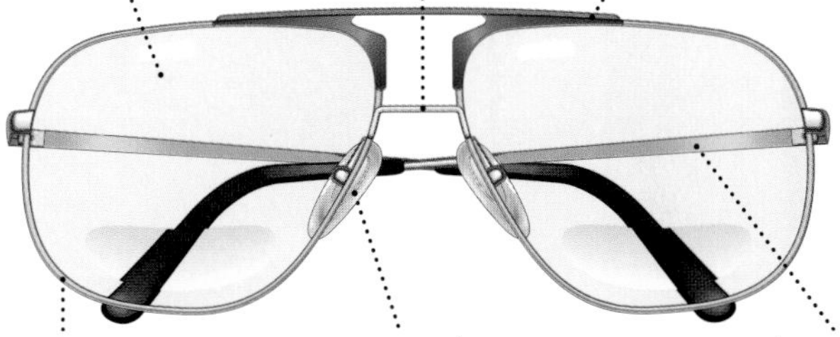
glass lens
bridge
bar
rim
nose pad
temple

UMBRELLA

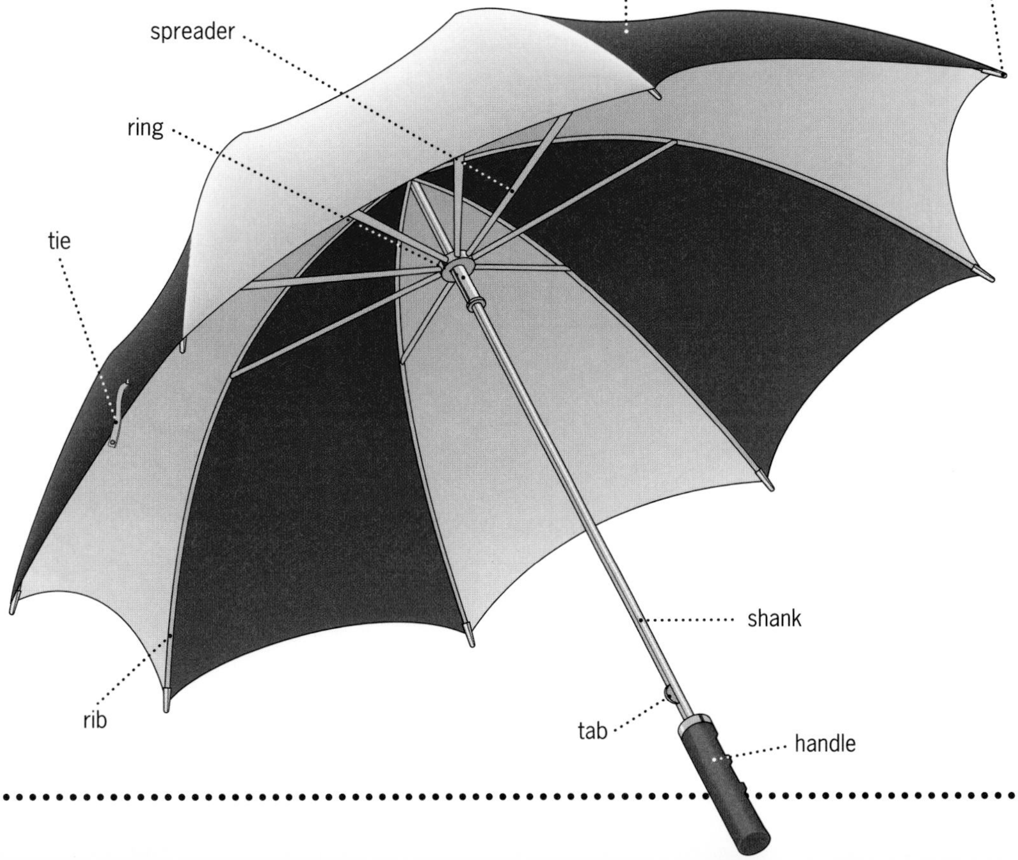
canopy
tip
spreader
ring
tie
shank
rib
tab
handle

telescopic umbrella
cover

COMMUNICATION BY TELEPHONE

telephone set

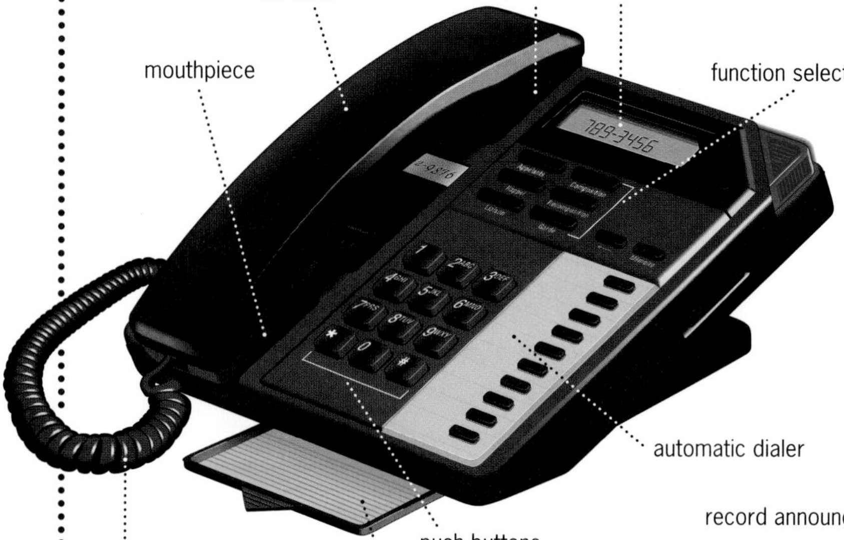
handset
earpiece
display
mouthpiece
function selectors
automatic dialer
push buttons
handset cord
telephone index

telephone answering machine

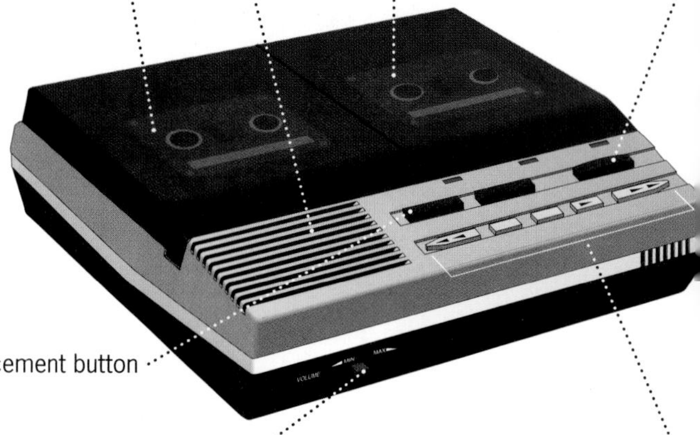
outgoing announcement cassette
incoming message cassette
speaker
listen button
record announcement button
volume control
cassette player controls

pay phone

coin slot
display
push buttons
handset
card reader
coin return tray

push-button telephone

portable cellular telephone

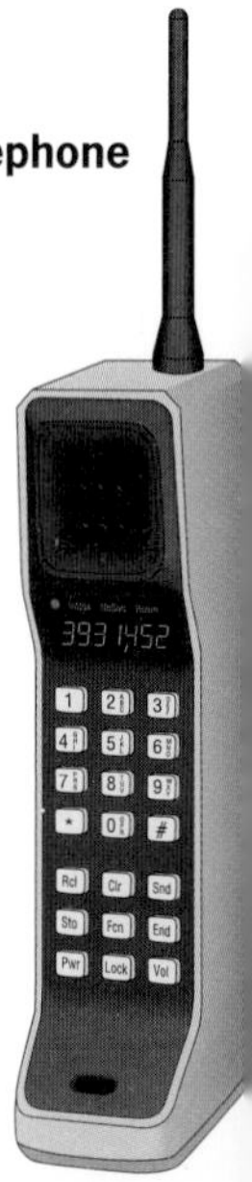

cordless telephone

PHOTOGRAPHY

single lens reflex (slr) camera

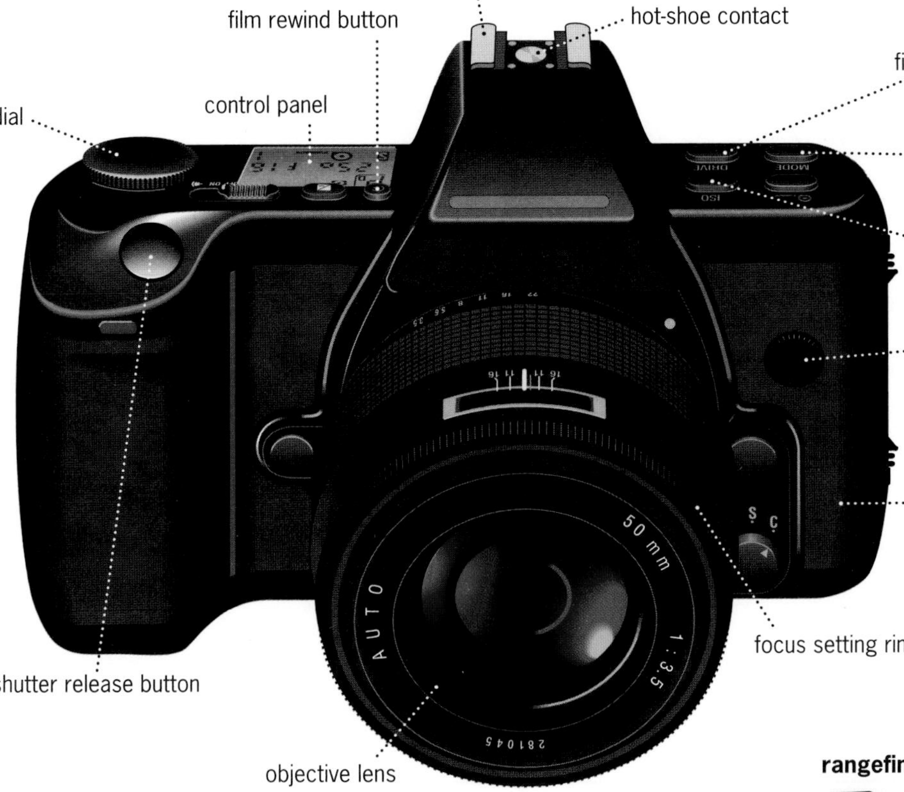
accessory shoe
film rewind button
hot-shoe contact
film advance button
control dial
control panel
exposure button
film speed
remote control terminal
camera body
focus setting ring
shutter release button
objective lens
50 mm
AUTO
1:3.5
281045
DRIVE
MODE
ISO

125

rangefinder; compact camera

electronic flash

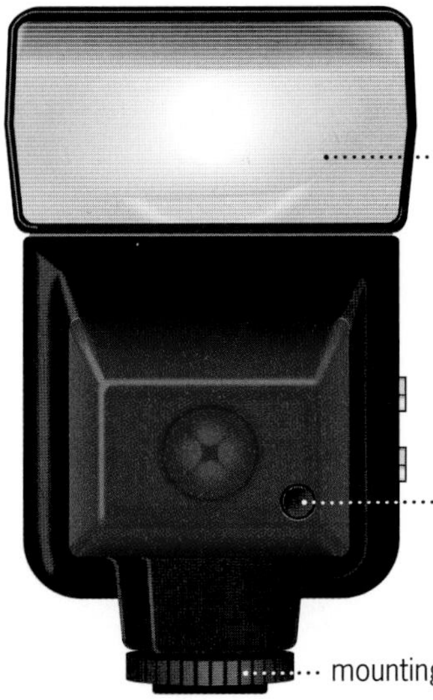
flashtube
photoelectric cell
mounting foot

cassette film

perforation
film leader

Polaroid® Land camera

pocket camera

cartridge film

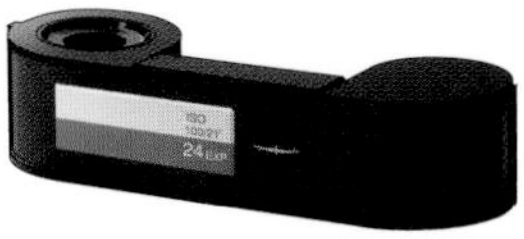

film pack

TELEVISION

television set

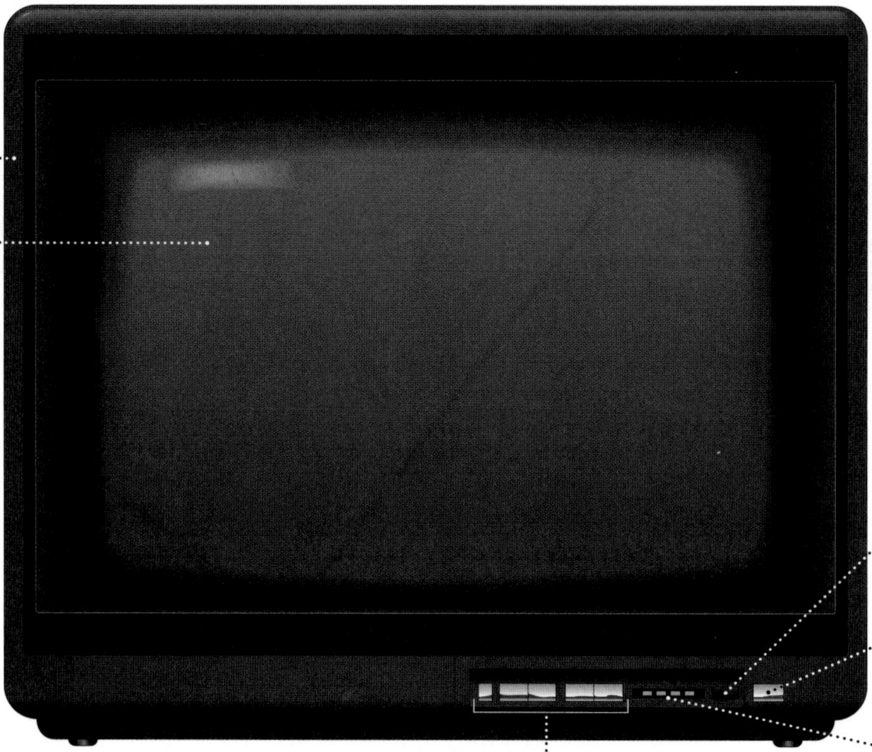
cabinet
screen
remote control sensor
on/off button
indicators
tuning controls

remote control

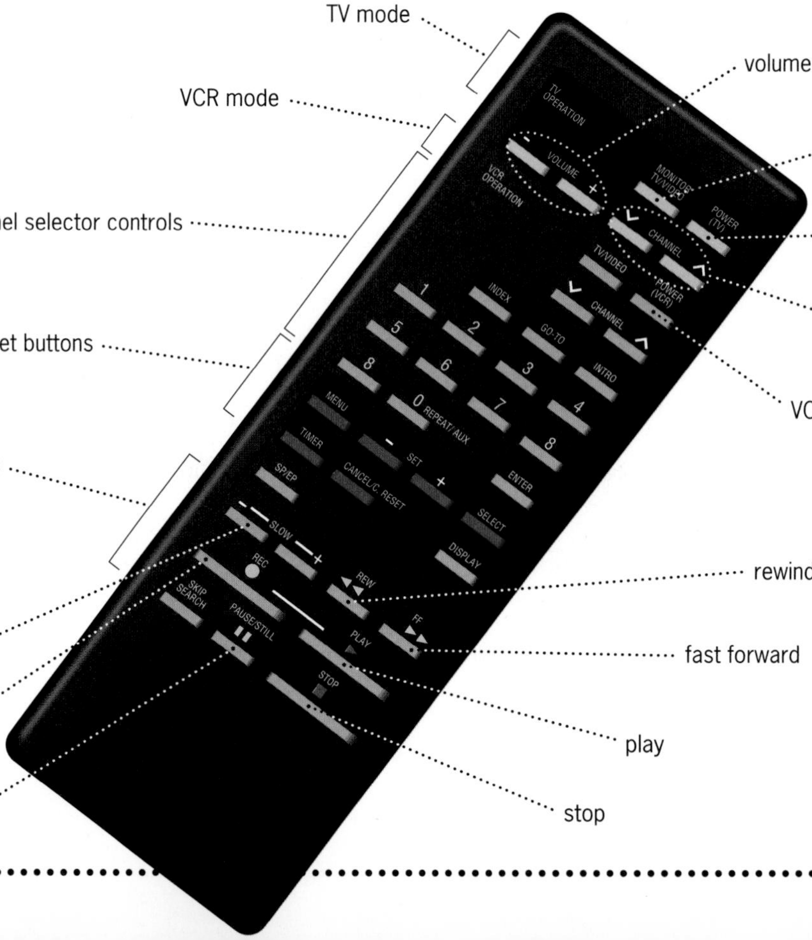
TV mode
volume control
VCR mode
TV/video button
channel selector controls
TV on/off button
channel scan buttons
preset buttons
VCR on/off button
VCR controls
rewind
slow-motion
fast forward
record
play
pause
stop
TV OPERATION
VCR OPERATION
VOLUME
MONITOR TV/VIDEO
POWER (TV)
CHANNEL
TV/VIDEO
POWER (VCR)
INDEX
GO-TO
INTRO
MENU
REPEAT/AUX
TIMER
SET
SP/EP
CANCEL/C. RESET
ENTER
SELECT
SLOW
DISPLAY
REC
REW
SKIP SEARCH
PAUSE/STILL
PLAY
FF
STOP

VIDEO

videocassette recorder (VCR)

on/off button
data display
preset buttons
cassette eject switch
controls
cassette compartment

video camera

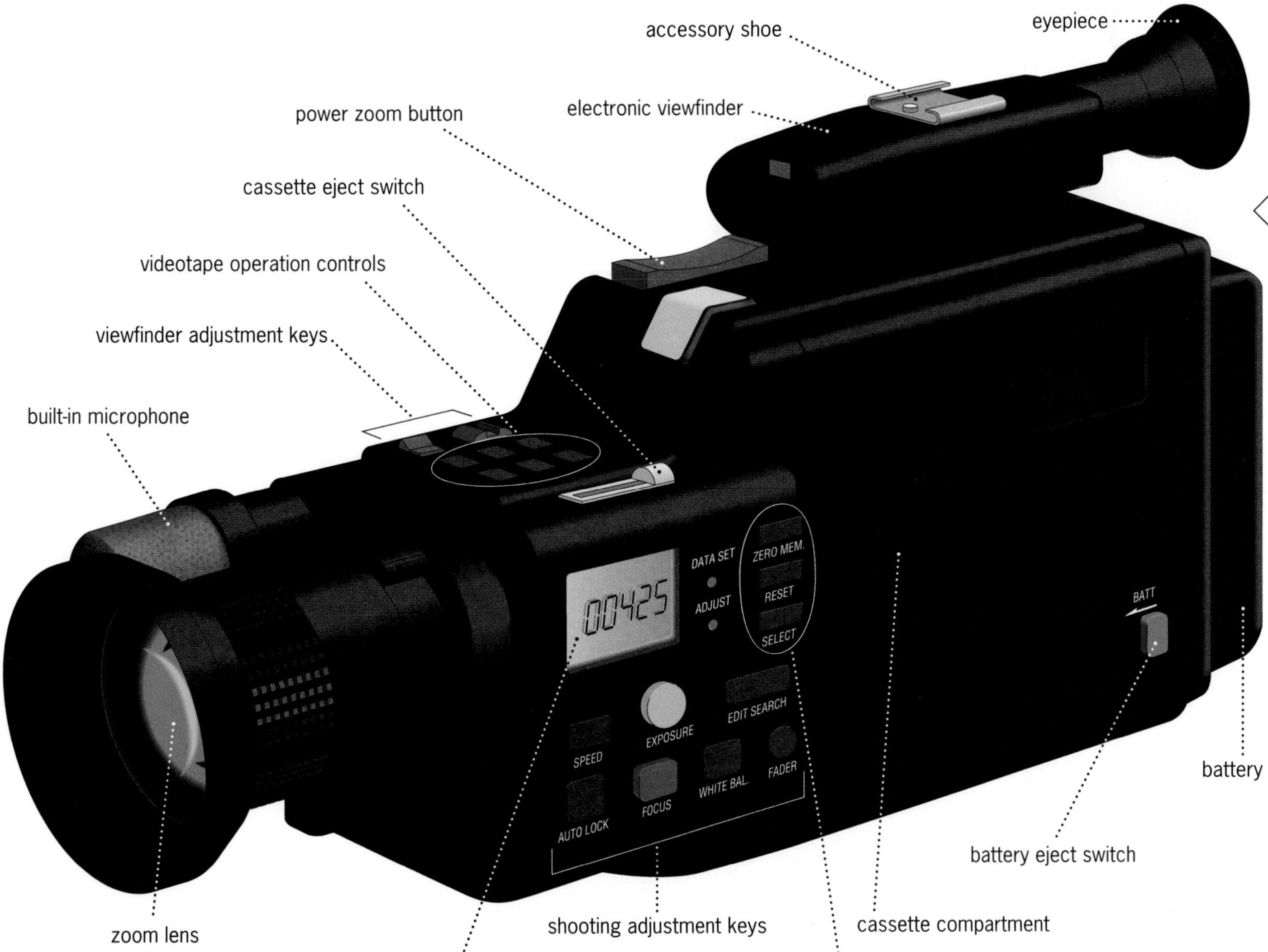
accessory shoe
eyepiece
electronic viewfinder
power zoom button
cassette eject switch
videotape operation controls
viewfinder adjustment keys
built-in microphone
DATA SET
ADJUST
ZERO MEM.
RESET
SELECT
00425
EDIT SEARCH
EXPOSURE
SPEED
FOCUS
WHITE BAL.
FADER
AUTO LOCK
BATT
battery
battery eject switch
zoom lens
shooting adjustment keys
cassette compartment
data display
edit/search buttons

STEREO SYSTEM

SYSTEM COMPONENTS

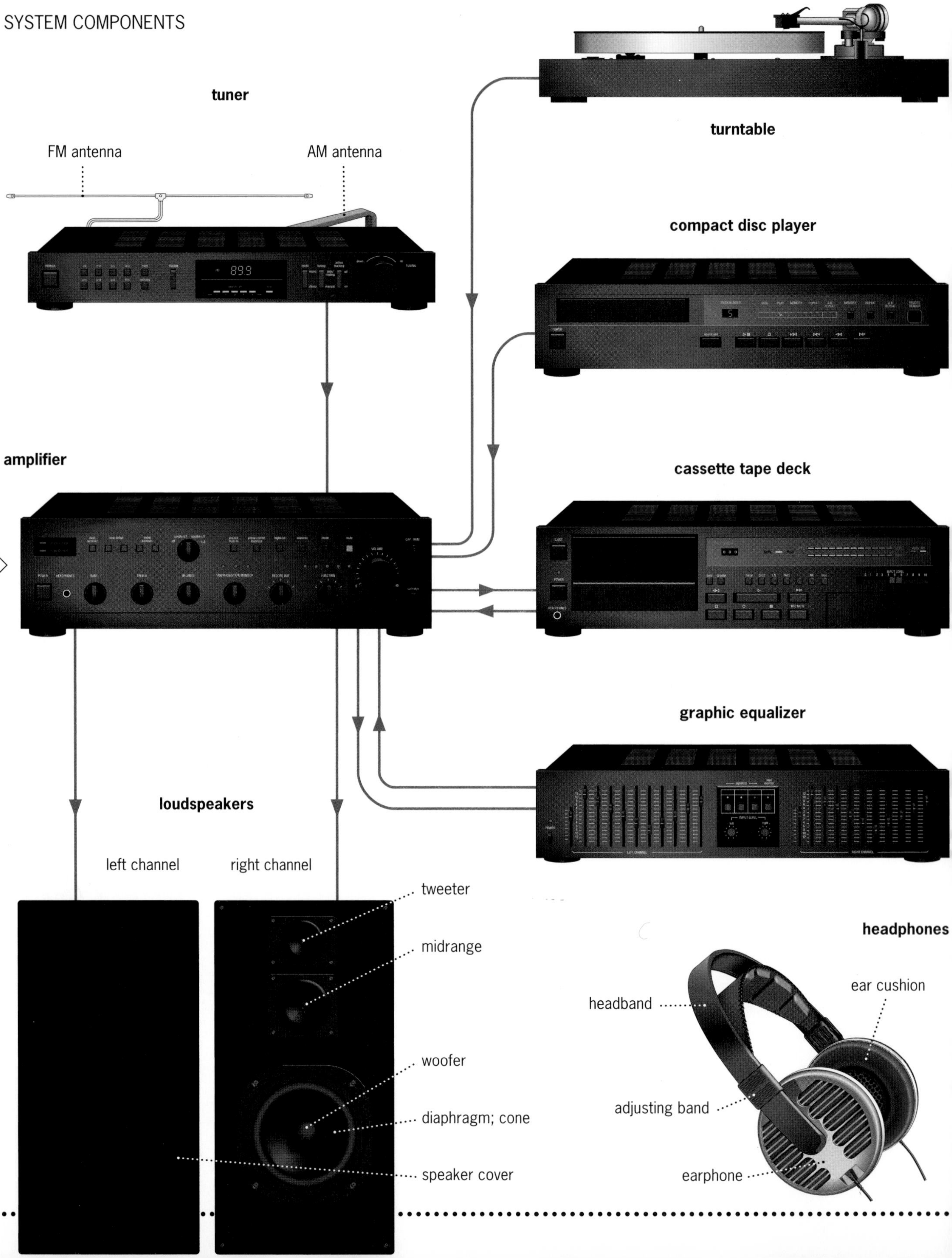
tuner
FM antenna
AM antenna
turntable
compact disc player
amplifier
cassette tape deck
graphic equalizer
loudspeakers
left channel
right channel
tweeter
midrange
woofer
diaphragm; cone
speaker cover
headphones
headband
ear cushion
adjusting band
earphone

PORTABLE SOUND SYSTEMS

portable CD AM/FM cassette recorder

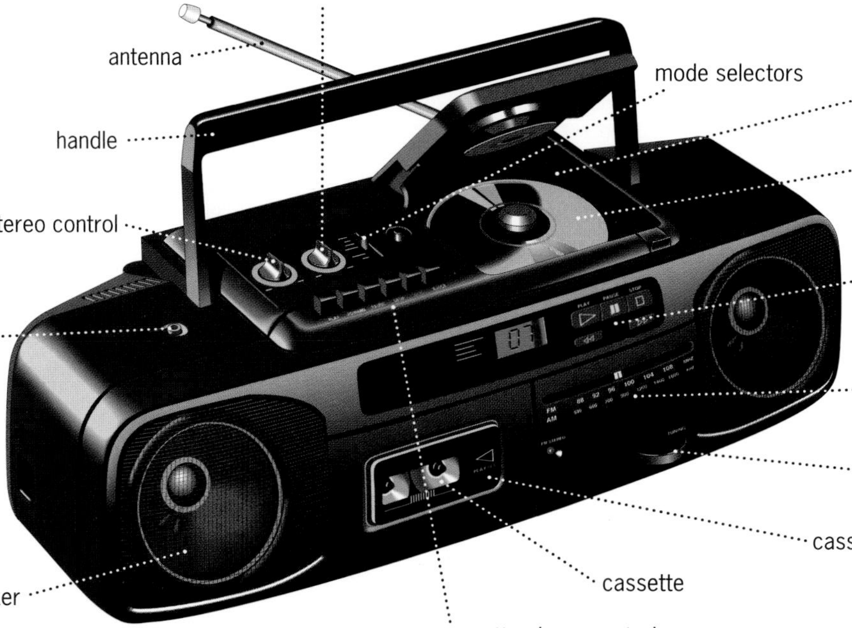
on/off/volume control
antenna
mode selectors
compact disc player
handle
compact disc
stereo control
disc player controls
headphone jack
tuner
tuning control
cassette player
speaker
cassette
cassette player controls

personal AM/FM cassette player; Walkman®

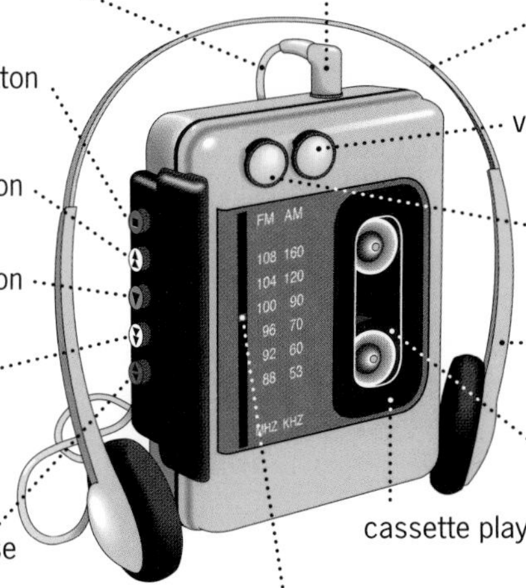
cable
headphone plug
headband
on/off button
volume control
rewind button
tuning control
play button
fast-forward button
headphones
cassette
auto reverse
cassette player
tuner

compact disc

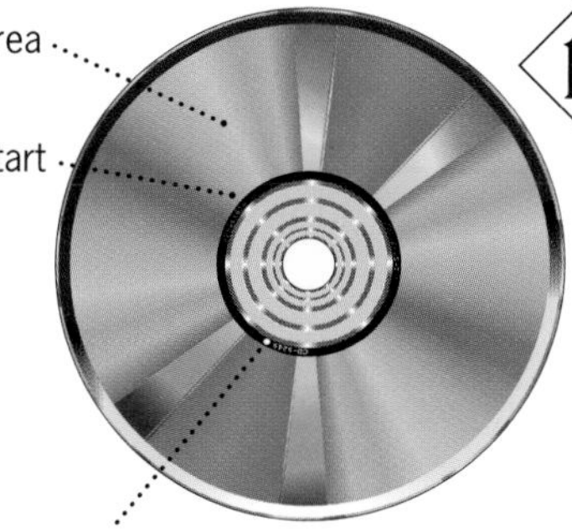
pressed area
reading start
technical identification band

cassette

housing
take-up reel
recording tape
tape guide
guide roller
playing window

record

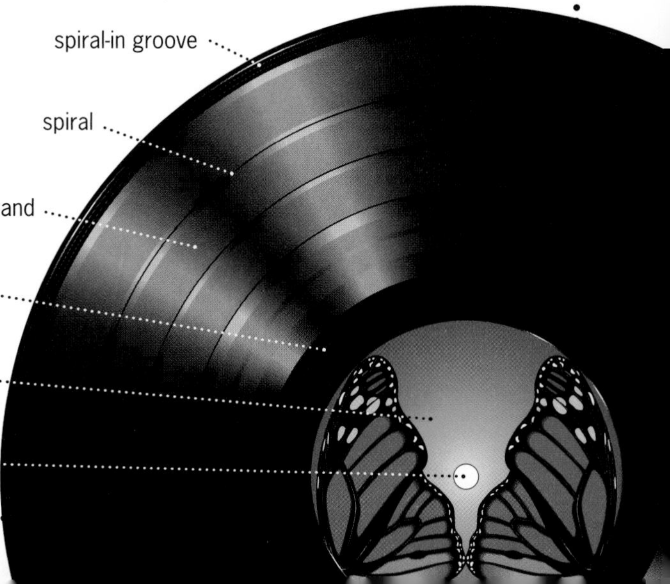
spiral-in groove
spiral
band
tail-out groove
label
center hole

CAR

body

windshield
windshield wiper
outside mirror
washer nozzle
hood
headlight
grille
bumper
fender

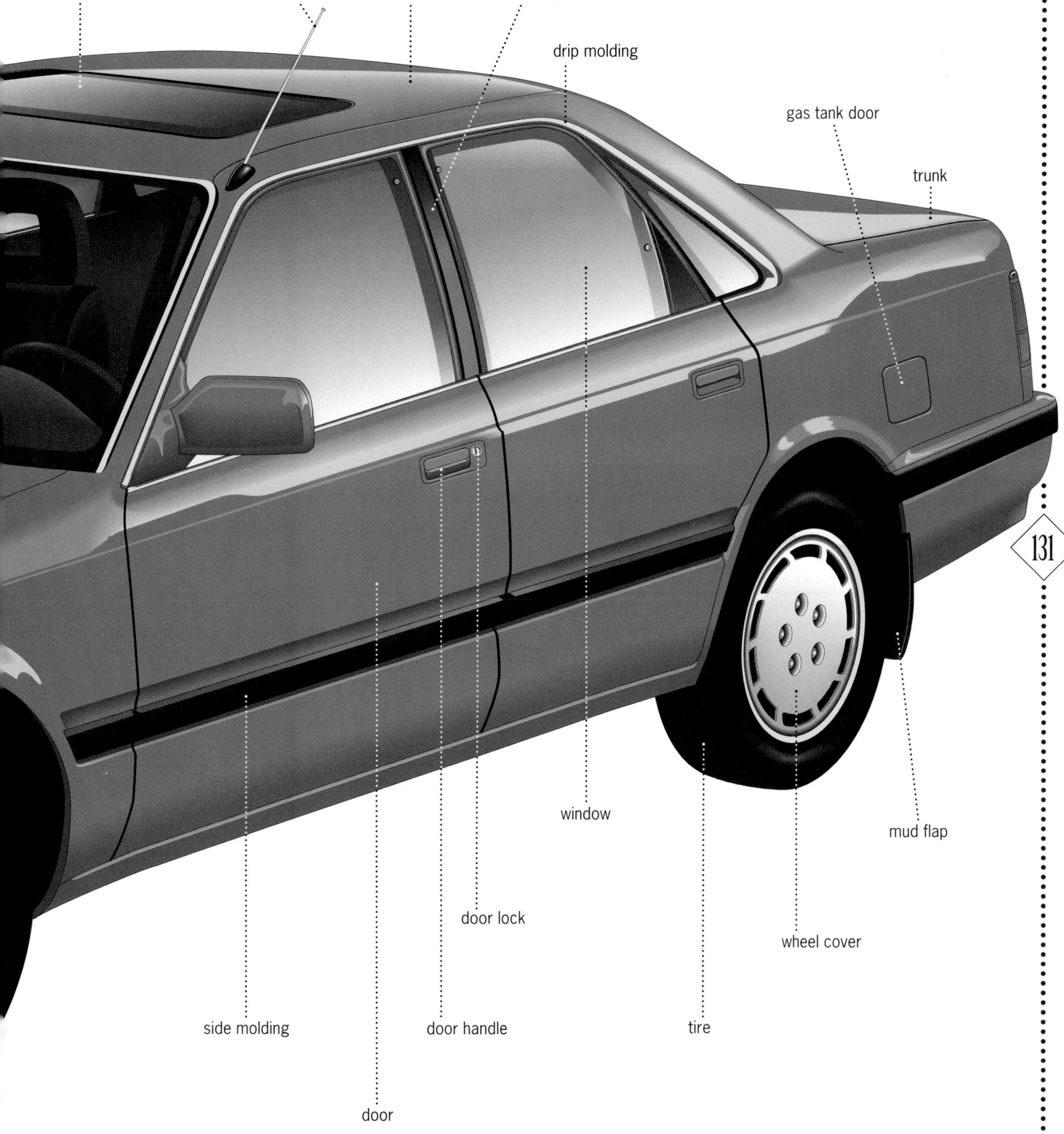
sunroof
antenna
roof
center post
drip molding
gas tank door
trunk
window
mud flap
door lock
wheel cover
side molding
door handle
tire
door

CAR

dashboard

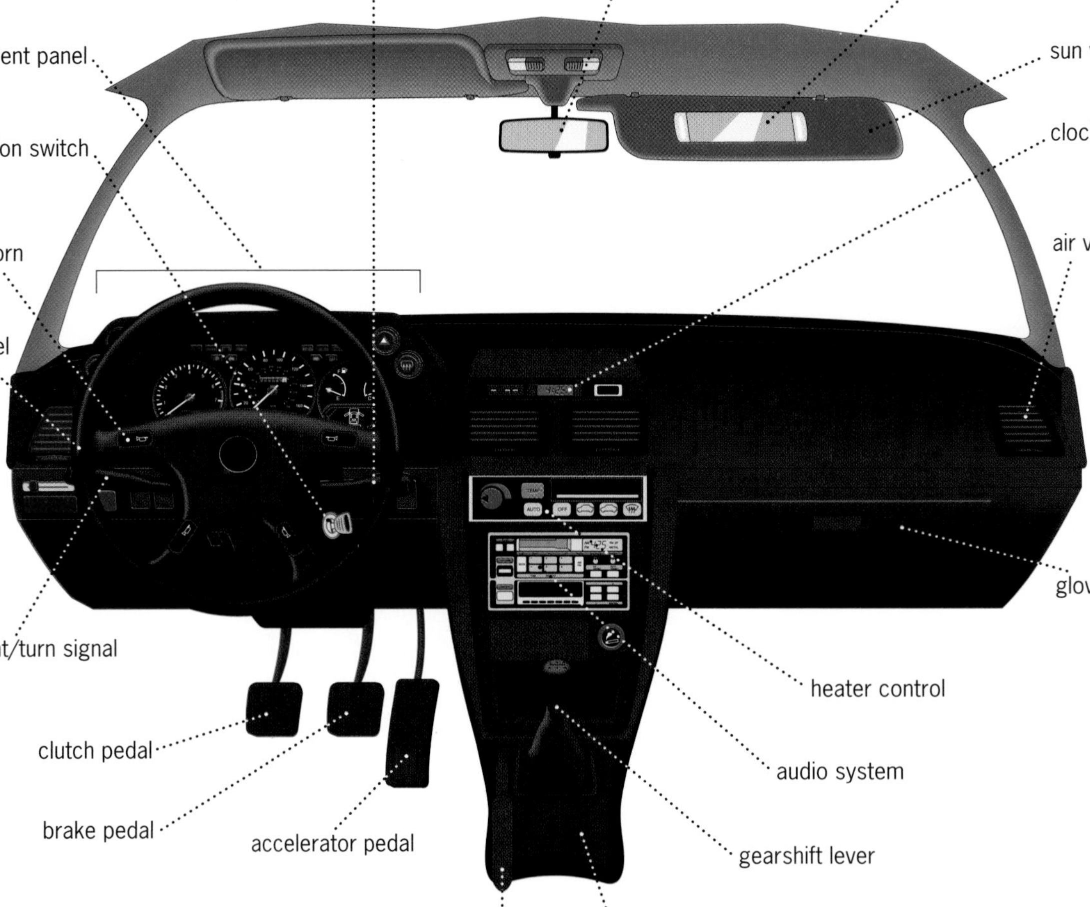
wiper switch
rearview mirror
vanity mirror
instrument panel
sun visor
ignition switch
clock
horn
air vent
steering wheel
glove compartment
headlight/turn signal
heater control
clutch pedal
audio system
brake pedal
accelerator pedal
gearshift lever
handbrake
center console

instrument panel

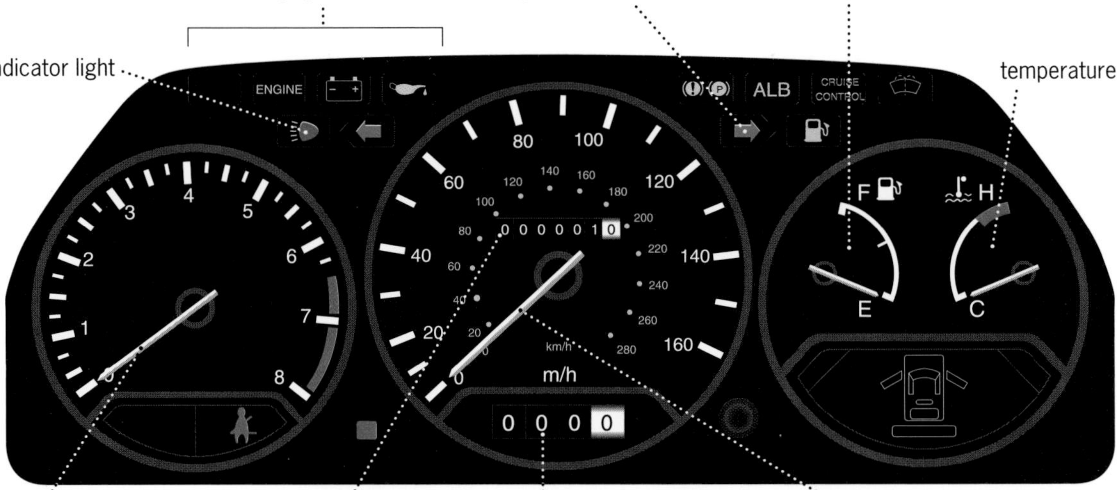
warning lights
turn signal indicator
fuel gauge
high beam indicator light
temperature gauge
ENGINE
ALB
CRUISE CONTROL
rev(olution) counter
odometer
trip odometer
speedometer

CAR LIGHTS

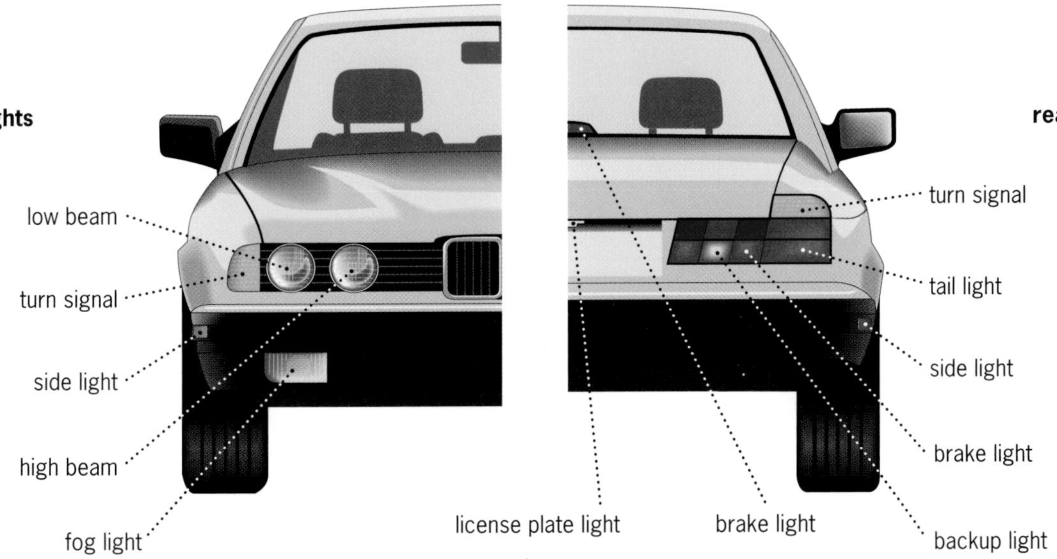
front lights
rear lights
low beam
turn signal
side light
high beam
fog light
license plate light
brake light
turn signal
tail light
side light
brake light
backup light

TYPES OF CAR BODIES

two-door sedan

sports car

hatchback

pickup truck

convertible

station wagon

four-door sedan

minivan

multipurpose vehicle

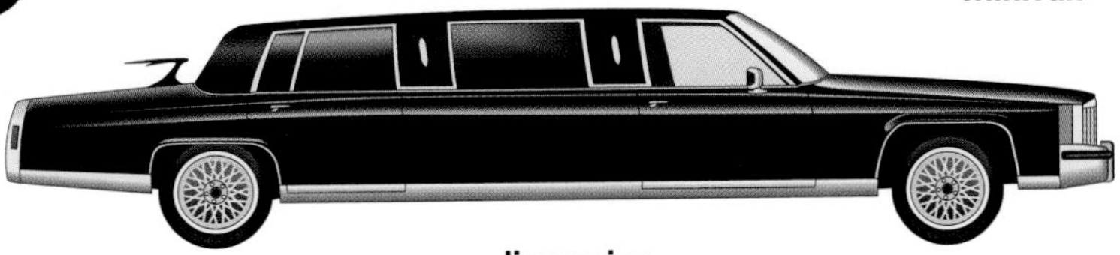

limousine

TRUCK

tractor unit

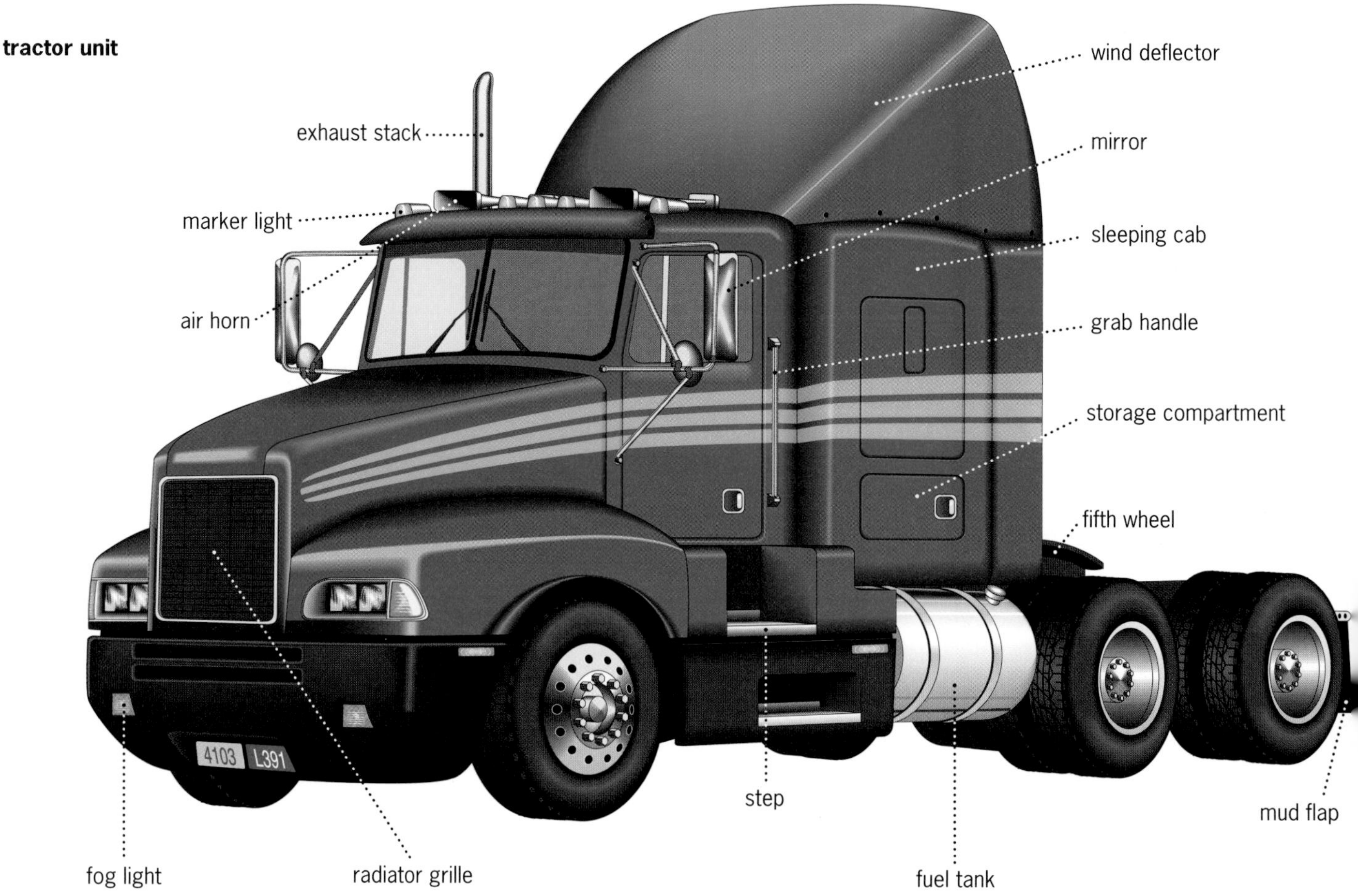
wind deflector
exhaust stack
mirror
marker light
sleeping cab
air horn
grab handle
storage compartment
fifth wheel
4103 L391
step
mud flap
fog light
radiator grille
fuel tank

service station

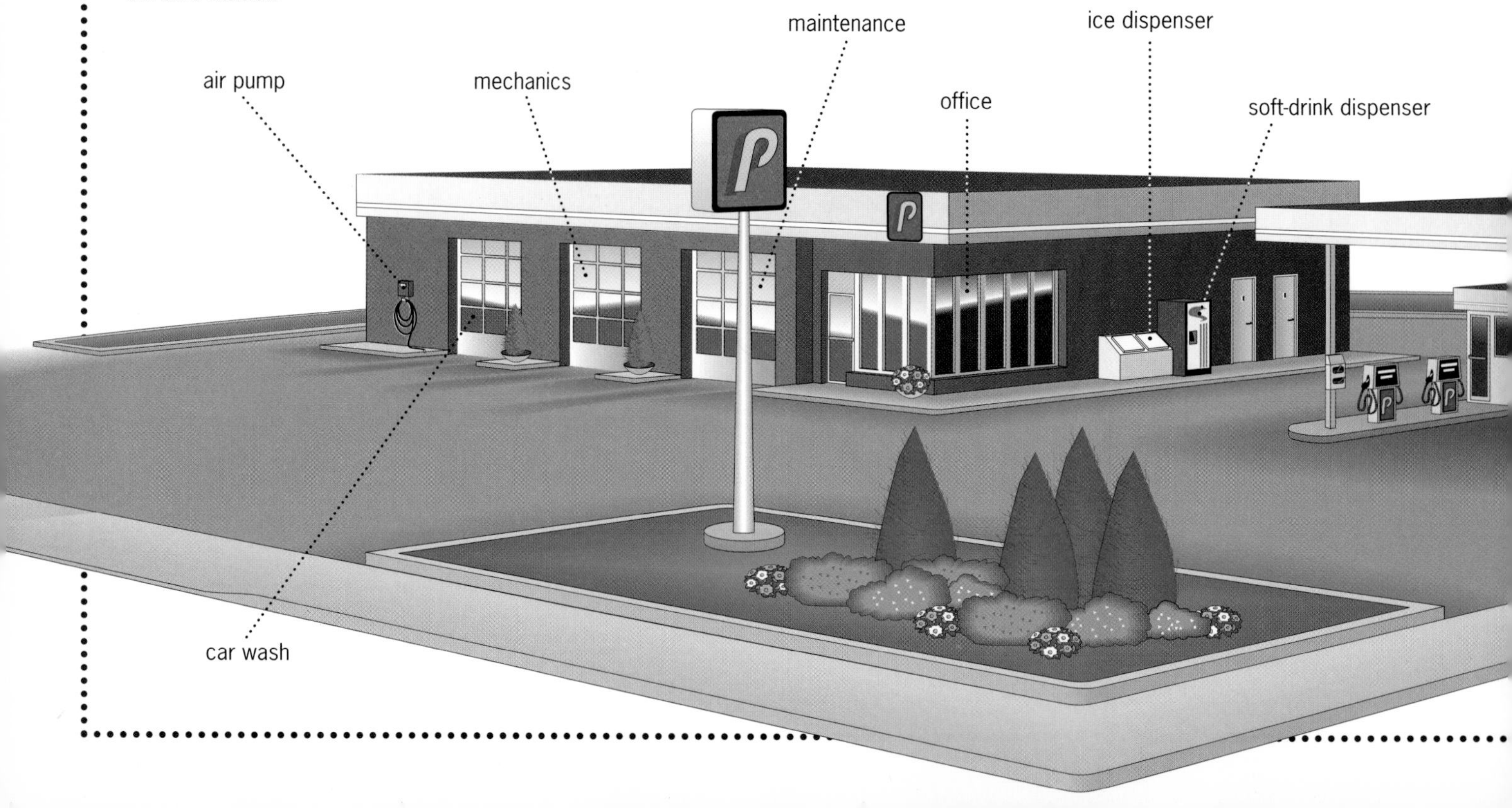
maintenance
ice dispenser
air pump
mechanics
office
soft-drink dispenser
car wash

MOTORCYCLE

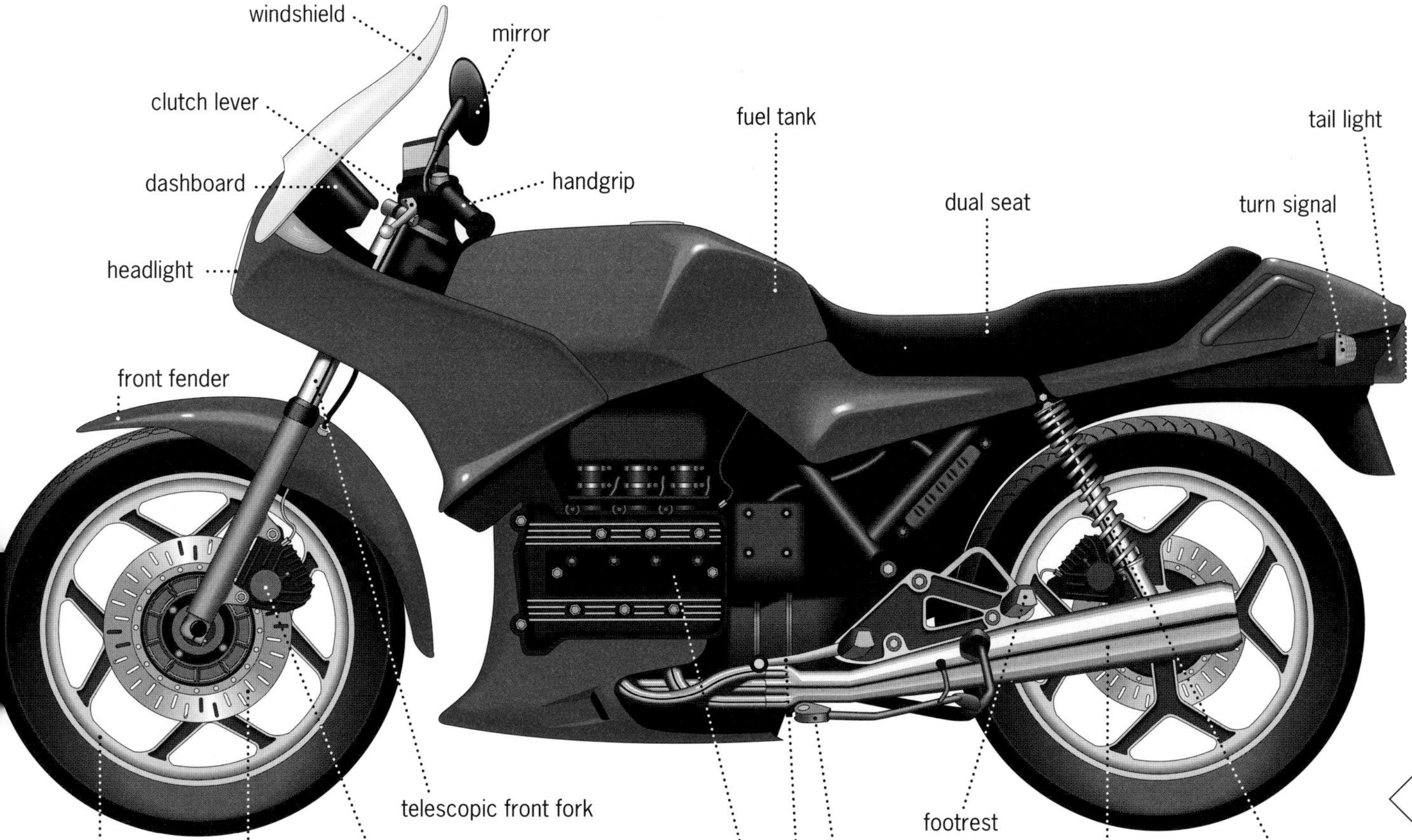
windshield
mirror
clutch lever
dashboard
handgrip
headlight
fuel tank
dual seat
tail light
turn signal
front fender
telescopic front fork
footrest
rear shock absorber
rim
brake caliper
engine
stand
disc brake
gearchange pedal
exhaust pipe

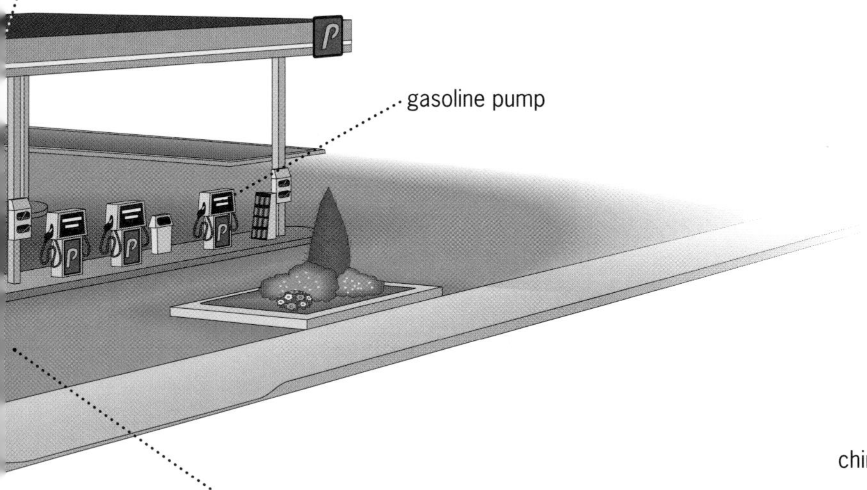
kiosk
gasoline pump
pump island

protective helmet

bubble
visor
chin protector

BICYCLE

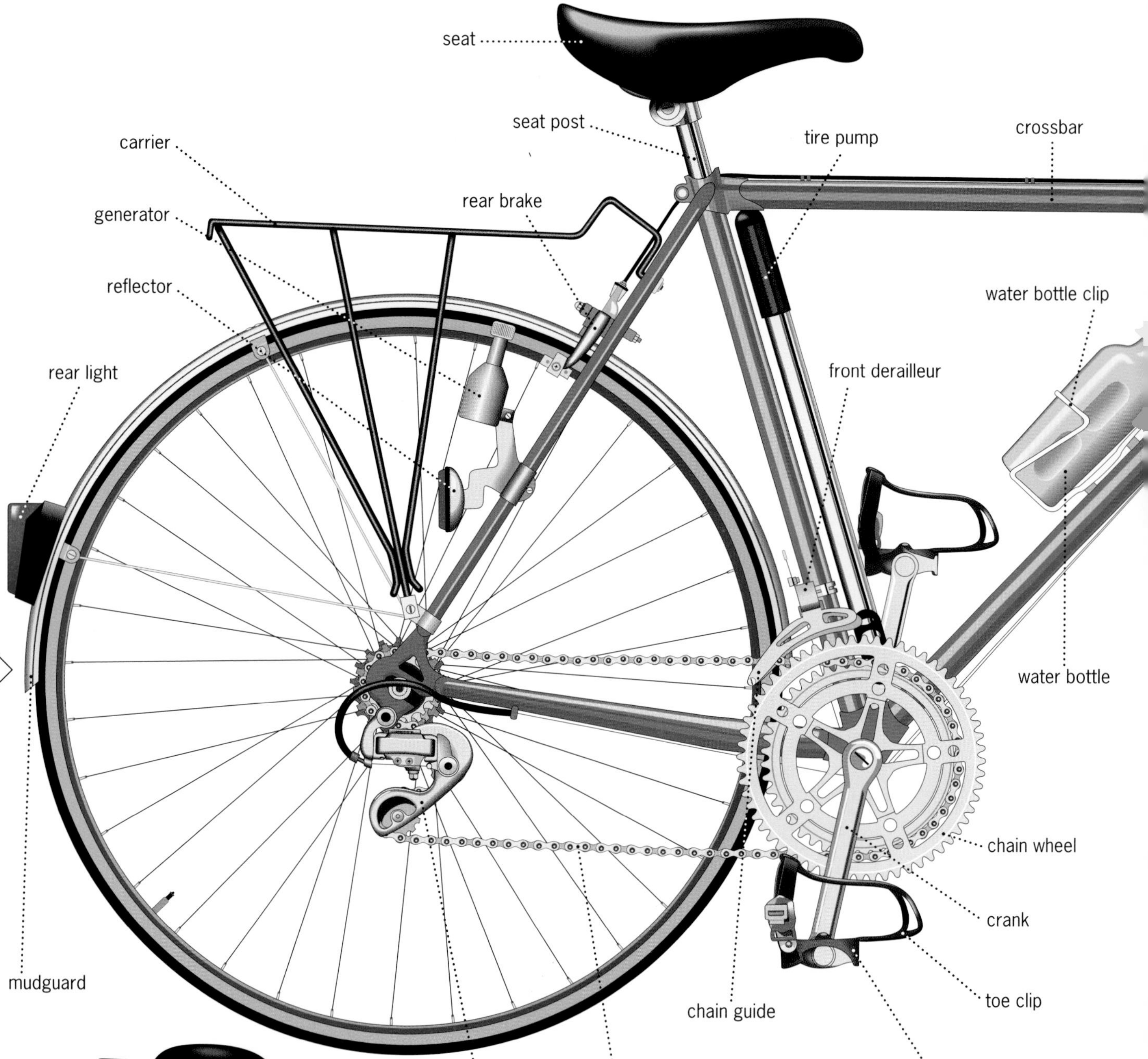
seat
seat post
carrier
generator
rear brake
tire pump
crossbar
reflector
water bottle clip
rear light
front derailleur
water bottle
chain wheel
crank
mudguard
toe clip
chain guide
pedal
rear derailleur
drive chain

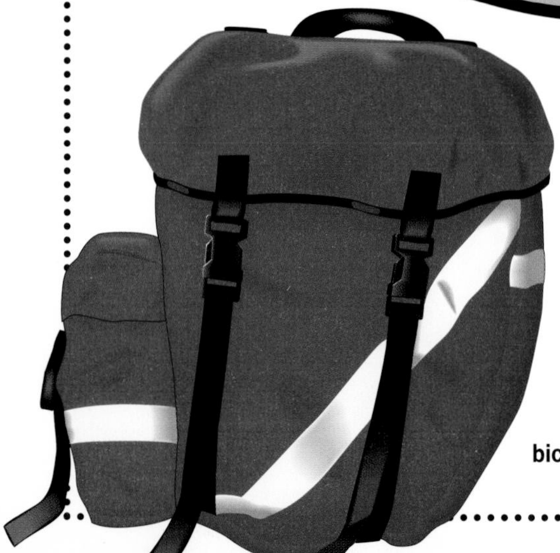

bicycle bag

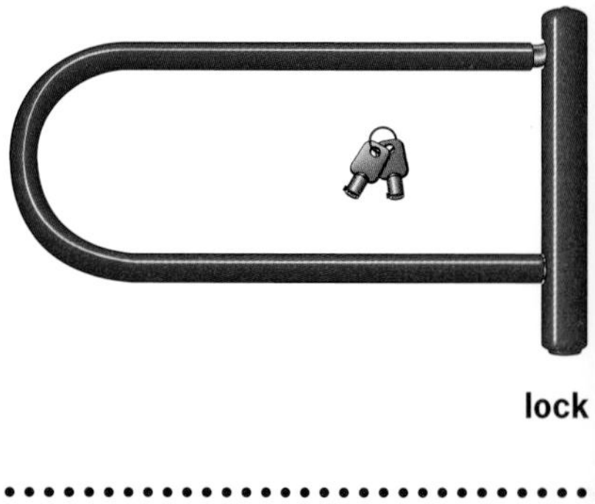

lock

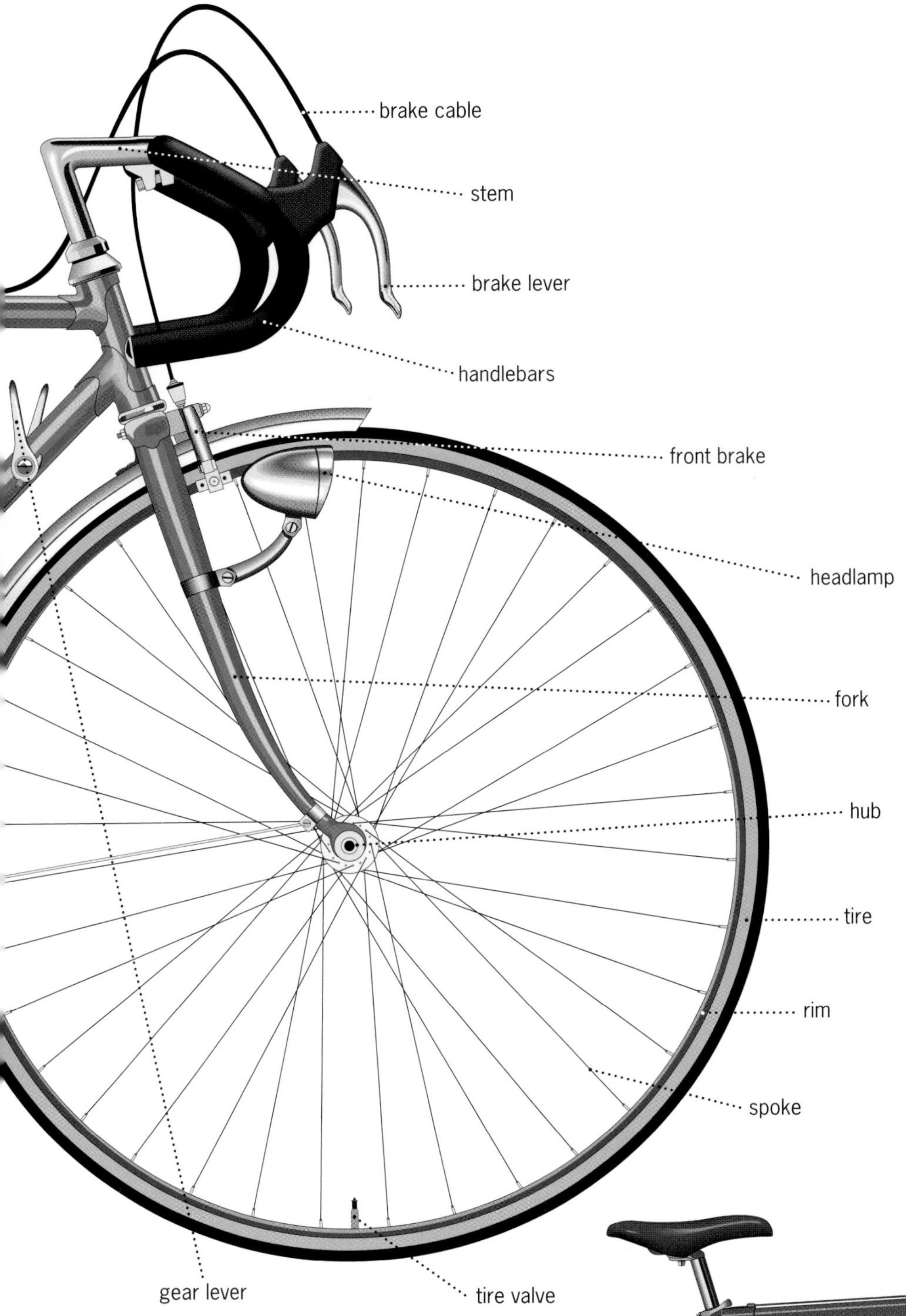
brake cable
stem
brake lever
handlebars
front brake
headlamp
fork
hub
tire
rim
spoke
gear lever
tire valve

protective helmet

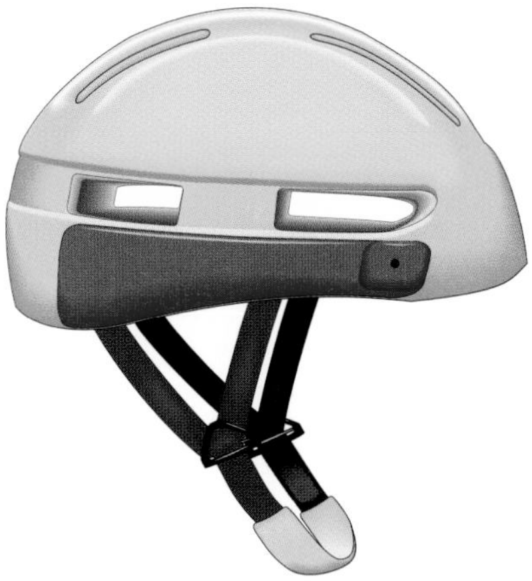

mountain bike

DIESEL-ELECTRIC LOCOMOTIVE

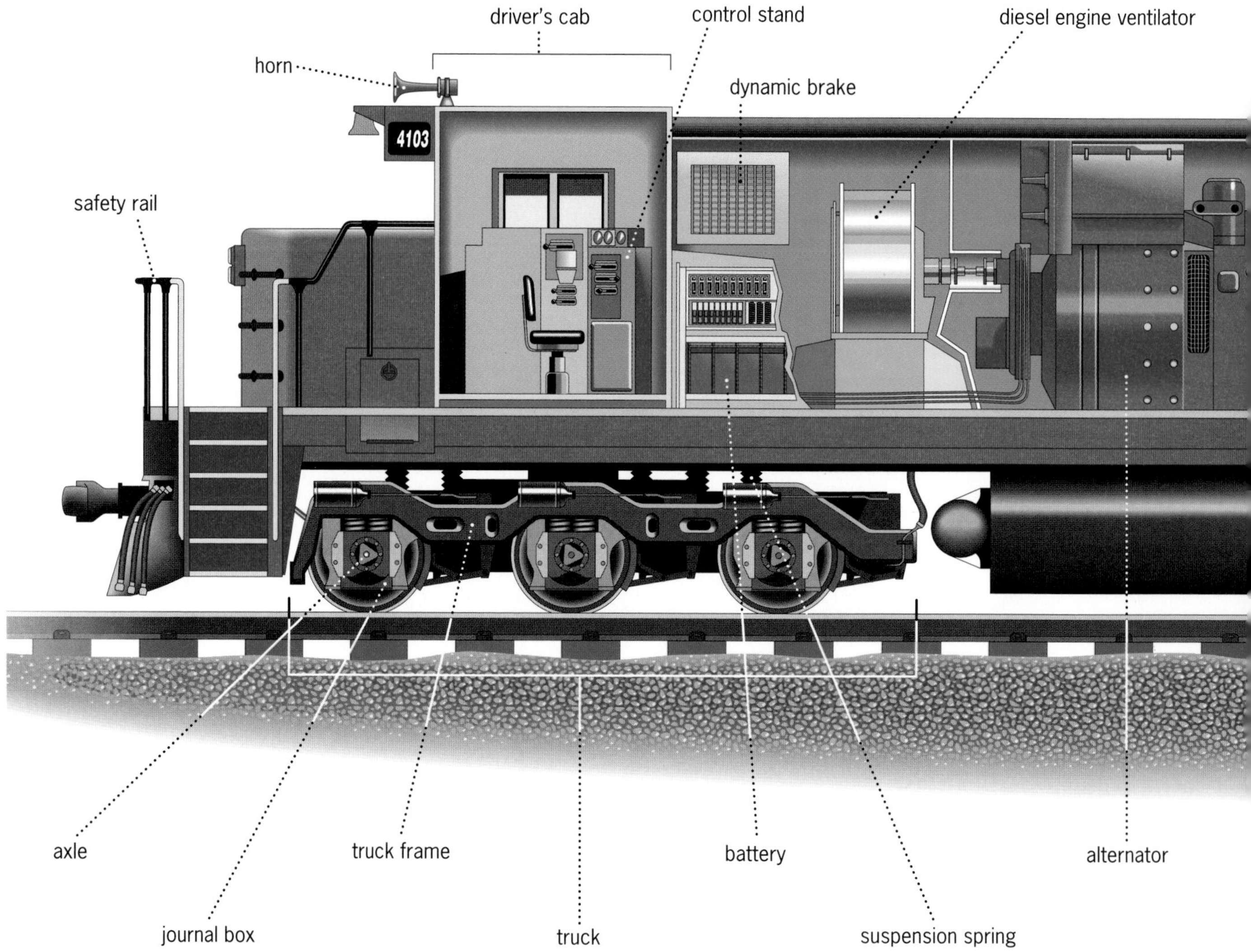
driver's cab
control stand
diesel engine ventilator
horn
dynamic brake
4103
safety rail
axle
truck frame
battery
alternator
journal box
truck
suspension spring

TYPES OF FREIGHT CARS

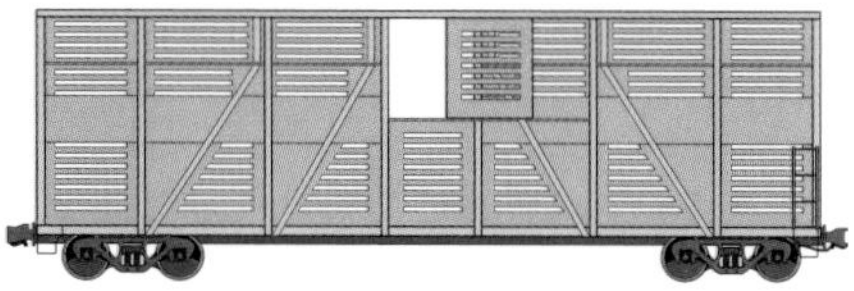
livestock car

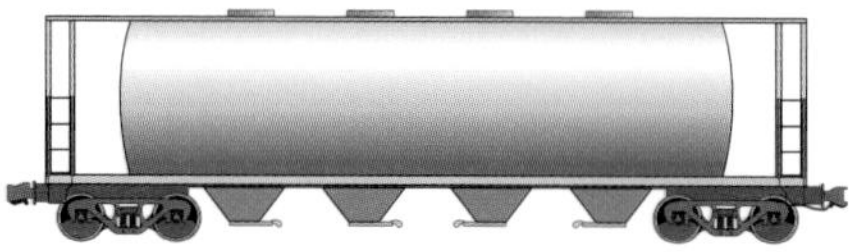
hopper car

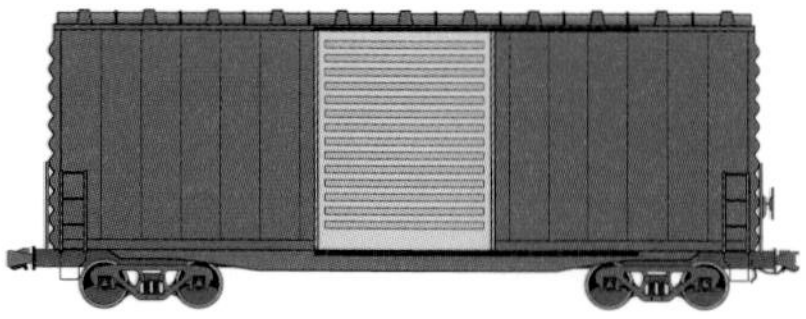
box car

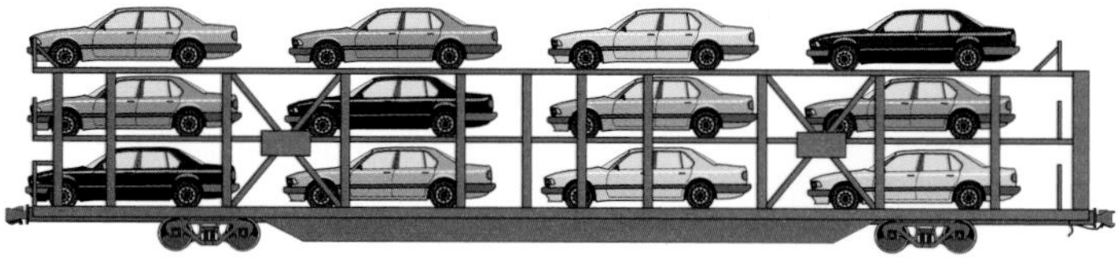
automobile car

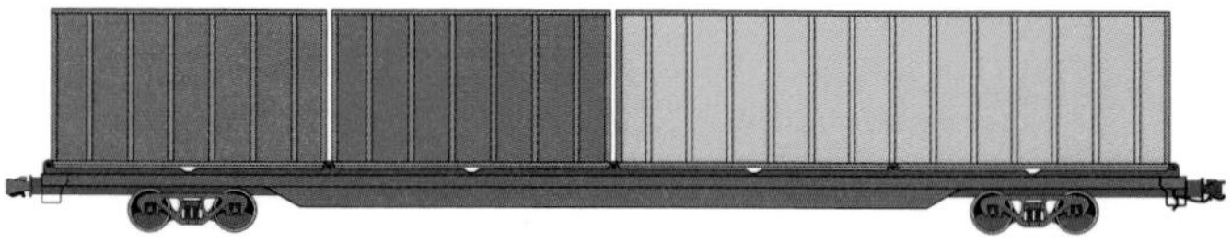
container car

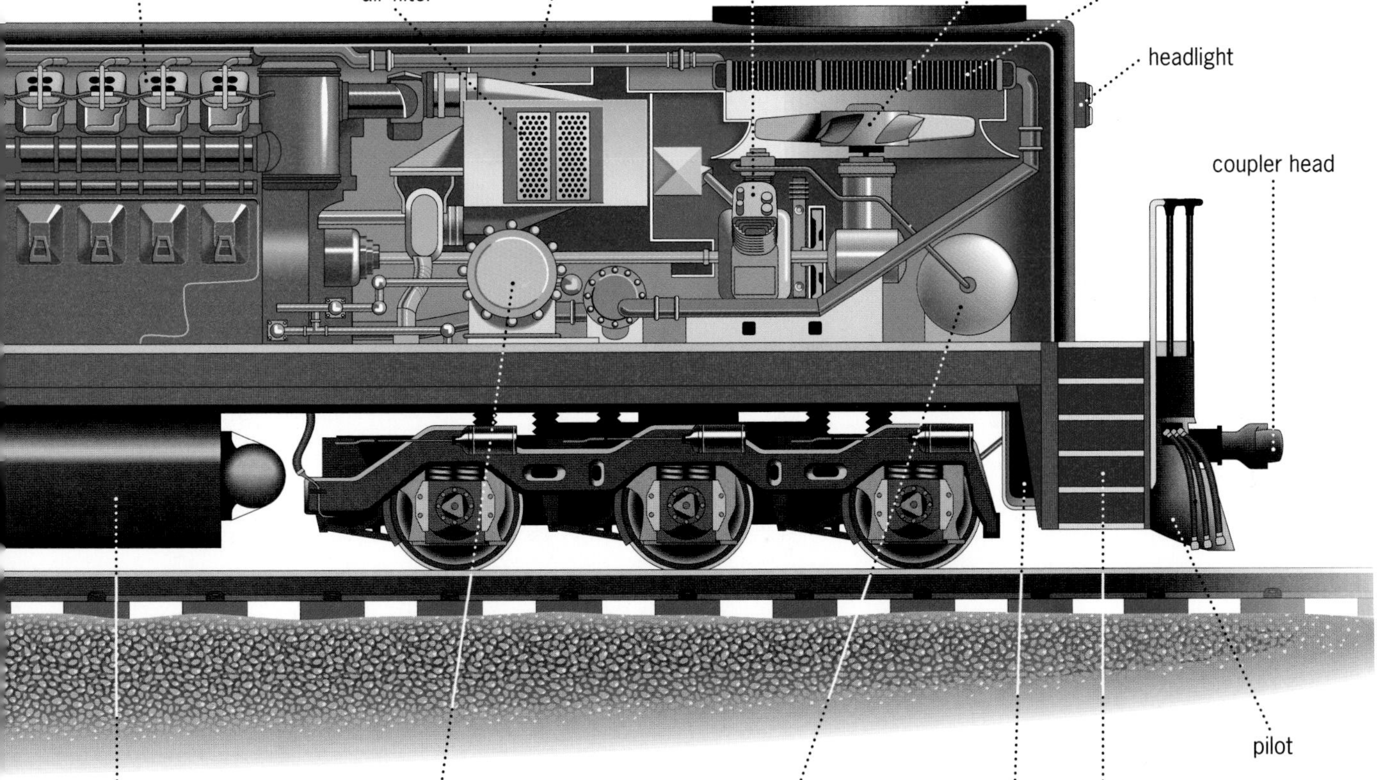
diesel engine
water tank
air compressor
ventilating fan
radiator
air filter
headlight
coupler head
pilot
fuel tank
lubricating system
compressed air reservoir
side footboard
sandbox

bulkhead flat car

tank car

flat car

depressed center flat car

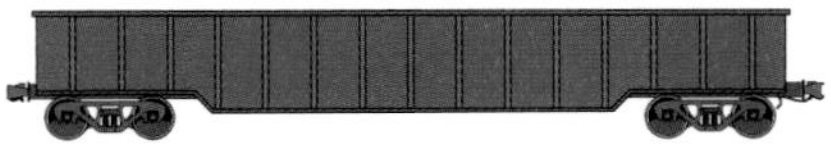

gondola car

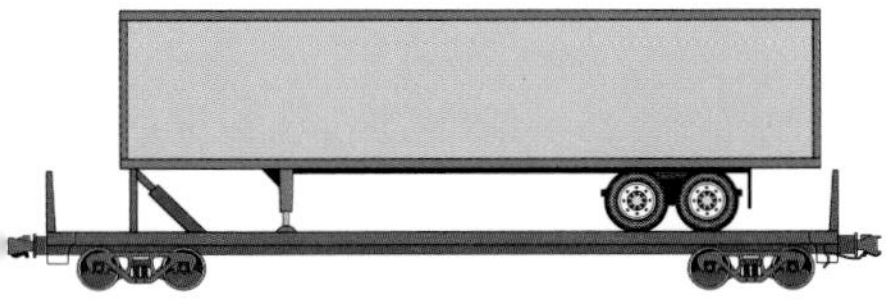

piggyback car

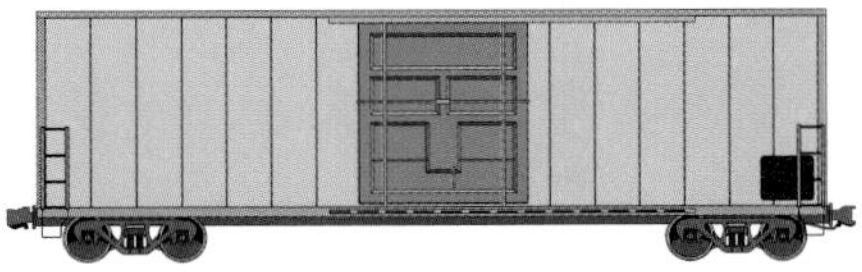

refrigerator car

caboose

HIGHWAY CROSSING

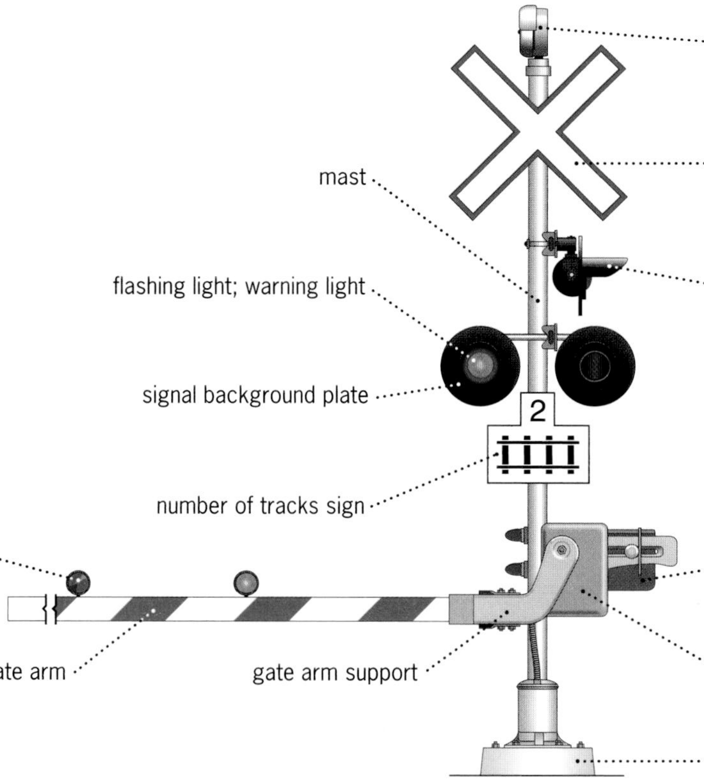
highway crossing bell
crossbuck sign
mast
visor
flashing light; warning light
signal background plate
2
number of tracks sign
gate arm lamp
counterweight
gate arm
gate arm support
crossing gate mechanism
base

HIGH-SPEED TRAIN

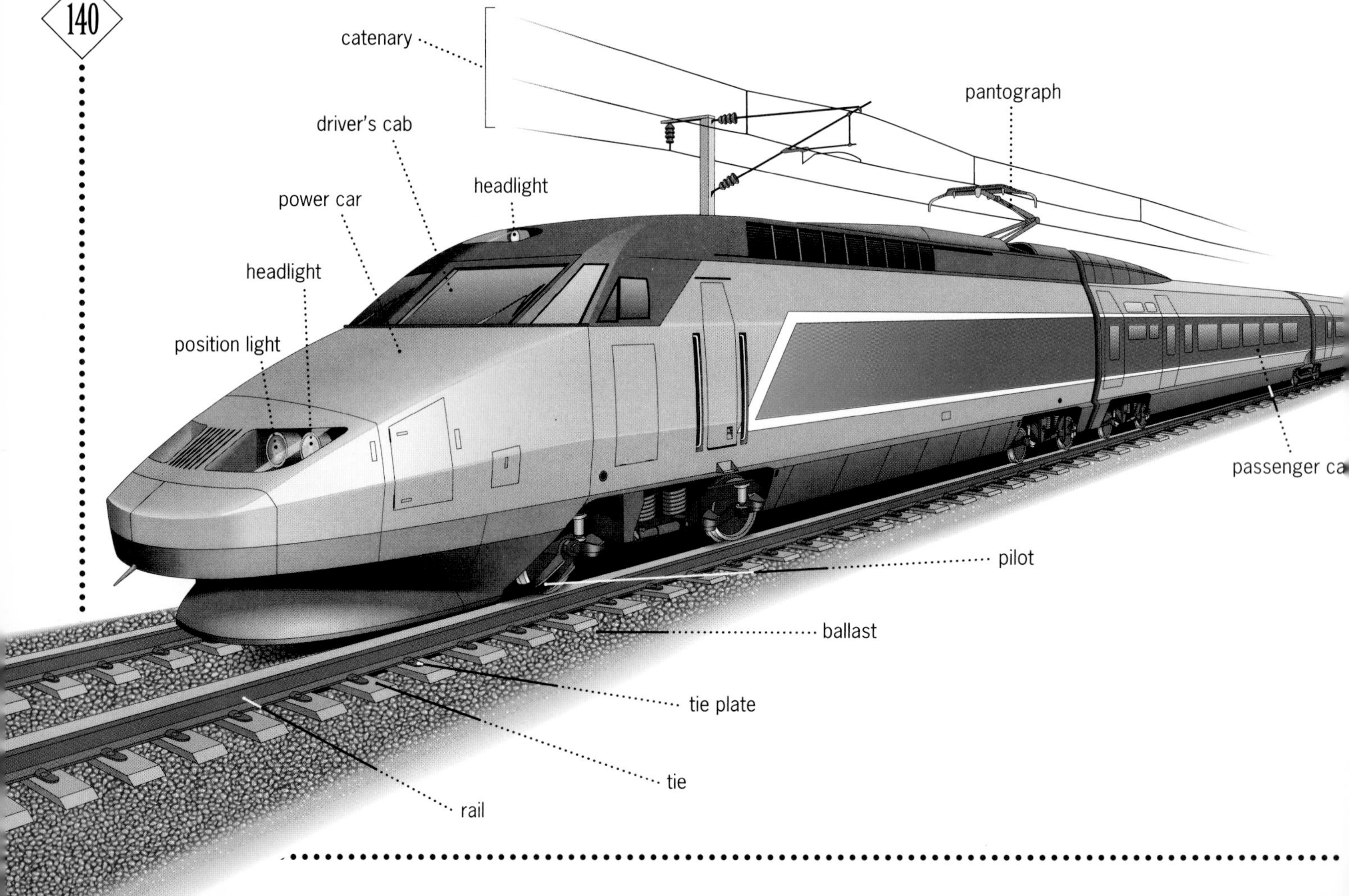
catenary
pantograph
driver's cab
headlight
power car
headlight
position light
passenger ca
pilot
ballast
tie plate
tie
rail

FOUR-MASTED BARK

mizzenmast
mainmast
foremast
fore royal sail
jigger topgallant staysail
upper fore topgallant sail
aftermast
lower fore topgallant sail
upper fore topsail
flying jib
bowsprit
gaff topsail
jigger topmast staysail
shroud
stem
spanker
sheet
foresail
gaff sail boom
mainsail
lower fore topsail
poop
lifeboat
side

HOVERCRAFT

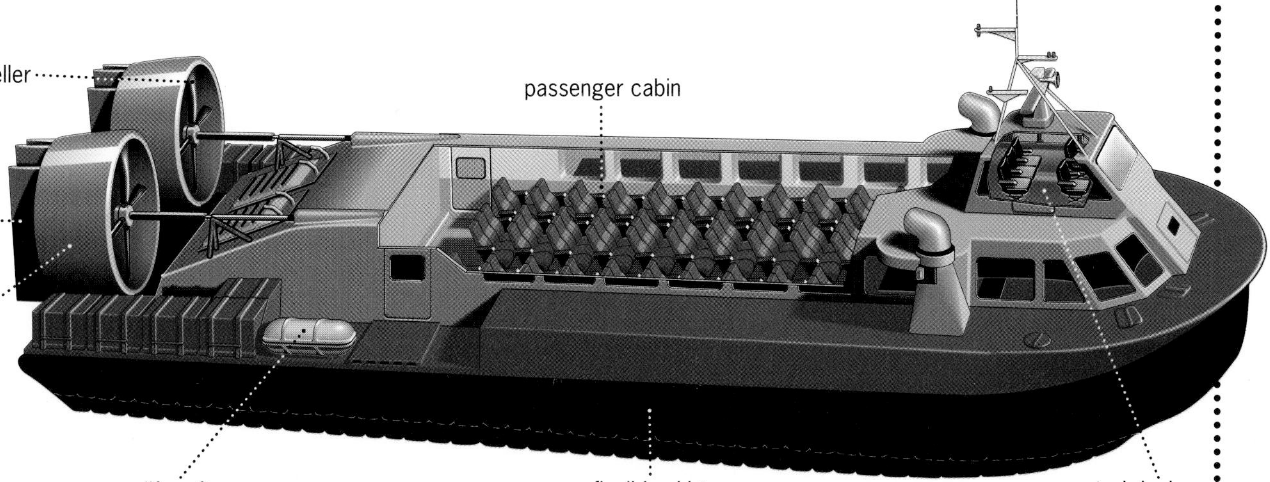
dynamics propeller
passenger cabin
rudder
propeller duct
life raft
flexible skirt
control deck

CRUISE LINER

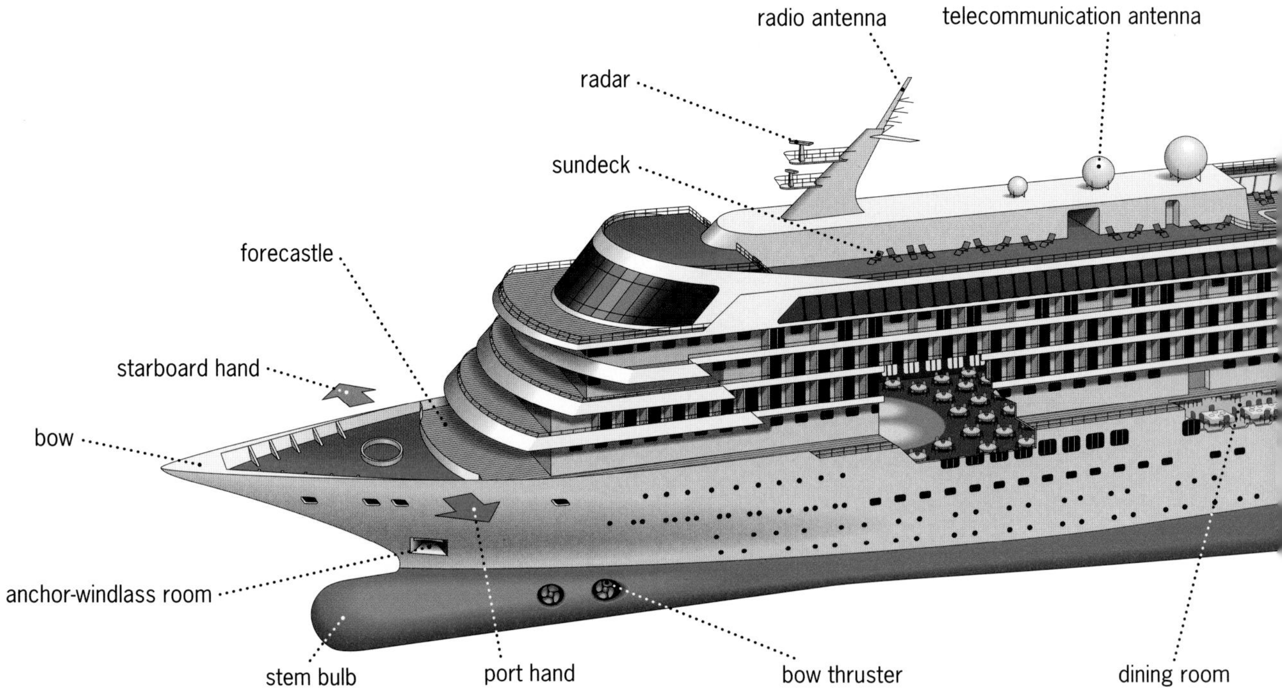
radio antenna
telecommunication antenna
radar
sundeck
forecastle
starboard hand
bow
anchor-windlass room
stem bulb
port hand
bow thruster
dining room

HARBOR

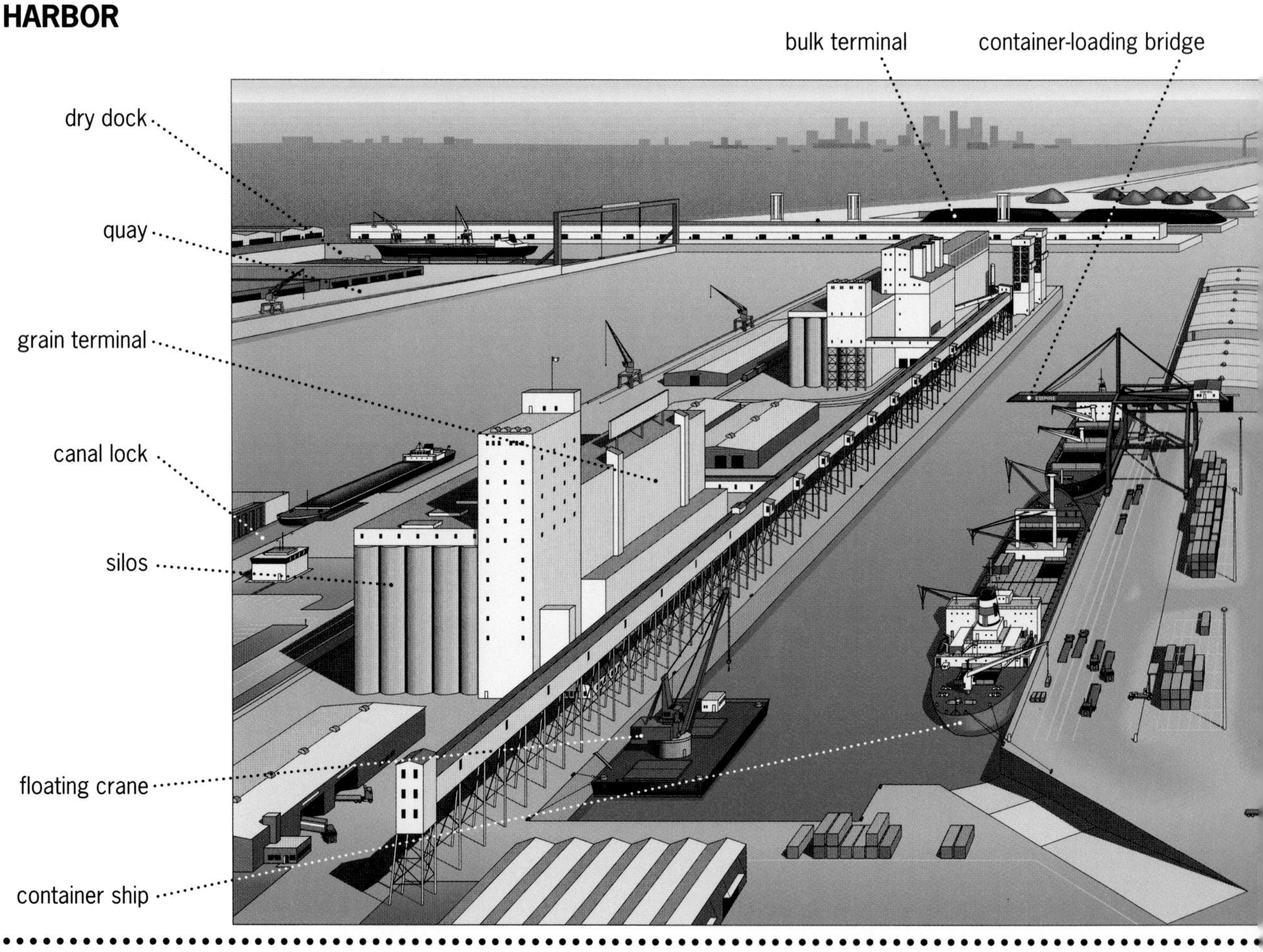
bulk terminal
container-loading bridge
dry dock
quay
grain terminal
canal lock
silos
floating crane
container ship

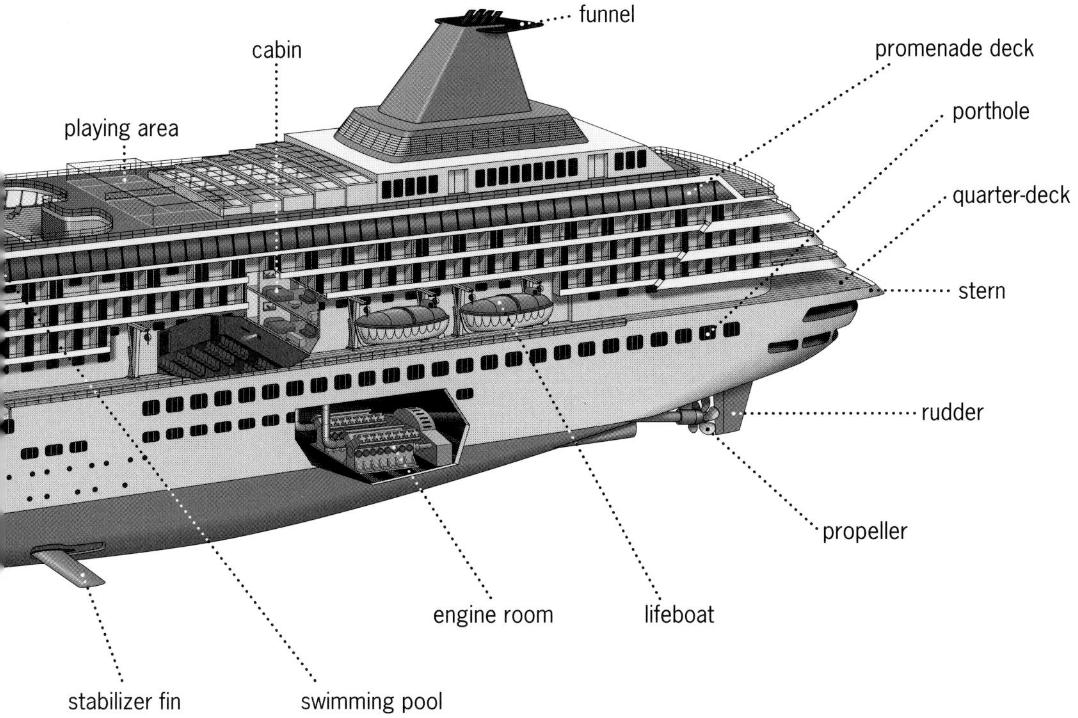
funnel
cabin
promenade deck
porthole
playing area
quarter-deck
stern
rudder
propeller
engine room
lifeboat
stabilizer fin
swimming pool

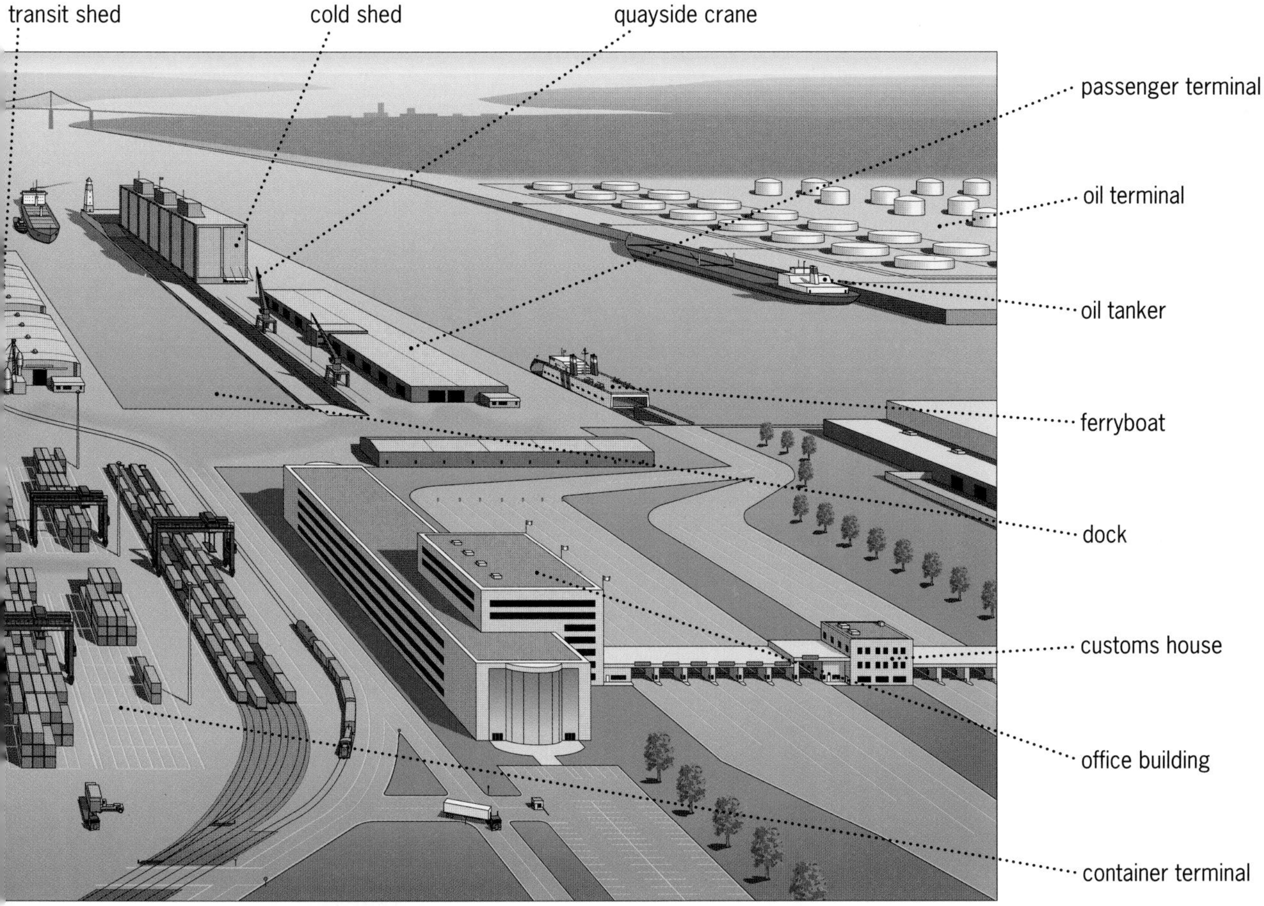
transit shed
cold shed
quayside crane
passenger terminal
oil terminal
oil tanker
ferryboat
dock
customs house
office building
container terminal

PLANE

TYPES OF WING SHAPES

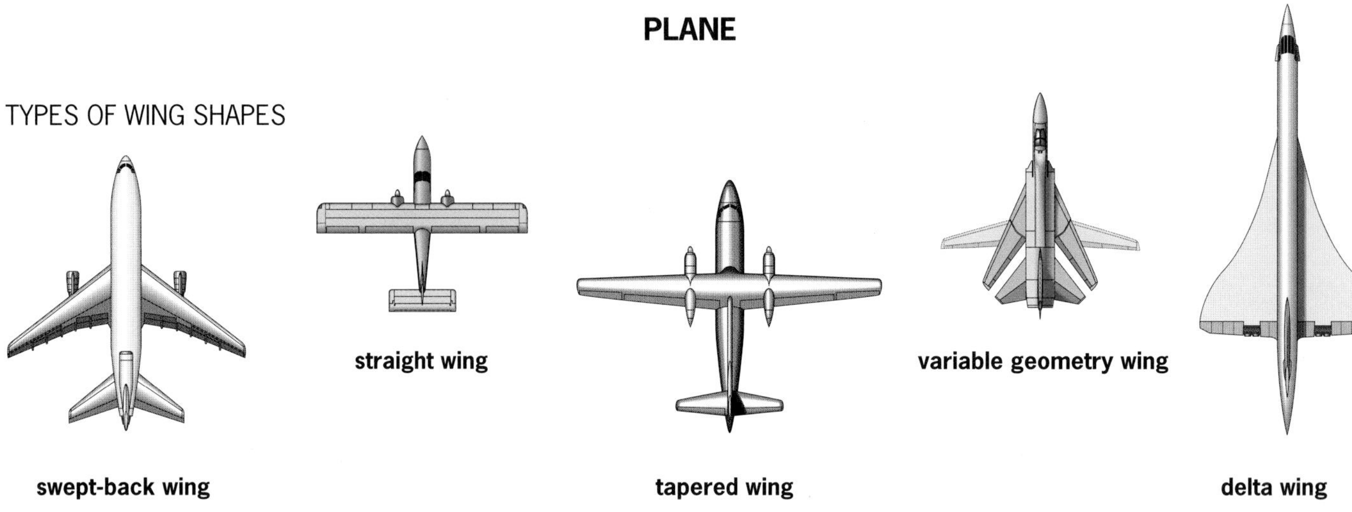
swept-back wing
straight wing
tapered wing
variable geometry wing
delta wing

long-range jet

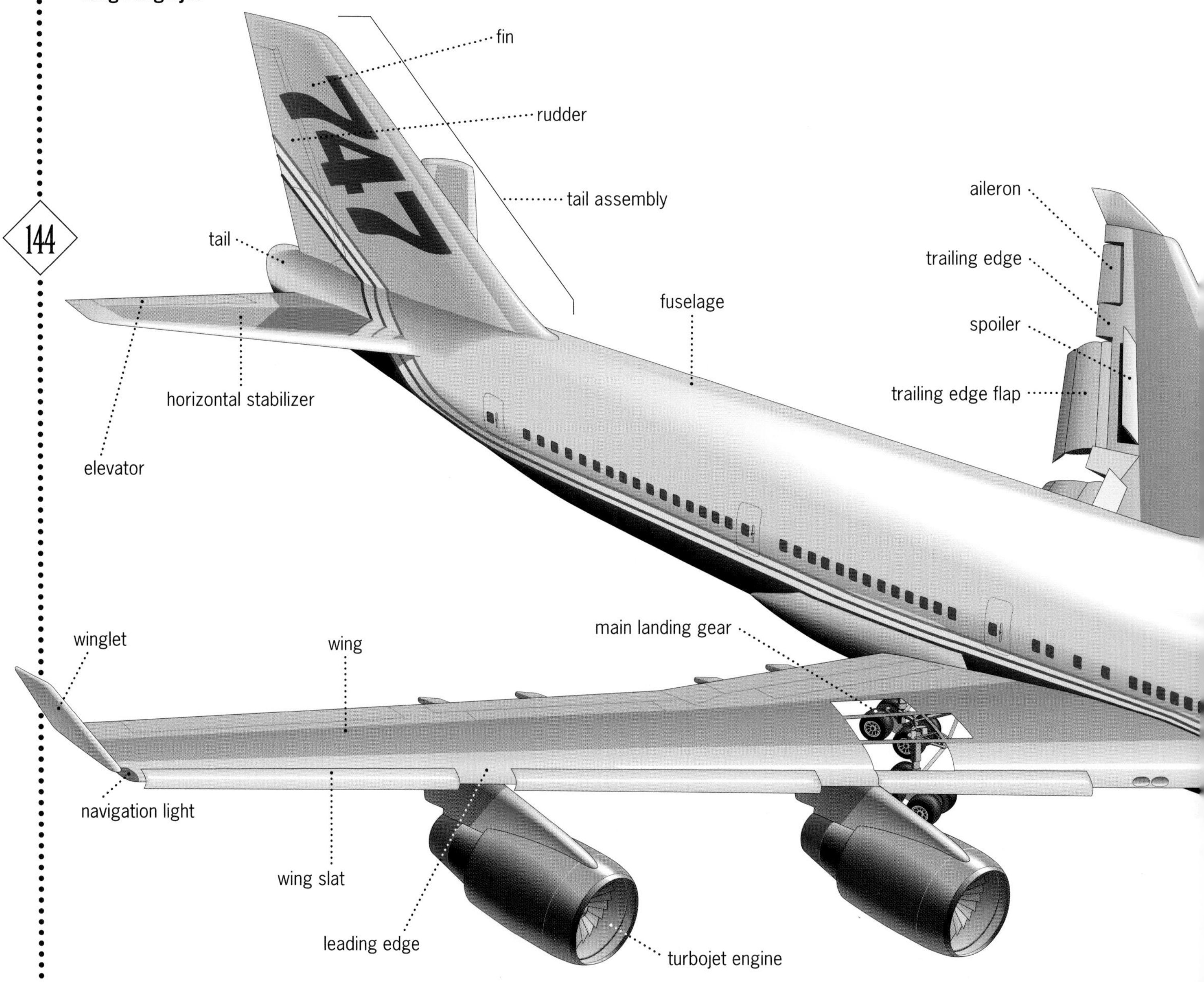
fin
rudder
tail assembly
tail
horizontal stabilizer
elevator
fuselage
aileron
trailing edge
spoiler
trailing edge flap
winglet
wing
main landing gear
navigation light
wing slat
leading edge
turbojet engine

HELICOPTER

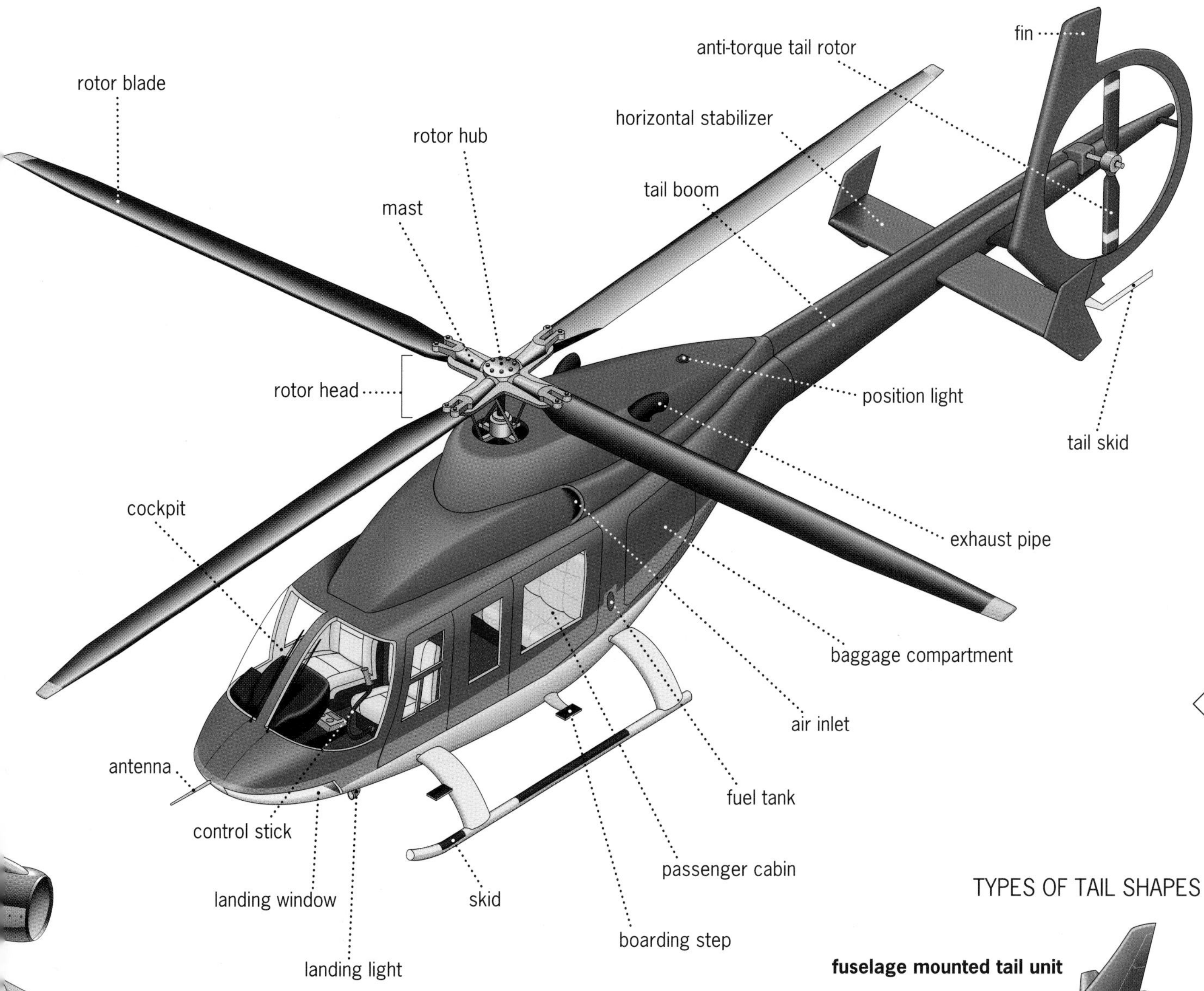
fin
anti-torque tail rotor
rotor blade
horizontal stabilizer
rotor hub
tail boom
mast
rotor head
position light
tail skid
cockpit
exhaust pipe
baggage compartment
air inlet
antenna
fuel tank
control stick
passenger cabin
landing window
skid
boarding step
landing light

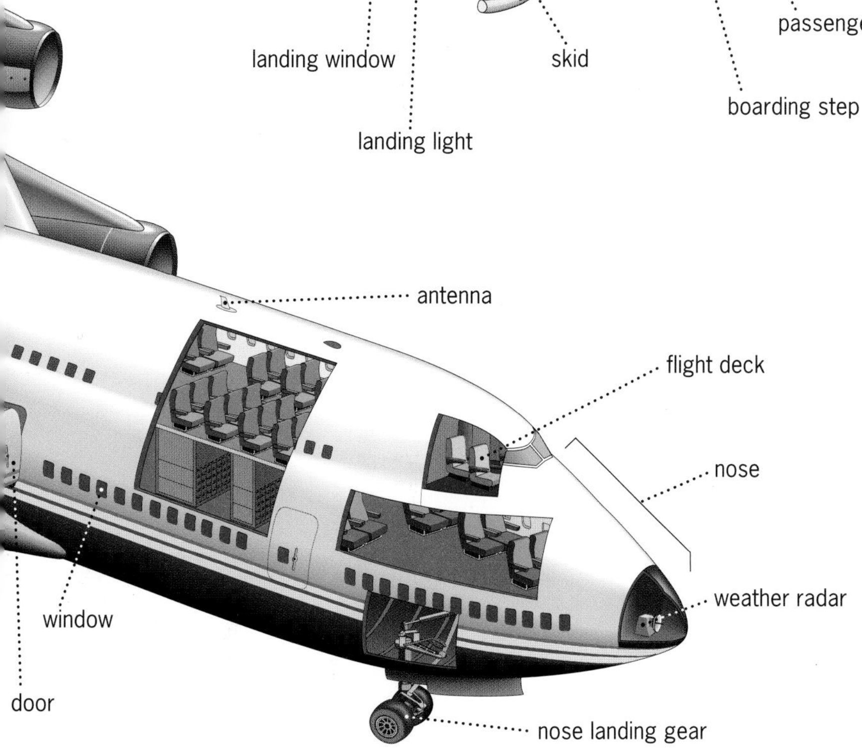
antenna
flight deck
nose
window
weather radar
door
nose landing gear

TYPES OF TAIL SHAPES

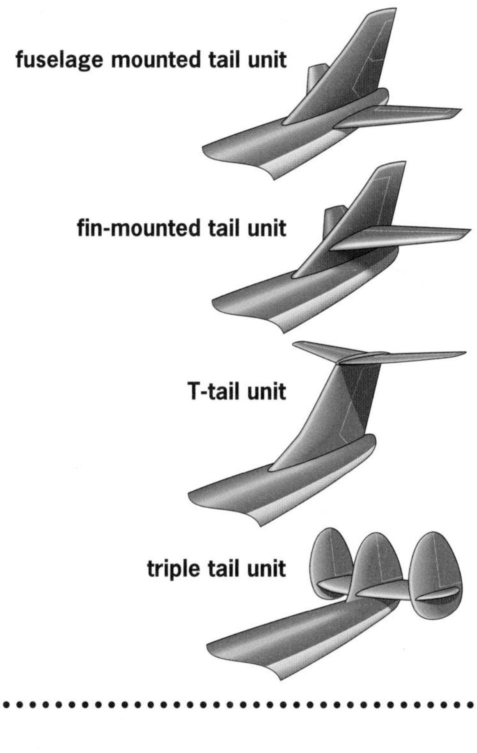
fuselage mounted tail unit
fin-mounted tail unit
T-tail unit
triple tail unit

AIRPORT

control tower
control tower cab
access road
high-speed exit runway
by-pass runway
apron
apron
service road
runway

AIRPORT GROUND EQUIPMENT

tow bar

tow tractor

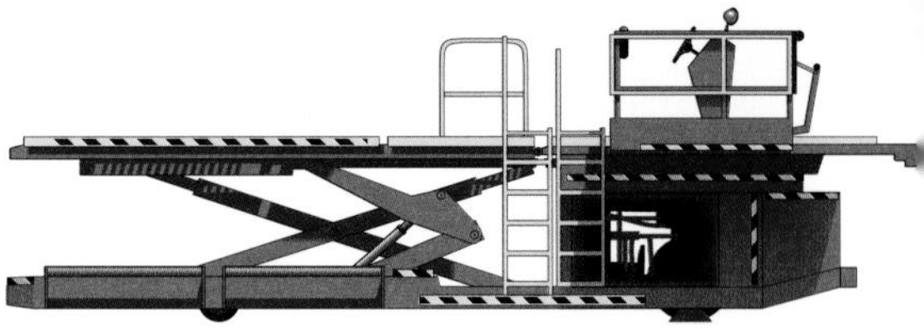

container/pallet loader

universal step

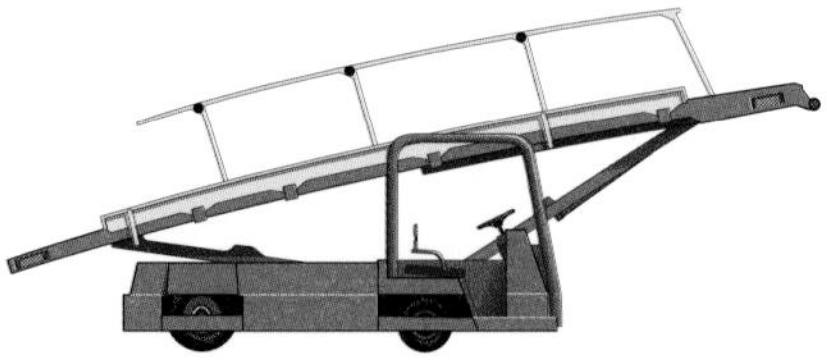

baggage conveyor

wheel chock

127

maintenance hangar
parking area
passenger terminal
boarding walkway
radial passenger loading area
telescopic corridor
service area
runway line

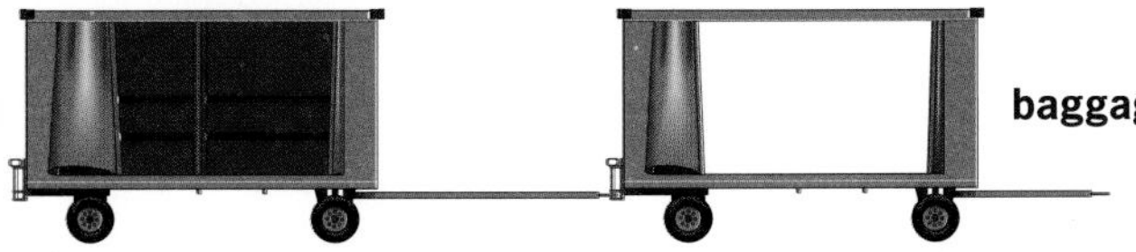

baggage trailer

tow tractor

189
189

passenger transfer vehicle

catering vehicle

SPACE SHUTTLE

space shuttle at takeoff

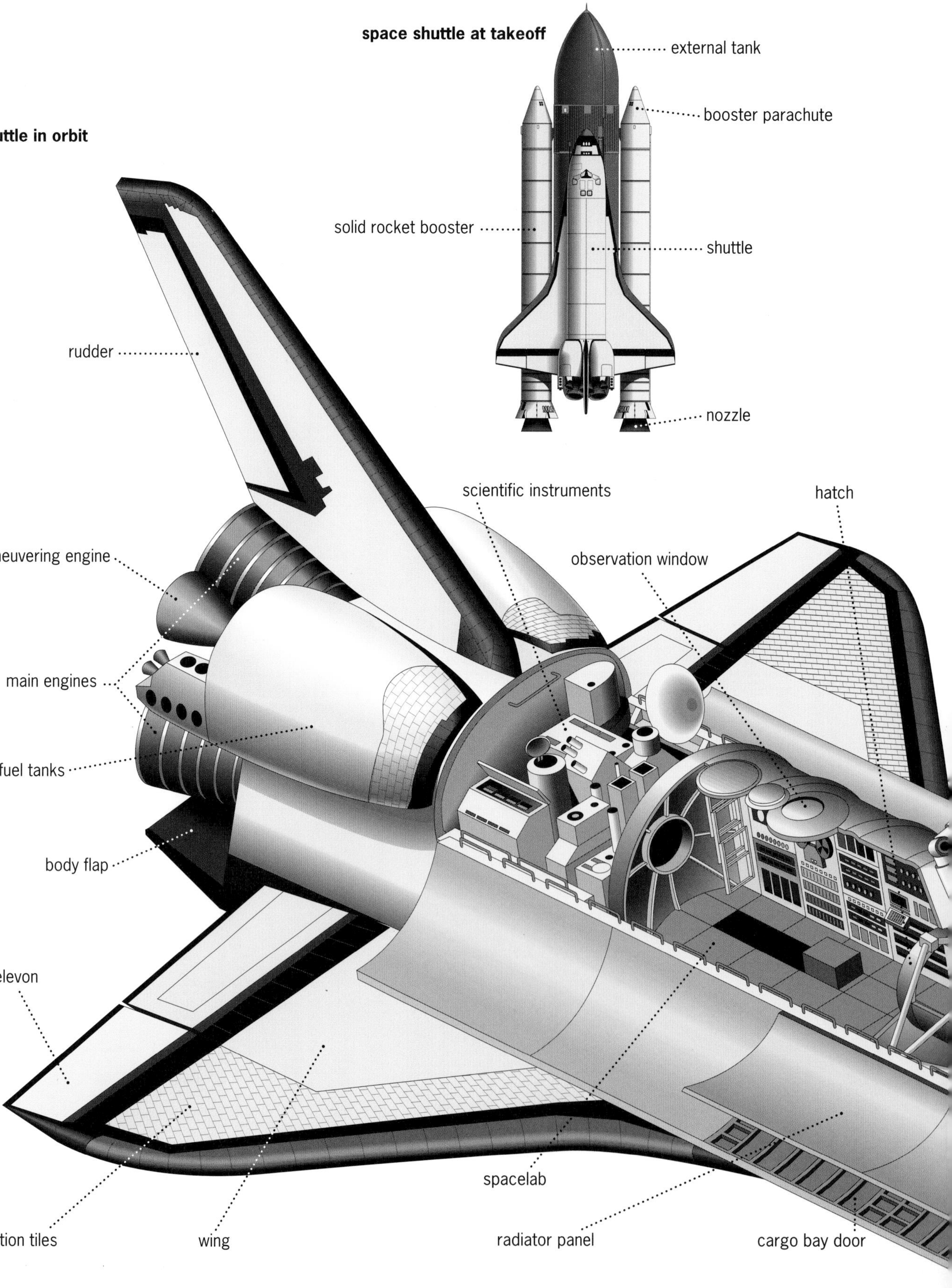
external tank
booster parachute
solid rocket booster
shuttle
nozzle
space shuttle in orbit
rudder
maneuvering engine
main engines
fuel tanks
body flap
elevon
insulation tiles
wing
scientific instruments
observation window
hatch
spacelab
radiator panel
cargo bay door

SPACESUIT

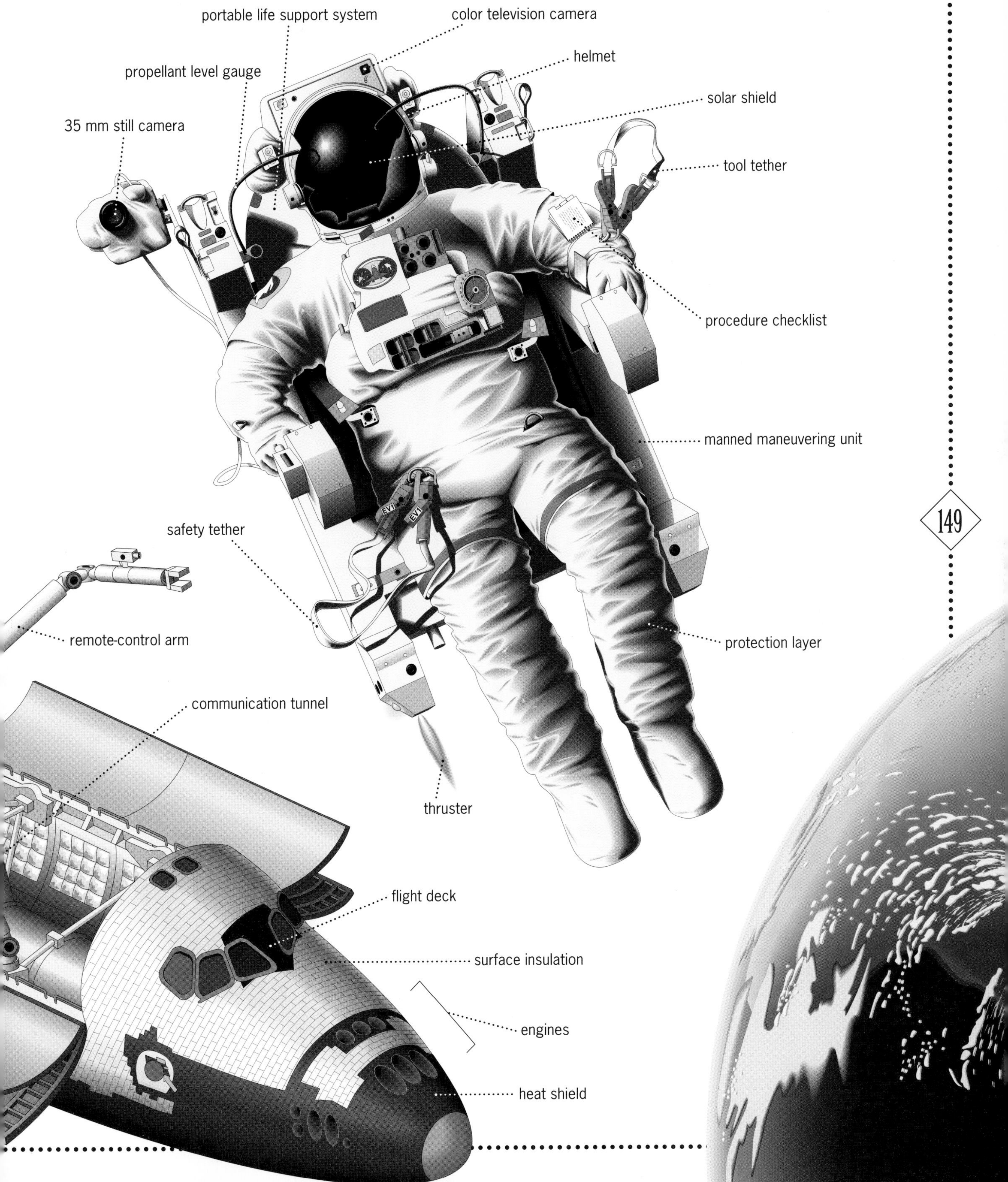
portable life support system
color television camera
helmet
propellant level gauge
solar shield
35 mm still camera
tool tether
procedure checklist
manned maneuvering unit
safety tether
remote-control arm
protection layer
communication tunnel
thruster
flight deck
surface insulation
engines
heat shield
EV1

SCHOOL SUPPLIES

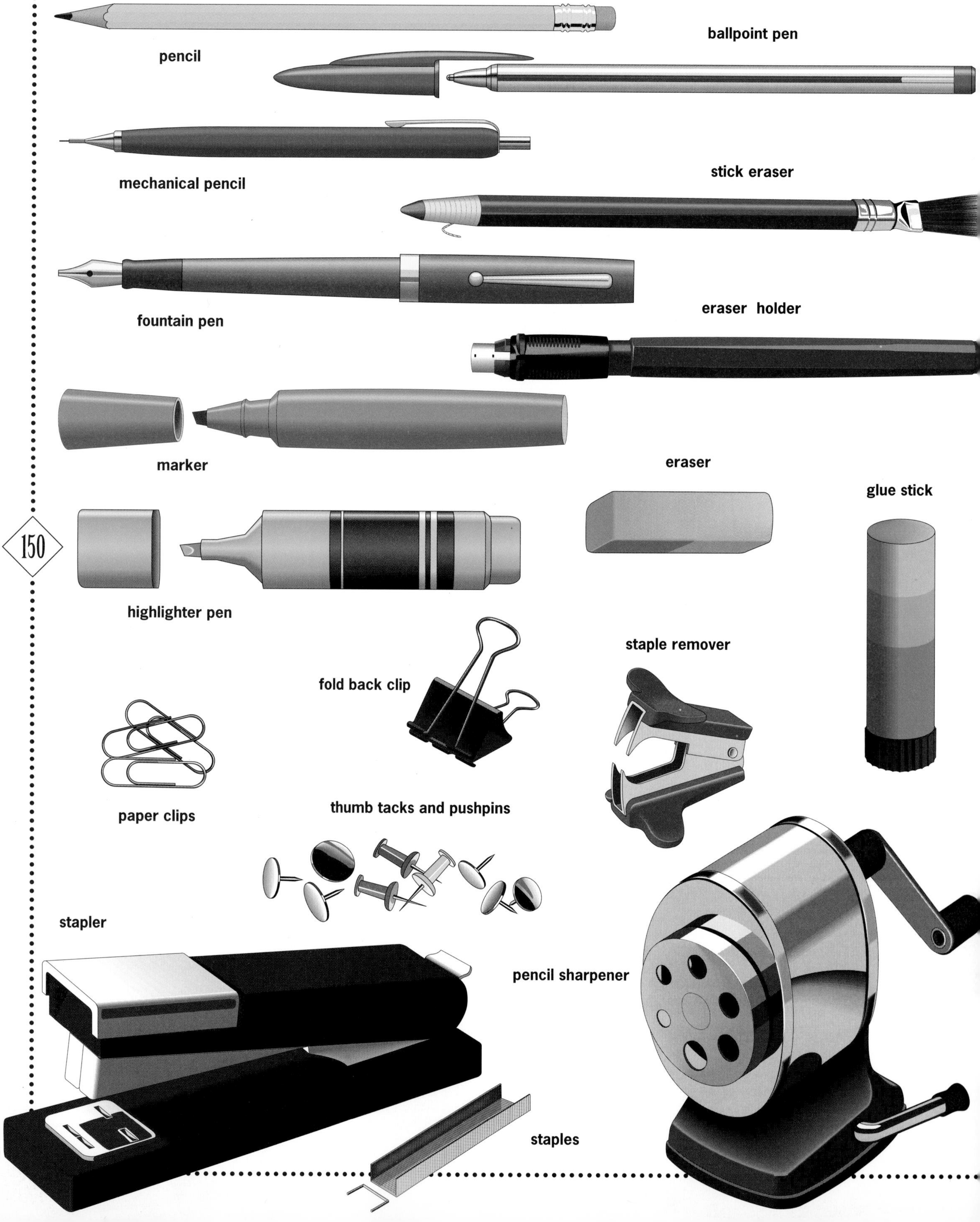
pencil
ballpoint pen
mechanical pencil
stick eraser
fountain pen
eraser holder
marker
eraser
glue stick
highlighter pen
staple remover
fold back clip
paper clips
thumb tacks and pushpins
stapler
pencil sharpener
staples

ruler
protractor
set square
tape dispenser
ring binder
spiral bound notebook
loose-leaf paper
notebook
notepad
briefcase
book bag

SCHOOL EQUIPMENT

blackboard

a b c
1 2 3

overhead projector

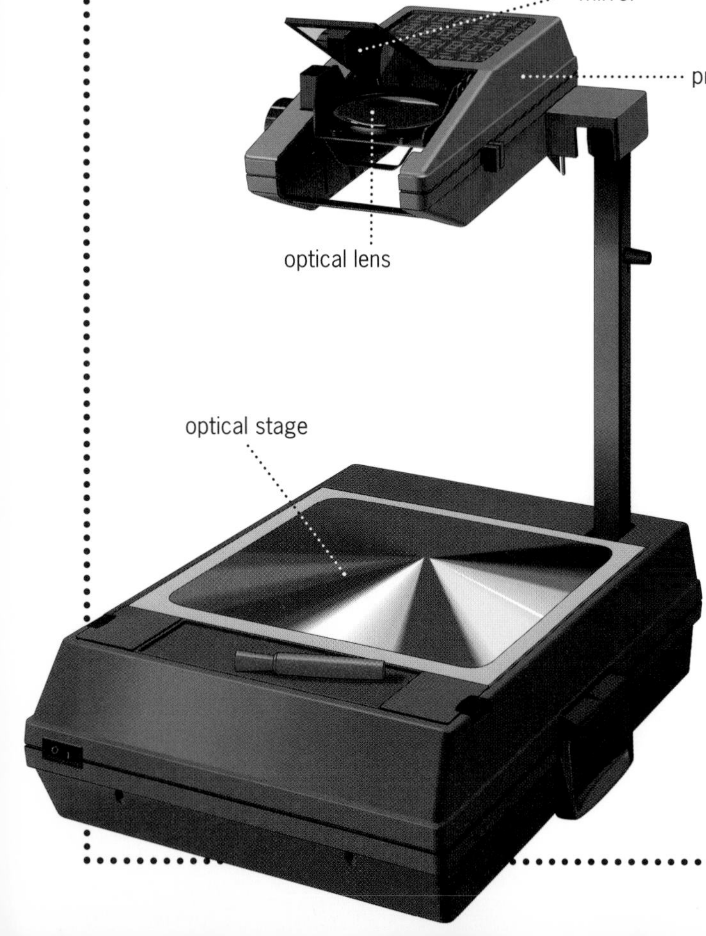
mirror
projection head
optical lens
optical stage

globe of Earth

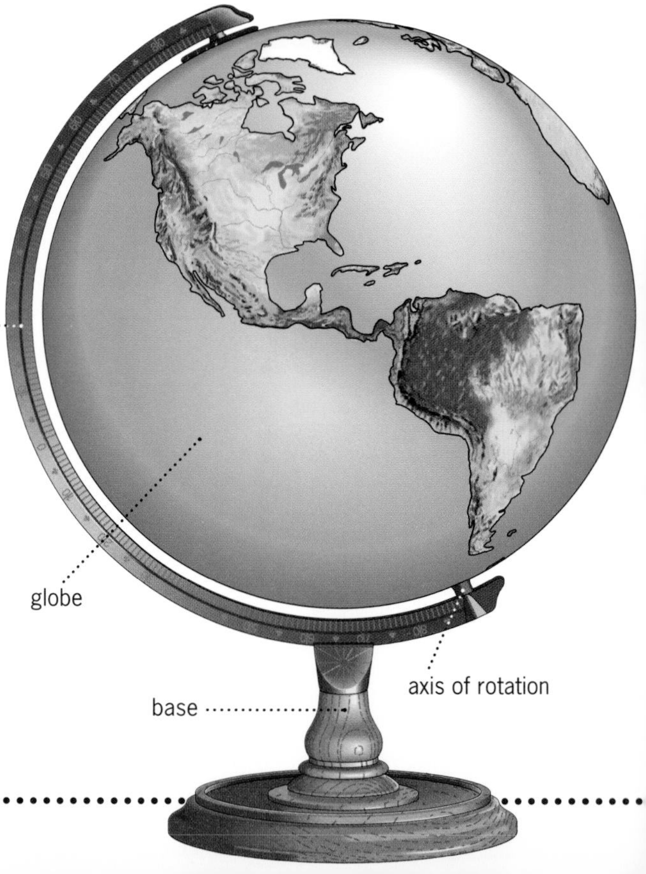
meridian band
globe
axis of rotation
base

slide projector

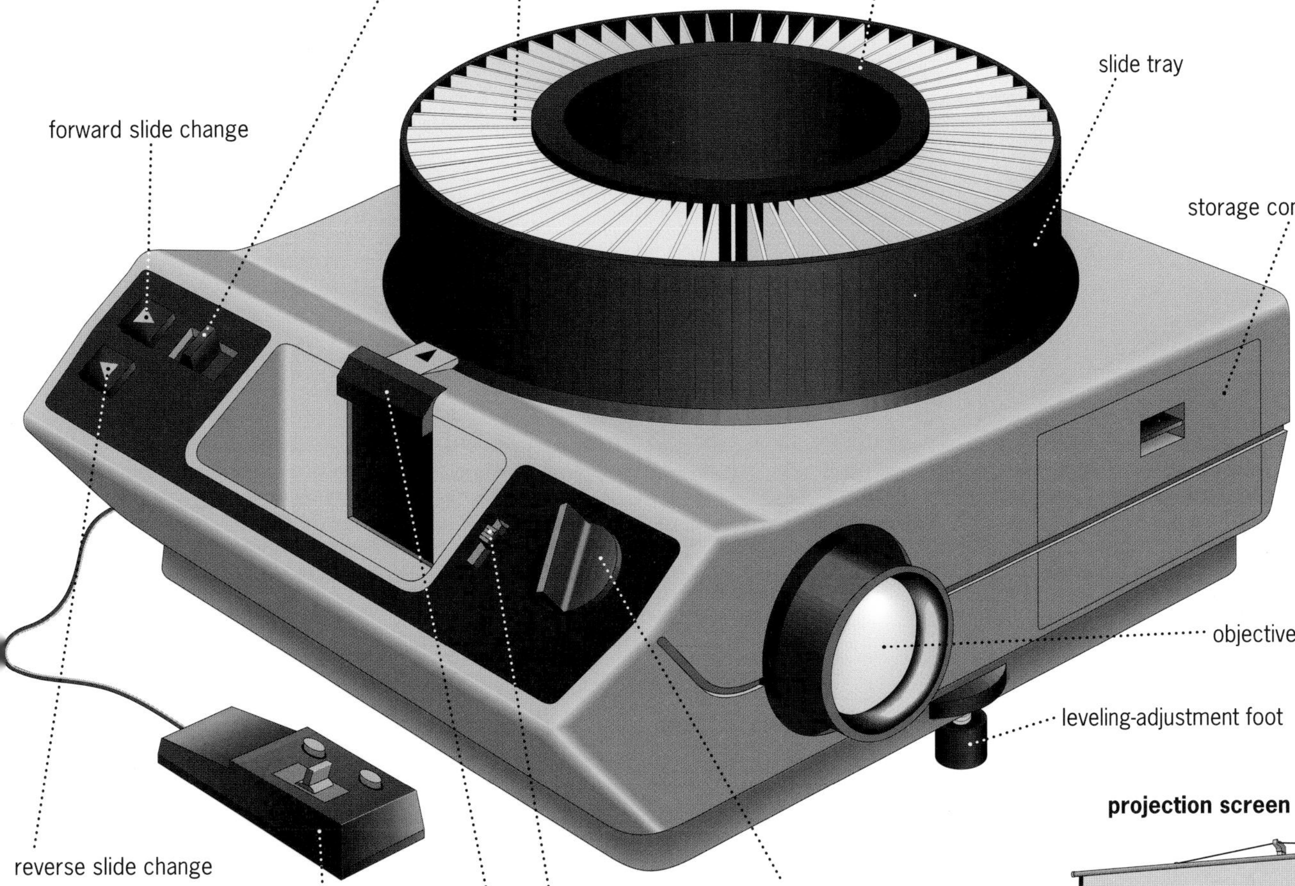
on/off switch
slide
lock ring
slide tray
forward slide change
storage compartment
objective lens
leveling-adjustment foot
reverse slide change
manual focusing knob
autofocus on/off switch
remote control
slide-select bar

projection screen

SLIDE

transparency

slide mount

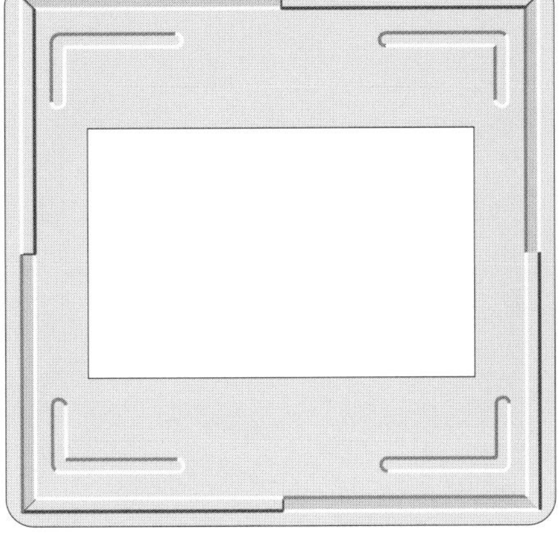

SCHOOL EQUIPMENT

pocket calculator

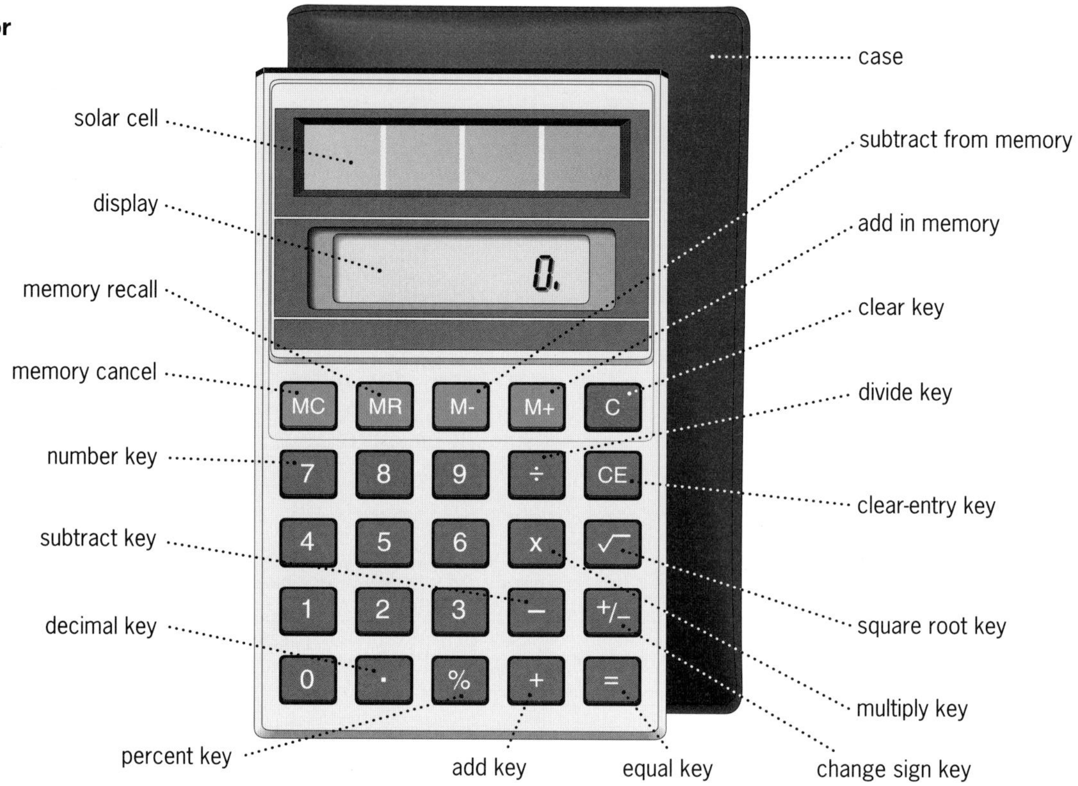
case
solar cell
subtract from memory
display
add in memory
memory recall
clear key
memory cancel
divide key
number key
clear-entry key
subtract key
square root key
decimal key
multiply key
percent key
add key
equal key
change sign key
0.
MC
MR
M-
M+
C
7
8
9
÷
CE
4
5
6
x
1
2
3
–
+/–
0
.
%
+
=

personal computer

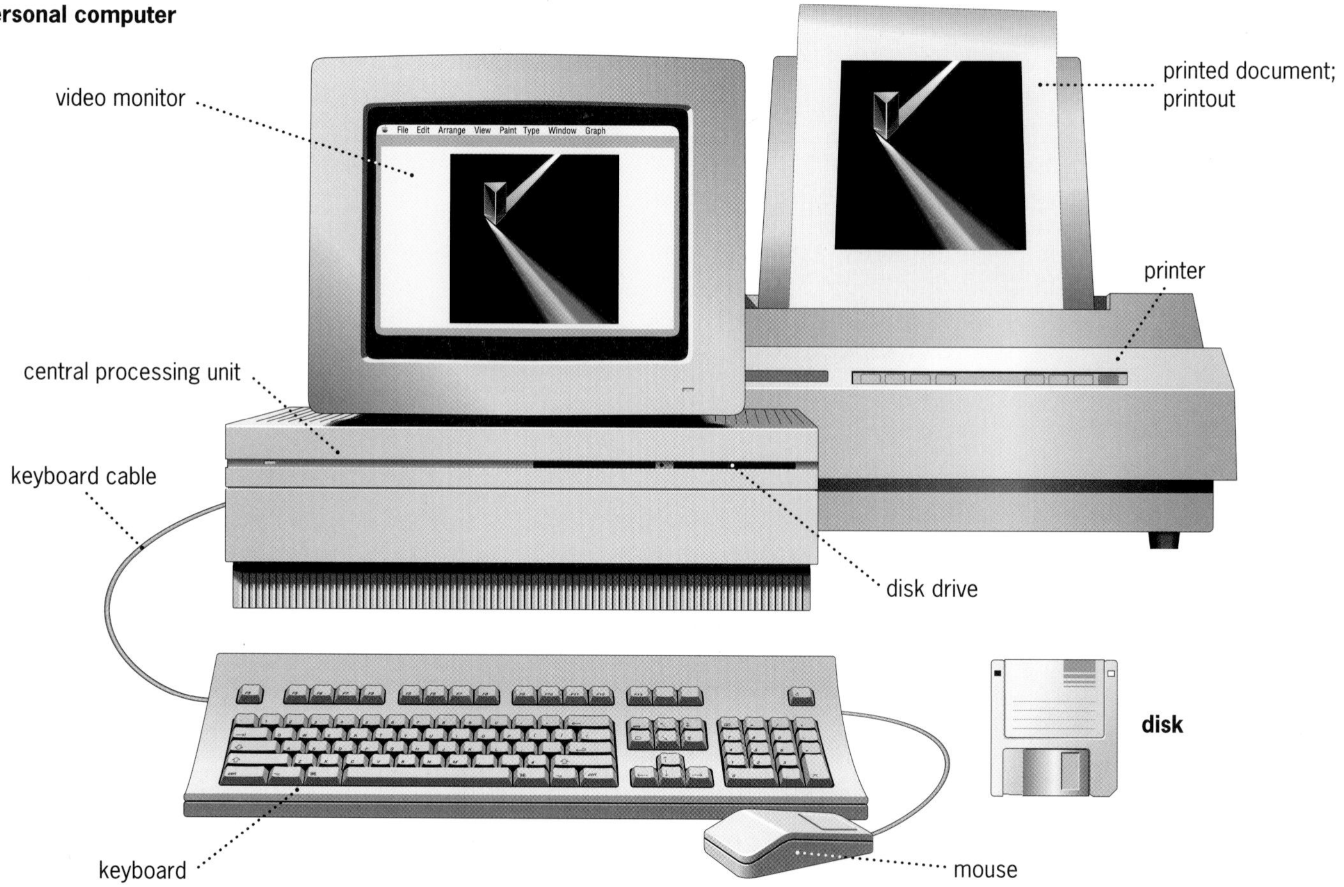
video monitor
printed document; printout
printer
central processing unit
keyboard cable
disk drive
disk
keyboard
mouse
File Edit Arrange View Paint Type Window Graph

magnifying glass

test tube

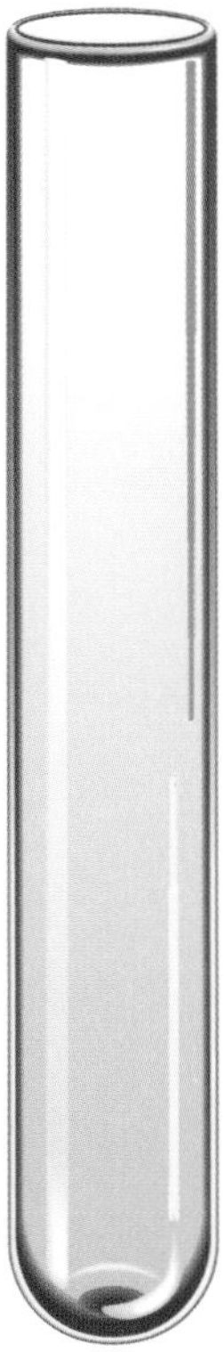

microscope

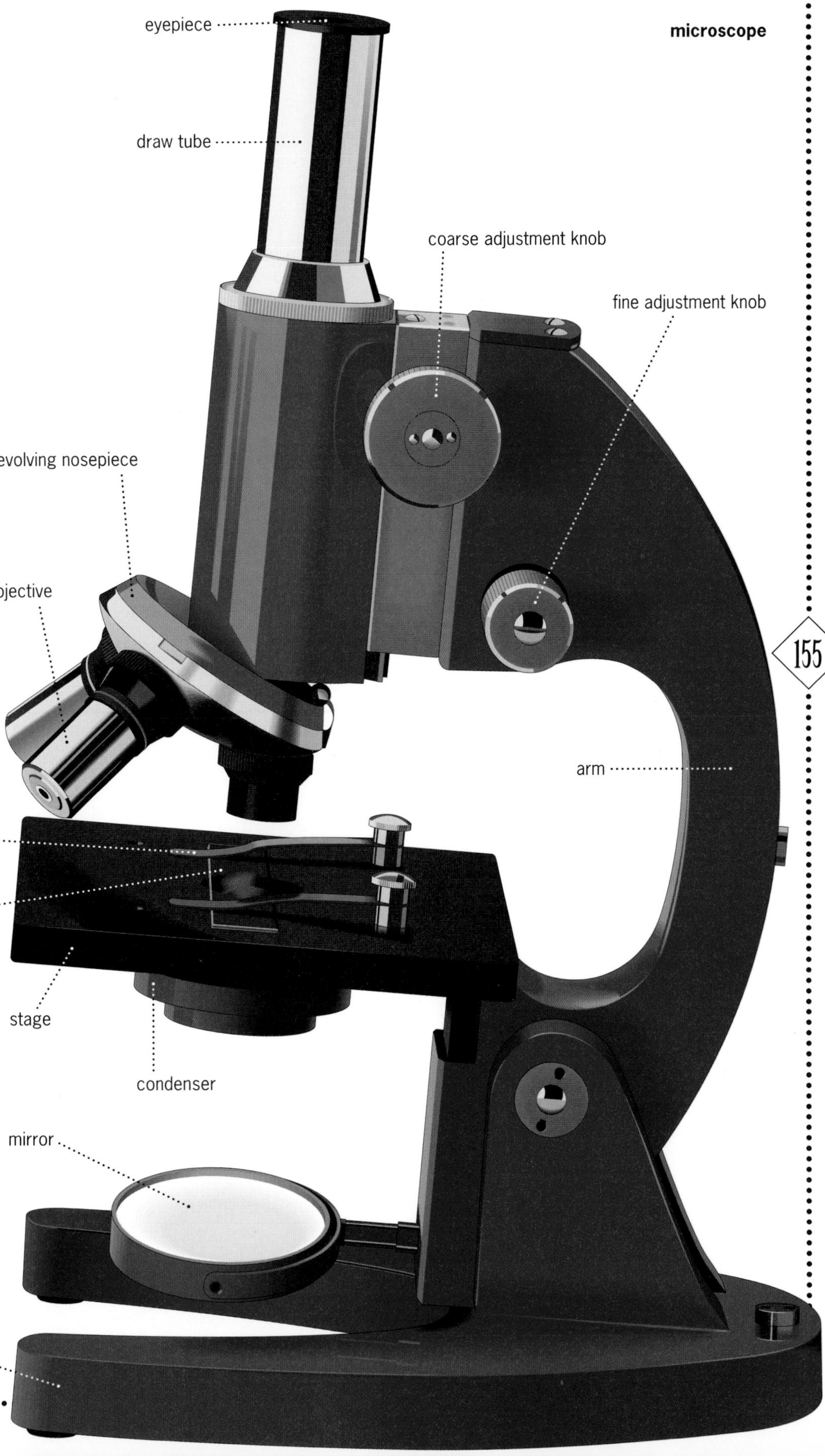
eyepiece
draw tube
coarse adjustment knob
fine adjustment knob
revolving nosepiece
objective
arm
stage clip
glass slide
stage
condenser
mirror
base

GEOMETRY

PLANE SURFACES

circle

square

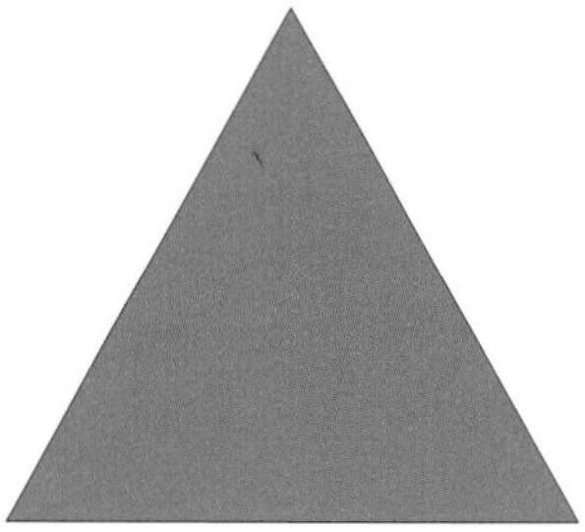

triangle

rhombus

rectangle

trapezoid

parallelogram

SOLIDS

sphere

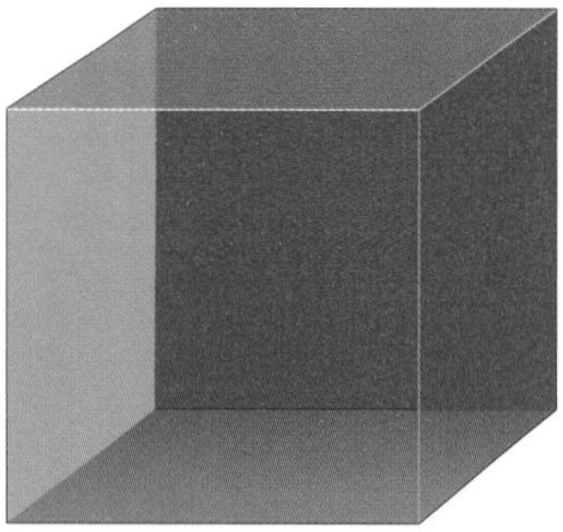

cube

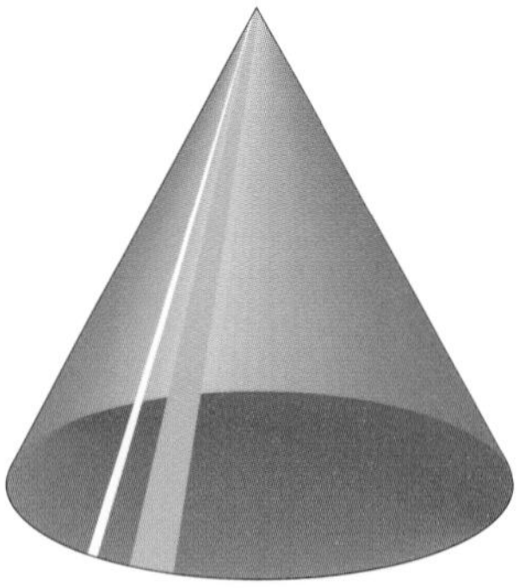

cone

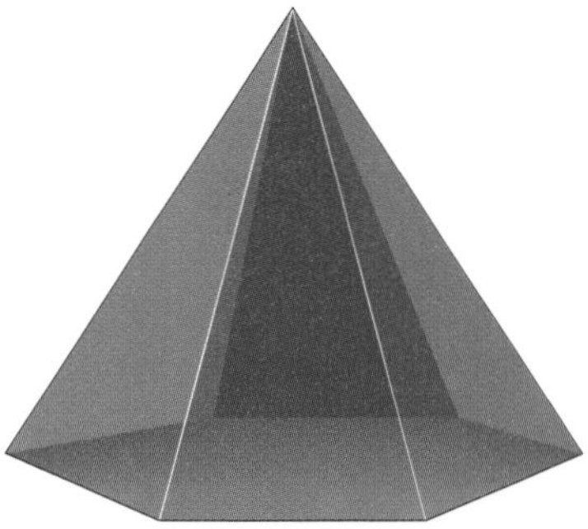

pyramid

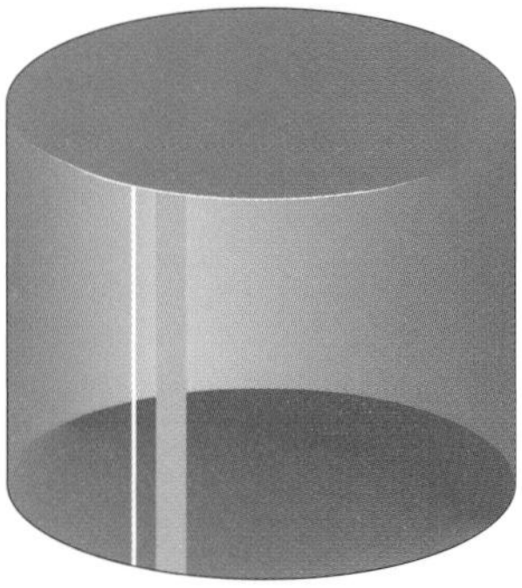

cylinder

parallelepiped

prism

DRAWING

COLOR CIRCLE

primary colors

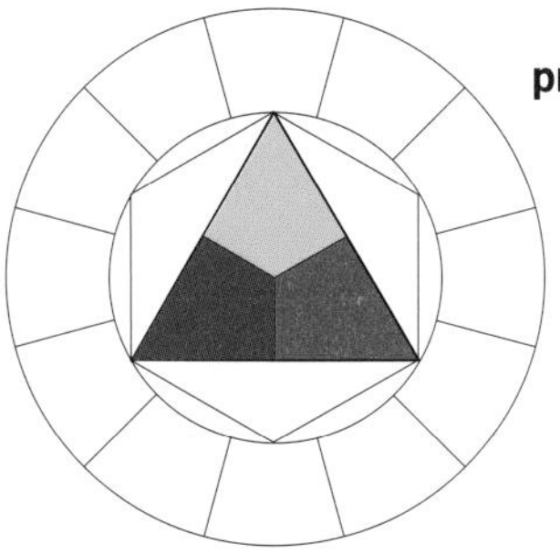

secondary colors

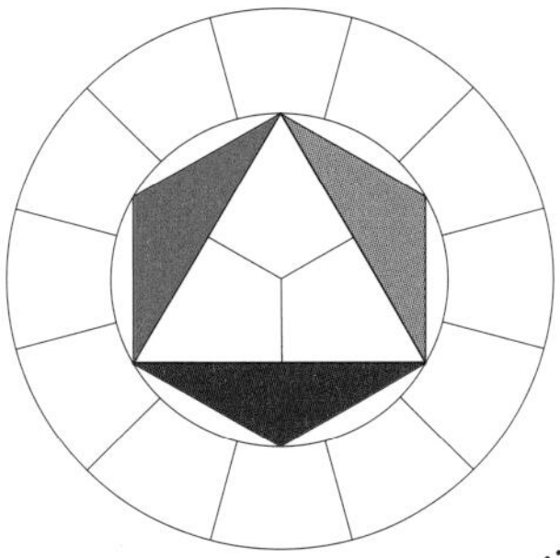

tertiary colors

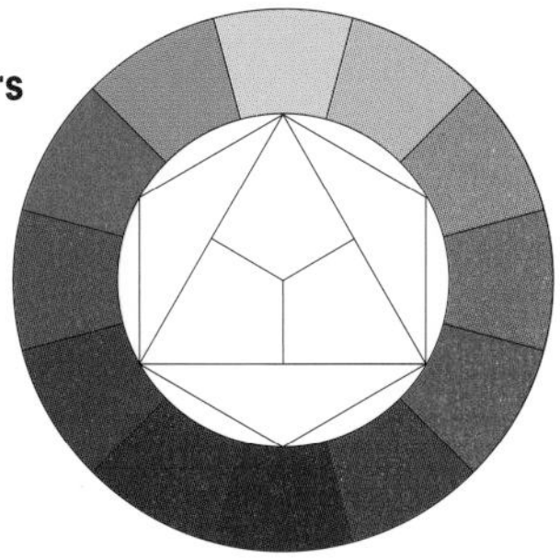

yellow

yellow-green

orange-yellow

green

orange

blue-green

orange-red

blue

red

violet-blue

red- violet

violet

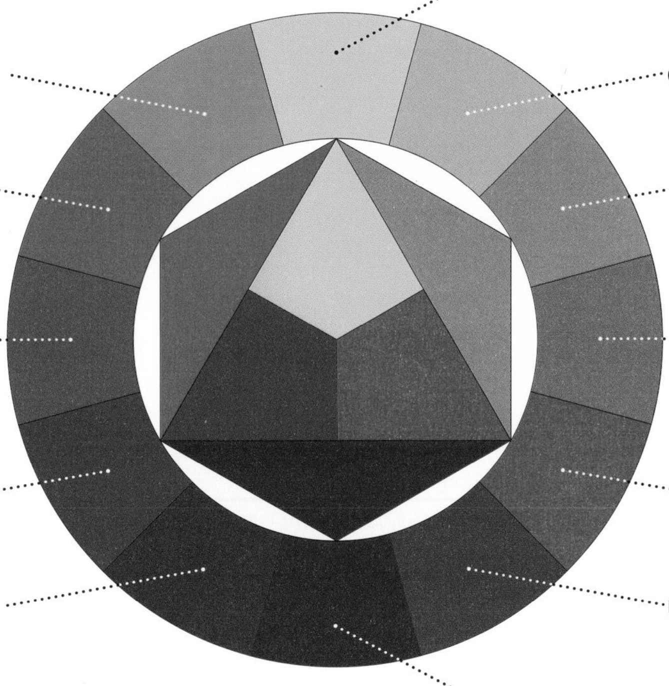

paintbrush

flat brush

colored pencils

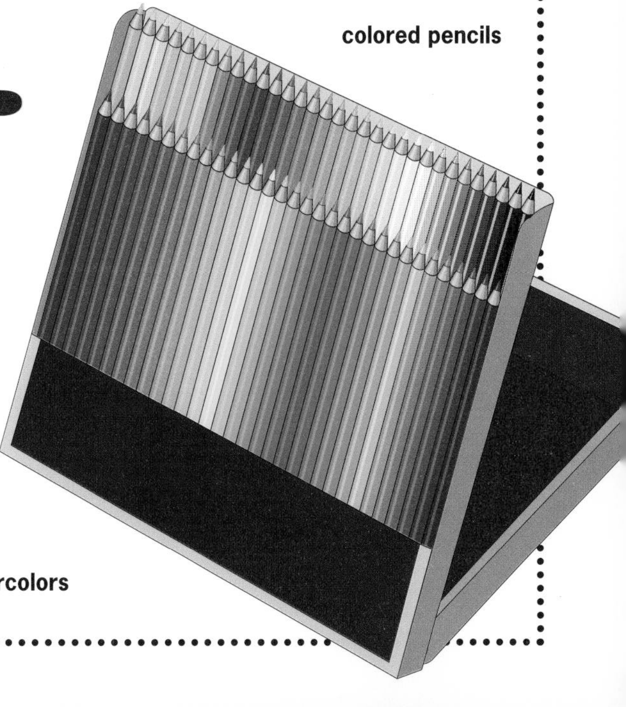

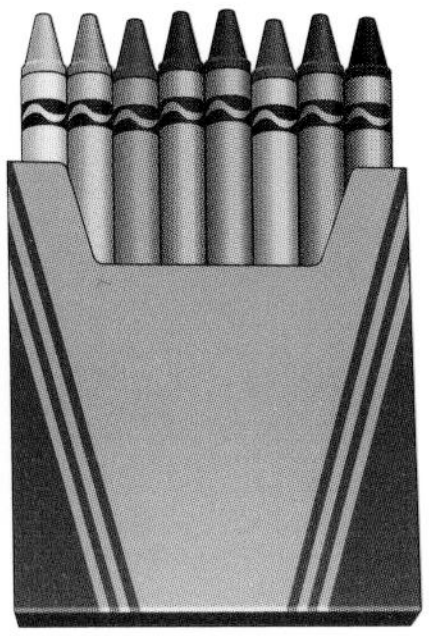

crayons

watercolors

TRADITIONAL MUSICAL INSTRUMENTS

balalaika

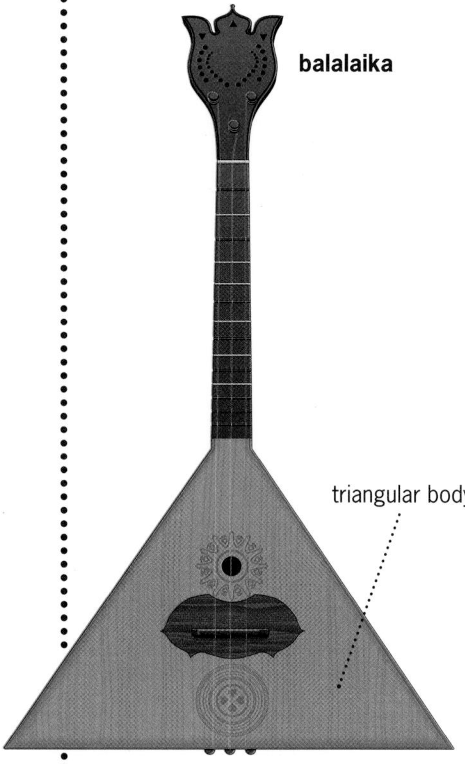
triangular body

mandolin

pear-shaped body

zither

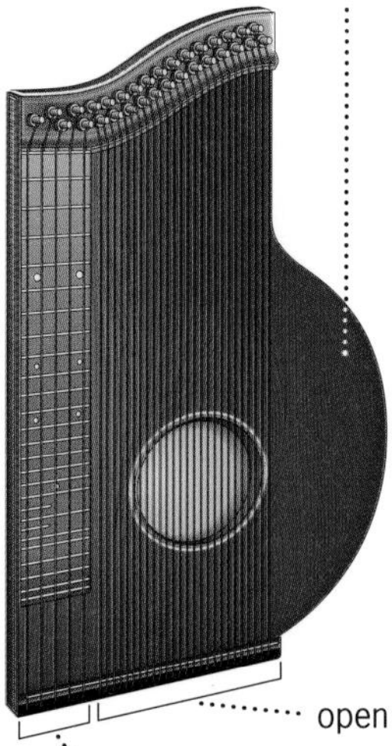
soundboard
open strings
melody strings

lyre

banjo

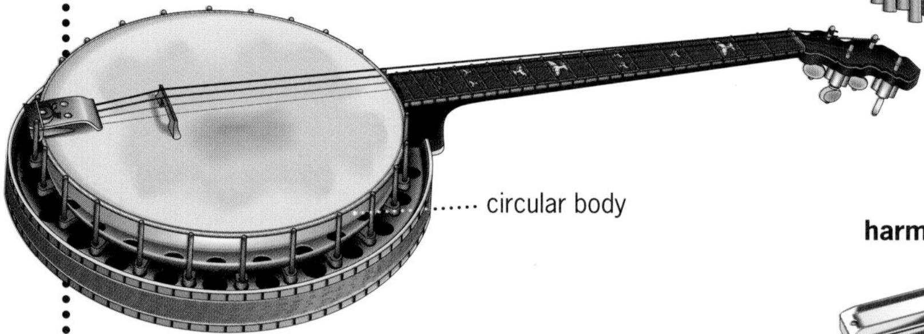
circular body

panpipes

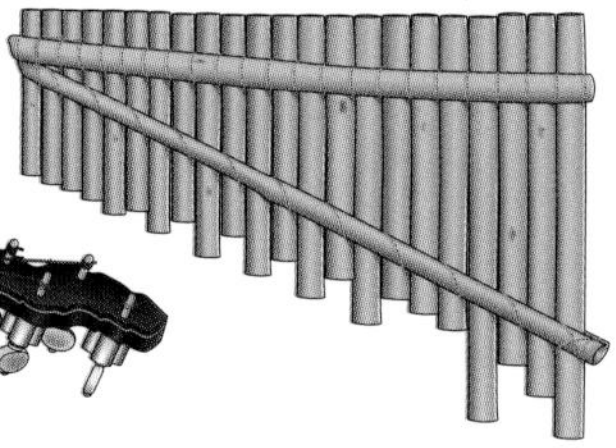

harmonica

bagpipes

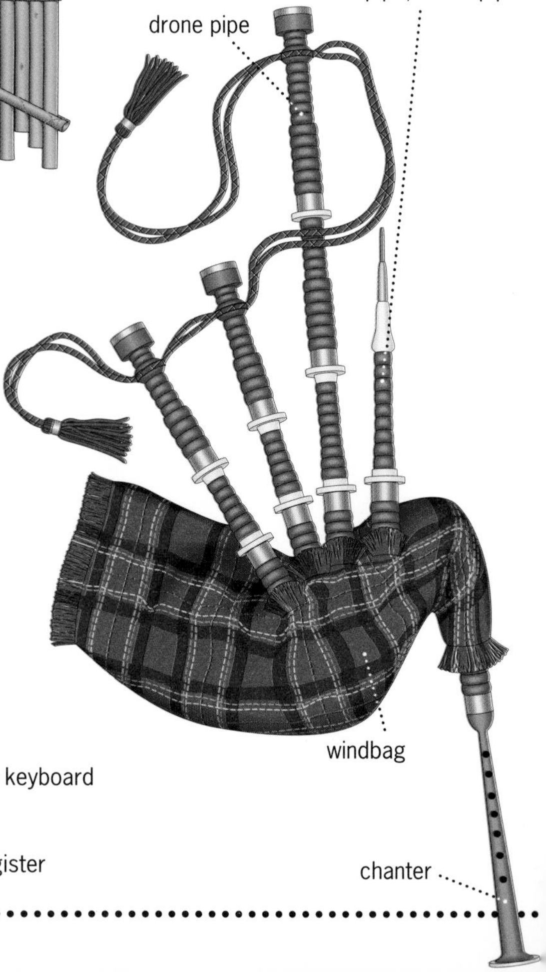
blowpipe; mouthpipe
drone pipe
windbag
chanter

accordion

bellows
treble keyboard
treble register
bass keyboard
bass register

KEYBOARD INSTRUMENT

upright piano

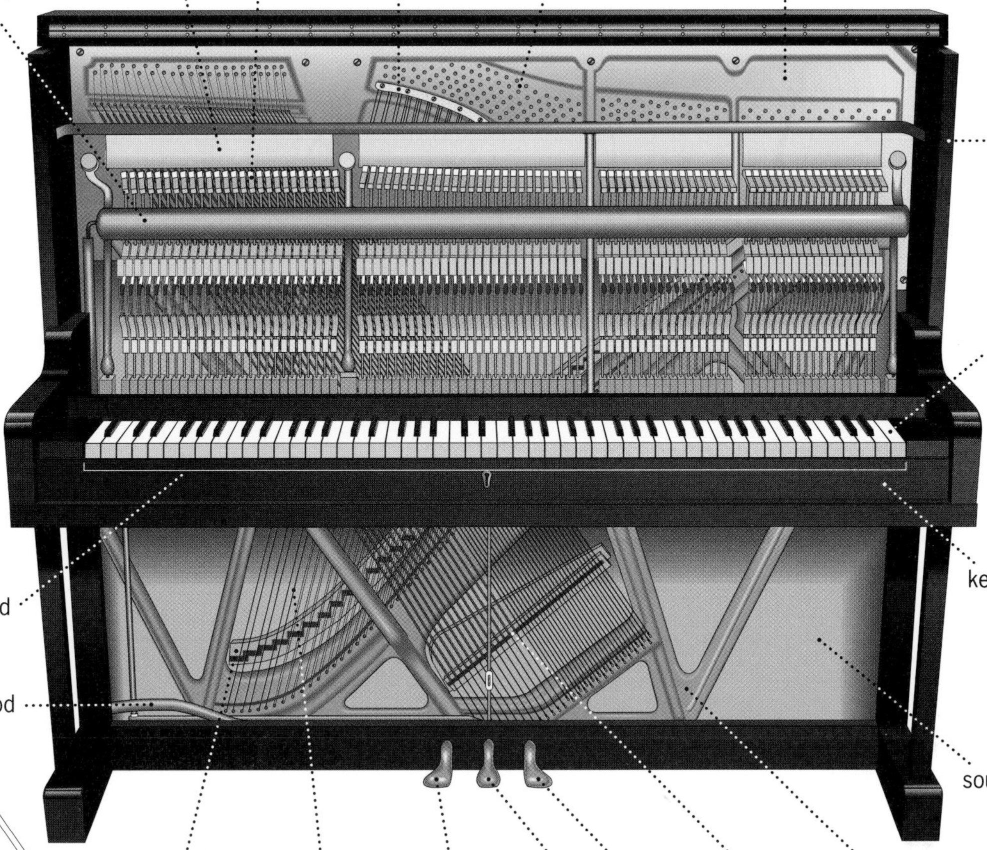
muffler felt
hammer
tuning pin
hammer rail
pressure bar
pin block
case
key
keybed
keyboard
pedal rod
soundboard
treble bridge
soft pedal
metal frame
strings
muffler pedal
bass bridge
damper pedal

MUSICAL ACCESSORIES

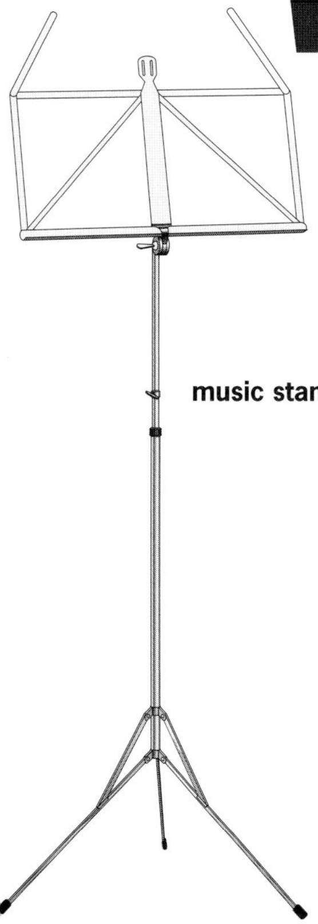

music stand

metronome

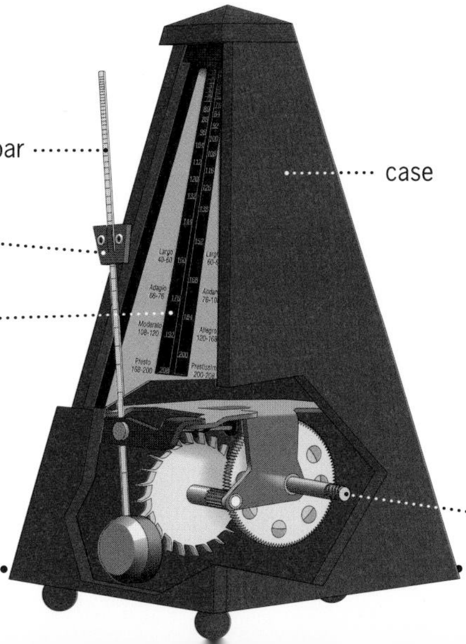
pendulum bar
case
sliding weight
tempo scale
key

tuning fork

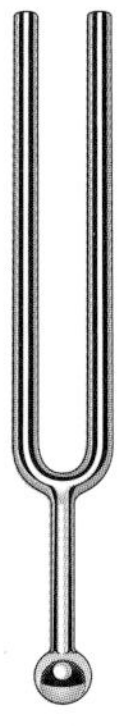

MUSICAL NOTATION

staff

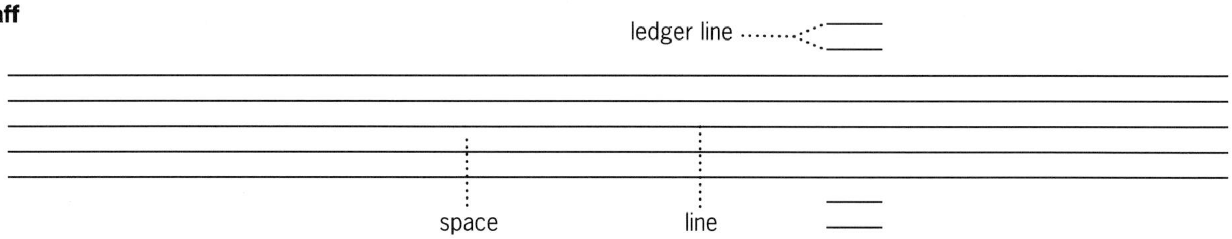
ledger line
space
line

clefs

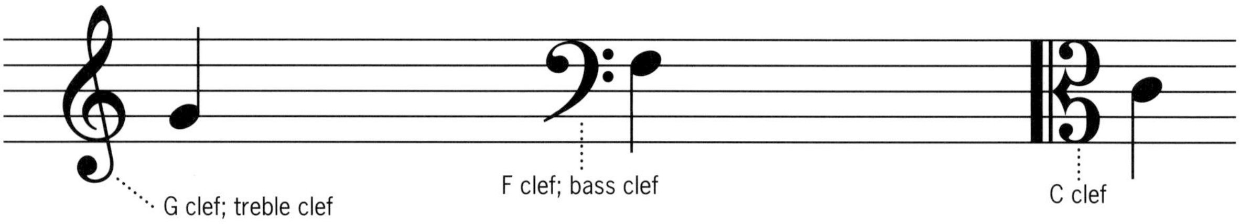
G clef; treble clef
F clef; bass clef
C clef

time signatures

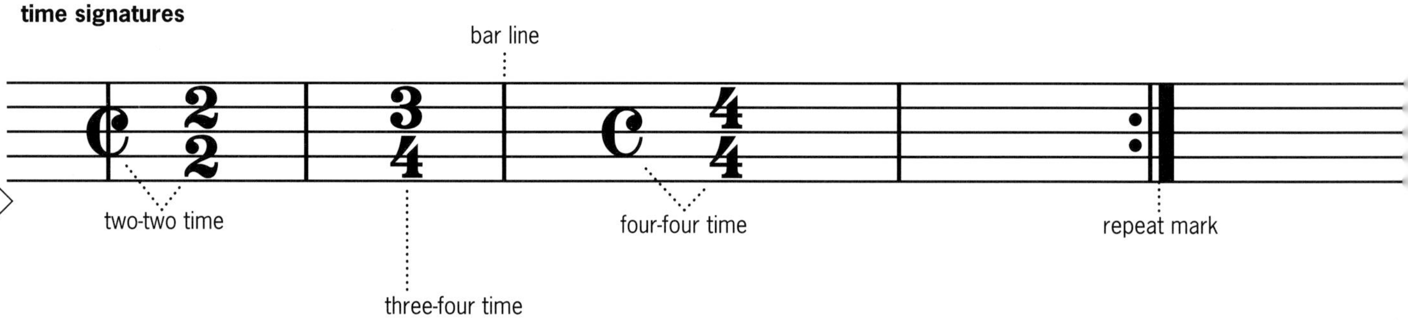
bar line
two-two time
three-four time
four-four time
repeat mark

scale

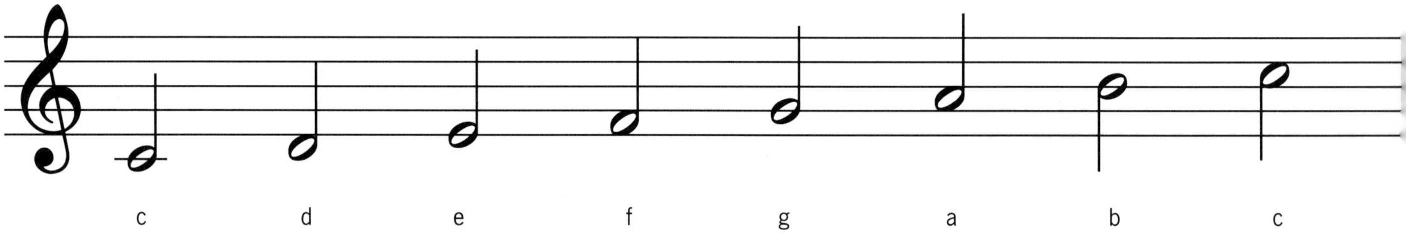
c
d
e
f
g
a
b
c

intervals

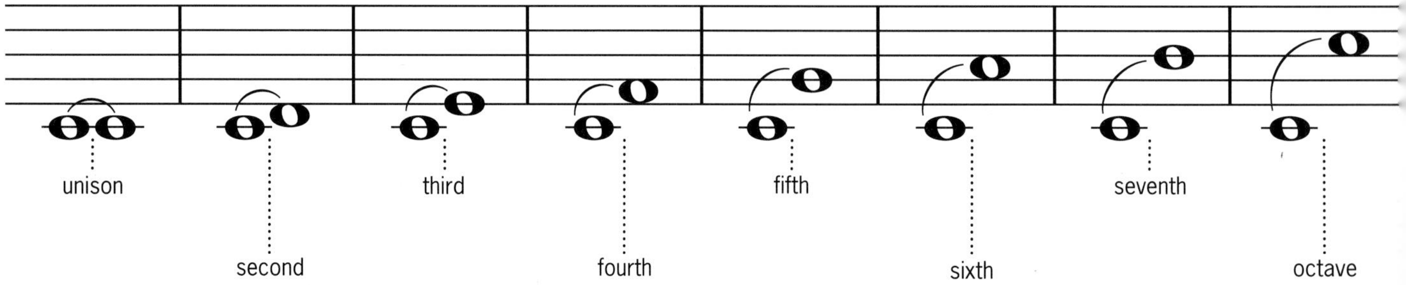
unison
second
third
fourth
fifth
sixth
seventh
octave

note symbols

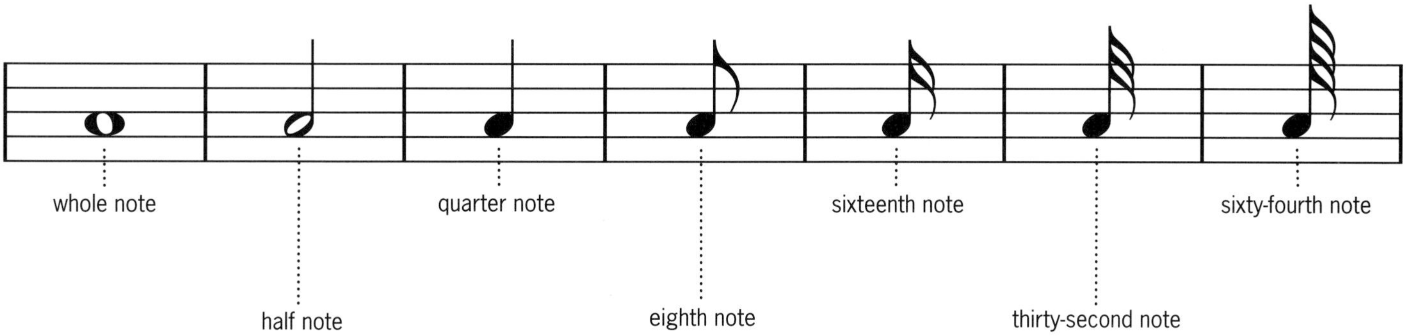
whole note
half note
quarter note
eighth note
sixteenth note
thirty-second note
sixty-fourth note

rest symbols

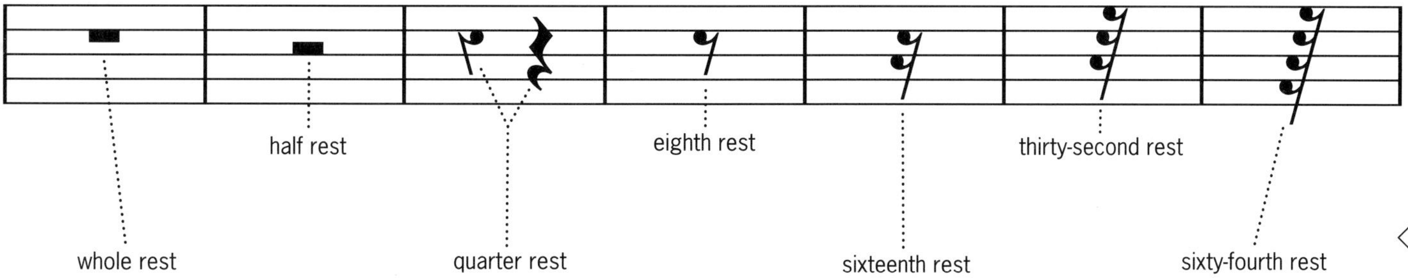
whole rest
half rest
quarter rest
eighth rest
sixteenth rest
thirty-second rest
sixty-fourth rest

accidentals

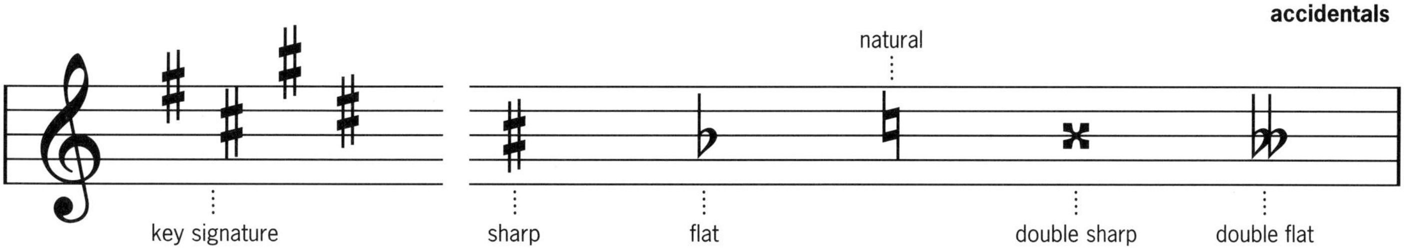
key signature
sharp
flat
natural
double sharp
double flat

ornaments

appoggiatura
trill
tr
turn
mordent

STRINGED INSTRUMENTS

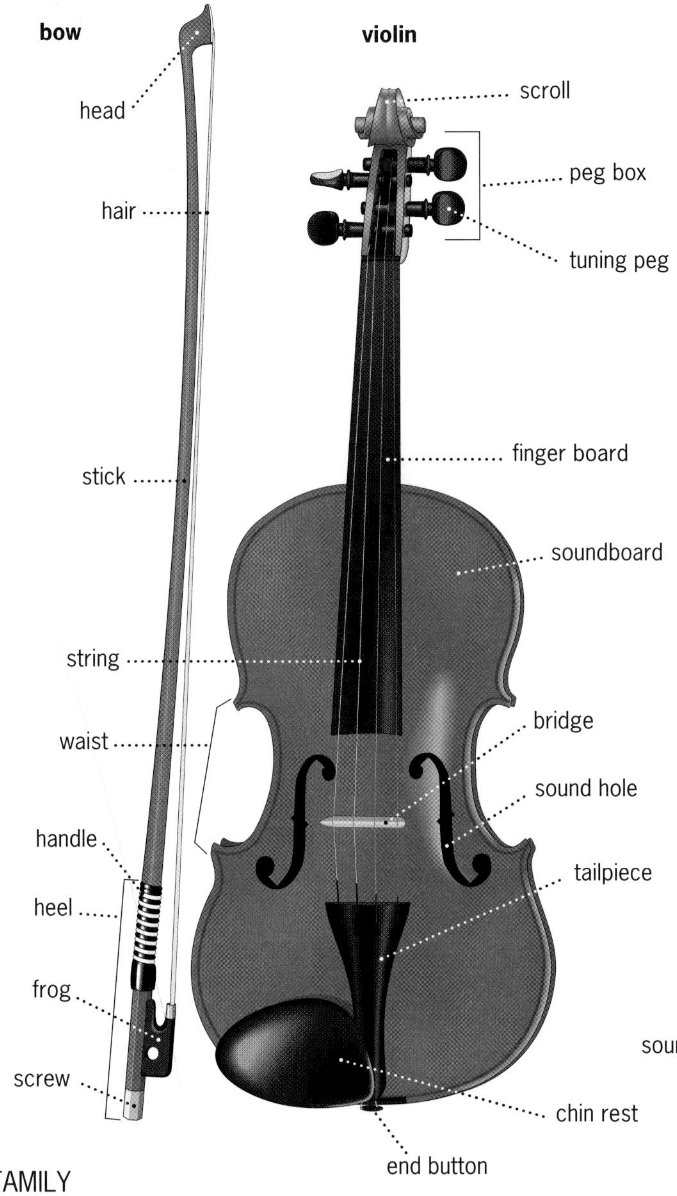
bow
head
hair
stick
string
waist
handle
heel
frog
screw
violin
scroll
peg box
tuning peg
finger board
soundboard
bridge
sound hole
tailpiece
chin rest
end button

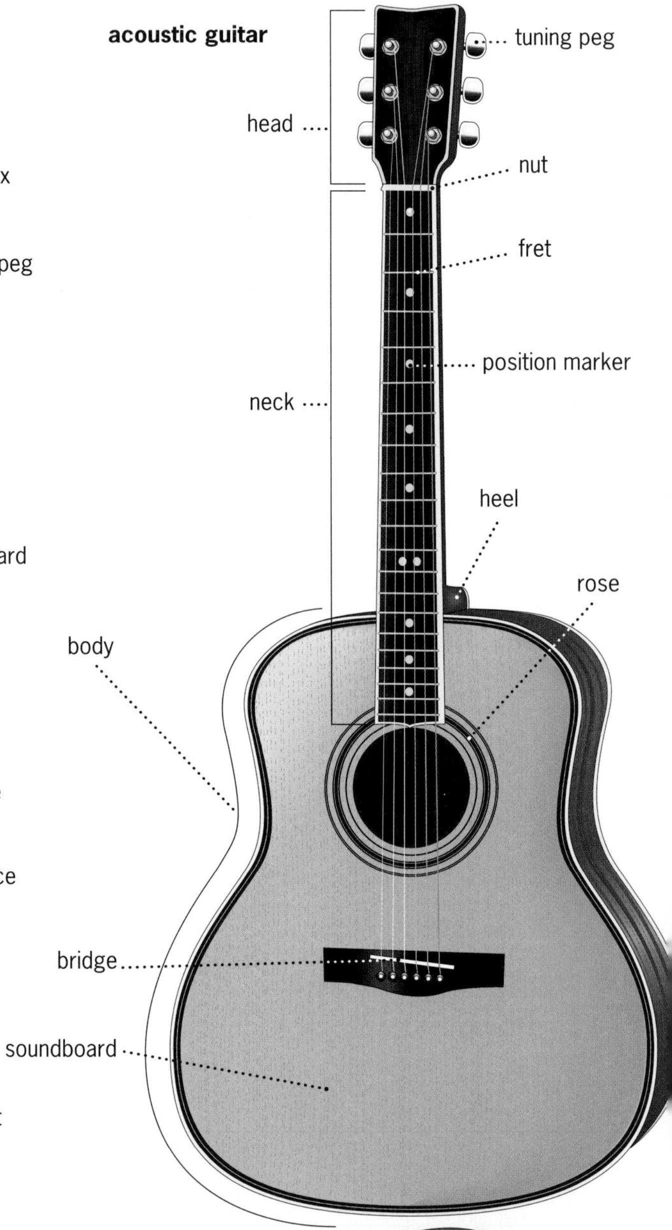
acoustic guitar
tuning peg
head
nut
fret
position marker
neck
heel
rose
body
bridge
soundboard

VIOLIN FAMILY

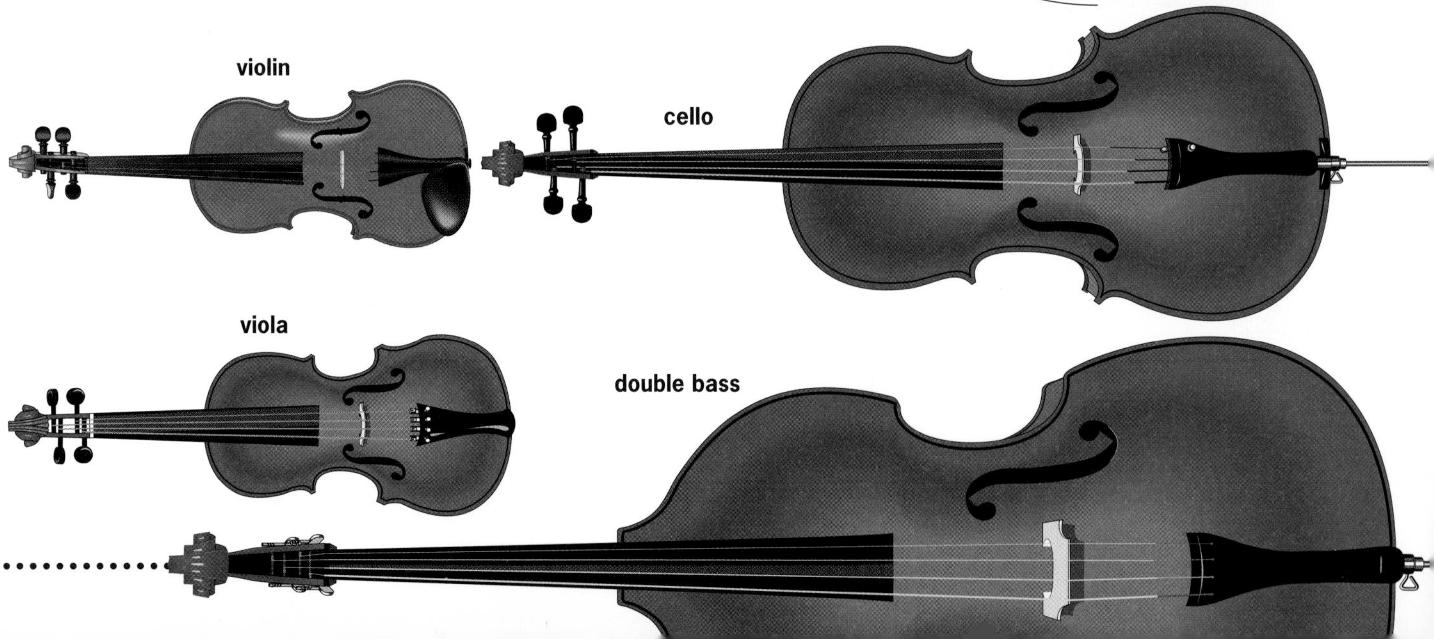
violin
cello
viola
double bass

electric guitar

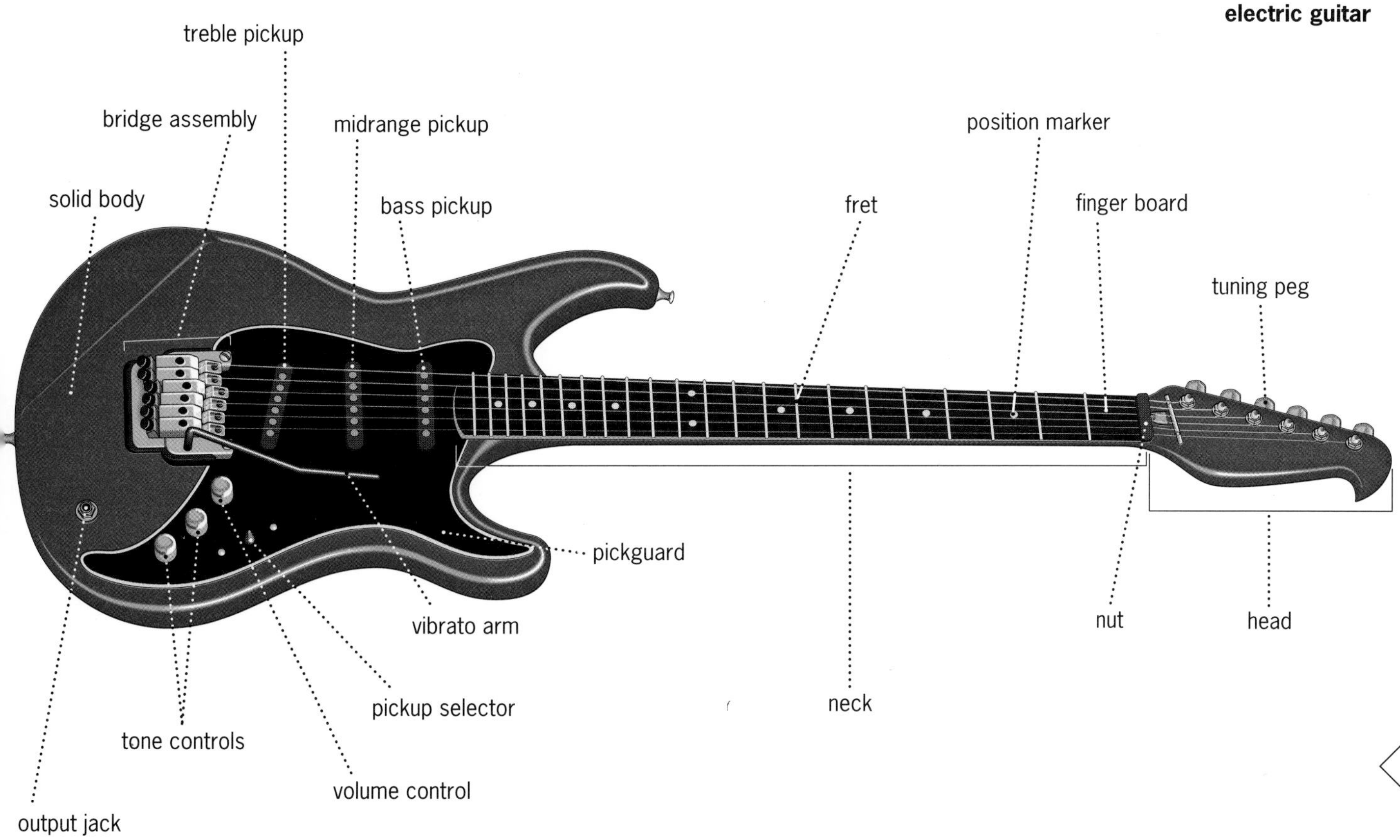
treble pickup
bridge assembly
midrange pickup
position marker
solid body
bass pickup
fret
finger board
tuning peg
pickguard
vibrato arm
nut
head
pickup selector
neck
tone controls
volume control
output jack

bass guitar

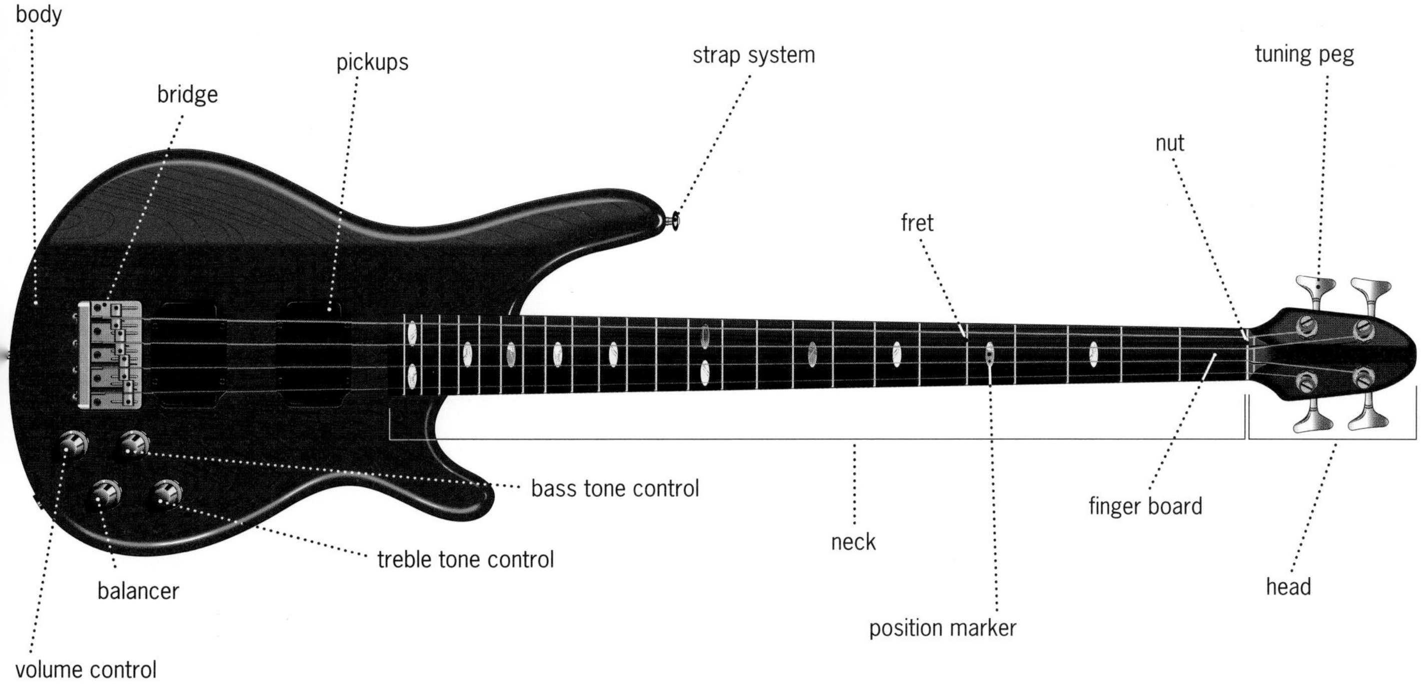
body
pickups
strap system
tuning peg
bridge
nut
fret
bass tone control
finger board
treble tone control
neck
balancer
head
position marker
volume control

WIND INSTRUMENTS

trumpet

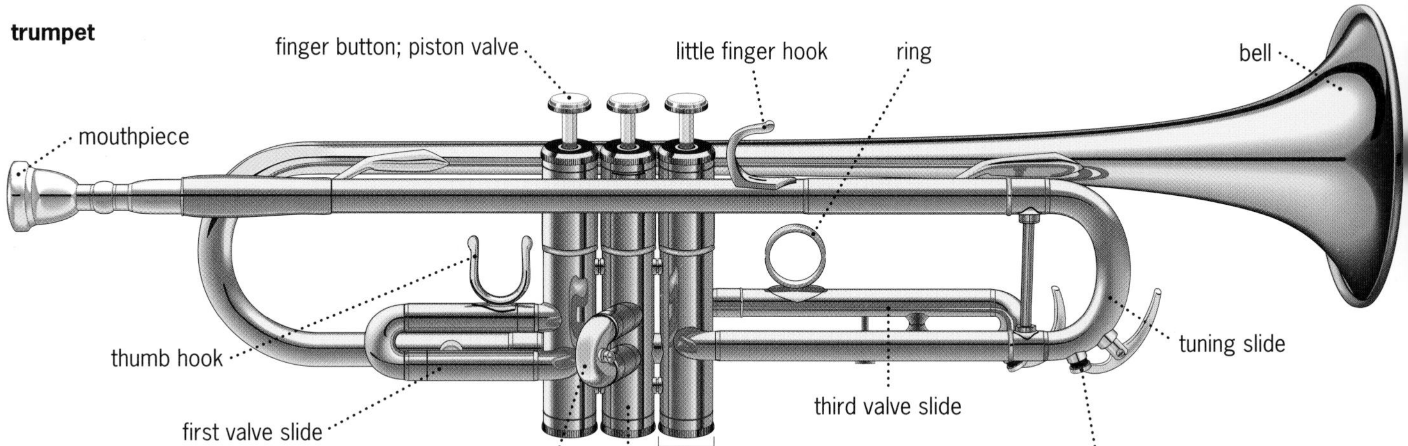
finger button; piston valve
little finger hook
ring
bell
mouthpiece
thumb hook
tuning slide
first valve slide
third valve slide
second valve slide
valve
water key
valve casing

BRASS FAMILY

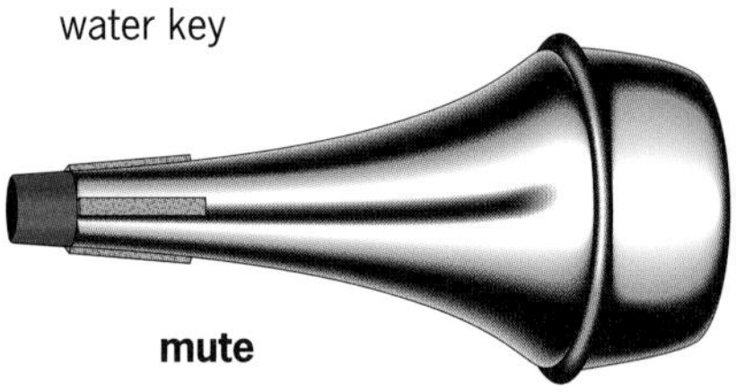

mute

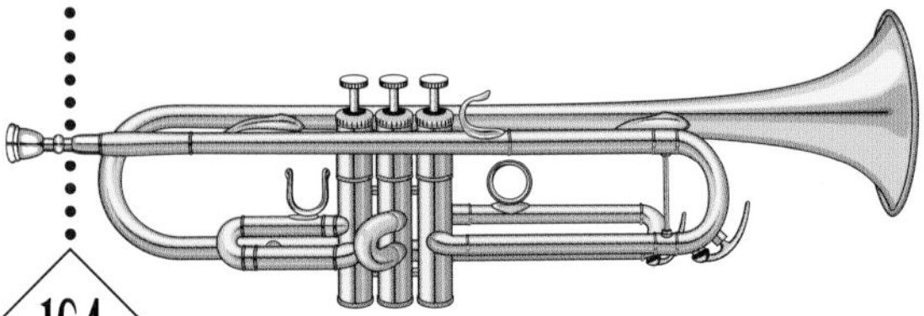

trumpet

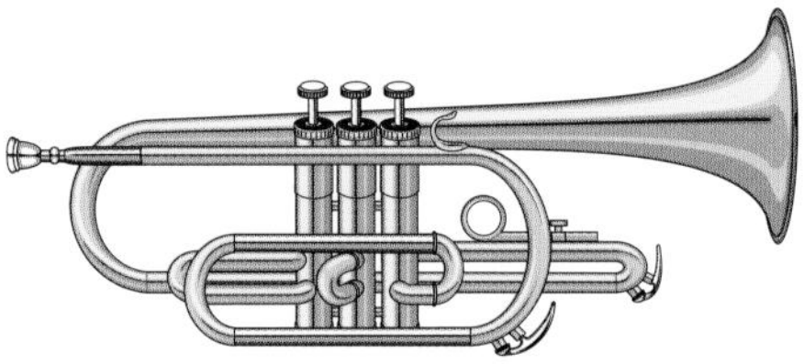

cornet

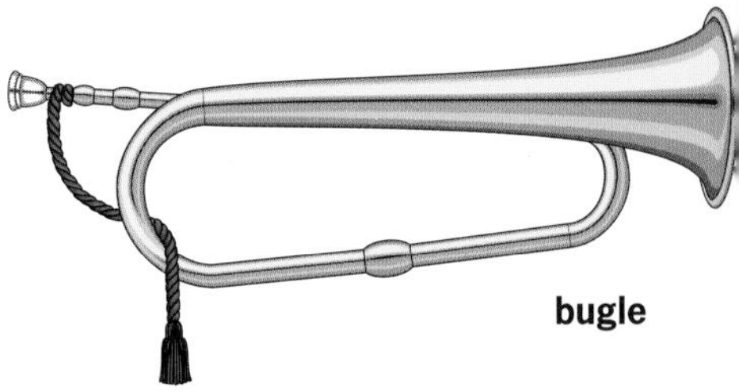

bugle

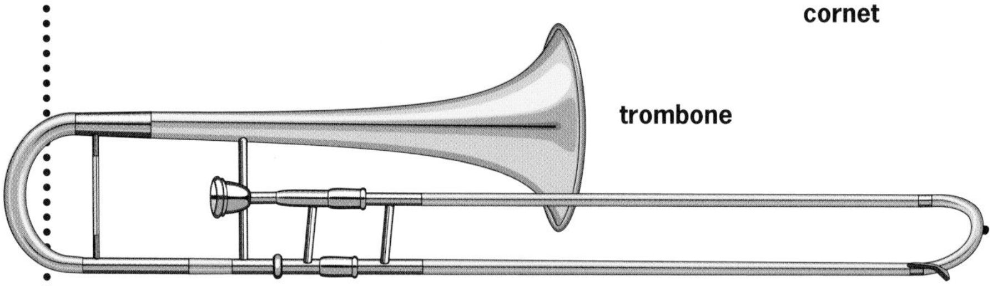

trombone

tuba

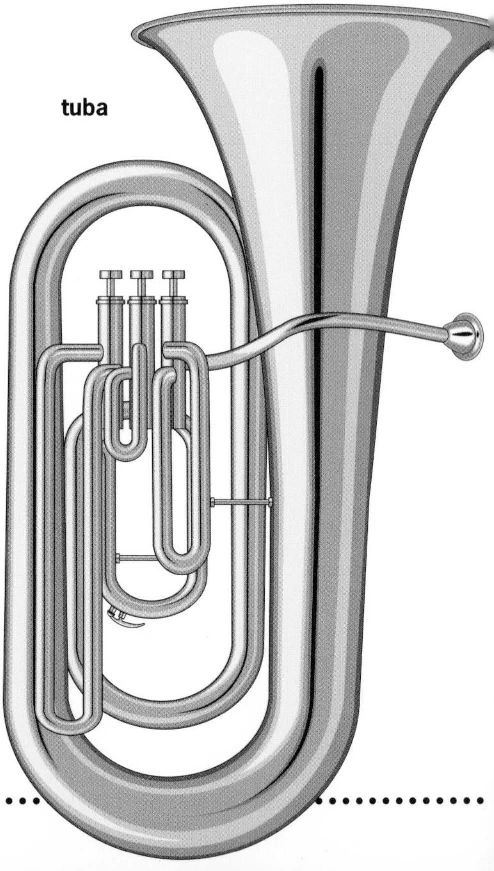

saxhorn

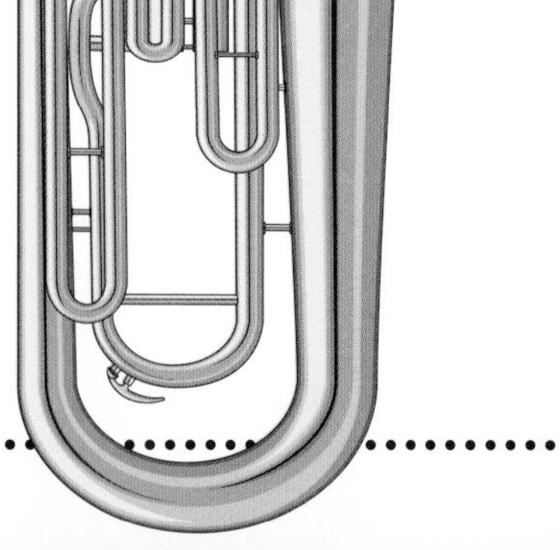

French horn

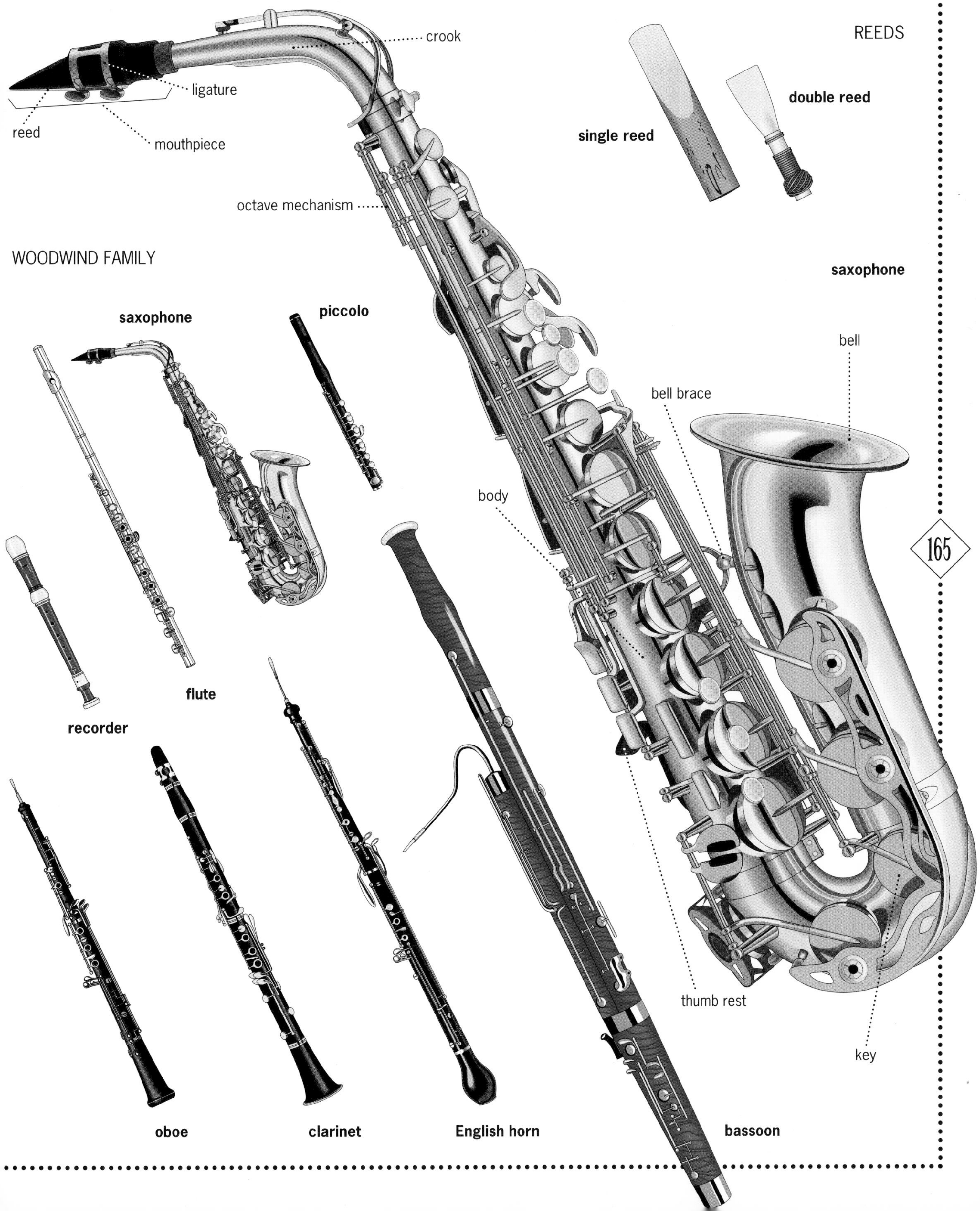
crook
ligature
reed
mouthpiece
octave mechanism
REEDS
double reed
single reed
WOODWIND FAMILY
saxophone
saxophone
piccolo
bell
bell brace
body
flute
recorder
thumb rest
key
oboe
clarinet
English horn
bassoon

PERCUSSION INSTRUMENTS

drums

cymbal
tom-toms
Charleston cymbal; hi-hat cymbal
batter head
snare drum
tripod stand
bass drum
stand
pedal
mallet
tenor drum

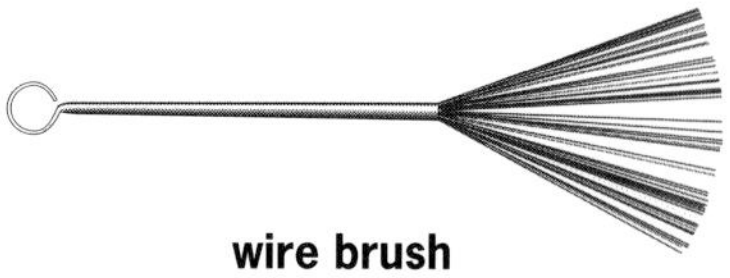

wire brush

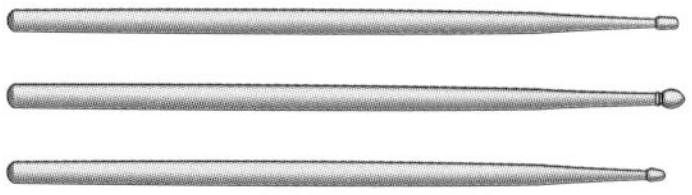

sticks

mallets

triangle

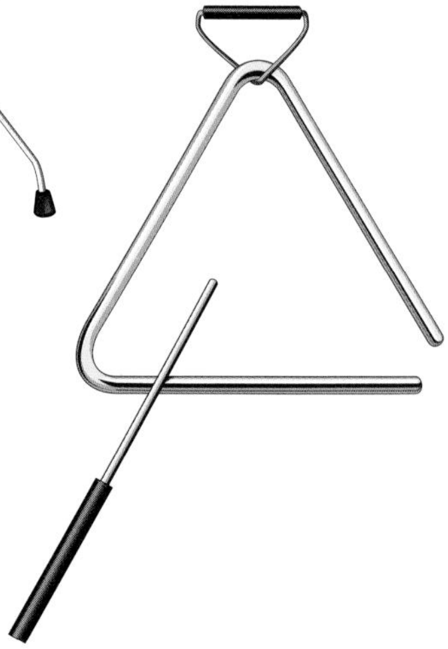

sistrum

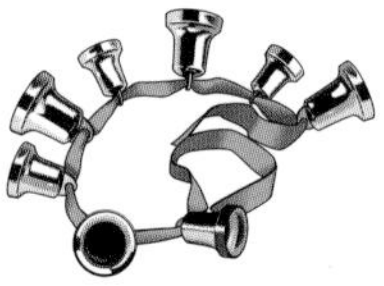

set of bells

sleigh bells

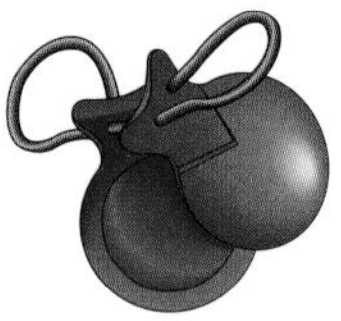

castanets

bongos

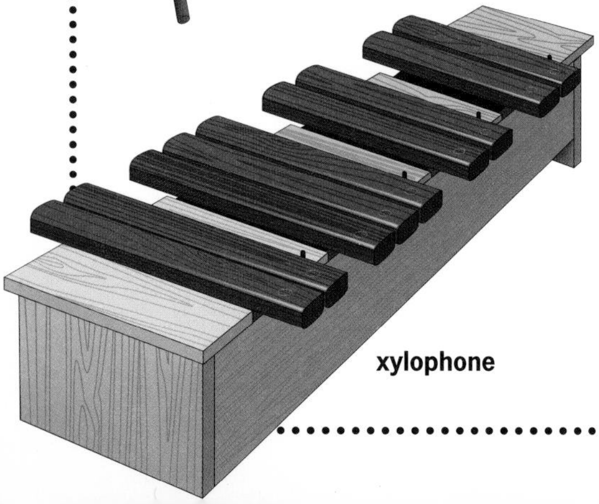

xylophone

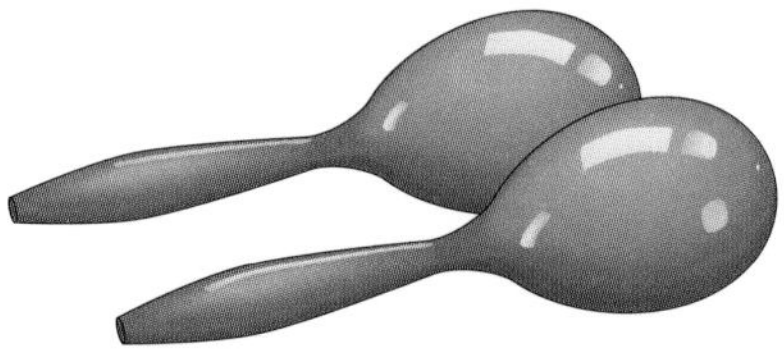

maracas

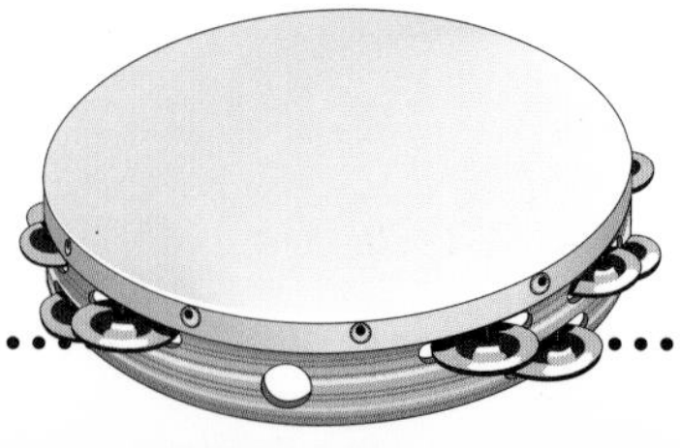

tambourine

SYMPHONY ORCHESTRA

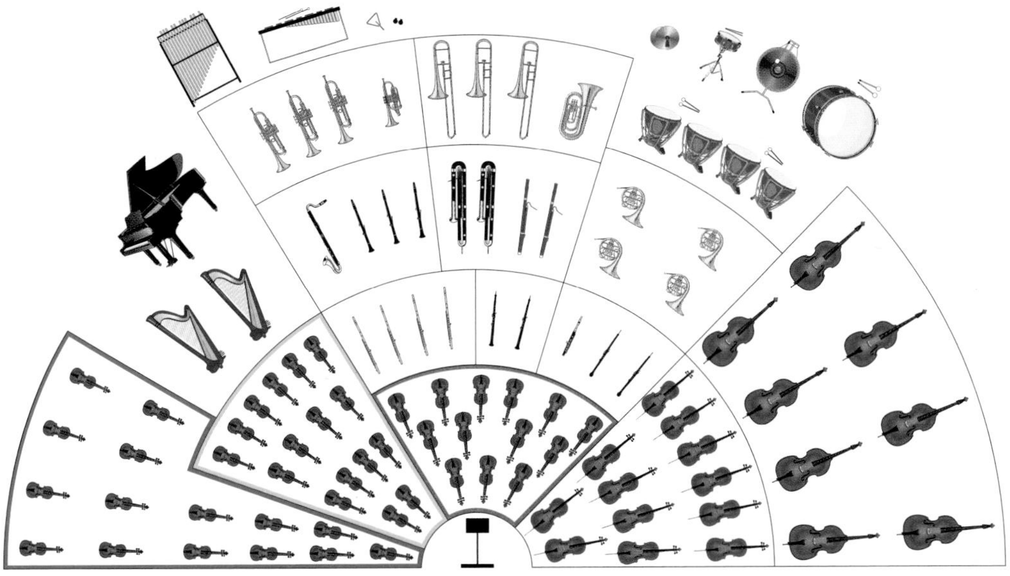
conductor's podium

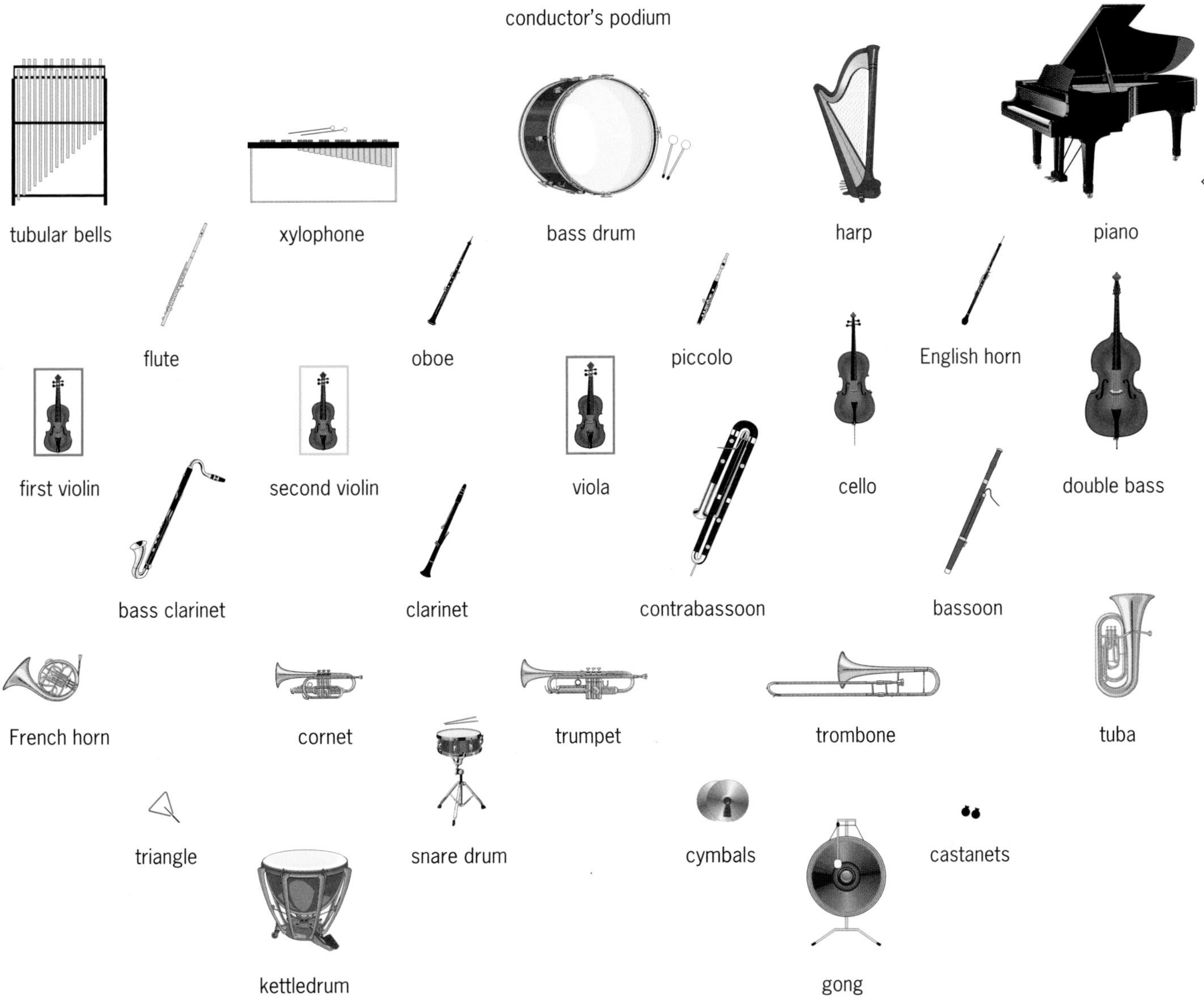
tubular bells
xylophone
bass drum
harp
piano
flute
oboe
piccolo
English horn
first violin
second violin
viola
cello
double bass
bass clarinet
clarinet
contrabassoon
bassoon
French horn
cornet
trumpet
trombone
tuba
triangle
snare drum
cymbals
castanets
kettledrum
gong

BASEBALL

fielder's glove

web
strap
thumb
finger
palm
heel
lace

bat

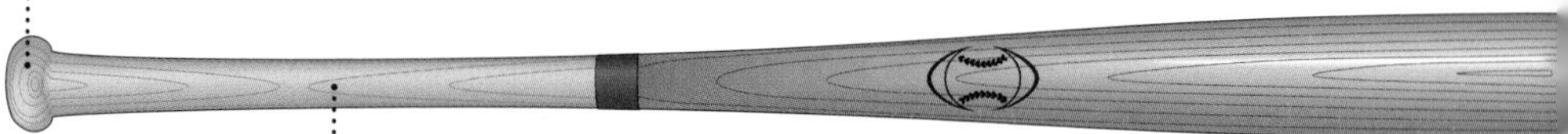
knob
handle
hitting area

baseball

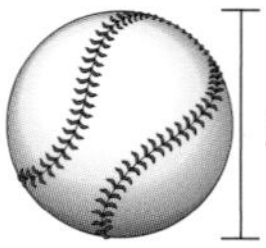
2 9/10 in

batter

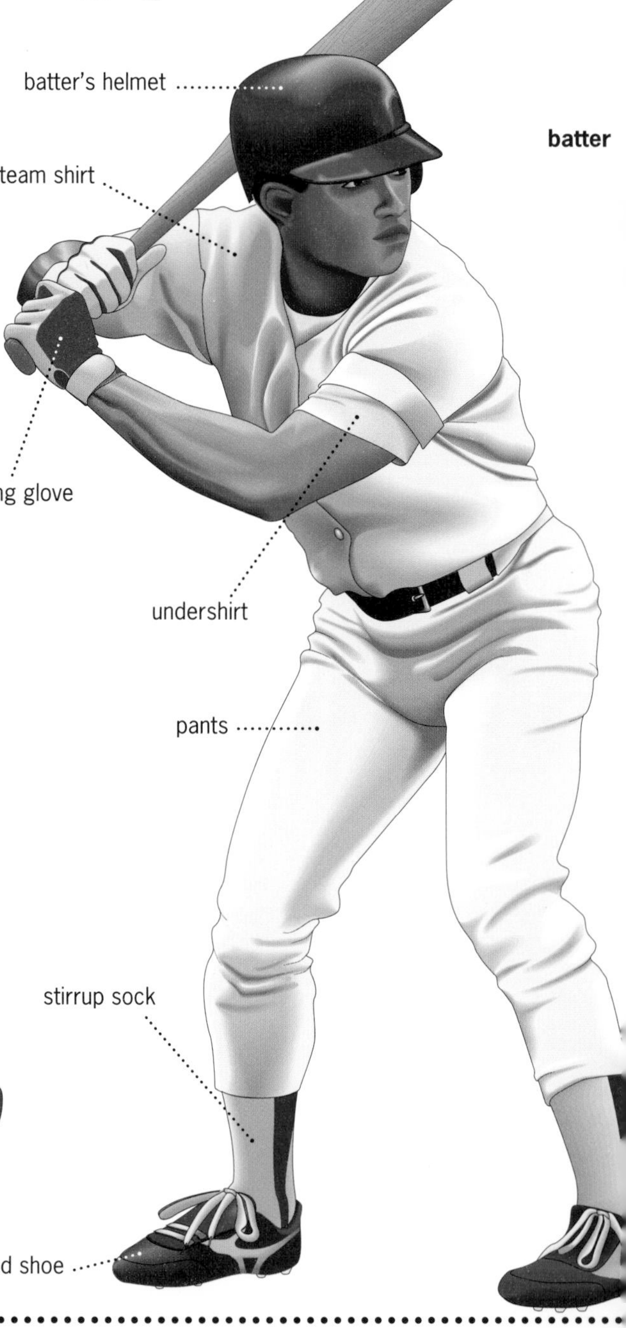
batter's helmet
team shirt
batting glove
undershirt
pants
stirrup sock
spiked shoe

catcher

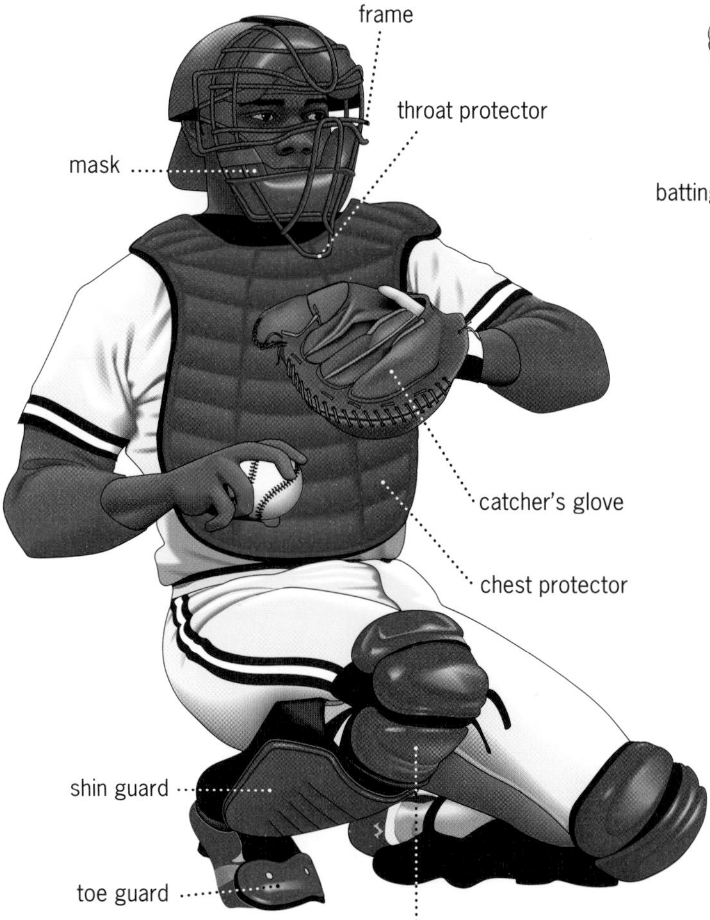
frame
throat protector
mask
catcher's glove
chest protector
shin guard
toe guard
knee pad

field

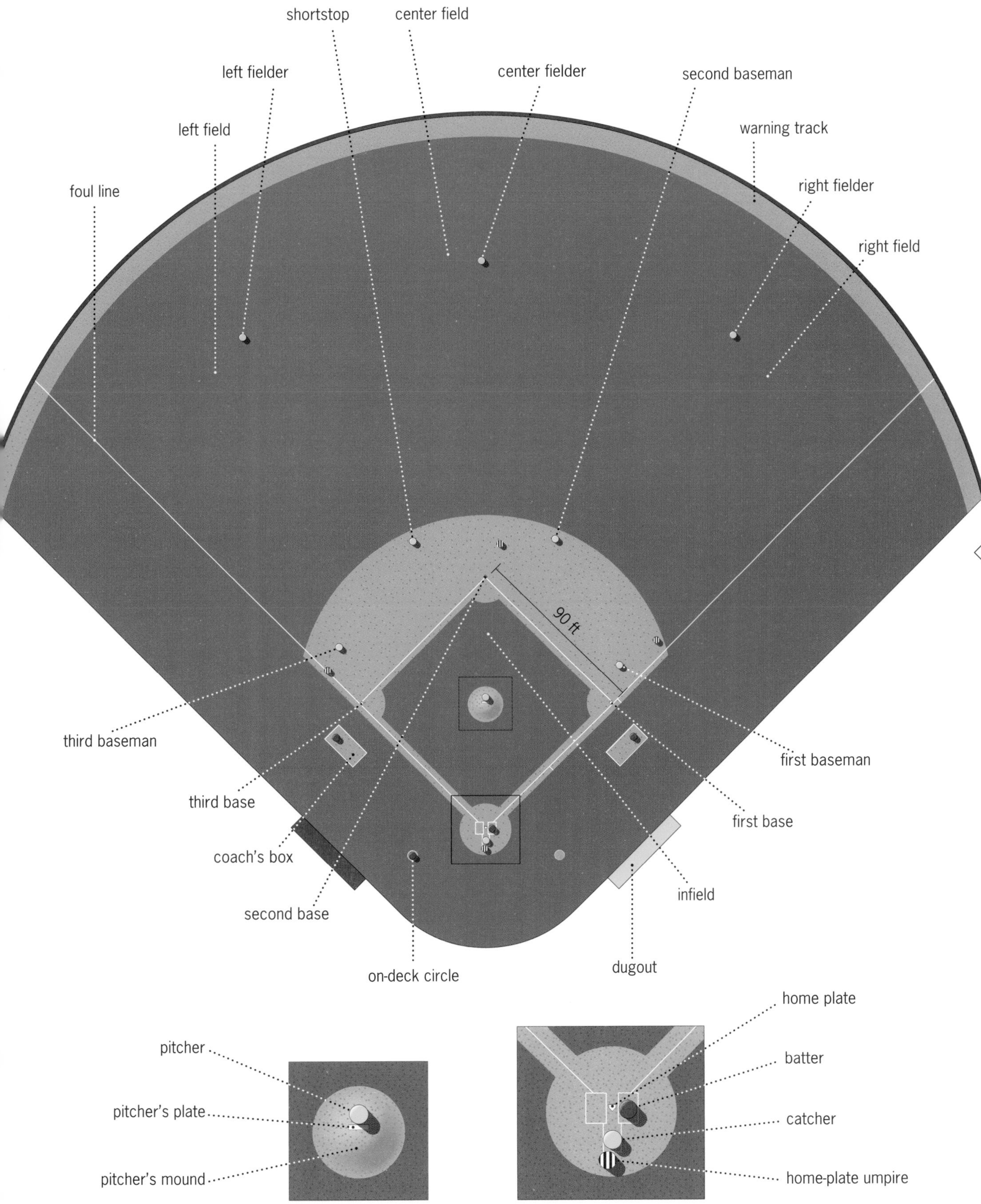
shortstop
center field
left fielder
center fielder
second baseman
left field
warning track
foul line
right fielder
right field
90 ft
third baseman
first baseman
third base
first base
coach's box
infield
second base
on-deck circle
dugout
home plate
pitcher
batter
pitcher's plate
catcher
pitcher's mound
home-plate umpire

FOOTBALL

football player

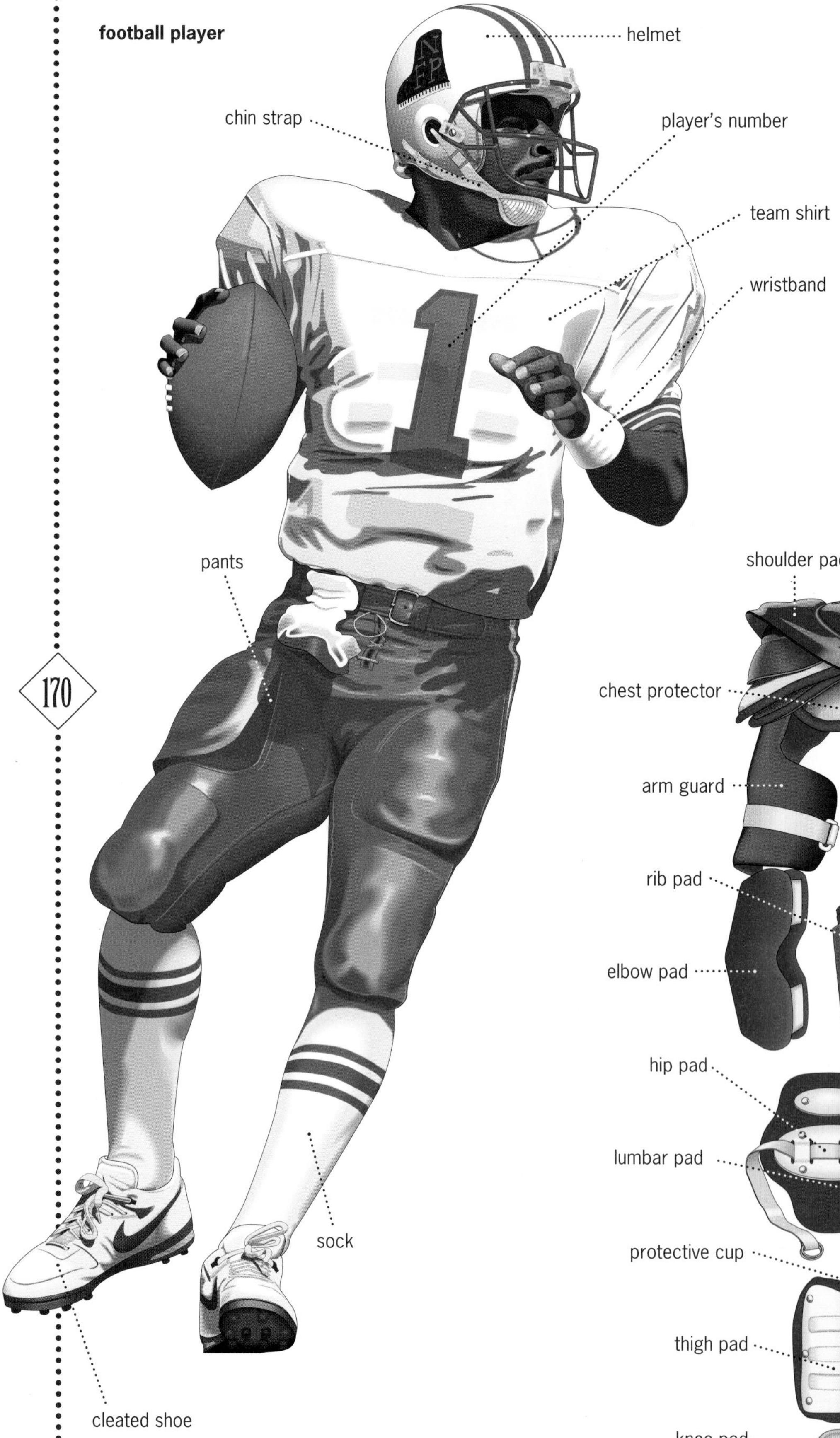
helmet
chin strap
player's number
team shirt
wristband
pants
sock
cleated shoe

football

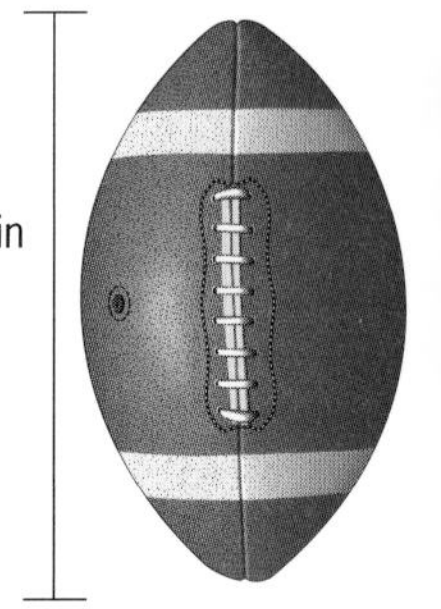
11 – 11 ¼ in

protective equipment

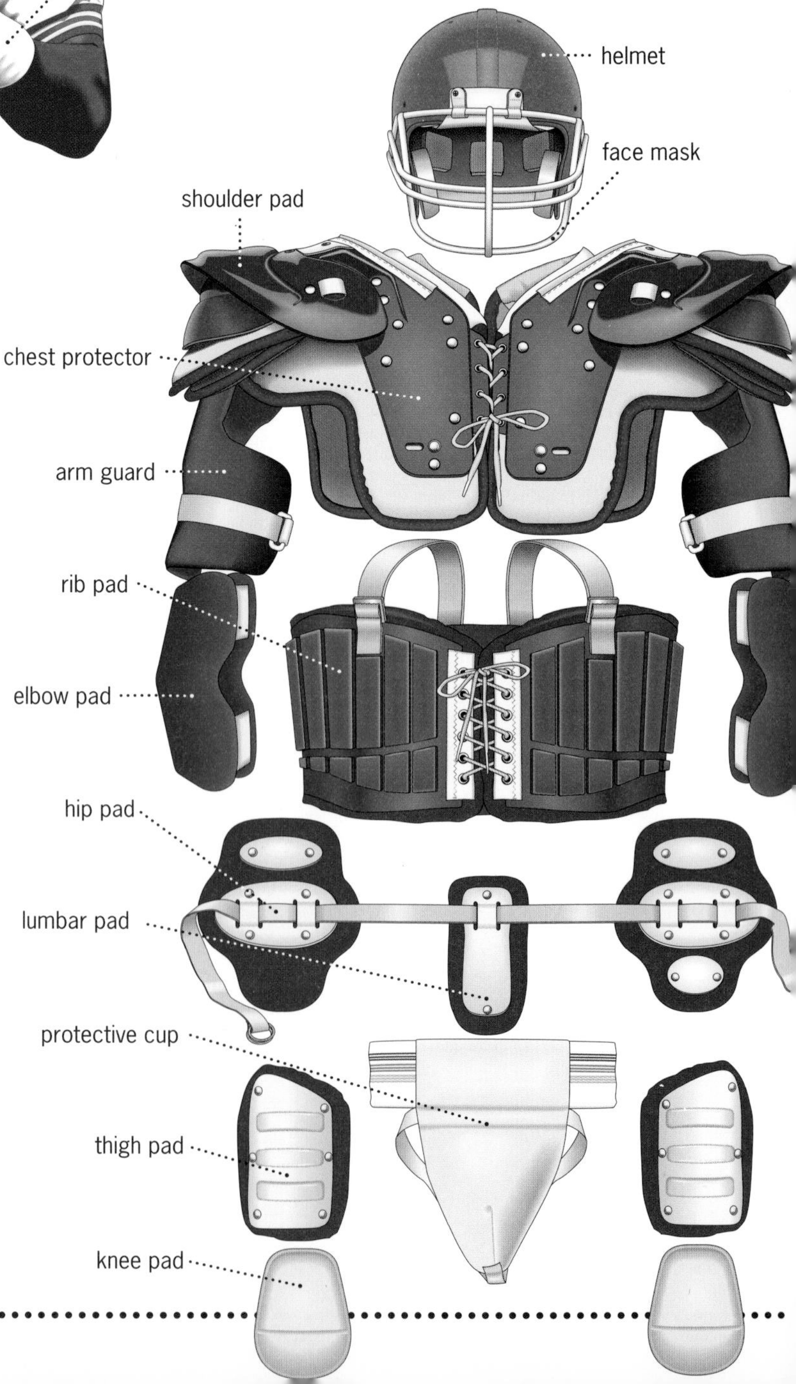
helmet
face mask
shoulder pad
chest protector
arm guard
rib pad
elbow pad
hip pad
lumbar pad
protective cup
thigh pad
knee pad

scrimmage

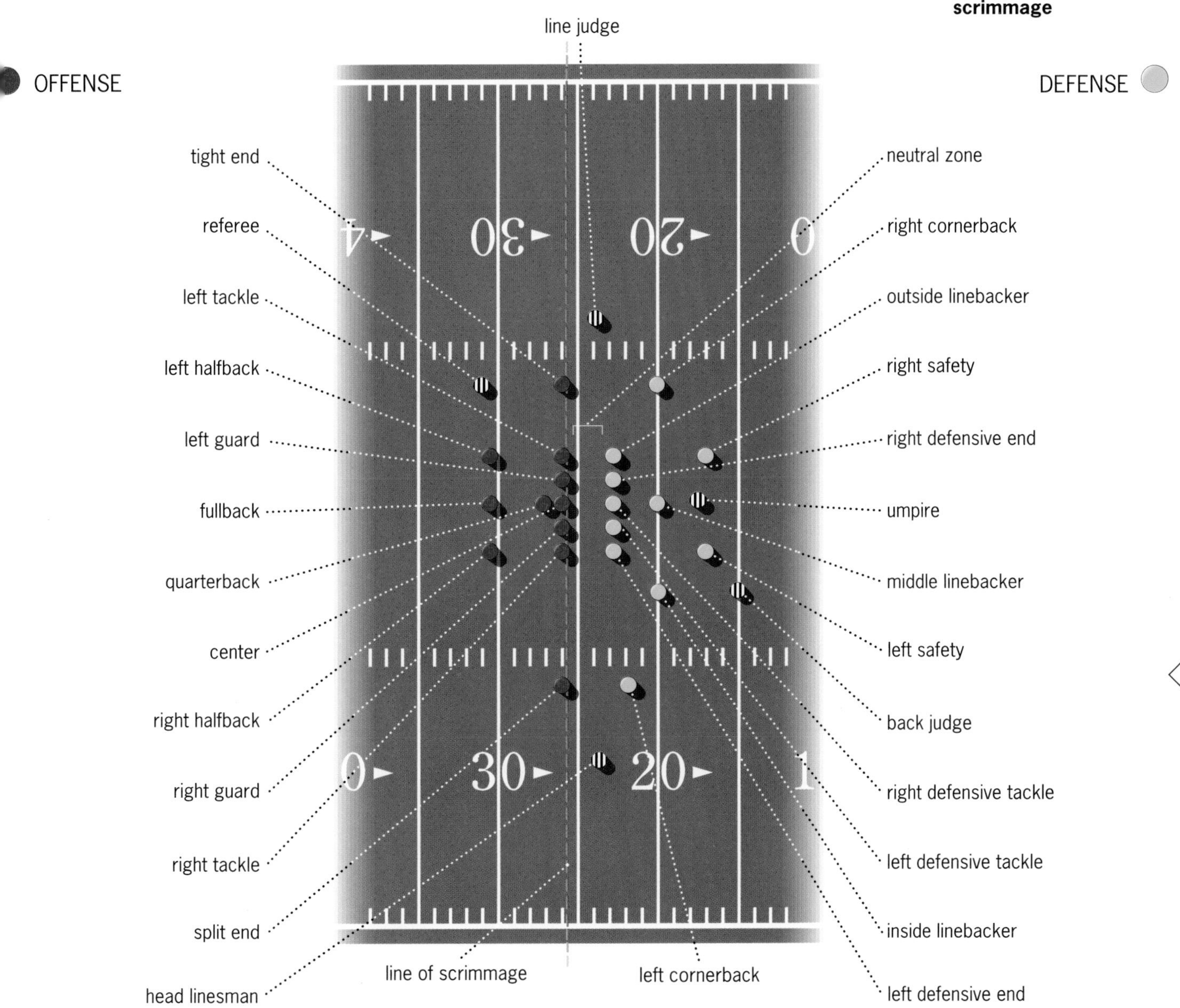
line judge
OFFENSE
DEFENSE
tight end
referee
left tackle
left halfback
left guard
fullback
quarterback
center
right halfback
right guard
right tackle
split end
head linesman
line of scrimmage
left cornerback
neutral zone
right cornerback
outside linebacker
right safety
right defensive end
umpire
middle linebacker
left safety
back judge
right defensive tackle
left defensive tackle
inside linebacker
left defensive end
30
20

playing field for football

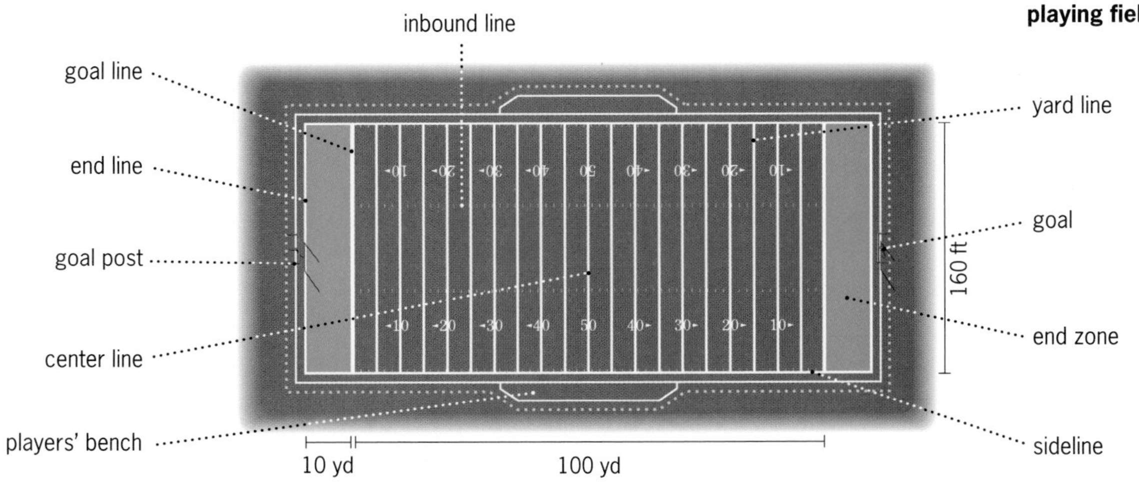
inbound line
goal line
end line
goal post
center line
players' bench
yard line
goal
160 ft
end zone
sideline
10 yd
100 yd

SOCCER

soccer player

team shirt
shorts
shin guard
soccer shoe
interchangeable studs

soccer ball

8 3/5 - 8 9/10 in

playing field

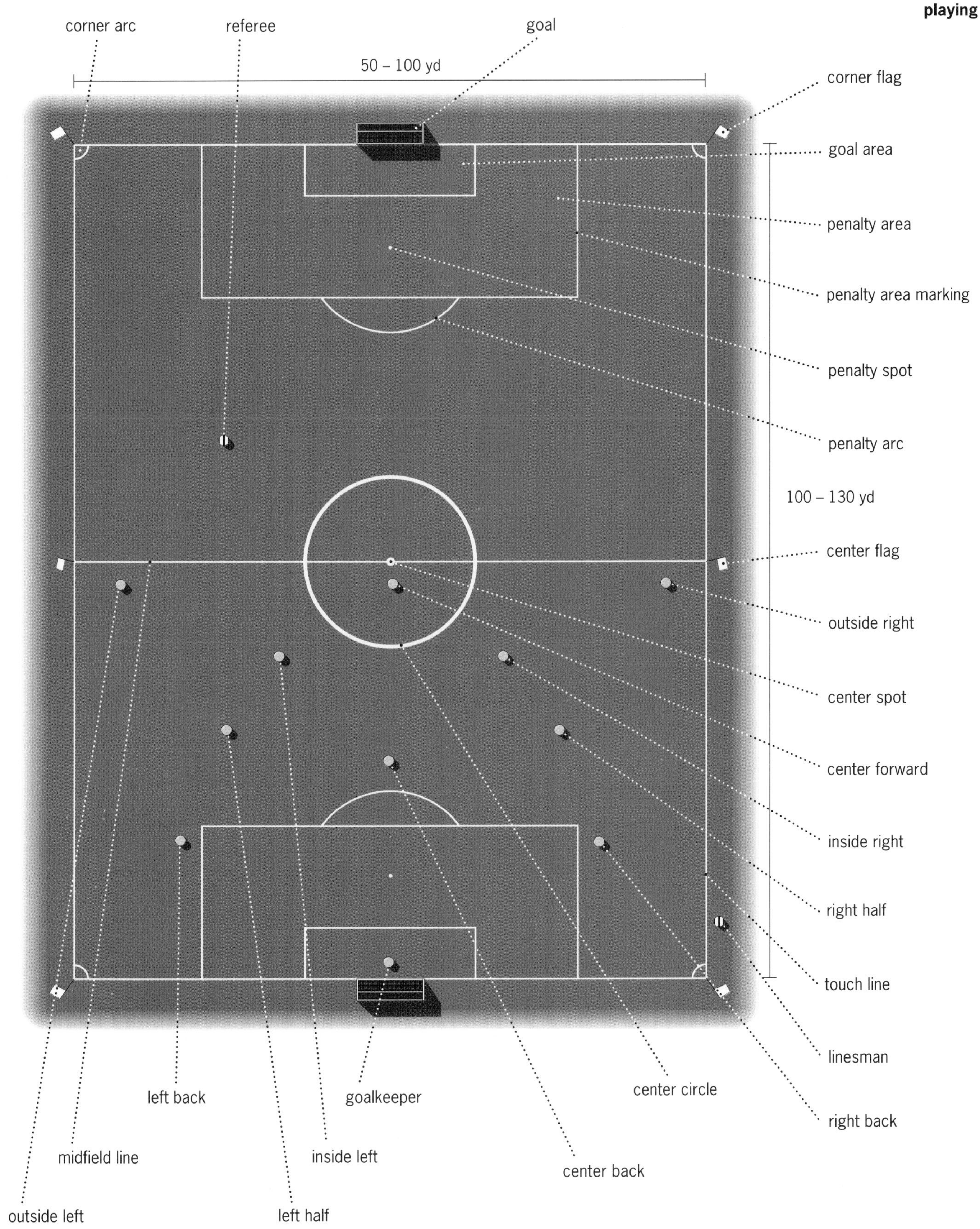
corner arc
referee
goal
50 – 100 yd
corner flag
goal area
penalty area
penalty area marking
penalty spot
penalty arc
100 – 130 yd
center flag
outside right
center spot
center forward
inside right
right half
touch line
linesman
right back
center circle
center back
goalkeeper
left back
inside left
midfield line
outside left
left half

VOLLEYBALL

court

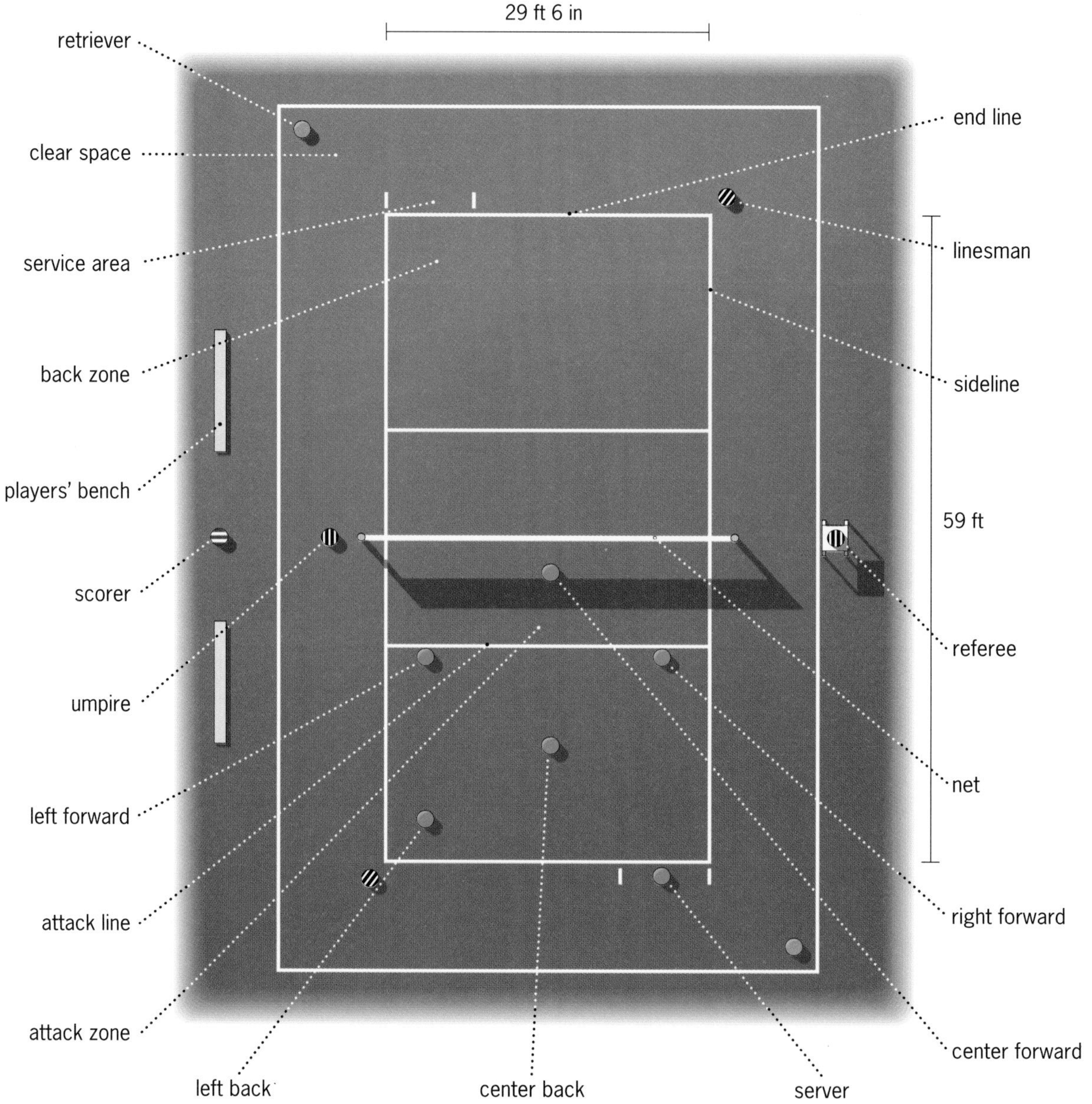
29 ft 6 in
retriever
clear space
service area
back zone
players' bench
scorer
umpire
left forward
attack line
attack zone
left back
center back
server
center forward
right forward
net
referee
59 ft
sideline
linesman
end line

net

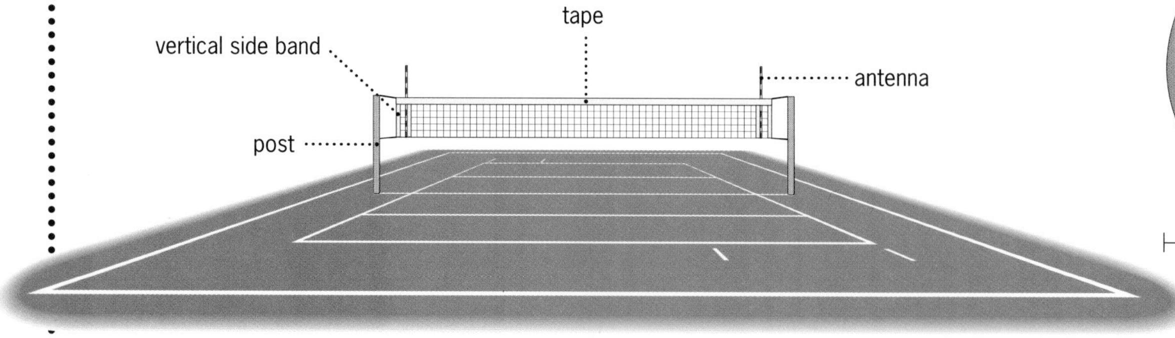
tape
vertical side band
antenna
post

volleyball

8 ¼ in

FIELD HOCKEY

playing field

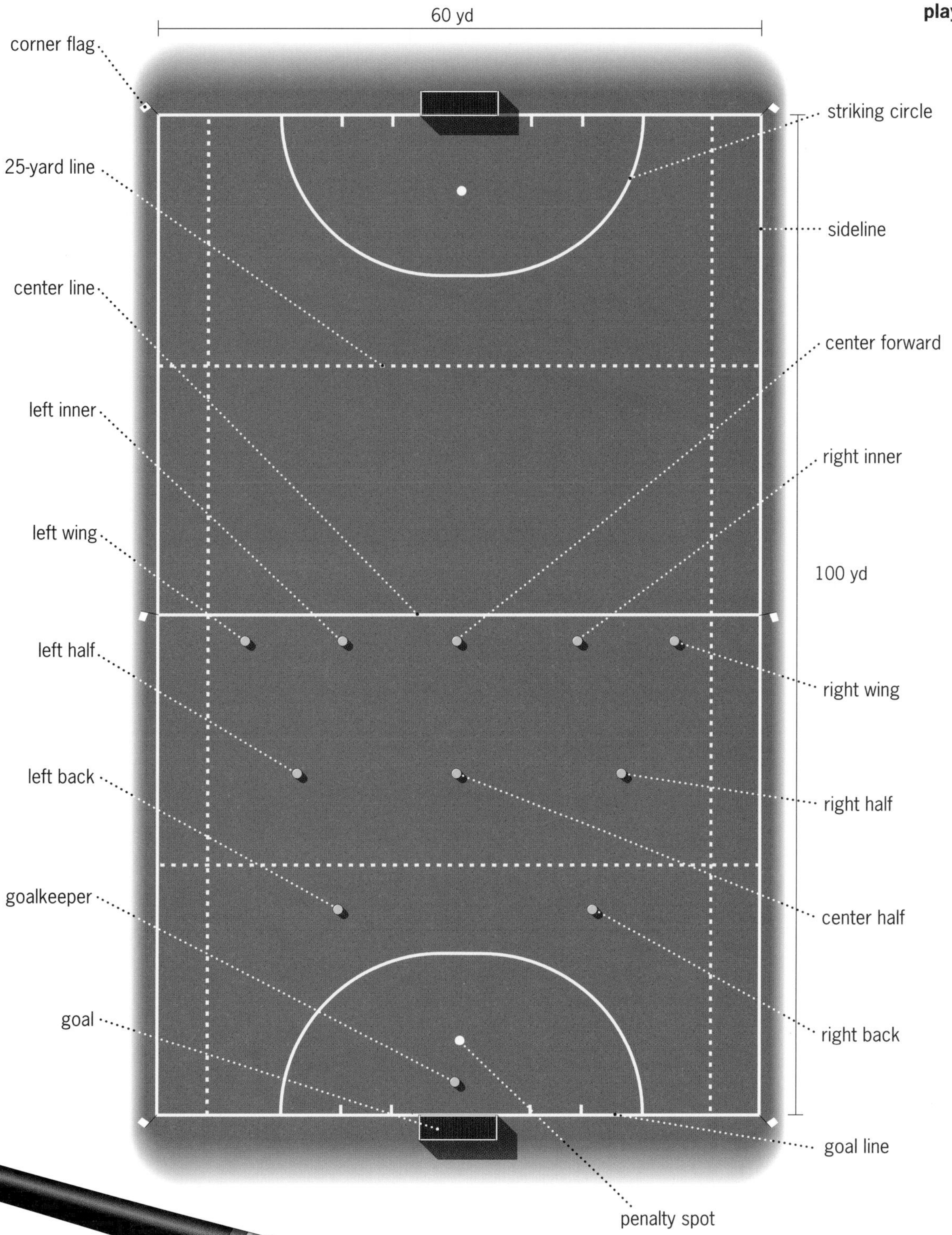
60 yd
100 yd
corner flag
25-yard line
center line
left inner
left wing
left half
left back
goalkeeper
goal
striking circle
sideline
center forward
right inner
right wing
right half
center half
right back
goal line
penalty spot

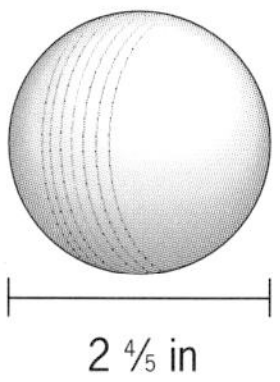
2 ⅘ in

hockey ball

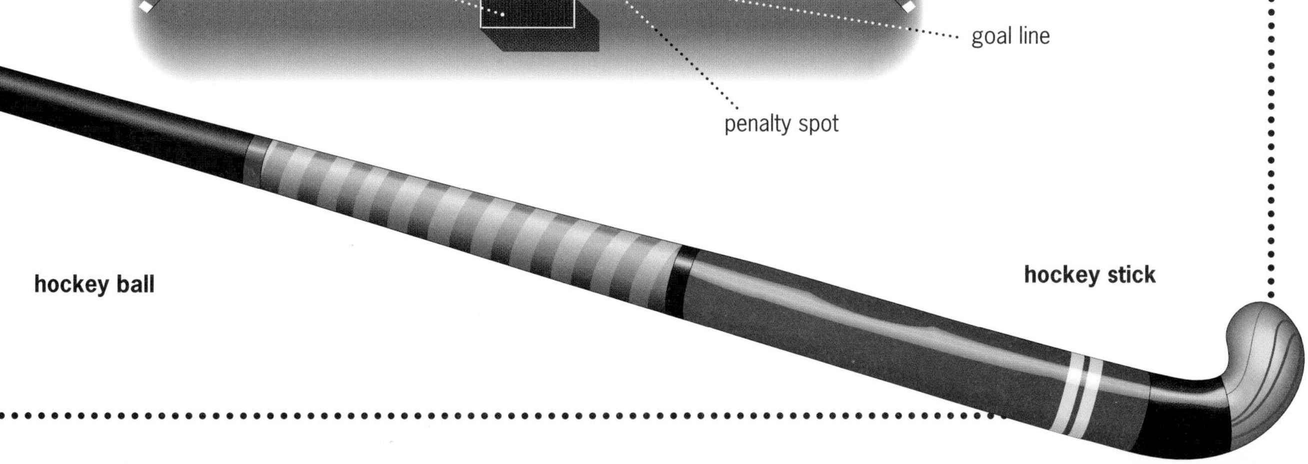

hockey stick

ICE HOCKEY

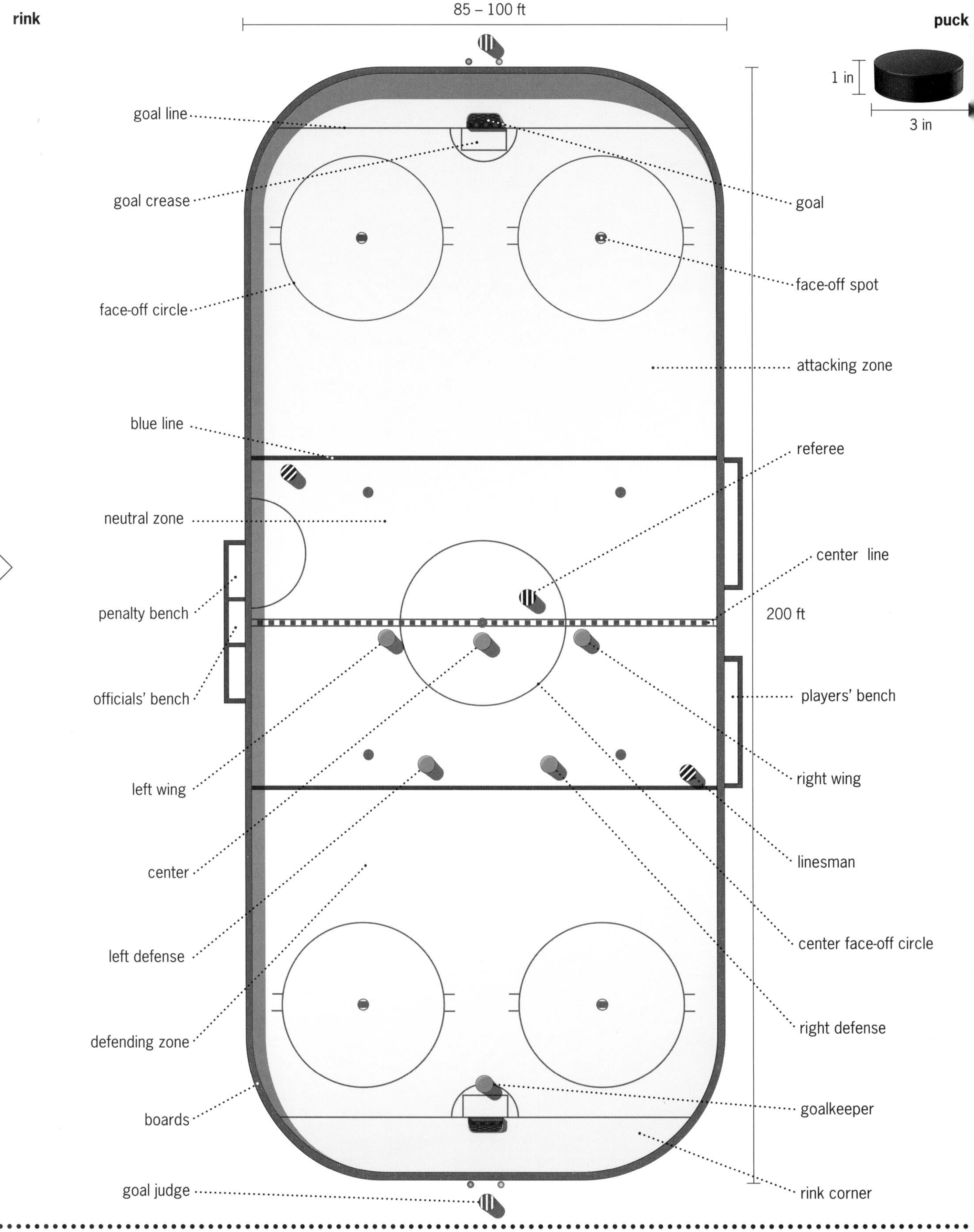
rink
85 – 100 ft
goal line
goal crease
face-off circle
blue line
neutral zone
penalty bench
officials' bench
left wing
center
left defense
defending zone
boards
goal judge
goal
face-off spot
attacking zone
referee
center line
200 ft
players' bench
right wing
linesman
center face-off circle
right defense
goalkeeper
rink corner
puck
1 in
3 in

player's stick

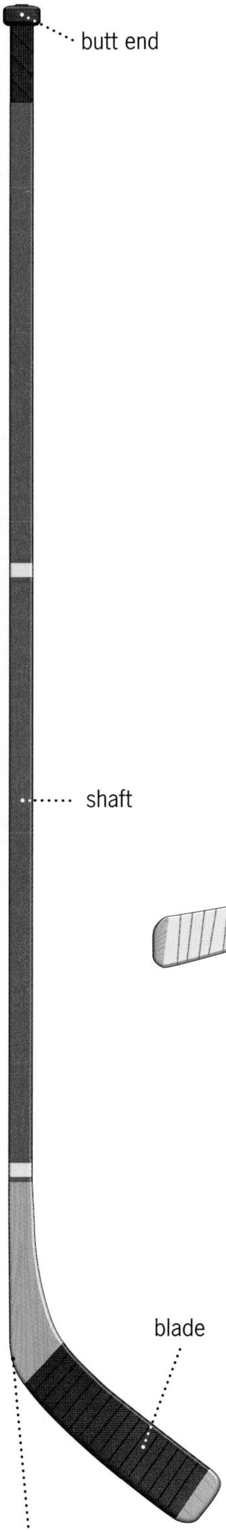
butt end
shaft
blade
heel

ice hockey player

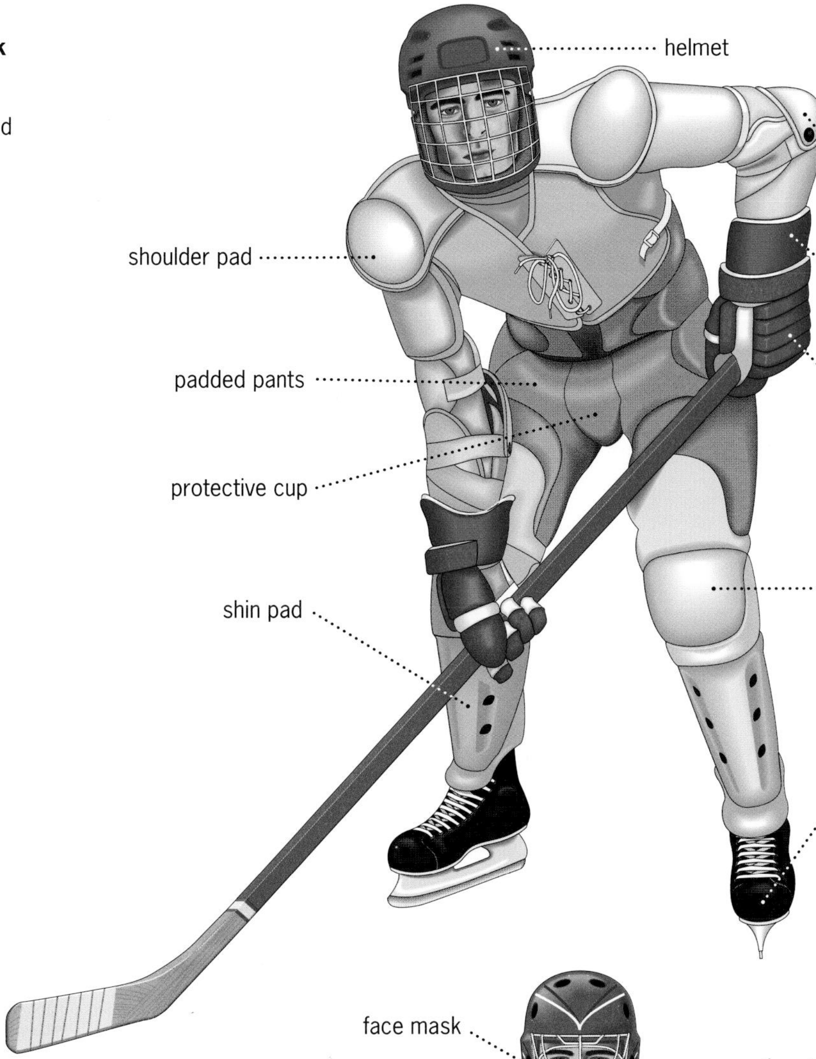
helmet
elbow pad
shoulder pad
cuff
padded pants
glove
protective cup
knee pad
shin pad
skate

goalkeeper

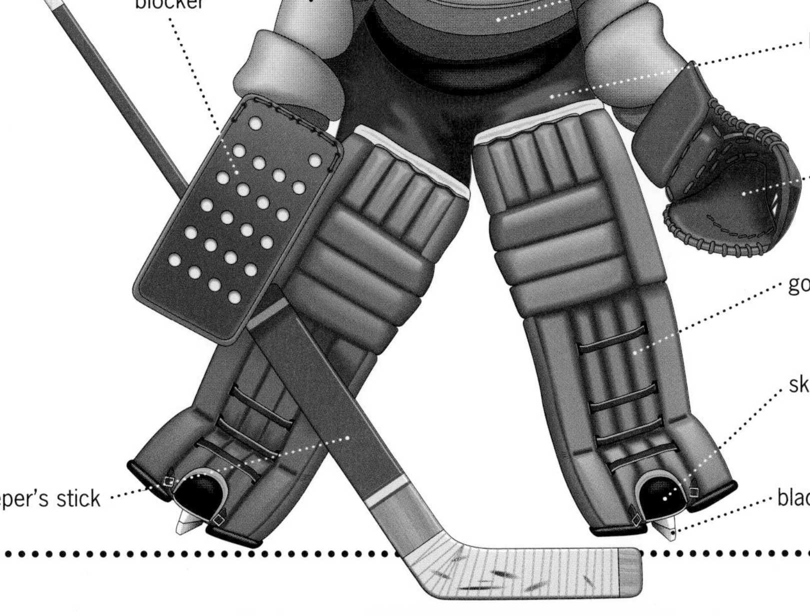
face mask
throat protector
arm pad
body pad
blocker
pants
catching glove
goalkeeper's pad
skate
goalkeeper's stick
blade

BASKETBALL

court

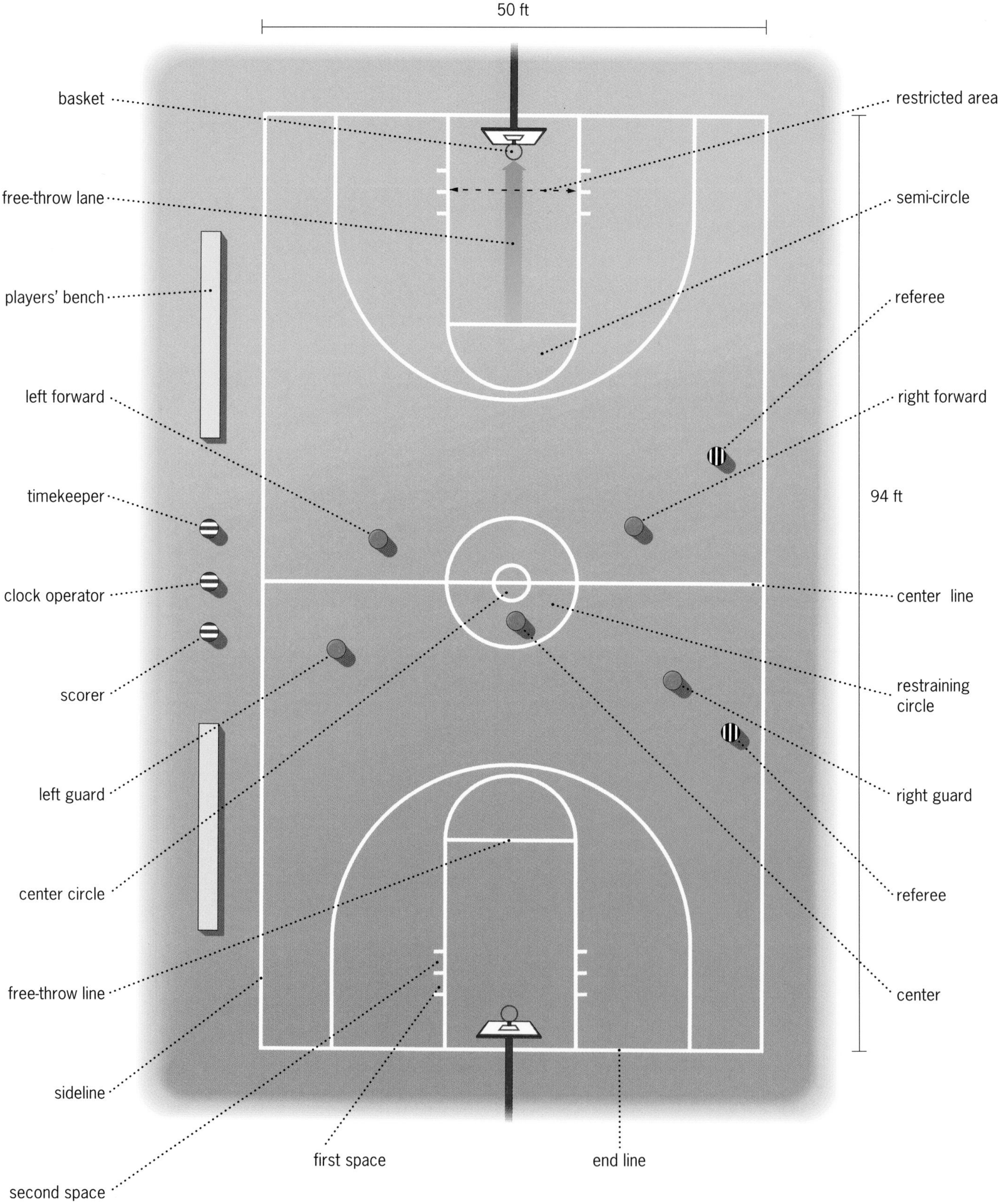
50 ft
basket
free-throw lane
players' bench
left forward
timekeeper
clock operator
scorer
left guard
center circle
free-throw line
sideline
second space
first space
end line
restricted area
semi-circle
referee
right forward
94 ft
center line
restraining circle
right guard
referee
center

basket

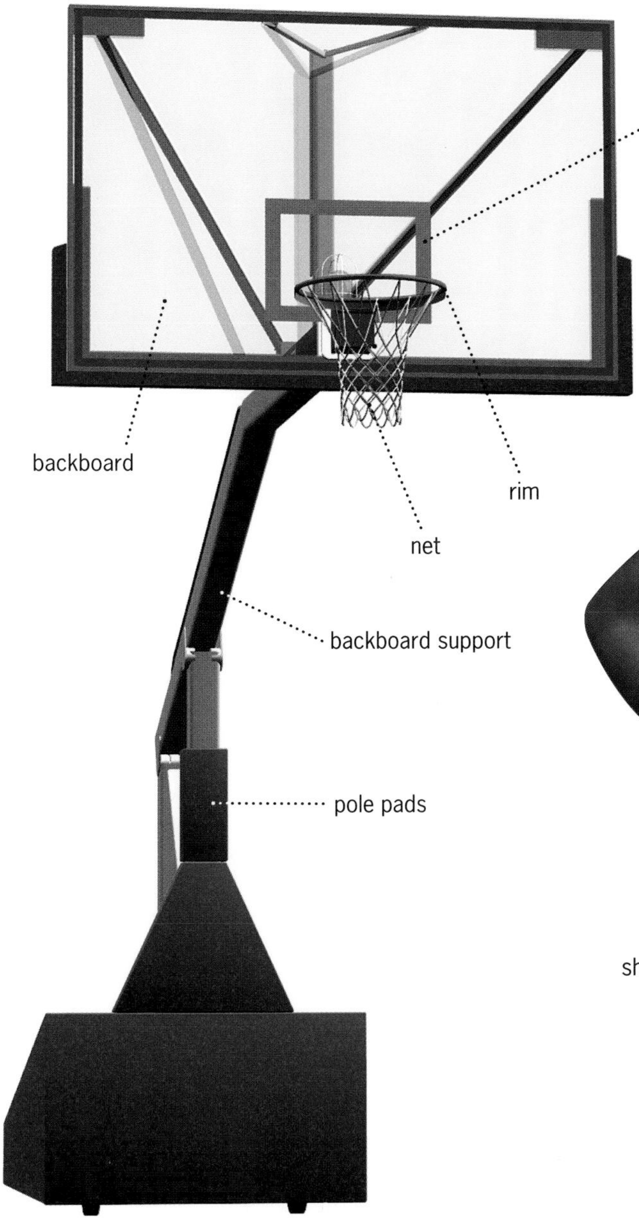
target rectangle
backboard
rim
net
backboard support
pole pads

basketball player

shirt
shorts
basketball
number
sneakers

basketball

9 9/16 in

TENNIS

court

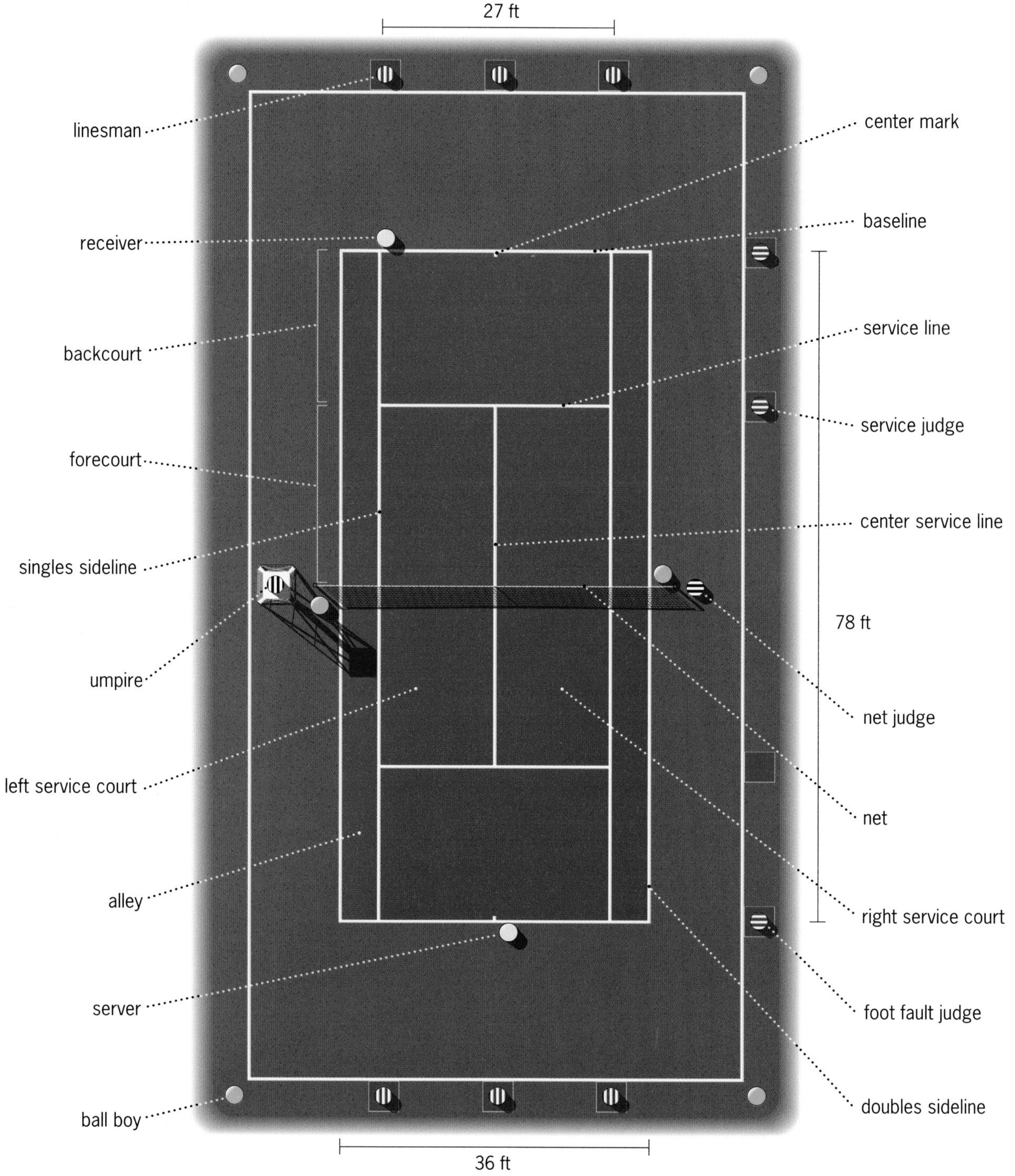
27 ft
linesman
center mark
receiver
baseline
backcourt
service line
service judge
forecourt
center service line
singles sideline
78 ft
umpire
net judge
left service court
net
alley
right service court
server
foot fault judge
ball boy
doubles sideline
36 ft

net

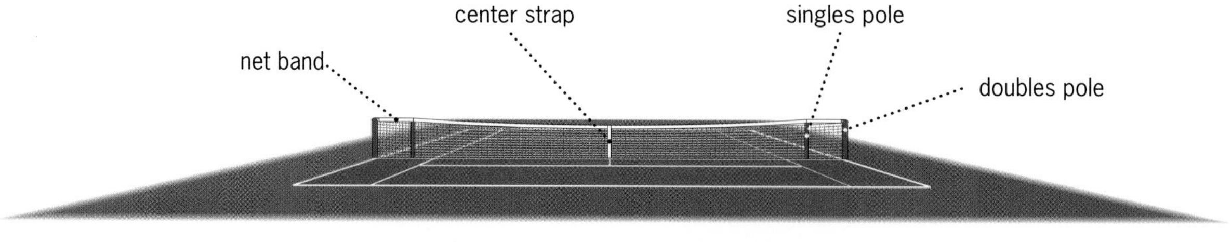
center strap
singles pole
net band
doubles pole

tennis ball

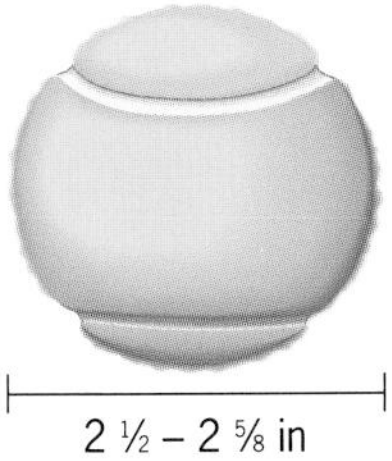
2 ½ – 2 ⅝ in

tennis player

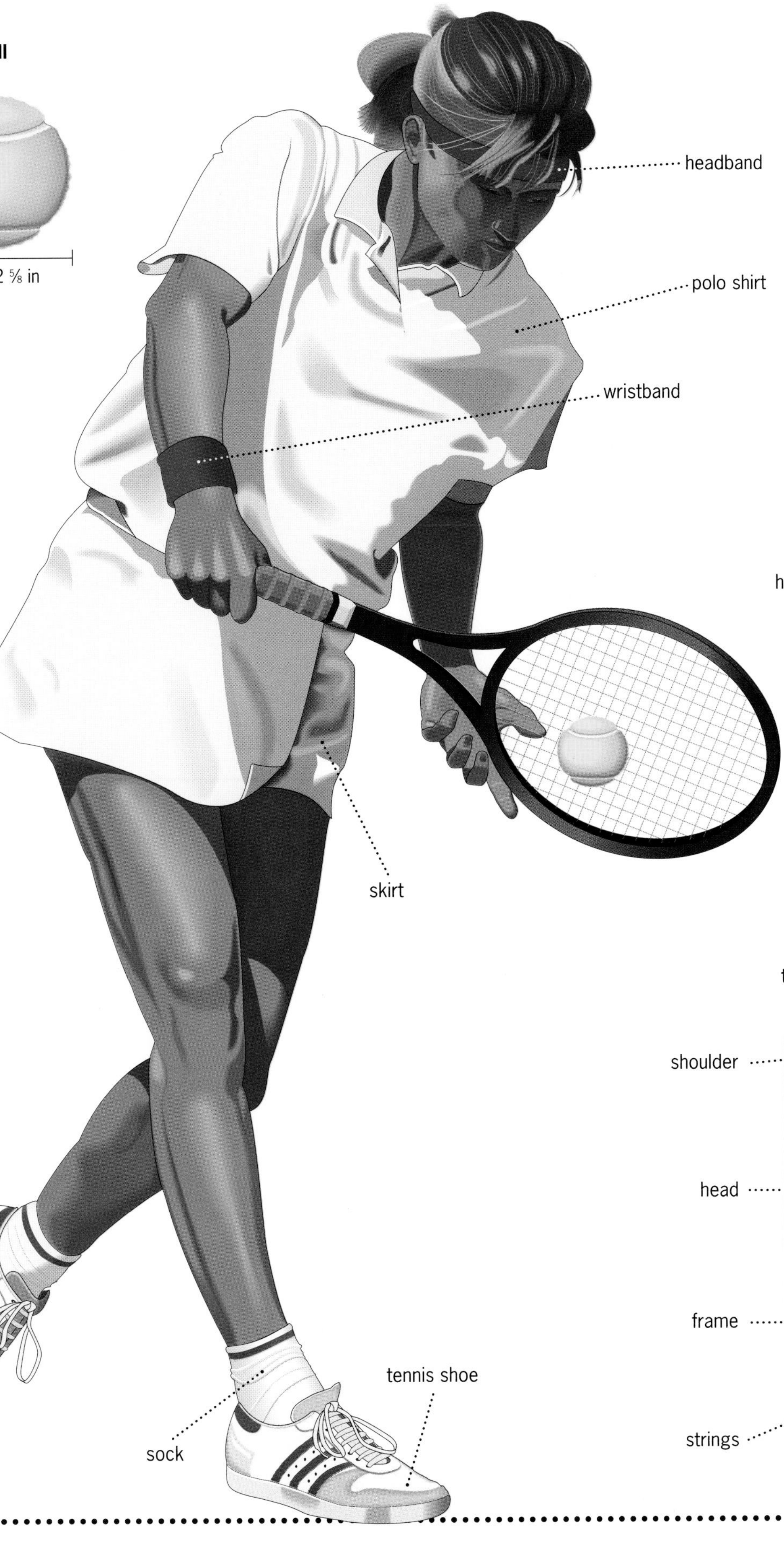
headband
polo shirt
wristband
skirt
sock
tennis shoe

tennis racket

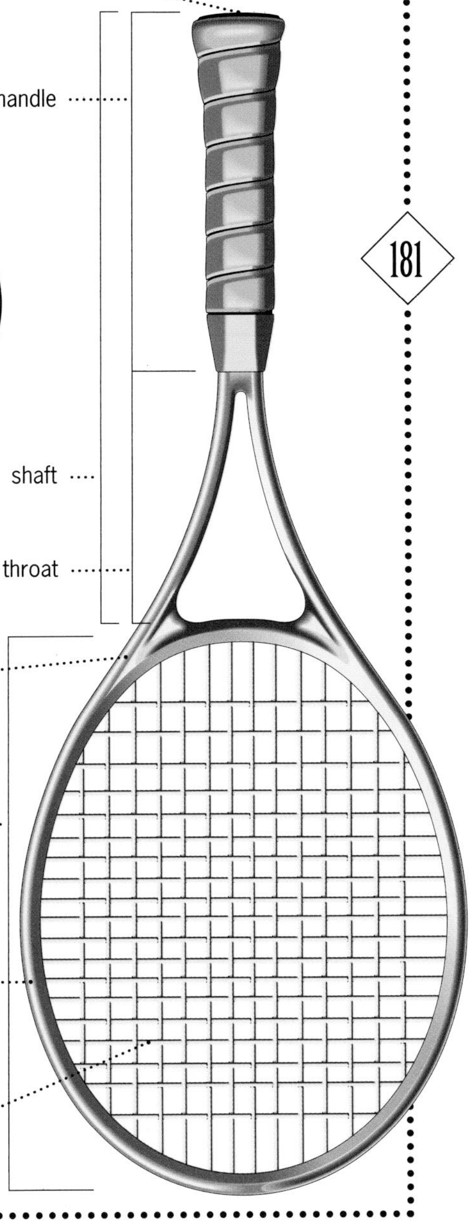
butt
handle
shaft
throat
shoulder
head
frame
strings

SWIMMING

competitive course

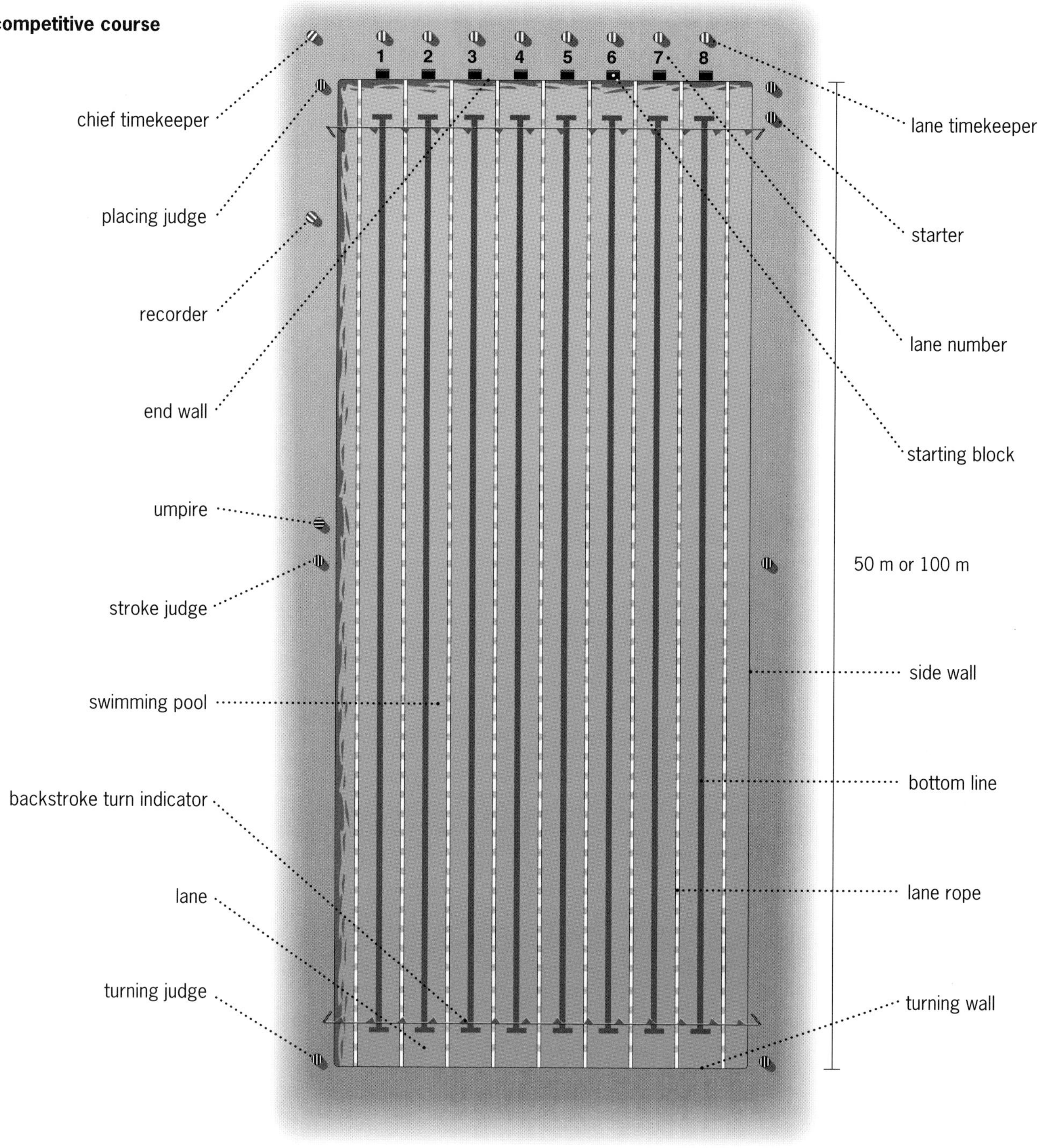
1
2
3
4
5
6
7
8
chief timekeeper
placing judge
recorder
end wall
umpire
stroke judge
swimming pool
backstroke turn indicator
lane
turning judge
lane timekeeper
starter
lane number
starting block
50 m or 100 m
side wall
bottom line
lane rope
turning wall

starting block

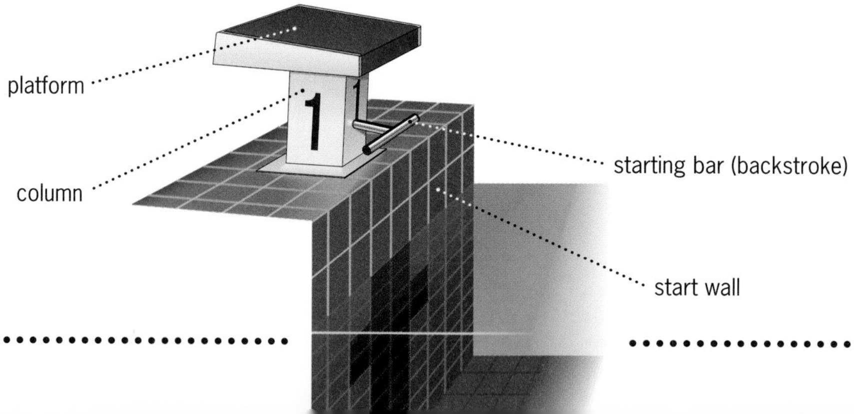
platform
column
1
starting bar (backstroke)
start wall

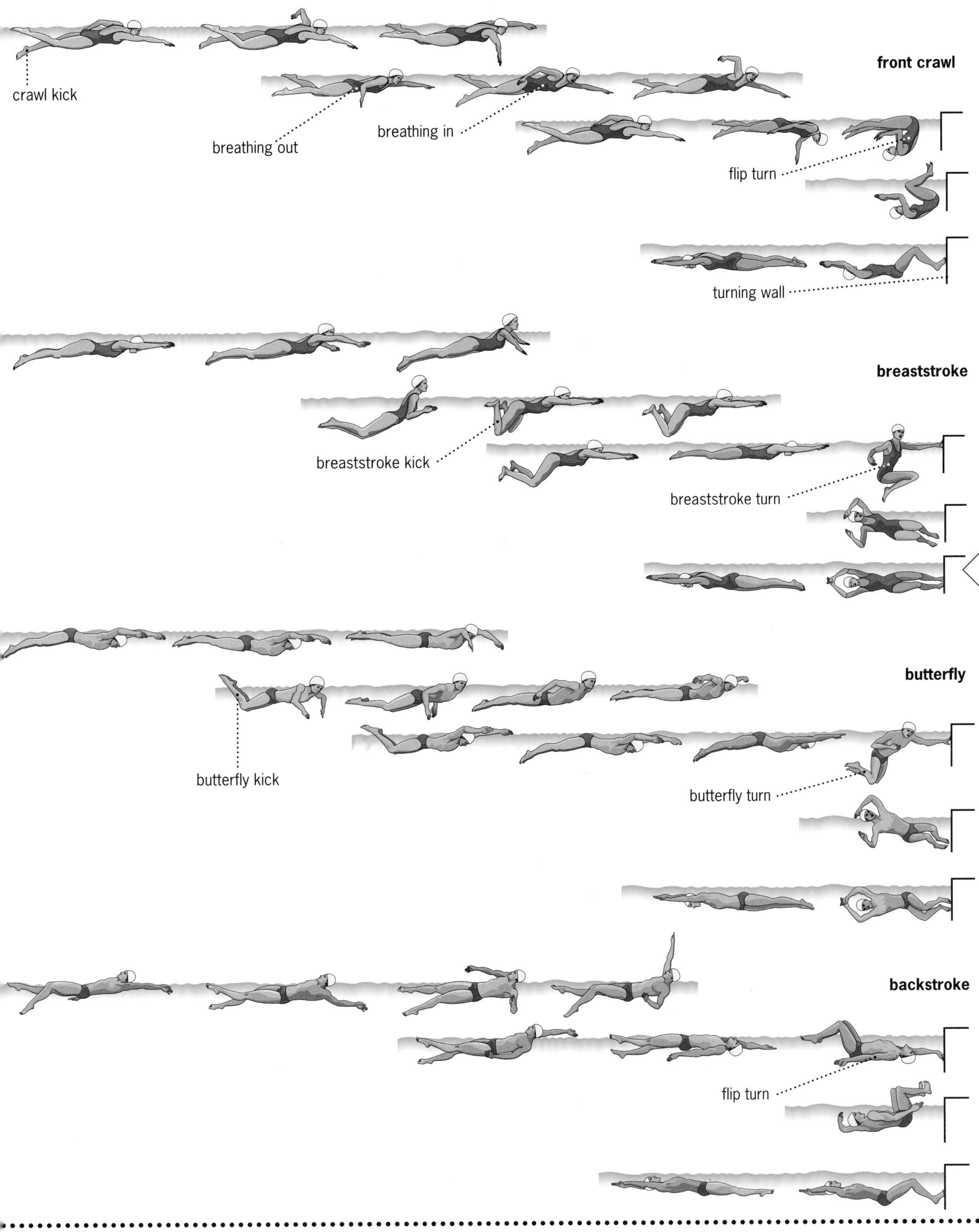
front crawl
crawl kick
breathing out
breathing in
flip turn
turning wall
breaststroke
breaststroke kick
breaststroke turn
butterfly
butterfly kick
butterfly turn
backstroke
flip turn

SAILBOARD

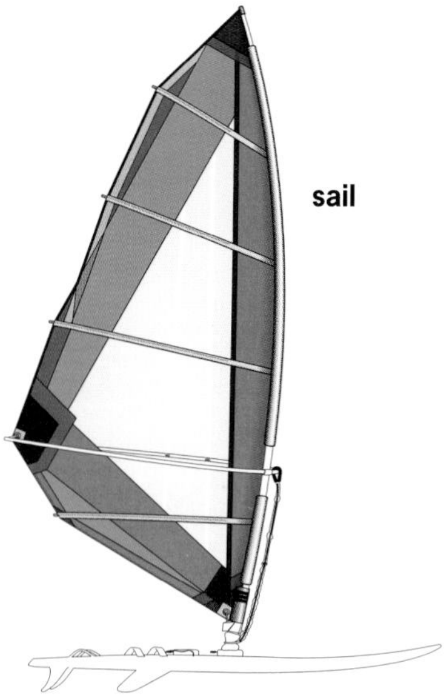
sail

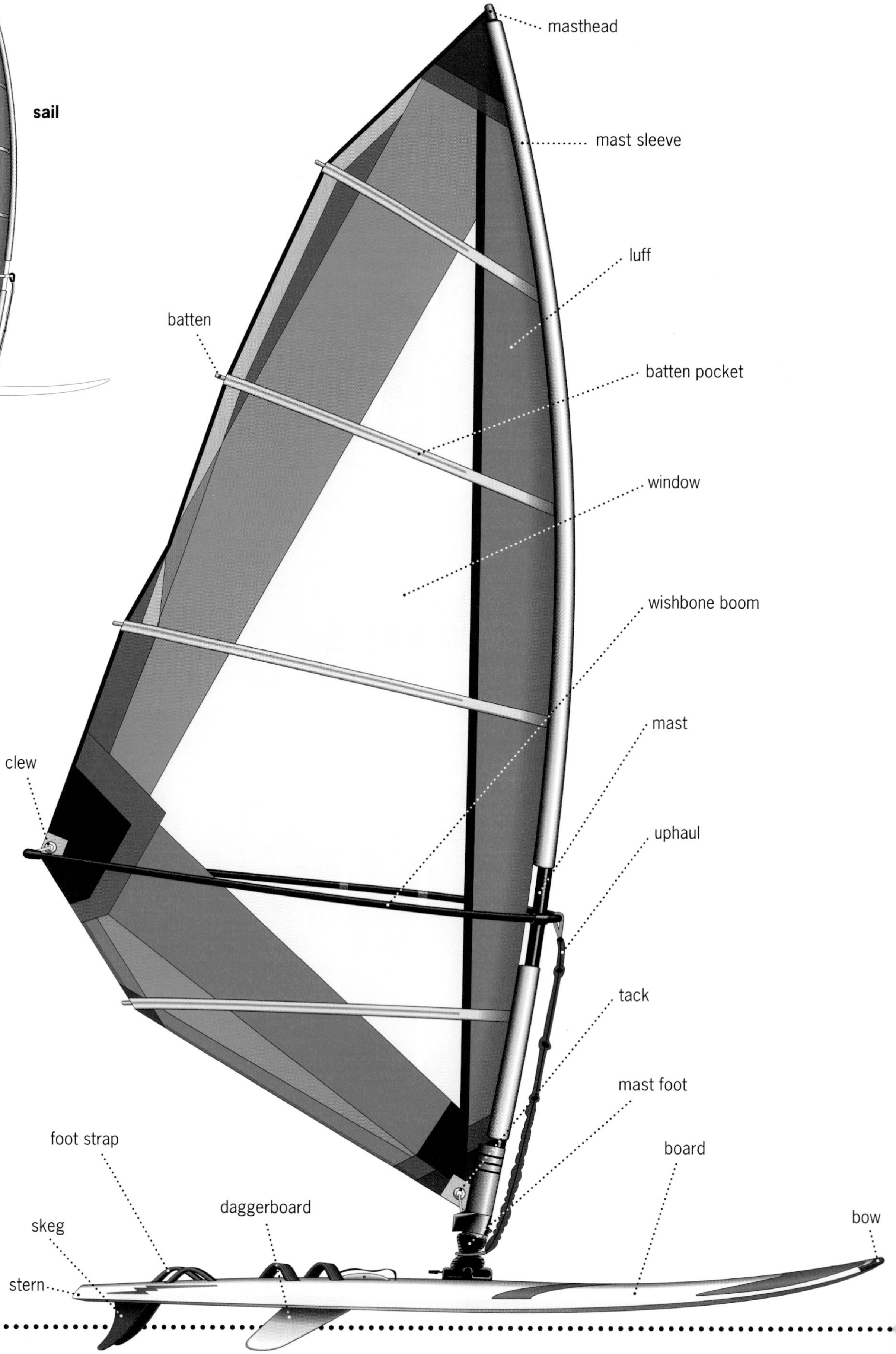
masthead
mast sleeve
luff
batten
batten pocket
window
wishbone boom
mast
clew
uphaul
tack
mast foot
foot strap
board
daggerboard
skeg
bow
stern

SKATING

in-line skate

inner boot
upper shell
adjusting buckle
boot
axle
wheel
truck
heel stop

speed skate

hockey skate

tendon guard
boot
toe box
point
blade

figure skate

tongue
hook
backstay
eyelet
boot
lace
stanchion
edge
blade
sole
toe pick

skate guard

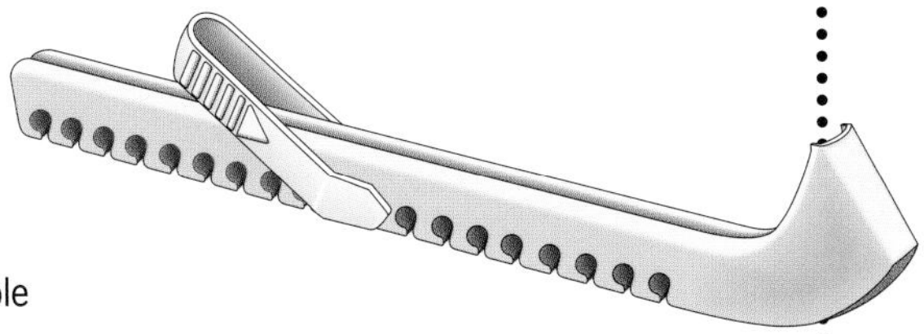

SKIING

alpine skier

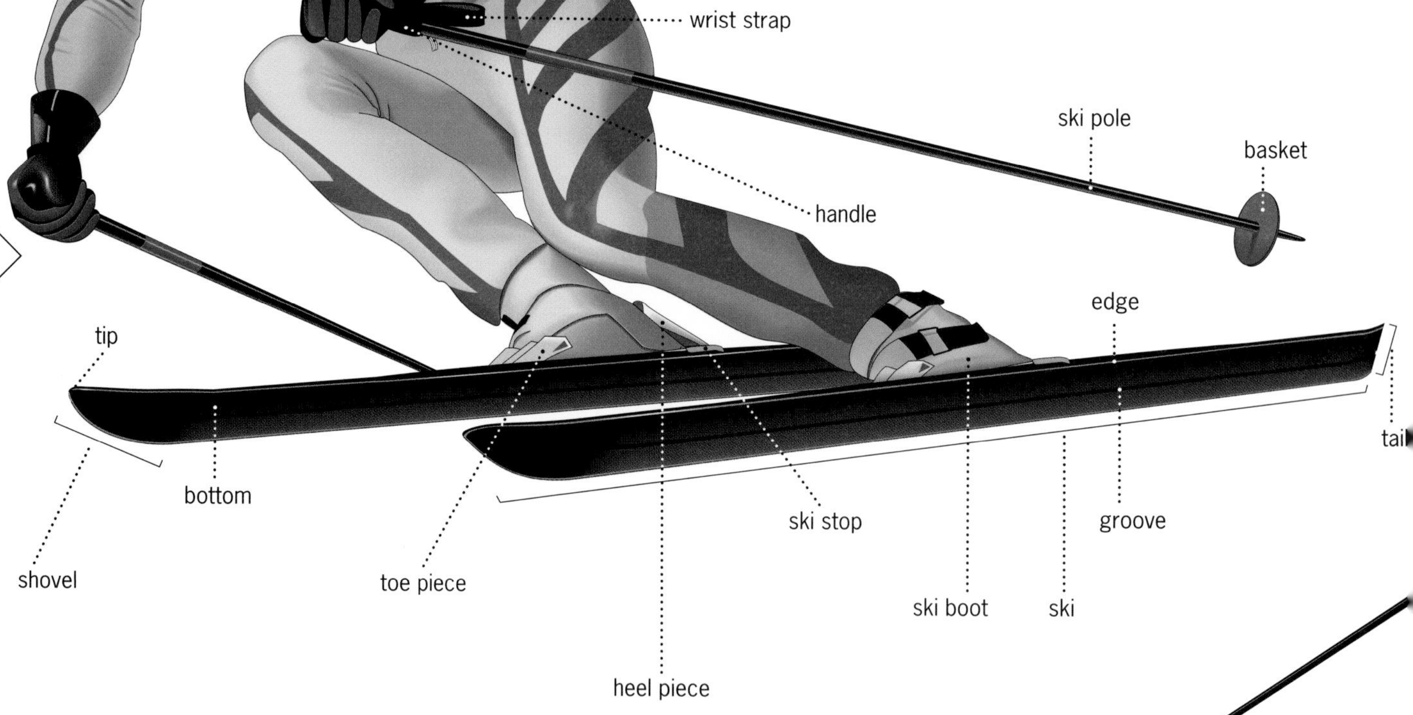
ski hat
ski goggles
ski suit
ski glove
wrist strap
ski pole
basket
handle
tip
edge
tail
bottom
shovel
toe piece
ski stop
groove
ski boot
ski
heel piece

ski boot

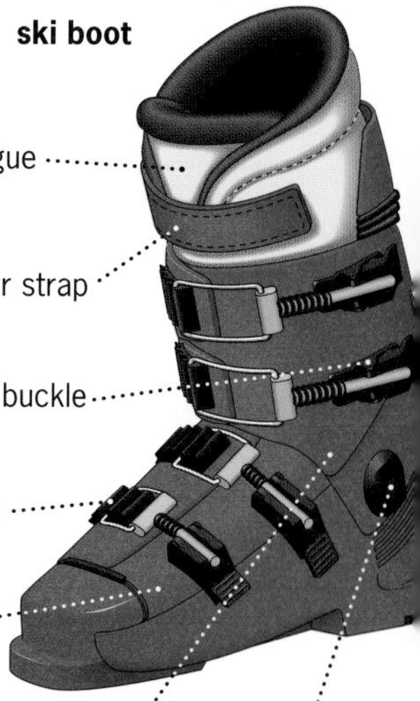
tongue
upper strap
buckle
adjusting catch
lower shell
upper shell
hinge

cross-country ski

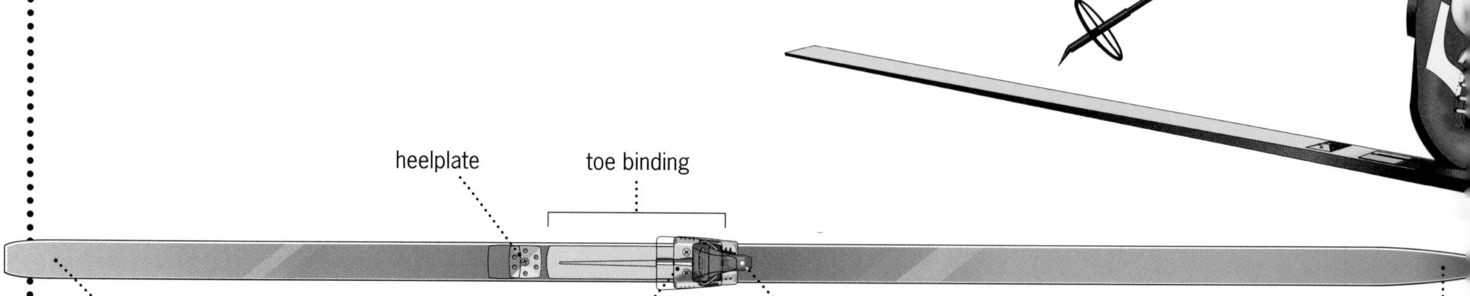
heelplate
toe binding
tail
toeplate
clamp
shovel

safety binding

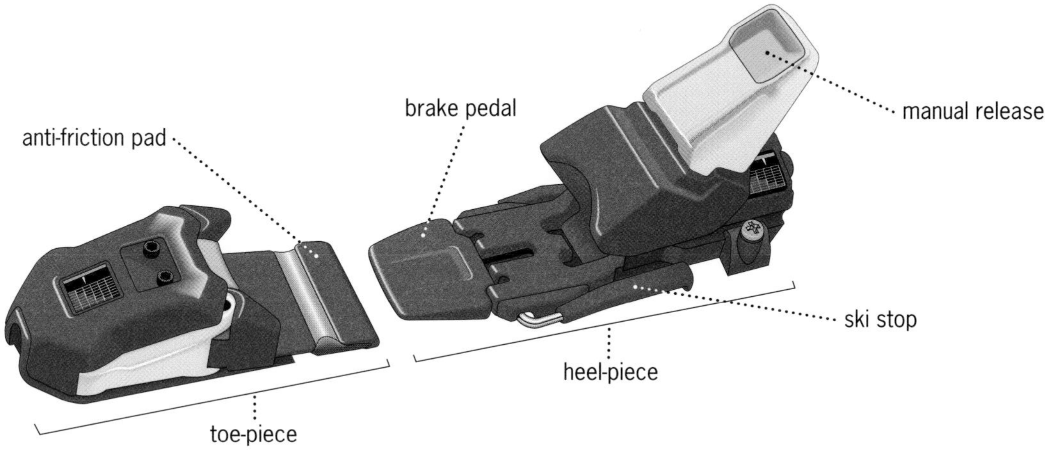
brake pedal
anti-friction pad
manual release
ski stop
heel-piece
toe-piece

cross-country skier

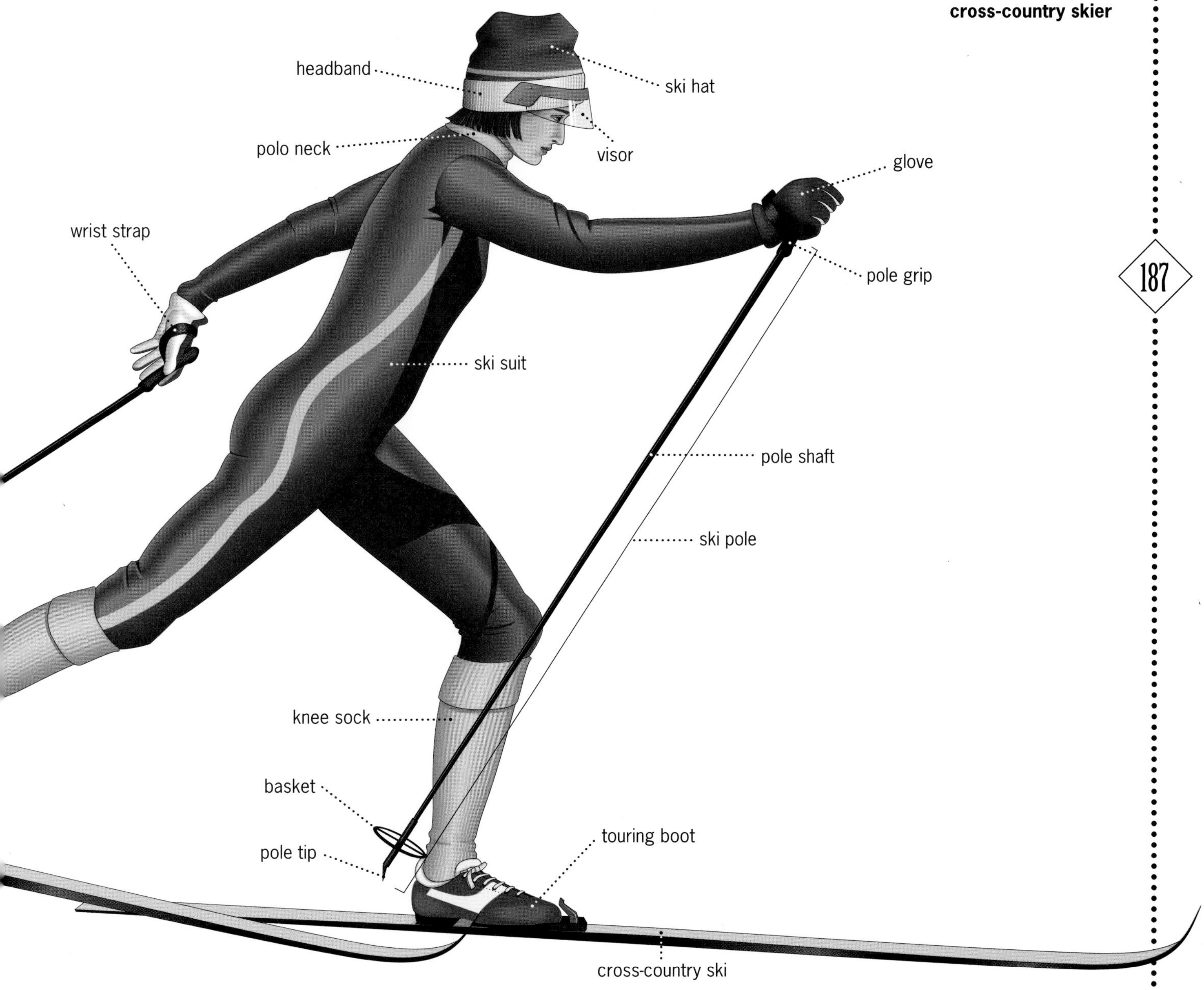
headband
ski hat
polo neck
visor
glove
wrist strap
pole grip
ski suit
pole shaft
ski pole
knee sock
basket
touring boot
pole tip
cross-country ski

GYMNASTICS

pommel horse

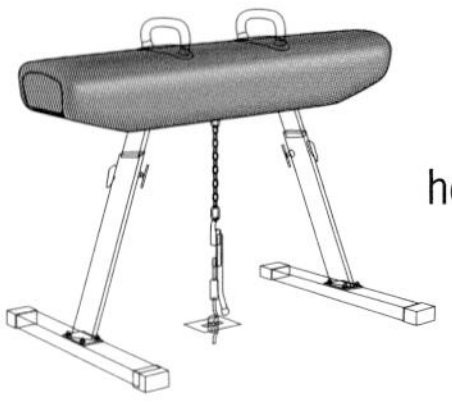
horse

base

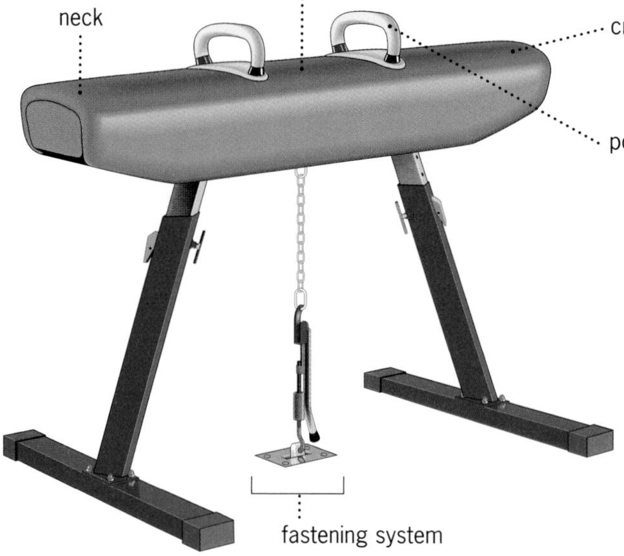
saddle
neck
croup
pommel
fastening system

vault

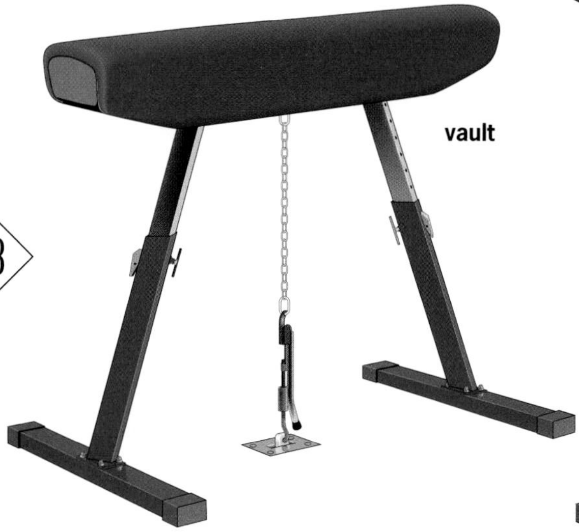

balance beam

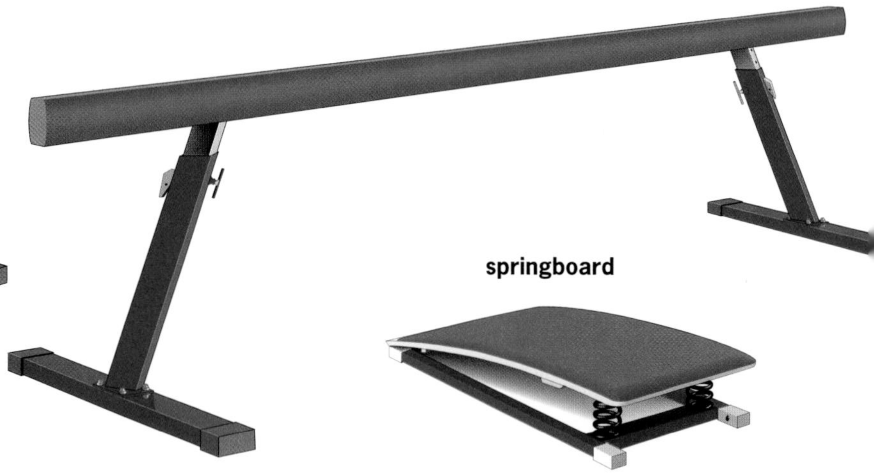

springboard

trampoline

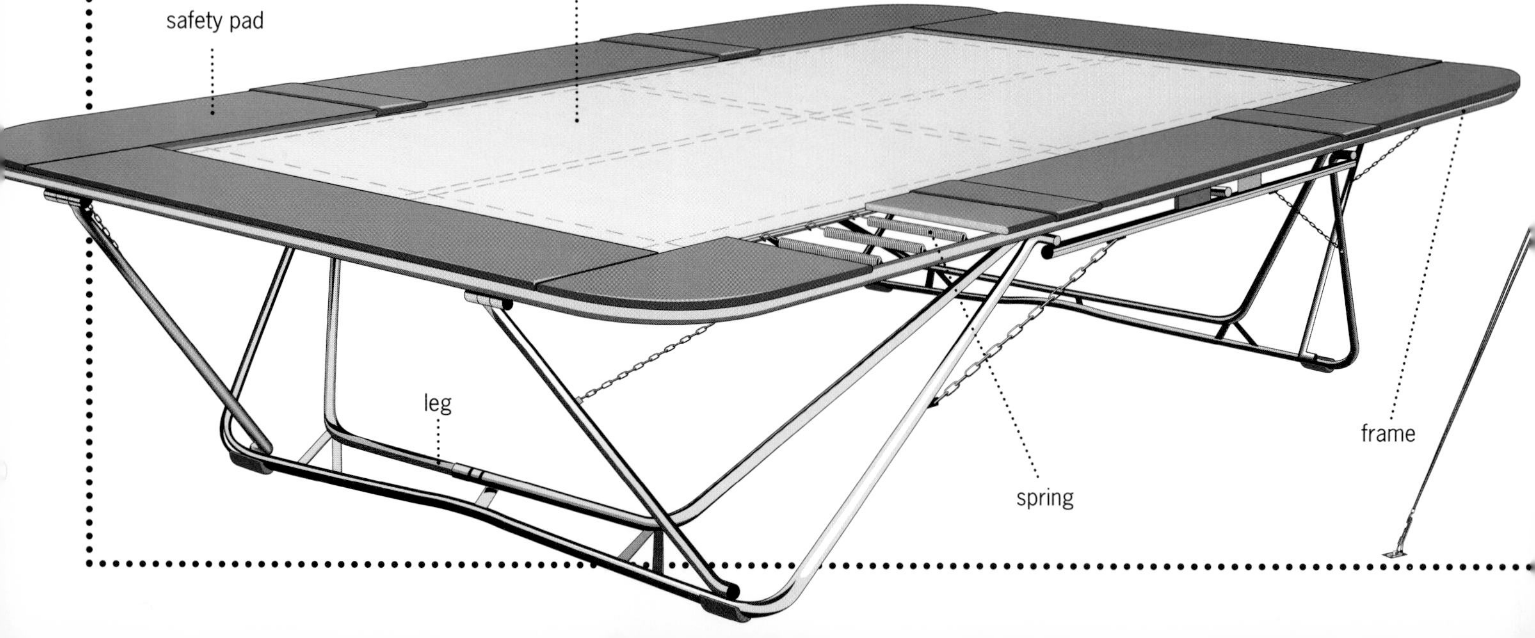
bed
safety pad
leg
spring
frame

uneven bars

horizontal bar; high bar

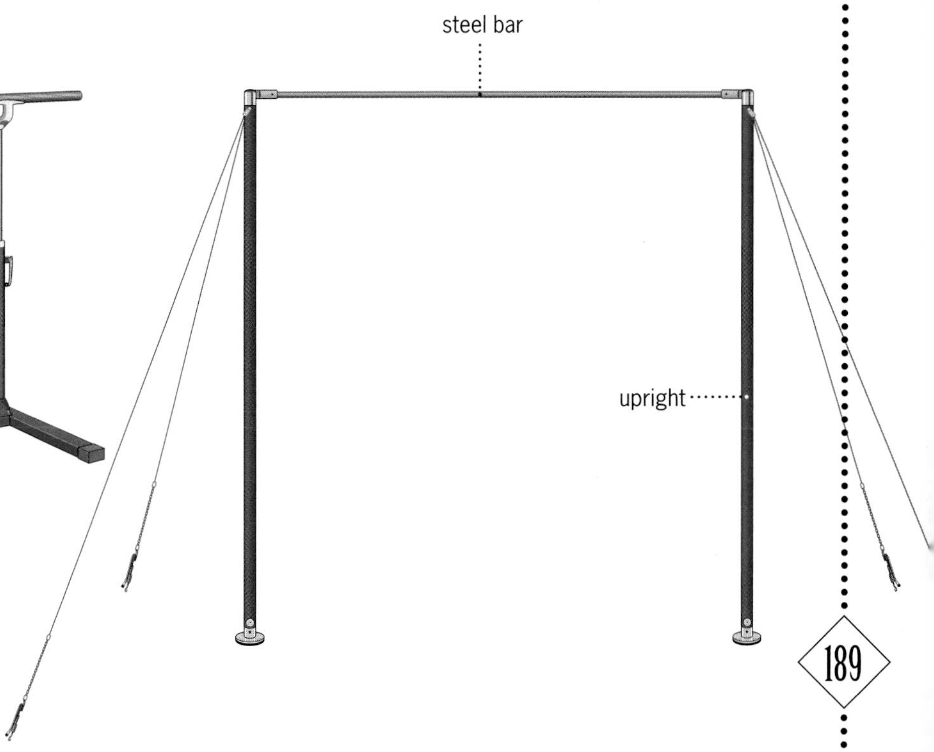
steel bar
upright

rings

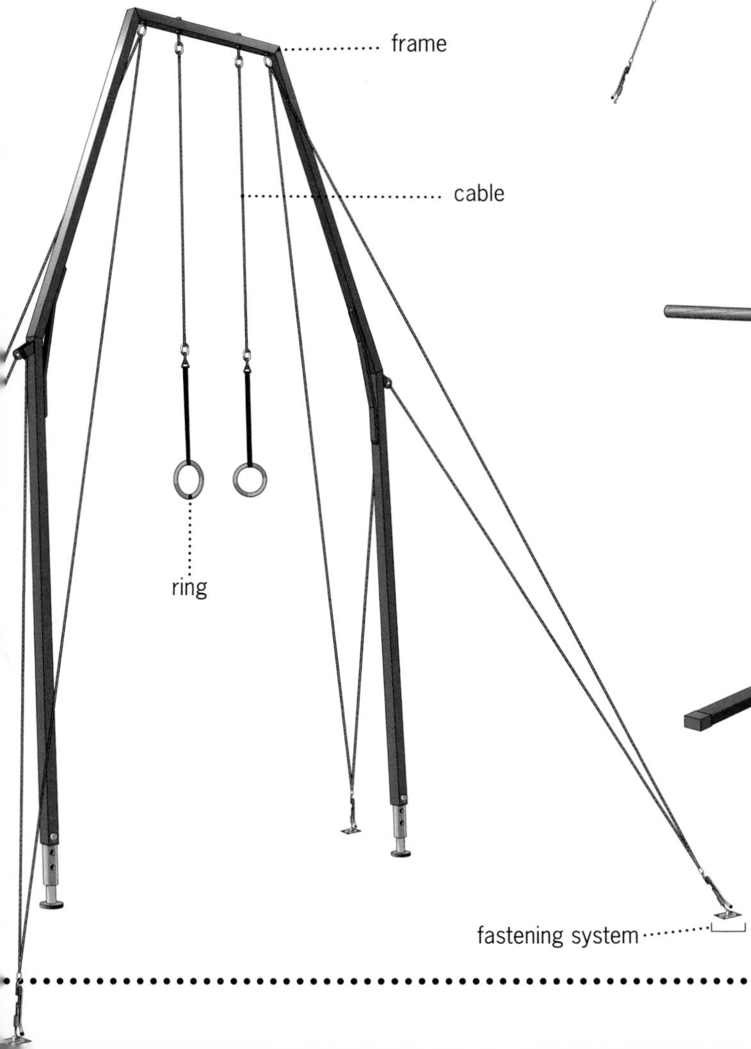
frame
cable
ring
fastening system

parallel bars

TENTS

two-person tent

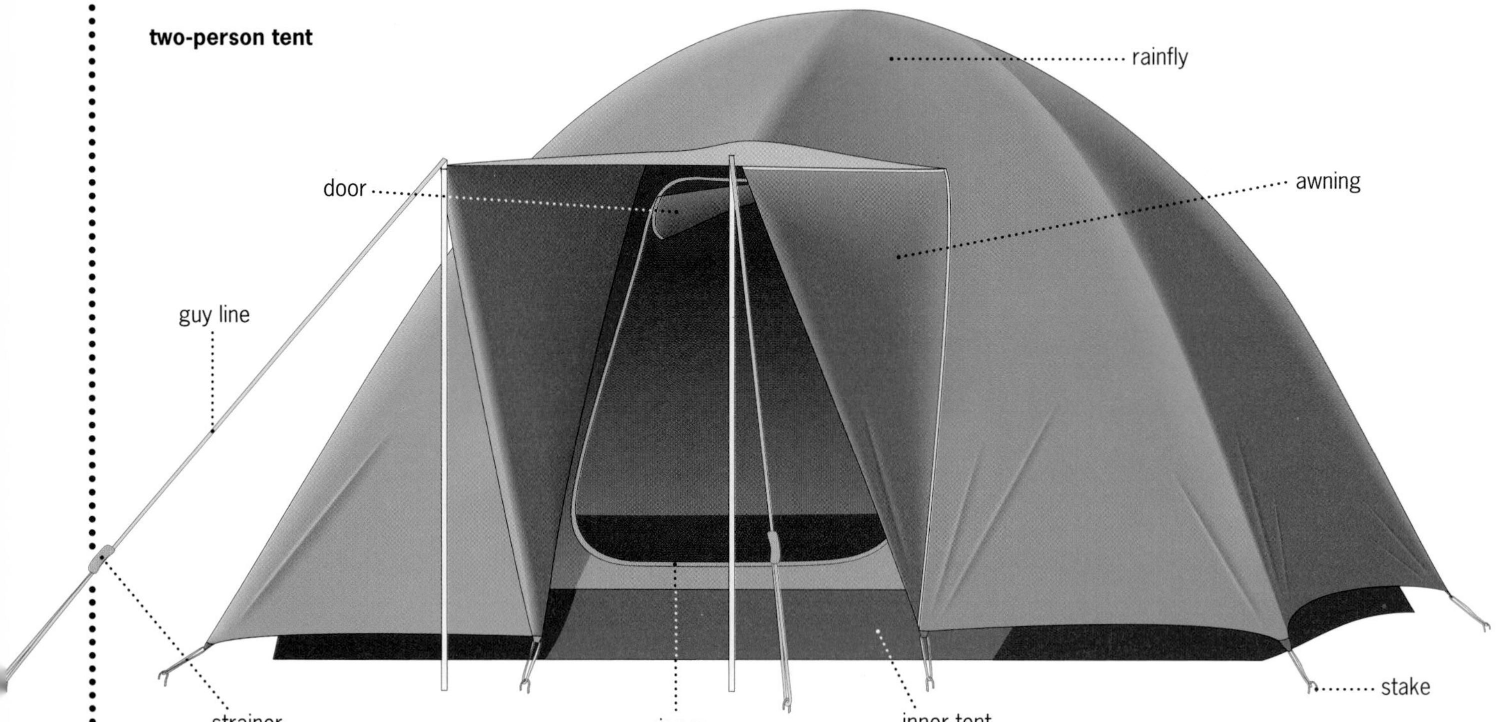
rainfly
door
awning
guy line
strainer
zipper
inner tent
stake

190 MAJOR TYPES OF TENTS

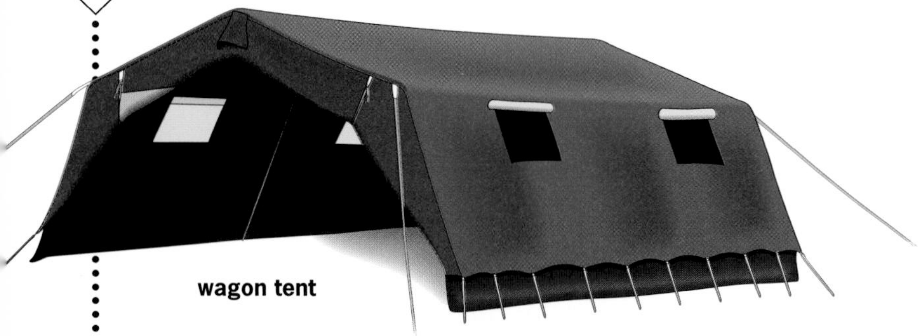

wagon tent

wall tent

pup tent

dome tent

pop-up tent

family tent

one-person tent

SLEEPING EQUIPMENT

BEDS AND MATTRESSES

foam pad

self-inflating mattress

inflator

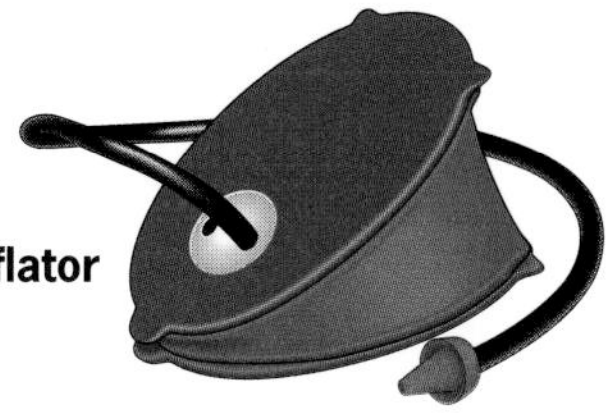

inflator-deflator

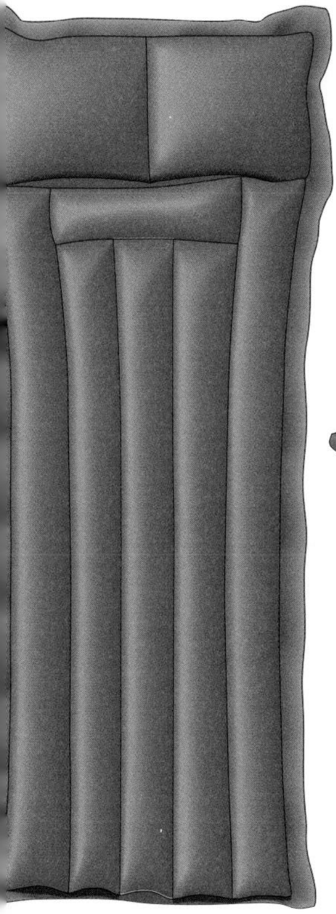

air mattress

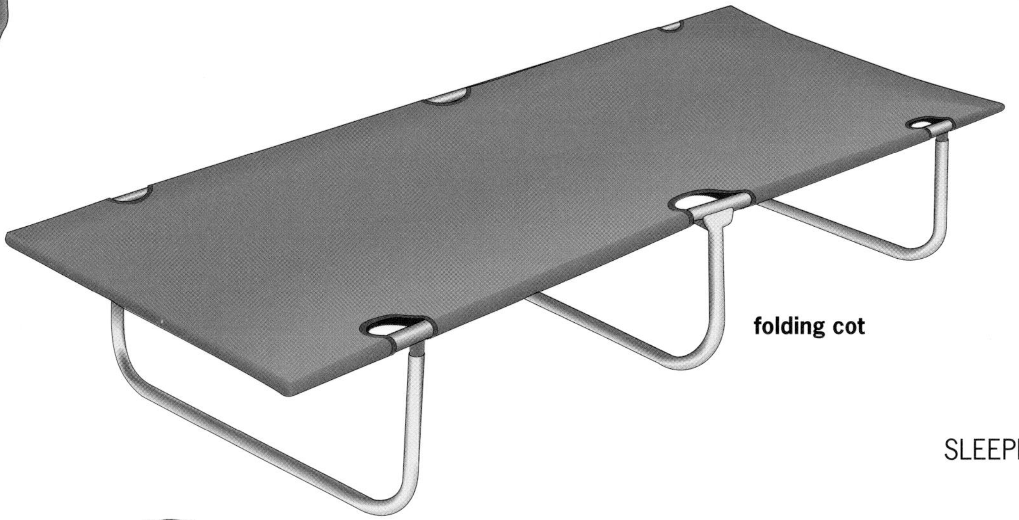

folding cot

SLEEPING BAGS

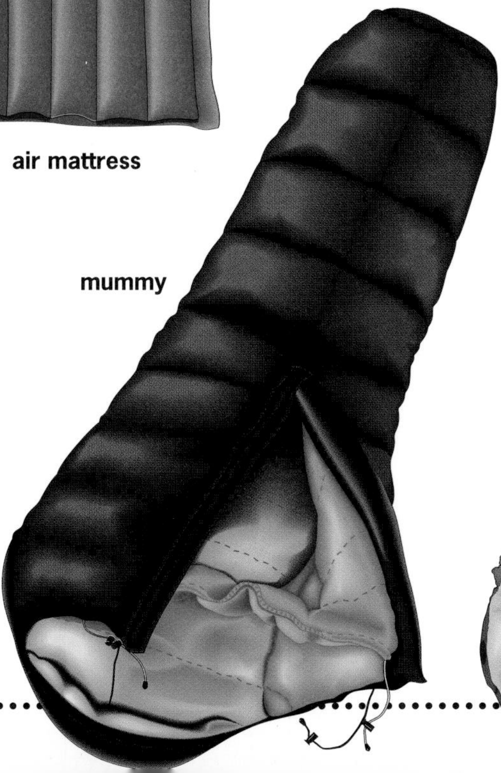

mummy

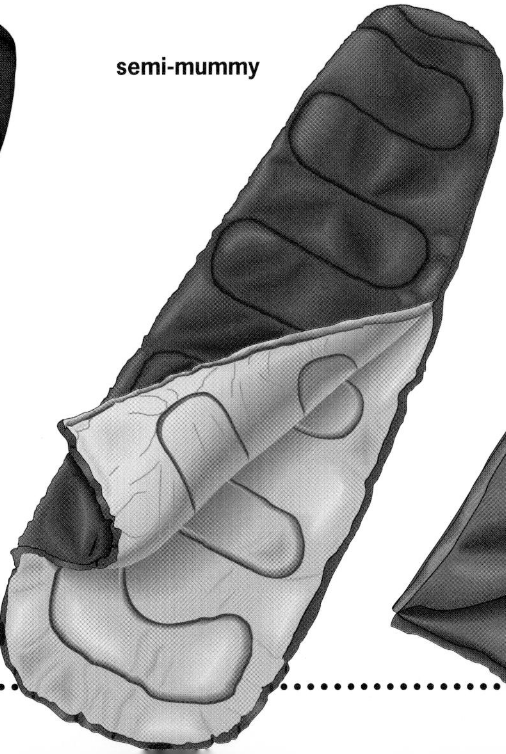

semi-mummy

rectangular

CAMPING EQUIPMENT

Swiss army knife

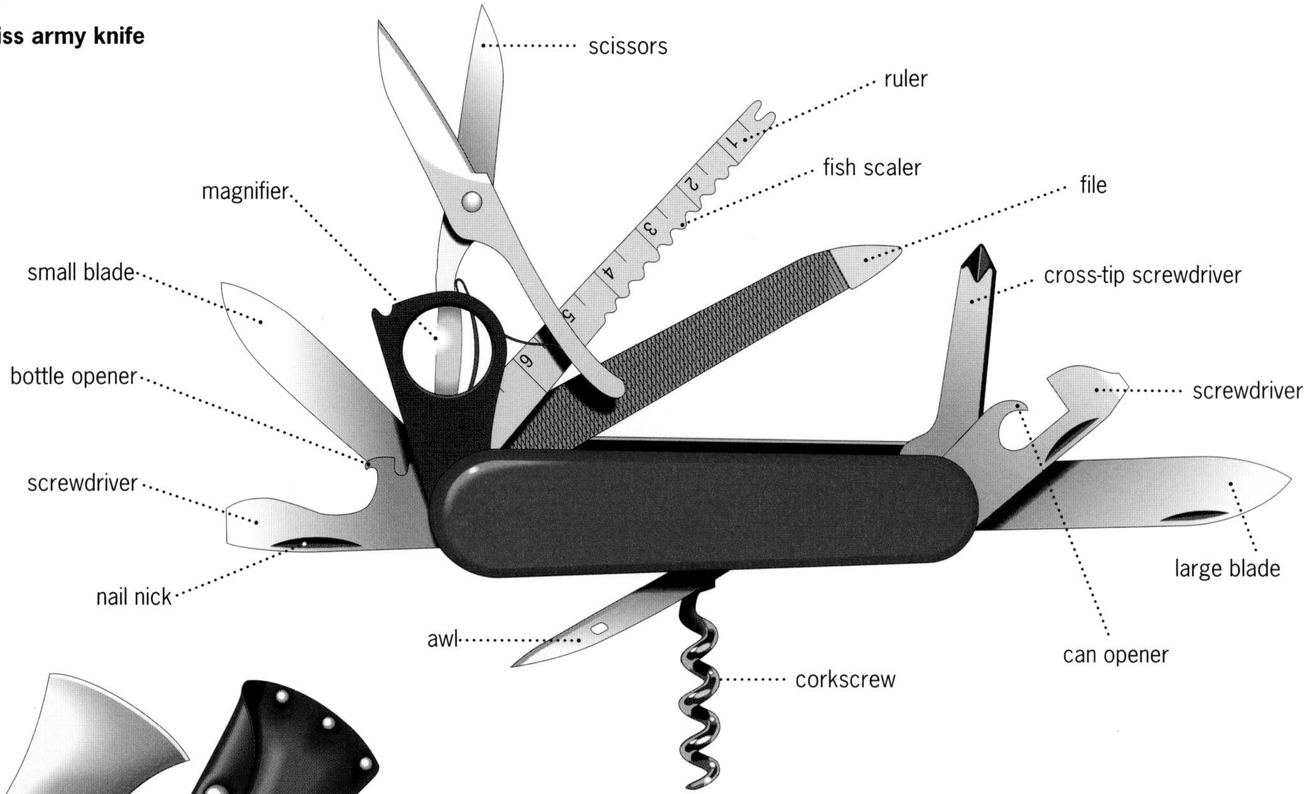
scissors
ruler
fish scaler
file
magnifier
small blade
cross-tip screwdriver
bottle opener
screwdriver
screwdriver
large blade
nail nick
awl
can opener
corkscrew

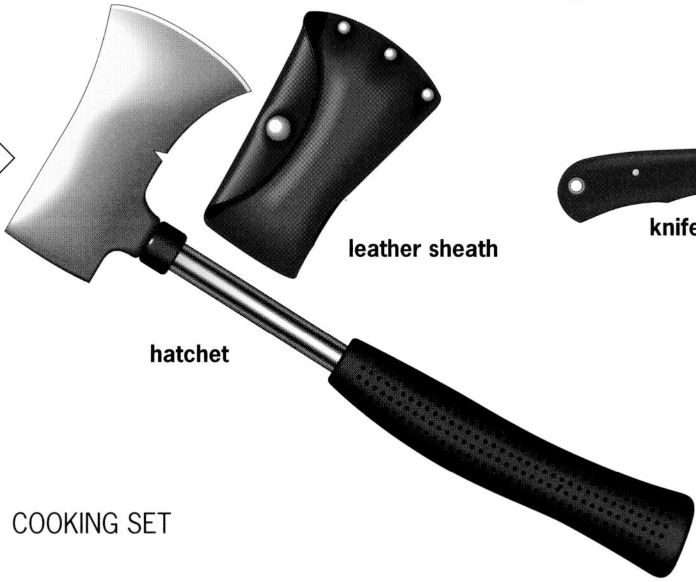
hatchet

leather sheath

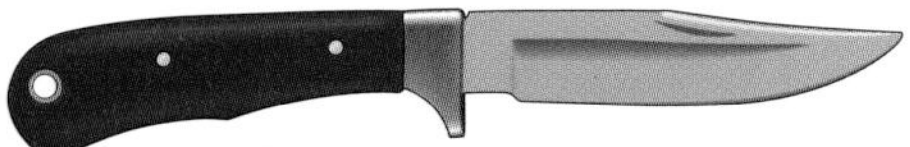
knife

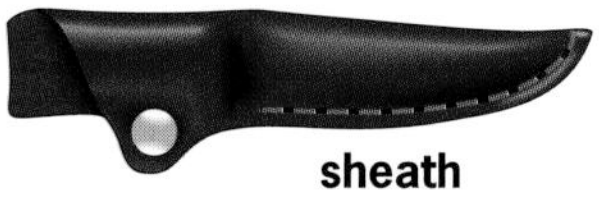
sheath

flashlight

COOKING SET

coffee pot

plate

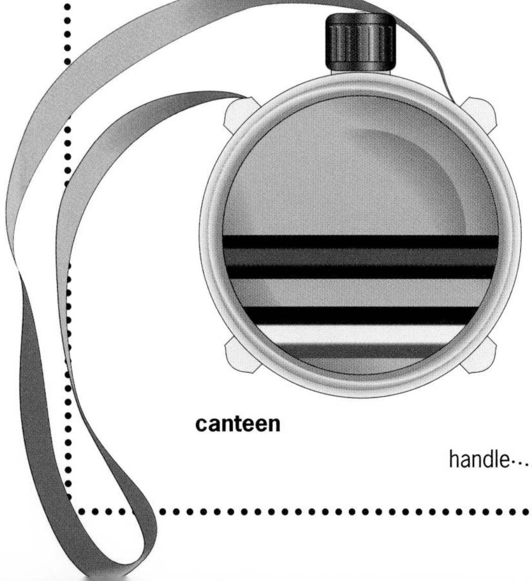
canteen

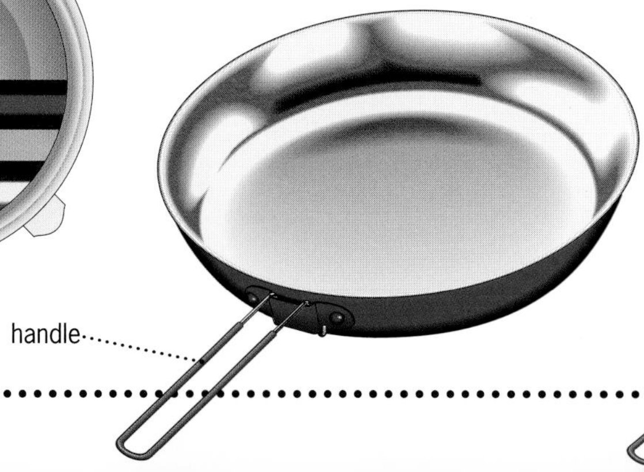
handle
frying pan

cup

saucepan

backpack

top flap
shoulder strap
tightening buckle
side compression strap
strap loop
internal frame
front compression strap
waist belt

first aid kit

magnetic compass

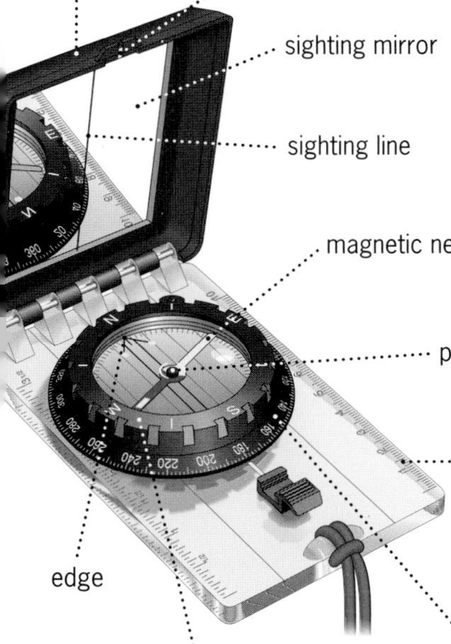
sight
cover
sighting mirror
sighting line
magnetic needle
pivot
scale
edge
compass card
graduated dial

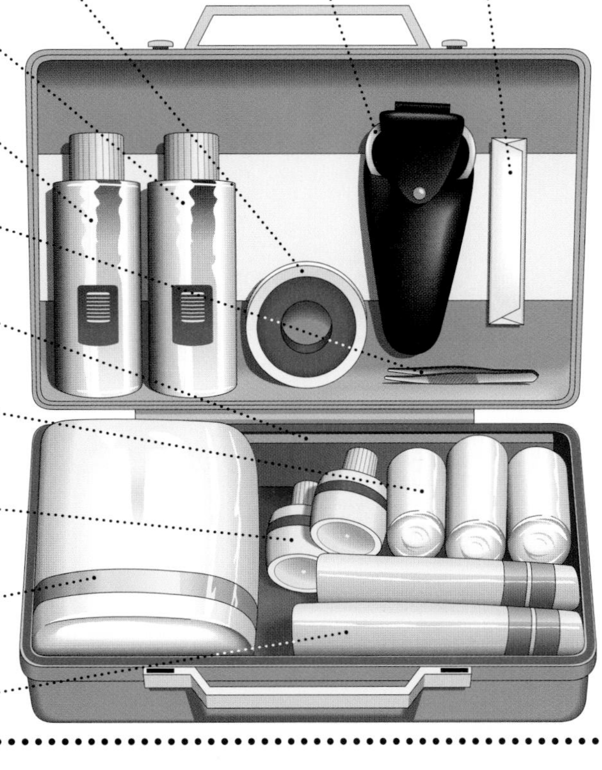
adhesive tape
scissors
small bandage
antiseptic lotion
antiseptic
tweezers
splint
gauze roller bandage
multipurpose bottle
cotton roll
sterile dressing

CARD GAMES

heart
diamond
club
spade

Joker
Ace
King
Queen
Jack

DICE

poker die

ordinary die

DOMINOES

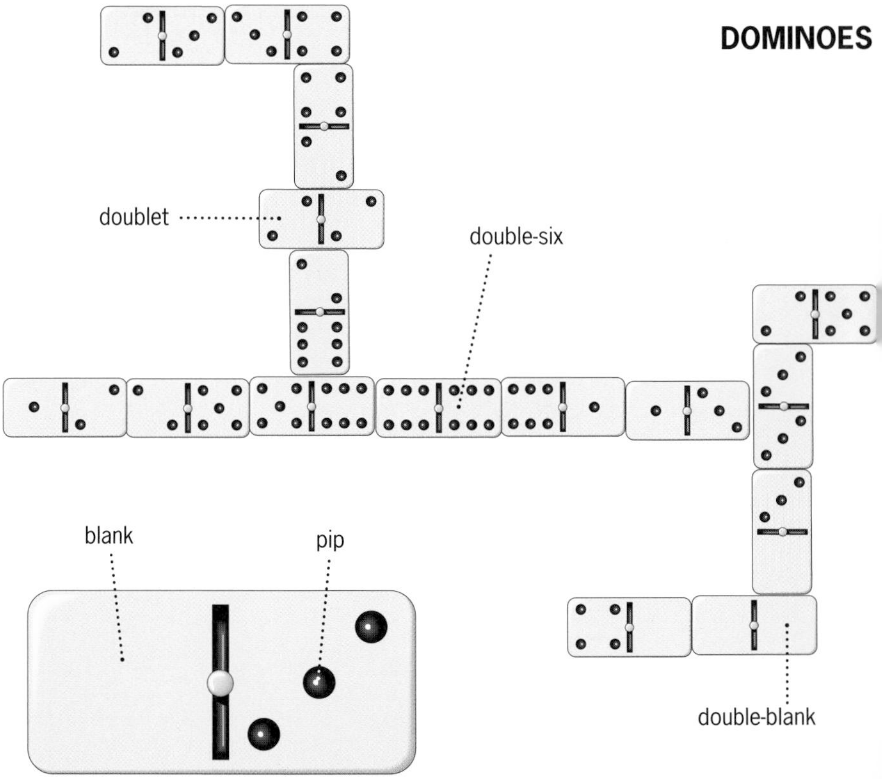
doublet
double-six
blank
pip
double-blank

CHESS

chessboard

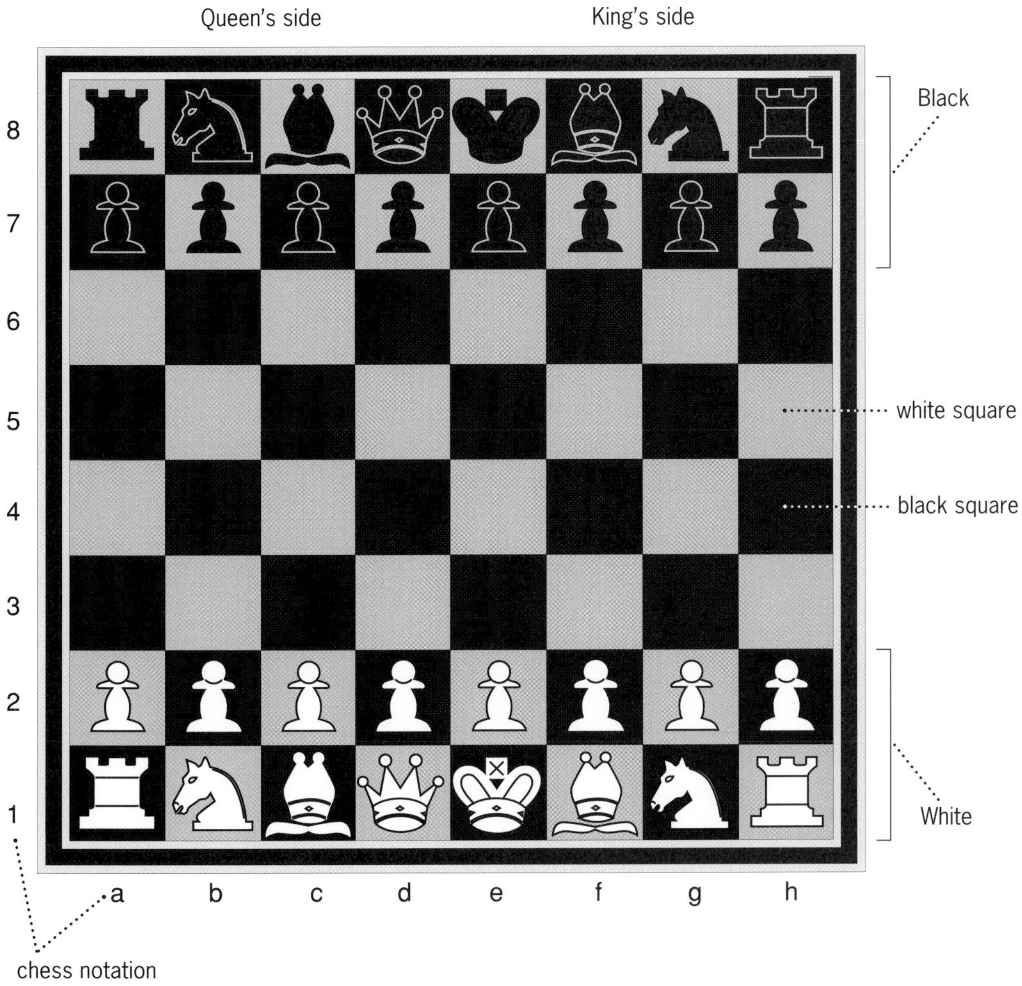
Queen's side
King's side
Black
white square
black square
White
8
7
6
5
4
3
2
1
a
b
c
d
e
f
g
h
chess notation

MEN

Pawn
Knight
Bishop
Rook
Queen
King

types of movements

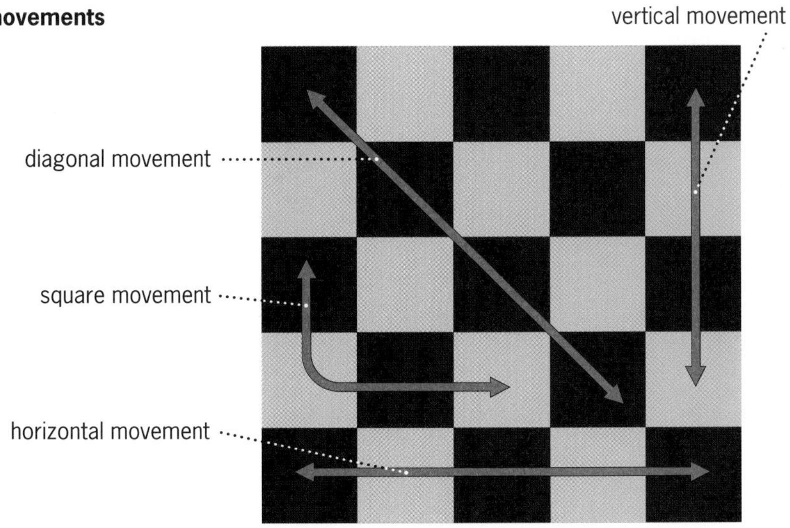
vertical movement
diagonal movement
square movement
horizontal movement

BACKGAMMON

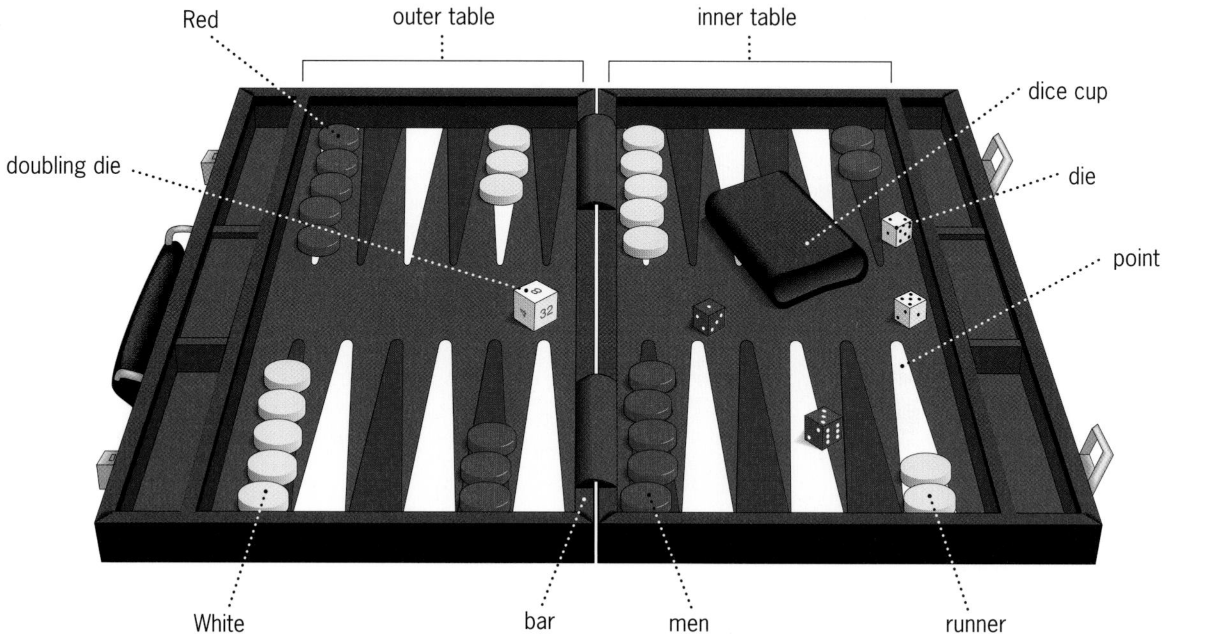
Red
outer table
inner table
dice cup
doubling die
die
point
White
bar
men
runner

CHECKERS

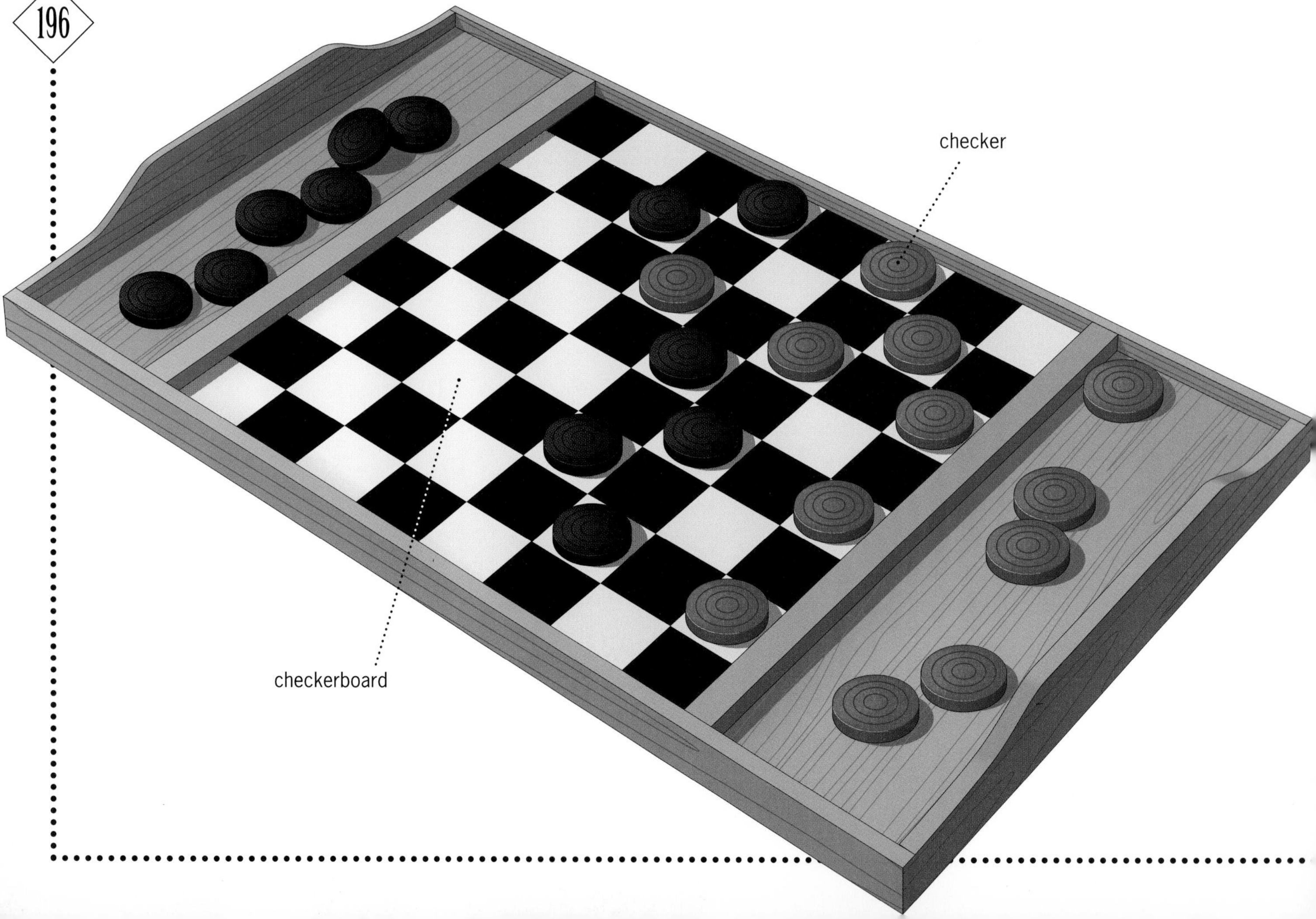
checker
checkerboard

VIDEO ENTERTAINMENT SYSTEM

visual display
game cartridge
control deck
function button
control pad

GAME OF DARTS

dart

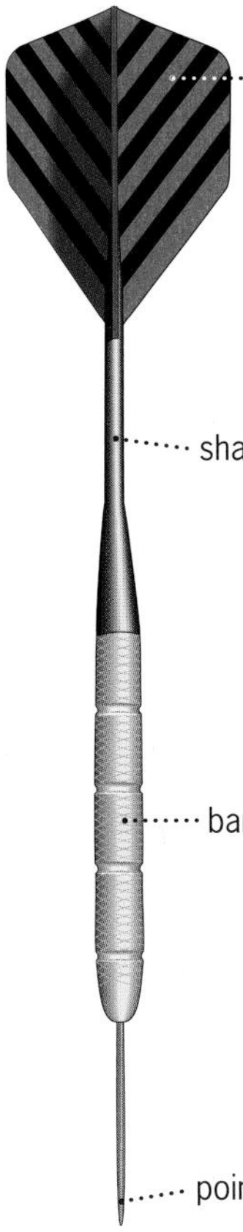
flight
shaft
barrel
point

dartboard

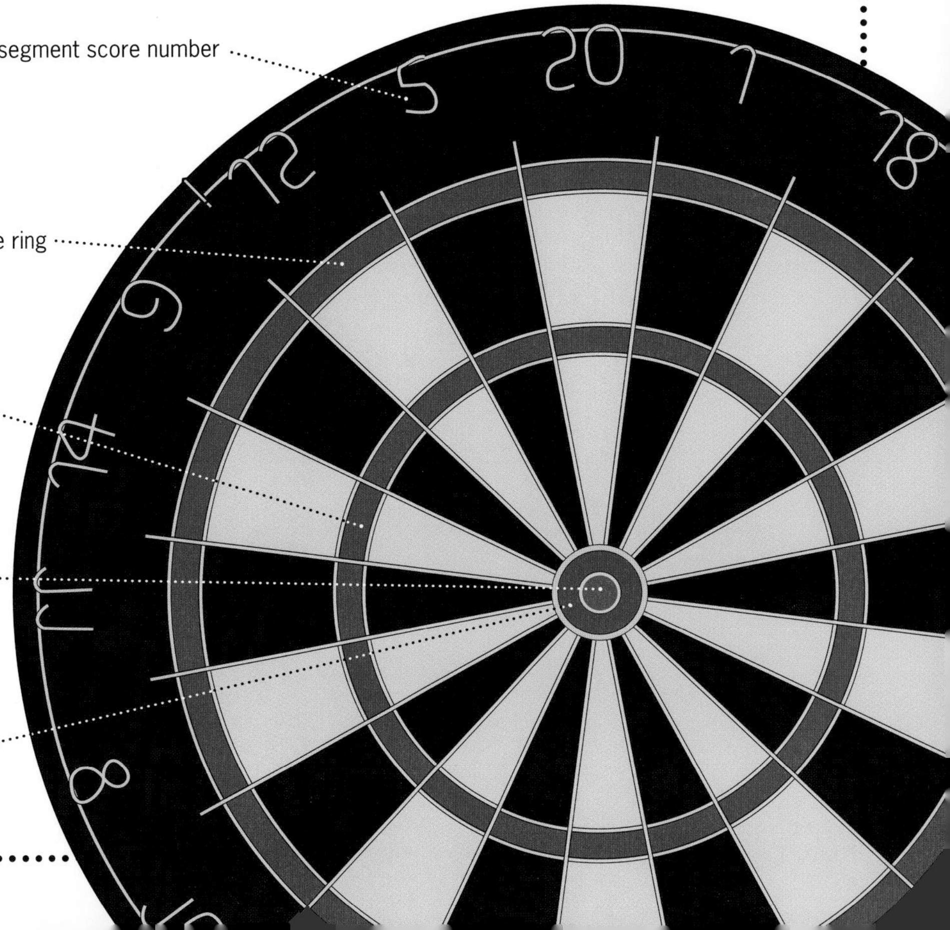
segment score number
double ring
triple ring
bull's-eye
25 ring
20
1
18
5
12
9
14
11
8

MEASURE OF TIME

stopwatch

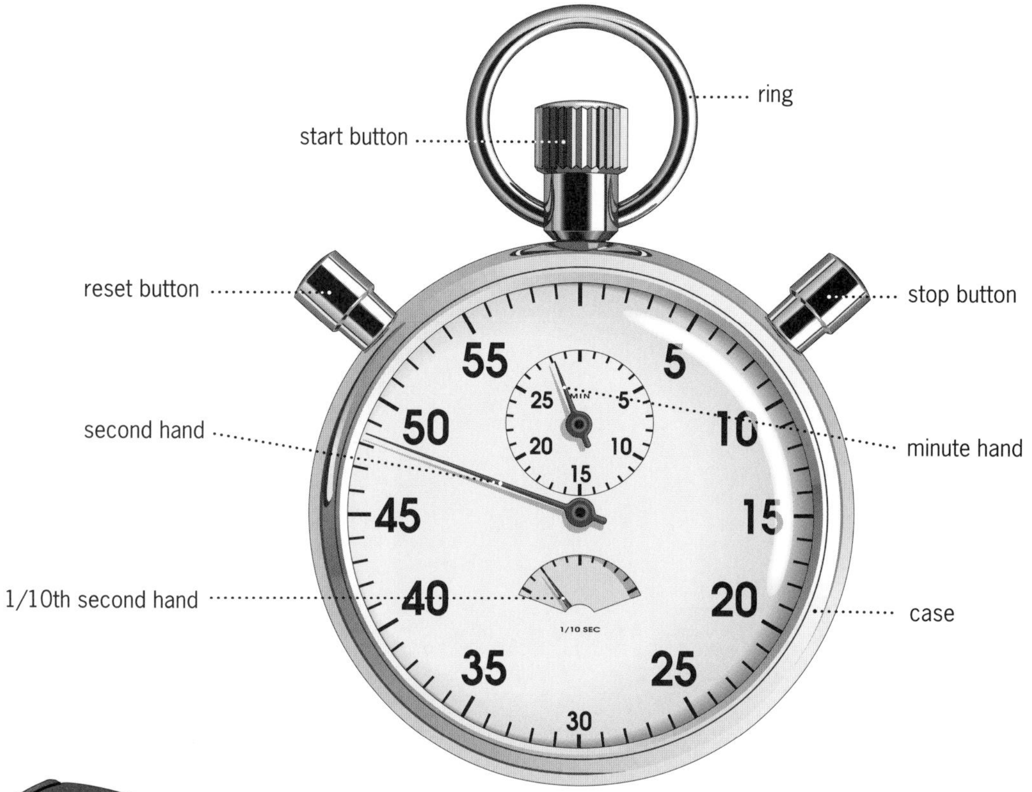
ring
start button
reset button
stop button
second hand
minute hand
1/10th second hand
case
55
5
50
10
45
15
40
20
35
25
30
25
MIN
5
20
10
15
1/10 SEC

analog watch

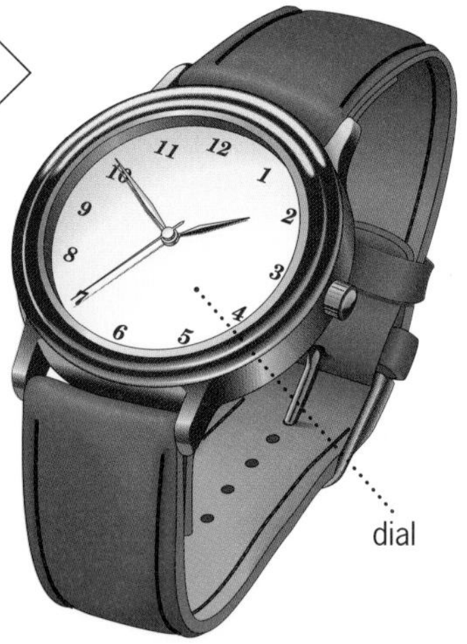
dial

kitchen timer

egg timer

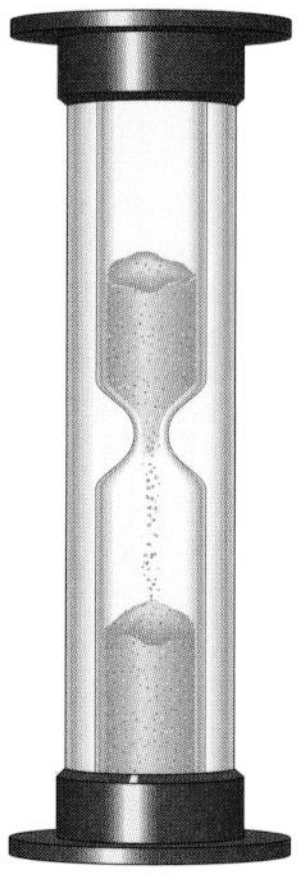

digital watch

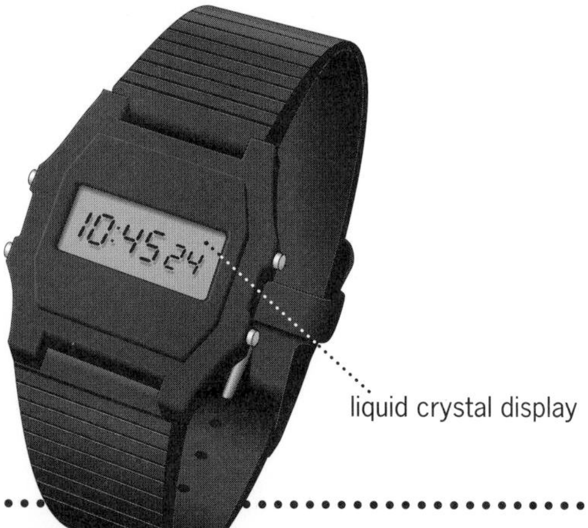
10:45 24
liquid crystal display

sundial

gnomon
shadow
dial

MEASURE OF TEMPERATURE

room thermostat

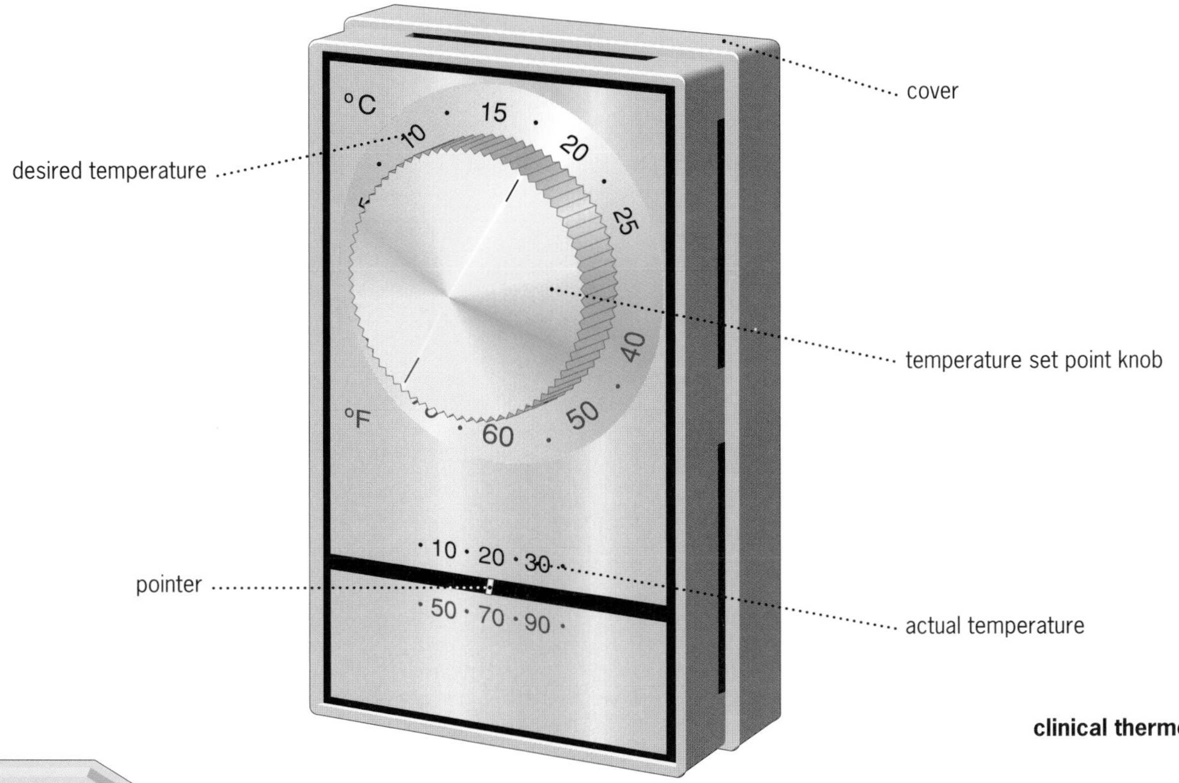
cover
°C
15
10
20
25
40
50
60
°F
desired temperature
temperature set point knob
10 · 20 · 30
50 · 70 · 90
pointer
actual temperature

thermometer

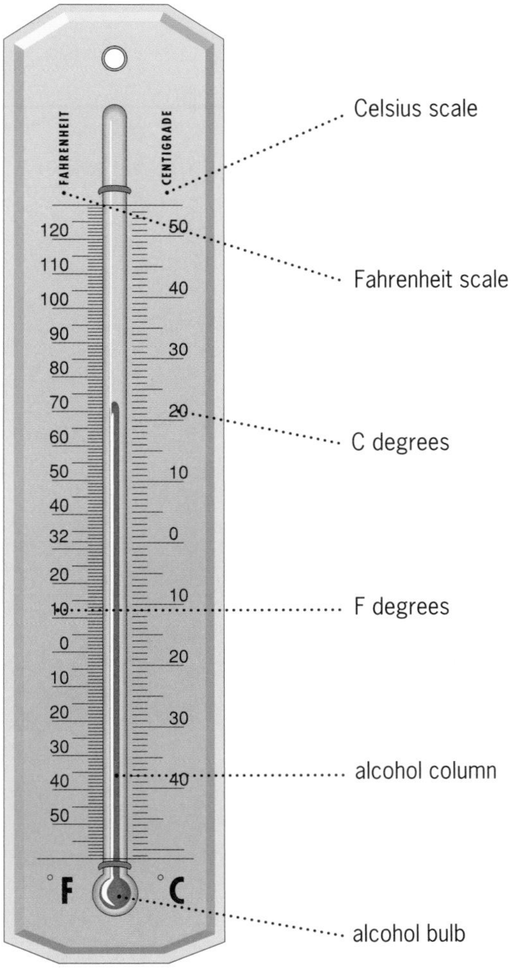
FAHRENHEIT
CENTIGRADE
Celsius scale
Fahrenheit scale
C degrees
F degrees
alcohol column
alcohol bulb
°F
°C

clinical thermometer

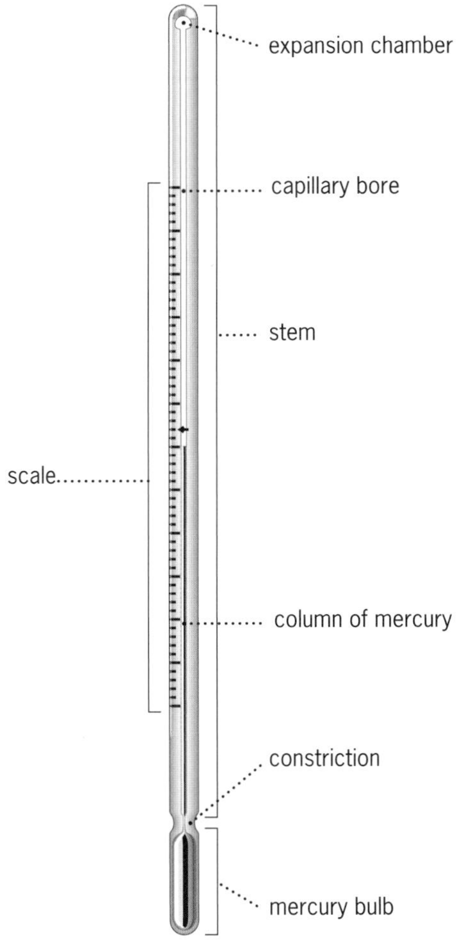
expansion chamber
capillary bore
stem
scale
column of mercury
constriction
mercury bulb

MEASURE OF WEIGHT

balance

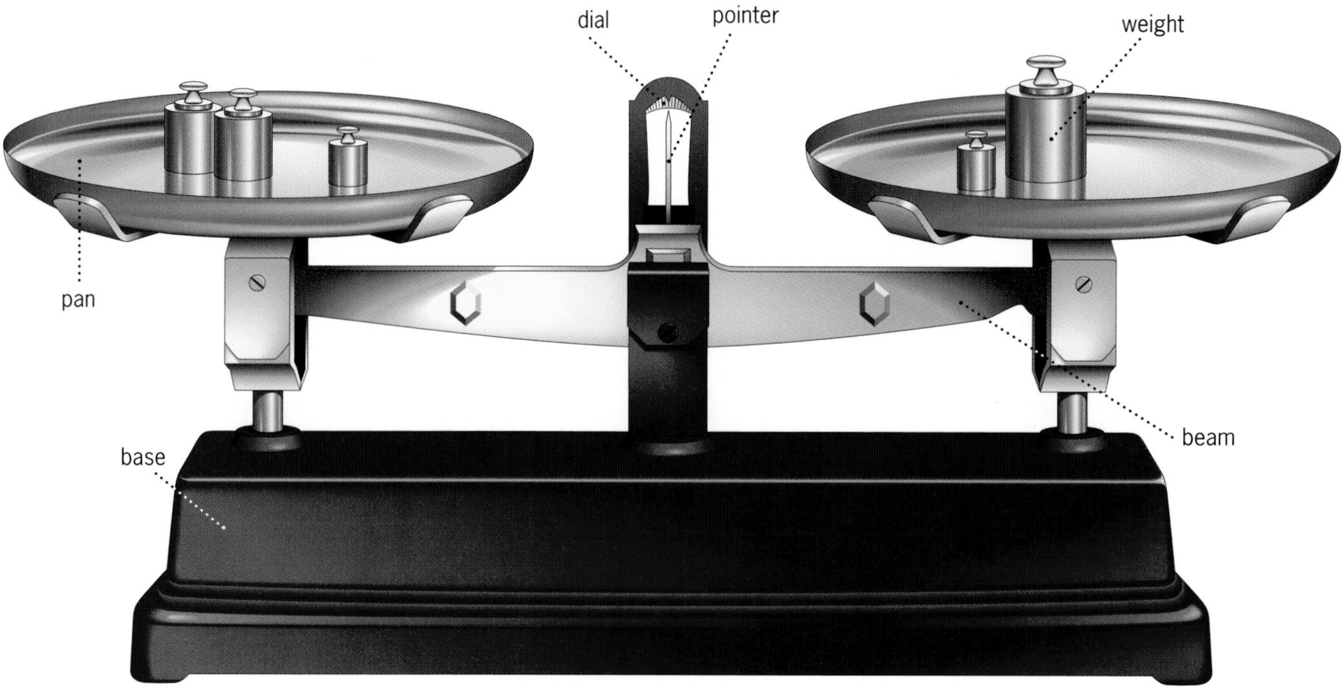
dial
pointer
weight
pan
beam
base

steelyard

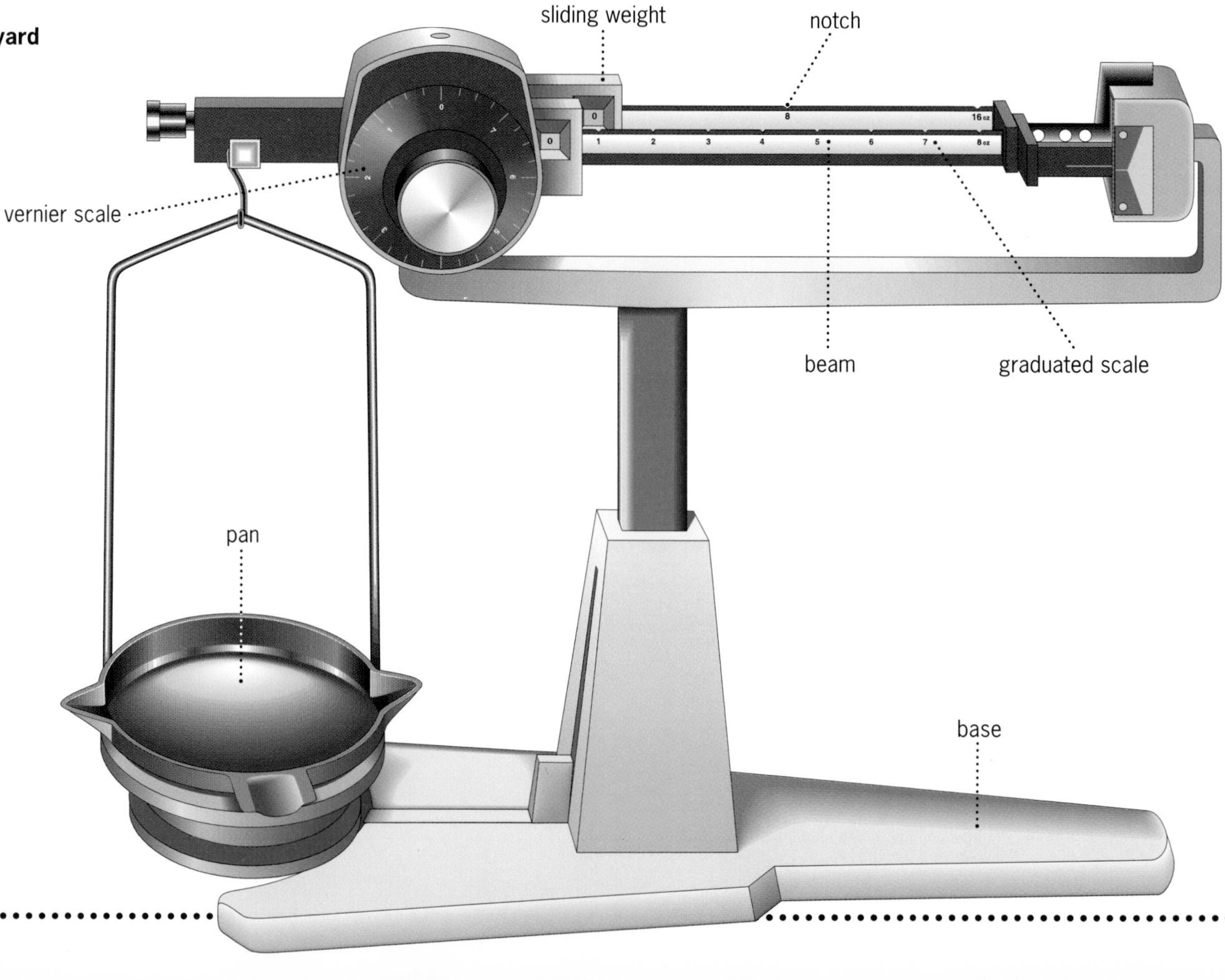
sliding weight
notch
vernier scale
beam
graduated scale
pan
base

spring balance

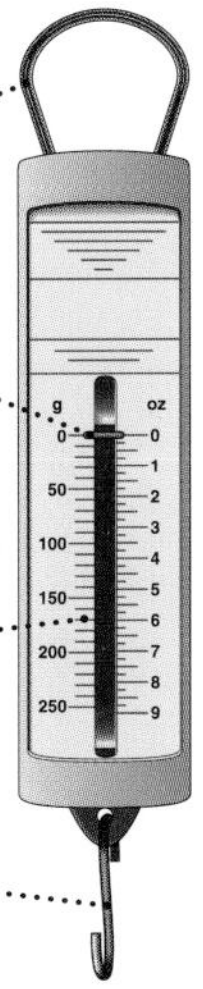
ring
pointer
graduated scale
hook

electronic scale

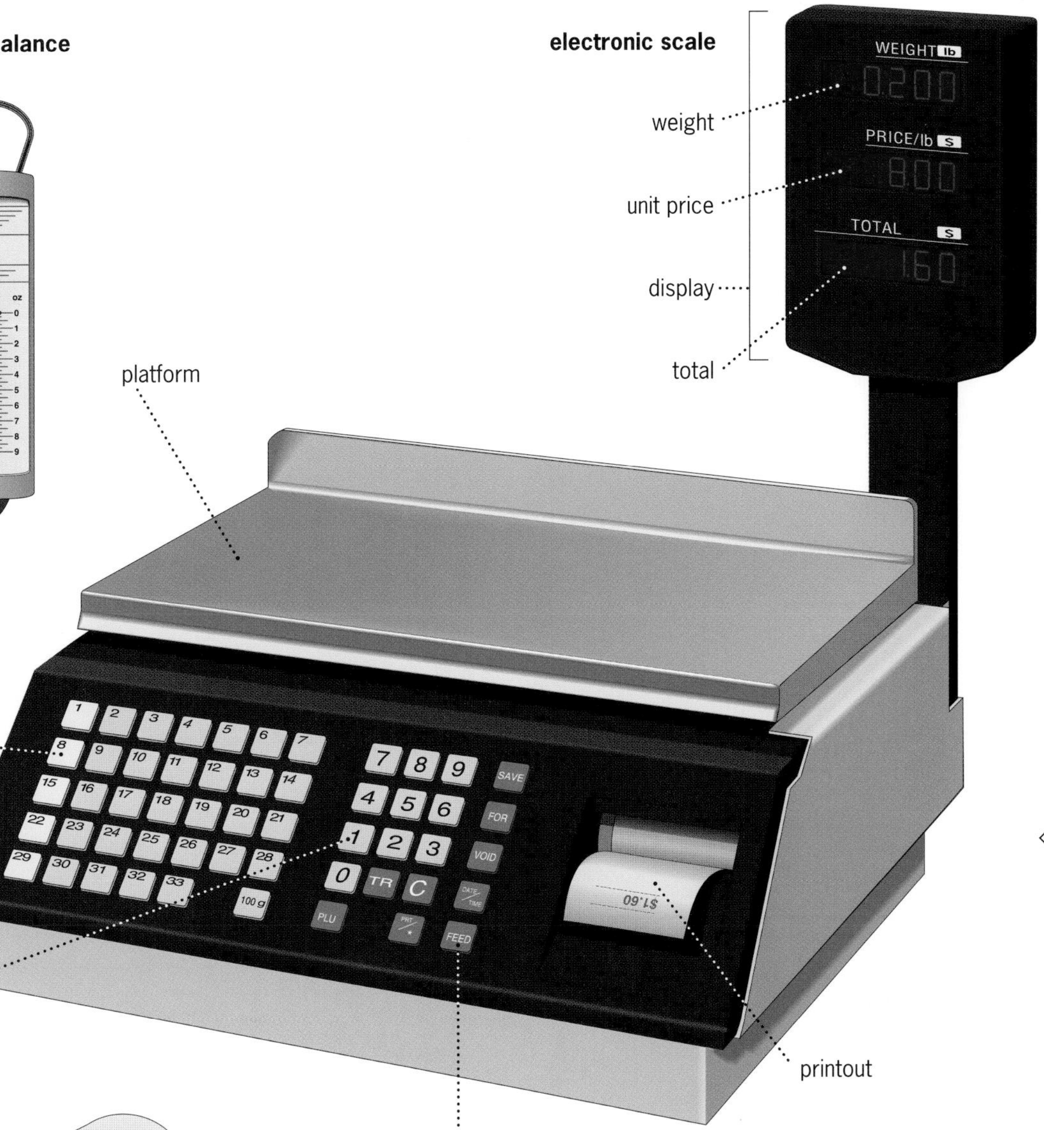
weight
unit price
display
total
platform
product code
numeric keyboard
function keys
printout
WEIGHT lb
PRICE/lb $
TOTAL $

bathroom scale

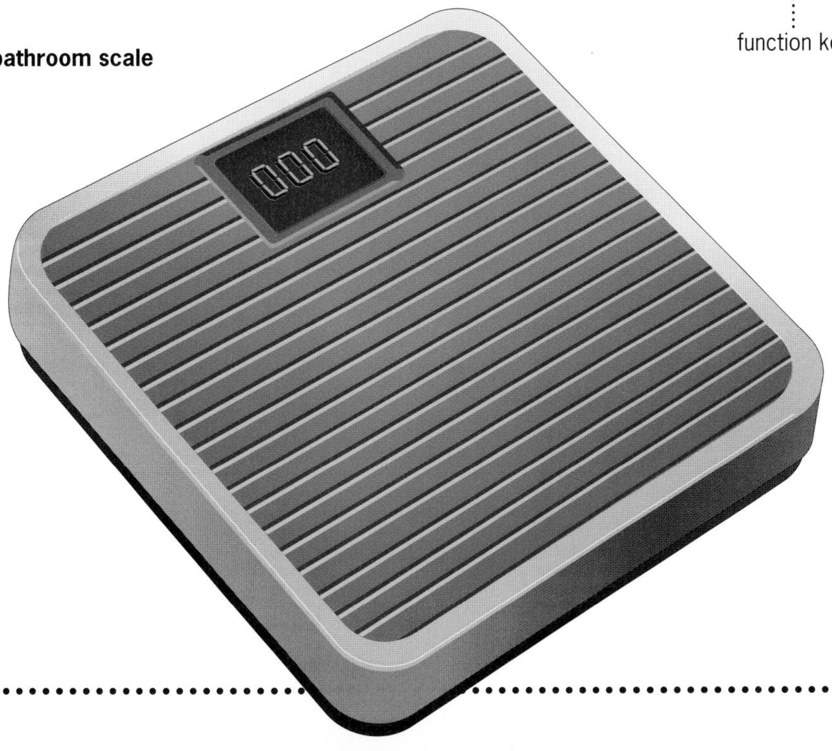

kitchen scale

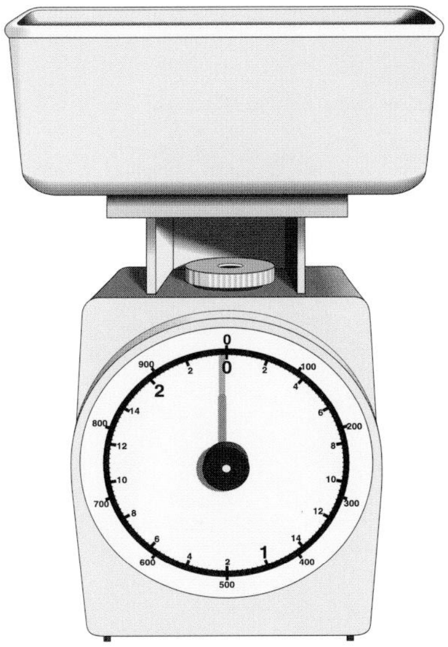

OIL

GROUND TRANSPORT

pipeline

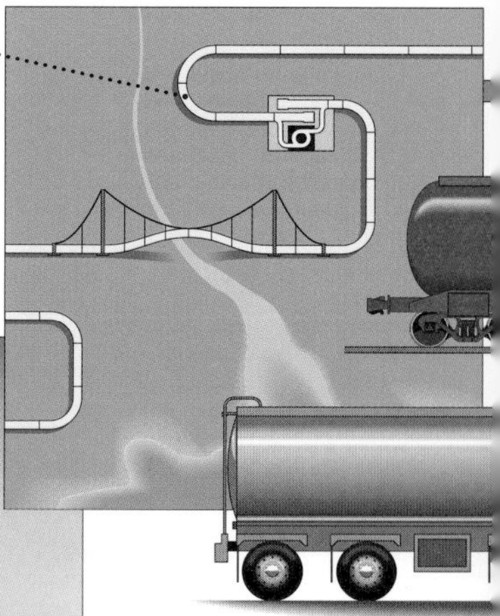

tank trailer

PROSPECTING

surface prospecting

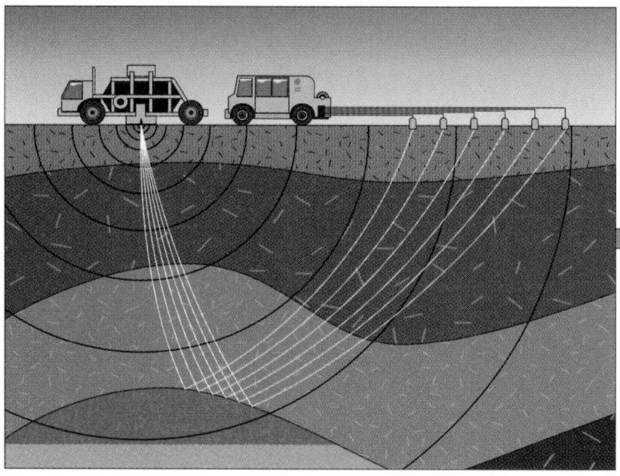

DRILLING

drilling rig

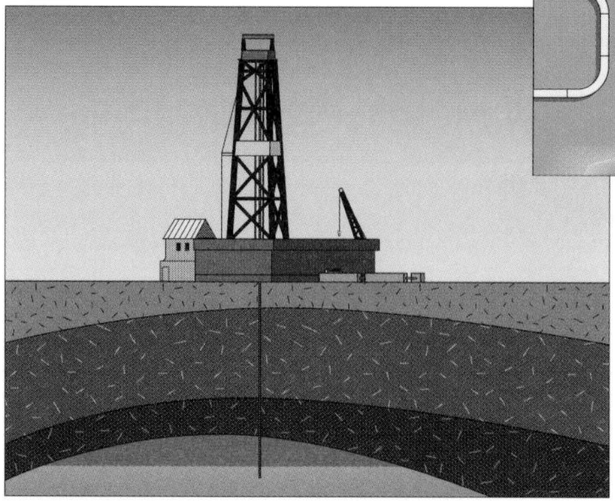

offshore prospecting

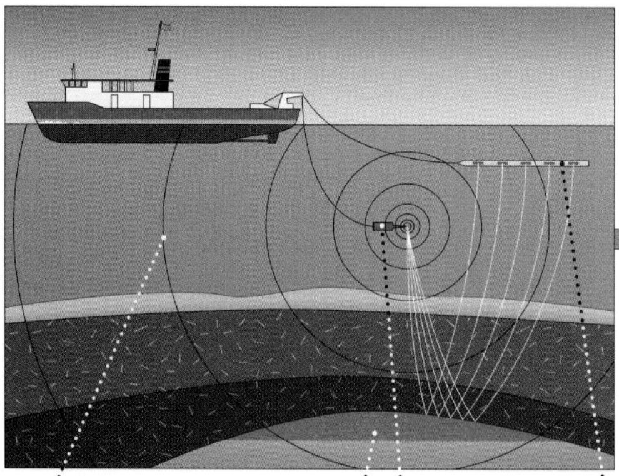

shock wave

seismographic recording

petroleum trap

blasting charge

production platform

MARITIME TRANSPORT

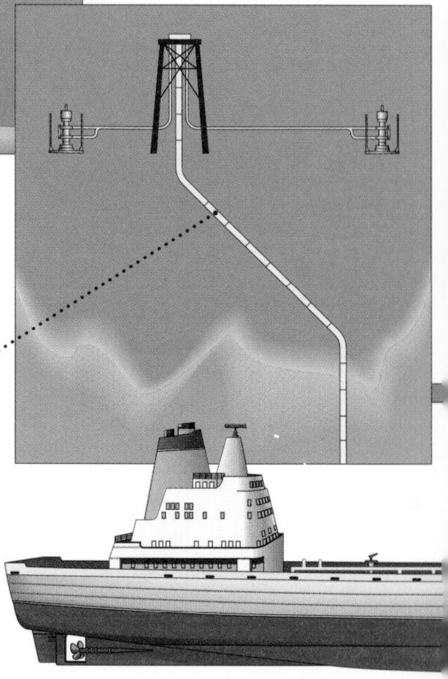

submarine pipeline

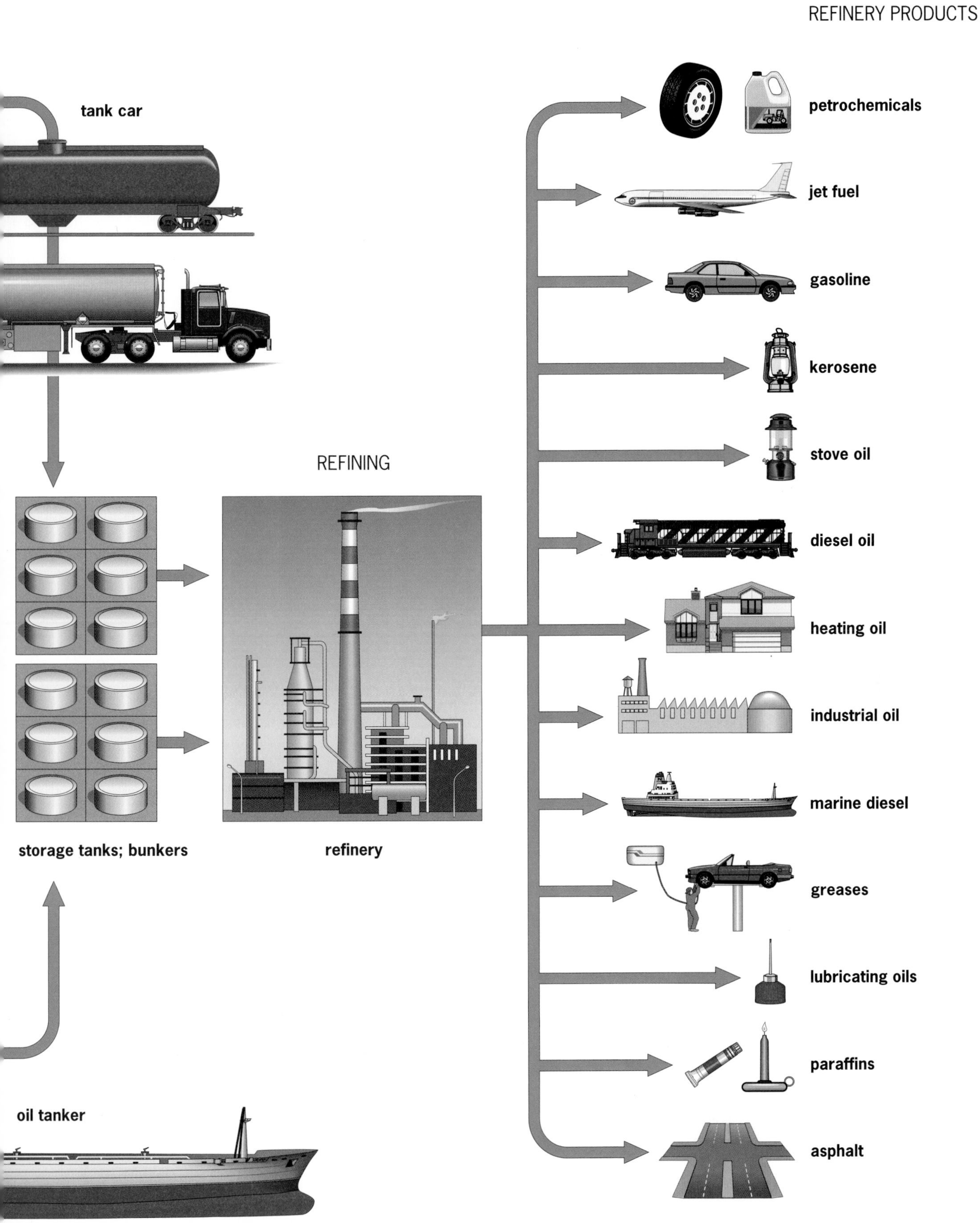
REFINERY PRODUCTS
tank car
petrochemicals
jet fuel
gasoline
kerosene
stove oil
REFINING
diesel oil
heating oil
industrial oil
marine diesel
storage tanks; bunkers
refinery
greases
lubricating oils
paraffins
oil tanker
asphalt

HYDROELECTRIC ENERGY

hydroelectric complex

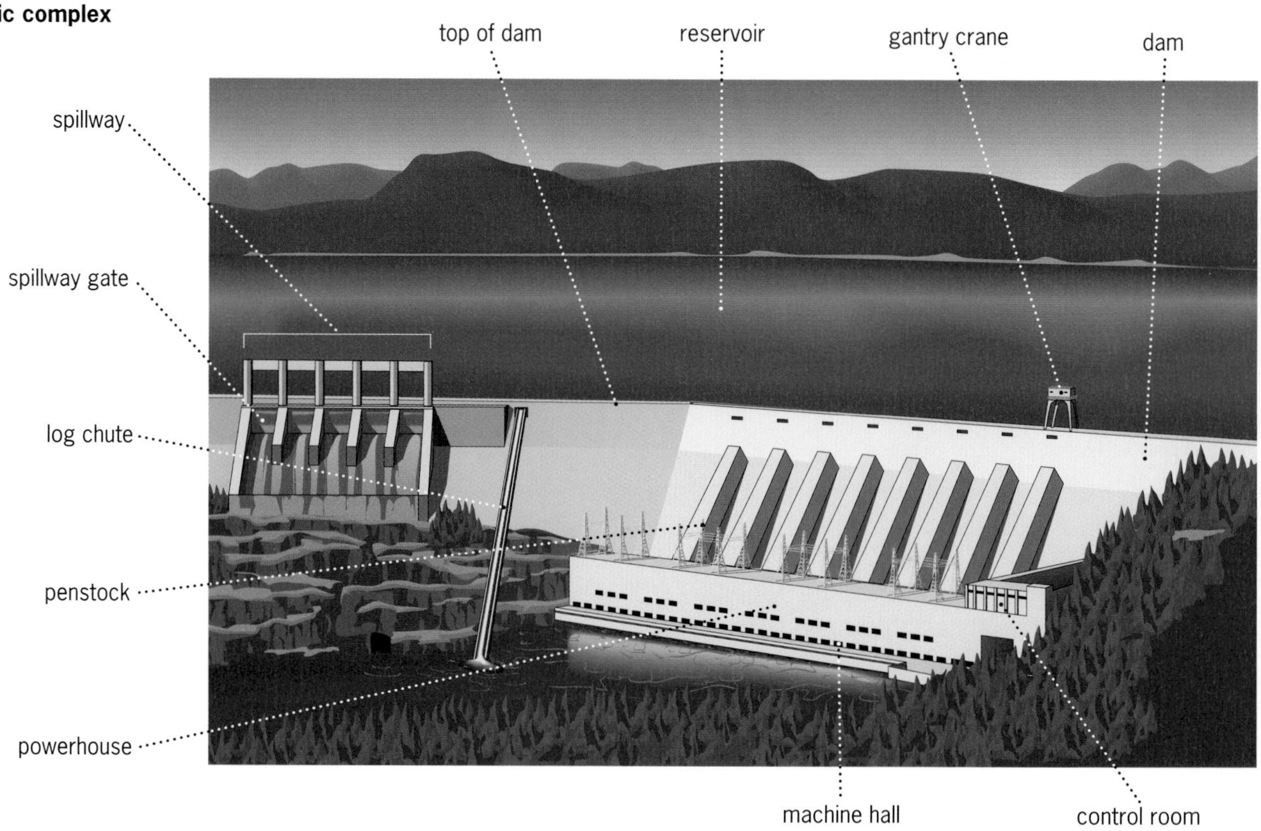
top of dam
reservoir
gantry crane
dam
spillway
spillway gate
log chute
penstock
powerhouse
machine hall
control room

cross section of hydroelectric power station

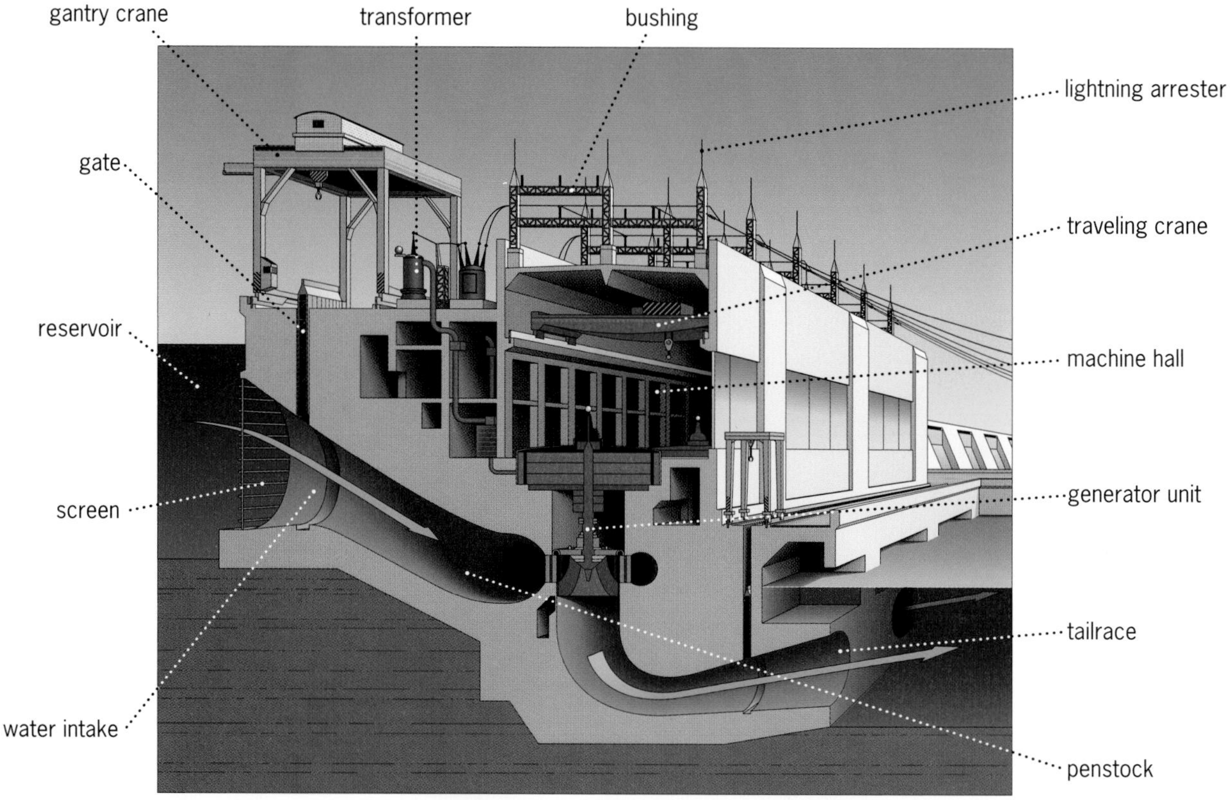
gantry crane
transformer
bushing
lightning arrester
gate
traveling crane
reservoir
machine hall
screen
generator unit
tailrace
water intake
penstock

electric circuit

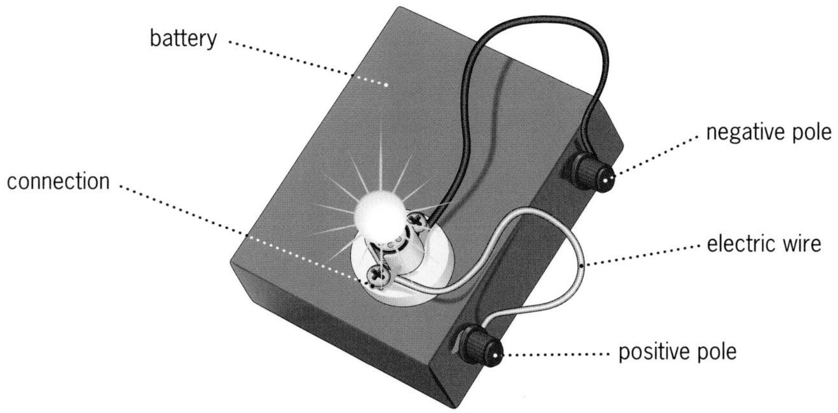
battery
negative pole
connection
electric wire
positive pole

steps in production of electricity

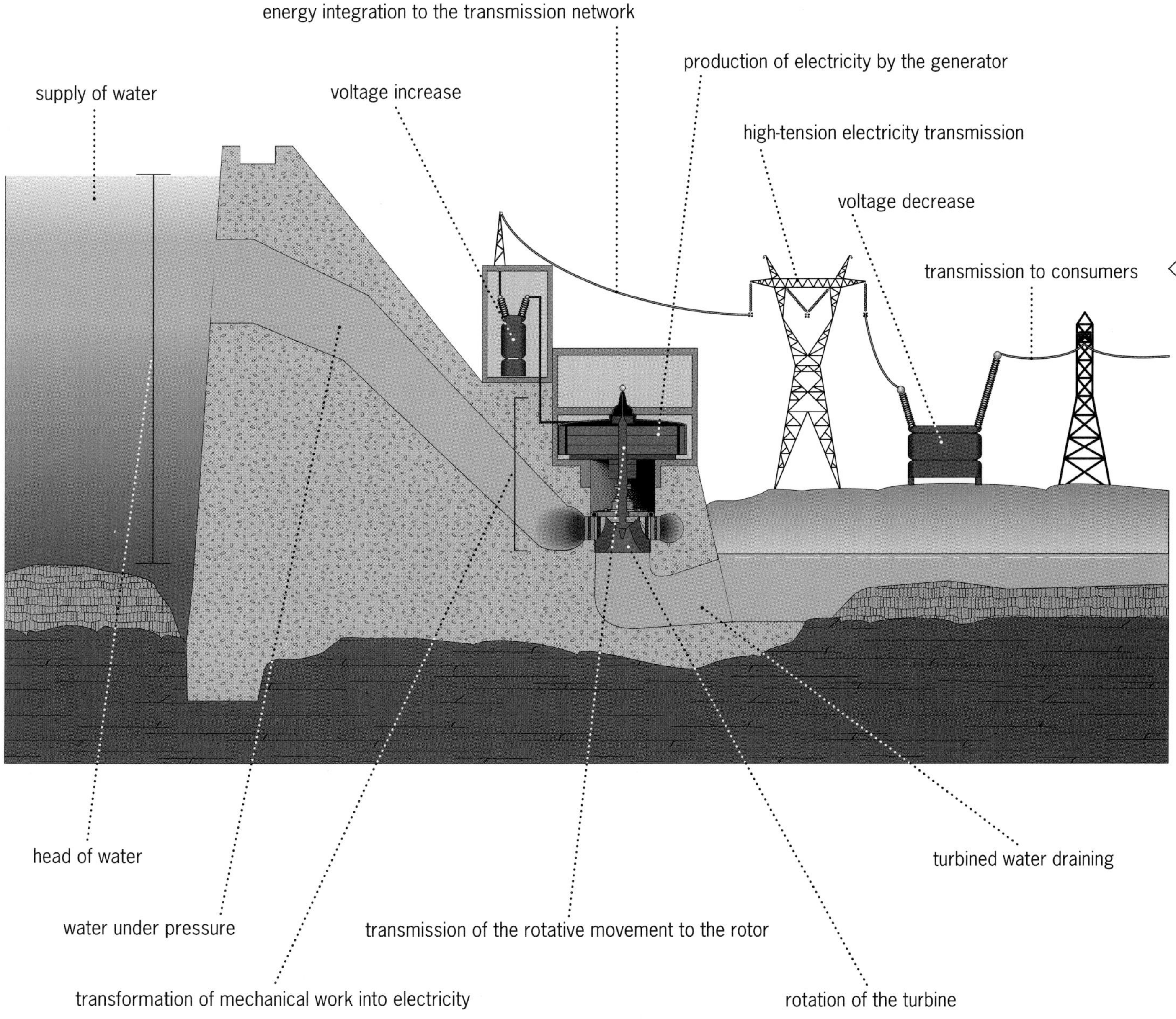
energy integration to the transmission network
production of electricity by the generator
supply of water
voltage increase
high-tension electricity transmission
voltage decrease
transmission to consumers
head of water
turbined water draining
water under pressure
transmission of the rotative movement to the rotor
transformation of mechanical work into electricity
rotation of the turbine

NUCLEAR ENERGY

nuclear power station

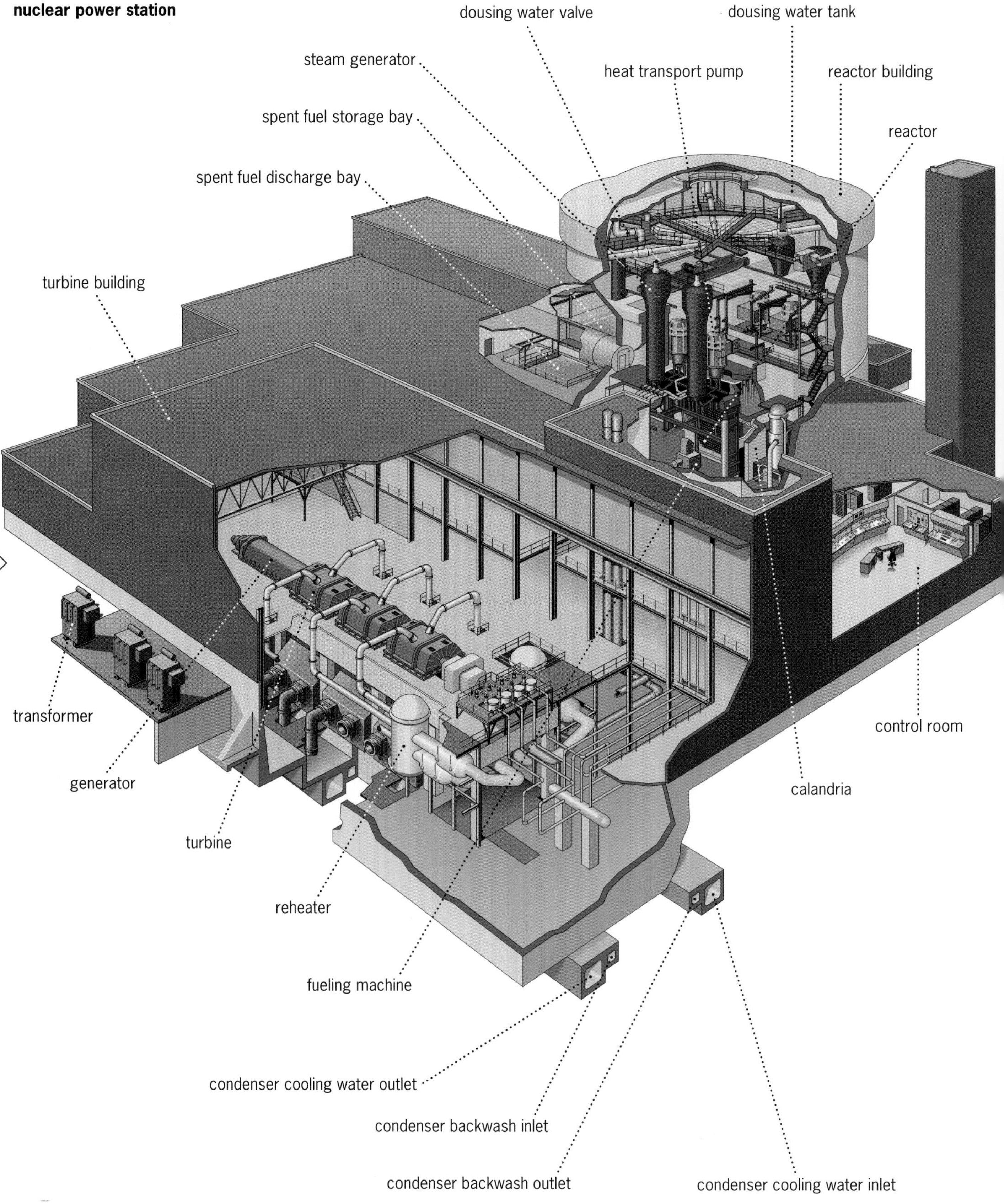
dousing water valve
dousing water tank
steam generator
heat transport pump
reactor building
spent fuel storage bay
reactor
spent fuel discharge bay
turbine building
transformer
generator
turbine
reheater
fueling machine
control room
calandria
condenser cooling water outlet
condenser backwash inlet
condenser backwash outlet
condenser cooling water inlet

production of electricity from nuclear energy

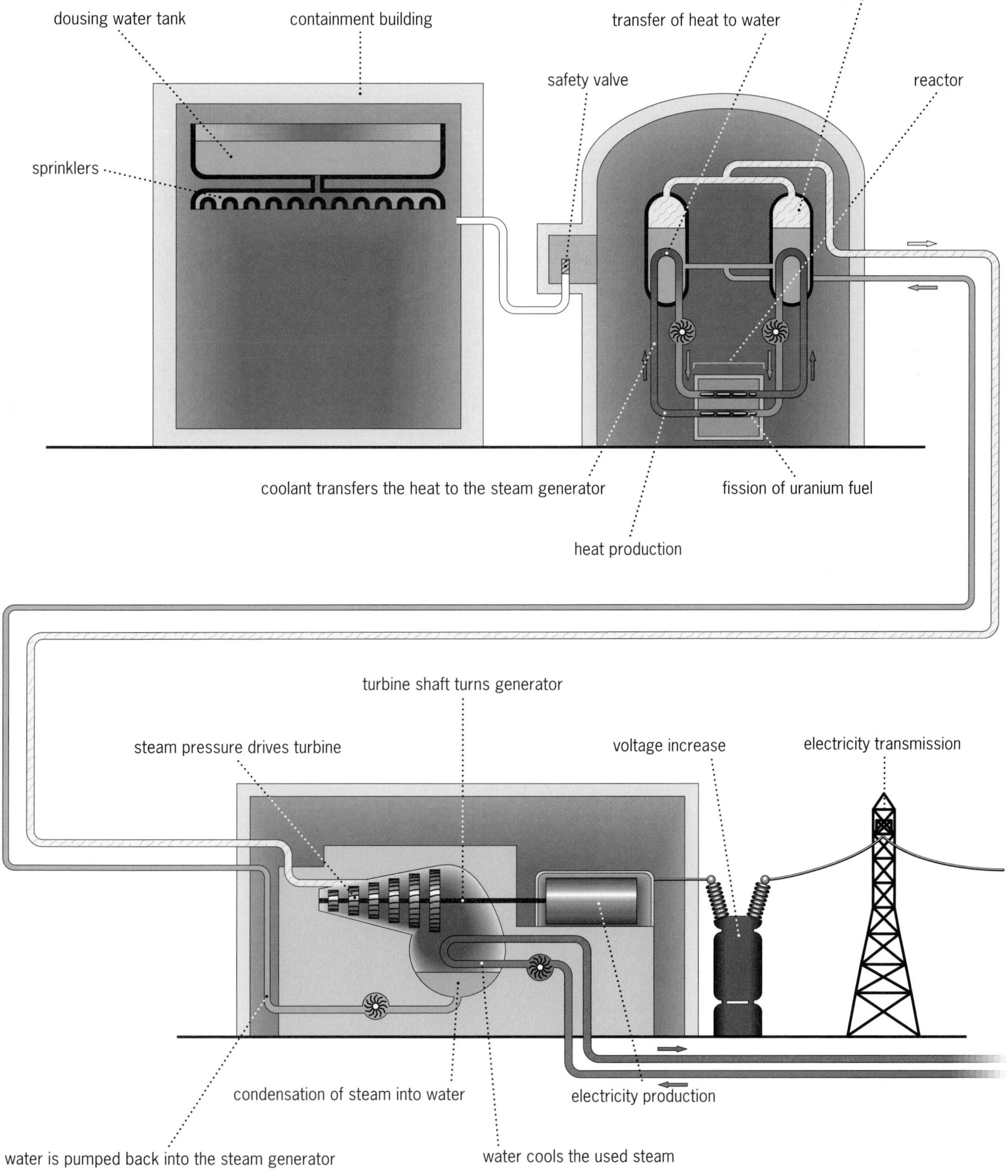
water turns into steam
dousing water tank
containment building
transfer of heat to water
safety valve
reactor
sprinklers
coolant transfers the heat to the steam generator
fission of uranium fuel
heat production
turbine shaft turns generator
steam pressure drives turbine
voltage increase
electricity transmission
condensation of steam into water
electricity production
water is pumped back into the steam generator
water cools the used steam

SOLAR ENERGY

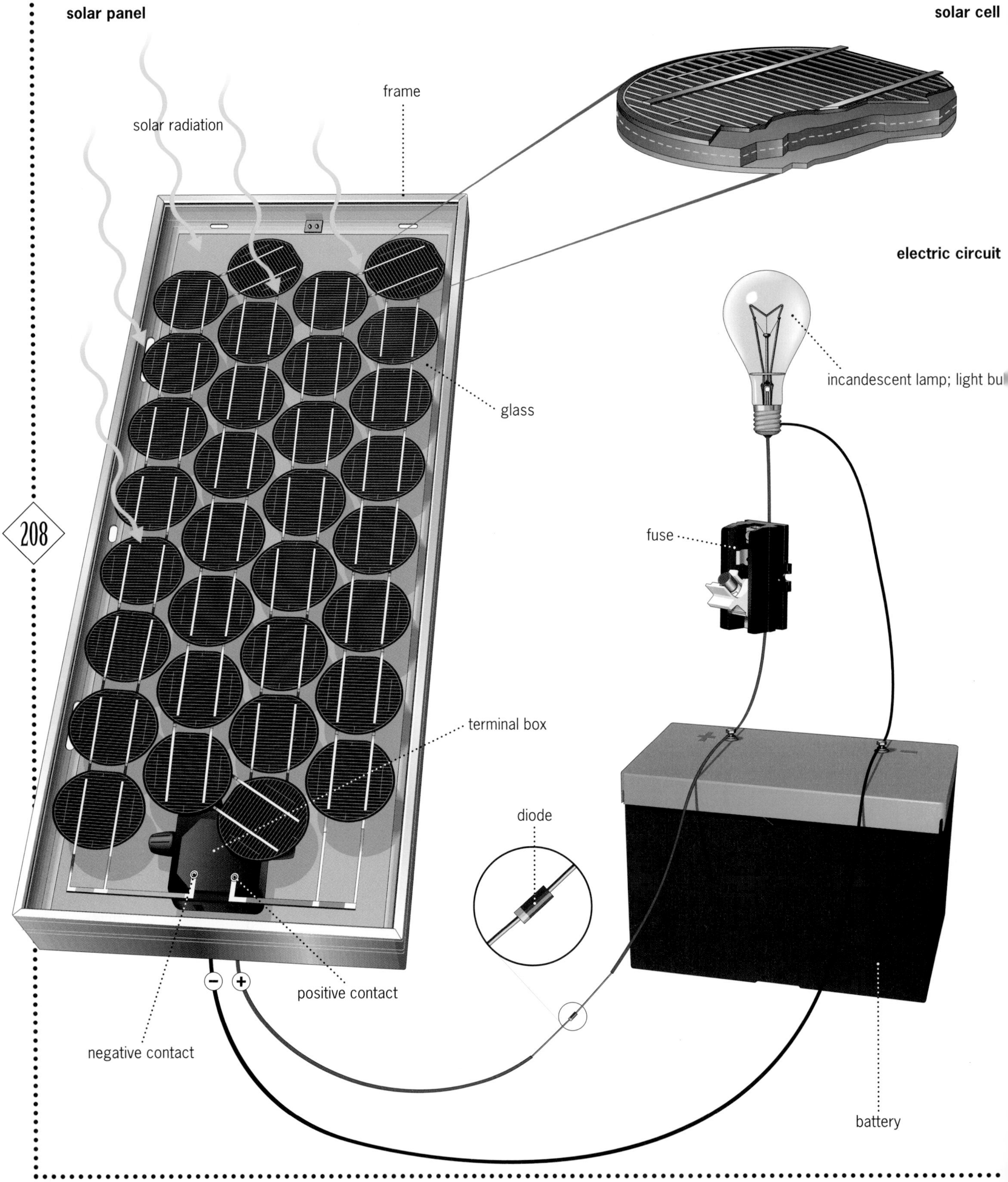

solar panel
solar cell
frame
solar radiation
electric circuit
incandescent lamp; light bu
glass
fuse
terminal box
diode
positive contact
negative contact
battery

WIND ENERGY

horizontal-axis wind turbine

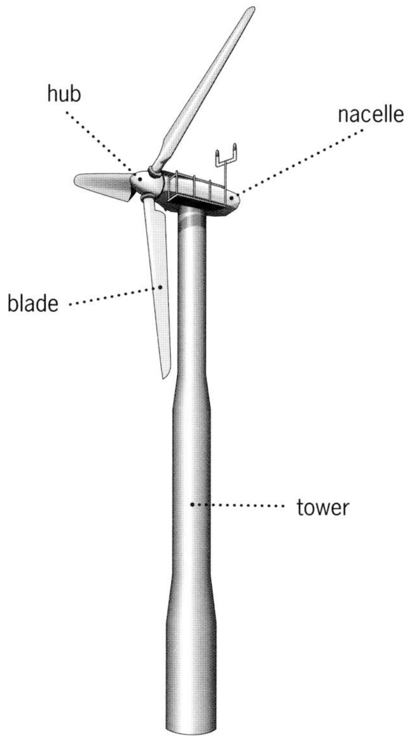
hub
nacelle
blade
tower

vertical-axis wind turbine

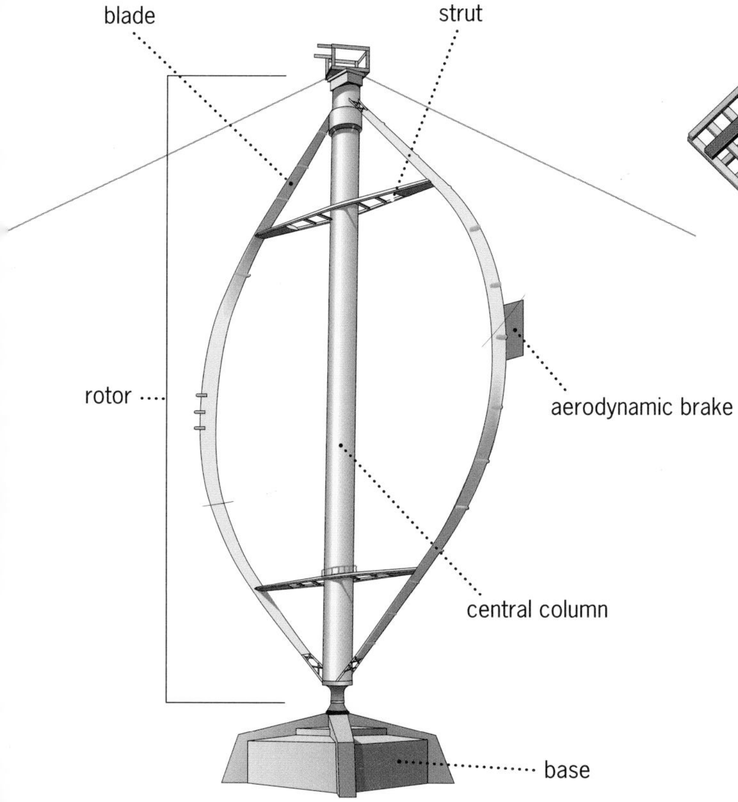
blade
strut
rotor
aerodynamic brake
central column
base

windmill

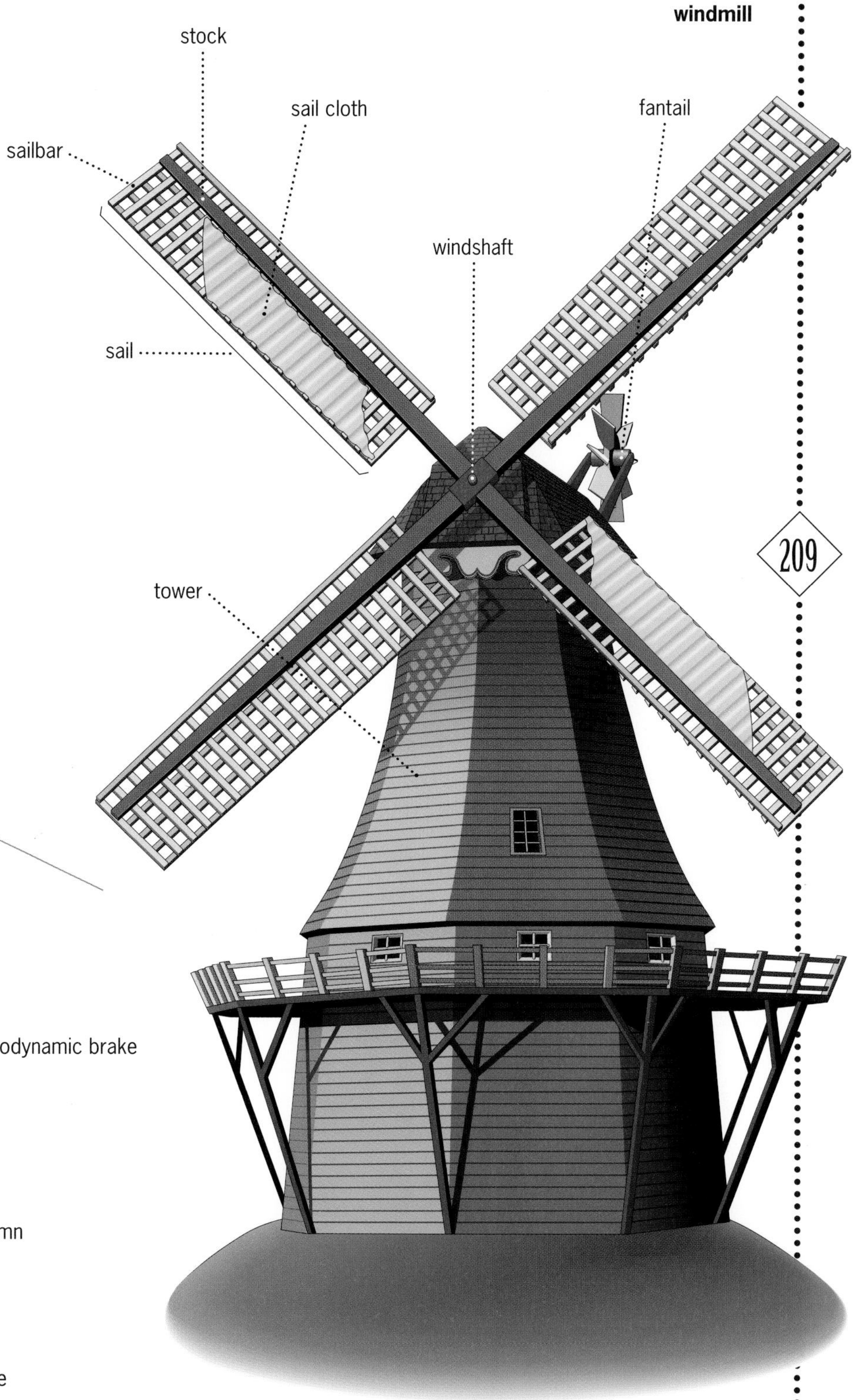
stock
sail cloth
fantail
sailbar
windshaft
sail
tower

FIRE PREVENTION

fire hose

portable fire extinguisher

fire hydrant

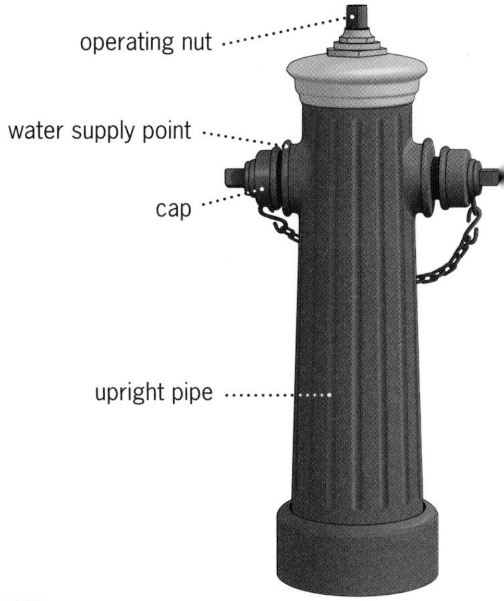
operating nut
water supply point
cap
upright pipe

fire engine

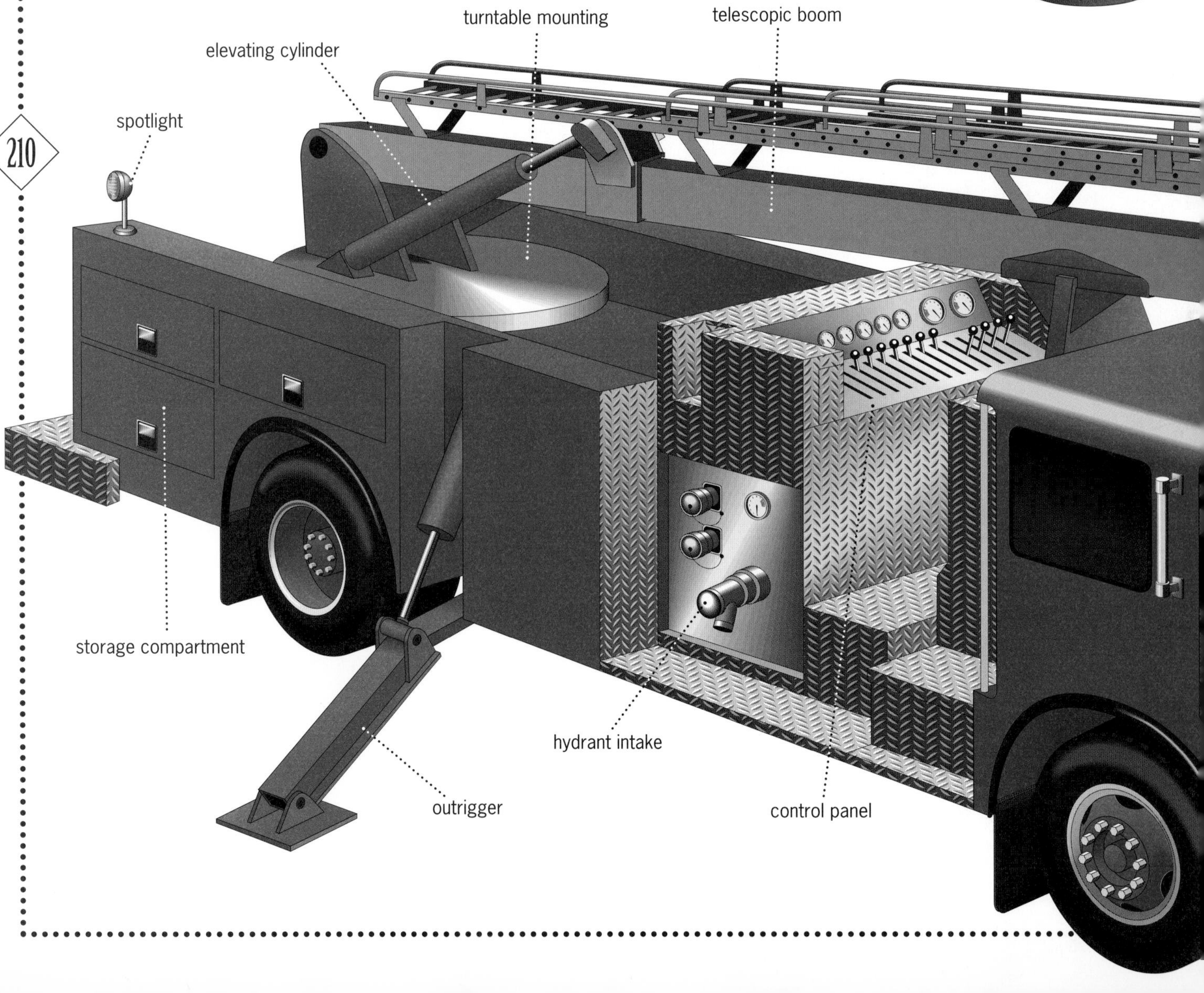
turntable mounting
telescopic boom
elevating cylinder
spotlight
storage compartment
hydrant intake
outrigger
control panel

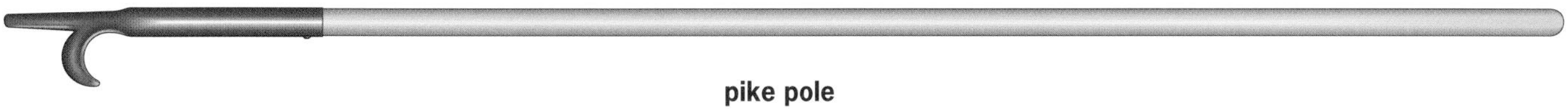

pike pole

fire-fighter's hatchet

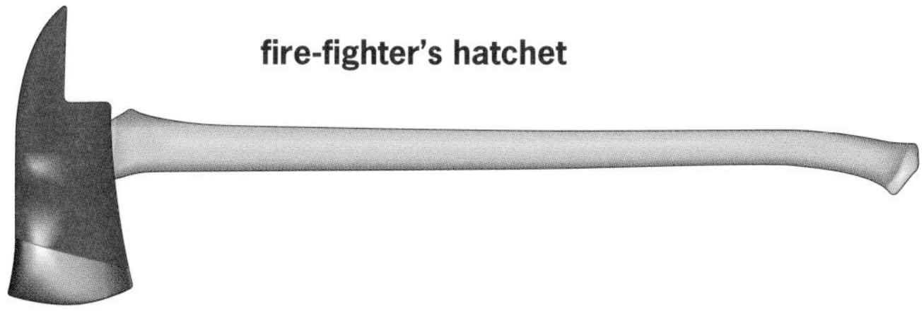

fire-fighter

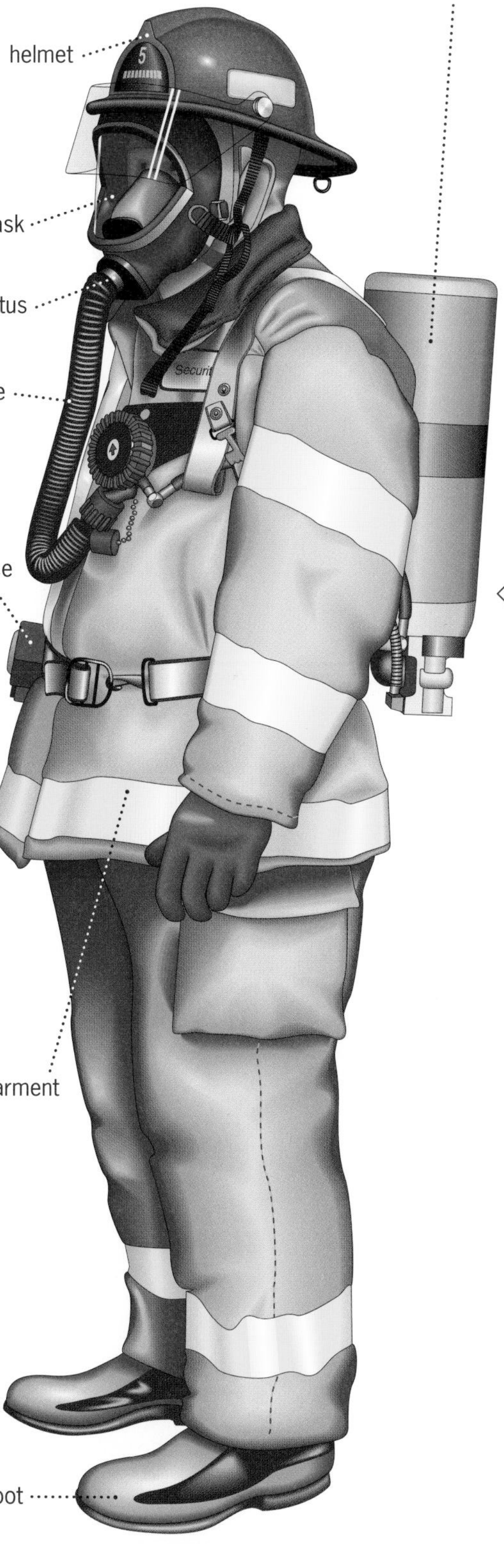
compressed-air cylinder
helmet
full face mask
self-contained breathing apparatus
air-supply tube
warning device
fireproof and waterproof garment
rubber boot

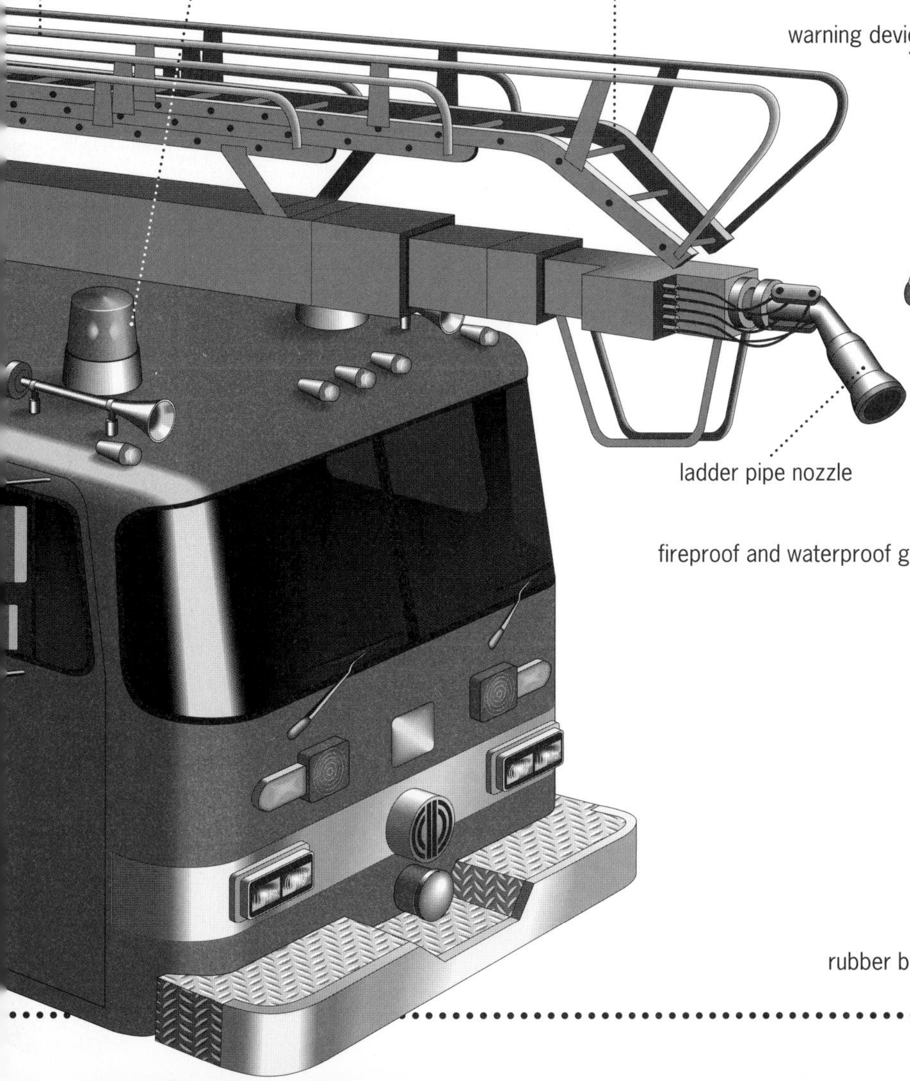
tower ladder
flashing light
top ladder
ladder pipe nozzle

HEAVY VEHICLES

loader

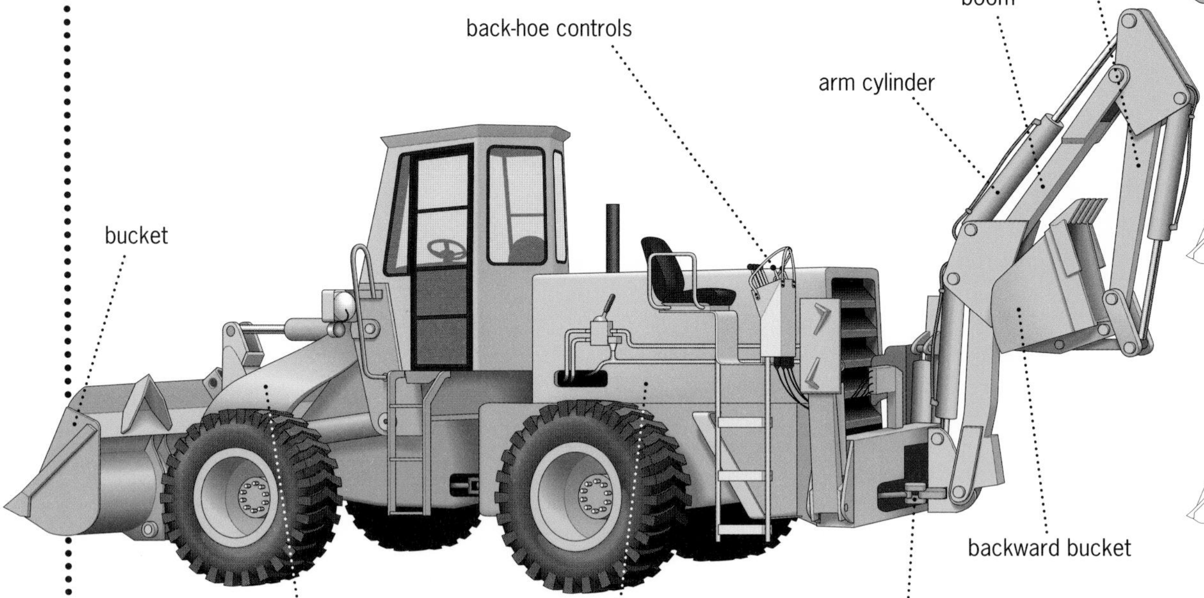
arm
boom
back-hoe controls
arm cylinder
bucket
backward bucket
lift arm
diesel engine
bucket hinge pin

front-end loader

wheel tractor

back-hoe

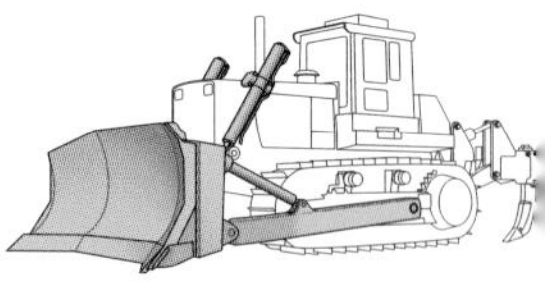

blade

bulldozer

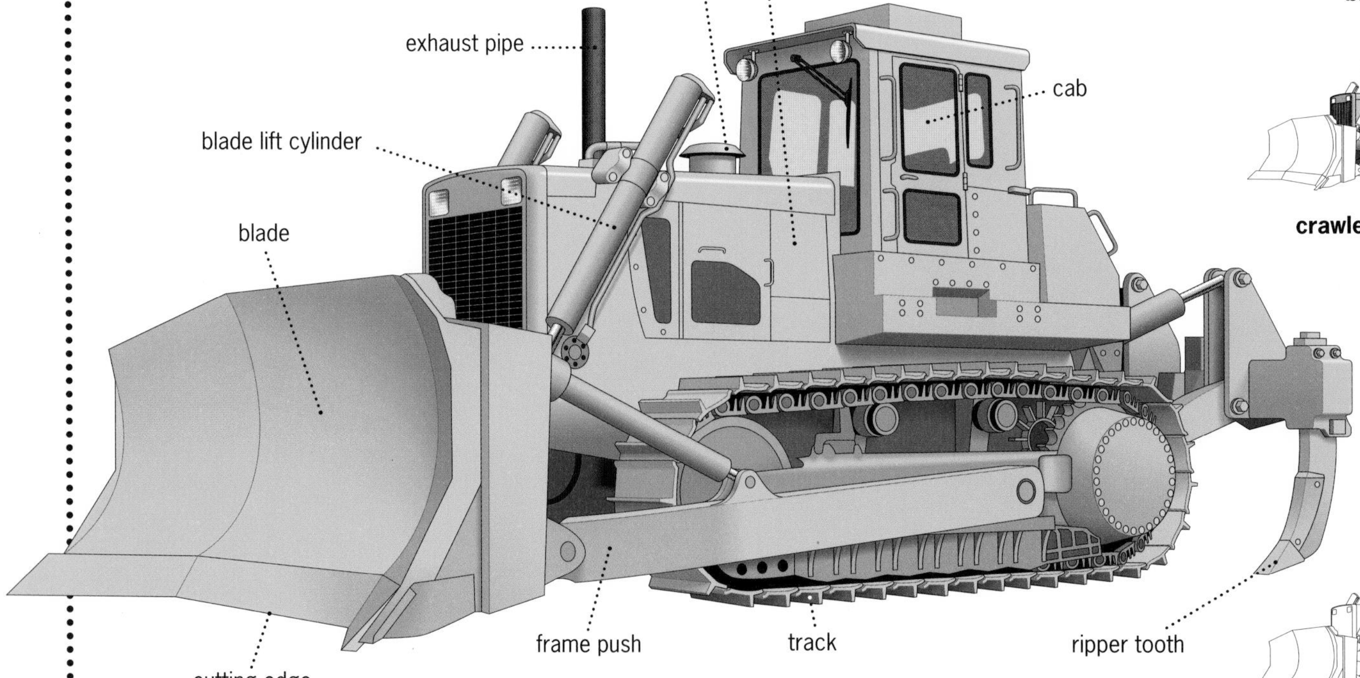
air filter
diesel engine
exhaust pipe
cab
blade lift cylinder
blade
frame push
track
ripper tooth
cutting edge

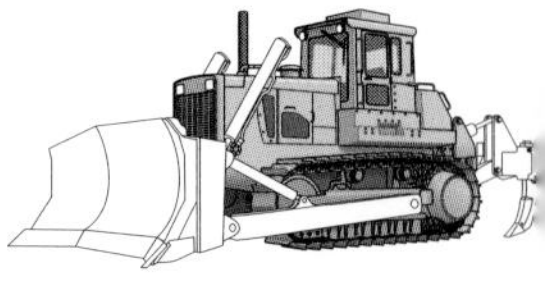

crawler tractor

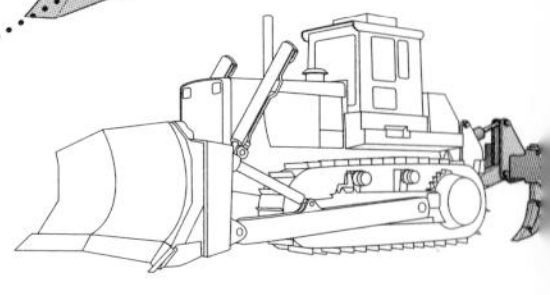

ripper

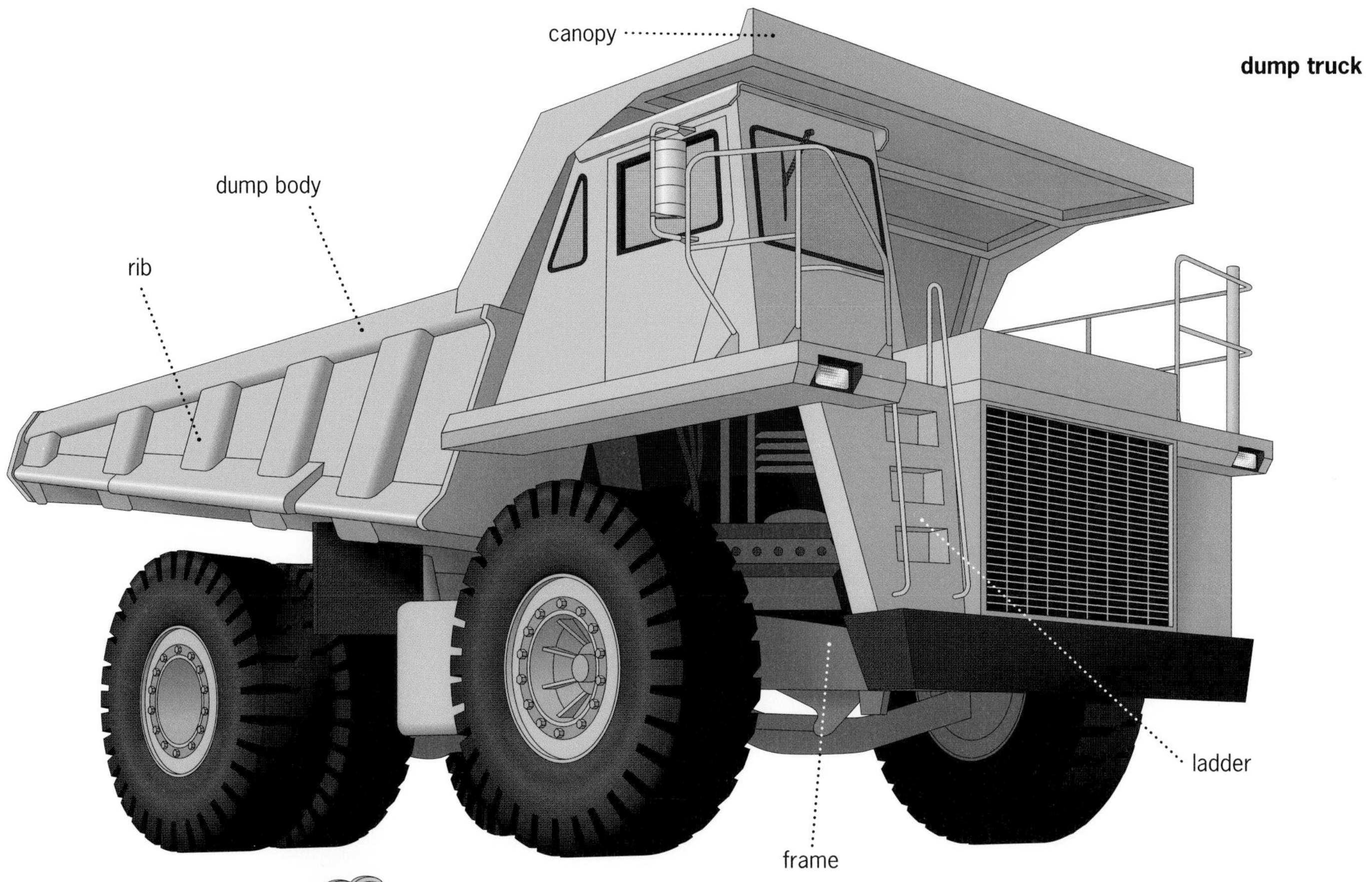
dump truck
canopy
dump body
rib
ladder
frame

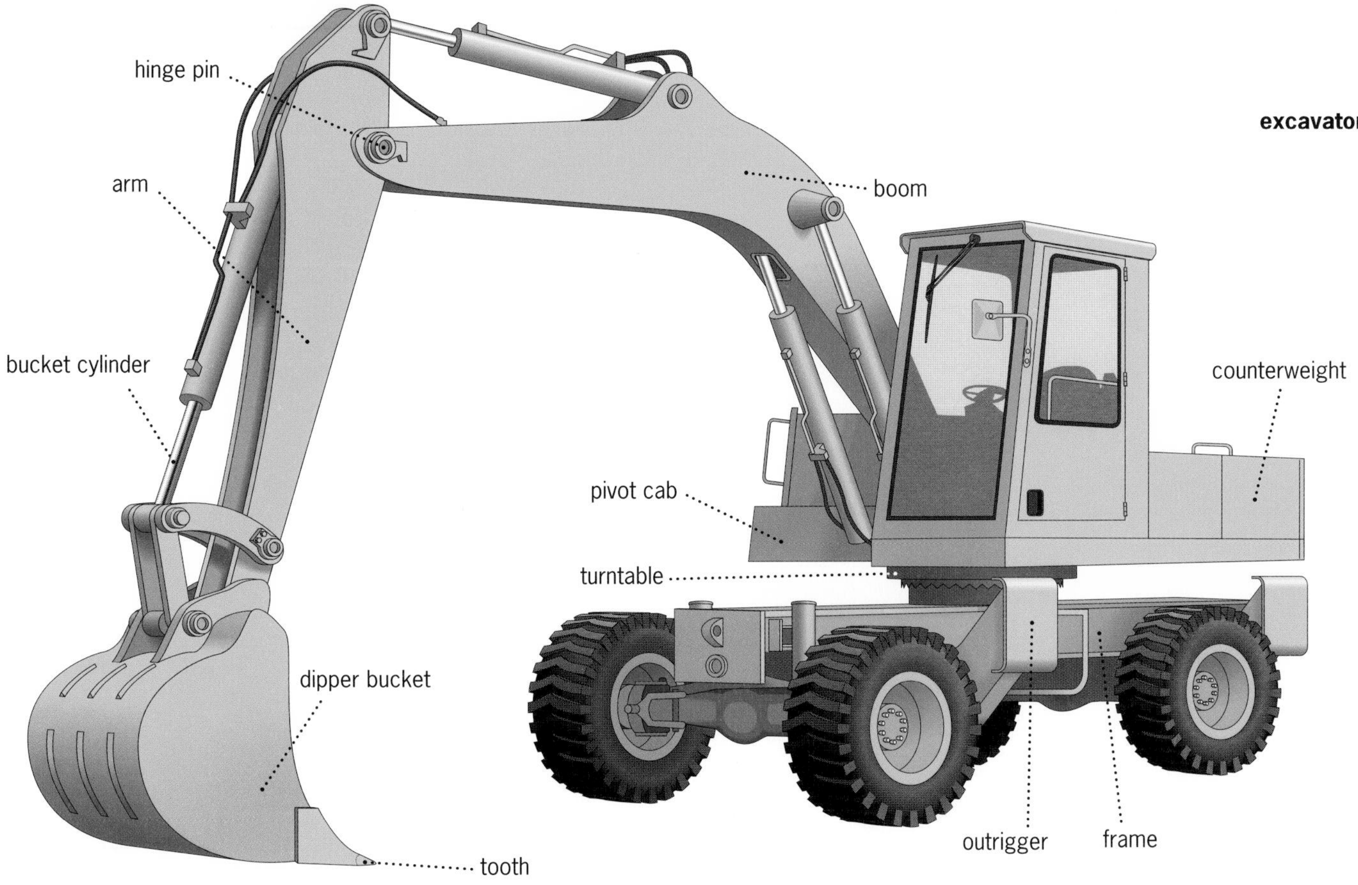
excavator
hinge pin
arm
boom
bucket cylinder
counterweight
pivot cab
turntable
dipper bucket
tooth
outrigger
frame

HEAVY MACHINERY

tower crane

street sweeper

snowblower

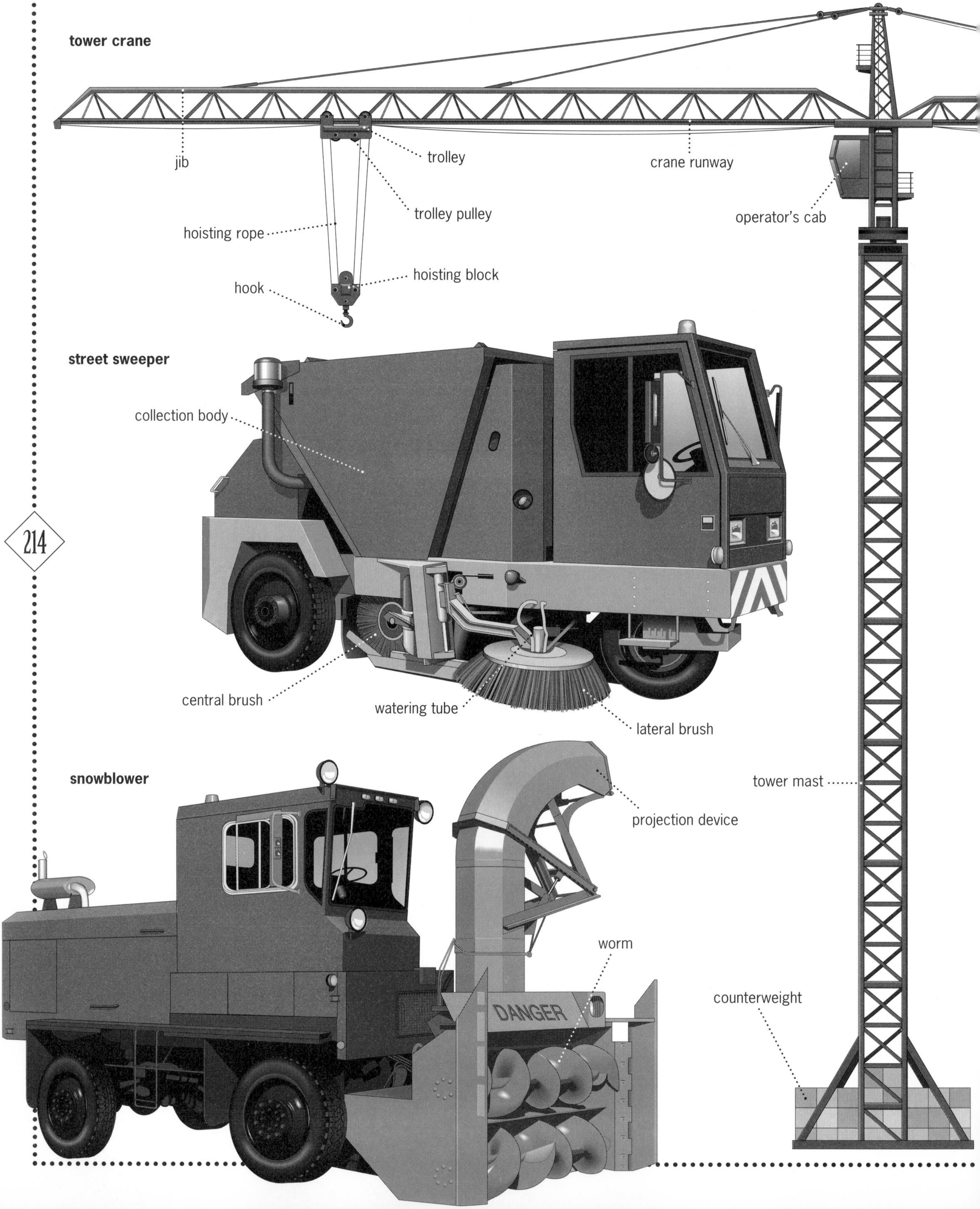
jib
trolley
crane runway
trolley pulley
operator's cab
hoisting rope
hoisting block
hook
collection body
central brush
watering tube
lateral brush
tower mast
projection device
worm
DANGER
counterweight

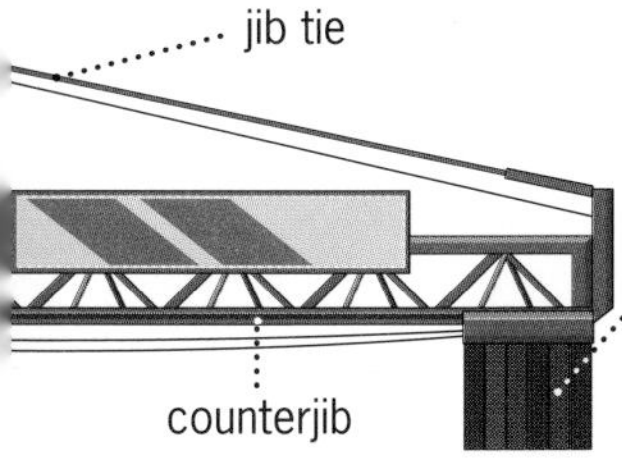
jib tie
counterjib ballast
counterjib

sanitation truck

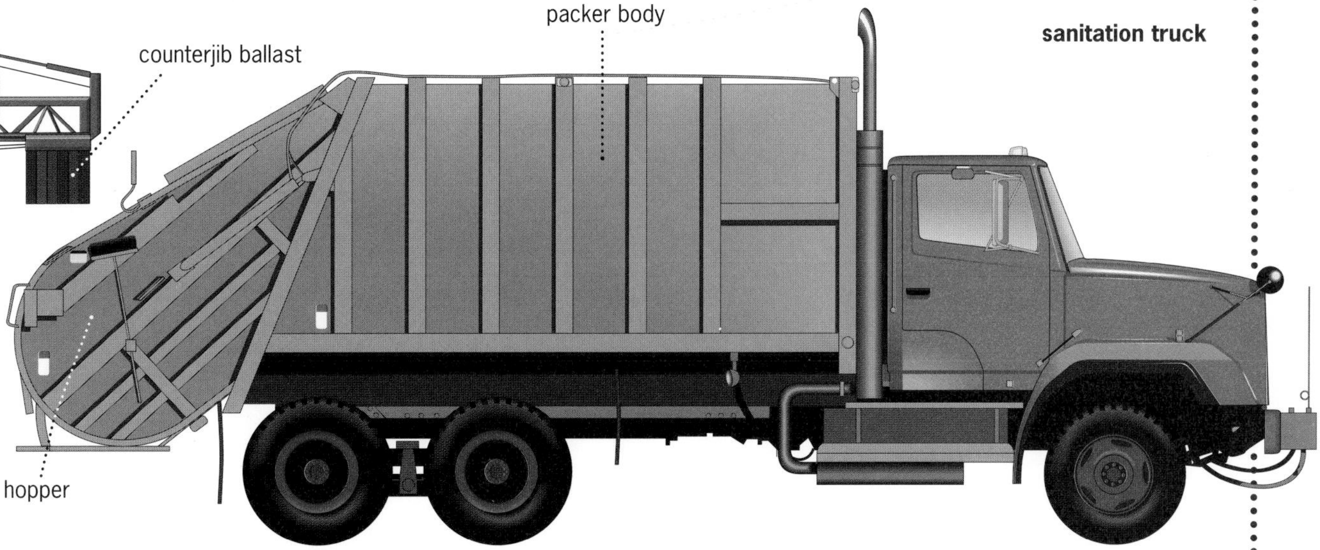
packer body
loading hopper

truck crane

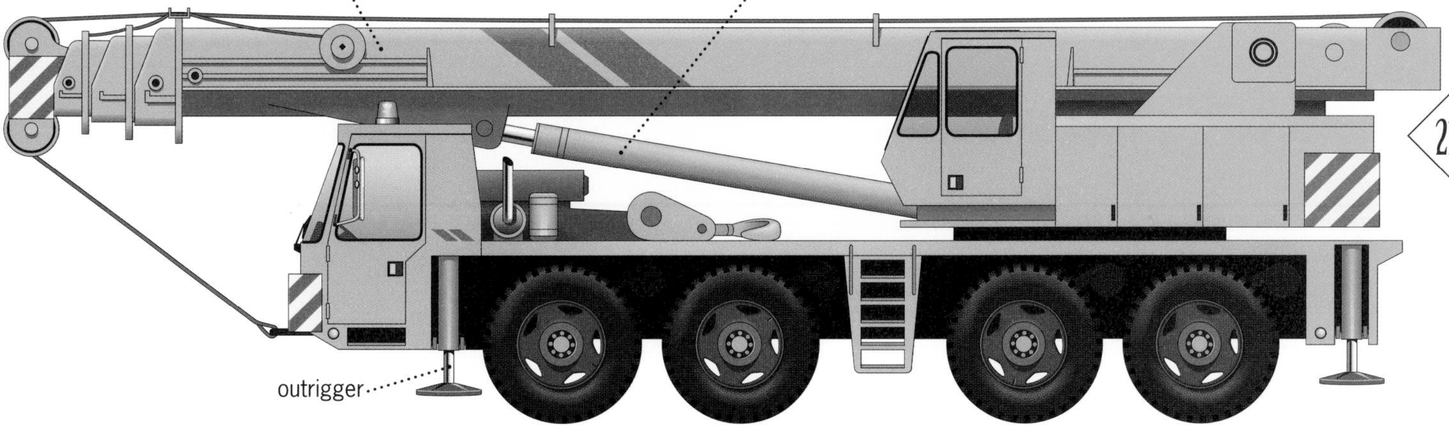
telescopic boom
elevating cylinder
outrigger

tow truck

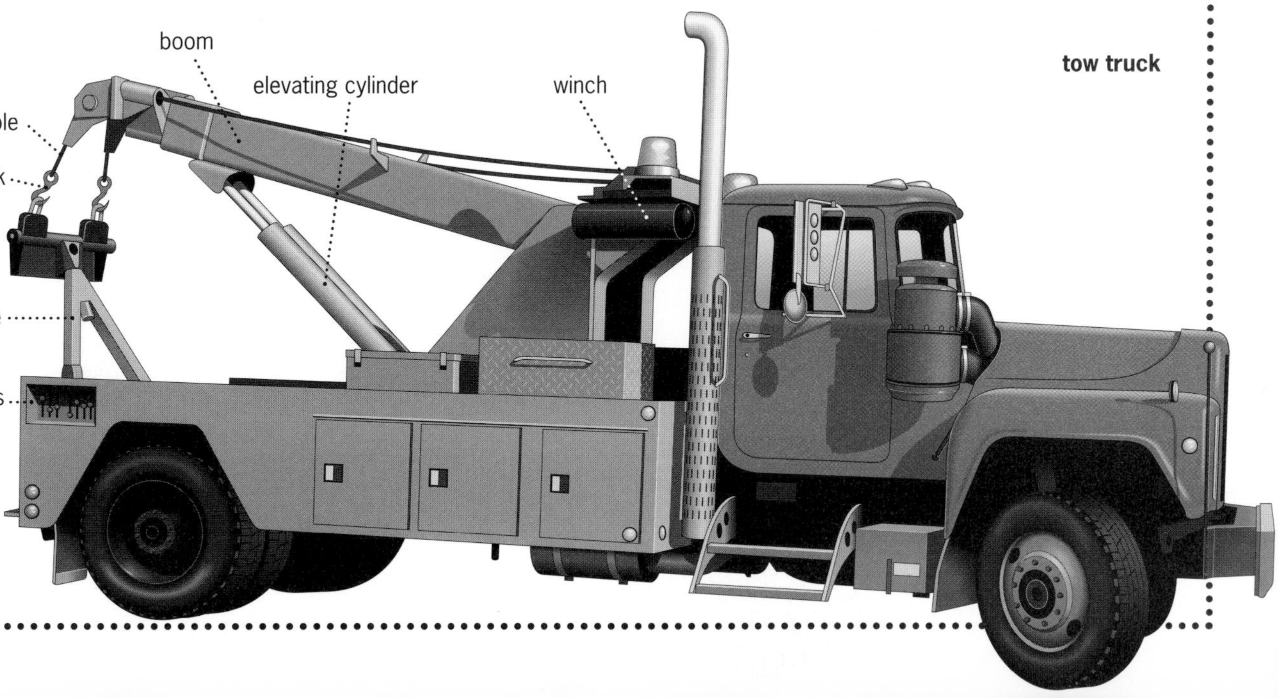
boom
elevating cylinder
winch
cable
hook
towing device
winch controls

COMMON SYMBOLS

women's rest room

men's rest room

wheelchair access

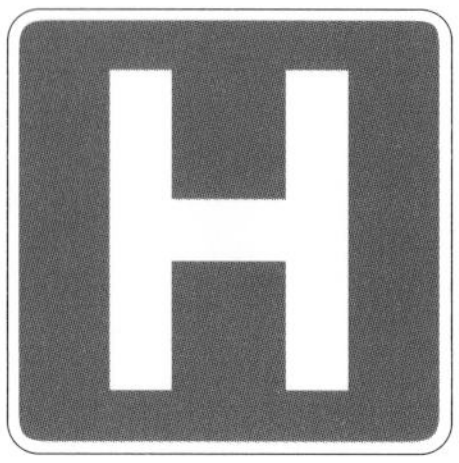
hospital

telephone

no smoking

camping (tent)

camping prohibited

stop at intersection

SAFETY SYMBOLS

corrosive

electrical hazard

explosive

flammable

radioactive

poisonous

PROTECTION

eye protection

ear protection

head protection

hand protection

foot protection

respiratory system protection

The terms in **bold type** correspond to an illustration; those in CAPITALS indicate a title.

D

The terms in **bold type** correspond to an illustration; those in CAPITALS indicate a title.

E

F

G

The terms in **bold type** correspond to an illustration; those in CAPITALS indicate a title.

The terms in **bold type** correspond to an illustration; those in CAPITALS indicate a title.

The terms in **bold type** correspond to an illustration; those in CAPITALS indicate a title.

Q

R

S

The terms in **bold type** correspond to an illustration; those in CAPITALS indicate a title.

T

The terms in **bold type** correspond to an illustration; those in CAPITALS indicate a title.

U

V

W

X

Y

Z

The terms in **bold type** correspond to an illustration; those in CAPITALS indicate a title.